Teaching in Today's Inclusive Classrooms

A Universal Design for Learning Approach

Richard M. Gargiulo
University of Alabama at Birmingham

Deborah J. Metcalf
Pitt County Schools, NC, and East Carolina University

WADSWORTH
CENGAGE Learning™

Australia • Brazil • Japan • Korea • Mexico • Singapore • Spain • United Kingdom • United States

WADSWORTH
CENGAGE Learning

Teaching in Today's Inclusive Classrooms: A Universal Design for Learning Approach
Richard M. Gargiulo and
Deborah J. Metcalf

Acquisitions Editor: Christopher Shortt

Developmental Editor: Tangelique Williams

Assistant Editor: Caitlin Cox

Editorial Assistant: Linda Stewart

Media Editor: Ashley Cronin

Marketing Manager: Kara Parsons

Marketing Assistant: Ting Jian Yap

Marketing Communications Manager: Martha Pfeiffer

Content Project Manager: Tanya Nigh

Creative Director: Rob Hugel

Art Director: Maria Epes

Print Buyer: Linda Hsu

Rights Acquisitions Account Manager, Text: Roberta Broyer

Rights Acquisitions Account Manager, Image: Robyn Young

Production Service: Newgen–North America

Text Designer: Diane Beasley

Photo Researcher: PrePress

Copy Editor: Kathy Finch

Illustrator: Newgen

Cover Designer: Bartay Studio

Compositor: Newgen

For product information and technology assistance, contact us at
**Cengage Learning Customer & Sales Support,
1-800-354-9706.**
For permission to use material from this text or product,
submit a requests online at **http://www.cengage.com/permissions.**
Further permissions questions can be e-mailed to
permissionrequest@cengage.com.

Library of Congress Control Number: 2008937399

ISBN-13: 978-0-495-09715-0
ISBN-10: 0-495-09715-2

Wadsworth
10 Davis Drive
Belmont, CA 94002-3098
USA

Cengage Learning is a leading provider of customized learning solutions with office locations around the globe, including Singapore, the United Kingdom, Australia, Mexico, Brazil, and Japan. Locate your local office at **www.cengage.com/international.**

Cengage Learning products are represented in Canada by Nelson Education, Ltd.

To learn more about Wadsworth, visit **www.cengage.com/Wadsworth**

Purchase any of our products at your local college store or at our preferred online store **www.ichapters.com.**

Printed in the United States of America
1 2 3 4 5 6 7 13 12 11 10 09

This book is dedicated with respect and admiration to all of the teachers who strive daily to make a difference in the lives of their students.

RMG
DJM
October 2008

About the Authors

Richard M. Gargiulo is currently a professor in the Department of Educational Leadership, Special Education, and Foundations at the University of Alabama at Birmingham (UAB). Prior to receiving his Ph.D. degree in educational psychology from the University of Wisconsin, Richard taught fourth graders as well as young children with mental retardation in the Milwaukee Public Schools. Upon receiving his doctorate he joined the faculty of Bowling Green State University, Bowling Green, Ohio. He has been a teacher educator at UAB for more than 25 years.

A frequent contributor to the professional literature, Richard has authored or coauthored approximately 100 publications, including several books. He has twice served as President of the Alabama Federation, Council for Exceptional Children and also as President of the Division of International Special Education and Services (DISES), Council for Exceptional Children. Teaching, however, has always been Richard's passion. In 1999 he received UAB's President's Award for Excellence in Teaching. In 2007 he was honored by the Alabama Federation, Council for Exceptional Children, with the Jasper Harvey Award in recognition of being named the outstanding teacher educator in the state.

Debbie Metcalf currently works in partnership with Pitt County Schools and East Carolina University in Greenville, North Carolina. She is an Intervention Specialist for Pitt County Schools and serves as a Teacher-in-Residence in the Department of Curriculum and Instruction at East Carolina University. She teaches methods courses and works in the classroom with undergraduate preservice teachers. Debbie received a Master of Arts in Education degree from San Diego State University and is certified in both general and special education, including assistive technology. She became a National Board Certified Teacher in 1997. In 2004, she was awarded the Clarissa Hug Teacher of the Year Award from the International Council for Exceptional Children.

Debbie has taught students of all ages for over 30 years in California, New Mexico, Hawaii, Michigan, and North Carolina. She continues to mentor new teachers and teachers pursuing National Board Certification. Her primary research areas include access to the general curriculum for students with exceptionalities, collaborative teaching models, alternate assessment models for diverse learners, curriculum revision, alignment, and service learning.

Brief Contents

CHAPTER 1 Teaching in Today's Classrooms   1

CHAPTER 2 Special Education Procedures, Policies, and Process   31

CHAPTER 3 Today's Learners I: Students with High Incidence Disabilities and Gifts and Talents   51

CHAPTER 4 Today's Learners II: Students with Low Incidence Disabilities and Other Special Needs   87

CHAPTER 5 Collaboration and Cooperative Teaching: Tools for Teaching All Learners   127

CHAPTER 6 Assistive Technologies and Innovative Learning Tools   153

CHAPTER 7 Universal Design for Learning   179

CHAPTER 8 Assessing and Evaluating Learner Progress   207

CHAPTER 9 Selecting Instructional Interventions for Teaching All Learners   233

CHAPTER 10 Designing Learning that Works for All Students   267

CHAPTER 11 Creating Literacy-Rich Environments for All Learners   301

CHAPTER 12 Developing an Understanding of Mathematics in All Learners   331

CHAPTER 13 Teaching Critical Content in Science and Social Studies to All Learners   365

CHAPTER 14 Selecting Behavioral Supports for All Learners   401

Appendix A Interstate New Teacher Assessment and Support Consortium (INTASC) Standards   435

Appendix B Council for Exceptional Children Knowledge and Skill Base Standards for All Entry-Level Special Education Teachers   436

Glossary   442

Index   451

Detailed Contents

Preface   xvii

CHAPTER 1

Teaching in Today's Classrooms   1

Schooling in America   2
Learners in Need of Special Services   3
By the Numbers: A Quick Look   5
Service Delivery Options: Where Children with Special Needs Are Served   5
Educational Placements   6
A Cascade of Service Delivery Options   7
A Contemporary Challenge   8
Inclusionary Practices and Thinking   10
Summary of Key Litigation and Legislation   11
Key Judicial Decisions   12
Individuals with Disabilities Education Act: 1975–1997   12
Section 504 of the Rehabilitation Act of 1973   18
Americans with Disabilities Act   19
Educational Reform: Standards-Based Education   20
No Child Left Behind Act of 2001   20
Individuals with Disabilities Education Improvement Act of 2004   21
Introducing Universal Design for Learning   25
Thematic Summary   26
Making Connections for Inclusive Teaching   26
Learning Activities   27
Looking at the Standards   27
Key Concepts and Terms   28
References   28

CHAPTER 2

Special Education Procedures, Policies, and Process   31

Identification and Assessment of Individual Differences   32
Referral and Assessment for a Special Education   33
Prereferral   33
Referral   34
Assessment   36
Instructional Programming and Appropriate Placement   37
The Individualized Education Program   38
Related Services   42
Section 504 Accommodation Plan   43
Who Is Protected by Section 504?   44
Providing a Free, Appropriate Public Education   44
Section 504 Eligibility Determination   45
Accommodation Plans   46

Thematic Summary   46

Making Connections for Inclusive Teaching   48

Learning Activities   48

Looking at the Standards   48

Key Concepts and Terms   49

References   49

CHAPTER 3

Today's Learners I: Students with High Incidence Disabilities and Gifts and Talents   51

Learners with Mental Retardation   53

Defining Mental Retardation   54

Classification of Learners with Mental Retardation   57

How Many Learners Are Mentally Retarded?   57

What Are Some of the Causes of Mental Retardation?   57

Selected Learning and Behavioral Characteristics of Learners with Mental Retardation   58

Learners with Learning Disabilities   58

Defining Learning Disabilities   60

How Many Learners Are Learning Disabled?   62

What Are Some of the Causes of Learning Disabilities?   63

Selected Learning and Behavioral Characteristics of Learners with Learning Disabilities   63

Learners with Speech and Language Disorders   64

Defining Speech and Language   64

Classifying Learners with Speech and Language Disorders   65

How Many Learners Have Speech and Language Disorders?   66

What Are Some of the Causes of Speech and Language Disorders?   66

Selected Characteristics of Learners with Speech and Language Disorders   66

Learners with Emotional or Behavioral Disorders   67

Defining Emotional or Behavioral Disorders   69

Classification of Learners with Emotional or Behavioral Disorders   69

How Many Learners Exhibit Emotional or Behavioral Disorders?   70

What Are Some of the Causes of Emotional or Behavioral Disorders?   71

Selected Learning and Behavioral Characteristics of Learners with Emotional or Behavioral Disorders   71

Learners with Attention Deficit Hyperactivity Disorder   72

Defining Attention Deficit Hyperactivity Disorder   73

How Many Learners Have Attention Deficit Hyperactivity Disorder?   74

What Are Some of the Causes of Attention Deficit Hyperactivity Disorder?   74

Selected Learning and Behavioral Characteristics of Learners with Attention Deficit Hyperactivity Disorder   75

Learners with Gifts and Talents   77

Defining Giftedness   77

How Many Learners Are Gifted and Talented?   78

What Are Some of the Causes of Giftedness and Talent?   78

Selected Learning and Behavioral Characteristics of Learners with Gifts and Talents   79

Summary of Selected Learning and Behavioral Characteristics   79

Thematic Summary   81

Making Connections for Inclusive Teaching   81

Learning Activities   81
Looking at the Standards   82
Key Concepts and Terms   83
References   83

CHAPTER 4

Today's Learners II: Students with Low Incidence Disabilities and Other Special Needs   87

Learners with Hearing Impairments   89
  Defining Hearing Impairments   89
  Classification of Learners with Hearing Impairments   89
  How Many Learners Are Hearing Impaired?   91
  What Are Some of the Causes of Hearing Impairment?   92
  Selected Learning and Behavioral Characteristics of Learners with Hearing Impairment   93
Learners with Visual Impairments   94
  Defining Visual Impairments   94
  Classification of Learners with Visual Impairments   94
  How Many Learners Are Visually Impaired?   95
  What Are Some of the Causes of Visual Impairment?   95
  Selected Learning and Behavioral Characteristics of Learners with Visual Impairment   96
Learners with Autism Spectrum Disorders   97
  Defining Autism Spectrum Disorders   98
  How Many Learners Exhibit Autism Spectrum Disorders?   99
  What Are Some of the Causes of Autism Spectrum Disorders?   99
  Selected Learning and Behavioral Characteristics of Learners with Autism Spectrum Disorders   100
Learners with Physical Disabilities, Health Disabilities, or Traumatic Brain Injury   100
  Defining Physical Disabilities, Health Disabilities, and Traumatic Brain Injury   101
  Conditions Associated with Physical and Health Disabilities   102
  How Many Learners Have Physical Disabilities, Health Disabilities, or Traumatic Brain Injury?   107
  What Are Some of the Causes of Physical Disabilities, Health Disabilities, and Traumatic Brain Injury?   107
  Selected Learning and Behavioral Characteristics of Learners with Physical Disabilities, Health Disabilities, or Traumatic Brain Injury   108
Learners Who Are Culturally and Linguistically Diverse   110
  Terminology of Cultural Differences   111
  Bilingual Education: Concepts and Characteristics   112
  Cultural and Linguistic Diversity and Special Education   112
Learners Who Are at Risk for Failure in School   114
  Defining At Risk   115
  Family Poverty   115
  Homelessness   116
  Child Abuse and Neglect   118
Summary of Selected Learning and Behavioral Characteristics   121
Thematic Summary   121
Making Connections for Inclusive Teaching   122
Learning Activities   122

Looking at the Standards   123
Key Concepts and Terms   124
References   124

CHAPTER 5

Collaboration and Cooperative Teaching: Tools for Teaching All Learners   127

Collaboration   128
   Collaboration Between General and Special Educators   129
   Collaborating with Paraprofessionals   130
   Collaborating with Parents/Families   132
Collaborative Consultation   136
Teaming Models   137
   Multidisciplinary Teams   138
   Interdisciplinary Teams   139
   Transdisciplinary Teams   139
Cooperative Teaching   140
   Cooperative Teaching Options   141
   Research Support   144
   Suggestions for Building Successful Cooperative Teaching Arrangements   144
Thematic Summary   148
Making Connections for Inclusive Teaching   149
Learning Activities   149
Looking at the Standards   149
Key Concepts and Terms   150
References   150

CHAPTER 6

Assistive Technologies and Innovative Learning Tools   153

Digital Native or Digital Immigrant?   155
Technology Myths and Facts   156
Technology for People with Disabilities   158
The Definition of Assistive Technology   160
Examples of Assistive Technology   160
   Communication Aids   161
   Daily Living Aids   161
   Ergonomic Aids   162
   Environmental Aids   162
   Sensory Aids   162
   Mobility and Transportation Aids   162
   Seating and Positioning Aids   163
   Sports, Recreation, and Leisure Aids   163
   Computer Access Aids   163
   Education and Learning Aids   163
Assistive Technology: Key to Accessing the General Education Curriculum   164
   Academic Outcomes   164
   Learner Needs and Preferences   165
   Differentiated Instruction and Assistive Technology   166
   Function over Disability   167

A Framework for Selecting Assistive Technology   167
    The Student   167
    The Environment(s)   167
    The Task(s)   168
    The Tool(s)   168
Active Learning through Innovative Technology   168
Social Software Tools   169
Visual and Media Literacy Tools   171
Opportunities through Technology   173
Thematic Summary   174
Making Connections for Inclusive Teaching   175
Learning Activities   175
Looking at the Standards   176
Key Concepts and Terms   176
References   177

CHAPTER 7

Universal Design for Learning   179

The Concept of Universal Design   181
    Background in Architecture   181
    The Seven Principles of Universal Design   182
    Universal Design Applications in Society   182
    Implications for Today's Classrooms   183
The Development of Universal Design for Learning   183
    Brain-Based Research: Recognition, Strategic, Affective Systems   184
    Cognitive-Social Learning Theories   185
    Multiple Intelligences and Learning Preferences   189
    Implications for Teaching and Learning   190
Three Essential Qualities of UDL: Representation, Engagement, and Expression   192
    Multiple Means of Representation   193
    Multiple Means of Engagement   195
    Multiple Means of Expression   196
UDL and Differentiated Instruction   199
The Benefits of Flexible Options   200
Thematic Summary   202
Making Connections for Inclusive Teaching   202
Learning Activities   203
Looking at the Standards   203
Key Concepts and Terms   204
References   204

CHAPTER 8

Assessing and Evaluating Learner Progress   207

The Importance of Classroom Assessment   208
    Large-Scale Assessments   208
    Ongoing Assessment   209
    UDL Applied to Assessment   210

Effective Classroom Assessment Approaches   210
  Approaches to Initial Assessment That Increase Learner Engagement   210
  Review of School Records   210
  Formal and Informal Assessment   210
  Applying Inventories   211
  Working Collaboratively   216
  Interpreting Standardized Tests   217
  Interpreting Behavior Rating Scales   218
  Positive Behavior Supports   218
  Functional Behavior Assessments   218
Assessment Organization   218
  Planning for Ongoing Assessment   218
  Formative Assessments   219
  Summative Assessments   219
  Organizational Systems for Assessment   219
Recording Assessments   220
  Probes   220
  Curriculum-Based Measurement   220
  Rubrics   220
Methods for Ongoing Assessment   222
  High-Tech and Low-Tech Materials   222
  Computerized Assessments   222
Multiple Means of Engagement in Assessment   223
  Fostering Motivation   223
  Providing Student Feedback   223
Multiple Means of Representation in Assessment   224
  High-Tech and Low-Tech Options   225
  Presenting Testing Accommodations   225
Student Expression in Assessment   225
  High-Tech and Low-Tech Options   226
  Multimedia Projects   227
  Portfolios   228
Final Thoughts   230
Thematic Summary   230
Making Connections for Inclusive Teaching   230
Learning Activities   231
Looking at the Standards   231
Key Concepts and Terms   232
References   232

CHAPTER 9

**Selecting Instructional Interventions for Teaching
All Learners   233**

Considering Stages of Learning in Intervention Selection   235
  Acquisition Stage   235
  Proficiency   236
  Maintenance   236
  Generalization   236
  Adaptation   237
Using Curricular Design Principles in Intervention Selection   238
  Begin with Big Ideas   238
  Activate Prior Knowledge   238

Integrate Learning Goals   239
Use Conspicuous Strategies   243
Apply Mediated Scaffolding   246
Provide Purposeful and Cumulative Review   250
Considering Specific Learning Domains in General Intervention Selection   252
Cognitive/Generalization   252
Giftedness   253
Language/Speech   254
Memory   255
Study Skills, Organization, and Test Taking   255
Attention Disorders/Hyperactivity/Impulsivity   257
Social/Emotional/Motivational Challenges   257
Physical/Motor/Sensory Challenges   258
Using Classroom Websites and Other Web Tools   260
Thematic Summary   261
Making Connections for Inclusive Teaching   261
Learning Activities   261
Looking at the Standards   262
Key Concepts and Terms   263
References   263

CHAPTER 10

Designing Learning that Works for All Students   267

Four Components of Universally Designed Curriculum   268
Designing Academic Learning for Access   269
Goals   269
Materials and Resources   277
Methods   278
Assessment   280
The UDL Lesson Plan   281
Designing Physical Learning Environments   281
Physical Environment Considerations   283
Designing Social Learning Environments   288
ACCESS to the Social Environment   289
Positive Behavior Support (PBS) and UDL   293
Using Adaptations to Support Universally Designed Learning Environments   294
Accommodations   294
Modifications   294
Collaboration in Planning Universally Designed Environments   296
Collaborative Planning and Teaching   296
Collaborative Problem Solving   296
Thematic Summary   297
Making Connections for Inclusive Teaching   298
Learning Activities   298
Looking at the Standards   299
Key Concepts and Terms   299
References   300

CHAPTER 11

Creating Literacy-Rich Environments for All Learners   301

Goals: Literacy Instruction Big Ideas   303

Phonemic Awareness, Phonics, and Word Recognition   304

Fluency with Text   305

Vocabulary   305

Comprehension   306

Writing/Spelling/Handwriting   306

Literacy Assessment   307

Formal Assessments   307

Reading Interest Inventories   307

Informal Assessments   309

Ongoing Assessments   310

Methods, Materials, and Resources that Promote Literacy for All Learners   310

Fostering Phonemic Awareness, Phonics, and Word Recognition   311

Increasing Fluency with Text   312

Developing Vocabulary   313

Building Comprehension   314

Assisting with Writing/Spelling/Handwriting   317

Applying UDL to Reading in the Content Areas   321

Eliminate the Reading Requirement Entirely   321

Modify the Reading Level of the Text   322

Adapt the Format of the Text/Print Material   323

Adapt the Presentation of the Text   323

Other Possible Barriers to Reading   325

Vision   325

Social Emotional   325

ADHD and Motivational   325

Academically Gifted   326

Fostering Literacy Collaboration   326

Thematic Summary   327

Making Connections for Inclusive Teaching   327

Learning Activities   327

Looking at the Standards   328

Key Concepts and Terms   329

References   329

CHAPTER 12

Developing an Understanding of Mathematics in All Learners   331

Establish Learning Goals: Big Ideas in Mathematics Instruction   333

Problem Solving   333

Mathematic Communication   334

Numbers and Operations   334

Algebra   335

Geometry and Spatial Sense   336

Measurement   336

Data Analysis and Probability   337

Assessment of Mathematics   337
    Formal Assessment   337
    Informal Assessment   338
**Methods, Materials, and Resources that Promote Mathematics for
All Learners   339**
    Problem Solving   341
    Communication of Mathematic Ideas   342
    Numbers and Operations   344
    Algebra   348
    Geometry and Spatial Sense   352
    Measurement   354
    Data Analysis and Probability   357
Fostering Collaboration in Mathematics Instruction   359
Thematic Summary   360
Making Connections for Inclusive Teaching   360
Learning Activities   360
Looking at the Standards   361
Key Concepts and Terms   362
References   362

CHAPTER 13

Teaching Critical Content in Science and Social Studies to All Learners   365

Challenges for Diverse Learners in Science and Social Studies   367
Establishing Learning Goals   368
    Focusing on Big Ideas in Science   368
    Focusing on Big Ideas in Social Studies   370
Assessing Science and Social Studies Content Areas   371
    Using Rubrics   372
    Applying UDL to Science and Social Studies Assessments   373
Planning Instruction   375
    Brainstorming with a Graphic Organizer   375
    Differentiating Instruction   376
    Identifying Methods, Tools, Materials, and Resources   377
    Preparing Lessons   379
Varying Representation in Science and Social Studies Instruction   384
    Implementing Inquiry-Based Instruction   384
    Using an Activities-Oriented Approach   384
    Providing Field Trips and Community-Based Experiences   385
    Working with Vocabulary and Readability   385
    Applying Memory Strategies   386
Increasing Engagement in Science and Social Studies   388
    Implementing Cooperative Learning   388
    Involving Peers   389
Expanding Expression Opportunities in Science and Social Studies   391
    Providing Opportunities to Practice with Support   391
    Offering Flexible Ways to Demonstrate Skill   391
Making Adaptations   392
    Considering the Social and Physical Environment   392
    Considering the Academic Environment   393

Fostering Collaboration in Science and Social Studies Instruction   395
  Collaborative Planning   395
  Co-teaching   395
  Building Community Support   396
Thematic Summary   396
Making Connections for Inclusive Teaching   396
Learning Activities   397
Looking at the Standards   397
Key Concepts and Terms   398
References   398

CHAPTER 14

Selecting Behavioral Supports for All Learners   401

Establish Learning Goals: Big Ideas for Behavioral Support   403
  Teacher Expectations and Challenging Behaviors   403
  Students with Exceptionalities and Other Diverse Learners   403
  Multiple Meanings of Challenging Behavior   405
  Using Positive Behavior Support   406
Assessment of Behavior   407
  Targeting the Behavior   408
  Tracking the Behavior   408
  Recording Behavior   409
  Analyzing Behavior   413
Methods, Materials, and Resources that Promote Positive Behavior for All Learners   414
  Understanding Terminology   414
  Increasing Appropriate Behavior   415
  Decreasing Inappropriate Behavior   417
  Teaching New Behavior   420
  Maintenance and Generalization   423
  Peers and School Personnel   424
  Collaborating with Parents   425
  Culturally Diverse Families   426
Summary—Putting It All Together   428
Thematic Summary   430
Making Connections for Inclusive Teaching   430
Learning Activities   431
Looking at the Standards   432
Key Concepts and Terms   432
References   433

Appendix A   Interstate New Teacher Assessment and Support Consortium (INTASC) Standards   435

Appendix B   Council for Exceptional Children Knowledge and Skill Base Standards for All Entry-Level Special Education Teachers   436

Glossary   442

Index   451

Preface

Recent legislative enactments and legal imperatives have resulted in a growing number of students with a broad range of special needs seeking services in general education classrooms. Because of this growing national trend, general educators are confronted with creating learning environments that are responsive to the needs of *all* learners. Success in this endeavor calls for, among other factors, a well-prepared teacher workforce. Regrettably, some general educators feel inadequately prepared to meet the needs of an increasingly diverse population of learners, a group that often includes not only pupils with disabilities but also individuals who are gifted or talented, those at risk for school failure, and students from culturally and linguistically diverse backgrounds. In addition to a changing clientele, teachers are encountering demands for greater accountability for the performance of *all* learners. Consequently, increased attention is being focused on what students are being taught as well as how they are being instructed.

Our purpose in writing this book is to provide general educators (as well as special educators) with practical, researched-based teaching and learning strategies that form an overall framework for effective instruction and management appropriate to the realities and challenges of schools in the 21st century. We have chosen to adopt a universal design approach for accomplishing this task. Unlike other books, *Teaching in Today's Inclusive Classrooms* focuses on best practices appropriate to teaching *all* children in general education classrooms. Our book embraces a teaching philosophy of "Teachers teach students, not disability labels"; "If a child doesn't learn the way we teach, then we better teach the way the child learns"; and "Good teaching is good teaching." Universal design reflects this belief. Simply stated, our aim is to offer preservice educators and other professionals working in our schools a foundation for creating effective co-teaching (collaborative) situations by examining such critical variables as teaming, common planning, and a shared responsibility for instruction and assessment. *Teaching in Today's Inclusive Classrooms* considers the integration of teaching skills, instructional content, and the individuals (for example, teachers, paraprofessionals, and parents) needed to successfully sustain learning environments that meet the needs of every pupil.

The six chapters of Part I, Foundations for Educating All Learners, establishes the groundwork for understanding the challenges and opportunities afforded educators in today's classrooms. This section of the book addresses historical and contemporary perspectives on teaching, the importance of teaming and collaboration, partnerships with parents, and the vital role of technology as an instructional tool. Part I also provides a description of students with disabilities and those with gifts and talents, pupils who are culturally or linguistically diverse, and learners considered to be at risk for success in school. Collectively these chapters secure a solid foundation for Parts II and III.

Part II, Designing Curriculum for Teaching All Learners, consisting of four chapters, introduces the reader to the concept of Universal Design for Learning (UDL). The UDL framework, which is based on principles from the field of architecture, holds great promise for moving schools forward in the 21st century. It provides teachers with a flexible, "hands-on" structure for planning effective ways to meet the standards-based goals of today's schools. Part II applies UDL principles to assessment, teaching methodology, and environmental design. This design addresses academic, physical, and social environments that can be prepared "up front" to maximize access to the curriculum for *all* students.

The four chapters of Part III, Effective Instructional Practices for All Learners, offer research-based interventions and examples for teaching reading, mathematics, science and social studies, as well as social/behavioral support. These principles and techniques can be applied to other content areas as well. Sample lesson plans using UDL applications are included. These examples also demonstrate how instruction can be differentiated and how individual needs can be planned for and implemented by applying UDL principles. These guiding principles can be applied across all grade levels. The interventions highlighted in these chapters will be helpful to schools implementing Response-to-Intervention practices. The connections are seamless.

Some of the unique features found in *Teaching in Today's Inclusive Classrooms*, include:

- Teaching All Students—a selection of instructional tips, strategies, and practical information
- Universal Design for Learning—the three elements of UDL are color coded and highlighted consistently throughout Parts II and III to show how they can positively impact goal setting, planning, assessment, and implementation of effective instruction that can meet the needs of all learners
- Teacher Voices—practical ideas, suggestions, and instructional commentary provided by award-winning classroom teachers
- Chapter content aligned with INTASC (Interstate New Teacher Assessment and Support Consortium) and CEC (Council for Exceptional Children) professional standards
- A sample IEP (individualized education program)

Acknowledgments

Writing a textbook is a tremendous undertaking, a task that requires immense teamwork and collaboration (along with small dose of insanity). We are especially grateful to Tara Jeffs, East Carolina University, who authored the chapter on assistive technology. We also deeply appreciate the valuable contribution of Jennifer Bautel Williams, East Carolina University, who wrote the assessment chapter. Lastly, we acknowledge the expertise and assistance of Chan Evans, East Carolina University, who collaborated with the second author on several chapters found in Parts II and III, especially Chapter 14. The contributions and talents of these three professionals immeasurably added to the significance of our book. We are also indebted to our students who provided constant feedback, reality checks, and creative ideas and suggestions.

We are also grateful to those individuals who reviewed the many drafts of this work. Their expertise and guidance along with their thoughtful suggestions contributed to a book that we are very proud of. We deeply appreciate the invaluable assistance of the reviewers:

Sarah Williams, East Carolina University
Robbie Ludy, Buena Vista University
Liz Kramer, Florida International University
Sandy Ritter, California State University, Northridge
John Somers, University of Indianapolis
Sue Houdyshell, Virginia Commonwealth University
Nancy Yost, Indiana University of Pennsylvania
Shirley McKinney, Arizona State University
Delar Singh, Eastern Connecticut State University
Maurice Miller, Indiana State University
Elizabeth Ankeny, St. Cloud State University
Mary Hilsenbeck, University of Louisville
Billie Friedland, Delaware State University

Gay Goodman, University of Houston
Deborah Webster, Cleveland State University
L. Cheri Bradley, Fairmont State University
Patrice Hallock, Utica College
Diane Taylor, Tarleton State University
Melanie Presnell, Florida State University
Anita Solarski, University of West Florida
Frank Lilly, California State University, Sacramento

We would like to thank the outstanding teachers who contributed to the "Teacher Voices" sections and lesson plans. Some of the greatest joys of teaching can be found by surrounding oneself with "giants." These contributors are all truly giants in this profession and we are honored to work with them and showcase their ideas and efforts. Each one of them is selflessly dedicated to helping each and every student reach his or her full potential.

We would be remiss if we did not thank the talented editorial and production team at Wadsworth/Cengage Learning who worked with us to bring our ideas and vision to life. The leadership, direction, and belief in this project exhibited by our editor, Chris Shortt, is gratefully acknowledged. We also wish to sincerely thank our development editor, Tangelique Williams, who worked with us from the very beginning. Her expertise, pleasant demeanor, insightful observations, and attention to detail helped make this book a reality. We tip our hats to you, Tangelique! We were also very fortunate to work with an outstanding copy editor, Kathy Finch, who had the difficult task of keeping us grammatically and stylistically accurate and whose judicious editing and meticulous attention to detail ensured the readability of our book. We also thank Ashley Cronin, Technology Project Manager; Caitlin Cox, Assistant Editor; Janice Bockelman and Linda Stewart, Editorial Assistants; Tanya Nigh, Production Manager; and Kara Parsons, Marketing Manager.

Lastly, this book would not be possible if it weren't for the unwavering support of our families. Over the past three years they were, at times, ignored because of "the book." Their understanding, encouragement, patience, and love helped make this book possible. Our families truly are the unnamed coauthors.

LifeStock/PhotoSpin

1

Teaching in Today's Classrooms

Schooling in America
Learners in Need of Special Services
By the Numbers: A Quick Look
Service Delivery Options: Where Children with Special Needs are Served
Educational Placements
A Cascade of Service Delivery Options
A Contemporary Challenge
Inclusionary Practices and Thinking

Summary of Key Litigation and Legislation
Key Judicial Decisions
Individuals with Disabilities Education Act: 1975–1997
Section 504 of the Rehabilitation Act of 1973
Americans with Disabilities Act

Educational Reform: Standards-Based Education
No Child Left Behind Act of 2001
Individuals with Disabilities Education Improvement Act of 2004

Introducing Universal Design for Learning

Learning Outcomes

After studying this chapter, you should be able to:

- Trace the evolution of services for children with special needs.
- Describe the concept of least restrictive environment and placement options for educating students with special needs.
- Explain the role that the courts have played in the education of children with special needs.
- Summarize the major provisions contained in the Individuals with Disabilities Education Act and IDEA 2004.
- Discuss the impact of the Americans with Disabilities Act and Section 504 on contemporary society.
- Describe how the educational reform movement has affected the education of children with special needs and the preparation of teachers.
- Explain the concept of universal design for learning (UDL).

Each and every one of us is a unique human being. Some of our differences are obvious like the length and color of our hair or whether we are considered to be tall or short. These, and other features, contribute to making us distinct and interesting individuals. Some aspects of our individuality, however, are not easily recognizable; for instance, our ability to solve quadratic equations or throw a football in a perfect spiral. Of course, some characteristics are more important than others. Most people would attach greater significance to intellectual abilities than eye color. Luckily, the recognition and appreciation of individual difference is one of the cornerstones of contemporary society.

Most of us would consider ourselves to be normal or typical (however defined); yet, for millions of school-age children and adolescents this label does not apply. They have been identified and/or perceived to be "different." These differences might be the result of behavioral deficiencies, language differences, intellectual abilities, one's cultural heritage, or sensory impairments, along with a host of other possible reasons. This textbook is about these individuals who compose today's student population. Although many children are viewed as typical, some pupils may require a special education, others may be at risk for learning difficulties, and still others might be seen as gifted or talented. Our goal is to assist you to in developing an understanding and an appreciation for *all* the learners you will encounter in the classrooms of the 21st century.

Finally, as you begin to read and learn about the children and young adults enrolled in our schools, you will notice we have purposefully adopted a people-first perspective when talking about individuals with disabilities or other special needs. We have deliberately chosen to focus on the person, not the disability or impairment. Thus, instead of describing an adolescent as a "retarded student," we will say a "student with mental retardation"; rather than an "at risk learner," we say a "learner who is at risk"; and finally, rather than a "gifted child," we say a "child who is gifted." This writing style reflects more than just a change in word order, it reflects an attitude and a belief in the value, dignity, and potential found within all of our students. The individuals described in this book are first and foremost people, as educators we need to focus on their assets and abilities not their limitations or deficits.

Schooling in America

If a teacher who retired in the early 1970s was to visit a classroom today, he or she would be truly astonished by the diversity of students. Our schools are a microcosm of the changing face of American society. A diverse population of learners is no longer the exception, today it is the norm. It is not uncommon to find over 100 languages spoken in our schools, the integration of students with disabilities in general education classrooms (Council for Exceptional Children, 2005), or pupils whose cultural beliefs and practices vary significantly in important ways from mainstream American customs. One of the challenges confronting today's teachers and other professionals is how best to meet the needs of a changing and expanding population of learners. We think this growing diversity is something to be valued and appreciated, an opportunity for students to respect and understand their classmates for their differences.

Public education in the United States, in contrast to other nations, is an amazing system. It is purposely designed to provide educational opportunities to all youth. Yet, this was not always the case, exclusionary practices rather than inclusionary policies characterized public education in this country for many decades. Generally speaking, from a historical perspective, publicly funded education was provided only to a rather exclusive group of students—white males from affluent families. Public schooling was usually unavailable to other children. Females, for instance, did not routinely attend school until the early 1900s. Furthermore, it was not until the second half of the 19th century and the early years of the 20th century, that classes for students with special needs began to appear in public schools (Gargiulo, 2009). Greater access to public education for youth viewed as "different" (the poor, those with disabilities, or non-English speaking children) slowly came about due to the efforts of enlightened educational reformers, parental advocacy, and political activism coupled with litigation and federal legislation.

Teachers, today, are charged with providing effective instruction to a diverse population of learners who bring to the classroom a wide variety of cultures, languages, learning styles, and abilities as well as disabilities. This diversity heightens the need for inclusionary practices coupled with instructional strategies capable of meeting the compelling and oftentimes complex needs of the full range of students attending our schools (Council for Exceptional Children, 2005).

Learners in Need of Special Services

As we stated previously, diversity in our classrooms is the norm rather than the exception. Probably the largest group of diverse learners are **students with disabilities**. According to the Individuals with Disabilities Education Improvement Act of 2004 (PL 108-446), commonly called IDEA 2004, pupils with disabilities include individuals who exhibit

> mental retardation, hearing impairment (including deafness), speech or language impairment, visual impairments (including blindness), emotional disturbance, orthopedic impairments, autism, traumatic brain injury, other health impairments, or specific learning disabilities. (Sec. 602 (3) (A) (i))

We will talk about these disability categories in greater detail in Chapters 3 and 4. Table 1.1 provides a brief description of the various disabilities recognized by the federal government.

Of course, children with disabilities (in addition to their typical classmates) are not the only types of children with special needs found in today's classrooms. Three other groups of learners are also common—students who are gifted and talented; culturally and linguistically diverse individuals; and pupils who are at risk for future learning difficulties, school failure, and/or becoming a school dropout. Let us briefly examine each group:

- **Students who are gifted and talented.** Pupils who are gifted and talented are not considered disabled but are viewed as *exceptional* because of their overall intellectual abilities, creativity, leadership abilities, athleticism, and/or talents in the visual and performing arts (Gargiulo, 2009). Even though learning problems are generally not an issue for these students, they do require specialized and effective instruction if their full potential and abilities are to be expressed. Interestingly, pupils who are gifted and talented are not included in federal special education legislation (review Table 1.1). Many states, however, have enacted legislation providing for the identification and education of children with special gifts and talents.
- **Students who are culturally and linguistically diverse.** This group of learners generally includes pupils whose values, attitudes, norms, folkways, traditions, and belief systems are in contrast to mainstream U.S. culture. These students may or may not speak English. Regrettably, in too many instances, culturally and linguistically diverse children are thought to be less capable than their classmates. As educators working in increasingly diverse schools, we must model respect for and sensitivity to the cultural and linguistic characteristics represented by our students and their families.
- **Students who are at risk.** Unfortunately, some students encounter life experiences that make them more likely than their classmates to fail in school. Although these pupils are ineligible for special education services, their success in school is often jeopardized by a variety of sociocultural factors. These problems, which are frequently interrelated, may include

Table 1.1	Federal Disability Categories
Category	**Brief Description**
Autism	A life-long disorder significantly affecting communication, social interactions, and learning. Onset typically prior to age 3. Repetitive and stereotyped movements are common.
Deafness	A hearing loss that is so severe that the individual experiences difficulty in processing linguistic information, with or without amplification. Loss may range from slight to profound; adversely affects educational performance.
Deaf-blindness	Significant and simultaneous loss of hearing and vision; major impact on learning, communication, and other developmental needs.
Emotional disturbance (ED)	Long-term difficulties with interpersonal relationships, display of inappropriate behaviors or feelings, pervasive unhappiness, a tendency to develop physical symptoms or fears associated with personal or school problems. Term also includes schizophrenia. Educational performance is adversely affected.
Hearing impairment (HI)	Individuals with permanent or fluctuating hearing loss to such a degree that educational performance is negatively impacted.
Mental retardation (MR)	Significantly subaverage cognitive abilities coupled with impairments in adaptive behavior. Onset prior to age 18. Limitations may range from mild to profound.
Multiple disabilities	Simultaneous occurrence of two or more disabilities, primary impairment is unable to be identified (e.g., mental retardation and cerebral palsy). Term does not include deaf-blindness.
Orthopedic impairment (OI)	Typically associated with physical conditions that affect movement or motor activities. Disability adversely affects educational performance.
Other health impairment (OHI)	Chronic or acute health issues that impact a pupil's strength, alertness, and vitality. Examples range from diabetes to leukemia to attention deficit hyperactivity disorder (ADHD).
Specific learning disability (SLD)	A controversial definition, generally refers to difficulty in processing information to such a degree that many areas of school performance are negatively affected. Discrepancy between achievement and assumed potential. Typically defined by eliminating other etiological possibilities for learning problems.
Speech or language impairment	A communication disorder affecting, in some instances, the production of speech or a significant limitation in using oral language as a means of communication. Stuttering and articulation problems are but two examples.
Traumatic brain injury (TBI)	Acquired trauma to the brain typically associated with accidents or injury. Open or closed head injuries associated with learning, language, behavior, and/or social skill deficits. Impact on classroom performance may range from mild to significant.
Visual impairment (VI)	A loss of vision that even often correction adversely affects educational performance. Term includes persons who are blind or partially sighted (capable of reading large print).
Developmental delay (DD)	Although considered a disability category, the federal government did not define this term. A state-specific definition applied to children 3–9 years of age. In many instances, a quantitative definition based on standardized developmental assessments is used.

domestic violence, homelessness, exposure to drug and alcohol abuse, poverty, and child abuse to mention only a few risk factors. It is important to note that exposure to these conditions does *not* automatically guarantee learning or behavioral problems in school; only that the probability of experiencing difficulties is heightened.

Many of the children we have just identified will primarily be educated in the general education classroom. This means that the general educator, often working in conjunction with other school personnel, must develop and implement instructional programs designed to meet the needs of a very heterogeneous group of learners. One of the purposes of this book is to help you successfully meet this challenge.

By the Numbers: A Quick Look

We have argued that the number of students with special needs in our classrooms is growing. Although statistics don't always paint a complete picture, the following information gives a hint of the changing demographics confronting educators and policy makers alike.

- Almost 6,082,000 students, ages 6–21, were receiving a special education during the 2006–2007 school year. These pupils represent approximately 11 percent of the public school enrollment in the United States (U.S. Department of Education, 2008). Over the past decade the number of individuals receiving a special education has increased by 16 percent.
- Educators believe that approximately 3–5 percent of the school-age population is gifted or talented. Of course, the number of students identified as gifted or talented depends on the definition of giftedness used by each state (Gargiulo, 2009).
- By the year 2020, students of color are projected to make up almost half of all school-age youth (Gollnick & Chinn, 2009).
- About one in five residents, or approximately 19 percent of the U.S. population over the age of 5, speaks a language other than English at home (U.S. Census Bureau, 2007).
- Approximately 11 percent of young adults (ages 16–24) in the United States do not possess a high school diploma (National Center for Education Statistics, 2007).
- In 2004 almost 20 percent of children under the age of 6 lived in poverty (Children's Defense Fund, 2005).
- More than 900,000 children, or one youngster every 35 seconds, was abused or neglected in 2003 (Children's Defense Fund, 2005).

Service Delivery Options: Where Children with Special Needs Are Served

With such diversity evident in today's classrooms, where are students with special needs typically served? As you will soon see, this is not an easy question to answer. In fact, the response to this inquiry has evolved over several decades. Generally speaking, the majority of learners with special needs are being educated in general education classrooms; this includes pupils with special abilities as well as the their classmates with disabilities, those children viewed as being at risk for school failure, and students who are culturally and linguistically diverse.

We have chosen to frame our discussion about where children with special needs are served around individuals receiving a special education. We adopted this tactic for two reasons. First, students with disabilities represent the largest population of learners with special needs. Second, it is because of the advocacy efforts, litigation, and legislation on behalf of students with disabilities that the right to be educated in what is commonly called the **least restrictive environment (LRE)** was secured. Educationally speaking, this usually means the general education classroom. It is because of these efforts, that many other learners with special needs are now routinely educated in the general education classroom.

The issue of appropriate placement of children with disabilities has generated considerable controversy and debate. In fact, it has been a point of contention among special educators for almost 40 years. Federal legislation mandates that services be provided to students in the least restrictive setting. The idea of least restrictive environment is a relative concept; it must be determined individually for each pupil. We interpret this principle to mean that students with disabilities should be educated in the setting that most closely approximates the general education classroom *and* still meets the unique needs of the individual. For a growing

Creatas/Jupiter Images

Federal legislation requires that pupils with disabilities be educated in the least restrictive environment.

number of students, this setting is the general education classroom. The concept of LRE calls for maximum opportunity for meaningful involvement and participation with classmates who are nondisabled. One of its inherent difficulties is the required balancing of maximum integration with the delivery of an education appropriate to their unique needs. It is important to remember that the degree of involvement and participation is determined individually for each pupil. No one arrangement is appropriate for each and every child (Gargiulo, 2009).

Educational Placements

The federal government acknowledges that children with disabilities are unique learners, thus requiring educational placements that are appropriate to their individual needs. The U.S. Department of Education annually monitors the various settings in which pupils with disabilities receive a special education. Figure 1.1 illustrates

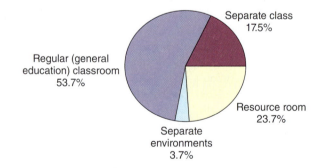

Separate class
17.5%

Regular (general education) classroom
53.7%

Resource room
23.7%

Separate environments
3.7%

Figure 1.1 **Percentage of Children with Disabilities Served in Various Educational Settings**

Notes: Data are for students ages 6–21 enrolled in special education during the 2006–2007 school year. Information based on data from the 50 states, District of Columbia, Puerto Rico, and the outlying areas. Separate environments include students receiving an education in residential facilities, separate schools, or hospital/homebound programs.

Source: Adapted from U.S. Department of Education. (2008). *IDEA data.* Available at https://www.ideadata.org/PartBReport.asp

the percentage of students in each of the four educational environments currently recognized by the federal government.

A Cascade of Service Delivery Options[1]

As we have just seen, the federal government recognizes that no one educational setting is appropriate for meeting the needs of all children with disabilities. Effective delivery of a special education requires an array or continuum of placement possibilities customized to the individual requirements of each pupil. The concept of a continuum of educational services has been part of the fabric of American special education for almost four decades. Reynolds (1962) originally described the concept of a range of placement options in 1962. His thinking was later elaborated on and expanded by Deno (1970), who constructed a model offering a "cascade" or continuum of settings. A traditional view of service delivery options is portrayed in Figure 1.2.

In this model, the general education classroom is viewed as the most normalized or typical setting; consequently, the greatest number of students are served in this environment. This placement would be considered the least restrictive option. Deviation from the general education classroom should occur only when it is educationally necessary for the pupil to receive an appropriate education. Each higher level depicted in Figure 1.2 represents a progressively more restrictive setting. Movement up the hierarchy generally leads to the delivery of more intensive services to children with more severe disabilities, who are fewer in number. However, intensive supports are now being provided in general education classrooms with increasing frequency. Environments at the upper levels are considered to be the most restrictive and least normalized; yet, as we will see shortly, they may be the most appropriate placement for a particular individual.

As originally conceived, the natural flow of this cascade of service delivery options would be in a downward movement from more restrictive settings to those viewed as least restrictive, such as the general education classroom with or without support services. Contemporary thinking, however, suggests that pupils should begin in the general education classroom and ascend the model, reaching a

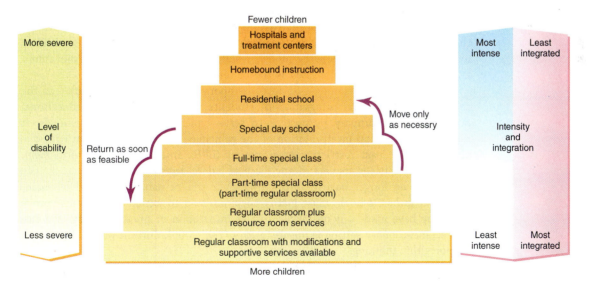

Figure 1.2 A Traditional View of Service Delivery Options
Source: Adapted from S. Graves, R. Gargiulo, and L. Sluder, *Young Children: An Introduction to Early Childhood Education* (St. Paul, MN: West, 1996), p. 398.

[1]From R. Gargiulo, *Special Education in Contemporary Society*, 3rd ed. (Thousand Oaks, CA: Sage, 2009).

level that meets their unique needs. A key feature of this model, too often overlooked, is that a particular placement is only temporary; flexibility or freedom of movement is what makes this model work. The settings must be envisioned as fluid rather than rigid. As the needs of the pupil change, so should the environment; this is why there is an array of service delivery possibilities.

A Contemporary Challenge

At the present time, the field of special education is confronting the challenge of calls for greater inclusion of individuals with disabilities into all aspects of society, especially educational programs. Simply stated, some advocates for people with disabilities (and some parents as well) dismiss the long-standing concept of a continuum of service delivery possibilities and argue that all pupils with disabilities, regardless of the type or severity of their impairment, should be educated in general education classrooms at neighborhood schools. They argue further that students should be served on the basis of their chronological age rather than academic ability or mental age. This is truly an explosive proposal. The debate surrounding this issue is an emotionally charged one with great potential for polarizing the field of special education as other professionals, advocates and parents argue fervently against this thinking. According to Gargiulo and Kilgo (2005), supporters of this movement see it as the next great revolution in special education, whereas opponents consider it the start of a return to the "dark ages" of special education—the era before legislation was enacted protecting the educational rights of learners with disabilities. We suspect that the truth lies somewhere between these two extremes.

The intensity of this debate is fueled by several factors, one of which is the inconsistent use of terminology. As frequently happens in arguments, people are often saying the same thing but using different words. Therefore, we offer the following interpretations of key terms frequently encountered in describing this movement.

Mainstreaming

The first potentially confusing term is **mainstreaming**, which first appeared on the educational scene more than 30 years ago. It evolved from an argument put forth by Dunn (1968) who, in a classic essay, questioned the pedagogical wisdom of serving children with mild mental retardation in self-contained classrooms, which was then common practice. Other professionals soon joined with Dunn in his call for a more integrated service delivery model, resulting in the beginning of a movement away from isolated special classes as the placement of choice.

We define mainstreaming—or, in contemporary language, **integration**—as the social and instructional integration of students with disabilities into educational programs whose primary purpose is to serve typically developing individuals. It represents a common interpretation of the principle of educating children with disabilities in the least restrictive environment (LRE). Interestingly, the term *mainstreaming* itself never appears in any piece of federal legislation.

Parents no longer have to prove that their son or daughter should be mainstreamed; rather, schools must justify their position to exclude. They must prove that they have made a good faith effort at integration or present strong evidence that an inclusionary setting is unsatisfactory (Yell, 2006). Current federal legislation supports this thinking.

Mainstreaming must provide the student with an appropriate education based on the unique needs of the child. It is our opinion that policy makers never envisioned that mainstreaming would be interpreted to mean that all children with special needs must be placed in integrated placements; to do so would mean abandoning the idea of determining the most appropriate placement for a particular child. IDEA 2004 (to be discussed shortly) clearly stipulates that, to the maximum extent appropriate, children with disabilities are to be educated with their typical peers. We interpret this provision to mean that, for some individuals, an integrated or main-stream setting, even with supplementary aids and services, might be an inappropriate placement in light of the child's unique characteristics. A least restrictive environment does not automatically mean placement with typical learners. As educators, we need to make the distinction between appropriateness and restrictiveness.

Least Restrictive Environment

Least restrictive environment (LRE) is a legal term often interpreted to say individuals with disabilities are to be educated in environments as close as possible to the general education classroom setting. An LRE is not a place but a concept.

Determination of the LRE is made individually for each child. An appropriate placement for one student could quite easily be inappropriate for another. The LRE is based on the pupil's educational needs, not on his or her disability. It applies equally to children of school age and to preschoolers. Even infants and toddlers with disabilities are required by law (PL 102-119) to have services delivered in normalized settings.

Inherent within the mandate of providing a special education and/or related services within the LRE is the notion of a continuum of service delivery possibilities. Figure 1.2 reflects varying degrees of restrictiveness, or amount of available contact with typical learners. Being only with children with disabilities is considered restrictive; placement with peers without disabilities is viewed as least restrictive. As we ascend the continuum, the environments provide fewer and fewer opportunities for interaction with typically developing agemates—hence the perception of greater restrictiveness. Despite a strong preference for association with students who are typical, this desire must be balanced by the requirement of providing an education appropriate to the unique needs of the individual. Consequently, an integrative environment may not always be the most appropriate placement option. Each situation must be individually assessed and decided on a case-by-case basis. The educational setting must meet the needs of the learner. The philosophy of the LRE should guide rather than dictate educational decision-making.

We recognize, as do many other special educators, that maximum integration with typically developing children is highly desirable and should be one of our major goals. The question is when, where, with whom, and to what extent are individuals with disabilities to be integrated.

Regular Education Initiative

The third concept that requires our attention is the **regular education initiative**, or as it is commonly called, **REI**. REI is an important link in the evolution of the full inclusion movement. The term was introduced in 1986 by former Assistant Secretary of Education (Office of Special Education and Rehabilitative Services) Madeline Will, who questioned the legitimacy of special education as a separate system of education and called for a restructuring of the relationship between general (regular) and special education. She endorsed the idea of shared responsibility—a partnership between general and special education resulting in a coordinated delivery system (Will, 1986b). Will recommended that general educators assume greater responsibility for students with disabilities. She envisioned a meaningful partnership whereby general and special educators would "cooperatively assess the educational needs of students with learning problems and cooperatively develop effective educational strategies for meeting those needs" (Will, 1986a, p. 415). Will (1986b) also believes that educators must "visualize a system that will bring the program to the child rather than one that brings the child to the program" (p. 21). As special educators, most of us can embrace this idea. Few professionals would dispute that the delivery of special education services would be significantly enhanced if there were greater coordination, cooperation, and collaboration between general and special educators.

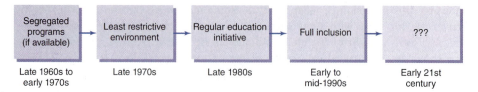

Figure 1.3 The Evolution of Placement Options for Children with Disabilities

Source: R. Gargiulo and J. Kilgo, *Young Children with Special Needs: An Introduction to Early Childhood Special Education,* 2nd ed. (Clifton Park, NY: Delmar, 2005), p. 165.

Full Inclusion

We see the movement toward **full inclusion** as an extension of REI and earlier thinking about where children with disabilities should be educated. Full inclusion represents the latest trend in meeting the requirement of providing an education in the least restrictive environment (Bennett, DeLuca, & Bruns, 1997). Figure 1.3 illustrates the evolution of this thought process.

Full inclusion is a potentially explosive issue, with vocal supporters as well as detractors. It has emerged as one of the most controversial and complex subjects in the field of special education. As with other controversial topics, an agreed upon definition is difficult to develop. We offer the following succinct interpretation: Full inclusion is a belief that *all* children with disabilities should be taught exclusively (with appropriate supports) in general education classrooms at neighborhood schools—that is, in the same school and age/grade appropriate classrooms they would attend if they were not disabled.

Although the trend in judicial interpretations is tilted toward inclusionary practices, the LRE mandate does *not* require that all pupils be educated in general education classrooms or at their neighborhood schools. The framers of IDEA never envisioned, according to Kauffman (1995), that the general education classroom located in a neighborhood school would be the least restrictive setting for all pupils. In fact, policy makers believed that a cascade of placement options would be required in order to provide an appropriate education for students with disabilities.

Advocates of full inclusion (Kennedy & Horn, 2004; Petterson & Hittie, 2003; Sailor, 2002) argue that the present pullout system of serving students with special needs is ineffective. They contend that children are labeled and stigmatized, their programming is frequently fragmented, and general educators often assume little or no ownership for students in special education (a "your" kids versus "my" kids attitude). Placement in a general education classroom, with a working partnership between special education teachers and general educators, would result in a better education for all pupils, not just those with special needs, and would occur within the context of the least restrictive environment.

When correctly instituted, full inclusion is characterized by its virtual invisibility. Students with disabilities are not segregated but dispersed into classrooms they would normally attend if they were not disabled. They are seen as full-fledged members of, not merely visitors to, the general education classroom. Special educators provide an array of services and supports in the general education classroom alongside their general education colleagues, often using strategies such as cooperative teaching in an effort to meet the needs of the pupils. Table 1.2 summarizes the key components of most models of full inclusion.

Inclusionary Practices and Thinking

In many instances, the general education classroom is becoming the placement of choice for a growing number of learners with special needs. A diverse learning community is no longer the exception but rather the norm. One result of the changing face or composition of our classrooms is the trend toward inclusion. Unfortunately, a clear understanding of this term has proven elusive. We simply see **inclusion** as

Table 1.2	Key Elements of Full Inclusion Models

- **"Homeschool" attendance.** Defined as the local school the child would attend if not disabled.
- **Natural proportion at the school site.** The percentage of children with special needs enrolled in a particular school is in proportion to the percentage of pupils with exceptionalities in the entire school district; in general education classes, this would mean approximately two to three students with disabilities.
- **Zero rejection.** All students are accepted at the local school, including those with severe impairments; pupils are not screened out or grouped separately because of their disability.
- **Age/grade-appropriate placement.** A full-inclusion model calls for serving children with special needs in general education classrooms according to their chronological age rather than basing services on the child's academic ability or mental age.
- **Site-based management or coordination.** Recent trends in school organizational reform suggest a movement away from central office administration for special education programs to one where the building principal (or other administrator) plays a large role in planning and administering programs for all children in the school.
- **Use of cooperative learning and peer instructional models.** Instructional practices that involve children learning in a cooperative manner rather than in a competitive fashion and using students to assist in the instruction of classmates with disabilities can be effective strategies for integrating exceptional learners in the general education classroom.

Source: R. Gargiulo, *Special Education in Contemporary Society*, 3rd ed. (Thousand Oaks, CA: Sage, 2009).

the movement toward, and the practice of, educating students with disabilities and other learners with exceptionalities in general education classrooms alongside their typical peers with appropriate supports and services provided as necessary. One of the underlying assumptions of inclusion is the belief that *all* students are part of or belong in the general education classroom. Yet, it is important to note,

> That the physical placement of students in general education classroom is not an end in and of itself but rather a means to an end. *Inclusion* does not refer to a physical space, it refers to a condition or state of being. The concept of inclusion implies a sense of belonging and acceptance. Hence, inclusion has more to do with how educators respond to individual differences than it has to do with specific instructional configurations . . . [Inclusion emphasizes] the creation of instructional environments that promote educational success and a sense of belonging for all students. (Voltz, Brazil, & Ford, 2001, p. 24)

Successful inclusion requires a new attitude or fresh thinking about how students with special needs should be educated.

Summary of Key Litigation and Legislation

Over the past several decades, the field of education, especially special education, has been gradually transformed and restructured, largely as a result of judicial action and legislative enactments. These two forces have been powerful tools in securing many of the benefits and educational rights presently enjoyed by pupils with disabilities and other students with special needs. Securing the opportunity for an education has been a slowly evolving process for students with disabilities. What is today seen as a fundamental right for these children was, at one time, viewed strictly as a privilege.

In the 1954 landmark school desegregation case, *Brown v. Board of Education of Topeka* (347 U.S. 483), the U.S. Supreme Court reasoned that it was unlawful to discriminate against a group of individuals for arbitrary reasons. The Court specifically ruled that separate schools for black and white students were inherently unequal, contrary to the Fourteenth Amendment, and thus unconstitutional. Furthermore, education was characterized as a fundamental function of government that should be afforded to all citizens on an equal basis. Though primarily recognized as striking down racial segregation, the thinking articulated in *Brown* had major implications for children with disabilities. Much of contemporary litigation and legislation affecting special education is legally, as well as morally, grounded in the precedents established by *Brown*.

iofoto/Fotolia

Students with disabilities as well as learners with other special needs have greatly benefited from judicial and legislative actions.

The movement to secure equal educational opportunity for children with disabilities was also aided by the U.S. civil rights movement of the 1960s. As Americans attempted to deal with issues of discrimination, inequality, and other social ills, advocates for individuals with disabilities also pushed for equal rights. Parental activism was ignited. Lawsuits were filed and legislation enacted primarily as a result of the untiring, vocal, collaborative efforts of parents and politically powerful advocacy groups. The success of these tactics was felt at the local, state, and eventually, national level.

It is exceedingly difficult to say which came first, litigation or legislation. Both of these forces have played major roles in the development of state and federal policy concerning special education. They enjoy a unique and almost symbiotic relationship—one of mutual interdependence. Litigation frequently leads to legislation, which in turn spawns additional judicial action as the courts interpret and clarify the law, which often leads to further legislation. Regardless of the progression, much of special education today has a legal foundation.

Key Judicial Decisions

Since the 1960s and early 1970s, a plethora of state and federal court decisions have helped to shape and define a wide range of issues affecting contemporary special education policies and procedures. Although a thorough review of this litigation is beyond the scope of this chapter, Table 1.3 summarizes, in chronological order, a few of the landmark cases affecting the field of special education. Several of the judicial remedies emanating from these lawsuits serve as cornerstones for both federal and state legislative enactments focusing on both students with disabilities and their classmates with special needs. As you will see shortly, many of today's accepted practices in special education, such as nondiscriminatory assessments and due process procedures, can trace their roots to various court decisions.

Individuals with Disabilities Education Act: 1975–1997

Federal legislative intervention in the lives of persons with disabilities is of relatively recent origin. Before the late 1950s and early 1960s, little federal attention was paid to citizens with special needs. When legislation was enacted, it primarily assisted specific groups of individuals, such as those who were deaf or mentally retarded. The past 30 years, however, have witnessed a flurry of legislative activity that has aided the growth of special education and provided educational benefits and other opportunities and rights to children and adults with disabilities. We will examine four public laws[2] that have dramatically affected the educational opportunities of infants, toddlers, preschoolers, school-age children, and young adults with disabilities. Our initial review will focus on PL 94-142, the Education for All Handicapped Children Act, or as it is now called, the Individuals with Disabilities Education Act (IDEA). This change in legislative titles resulted from the enactment on October 30, 1990, of PL 101-476, which will be reviewed later.

Public Law 94-142

The Individuals with Disabilities Education Act is viewed as a "Bill of Rights" for children with exceptionalities and their families; it is the culmination of many years of dedicated effort by both parents and professionals. Like many other special educators, we consider this law to be one of the most important, if not the most important, pieces of federal legislation ever enacted on behalf of children with special needs. PL 94-142 may rightfully be thought of as the legislative heart of special education.

---

[2]National legislation, or public laws (PL), are codified according to a standardized format. Legislation is thus designated by the number of the session of Congress that enacted the law followed by the number of the particular bill. PL 94-142, for example, was enacted by the 94th session of Congress and was the 142nd piece of legislation passed.

Table 1.3	A Synopsis of Selected Court Cases Influencing Special Education		
Case	**Year**	**Issue**	**Judicial Decision**
Brown v. Board of Education of Topeka, Kansas	1954	Educational segregation	Segregation of students by race ruled unconstitutional; children deprived of equal educational opportunity. Effectively ended "separate but equal" schools for white and black pupils. Used as a precedent for arguing that children with disabilities cannot be excluded from a public education.
Hobson v. Hansen	1967	Classifying students	Ability grouping or "tracking" of students on the basis of nationally normed tests, which were found to be biased, held to be unconstitutional. Tracking systems discriminated against poor and minority children, thus denying them an equal educational opportunity. Equal protection clause of Fourteenth Amendment violated.
Diana v. State Board of Education	1970	Class placement	Linguistically different students must be tested in their primary language as well as in English. Students cannot be placed in special education classes on the basis of IQ tests that are culturally biased. Verbal test items to be revised so as to reflect students' cultural heritage. Group-administered IQ tests cannot be used to place children in programs for individuals with mental retardation.
Pennsylvania Association for Retarded Children v. Commonwealth of Pennsylvania	1972	Right to education	State must guarantee a free public education to all children with mental retardation ages 6–21 regardless of degree of impairment or associated disabilities. Students to be placed in the most integrated environment. Definition of education expanded. Case established the right of parents to participate in educational decisions affecting their children. State to engage in extensive efforts to locate and serve ("child-find") all students with mental retardation. Preschool services to be provided to youngsters with mental retardation if local school district serves preschoolers who are not retarded.
Mills v. Board of Education, District of Columbia	1972	Right to education	Extended the Pennsylvania decision to include all children with disabilities. Specifically established the constitutional right of children with exceptionalities to a public education regardless of their functional level. Students have a right to a "constructive education" matched to their needs, including specialized instruction. Presumed absence of fiscal resources is not a valid reason for failing to provide appropriate educational services to students with disabilities. Elaborate due process safeguards established to protect the rights of the child, including parental notification of pending initial evaluation, reassignment, or planned termination of special services.
Larry P. v. Riles	1972, 1979	Class placement	A landmark case parallel to the *Diana* suit. African American students could not be placed in classes for children with mild mental retardation solely on the basis of intellectual assessments found to be culturally and racially biased. The court instructed school officials to develop an assessment process that would not discriminate against minority children. Failure to comply with this order resulted in a 1979 ruling that completely prohibited the use of IQ tests for placing African American students in classes for children with mild mental retardation. Ruling applies only to the state of California.
Lau v. Nichols	1974	Equal educational opportunity	A milestone case in the field of bilingual education. A U.S. Supreme Court ruling that noted "there is not equality in treatment merely by providing students with the same facilities, textbooks, teachers, and curriculum, for students who do not understand English are effectively foreclosed from a meaningful education." Decision significantly affected the education of culturally and linguistically diverse learners. Although the Court did not stipulate a specific method of instruction for non-English-speaking or limited-English-speaking pupils, it did require schools to offer special language programs if schools were to confer equal educational opportunity.
Tatro v. State of Texas	1980	Related services	U.S. Supreme Court held that catheterization qualified as a related service under PL 94-142. Catheterization was not considered an exempted medical procedure, as it could be performed by a health care aide or school nurse. Court further stipulated that only those services that allow a student to benefit from a special education qualify as related services.
Board of Education of the Hendrick Hudson Central School District v. Rowley	1982	Appropriate education	First U.S. Supreme Court interpretation of PL 94-142. Court addressed the issue of what constitutes an "appropriate" education for a student with hearing impairments making satisfactory educational progress. Supreme Court ruled that an appropriate education does not necessarily mean an education that will allow for the maximum possible achievement; rather, students must be given a reasonable opportunity to learn. Parents' request for a sign language interpreter, therefore, was denied. An appropriate education is not synonymous with an optimal educational experience.

Table 1.3   A Synopsis of Selected Court Cases Influencing Special Education (Continued)

Case	Year	Issue	Judicial Decision
Daniel R.R. v. State Board of Education	1989	Class placement	Fifth Circuit Court of Appeals held that a segregated class was an appropriate placement for a student with Down syndrome. Preference for integrated placement viewed as secondary to the need for an appropriate education. Court established a two-prong test for determining compliance with the least restrictive environment (LRE) mandate for students with severe disabilities. First, it must be determined if a pupil can make satisfactory progress and achieve educational benefit in the general education classroom through curriculum modification and the use of supplementary aids and services. Second, it must be determined whether the pupil has been integrated to the maximum extent appropriate. Successful compliance with both parts fulfills a school's obligation under federal law. Ruling affects LRE cases in Louisiana, Texas, and Mississippi, but has become a benchmark decision for other jurisdictions as well.
Oberti v. Board of Education of the Borough of Clementon School District	1982	Least restrictive environment	Placement in a general education classroom with supplementary aids and services must be offered to a student with disabilities prior to considering more segregated placements. Pupil cannot be excluded from a general education classroom solely because curriculum, services, or other practices would require modification. A decision to exclude a learner from the general education classroom necessitates justification and documentation. Clear judicial preference for educational integration established.
Cedar Rapids Community School District v. Garret F.	1999	Related services	U.S. Supreme Court expanded and clarified the concept of related services. Affirmed that intensive and continuous school health care services necessary for a student to attend school, if not performed by a physician, qualify as related services.
Schaffer v. Weast	2005	Burden of proof	A U.S. Supreme Court ruling addressing the issue of whether the parent(s) or school district bears the burden of proof in a due process hearing. The specific question before the Court was whether the parent(s), acting on behalf of their son or daughter, must prove that their child's individualized education program (IEP) is inappropriate or whether the school district must prove that the IEP is appropriate. The court ruled that the burden of proof is placed upon the party seeking relief.

Source: Adapted from R. Gargiulo and J. Kilgo, *Young Children with Special Needs: An Introduction to Early Childhood Special Education*, 2nd ed. (Clifton Park, NY: Delmar, 2005), pp. 31–34.

The purpose of this bill, which was signed into law by President Gerald Ford on November 29, 1975, is

> to assure that all handicapped children have available to them . . . a free appropriate public education which emphasizes special education and related services designed to meet their unique needs, to assure that the rights of handicapped children and their parents or guardians are protected, to assist States and localities to provide for the education of all handicapped children, and to assess and assure the effectiveness of efforts to educate handicapped children. [Section 601(c)]

In pursuing these four purposes, this legislation incorporates six major components and guarantees that have forever changed the landscape of education across the United States. Despite legislative and court challenges over the past three decades, the following principles have endured to the present day:

- **A free appropriate public education (FAPE).** All children, regardless of the severity of their disability (a "zero reject" philosophy), must be provided an education appropriate to their unique needs at no cost to the parent(s)/ guardian(s). Included in this principle is the concept of related services, which requires that children receive, for example, occupational therapy as well as other services as necessary in order to benefit from special education.
- **The least restrictive environment (LRE).** Children with disabilities are to be educated, to the maximum extent appropriate, with students without disabilities. Placements must be consistent with the pupil's educational needs.

- **An individualized education program (IEP).** This document, developed in conjunction with the parent(s)/guardian(s), is an individually tailored statement describing an educational plan for each learner with exceptionalities. The IEP, which will be fully discussed in Chapter 2, is required to address (1) the present level of academic functioning; (2) annual goals and accompanying instructional objectives; (3) educational services to be provided; (4) the degree to which the pupil will be able to participate in general education programs; (5) plans for initiating services and length of service delivery; and (6) an annual evaluation procedure specifying objective criteria to determine if instructional objectives are being met.

- **Procedural due process.** The Act affords parent(s)/guardian(s) several safeguards as it pertains to their child's education. Briefly, parent(s)/guardian(s) have the right to confidentiality of records; to examine all records; to obtain an independent evaluation; to receive written notification (in parents' native language) of proposed changes to their child's educational classification or placement; and the right to an impartial hearing whenever disagreements arise regarding educational plans for their son/daughter. Furthermore, the student's parent(s)/guardian(s) have the right to representation by legal counsel.

- **Nondiscriminatory assessment.** Prior to placement, a child must be evaluated by a multidisciplinary team in all areas of suspected disability by tests that are neither racially, culturally, nor linguistically biased. Students are to receive several types of assessments, administered by trained personnel; a single evaluation procedure is not permitted for either planning or placement purposes.

- **Parental participation.** PL 94-142 mandates meaningful parent involvement. Sometimes referred to as the "Parent's Law," this legislation requires that parents participate fully in the decision-making process that affects their child's education.

Congress indicated their desire by September 1, 1980, to provide a free appropriate public education for all eligible children ages 3–21. The law, however, did not require services to preschool children with disabilities. Because many states were not providing preschool services to typical children, an education for young children with special needs, in most instances, was not mandated. Although this legislation failed to require an education for younger children, it clearly focused attention on the preschool population and recognized the value of early education.

PL 94-142 did contain some benefits for children under school age. It offered small financial grants (Preschool Incentive Grants) to the individual states as an incentive to serve young children with disabilities. It also carried a mandate for schools to identify and evaluate children from birth through age 21 suspected of evidencing a disability. Finally, PL 94-142 moved from a census count to a child count of the actual number of individuals with disabilities being served. The intent was to encourage the states to locate and serve children with disabilities.

Public Law 99-457 (1986 Amendments to PL 94-142)

In October 1986, Congress passed one of the most comprehensive pieces of legislation affecting young children with special needs and their families—PL 99-457. This law changed both the scope and intent of services provided to preschoolers with special needs and formulated a national policy for infants and toddlers at risk for and with identified disabilities.

Simply stated, this law is a downward extension of PL 94-142, including all its rights and protections. This legislation does not require that preschoolers be identified with a specific disability label. It does demand that, as of the 1991–1992 school year, all preschoolers with special needs, ages 3–5 inclusive, are to receive a free and appropriate public education. This element of the law is a mandated requirement;

Preschoolers who have a disability are entitled to receive a free and appropriate public education.

states will lose significant amounts of federal preschool funding if they fail to comply. The goal of this legislation was finally accomplished in the 1992–1993 school year, when all states had mandates in place establishing a free and appropriate public education for all children with disabilities ages 3–5.

Title I of PL 99-457 created the Handicapped Infants and Toddlers Program (Part H), a new provision aimed at children from birth through age 2 with developmental delays or disabilities. This component of the legislation is voluntary; states are not compelled to comply. This part of the statute creates a discretionary program that assists states in implementing a statewide, comprehensive, coordinated, multidisciplinary, interagency program of services for very young children and their families who are experiencing developmental delays or who evidence a physical or mental condition that has a high probability of resulting in a delay, such as cerebral palsy or Down syndrome. (At the state's discretion, youngsters who are at risk for future delays may also be served.) As of September 30, 1994, all states had plans in place for the full implementation of Part H (U.S. Department of Education, 1995).

Eligible children and their families must receive a multidisciplinary assessment conducted by qualified professionals and a written individualized family service plan, or IFSP. An IFSP must be reviewed every six months (or sooner if necessary) to assess its continued appropriateness. The law requires that each infant or toddler be reevaluated annually. Regulations further stipulate that an IFSP must be developed within 45 days after a referral for services is made.

PL 99-457 is the product of a decade of hard work by parents, professionals, advocates, and legislators. It represents an opportunity to intervene and effect meaningful change in the lives of our nation's youngest and most vulnerable children.

Public Law 101-476 (1990 Amendments to PL 94-142)

Arguably, one of the most important changes contained in this legislation was the renaming of PL 94-142 as the Individuals with Disabilities Education Act (IDEA). "Children" was replaced with the term "individuals" and "handicapped" became "with disabilities." This phrase signifies a change in attitude to a more appropriate person-first point of view. We now realize that an individual's disability is but one aspect of his or her personhood.

Congress also recognized the importance of preparing adolescents for a productive life after they exit from public school. These amendments required that each student have, no later than age 16, an individual transition plan (ITP) as part of his/her IEP. This plan allows for a coordinated set of activities and interagency linkages designed to promote the student's movement to postschool functions such as independent living, vocational training, and additional educational experiences.

PL 101-476 also expanded the scope of the related services provision by adding two services: social work and rehabilitation counseling. Another element of this legislation was the identification of autism and traumatic brain injury as distinct disability categories. Previously, these disabilities had been subsumed under other disability labels. Lastly, Congress repealed states' immunity from lawsuits for violating IDEA. This part of the Act allows parents and others to sue a state in federal court for noncompliance with the provisions of the law.

Public Law 105-17 (1997 Amendments to IDEA)

After more than two years of intense and sometimes difficult negotiations, Congress was finally able to pass a comprehensive revision to IDEA. The IDEA Act Amendments of 1997 (IDEA '97) was overwhelmingly supported by both houses of the 105th Congress and was signed into law by President Bill Clinton on June 4, 1997.

This law restructures IDEA into four parts, revises some definitions, and revamps several key components, ranging from funding to disciplining students with disabilities to how IEPs are to be developed. Here are some of the more significant changes:

- Students with disabilities who bring weapons to school, possess or use illegal drugs, or pose a serious threat of injury to other pupils or themselves may be removed from their current placement only after a due process hearing and for no more than 45 days. Students who are suspended or expelled are still entitled to receive a free and appropriate public education in accordance with their IEP.
- Pupils with disabilities who exhibit less serious infractions of school conduct may be disciplined in ways similar to children without disabilities (including a change in placement) provided that the misbehavior was not a manifestation of the student's disability.
- IEPs are now required to state how the student with disabilities will be involved with and progress in the general education curriculum. Other provisions stipulate that transition planning will begin at age 14 instead of age 16, general educators will become part of the IEP team, benchmarks and measurable annual goals will be emphasized, and the assistive technology needs of each learner must be considered by the IEP team.
- Orientation and mobility services for children with visual impairments are now included in the definition of related services.
- The present mandate of comprehensive triennial reevaluation of pupils with disabilities is lifted if school authorities and the student's parents both agree that this process is unnecessary.
- A new section on mediation requires states to offer mediation services to help resolve disputes as an alternative to using more costly and lengthy due process hearings. Parental participation is voluntary, and parents still retain their right to a due process hearing.
- The category of developmental delay may now be used when describing children ages 3–9. The use of this term is at the discretion of the state and local education agency.
- Initial evaluations and reevaluations are not restricted to the use of formal, standardized tests. A variety of assessment tools and strategies are to be used in an effort to gather relevant functional and developmental information. Curriculum-based tests, portfolio reviews, parental input, and the

observations of teachers and related service providers may be considered in determining whether or not the student has a disability and in developing the content of the IEP. A student may not be considered eligible for a special education if educational difficulties are primarily the result of limited proficiency in English or lack of adequate instruction in math and/or reading.

- The reauthorization of IDEA requires schools to establish performance goals for students with disabilities in an effort to assess their academic progress. Additionally, these youngsters are to be included in statewide and district-wide assessment programs or given alternative assessments that meet their unique needs.

Section 504 of the Rehabilitation Act of 1973

The four pieces of legislation that we just examined are representative special education laws. PL 93-112, the Rehabilitation Act of 1973, however, is a *civil rights* law. Section 504 of this enactment is the first public law specifically aimed at protecting children and adults against discrimination due to a disability. It said that no individual can be excluded, solely because of his or her disability, from participating in or benefiting from any program or activity receiving federal financial assistance, which includes schools (*CEC Today,* 1997).

Unlike IDEA, this Act uses a functional rather than a categorical model for determining a disability. According to this law, an individual is eligible for services if they:

1. have a physical or mental impairment that substantially limits one or more life activities;
2. have a record of such impairment; or
3. are regarded as having such an impairment by others.

"Major life activities" are broadly defined and include, for example, walking, seeing, hearing, working, and learning.

To fulfill the requirements of Section 504, schools must make "reasonable accommodations" for pupils with disabilities so that they can participate in educational programs provided to other students. Reasonable accommodations might include modifications of the general education program, the assignment of an aide, a behavior management plan, or the provision of special study areas (Smith, 2002; Smith & Patton, 1998). Students may also receive related services such as occupational or physical therapy even if they are not receiving a special education through IDEA.

Because the protections afforded by this law are so broad, an individual who is ineligible for a special education under IDEA may qualify for special assistance or accommodations under Section 504. An adolescent with attention deficit hyperactivity disorder (ADHD) or a student with severe allergies, for example, would be eligible for services via Section 504, whereas they are likely to be ineligible to receive services under IDEA (*CEC Today,* 1997). All students who are eligible for a special education and related services under IDEA are also eligible for accommodations under Section 504; the converse, however, is *not* true.

Similar to IDEA, there is a mandate contained within Section 504 to educate pupils with special needs with their typical peers to the maximum extent possible. Additionally, schools are required to develop an accommodation plan (commonly called a "504 plan") customized to meet the unique needs of the individual. This document should include a statement of the pupil's strengths and weaknesses, a list of necessary accommodations, and the individual(s) responsible for ensuring implementation. The purpose of this plan is to enable the student to receive a free, appropriate public education (Smith, 2002).

Finally, unlike IDEA, which offers protections for students only between the ages 3–21, Section 504 covers the individual's lifespan. See Table 1.4 for a companion of some of the key provisions of IDEA and Section 504.

Table 1.4	**A Comparison of Key Features of IDEA and Section 504**	
Provision	**IDEA**	**Section 504**
Purpose	Provides a free and appropriate public education to children and youth with specific disabilities.	Prohibits discrimination on the basis of a person's disability in all programs receiving federal funds.
Ages Covered	Individuals 3–21 years old.	No age restriction.
Definition of Disability	Twelve disabilities defined according to federal regulations plus state/local definition of *developmentally delayed*.	Broader interpretation of a disability than found in IDEA—a person with a physical or mental impairment that substantially limits a major life activity, has a record of such impairment, or is regarded as having such an impairment.
Funding	States receive some federal dollars for excess cost of educating students with disabilities.	Because this is a civil rights law, no additional funding is provided.
Planning Documents	Individualized education program (IEP).	Accommodation plan (commonly referred to as a "504 plan").
Assessment Provisions	A comprehensive, nondiscriminatory eligibility evaluation in all areas of suspected disability conducted by a multidisciplinary team; reevaluations every three years unless waived.	Eligibility determination requires nondiscriminatory assessment procedures; requires reevaluation prior to a "significant change" in placement.
Due Process	Extensive rights and protections afforded to student and parents.	Affords parents impartial hearing, right to inspect records, and representation by counsel. Additional protections at discretion of local school district.
Coordination	No provision.	School district required to identify a 504 coordinator.
Enforcement	U.S. Department of Education, Office of Special Education Programs	Office for Civil Rights, U.S. Department of Education

Americans with Disabilities Act

Probably the most significant civil rights legislation affecting individuals with disabilities, the Americans with Disabilities Act (ADA) (PL 101-336) was signed into law on July 26, 1990, by President George Bush, who stated, "Today, America welcomes into the mainstream of life all people with disabilities. Let the shameful wall of exclusion finally come tumbling down." This far-reaching enactment, which parallels Section 504 of PL 93-112, forbids discrimination against persons with disabilities in both the public and private sectors. Its purpose, according to Turnbull (1993), is to "provide clear, strong, consistent, and enforceable standards prohibiting discrimination against individuals with disabilities without respect for their age, nature or extent of disability" (p. 23).

The ADA goes far beyond traditional thinking of who is disabled and embraces, for instance, people with AIDS, individuals who have successfully completed a substance abuse program, and persons with cosmetic disfigurements. In fact, any person with an impairment that substantially limits a major life activity is covered by this legislation. It extends protections and guarantees of civil rights in such diverse arenas as private sector employment, transportation, telecommunications, public and privately owned accommodations, and the services of local and state government.

Examples of the impact of this landmark legislation include the following:

- Employers of 15 or more workers must make "reasonable accommodations" so that an otherwise qualified individual with a disability is not discriminated against. Accommodations might include a Braille computer keyboard for a worker who is visually impaired or wider doorways to allow easy access for an employee who uses a wheelchair. Furthermore, hiring, termination, and promotion practices may not discriminate against an applicant or employee who has a disability.
- Mass transit systems, such as buses, trains, and subways, must be accessible to citizens with disabilities.
- Hotels, fast-food restaurants, theaters, hospitals, early childhood centers, banks, dentists' offices, retail stores, and the like may not discriminate

Bonnie Kamin/PhotoEdit

The Americans with Disabilities Act protects the rights of individuals with disabilities.

against individuals with disabilities. These facilities must be accessible, or alternative means for providing services must be available.

- Companies that provide telephone service must offer relay services to individuals with hearing or speech impairments.

Think what this legislation means for the field of special education in general, and specifically for adolescents with disabilities as they prepare to leave high school and transition to the world of adults as independent citizens able to participate fully in all aspects of community life. Thanks to this enactment, the future of the almost 54 million Americans with disabilities is definitely brighter and more secure.

Educational Reform: Standards-Based Education

Over the past two decades, there has been a growing movement toward greater educational accountability with accompanying calls for educational reform or restructuring resulting in enhanced academic excellence. (See, for example, President Clinton's Goals 2000: Educate America Act of 1994 [PL 103-227]). As a result of this trend, many states initiated challenging academic standards and more stringent graduation requirements for their students, and several professional organizations published performance indicators in various content areas, such as mathematics, language arts, and science. Likewise, many state departments of education are moving toward performance-based standards when establishing teacher licensure/certification requirements thus linking student success with teacher qualifications. The overall focus of this movement, fueled by various political, social, and economic forces, was a concern over the learning outcomes of our students. It is equally concerned with establishing educational equity among all learners.

Educational standards, which are "general statements of what students should know or be able to do as a result of their public school education" (Nolet & McLaughlin, 2005, p. 5), are important for a couple of reasons. First, "they are intended," according to Nolet and McLaughlin, "to create equity across schools and classrooms in that they define what all teachers should teach and . . . [they] also define the content that will be assessed and for which schools will be held accountable" (p. 5). Recent federal legislation embraces this thinking. The importance attached to standards driven reform is clearly evident in the No Child Left Behind Act of 2001.

No Child Left Behind Act of 2001

In 2001 Congress reauthorized the Elementary and Secondary Education Act, popularly known as the No Child Left Behind Act of 2001 (PL 107-110). This legislation reflects President Bush's commitment to educational reform and accountability. A brief synopsis of this ambitious law reveals that eventually all pupils, including those in special education, are expected to demonstrate proficiency in mathematics and reading, with science eventually being included. Annual testing of children in grades 3–8 is required, with students in grades 10–12 assessed at least once. Schools are expected to show adequate yearly progress toward the goal of 100 percent proficiency by 2014. (A small percentage of students may be excused from participating in state- and districtwide achievement tests if their IEP provides for their exemption.) Because this law is concerned with the achievement of *all* students, test scores must be disaggregated according to the pupil's disability, socioeconomic status, race, ethnicity, and English language proficiency. The anticipated benefit of this requirement is that assessment results will directly translate into instructional accommodations, further aligning special education and general education into a unified delivery system responsible for serving all learners (Salend, 2008).

Schools that experience difficulty attaining the goal of adequate yearly progress will be provided technical and financial assistance. If a school fails to demonstrate adequate yearly progress for three consecutive years, the local school district is required to offer supplemental instructional services such as tutoring, after school classes, and summer programs (Council for Exceptional Children, 2003). Parents of children in "failing" schools will be given the opportunity to transfer their child to another school, including private and parochial schools.

In addition to stressing student educational accomplishment, other aspects of this law require that the public as well as parents be informed of individual school performance in addition to the qualifications of teachers. All elementary and secondary school teachers were expected to be "highly qualified" by the end of the 2005–2006 school year according to state criteria. Rigorous standards are also being imposed on teacher aides.

What are the implications of this law for general as well as special educators? How competently will students with special needs perform in this age of educational reform and standards-based education? Obviously, PL 107-110 emphasizes academic achievement as measured by student performance on standardized tests. The expectation seems to be that effective instructional strategies can compensate for a student's disability. The enactment of this law has ushered in an era of what is now commonly referred to as "high-stakes testing." Greater emphasis will most likely be placed on ensuring that pupils in special education are exposed to the general education curriculum. One can also anticipate that greater attention will be focused on aligning IEP goals with the content standards of the general education curriculum (Council for Exceptional Children, 2003). Finally, how colleges and universities prepare future teachers will also likely undergo significant change in an effort to ensure that graduates are highly qualified professionals.

Individuals with Disabilities Education Improvement Act of 2004

On November 19, 2004 Congress passed legislation reauthorizing the Individuals with Disabilities Education Act. The new version of this law is called the Individuals with Disabilities Education Improvement Act of 2004, commonly referred to as IDEA 2004. President George W. Bush signed this bill (PL 108-446) into law on December 3, 2004. Many of the provisions of this legislation became effective on July 1, 2005; some elements of the law became effective, however, on the date the President signed the bill.

The impact of this legislation will unfold over the coming years. It is safe to say that IDEA 2004 will significantly affect the professional lives of both general education teachers and special educators. Parents of children with disabilities will also encounter new roles and responsibilities as a result of this law.

> The Individuals with Disabilities Education Improvement Act of 2004 (IDEA) [has] increased the focus of special education from simply ensuring access to education to improving the educational performance of students with disabilities and aligning special education services with the larger national school improvement efforts that include standards, assessments, and accountability [i.e., greater conformity with the No Child Left Behind Act]. (Nolet & McLaughlin, 2005, pp. 2–3)

Listed below you will find highlights of some of the significant issues addressed in this historic document.

Individualized Education Program (IEP) Process
- Short-term objectives and benchmarks will no longer be required except for those pupils who are evaluated via alternate assessments aligned to alternate achievement standards.
- Assessment of the progress that a student is making toward meeting annual goals, which must be written in measurable terms, is still required. Reference, however, to the current requirement of reporting to the "extent to which progress is sufficient to enable the child to achieve goals by the end of

the year" is eliminated. IEPs will now need to describe how the individual's progress toward achieving annual goals will be measured and when these progress reports will be made.

- A new provision of the legislation allows for members of the IEP team to be excused from participating in all or part of the meeting if the parents and school district agree that attendance is not necessary because the individual's area of curriculum or related service is not being reviewed or modified. The team member will be required, however, to submit written input into the development of the IEP prior to the meeting.
- PL 108-446 allows for alternatives to physical IEP meetings such as video conferencing and conference telephone calls.
- Once an IEP is established, IDEA 2004 will allow for changes to be made via a written plan to modify the document without convening the entire team and redrafting the whole IEP.
- The new legislation deletes references to transition services beginning at age 14. Now, transition services are to begin no later than the first IEP in effect when the student turns 16 (and updated annually). It also establishes a new requirement for postsecondary goals pertaining to appropriate education, training, employment, and independent living skills.
- School districts will be allowed, with parental consent, to develop multiyear IEPs (not to exceed three years).
- The U.S. Department of Education is charged with developing and disseminating model IEP forms and model IFSP (individualized family service plan) forms.

Identifying Students with Specific Learning Disabilities

Under IDEA '97, when identifying an individual for a possible learning disability, educators typically looked to see if the student exhibited a severe discrepancy between achievement and intellectual ability. IDEA 2004 removed this discrepancy provision. School districts will now be able, if they so choose, to use a process that determines if the pupil responds to empirically validated, scientifically based interventions; a procedure known as response-to-intervention (treatment). Under the new guidelines, rather than comparing IQ with performance on standardized achievement tests, general education teachers can offer intensive programs of instructional interventions. If the child fails to make adequate progress, a learning disability is assumed to be present and additional assessment is warranted.

Highly Qualified Special Education Teachers

The language contained in IDEA 2004 concerning who is considered a "highly qualified" special educator is complementary to the standards promulgated in the No Child Left Behind Act (NCLB) of 2001, PL 107-110.

- All special education teachers must hold at least a bachelor's degree and be fully certified or licensed in the field of special education in order to be deemed "highly qualified." Special educators employed as of July 1, 2005 were required to meet this standard.
- Special educators who teach core subjects in elementary schools can obtain highly qualified status by passing their state's licensing or certification exam.
- Teachers of middle- or high-school-aged students with significant cognitive deficits, that is, pupils whose progress will be assessed via alternate achievement standards, may be considered highly qualified if they meet the NCLB standards for *elementary* school teachers. The effective date of this provision was December 3, 2004.
- Currently employed special educators who teach multiple core academic subjects exclusively to students with disabilities, may be designated "highly

qualified" after successfully passing "a single, high objective uniform State standard of evaluation" (HOUSSE), which addresses multiple subjects.

- A special education teacher who is new to the field, but is already deemed highly qualified in a single core academic area (such as science, reading or language arts, mathematics, foreign languages, or history), may become highly qualified by successfully completing the HOUSSE requirement for the remaining subjects taught. This requirement must be fulfilled within two years of their hire date. This provision, like the preceding one, became effective on December 3, 2004.

- This legislation does not address "highly qualified" requirements for early childhood special educators.

Discipline

- PL 108-446 stipulates that when a student is removed from their current educational setting, the pupil is to continue to receive those services that enable him or her to participate in the general education curriculum and to ensure progress toward meeting their IEP goals.

- IDEA '97 allowed school authorities to unilaterally remove a student to an interim alternative educational setting (IASE) for up to 45 days for offenses involving weapons or drugs. IDEA 2004 now permits school officials to remove any pupil (including those with and without disabilities) to an IASE for up to 45 days for inflicting "serious bodily injury."

- Removal to an IASE will now be for 45 *school* days rather than 45 calendar days.

- Behavior resulting in disciplinary action still requires a manifestation review; however, language requiring the IEP team to consider whether the pupil's disability impaired their ability to control their behavior or comprehend the consequences of their actions has been eliminated. IEP teams will now only need to ask two questions:
    1. Did the disability cause or have a direct and substantial relationship to the offense?
    2. Was the violation a direct result of the school's failure to implement the IEP?

- IDEA 2004 modifies the "stay put" provision enacted during an appeals process. When either the LEA or parent requests an appeal of a manifestation determination or placement decision, the pupil is required to remain in the current IASE until a decision is rendered by the hearing officer or until the time period for the disciplinary violation concludes. A hearing must be held within 20 school days of the date of the appeal.

Due Process

- Parents will encounter a two-year statute of limitations for filing a due process complaint from the time they knew or should have known that a violation occurred. Alleged violations might involve identification, assessment, or placement issues or the failure to provide an appropriate education.

- A mandatory "resolution session" is now required prior to proceeding with a due process hearing. (The parents and school district may waive this requirement and directly proceed to mediation.) School districts must convene a meeting with the parents and IEP team members within 15 days of receiving a due process compliant. If the complaint is not satisfactorily resolved within 30 days of the filing date, the due process hearing may proceed.

- Under provisions of IDEA '97, parents who prevailed in due process hearings and/or court cases could seek attorney's fees from the school district. IDEA 2004 now permits school districts to seek attorney's fees from the parents' attorney (or the parents themselves) if the due process compliant or lawsuit is deemed frivolous, unreasonable or without foundation or the attorney continues to litigate despite these circumstances. Reasonable attorney fees can also be awarded by the court if the complaint or lawsuit was filed for an improper purpose such as to harass, cause unnecessary delay, or needlessly increase the cost of litigation.

Evaluation of Students

- School districts will be required to determine the eligibility of a student to receive a special education and the educational needs of the child within a 60-day time frame. (This provision does not apply if the state has already established a timeline for accomplishing this task.) The 60-day rule commences upon receipt of parental permission for evaluation.

Teaching All Students

IDEA Highlights: 1975–2004

Year	Public Law	Key Components
1975	PL 94-142	• All students, regardless of the severity of their disability, are provided an education appropriate to their unique needs • Children with disabilities are to be educated, to the maximum extent appropriate, with their typical peers • Individualized education program (IEP) provided for each learner • Procedural due process safeguards established • Nondiscriminatory assessments conducted by a multidisciplinary team • Meaningful parental involvement in decision making process
1986	PL 99-457	• Mandated services for preschoolers with disabilities, ages 3–5 • Permissive early intervention services for infants and toddlers, birth through age 2 • Individualized family service plan (IFSP) established for infants and toddlers • "Developmentally delayed" label created
1990	PL 101-476	• Name of legislation changed to Individuals with Disabilities Education Act (IDEA) • Autism and traumatic brain injury identified as discrete disability categories • Rehabilitation counseling and social work considered related services • Established the requirement of an individual transition plan (ITP) by age 16
1997	PL 105-17	• Students with disabilities required to participate in state-and districtwide assessments • Transition planning commences at age 14 • Orientation and mobility included as a related service • Discretionary use of developmentally delayed label for pupils ages 3–9 • General educators required to participate on IEP team • Students with disabilities are to be involved in and have access to general education curriculum • Mediation offered as a means of resolving disputes • Benchmarks and measurable annual goals emphasized • Pupils who violate student code of conduct may be removed from current educational placement after a due process hearing • Assistive technology needs of each learner must be assessed
2004	PL 108-446	• Modified criteria for identifying students with specific learning disabilities • Educators must be "highly qualified" • Eliminates use of short-term objectives in IEPs • Relaxes requirements for participation in IEP meetings • Resolution session required prior to a due process hearing • Statute of limitations imposed on parents for filing complaints • Multiyear IEPs are permissible • Transition planning to begin with first IEP in effect once student reaches age 16 • IEPs to incorporate research-based interventions • Students with disabilities may be removed to an interim alternative educational setting for up to 45 school days for offenses involving weapons or drugs or inflicting serious bodily injury

- Reevaluation of eligibility for a special education may not occur more than once per year (unless agreed to by the school district and parent); and it must occur at least once every three years unless the parent and school district agree that such a reevaluation is unnecessary.
- IDEA 2004 modifies the provision pertaining to native language and preferred mode of communication. New language in the bill requires that evaluations are to be "provided and administered in the language and form most likely to yield accurate information on what the child knows and can do academically, developmentally, and functionally, unless it is not feasible to so provide or administer."
- School districts are not allowed to seek dispute resolution when parents refuse to give their consent for special education services. If parents refuse to give consent, then the school district is not responsible for providing a free and appropriate public education.

Assessment Participation

- PL 108-446 requires that *all* students participate in all state- and districtwide assessments (including those required under the No Child Left Behind Act, PL 107-110), with accommodations or alternative assessments, if necessary, as stipulated in the pupil's IEP. States are permitted to assess up to 1 percent of students (generally those pupils with significant cognitive deficits) with alternative assessments aligned with alternative achievement standards. This cap represents approximately 9 percent of all students with disabilities. IDEA 2004 further requires that assessments adhere to the principles of universal design when feasible.

The coming years will be ones of exciting opportunities and challenges as the entire educational community responds to the mandates of PL 107-110 and PL 108-446. These laws, like PL 94-142 over 30 years ago, will dramatically change the educational landscape for both general education and special education.

Introducing Universal Design for Learning

With the growing movement toward serving all learners in the general education classroom coupled with legislative mandates that pupils with disabilities be involved with and progress in the general education curriculum, it is not uncommon to find teachers searching for ways to (1) adapt curriculum; (2) modify instructional strategies; and (3) assess students in ways that permit them to demonstrate their mastery of what they've been taught. One solution to this quest is the emerging best practice of **universal design for learning**, commonly known by its acronym, **UDL**.

Originally developed for architects and consumer product designers, the principles of UDL have been adapted to the field of education. We offer the following concise description of UDL:

> The central practical premise of UDL [universal design for learning] is that a curriculum should include alternatives to make it accessible and appropriate for individuals with different backgrounds, learning styles, abilities, and disabilities in widely varied learning contexts. The "universal" in universal design does not imply one optimal solution for everyone. Rather, it reflects an awareness of the unique nature of each learner and the need to accommodate differences, create learning experiences that suit the learner, and maximize his or her ability to progress. (Rose & Meyer, 2002, p. 70)

Essentially, UDL is an educational model or approach to designing instructional methods, materials, activities, and evaluation procedures in an effort to assist individuals with "wide differences in their abilities to see, hear, speak, move, read, write, understand English, attend, organize, engage, and remember" (Orkwis, 2003, n.p.).

Universal design for learning is accomplished by means of flexible curriculum materials and activities that offer alternatives to pupils with widely varying abilities and backgrounds. These adaptations are built into instructional design rather than added on later as an afterthought. Universal design for learning provides equal access to learning, not simply equal access to information. It allows the student to determine the most appropriate method for accessing information while the teacher monitors the learning process (Ohio State University Partnership Grant, 2008). UDL assumes that there is no one method of presentation or expression that provides equal access for all learners. Learning activities and materials are purposely designed to allow for flexibility and offer various ways to learn (Rose & Meyer, 2002; Scott, McGuire, & Shaw, 2003). These accommodations are "designed-in" or built "directly into the materials so that *all* [italics added] students with differing abilities can use the same material, but in a way tailored to their strengths and instructional needs" (Freund & Rich, 2005, p. 81).

Universal design for learning is envisioned an instructional resource, a vehicle for diversifying instruction in order to deliver the general education curriculum to each pupil (Orkwis & McLane, 1998). UDL does not remove academic challenges; it removes barriers to access. Simply stated, universal design for learning is just good teaching (Ohio State University Partnership Grant, 2008). The greatest promise of UDL is that of flexible, equitable, and accessible ways to teach. With this approach "teachers can reach each individual student, disabled or nondisabled, providing a platform for each to interact with the curriculum—in ways that best support unique learning styles" (Council for Exceptional Children, 2005, p. 2). Some of the beneficiaries of this strategy include, for example, individuals who speak English as a second language, pupils with disabilities, and students whose preferred learning style is inconsistent with their teacher's teaching style (Ohio State University Partnership Grant).

Because UDL serves as the philosophical and pedagogical anchor for our text, we will have much more to say about this instructional model in the following chapters.

Web Resources

For additional information about universal design for learning, visit the following websites:

- Trace Research and Development Center, **http://www.trace.wisc.edu**
- Center for Applied Special Technology, **http://www.cast.org**
- National Early Childhood Technical Assistance Center, **http://www.nectac.org/topics/atech/udl.asp**

Access to these websites is available on this text's companion website, **http://academic.cengage.com/education/gargiulo**.

Thematic Summary

- Today's classrooms evidence an increasingly diverse student population. Teachers are confronted with the challenge of teaching students with disabilities, learners who are culturally and linguistically diverse, and pupils recognized as gifted and talented as well as the typical child.
- It is becoming increasingly common to serve all individuals with special learning needs in the general education classroom.
- State and federal courts have played a large role in securing educational rights and protections for students with disabilities and other learners with special needs.
- Thanks to federal legislation, students and adults with disabilities have secured, over the past several decades, unprecedented educational and civil rights.
- Calls for reform and greater educational accountability currently characterize the educational climate in the United States.
- Universal design for learning is seen as one vehicle for ensuring that teachers are able to meet the needs of students who exhibit widely varying learning requirements.

Making Connections for Inclusive Teaching

1. All students with special needs should be educated in the general education classroom. Do you agree or disagree with this statement? Defend your viewpoint.

2. Discuss how litigation and legislation have worked together to enhance educational opportunities for learners with disabilities and pupils with other special needs.
3. Describe how the No Child Left Behind Act of 2001 in conjunction with the Individuals with Disabilities Education Improvement Act is currently affecting education in the United States.
4. Explain how universal design for learning benefits all students.

Learning Activities

1. Interview a veteran general education teacher or a special educator (someone who has been teaching since the late 1970s). Ask this person how the field of education has changed over the past decades. In what ways are things still the same? What issues and challenges does this teacher confront in his or her career? What is this person's vision of the future of education?
2. Interview an administrator from your local school district. Find out how court decisions and legislative requirements have affected the delivery of special education services. Here are some suggested topics for discussion:
   - How has special education changed over the past several years as a result of judicial and legislative mandates?
   - How is the school district meeting the requirement of educating pupils with disabilities in the least restrictive environment?
   - What are the perceived advantages and disadvantages of the No Child Left Behind Act of 2001 and IDEA at the local level?
3. Visit an elementary and secondary school in your area and interview several general educators. What types of students do they have in their classrooms? How do they feel about teaching students with special needs? What do they see as the advantages and disadvantages of inclusion?
4. Obtain and copy your state's special education laws. How do the requirements and provisions of the law compare with IDEA 2004?

Looking at the Standards

There is a growing expectation in education circles that teachers are responsible for effectively providing an appropriate education to *all* learners. Many teacher preparation programs have aligned their standards and practices to reflect this philosophy. Additionally, just as school-age students are expected to demonstrate their mastery of the curriculum, individuals desiring to become teachers (general educators or special educators) are encountering standard-based licensure/certification requirements as part of the educational reform movement that seeks to improve the quality of *all* teachers working in today's classrooms. Colleges and universities that prepare teachers, as well as several state departments of education, have turned to professional organizations and associations for direction and guidance in meeting this challenge. Two representative groups are the Council for Exceptional Children (CEC) and the Interstate New Teacher Assessment and Support Consortium (INTASC). Together, these national organizations have, over the years, developed, refined, and aligned statements of what beginning educators should know and be able to do in order to be effective teachers.

Appendix A presents the INTASC standards that reflect the knowledge, attitudes, and skills that *all* teachers are expected to master as they commence their career. Appendix B illustrates the CEC standards appropriate for beginning teachers of students with exceptionalities.

In this chapter, and all of the following chapters, we identify specific standards that each of our chapters address. The content of this chapter most closely aligns itself with the following set of standards:

INTASC Standards

- *Student Development.* The teacher understands how students differ in their approaches to learning and creates instructional opportunities that are adapted to diverse learners.

Council for Exceptional Children

Special educators are to have knowledge of the following:

- CCIK1: Models, theories, and philosophies that form the basis for special education practice.
- CC1K3: Relationship of special education to the organization and function of educational agencies.
- GC1K4: Legal, judicial, and educational systems to assist individuals with disabilities.
- GC1K5: Continuum of placement and services available for individuals with disabilities.
- GC1K8: Principles of normalization and concept of least restrictive environment.

Key Concepts and Terms

students with disabilities	integration	inclusion
least restrictive environment (LRE)	regular education initiative (REI)	universal design for learning
mainstreaming	full inclusion	

References

Bennett, T., DeLuca, D., & Bruns, D. (1997). Putting inclusion into practice: Perspectives of teachers and parents. *Exceptional Children, 64*(1), 115–131.

CEC Today. (1997). What every teacher needs to know: A comparison of Section 504, ADA, and IDEA. 4(4), 1, 3, 15.

Children's Defense Fund. (2005). *The state of children in America's union.* Washington, DC: Author.

Council for Exceptional Children. (2003). *No Child Left Behind Act of 2001: Reauthorization of the Elementary and Secondary Education Act* (technical assistance resource). Arlington, VA: Author.

Council for Exceptional Children. (2005). *Universal design for learning: A guide for teachers and education professionals.* Arlington, VA: Author.

Deno, E. (1970). Special education as developmental capital. *Exceptional Children, 37*(3), 229–237.

Dunn, L. (1968). Special education for the mildly retarded—Is much of it justifiable? *Exceptional Children, 35*(1), 5–22.

Freund, L., & Rich, R. (2005). *Teaching students with learning problems in the inclusive classroom.* Upper Saddle River, NJ: Pearson Education.

Gargiulo, R. (2009). *Special education in contemporary society: An introduction to exceptionality* (3rd ed.). Thousand Oaks, CA: Sage.

Gargiulo, R., & Kilgo, J. (2005). *Young children with special needs: An introduction to early childhood special education* (2nd ed.). Clifton Park, NY: Delmar.

Gollnick, D., & Chinn, P. (2009). *Multicultural education in a pluralistic society* (8th ed.). Upper Saddle River, NJ: Pearson Education.

Kauffman, J. (1995). Why we must celebrate a diversity of restrictive environments. *Learning Disabilities Research & Practice, 10*(4), 225–232.

Kennedy, C., & Horn, E. (Eds.). (2004). *Including students with severe disabilities.* Boston: Allyn & Bacon.

National Center for Education Statistics. (2007). *Digest of education statistics, 2006.* Washington, DC: U.S. Government Printing Office.

Nolet, V., & McLaughlin, M. (2005). *Accessing the general education curriculum* (2nd ed.). Thousand Oaks, CA: Corwin Press.

Ohio State University Partnership Grant. (2008). *Fast facts for faculty: Universal design for learning.* Retrieved March 4, 2008, from http://ada.OSU.edu/resources/fastfacts/Universal _Design.htm

Orkwis, R. (2003). *Universally designed instruction*. Retrieved March 8, 2008 from http://www.cec.sped.org/AM/Template .cfm?Section=Search&template=/CM/HTMLDisplay .cfm&ContentID=2636

Orkwis, R., & McLane, K. (1998, Fall). *A curriculum every student can use: Design principles for student access*. ERIC/OSEP Topical Brief, ERIC Clearinghouse on Disabilities and Gifted. (ERIC Document Reproduction Service No. ED 423 654)

Petterson, J., & Hittie, M. (2003). *Inclusive teaching: Creating effective schools for all learners*. Boston: Allyn & Bacon.

Reynolds, M. (1962). A framework for considering some issues in special education. *Exceptional Children, 28*(7), 367–370.

Rose, D., & Meyer, A. (2002). *Teaching every student in the digital age: Universal design for learning*. Alexandria, VA: Association for Supervision and Curriculum Development.

Sailor, W. (Ed.). (2002). *Whole-school success and inclusive education: Building partnerships for learning, achievement, and accountability*. New York: Teachers College Press.

Salend, S. (2008). *Creating inclusive classrooms* (6th ed.). Upper Saddle River, NJ: Pearson Education.

Scott, S., McGuire, J., & Shaw, S. (2003). Universal design for instruction: A new paradigm for adult instruction in post-secondary education. *Remedial and Special Education, 24*(6), 369–379.

Smith, T. (2002). Section 504: Basic requirements for schools. *Intervention in School and Clinic, 37*(5), 259–266.

Smith, T., & Patton, J. (1998). *Section 504 and public schools*. Austin, TX: Pro-Ed.

Turnbull, H. (1993). *Free appropriate public education: The law and children with disabilities* (4th ed.). Denver: Love.

U.S. Census Bureau. (2007). *Statistical abstract of the United States: 2008* (127th ed.). Washington, DC: Author.

U.S. Department of Education. (1995). *Seventeenth annual report to Congress on the implementation of the Individuals with Disabilities Education Act*. Washington, DC: U.S. Government Printing Office.

U.S. Department of Education. (2008). *IDEA data*. Retrieved March 3, 2008 from https://www.ideadata.org/PartBReport .asp

Voltz, D., Brazil, N., & Ford, A. (2001). What matters most in inclusive education: A practical guide for moving forward. *Intervention in School and Clinic, 37*(1), 23–30.

Will, M. (1986a). Educating children with learning problems: A shared responsibility. *Exceptional Children, 52*(5), 411–415.

Will, M. (1986b). *Educating students with learning problems. A shared responsibility*. Washington, DC: U.S. Department of Education, Office of Special Education and Rehabilitative Services.

Yell, M. (2006). *The law and special education* (2nd ed.). Upper Saddle River, NJ: Pearson Education.

istockphoto.com

Special Education Procedures, Policies, and Process

Identification and Assessment of Individual Differences

Referral and Assessment for a Special Education

  Prereferral

  Referral

  Assessment

  Instructional Programming and Appropriate Placement

The Individualized Education Program

Related Services

Section 504 Accommodation Plan

  Who Is Protected by Section 504?

  Providing a Free, Appropriate Public Education

  Section 504 Eligibility Determination

  Accommodation Plans

Learning Outcomes

After studying this chapter, you should be able to:

- Distinguish between inter- and intraindividual differences.
- Describe the purpose of prereferral interventions.
- Explain the role and function of the multidisciplinary team.
- Discuss the differences between norm-referenced and criterion-referenced tests.
- Identify the required components of an individualized education program (IEP).
- Identify examples of related services for students with special needs.
- Summarize the purpose of Section 504 (of PL 93-112) and accommodation plans.

The purpose of this chapter is to describe and discuss the roles and responsibilities of both general education teachers and special educators as they work together to meet the needs of a diverse learning community. As you will soon see, teachers by necessity, work with a variety of professionals as well as parents in their attempt to provide an appropriate education for all students. Sometimes, however, despite teachers' best efforts, some children seem to continuously struggle in the classroom. What should a teacher do? How can you help these students? Is a special education always necessary? This chapter will answer these questions and others. Much of what teachers do in their endeavors to meet the unique needs of their students is driven by legislative mandates and legal requirements. We will examine these various provisions that often dictate how teachers respond to the learning requirements of their pupils. We begin with a discussion of recognizing the importance of individual differences.

Identification and Assessment of Individual Differences

One of the distinguishing characteristics of the field of education is the individuality and uniqueness of the students we serve. There is considerable wisdom in the maxim "No two children are alike." Experienced educators will quickly tell you that even though students may share a common label, such as gifted and talented, culturally diverse, or hearing impaired, that is where the similarity ends. These pupils are likely to be as different as day and night. Of course, the individuality of our students, both typical and atypical, has the potential for creating significant instructional and/or management concerns for the classroom teacher. Recall from Chapter 1 that today's schools are serving an increasingly diverse student population. At the same time, there is greater cooperation and more shared responsibility between general and special educators as well as service providers as they collectively plan appropriate educational experiences for all learners.

When teachers talk about the individuality of their students, they often refer to **interindividual differences** or the heterogeneity of their pupils. These differences

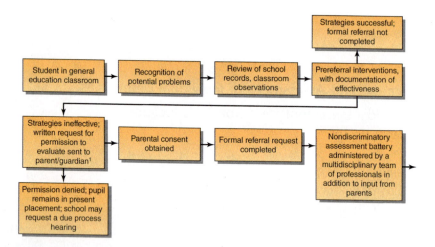

Figure 2.1 A Procedural Decision-Making Model for the Delivery of Special Education Services

[1] IDEA does not mandate parental consent for referral but does require consent for evaluation.

[2] Eligibility determination must occur within 60 days of referral.

[3] If parents refuse consent for a special education, school district is not responsible for providing a free and appropriate public education.

[4] IEP must be developed within 30 days of eligibility determination.

*Mandatory resolution session required prior to a due process hearing.

Source: R. Gargiulo, *Special Education in Contemporary Society*, 3rd ed. (Thousand Oaks, CA: Sage, 2009), pp. 62–63.

are what distinguish each student from his or her classmates. Interindividual differences are differences *between* pupils. Examples might include distinctions based on height, reading ability, athletic prowess, or intellectual competency. Some interindividual differences are more obvious and of greater educational significance than others.

Interindividual differences are frequently the reason for entry into special education programs. One child might be significantly above (or below) average in intellectual ability; another might exhibit a significant degree of vision loss. Categorization and placement decision making by school personnel revolve around interindividual differences. Stated another way, school authorities identify, label, and subsequently place a student in an instructional program on the basis of the student's interindividual differences.

However, not all pupils in a given program are alike. Children also exhibit **intraindividual differences**—a unique pattern of strengths and weaknesses. Intraindividual differences are differences *within* the child. Instead of looking at how students compare with their peers, teachers focus on the individual's abilities and limitations. We should point out that this is a characteristic of all pupils, not just those enrolled in special education programs. For example, Roberto, who is the best artist in his eighth grade class, is equally well known for his inability to sing. One of his classmates, Melinda, has a learning disability. Her reading ability is almost three years below grade level; yet she consistently earns very high grades in math.

Intraindividual differences are obviously of importance to teachers. A student's individualized education program (IEP) or Section 504 accommodation plan reflects this concern. Assessment data, derived from a variety of sources, typically profile a pupil's strengths and needs. This information is then used in crafting a customized instructional plan tailored to meet the unique needs of the learner.

Referral and Assessment for a Special Education

"Evaluation [assessment] is the gateway to special education, but referral charts the course to the evaluation process" (Turnbull, Turnbull, Erwin, & Soodak, 2006, p. 232). Litigation, legislative requirements, and today's best practices serve as our road map as we travel along the evaluation pathway to providing appropriate educational experiences for students with disabilities. This journey from referral to assessment to the development of an IEP and eventual placement in the most appropriate environment is a comprehensive process incorporating many different phases. Figure 2.1 illustrates this process. In the following sections, we examine several of the key elements involved in developing an individualized program plan.

Prereferral

Although evaluation may be the gateway to special education, a great deal of activity occurs prior to a student ever taking their first test. Careful scrutiny of our model

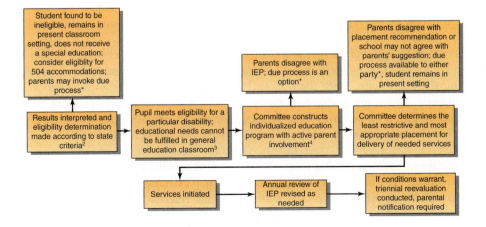

reveals an intervention strategy known as **prereferral intervention**, which occurs prior to initiating a referral for possible special education services. The purpose of this strategy is to reduce unwarranted referrals while providing individualized assistance to the student in an inclusive environment without the benefit of a special education. Although not mandated by IDEA, prereferral interventions have become increasingly common over the past two decades. In fact, IDEA 2004 permits the use of federal dollars to support these activities. Well over half of the states either require or recommend the use of this tactic with individuals suspected of having a disability (Buck, Polloway, Smith-Thomas, & Cook, 2003).

Prereferral interventions are preemptive by design. They call for collaboration between general educators and other professionals for the express purpose of developing creative, alternative instructional and/or management strategies designed to accommodate the specific needs of an individual learner. This process results in shared responsibility and joint decision making among general and special educators, related service providers, administrators, and other school personnel, all of whom possess specific expertise. Interestingly, in many instances, the pupil's parents are not involved in this early phase; although, their input could be invaluable. We believe that their participation should be encouraged.

The child's success or failure in school no longer depends exclusively on the pedagogical skills of the general educator; rather, it is now the combined responsibility of the school-based **intervention assistance team** (also commonly called teacher assistance teams, instructional support teams, or child/student study teams [Buck et al., 2003]). This group is charged with constructing academic accommodations or behavioral interventions for children believed to be at risk for school failure. Once the learning/behavioral accommodations are initiated, the student's progress is monitored for a prescribed period of time—often one grading period. If the strategies are successful, no further action is required as the desired outcomes were achieved. However, as beneficial as prereferral interventions often are, in some cases they are unsuccessful. Detailed documentation of the ineffectiveness of either the instructional adaptations or behavioral supports provides strong justification for the initiation of a formal referral for special education services. Figure 2.2 is one example of the type of planning document typically used by intervention assistance teams.

Referral

A referral is the first step in a long journey toward receiving a special education. As we have just seen, a referral may start as a result of unsuccessful prereferral interventions, or it may be the outcome of child-find efforts (IDEA-mandated screening and identification of individuals suspected of needing special education).

Simply stated, a referral is a written request to evaluate a student to determine whether or not the child has a disability. Typically, a referral begins with a general educator; it may also be initiated by a school administrator, related services provider, concerned parent, or other individual. Referrals typically arise from a concern about the child's academic achievement and/or social/behavioral problems. In some instances, a referral may be initiated because of a pupil's cultural or linguistic background; it may even be the result of problems caused by inappropriate teacher expectations or poor instructional strategies. Thus, the reasons for the referral may not always lie within the student. This is one reason why prereferral intervention strategies are so important. Only about 75 percent of the referrals for special education services actually result in placement; the remaining children are found ineligible (Ysseldyke, 2001).

Referral forms vary in their format. Generally, in addition to student demographic information, a referral must contain detailed reasons as to why the request is being made. Teachers must clearly describe the pupil's academic and/or social performance. Documentation typically accompanies the referral and may include test scores, checklists, behavioral observation data, and actual samples of the student's

Student: _____   Teacher: _____

Grade: _____   Date: _____

Intervention Plan

ACADEMIC MODIFICATIONS

What strategy/method is to be used?

_____

_____

How is it to be done?

_____

_____

Where will it be done?

_____

_____

When will it be done?

_____

_____

How long will it be done?

_____

_____

Who is responsible?

_____

_____

BEHAVIORAL STRATEGIES

_____

_____

PARENT/HOME ACTIVITIES

_____

_____

MOTIVATIONAL/INCENTIVE SYSTEM

_____

_____

DATA COLLECTION ACTIVITIES

How will effectiveness be assessed?

_____

_____

Who will collect the data?

_____

_____

How often will the data be collected?

_____

_____

FOLLOW-UP PLANS/PROCEDURES

How often will the team meet to monitor the plan?

_____

_____

What is our criteria for success?

_____

_____

Who will help the teacher implement the plan?

_____

_____

GENERAL COMMENTS

_____

_____

Figure 2.2 Sample Prereferral Intervention Planning Form

Source: Adapted from C. Ormsbee, "Effective Preassessment Team Procedures: Making the Process Work for Teachers and Students," *Intervention in School and Clinic, 36,* 2001, p. 151.

work. Teachers need to paint as complete a picture as possible of their concern(s), as well as their efforts to rectify the situation.

In most schools, the information that has been gathered is then reviewed by a committee, often known as the child study committee, special services team, or other such name. The composition of this group of professionals varies but typically includes an administrator, school psychologist, and experienced teachers. Other personnel may also be involved, depending on the nature of the referral. It is the job of this committee to review the available information and decide whether or not further assessment is warranted. If the team decides to proceed, a written request for permission to evaluate is sent to the child's parent(s). School authorities must obtain permission of the parent/guardian before proceeding with a formal evaluation. Interestingly, IDEA does not require parental consent for referrals. We believe, however, that it is wise to notify parents that a referral is being initiated, explain the reasons for the referral, and solicit their input and cooperation in the referral process.

Assessment

The first step in determining whether or not a student has a disability, and is in need of a special education, is securing the consent of the child's parent(s)/guardian(s) for the evaluation. As noted previously, this step is mandated by IDEA as part of the procedural safeguards protecting the legal rights of parent(s)/guardian(s). Under the provisions of IDEA, school officials must notify the pupil's parent(s)/guardian(s), in their native language, of the school's intent to evaluate (or refuse to evaluate) the student and the rationale for this decision; they must explain the assessment process and

In the Classroom

Assessment Accommodations

In order to accurately portray a pupil's abilities and needs, assessment accommodations are sometimes necessary. Accommodations are changes in how students access and demonstrate learning without changing the standards they are working toward. Accommodations must be individualized; not all pupils require them, nor do students with the same disability require the same type of accommodations. The need for accommodations may change over time; some individuals may require fewer accommodations, whereas in other situations additional support is required. Listed below are examples of accommodations that IEP teams may find beneficial.

Presentation accommodations let students access assignments, tests, and activities in ways other than reading standard print. Students with print disabilities (inability to visually decode standard print because of a physical, sensory, or cognitive disability) may require a combination of these accommodations:

- Visual: large print, magnification devices, sign language, visual cues
- Tactile: Braille, Nemeth code, tactile graphics
- Auditory: human reader, audiotape or CD, audio amplification device
- Visual and auditory: screen reader, videotape, descriptive video, talking materials

Response accommodations allow students to complete assignments, tests, and activities in different ways or solve or organize problems using an assistive device or organizer. Response accommodations include:

- Different ways to complete assignments, tests, and activities: expressing responses to a scribe through speech, sign language, pointing, or assistive communication device; typing on or speaking to a word processor, brailler, or tape recorder; writing in a test booklet instead of on an answer sheet
- Materials or devices to solve or organize responses: calculation devices; spelling and grammar assistive devices; visual or graphic organizers

Timing and scheduling accommodations give students the time and breaks they need to complete assignments, tests, and activities and may change the time of day, day of the week, or number of days over which an activity takes place. These include:

- Extended time
- Multiple or frequent breaks
- Changing the testing schedule or order of subtests
- Dividing long-term assignments

Setting accommodations change the location in which a student receives instruction or the conditions of the setting. Students may be allowed to sit in a different location than the majority of students to:

- Reduce distractions
- Receive distracting accommodations
- Increase physical access
- Use special equipment

Source: Adapted from S. Thompson, "Choosing and Using Accommodations on Assessments," *CEC Today, 10*(6), 2004, pp. 12, 18.

alternatives available to the parent/guardian, such as the right to an independent evaluation of their son or daughter. Many school districts automatically send parent(s)/guardian(s) a statement of their legal rights when permission to initially evaluate is sought.

Assessment, according to McLean, Wolery, and Bailey (2004), "is a generic term that refers to the process of gathering information for the purpose of making decisions" (p. 13). Educational assessment can rightly be thought of as an information gathering and decision-making process.

One of the goals of the assessment process is to obtain a complete profile of the student's strengths and needs. By law (IDEA), this requires the use of a **multidisciplinary team** of professionals, of which one member must be a teacher. The team is responsible for developing an individualized and comprehensive assessment package that evaluates broad developmental domains (cognitive, academic, achievement) as well as the specific areas of concern noted on the referral, such as social/emotional problems or suspected visual impairments.

Successful accomplishment of this task dictates the use of both formal and informal assessment tools. Once again, IDEA is very clear about this issue: No one procedure may be used as the sole basis of evaluation; a multitude of tests are required. IDEA regulations further require that the evaluations be presented in the pupil's native language or, when necessary, via other modes of communication such as sign language or Braille for students with a sensory impairment. Additionally, the selection and administration of the assessment battery must accurately reflect the child's aptitude and achievement and not penalize the student because of his or her impairment in sensory, manual, or speaking skills. The accompanying In the Classroom feature describes some accommodations that may be needed for accurate assessment.

School psychologists, educational diagnosticians, and other professionals responsible for evaluating the student have a wide variety of assessment instruments at their disposal. Evaluators attempt to gauge both inter- and intraindividual differences by using both norm- and criterion-referenced assessments. Simply stated, **norm-referenced** tests are standardized tests and are linked to interindividual differences. Norm-referenced tests compare a pupil's performance with that of a representative sample of children, providing the evaluator with an indication of the pupil's performance relative to other individuals of similar chronological age. Data are typically presented in terms of percentile ranks, stanines, or grade equivalent scores. Data gleaned from norm-referenced tests provide limited instructional information. In contrast, **criterion-referenced** tests are associated with intraindividual differences and can provide data that are useful for instructional planning. In this type of assessment procedure, a student's performance on a task is compared to a particular level of mastery. The criterion level is typically established by the classroom teacher. Criterion-referenced assessments are especially helpful for identifying the specific skills the pupil has already mastered as well as the skills that require additional instruction. Teachers are concerned with the individual's pattern of strengths and needs rather than how the student compares with his or her classmates.

As mentioned earlier, evaluators must put together a complete educational portrait of the student's abilities. This frequently requires multiple sources of information, which typically include standardized tests, work samples, and observational data, among other forms of input.

Table 2.1 summarizes some of the types of assessments increasingly being used by evaluation specialists to complement data derived from norm-referenced tests.

Instructional Programming and Appropriate Placement

When properly conducted, educational assessments lead to the development of meaningful IEPs. Measurable annual goals (and short-term objectives/benchmarks for pupils evaluated via alternative assessments) are crafted based upon data

Cengage Learning/Wadsworth

Formal and informal assessment tools may be used to determine a pupil's strengths and needs.

Table 2.1	Emerging Sources of Assessment Information
Source	**Description**
Naturalistic Observation	Documentation of qualitative as well as quantitative aspects of youngster's behavior in natural environment. Information may be recorded formally (rating scales, observational recording systems) or informally (anecdotal records, audio recordings). Data can be used to support or refute information gathered from other sources.
Interviews	Information obtained from significant individuals in student's life—parents, teachers, older siblings, or the pupil him/herself. Interviews are a planned and purposeful activity whose purpose is to gain insight or perspective on specific areas of interest, such as the child's background or possible reasons for behavioral problems. Format may be formal (interviewer follows a predetermined set of questions) or informal (interview proceeds according to the individual's responses). Data may be gathered orally or in writing.
Work Samples	Evidence of a pupil's actual classroom performance, typically focused on particular skill development. Sometimes referred to as a permanent product. Spelling tests, arithmetic fact sheets, and handwriting samples are examples of this information source. Work samples are especially useful when planning instructional intervention and modification. Requires teacher to think diagnostically and to look, for example, at error patterns or clarity of directions.
Portfolios	A type of authentic assessment, portfolios are an outgrowth of the familiar work folder concept. They include a wide range of examples of a student's emerging abilities and accomplishments over time. Qualitative and quantitative indicators of performance might include writing samples, audio/video recordings, worksheets, drawings, photographs, or other forms of evidence. Useful for student self-assessment.

gleaned from these evaluations. But first, the multidisciplinary team must determine whether or not the student is eligible to receive special education services according to specific state criteria. Eligibility standards differ from state to state, but most are framed around IDEA criteria.

If team members, working in concert with the child's parent(s), determine that the student fails to qualify for a special education, we suggest developing intervention strategies and recommendations for accommodations to address the referral concerns. We believe this is necessary because the pupil will remain in his or her present placement—the general education classroom. Additionally, the team might also wish to consider the pupil for a Section 504 accommodation plan if the student is eligible for such services. (We will address this topic in greater detail later in this chapter.) Parent(s)/guardian(s) must be sent written notification summarizing the evaluation and stating why their son or daughter is ineligible to receive a special education. If, however, it is determined that the pupil is eligible for a special education, the multidisciplinary team is then confronted with two monumental tasks: constructing the IEP and determining the most appropriate placement for the student.

The Individualized Education Program

Each student identified by a multidisciplinary child study team as having a disability and in need of a special education, must have an individualized program plan of specially designed instruction that addresses their unique needs. An individualized education program (IEP) is the guide to the design and delivery of customized services and instruction. It also serves as the vehicle for collaboration and cooperation between parents and professionals as they jointly devise appropriate educational experiences.

An IEP is part of an overall strategy designed to deliver services appropriate to the individual needs of pupils ages 3 and older. By the time we reach the IEP stage, the appropriate permissions have been gathered, assessments have been conducted, and a disability determination has been made. We are now at the point where the IEP is to be developed, followed by placement in the most appropriate and least restrictive setting. Bateman and Linden (2006) make a very important point about when the IEP is to be developed. They believe that IEPs are often written at the wrong time. Legally, the IEP is to be developed within 30 days following the evaluation and determination of the child's disability, but *before* a placement recommendation is formulated. Placement in the least restrictive and most normalized setting is based on a completed IEP, not the other way around. An IEP should not be limited by placement options or the availability of services. We believe it is best to see the IEP as a management tool or planning vehicle that provides instructional direction and ensures that children with disabilities receive an individualized education appropriate to their unique needs. This focus is in concert with both the intent and spirit of IDEA. IEPs are written by a team. At a minimum, participation must include a parent/guardian; the child's teachers, including a general education teacher and a special educator; a representative from the school district who is knowledgeable about special education, the general education curriculum, and the availability of resources in the local school district; and an individual able to interpret the instructional implications of the evaluation. When appropriate, the student, as well as other professionals who possess pertinent information or whose expertise is desired, may participate at the discretion of the parent or school. Parents have a legal right to participate meaningfully in this planning and decision-making process; they serve as the child's advocate. Although IDEA mandates a collaborative role for parents, it does not stipulate the degree or extent of their participation.

IEPs will vary greatly in their format and degree of specificity. Government regulations do not specify the level of detail considered appropriate, nor do they stipulate how the IEP is to be constructed—only that it be a written document. What is specified are the components (see the accompanying Teaching All Students feature).

Teaching All Students

Elements of a Meaningful IEP

- *Current Performance.* A statement of the student's present levels of educational and functional performance, including how a pupil's disability affects his or her involvement in the general education curriculum, or for preschoolers, how the disability affects participation in age-appropriate activities

- *Goals.* A statement of measurable annual goals that address the student's involvement and progress in the general education curriculum as well as the student's other education needs; short-term objectives or benchmarks are required for pupils who take alternate assessments aligned to alternate achievement standards

- *Special Education and Related Services.* A statement of special education, related services, and supplementary aids and services (based on peer-reviewed research) to be provided, including program modifications or supports necessary for the student to advance toward attainment of annual goals; to be involved and progress in the general education curriculum, extracurricular, and nonacademic activities; and to be educated and participate in activities with other children both with and without disabilities

- *Participation with Typical Students.* An explanation of the extent, if any, to which the student will *not* participate in the general education classroom

- *Participation in State- and Districtwide Assessments.* A statement of any individual modifications needed for the student to participate in state-or districtwide assessment; if student will not participate, a statement of why the assessment is inappropriate and how the pupil will be assessed

- *Dates and Places.* Projected date for initiation of services; expected location, duration, and frequency of such services

- *Transition Services.* Beginning at age 16, a statement of needed transition services identifying measurable post-school goals (training, education, employment, and, if appropriate, independent living skills), including a statement of interagency linkages and/or responsibilities

- *Measuring Progress.* A statement of how progress toward annual goals will be measured and how student's parents (guardians) will be regularly informed of such progress

- *Age of Majority.* At least one year before reaching age of majority, information regarding transfer of rights to student upon reaching age of majority

As stated previously, an IEP is, in essence, a management tool that stipulates *who* will be involved in providing a special education, *what* services will be offered, *where* they will be delivered, and for *how long*. In addition, an IEP gauges *how successfully* goals have been met. Although the IEP does contain a measure of accountability, it is not a legally binding contract; schools are not liable if goals are not achieved. Schools are liable, however, if they do not provide the services stipulated in the IEP. IEPs are to be reviewed annually, although parents may request an earlier review. A complete reevaluation of the pupil's eligibility for special education must occur every three years. PL 105-17 waived this requirement, however, if both the parents and school officials agree that such a review is not necessary.

The IEP is not meant to be so comprehensive that it serves as the entire instructional agenda, nor is it intended to dictate what the child is taught. They do have to be individualized, however, and address the unique learning and/or behavioral requirements of the student. It is for this reason that we find fault with the growing reliance on computer-generated goals and objectives. Although computer-managed IEPs may serve as a useful logistical tool, like Bateman and Linden (2006), we have grave doubts as to the educational relevancy of this procedure and question its legality. We hope teachers will use this resource only as a starting point for designing customized and individually tailored plans.

One of the challenges confronting the IEP team is ensuring that students have access to the general education curriculum as stipulated in the 1997 reauthorization of IDEA. But what is the general education curriculum? In most instances, it is the curriculum that typical learners are exposed to, which is often established by individual state boards of education. The IEP must address how the pupil's disability affects his or her involvement in and ability to progress in the general education curriculum. The underlying assumption seems to be that even if a child is receiving a special education, he or she should engage the general education curriculum. Documentation is required if the team believes that this curriculum is inappropriate for a particular student.

IDEA 2004 requires the IEP team to develop measurable annual goals while also emphasizing exposure to the general education curriculum. Goal statements are purposely broad. Their intent is to provide long-range direction to a student's educational program, not to define exact instructional tasks. Based on the pupil's current level of performance, goals are "written to reflect what a student needs in order to become involved in and to make progress in the general education curriculum" (Yell, 2006, p. 293). They represent reasonable projections or estimates of what the pupil should be able to accomplish within the academic year. They also answer the question, "What should the students be doing?" Annual goals can reflect academic functioning, social behavior, adaptive behavior, or life skills. Regardless of their emphasis, goal statements should be positive, student oriented, and relevant (Polloway, Patton, & Serna, 2008).

Measurable annual goals should include the following five components:

- The student . . . (the who)
- Will do what . . . (the behavior)
- To what level or degree . . . (the criterion)
- Under what conditions . . . (the conditions)
- In what length of time . . . (the time frame)

"Marvin will read 90–110 words of connected text per minute with 100% accuracy at the end of 36 weeks" is an example of a measurable annual goal (Alabama State Department of Education, 2006).

Short-term objectives or **benchmarks**, typically one to three months in duration, are only required in the IEPs of students with significant cognitive deficits— typically those learners who complete alternate assessments aligned to alternate achievement standards. These statements, written after goals have been crafted, describe the sequential steps the pupil will take to meet the intent of each goal

Cengage Learning/Wadsworth

Parents have a legal right to participate in the development of their child's individualized education program.

statement. Benchmarks are usually written by teachers and describe anticipated student accomplishment. Additionally, the IEP team is required to consider the unique needs of the student. In some instances, the IEP may need to address:

- behavior intervention strategies and positive behavior supports for pupils whose behavior impedes their learning or that of their classmates
- instruction in and the use of Braille for learners with visual impairments
- the need for assistive technology devices and services
- the language and communication needs for students with hearing impairments
- the need for services that extend beyond the typical school year
- for pupils whose language is other than English, the need for ESL (English as a second language) services

Quality IEPs largely depend on having well-written and appropriate goals (and objectives) that address the unique needs of the individual (see this text's companion website for an example of an IEP). IEPs are the primary means of ensuring that a specially designed educational program is provided. Table 2.2 provides a summary of the necessary components of an IEP, and the accompanying In the Classroom feature provides a sample agenda for an IEP team meeting.

Table 2.2	Components of an IEP
For All Students	**For Some Students**
• Present level of performance	• Transition—including transfer of rights at age of majority
• Measurable annual goals (and objectives if appropriate)	• Behavior intervention plan
• Assessment status	• ESL needs
• Participation with nondisabled peers	• Braille requirements
• Description of related services	• Communication needs
• Progress monitoring and reporting	• Assistive technology needs

Source: Adapted from B. Bateman and M. Linden, *Better IEPs: How to Develop Legally Correct and Educationally Useful Programs*, 4th ed. (Champaign, IL: Research Press, 2006), p. 57.

Related Services

Teachers today no longer work in isolation. In fact, because of tremendous student diversity, it is increasingly common for teachers to work in partnership with professionals from other disciplines. An IEP team is a good example of this partnership. Successfully meeting the needs of students with special needs in inclusive classrooms requires collaboration and cooperation between and among a wide variety of service providers. For those pupils with a disability, IDEA requires that their IEP provide **related services** if the student is to receive benefit from their special education. For example, a girl with orthopedic impairments might require physical therapy to aid in maintaining muscle tone and flexibility, a school bus equipped with a lift may also be necessary if she uses a wheelchair. Another student with autism might require services from a speech-language pathologist because of significant language delays. In other instances, school social workers might be involved if a teacher suspects one of the students is a victim of child abuse or neglect.

Related services, which essentially are noninstructional services, are obviously a key component of an individual's educational program. Examples of related services include:

- Physical therapy
- Audiology
- School nurse services
- Transportation
- Speech and language
- Psychology
- Recreational therapy
- Orientation mobility
- Interpretive services
- Occupational therapy
- Nutrition
- School social work
- Vocational education
- Rehabilitation counseling
- Parent counseling
- Health services

In the Classroom

Suggested Individualized Education Program Meeting Agenda

- Welcome and introduction of participants and their respective roles
- Statement of purpose
- Review of previous year's IEP (except for initial placement) and accomplishments
- Discussion of student's present level of performance and progress:
  - Assessment information
  - Strengths and emerging areas
- Consideration of specific needs:
  - Instructional modifications and accommodations
  - Participation in state- and districtwide assessments
  - Participation in general education curriculum and extra-curricular activities
- Related services
- Assistive technology needs
- Transition goals
- Behavior intervention plan
- Language needs for student with limited English proficiency
- Braille instruction for student who is visually impaired
- Development of annual goals (and benchmarks if appropriate)
- Recommendations and justification for placement in least restrictive environment
- Closing comments, securing of signatures
- Copies of IEP provided to all team members

Cengage Learning/Wadsworth

Related services are a critical component of a pupil's individualized education program.

The preceding list is neither complete nor exhaustive. Other services may be provided if deemed necessary by the IEP team.

Fortunately, there is a growing recognition among educators today of the importance of professionals working together regardless of the different disciplines they may represent. Because no one discipline or profession possesses all of the resources or skills needed to develop the educational experiences called for by learners with special needs, it is imperative that service providers work in a cooperative and collaborative fashion.

Section 504 Accommodation Plan

Recall from Chapter 1 that **Section 504** of the Rehabilitation Act of 1973 (PL 93-112) is a civil rights law designed to prohibit discrimination against individuals with disabilities The intent of this legislation, according to Smith (2002), is to create equal opportunities for persons with disabilities. Far-reaching in its intent and coverage, this law holds great significance for educators. Section 504 provides for, among other things, that students with disabilities (who are otherwise qualified) have equal access to programs, activities, and services, which are available to pupils without disabilities. This provision includes, for example, field trips, extracurricular activities, and academic courses (with appropriate accommodations) in addition to physical accessibility. Interestingly, because this law is an antidiscrimination statute, federal funds are not available to help schools meet the various requirements of Section 504. As this law pertains to education, PL 93-112 requires schools adhere to the following provisions:

- Annually identify and locate all children with disabilities who are unserved.
- Provide a "free, appropriate public education" to each student with a disability, regardless of the nature or severity of the disability. This means providing general or special education and related aids and services designed to meet the individual educational needs of persons with disabilities as adequately as the needs of nondisabled persons are met.
- Ensure that each student with disabilities is educated with nondisabled students to the maximum extent appropriate.

- Establish nondiscriminatory evaluation and placement procedures to avoid the inappropriate education that may result from the misclassification or misplacement of students.
- Establish procedural safeguards to enable parents and guardians to participate meaningfully in decisions regarding the evaluation and placement of their children.
- Afford children with disabilities an equal opportunity to participate in nonacademic and extracurricular services and activities. (Office for Civil Rights, 1989, p. 8)

Who Is Protected by Section 504?

Although 504 protections are afforded to persons with disabilities across their lifespan, our focus here is on school-age individuals. As we noted in Chapter 1, all students eligible for services under IDEA are also protected by Section 504. The converse of this statement is not true, however. Some examples of pupils eligible for services under Section 504 include:

- a student referred for special education services but who does not qualify under IDEA;
- individuals who are no longer eligible for services under IDEA or who transition out of a special education program;
- students with a history of substance abuse;
- victims of abuse and neglect;
- pupils with health needs, such as diabetes, asthma, severe allergies, hemophilia, or communicable diseases; and
- someone with a low IQ but who is not considered intellectually disabled.

Obviously, due to the broader scope of the definition of a disability incorporated in Section 504, significantly greater numbers of students are eligible to receive a free, appropriate public education via Section 504 then would be afforded services under IDEA.

Providing a Free, Appropriate Public Education

Similar to the requirements found in IDEA 2004, schools are required to provide a free, appropriate public education (FAPE) to pupils found eligible for Section 504 services and protections. This process involves the five areas of referral, evaluation, program planning, placement, and reevaluation. The specific requirements of the 504 FAPE process include:

- **Referral**—Schools are required to refer students who they think would be eligible for Section 504 services. A committee of knowledgeable individuals will make that determination. Parents or school personnel may make referrals.
- **Evaluation**—If the committee believes that the child would probably be eligible for Section 504 services, an evaluation of the area of suspected need must be completed. This evaluation must use nondiscriminatory procedures.
- **Eligibility Determination**—After the evaluation, the committee must determine if the student has a physical or mental impairment that substantially limits a major life activity.
- **Accommodation Plan Development**—If the committee determines that the student is eligible under Section 504, an accommodation plan must be developed.
- **Periodic Reevaluation**—The school must periodically reevaluate the student to determine continuing eligibility under Section 504. (Smith, 2002, p. 263)

The required steps for providing a free, appropriate public education are illustrated in Figure 2.3.

Section 504 Eligibility Determination

Anyone can refer a pupil for a Section 504 services with general educators and parents being the two most likely individuals. As found in IDEA, just because a pupil is referred does not mean that he or she will be eligible for services. A committee of school personnel who has knowledge of the student makes the eligibility determination (Smith, 2001).

As we saw earlier in Chapter 1, eligibility determination under Section 504 is not based on whether or not a student has a particular disability warranting a special education, but rather, whether there is a substantial limitation to a major life activity resulting from a physical or mental impairment. In many instances, this is a subjective process involving professional judgment. Observations, anecdotal information, and opinions are considered legitimate sources of assessment information. Norm-referenced assessments may be used but are *not* required as part of the evaluation process (Smith, 2001, 2002).

Making a determination as to whether or not a pupil is eligible for Section 504 services in the absence of test scores and other quantitative information may make some educators uncomfortable. Smith and Patton (1998) recommend that school personnel consider the duration and intensity of the student's impairment. They have developed a process for assisting teachers and other school personnel in their

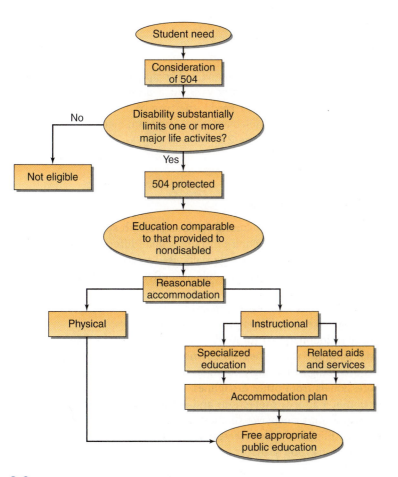

Figure 2.3 Section 504 Decision Making
Source: Adapted from *Student Access: A Resource Guide for Educators* (Albuquerque, NM: Council of Administrators of Special Education, 1992), p. 3a.

decision-making process. This procedure involves using a rating form incorporating a Likert-type scale for assessing the duration and intensity of various functional limitations. The use of this instrument offers school personnel a defensible position for their eligibility decision. Once a student has been found eligible for Section 504 services, an accommodation plan must be developed.

Accommodation Plans

Section 504 **accommodation plans** should be simple, inexpensive, and easy to use. The majority of accommodations will occur in the general education classroom. It is important to note that special educators are not liable for Section 504 accommodations; this responsibility belongs to general education teachers. Designed for an individual pupil, these plans should include the information necessary to enable the individual to have equal access to educational and extracurricular activities while also providing an equal opportunity to be successful (Smith, 2002). Many of the accommodations are common sense and will vary depending on the needs of the learner. Examples include:

- preferential seating
- extended test time
- rest periods during the school day
- tape-recorded lessons
- modified attendance policies
- oral testing options
- peer note-taker
- outlines and study guides
- textbooks kept at home

Accommodation plans do not have mandated components like IEPs do. The format of these plans will, therefore, greatly vary. At a minimum, this document should identify the pupil's strengths and needs, the type of accommodation required, the individual(s) responsible for implementation, and team members. A basic accommodation plan is illustrated in Figure 2.4.

Thematic Summary

- Effective instructional planning for learners with special needs requires that educators consider the pupil's intraindividual differences.
- Prereferral interventions are typically used to reduce unwarranted referrals for special education services while also offering assistance to the student in an inclusive setting.
- Educational assessments, incorporating both norm- and criterion-referenced tests, lead to the development of meaningful IEPs.
- An IEP is foundational to providing students with disabilities with an education appropriate to their unique needs.
- It is becoming increasingly common for teachers to work in partnership with professionals from other disciplines.
- Section 504 affords protections and services to students who have a physical or mental impairment which substantially limits a major life activity such as learning. Eligible pupils receive accommodations in the general education classroom via "504 plans."

Name: __Jason Wentworth__   Birthdate: __February 23, 1999__

School: __Greystone Elementary__   Grade: __3rd__

Teacher: __Mary Russell__   Date: __November 13, 2008__

Review Date: __At the end of the 6-week grading period__

General Strengths: Jason has above average intellectual ability. He is popular with his classmates. Discipline is generally not a problem. Supportive and involved parents.

General Weaknesses: Jason exhibits ADHD. He has difficulty concentrating (except for brief periods of time) and he is easily distracted. Classroom assignments and homework are frequently not completed. Recent evidence of growing frustration and loss of self-esteem.

Specific Accommodations

Accommodation #1

Class: __All classes__

Accommodation(s): __Worksheets will be modified so less material is presented on each page. Allow extra time for completion if necessary.__

Person Responsible for Implementation: __Mrs. Russell__

Accommodation #2

Class: __All classes__

Accommodation(s): __Jason will be given access to a study carrel when working on classroom assignments or taking tests.__

Person Responsible for Implementation: __Mrs. Russell__

Accommodation #3

Class: __All classes__

Accommodation(s): __Jason will record daily homework activities in assignment notepad. Teacher will check for accuracy and parents will sign notepad and return it to school.__

Person Responsible for Implementation: __Mrs. Russell__

Accommodation #4

Class: __All classes__

Accommodation(s): __Jason will receive praise and recognition for task completion and appropriate behavior. Teacher to provide immediate feedback whenever possible.__

Person Responsible for Implementation: __Mrs. Russell__

General Comments: __Weekly progress reports to parents via telephone or email.__

Accommodation Plan Team Members:

Name	Team Members' Signature	Position/Title
Ms. Claire Wentworth	*Claire Wentworth*	Parent/Guardian
Mr. Ralph Hastings	*Ralph Hastings*	Assistant Principal/ 504 Coordinator
Ms. Mildred Smith	*Mildred Smith*	School Counselor
Ms. Jennifer Jenkins	*Jennifer Jenkins*	Resource Teacher
Ms. Mary Russell	*Mary Russell*	General Educator

Copies: Parent

Classroom Teacher(s)

Cumulative File

Other: _____

Figure 2.4 Section 504 Accommodation Plan
Source: Form adapted from T. Smith and J. Patton, *Section 504 and Public Schools: A Practical Guide* (Austin, TX: Pro-Ed, 1998), p. 45.

Making Connections for Inclusive Teaching

1. How might prereferral interventions benefit a pupil suspected of requiring a special education?
2. Describe some of the alternatives to norm-referenced assessments. Why should teachers consider information from these sources?
3. "As a general educator, I don't have the time or the expertise to comply with the IEP accommodations of all my students; besides, this document is simply some paperwork to be placed in the students' file." Refute this statement. Why might some teachers express this belief?
4. How might an IEP and a Section 504 accommodation plan improve the quality of instruction for all students in an inclusive setting?

Learning Activities

1. Obtain examples of IEP forms and Section 504 accommodation plans from different school districts in your vicinity. In what ways do these forms differ? How are they the same? Do they fulfill the requirements of the law as outlined in your textbook?
2. Visit an elementary school and a middle or high school in your community. Talk to several general education teachers at each site who serve students with Section 504 accommodation plans. What types of accommodations do they typically provide their pupils? Are these teachers working with related service providers? If so, what is their role? What do they see as they advantages and disadvantages of including students with special needs in their classrooms?

Looking at the Standards

The content of this chapter most closely aligns itself with the following standards:

INTASC Standards

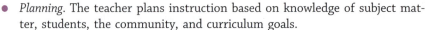

- *Planning.* The teacher plans instruction based on knowledge of subject matter, students, the community, and curriculum goals.
- *Assessment.* The teacher understands and uses formal and informal assessment strategies to evaluate and ensure continuous intellectual, social, and physical development of the learner.

Council for Exceptional Children

Special educators are to have knowledge of the following:

- CC1K4: Rights and responsibilities of students, parents, teachers, and other professionals, and schools related to exceptional learning needs.
- GC1K4: Legal, judicial, and educational systems to assist individuals with disabilities.
- CC7S2: Development and implementation of comprehensive, longitudinal individualized programs in collaboration with team members.
- CC8K3: Screening, prereferral, referral, and classification procedures.
- GC8K2: Laws and policies regarding referral and placement procedures for individuals with disabilities.

Key Concepts and Terms

interindividual differences
intraindividual differences
prereferral intervention
intervention assistance
   team

assessment
multidisciplinary team
norm-referenced
criterion-referenced
benchmarks

related services
Section 504
accommodation plans

References

Alabama State Department of Education. (2006). *Developing standards-based IEPs*. Montgomery, AL: Author.

Bateman, B., & Linden, M. (2006). *Better IEPs* (4th ed.). Champaign, IL: Research Press.

Buck, G., Polloway, E., Smith-Thomas, A., & Cook, K. (2003). Prereferral intervention processes: A survey of state practices. *Exceptional Children, 69*(3), 349–360.

McLean, M., Wolery, M., & Bailey, D. (2004). *Assessing infants and preschoolers with special needs* (3rd ed.). Upper Saddle River, NJ: Pearson Education.

Office for Civil Rights. (1989). *The civil rights of students with hidden disabilities under Section 504 of the Rehabilitation Act of 1973*. Washington, DC: Author.

Polloway, E., Patton, J., & Serna, L. (2008). *Strategies for teaching learners with special needs* (9th ed.). Upper Saddle River, NJ: Pearson Education.

Smith, T. (2001). Section 504, the ADA, and public schools: What educators need to know. *Remedial and Special Education, 22*(6), 335–343.

Smith, T. (2002). Section 504: What teachers need to know. *Intervention in School and Clinic, 37*(5), 259–266.

Smith, T., & Patton, J. (1998). *Section 504 and public schools: A practical guide*. Austin, TX: Pro-Ed.

Turnbull, A., Turnbull, R., Erwin, E., & Soodak, L. (2006). *Families, professionals, and exceptionality* (5th ed.). Upper Saddle River, NJ: Pearson Education.

Yell, M. (2006). *The law and special education* (2nd ed.). Upper Saddle River, NJ: Pearson Education.

Ysseldyke, J. (2001). Reflections on a research career: Generalization from 25 years of research on assessment and instructional decision making. *Exceptional Children, 67*(3), 295–309.

Jupiter Images

Today's Learners I: Students with High Incidence Disabilities and Gifts and Talents

Learners with Mental Retardation

Defining Mental Retardation
Classification of Learners with Mental Retardation
How Many Learners Are Mentally Retarded?
What Are Some of the Causes of Mental Retardation?
Selected Learning and Behavioral Characteristics of Learners with Mental Retardation

Learners with Learning Disabilities

Defining Learning Disabilities
How Many Learners Are Learning Disabled?
What Are Some of the Causes of Learning Disabilities?
Selected Learning and Behavioral Characteristics of Learners with Learning Disabilities

Learning Outcomes

After studying this chapter, you should be able to:

- Identify high incidence disability groups.
- Describe learners with attention deficit hyperactivity disorder and students considered gifted and talented.
- Define the terms: mental retardation, learning disabilities, speech or language impairments, emotional or behavioral disorders, attention deficit hyperactivity disorder, as well as gifted and talented.
- List possible etiological contributions to high incidence disabilities, attention deficit hyperactivity disorder, as well as giftedness and talent.
- Outline the learning and behavioral characteristics of students with high incidence disabilities, attention deficit hyperactivity disorder, and those learners considered gifted and talented.

51

Learners with Speech and Language Disorders

Defining Speech and Language

Classifying Learners with Speech and Language Disorders

How Many Learners Have Speech and Language Disorders?

What Are Some of the Causes of Speech and Language Disorders?

Selected Characteristics of Learners with Speech and Language Disorders

Learners with Emotional or Behavioral Disorders

Defining Emotional or Behavioral Disorders

Classification of Learners with Emotional or Behavioral Disorders

How Many Learners Exhibit Emotional or Behavioral Disorders?

What Are Some of the Causes of Emotional or Behavioral Disorders?

Selected Learning and Behavioral Characteristics of Learners with Emotional or Behavioral Disorders

Learners with Attention Deficit Hyperactivity Disorder

Defining Attention Deficit Hyperactivity Disorder

How Many Learners Have Attention Deficit Hyperactivity Disorder?

What Are Some of the Causes of Attention Deficit Hyperactivity Disorder?

Selected Learning and Behavioral Characteristics of Learners with Attention Deficit Hyperactivity Disorder

Learners with Gifts and Talents

Defining Giftedness

How Many Learners Are Gifted and Talented?

What Are Some of the Causes of Giftedness and Talent?

Selected Learning and Behavioral Characteristics of Learners with Gifts and Talents

Summary of Selected Learning and Behavioral Characteristics

As you learned in Chapter 1, today's teachers have the responsibility of providing effective instruction to an increasingly diverse population of learners. Many of these students frequently exhibit immense differences in learning abilities, languages, and cultures. Our focus in this chapter, however, will be on individuals with **high incidence disabilities**—speech or language impairments, learning disabilities, mental retardation, and emotional disturbance. As a group, these four categories account for 80 percent of children, ages 6–21, receiving a special education under IDEA (U.S. Department of Education, 2008). Students with high incidence disabilities are typically served in inclusive classrooms. Over half of all pupils with learning disabilities, for example, and approximately 85 percent of individuals with speech or language impairments are educated in the general education classroom (U.S. Department of Education). General educators, therefore, will usually have the primary instructional responsibility for ensuring that these learners have access to and success with the general education curriculum.

We will also examine two other large groups of students typically found in today's classrooms. In addition to pupils with high incidence disabilities, teachers may be challenged by individuals with **attention deficit hyperactivity disorder** (ADHD) and children who are recognized as **gifted and talented**. Interestingly, these two groups of learners are not specifically mentioned in IDEA legislation. Mandates to provide services to children and youth who are gifted and talented are the result of state rather than federal legislation. Likewise, ADHD is *not* recognized as a separate disability category under current IDEA legislation. Students with ADHD may be eligible for a special education and related services under the disability category "other health impairment" (OHI). Children with ADHD are also eligible for accommodations in general education classrooms under the protections afforded to them by Section 504 of PL 93-112 (Gargiulo, 2009). (See page 47 for an example of an accommodation plan for a youngster with ADHD.) Like all other pupils, these children have unique needs and learning styles as well as strengths. Because the vast majority of these students are served in general education classrooms, teachers must be able to provide the appropriate accommodations and instructional interventions if these learners are to experience success in school.

We have chosen to include these two groups of learners in this chapter because, like their classmates with high incidence disabilities, they represent large numbers of pupils receiving special services—frequently in inclusive classrooms. ADHD, for instance, is thought to affect anywhere from 3–5 percent of all school-age children (Barkley, 2006; National Institute of Mental Health, 2006). Even though there is little consensus as to the exact number of individuals who are considered gifted and talented, most educators believe that approximately 3–5 percent of the school-age population is gifted (Clark, 2008). Other professionals are of the opinion that upwards of 10 percent of school-age children can be thought of as gifted (Gargiulo, 2009).

Regardless of the exact numbers of students with high incidence disabilities and ADHD as well as those with special gifts and talents, it appears safe to say that the classrooms of the 21st century will present educators with a multitude of instructional challenges. We believe that one result of this situation is that teachers must adopt a new way of looking at their students. Instead of examining class rolls and seeing some pupils as typical and others as having IEPs or accommodation plans due to specific disabilities, in our opinion there is a great advantage in focusing on the *learner* and not a particular label. In this era of high-stakes assessment and enhanced accountability, teachers must focus on the strengths and similarities of their pupils and not their differences. Effective educators look at what their students can do, not what they cannot do. They also realize that children with disabilities and those with gifts and talents are more like their typical classmates than they are different. Today's educational climate calls for learning environments that are responsive to the needs of *all* learners. Teachers who concentrate on their students' strengths and similarities are well-positioned for creating successful inclusive classrooms.

For clarity of presentation, we will initially examine each of the six groups of learners[1] appropriate to this chapter before looking at similarities of needs across cognitive, language, and social domains.

Learners with Mental Retardation

Mental retardation is a complex and multifaceted concept. It is also a powerful and emotionally charged label, one that frequently conjures up various images of individuals with mental retardation. Do you know someone who is mentally retarded? What do you think of when you hear the term *mentally retarded*? In many instances, our images of someone with mental retardation are faulty and are subject to inaccuracies, misconceptions, and stereotypes. Consequently, individuals with mental retardation often encounter prejudice and discrimination simply because they are viewed as "different" from other people. Despite the great diversity encompassed by the term, we are firmly convinced that learners with mental retardation are first and foremost children and adolescents who are more like their nonretarded peers than they are different. Fortunately, very few individuals with mental retardation ever conform to our mistaken images; many, in fact, will frequently exceed our expectations.

[1]Content adapted from R. Gargiulo, *Special Education in Contemporary Society*, 3rd ed. (Thousand Oaks, CA: Sage, 2009).

Our understanding of mental retardation has been an evolving process.

Before defining the term *mentally retarded* we need to acknowledge that the term itself is subject to debate and controversy. Although the use of the term *mentally retarded* is widespread in the United States, in other regions of the world (and parts of this country) alternative labels such as *intellectual disability* or *cognitive impairments* are viewed as being more acceptable. Some professionals in the field and family members of individuals with mental retardation believe that the term is derogatory, stigmatizing, offensive, and one that promotes negative stereotypes (Gelb, 2002; Warren, 2000). Unfortunately, there is no consensus regarding an alternative term. Therefore, we will use the term *mental retardation* because it is currently used by the U.S. Department of Education, many state departments of education (Denning, Chamberlain, & Polloway, 2000), and major professional organizations such as the American Psychiatric Association.

Defining Mental Retardation

Developing an acceptable definition of mental retardation has been an evolving process spanning several decades. Historically speaking, mental retardation was often solely conceptualized as limitations or deficits in intellectual functioning. More contemporary definitions are characterized by limited intellectual abilities coupled with difficulty in meeting the social requirements or expectations of one's environment.

The two most commonly employed definitions today are the IDEA definition and the one championed by the American Association on Intellectual and Developmental Disabilities[2] (AAIDD), the leading professional organization in the field of mental retardation. The IDEA definition describes mental retardation as "significantly subaverage general intellectual functioning existing concurrently with deficits in adaptive behaviors and manifested during the developmental period that adversely affects a child's educational performance" (34 C.F.R. § 300.7[c][6]) (*Federal Register,* 2006). Interestingly, this definition mirrors a 1973 version of the definition crafted by the AAMR. The IDEA definition is currently used by most states when identifying students for special education services.

[2]Prior to January 1, 2007 this organization was known as the American Association on Mental Retardation (AAMR). We use the current name when appropriate.

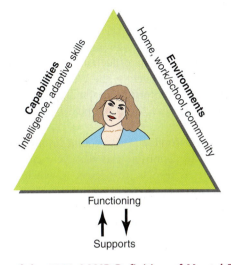

Figure 3.1 Structure of the 1992 AAMR Definition of Mental Retardation
Source: Mental Retardation: Definition, Classification, and Systems of Supports, 9th ed. (Washington, DC: American Association on Mental Retardation, 1992), p. 10.

The most recent attempt in an evolving understanding of mental retardation is the 2002 AAMR definition. This definition states that "mental retardation is a disability characterized by significant limitations both in intellectual functioning and in adaptive skills. This disability originates before age 18" (Luckasson et al., 2002, p. 1). Accompanying this description are five assumptions considered essential when applying this definition:

- Limitations in present functioning must be considered within the context of community environments typical of the individual's age, peers, and culture.
- Valid assessment considers cultural and linguistic diversity as well as differences in communication, sensory, motor, and behavioral factors.
- Within an individual, limitations often coexist with strengths.
- An important purpose of describing limitations is to develop a profile of needed supports.
- With appropriate personalized supports over a sustained period, the life functioning of the person with mental retardation will generally improve. (Luckasson et al., p. 1)

Like the ninth edition developed 10 years earlier, the 2002 AAMR definition retains a positive perspective toward individuals with mental retardation. It is a highly functional definition portraying mental retardation as a relationship among three key elements: the individual, the environment, and the type of support required for maximum functioning in various settings. It essentially reflects the "fit" between the person's capabilities and the structure and expectations of the environment. This version also represents a conceptual shift away from viewing mental retardation as an inherent trait to a perspective that considers the person's present level of functioning and the supports needed to improve it. The interaction among the individual, the environment, and support is depicted in Figure 3.1. The framers of the 1992 definition selected an equilateral triangle to represent their thinking because it shows the equality among the three elements.

The AAMR description of mental retardation stresses functioning in one's community rather than just focusing on the clinical aspect of the individual such as IQ or adaptive behavior. This definition is an optimistic one; it assumes that a person's performance will improve over time when appropriate supports are provided. Though certainly a unique portrayal of mental retardation, this definition retains an emphasis on intellectual performance coupled with impairments in adaptive skills.

The constructs of *intelligence* and *adaptive behavior* play key roles in our understanding of the concept of mental retardation. Both the IDEA and AAMR definitions talk about "significantly subaverage intellectual functioning" which often means an IQ score two or more standard deviations below the mean on an individually administered intelligence test such as the Wechsler Intelligence Scale for Children (Wechsler, 2003) or the Stanford-Binet Intelligence Scale (Roid, 2003). This generally translates into an IQ score of 70 or below. This represents 2.27 percent of the general population.

The notion of **adaptive behavior** is also found in both definitions. It was first introduced in the 1973 AAMR definition that was eventually codified into the IDEA definition. Adaptive behavior is seen as "the degree to which, and the efficiency with which, the individual meets the standards of maturation, learning, personal independence, and/or social responsibility that are expected for his or her age level and cultural group" (Grossman, 1983, p. 11). In continuing this thinking, the 2002 AAMR definition describes adaptive behavior as "the collection of conceptual, social, and practical skills that have been learned by people in order to function in their everyday society" (Luckasson et al., 2002, p. 73). Stated another way, it is how well a person copes with the everyday demands and requirements of his or her environment. The idea of context is important for understanding the concept of adaptive behavior. Because behavior is strongly influenced by cultural factors, age, and situation, appropriateness must always be considered within the setting in which it occurs. For example, a teenage girl who uses her fingers while eating might be viewed as exhibiting inappropriate behavior; however, this behavior is only maladaptive when considered within the context of Western cultures. Table 3.1 illustrates the three areas of adaptive behavior conceptualized within the 2002 AAMR definition.

Finally reference is made to the "developmental period," the time between conception and 18 years of age. This time limit is included to help distinguish mental

Table 3.1	Examples of Conceptual, Social, and Practical Adaptive Skills
Skill Area	**Examples of Behavior**
Conceptual	• Language (receptive and expressive) • Reading and writing • Money concepts • Self-direction
Social	• Interpersonal • Responsibility • Self-esteem • Gullibility (likelihood of being tricked or manipulated) • Naiveté • Follows rules • Obeys laws • Avoids victimization

Practical	• Activities of daily living:
	   • Eating
	   • Transfer/mobility
	   • Toileting
	   • Dressing
	 • Instrumental activities of daily living:
	   • Meal preparation
	   • Housekeeping
	   • Transportation
	   • Taking medication
	   • Money management
	   • Telephone use
	 • Occupational skills
	 • Maintains safe environments

Source: Adapted from *Mental Retardation: Definition, Classification, and Systems of Support*, 10th ed. (Washington, DC: American Association on Mental Retardation, 2002), p. 42.

Table 3.2	Classification of Mental Retardation According to Measured Intelligence	
	Measured IQ	
Classification Level	**Stanford-Binet and Wechsler IQ Tests**	**SD below Mean**
Mild retardation	55–70	2–3
Moderate retardation	40–55	3–4
Severe retardation	25–40	4–5
Profound retardation	<25	>5

Note: IQ scores represent approximate ranges. SD = standard deviation.

retardation from other disabilities such as traumatic brain injury, especially if the intellectual deficits appear after the age of 18.

Classification of Learners with Mental Retardation

A long-standing and popular classification scheme among psychologists and educators is one based on the severity of intellectual impairments as determined by an IQ test. This model is one of the most widely cited in the professional literature (Polloway, Smith, Chamberlain, Denning, & Smith, 1999) and, until recently, reflected the position of the AAIDD dating back to their 1973 definition of mental retardation. According to this system, deficits in intellectual functioning and related impairments in adaptive behavior result in individuals' being classified into one of four levels of mental retardation—mild, moderate, severe, or profound—with mild representing the highest level of performance for persons thought to be mentally retarded and profound the lowest. Intellectual competency is often the primary variable used in constructing these discriminations. Table 3.2 presents the IQ ranges typically used.

The most recent classification scheme is one that looks at the **level of support** an individual requires to be successful in different environments, rather than the severity of their intellectual impairment. The 2002 AAMR definition classifies persons with mental retardation according to four support levels (intermittent, limited, extensive, or pervasive) needed to effectively function across adaptive skill areas in various natural settings. The focus of this approach is to explain an individual's *functional* rather than intellectual limitations, a strategy that we believe has particular merit for students receiving services in inclusive classrooms. Table 3.3 illustrates the four levels currently recommended by the AAMR.

How Many Learners Are Mentally Retarded?

According to data from the U.S. Department of Education (2008), approximately 523,000 children between the ages of 6 and 21 were identified as mentally retarded and receiving a special education during the 2006–2007 school year. These students represent approximately 9 percent of all pupils with disabilities and about 1 percent of the total school-age population.

Within the population of individuals considered mentally retarded, persons with mild mental retardation constitute the largest proportion. It is estimated that approximately 90 percent of people with mental retardation function, to use a familiar term, at the mild level (IQ 50–70/75). The remaining 10 percent are classified as exhibiting moderate, severe, or profound mental retardation (Drew & Hardman, 2007). Mental retardation is the third largest disability category after learning disabilities and speech/language impairments.

What Are Some of the Causes of Mental Retardation?

Determining the cause, or **etiology**, of mental retardation is a difficult process. An individual may be mentally retarded for a multitude of reasons, and often the cause is unknown. In fact, in only about half of all cases of mental retardation can a

Table 3.3	Classification of Mental Retardation According to Intensities of Support	
Support Level	**Description**	**Examples**
Intermittent	Supports on an as-needed or episodic basis. Person does not always need the support(s), or person needs short-term supports during life-span transitions. When provided, intermittent supports may be of high or low intensity.	• Loss of employment • Acute medical crisis
Limited	Supports characterized by consistency over time, time-limited but not intermittent; may require fewer staff and less cost than more intense levels of support.	• Job training • Transitioning from school to adult status
Extensive	Supports characterized by regular involvement (e.g., daily) in at least some environments (such as work or home) and not time-limited.	• Ongoing home living assistance
Pervasive	Supports characterized by their constancy and high intensity; provided across all environments, potential life-sustaining nature. Pervasive supports typically involve more staff and intrusiveness than extensive or time-limited supports.	• Chronic medical situation

Source: Adapted from *Mental Retardation: Definition, Classification, and Systems of Supports,* 10th ed. (Washington, DC: American Association on Mental Retardation, 2002), p. 152.

specific cause be cited (Beirne-Smith, Patton, & Kim, 2006). Generally speaking, the less severe the retardation, the greater is the likelihood that a particular cause cannot be determined.

We would also like to point out that the etiology of a student's mental retardation, or for that matter, any other disability, is generally of little educational relevance. Educators are powerless to do anything about the cause of the child's disability. You will, however, have to deal with the results or consequences of their impairment in terms of unique learning, behavioral, and social characteristics. Remember, no two learners with mental retardation are alike, even if they share the same etiological factor.

Some representative causes of mental retardation are illustrated in Table 3.4 presented according to their time of onset: **prenatal** (occurring before birth), **perinatal** (occurring around the time of birth), and **postnatal** (occurring after birth).

Selected Learning and Behavioral Characteristics of Learners with Mental Retardation

Learners with mental retardation an especially heterogeneous population; interindividual differences are considerable. Many factors influence individual behavior and functioning, such as chronological age, the severity of the disability, its etiology, and educational opportunities. We urge you to remember that students with mental retardation are more like their nonretarded classmates than they are different, sharing many of the same social, emotional, and physical needs. Furthermore, pupils who are mentally retarded, especially those considered mildly mentally retarded, learn in the same way as the average or typical student; albeit, at a slower rate.

The most defining characteristic of someone identified as mentally retarded is impaired cognitive functioning. Yet, investigators are not typically concerned with the person's intellectual ability per se but rather with the impact that lower IQ has on the individual's ability to learn, acquire concepts, process information, and apply knowledge in various settings such as school, home, and community. Because learning is not a unitary variable—it is composed of many interrelated cognitive processes we have chosen to briefly outline several of the dimensions that researchers believe influence learning (see Table 3.5).

Learners with Learning Disabilities

Students with learning disabilities are a very heterogeneous group depicting individuals who typically have normal intelligence, but, for some reason, fail to learn as easily and efficiently as their classmates and peers. The idea that some people

Table 3.4	Representative Possible Causes of Mental Retardation	
Type	**Example**	**Characteristics and Considerations**
	Prenatal Contributions	
Chromosomal abnormality	Down syndrome	• Most common chromosomal abnormality • Distinctive physical characteristics • Generally mild to moderate mental retardation
	Fragile X syndrome	• One of the leading inherited causes of mental retardation • Predominantly affects males • Distinctive physical features • Wide variation in learning characteristics
Metabolic disorders	Phenylketonuria (PKU)	• Inborn error of metabolism, a recessive trait • Dietary intervention initiated shortly after birth prevents occurrence of mental retardation
Maternal infections	Rubella (German measles)	• One of the leading causes of multiple impairments in children • Exposure during first trimester of pregnancy usually results in severe consequences
Environmental conditions	Fetal alcohol syndrome	• One of the leading causes of mental retardation • Mild to moderate mental retardation with concomitant physical deformities
	Perinatal Contributions	
Gestational disorders	Low birth weight/ prematurity	• Infant at risk for serious problems at birth • Potential for learning problems as well as sensory and/or major impairments • More common in mothers living in poverty, teenage pregnancy, and women engaged in substance abuse
Neonatal complications	Anoxia (oxygen deprivation) Birth trauma Breach presentation Prolonged delivery	• Complicating factors surrounding birth *may* cause mental retardation and other developmental delays
	Postnatal Contributions	
Infectious and intoxicants	Meningitis	• Viral infection causing damage to the covering of the brain—the meninges • May result from typical childhood illness such as chicken pox or mumps • Mental retardation is a distinct possibility
	Lead poisoning	• Highly toxic substance • Infants/toddlers living in older homes in impoverished areas at risk for ingesting lead-based paint chips • Potential for causing seizures, central nervous system damage, and brain damage
Environmental factors	Malnutrition Environmental deprivation Child abuse/ neglect	• Correlates, but not necessarily causes, of mental retardation, especially instances of mild mental retardation • Best viewed as interacting psychosocial risk factors which heighten the vulnerability of some children for learning difficulties

Source: Adapted from R. Gargiulo, *Special Education in Contemporary Society*, 3rd ed. (Thousand Oaks, CA: Sage, 2009).

might possess a hidden or invisible disability is of relatively recent origin. The notion of learning disabilities is only about five decades old, but it has quickly grown and today represents the largest category of children and adolescents enrolled in special education.

For a large number of people with learning disabilities, their difficulties are chronic and will persist throughout life. It would be wrong to assume, however,

Table 3.5	Selected Learning and Behavioral Characteristics of Learners with Mental Retardation
Dimension	**Associated Attributes and Features**
Attention	• Inability to attend to critical or relevant features of a task • Diminished attention span • Difficulty ignoring distracting stimuli
Memory	• Deficits in memory correlated with severity of mental retardation • Limitations in ability to selectively process and store information • Inefficient rehearsal strategies • Difficulty with short-term (working) memory is common—recalling directions in sequence presented seconds earlier • Long-term retrieval (recalling telephone number) is similar to peers without mental retardation
Motivation	• History of and a generalized expectancy for failure—**learned helplessness**—effort is unrewarded, failure is inevitable • Exhibit **external locus of control**—belief that outcomes of behavior are the result of circumstances (fate, chance) beyond personal control rather than own efforts • Evidence **outer-directedness**, a loss of confidence, and a distrust of own abilities, reliance on others for cues and guidance
Generalization	• Difficulty applying knowledge or skills to new tasks, situations, or settings • Problem in using previous experience in novel circumstances • Teachers must explicitly plan for generalization; typically it does not occur automatically
Language Development	• Follow same sequence of language acquisition as nonretarded classmates; albeit at a slower rate • Strong correlation between intellectual ability and language development—the higher the IQ the less pervasive the language difficulty • Speech disorders (articulation errors, stuttering) more common then in peers without mental retardation • Vocabulary is often limited • Grammatical structure and sentence complexity are often impaired
Academic Development	• Generally exhibit difficulties in all academic areas with reading the weakest • Problem-solving difficulties in arithmetic
Social Development	• Typically lacking in social competence • Rejection by peers and classmates is common—poor interpersonal skills • Frequently exhibit socially inappropriate or immature behavior—difficulty establishing and maintaining friendships • Diminished self-esteem coupled with low self-concept

that these individuals are incapable of accomplishments and a life of quality. Some of the most distinguished individuals and brightest minds the world has ever known had extreme difficulty in learning and could easily be considered learning disabled. Some of these eminent people include Leonardo da Vinci, Auguste Rodin, Albert Einstein, Thomas Edison, Woodrow Wilson, Winston Churchill, Walt Disney, and Ernest Hemingway (Lerner & Kline, 2006; Smith, Polloway, Patton, & Dowdy, 2008). By all accounts, the preceding individuals were very successful persons; but they are exceptions. The vast majority of children and adolescents with learning disabilities will be frequently misunderstood and experience ongoing challenges and frustrations in their daily lives at school, at home, and in the community.

Defining Learning Disabilities

Students with learning disabilities have always been in our classrooms, but professionals have often failed to identify these pupils and recognize their special needs. These children have been known by a variety of confusing and sometimes controversial labels, including neurologically impaired, perceptually disordered, dyslexic, slow learner, remedial reader, and hyperactive. More than 35 years ago, Cruickshank (1972) published a list of some 40 terms used to describe students known as learning disabled. Deiner's (1993) more recent analysis found more than 90 terms used in professional literature to characterize individuals with learning disabilities.

Defining the term *learning disability* has proven to be problematic. At one time, Vaughn and Hodges (1973) identified 38 different definitions. Hammill (1990)

Cengage Learning/Wadsworth

Students who are learning disabled represent the largest category of individuals receiving a special education.

notes that 11 definitions have enjoyed varying degrees of official status in the field. Defining what a learning disability is has thus been an evolving process over the past 40 years.

After the Education for All Handicapped Children Act (PL 94-142) was enacted in 1975, the U.S. Office of Education spent two years developing the accompanying rules and regulations for identifying and defining individuals with learning disabilities. The following official federal definition of learning disabilities was published in the *Federal Register* in December 1977:

> "Specific learning disability" means a disorder in one or more of the basic psychological processes involved in understanding or in using language, spoken or written, which may manifest itself in an imperfect ability to listen, speak, read, write, spell, or to do mathematical calculations. The term includes such conditions as perceptual handicaps, brain injury, minimal brain dysfunction, dyslexia, and developmental aphasia. The term does not include children who have learning disabilities which are primarily the result of visual, hearing, or motor handicaps, or mental retardation, or emotional disturbance, or of environmental, cultural, or economic disadvantage. (U.S. Office of Education, 1977, p. 65083)

This definition was retained in the Individuals with Disabilities Education Act (PL 101-476), commonly called IDEA. It was also incorporated, with a few word changes, in both the 1997 (PL 105-17) and 2004 reauthorizations of IDEA, PL 108-446.

In the same issue of the *Federal Register,* the U.S. Office of Education issued the regulations and operational guidelines that were to be used by professionals as the criteria for identifying pupils suspected of being learning disabled. These regulations required that

(a) A team may determine that a child has a specific learning disability if:
  (1) The child does not achieve commensurate with his or her age and ability levels in one or more of the areas listed in paragraph (a) (2) of this section, when provided with learning experiences appropriate for the child's age and ability levels; and
  (2) The team finds that a child has a severe discrepancy between achievement and intellectual ability in one or more of the following areas:
     (i) Oral expression;
     (ii) Listening comprehension;

(iii) Written expression;
(iv) Basic reading skill;
(v) Reading comprehension;
(vi) Mathematics calculation; or
(vii) Mathematics reasoning.
 (U.S. Office of Education, 1977, p. 65083)

This definition of learning disabilities and its accompanying regulations describe a syndrome rather than a particular student. Unfortunately, the federal interpretation, while useful for classifying pupils, provides little information on how to instruct these learners.

The federal definition is not without its critics and controversy. Over the years, educators, professionals, and advocates for individuals with disabilities have raised several concerns about the IDEA definition. One particularly troubling aspect of the IDEA definition is the concept of a discrepancy between the student's academic performance and his or her estimated or assumed ability or potential. This discrepancy would not be anticipated on the basis of the pupil's overall intellectual ability—generally average to above average IQ. This discrepancy factor is considered by many professionals to be the most salient feature of the definition of learning disabilities. It explains how, for instance, a 10-year-old with above-average intelligence reads at a level two years below expectations for her chronological age. Generally speaking, in most instances, a discrepancy of two years or more below expected performance levels in one academic area is necessary for a designation of learning disabilities. Unfortunately, the federal government failed to stipulate what was meant by "a severe discrepancy." Early on, they attempted to quantify the notion of a discrepancy by offering several formulas, but their efforts only led to criticism and confusion (Council for Learning Disabilities, 1986; Reynolds, 1992).

With the enactment of the Individuals with Disabilities Education Improvement Act of 2004 (PL 108-446), the procedure for identifying an individual for a possible learning disability changed dramatically. States and local school districts will now be able, if they so choose, to use a process that determines if the pupil responds to empirically validated, scientifically based interventions: a procedure known as **response-to-intervention** (treatment). Under the new guidelines, rather than comparing IQ with performance on standardized achievement tests, general education teachers can offer intensive programs of instructional interventions. If the child fails to make adequate progress, a learning disability is assumed to be present and additional assessment is warranted. This alternative means of identifying students as learning disabled incorporates early identification and prevention rather than the "wait to fail" approach inherent within the ability-achievement discrepancy model (Bradley, Danielson, & Doolittle, 2007).

Despite its shortcomings, the IDEA definition, or some variation of it, is currently used by most of state departments of education in their efforts to define individuals who are learning disabled (Lerner & Kline, 2006).

How Many Learners Are Learning Disabled?

It is difficult to ascertain the percentage of students with learning disabilities because of variations used in determining eligibility for services. Current estimates range from 1 to 30 percent of the school population (Lerner & Kline, 2006). Recent statistics compiled by the federal government suggest that approximately 2.71 million pupils ages 6–21 are identified as learning disabled (U.S. Department of Education, 2008). Thus, learning disabilities is by far the largest category of special education, accounting for slightly less than one-half (45%) of all individuals receiving services. The U.S. Department of Education estimates that about 4 percent of the student population ages 6–21 is learning disabled.

What Are Some of the Causes of Learning Disabilities?

Despite intense research activity over the years, pinpointing the precise cause or causes of learning disabilities has remained an elusive goal. In fact, researchers have been unable to offer much in the way of concrete evidence as to the etiology of learning disabilities (Hallahan, Lloyd, Kauffman, Weiss, & Martinez, 2005). Many of the proposed causal factors remain largely speculative. In the vast majority of instances, the cause of a person's learning disability remains unknown. Just as there are many different types of learning disabilities, there appear to be multiple etiological possibilities. We should point out that the cause of an individual's learning difficulties is often of little educational relevance. In other words, knowing why a particular pupil is learning disabled does not necessarily translate into effective instructional strategies and practices. Nonetheless, investigators (Bender, 2008) posit four basic categories for explaining the etiology of learning disabilities:

- acquired trauma (central nervous system dysfunction)
- genetic/hereditary influences (some types of learning disabilities tend to "run in families")
- biochemical abnormalities (current clinical evidence does not support dietary restrictions or vitamin deficiencies as contributing to learning disabilities)
- environmental possibilities (maternal alcohol/illicit drug use, teratogens)

Selected Learning and Behavioral Characteristics of Learners with Learning Disabilities

There is probably no such entity as a "typical" person with learning disabilities; no two students possess the identical profile of strengths and weaknesses. The concept of learning disabilities covers an extremely wide range of characteristics. One pupil may have deficits in just one area while another exhibits deficits in several areas; yet both will be labeled learning disabled. Some children will experience cognitive difficulties, others may have problems with motor skills, and still others may exhibit social deficits. Most professionals agree, however, that the primary characteristics of students with learning disabilities are deficits in academic performance. A learning disability does not exist without impairments in academic achievement.

Over the years, parents, educators, and other professionals have identified a wide variety of characteristics associated with learning disabilities. One of the earliest profiles, developed by Clements (1966), and more recently validated by parents of children with learning disabilities (Ariel, 1992), includes the following 10 frequently cited attributes:

- Hyperactivity
- Perceptual-motor impairments
- Emotional lability
- Coordination problems
- Disorders of attention
- Impulsivity
- Disorders of memory and thinking
- Academic difficulties
- Language deficits
- Equivocal neurological signs

Lerner and Kline's (2006) contemporary list includes the following learning and behavioral characteristics of individuals with learning disabilities:

- Disorders of attention
- Poor motor abilities
- Psychological process deficits and information-processing problems

- Lack of cognitive strategies needed for efficient learning
- Oral language difficulties
- Reading difficulties
- Written language problems
- Quantitative disorders
- Social skills deficits

Not all students with learning disabilities will exhibit these characteristics, and many pupils who demonstrate these same behaviors are quite successful in the classroom. It is often the frequency, intensity, and duration of the behaviors that lead to problems in school and elsewhere. The way deficits are manifested also varies according to grade level. A language disorder may exhibit itself as delayed speech in a preschooler, as a reading problem in the elementary grades, and as a writing difficulty at the secondary level (Lerner & Kline, 2006).

Gender differences also play a role in the recognition of learning disabilities. Boys are four times more likely than girls to be identified as learning disabled. Lerner and Kline (2006) synthesize several lines of research suggesting that, in actuality, there are not fewer girls with learning disabilities, but girls are not as readily identified—perhaps because of differences in the kinds of disabilities they exhibit. These experts note that "boys tend to exhibit more physical aggression and loss of control . . . [while] girls with learning disabilities tend to have more cognitive, language, social problems, and to have severe academic achievement deficits in reading and math" (p. 17).

Learners with Speech and Language Disorders

We begin by differentiating the concepts *speech, language,* and *communication* so that you can be as precise as possible when you talk about speech and language disorders with other professionals. You are familiar with the three terms, but you may have used them interchangeably, and they have very distinct meanings. **Speech** is the expression of language with sounds—essentially the oral modality for language. Compared to other ways of conveying ideas and intentions (for example, manual signing, writing, gesturing), speech is probably the most difficult. Humans are not the only species to produce sound, but we are the only species with a vocal tract that permits production of the variety and complexity of sounds required for speech.

Language is a "rule-based method of communication involving the comprehension and use of signs and symbols by which ideas are represented" (Bryant, Smith, & Bryant, 2008, p. 56). In many ways language can be thought of as a code. It is a code in a sense that it is not a direct representation of the world, but, rather, is something with which to represent ideas and concepts and ideas about the world.

Communication is the exchange of ideas, information, thoughts, and feelings. It does not necessarily require speech or language. Examples of nonlinguistic communication behaviors are gestures, posture, eye contact, facial expression, and hand and body movement. Nonlinguistic communication modes may be used as the only method of communication, or they may be used in conjunction with linguistically encoded materials.

Defining Speech and Language

The Individuals with Disabilities Education Improvement Act of 2004 (PL 108-446) label for students with communication difficulties is "speech and language impairment." The regulations accompanying this legislation (*Federal Register,* 2006) indicate that pupils are eligible for services if they have "a communication disorder such as stuttering, impaired articulation, a language impairment, or a voice impairment, which adversely affects a child's educational performance" (§ 300.7 [c][11]).

The IDEA includes speech and language disorders under both special education and related services.

Another commonly used definition is one offered by the American Speech-Language-Hearing Association, the premiere organization for speech, language, and hearing professionals. This association defines a communication disorder as "an impairment in the ability to receive, send, process, and comprehend concepts or verbal, nonverbal, and graphic symbols systems. A communication disorder may be evident in the processes of hearing, language, and/or speech" (1993, p. 40).

Classifying Learners with Speech and Language Disorders

Speech Disorders

There are three basic types of speech impairments: articulation disorders, voice disorders, and fluency disorders.

Articulation disorders are errors in the production of speech sounds. It is one of the most common communication disorders in young children and school-age individuals. Most youngsters are able to correctly generate nearly all speech sounds, both individually and in combination by age eight. Four types of articulation problems are generally recognized:

- Omissions: a sound is omitted in a word (*Itly* for *Italy*)
- Distortions: a sound produced in a nonstandard fashion, sounds similar to another sound (*shlip* for *sip*)
- Substitutions: one sound replaced by another sound (*wabbit* for *rabbit*)
- Additions: extra sound inserted within a word (*laraynx* for *larynx*)

Each person's voice is unique and highly individualized. **Voice disorders** relate to the quality of the voice itself. There are two types of voice disorders, difficulties with **phonation** (or the production of sounds) and problems associated with **resonance** (or the direction of the sound). Voice disorders are not especially common in children.

- Phonation: includes deviations related to voice quality (hoarseness or breathiness), pitch (voice perceived to be too high or too low, speaking in a monotone), or loudness (speaking too loud or too soft)
- Resonance: generally characterized by **hypernasality** whereby too many sounds are emitted through the air passages of the nose (voice has a distinctive nasal "twang") or the opposite effect known as **hyponasality** where too few sounds are directed through the nose so that a person's speech sounds like they have a bad head cold or clamped their nose.

Fluency disorders are problems with the rate, flow, and rhythm of speech. Stuttering is the most familiar fluency disorder. It is a pattern of speaking in which the normal flow of the individual's speech is interrupted or broken by hesitations, repetitions, or prolongations, and it is frequently accompanied by struggle or avoidance behaviors ("W-W-Why did-didn't we go (go) to the s-s-store?"). Stuttering affects both the speaker and the listener with stuttering generally being more common in boys than in girls.

Language Disorders

Language has five components—**phonology, morphology, semantics, syntax,** and **pragmatics** that are present at both the receptive and expressive level (see Table 3.6). **Receptive language** refers to the ability to understand (the input) what is meant by spoken communication; **expressive language** involves the production (or output) of language that is understood by and meaningful to others. Language disorders occur when there is a delay or difficulties with mastery in one or more of the five aspects of language.

Table 3.6	Components of Language		
Component	**Definition**	**Receptive Level**	**Expressive Level**
Phonology	The sounds characteristic of a language, rules governing their distribution and sequencing, and the stress and intonations patterns that accompany sounds	Discrimination of speech sounds	Articulation of speech sounds
Morphology	The rules governing how words are formed from the basic element of meaning	Understanding of the grammatical structure of words	Use of grammar in words
Semantics	The linguistic realization of what the speaker knows about the world—the meanings of words and sentences	Understanding of word meanings and word relationships	Use of word meanings and word relationships
Syntax	Rules for how to string words together to form phrases and sentences—the relationships among elements of a sentence	Understanding of phrases and sentences	Use of grammar in phrases and sentences
Pragmatics	The social effectiveness of language in achieving desired functions—rules related to the use of language in social contexts	Understanding of social and contextual clues	Use of language to affect others

Source: Adapted from L.McCormick, "Introduction to Language Acquisition," in L. McCormick, D. F. Loeb, and R. L. Schiefelbusch (Eds.), *Supporting Children with Communication Difficulties in Inclusive Settings*, 2nd ed. (Boston: Allyn & Bacon, 2003), pp. 1–42.

How Many Learners Have Speech and Language Disorders?

According to the U.S. Department of Education (2008), approximately 19 percent of children receiving special education services are receiving services for speech and language disorders. This estimate does *not* include children who receive services for speech and language disorders that are secondary to other conditions such as deafness or mental retardation. It is estimated that one in ten persons in the United States has a speech and language disorder of one type or another (National Dissemination Center for Children with Disabilities, 2004). During the 2006–2007 school year approximately 1,161,000 students ages 6–21 were identified as having speech and language impairments (U.S. Department of Education).

What Are Some of the Causes of Speech and Language Disorders?

There are many different causes of speech and language impairments. Most of the reasons are broadly grouped into two categories: **organic** (an identifiable physical cause) or **functional** (without an obvious physical basis). Speech-language pathologists typically work with students who exhibit functional disorders.

The etiology of organic disorders are many and varied. Some of the causes may be due to prenatal factors (such as rubella), dental malformations, neurological dysfunction, exposure to teratogens, brain injury resulting from trauma or stroke (frequently associated with **aphasia**—the loss or impairment of language function), or structural abnormalities like **cleft palate** (a birth defect resulting in a gap in the soft palate or roof of the mouth).

Hearing loss, mental retardation, learning disabilities, and emotional disturbance are also commonly associated with communicative disorders and have implications for language as well as speech development.

Selected Characteristics of Learners with Speech and Language Disorders

Students with speech and language disorders represent a very diverse group of learners. Some children will only have speech difficulties (for example, stuttering). Others will exhibit language impairments (for example, expressive difficulties)

Mary Kate Denny/PhotoEdit

A speech-language pathologist works with pupils exhibiting a wide variety of speech and language impairments.

while a few individuals will have both speech and language disorders. The characteristics of these pupils, therefore, vary according to the type of impairment they manifest. Representative signs of speech impairments include:

- Developmentally inappropriate articulation errors
- Slurred speech
- Speaking in a voice that is too soft or too loud
- Overly nasal speech
- Speech lacking inflection—a monotone
- Age inappropriate hesitations and repetitions of sounds or word parts

It is also important that teachers be sensitive to the age of their student, his or her cultural heritage as well as the speech standards of the community. As an example, most educators would not make a referral for special education services because a second grader in Atlanta stated that she was, "fixin' to go to the library." Although technically this is an articulation error (omission), it would be viewed as normative in many southern cities.

Language impairments are typically categorized as being either expressive or receptive disorders. Table 3.7 presents some of the characteristics of children with this disorder.

In many instances, general educators are often the first professionals to recognize that a child may have a speech or language disorder. Because language impairments are generally viewed as more debilitating than speech disorders, it is important that teachers are cognizant of the possible signs of language impairment. Behaviors that may signal a closer examination by a speech-language pathologist are identified in Table 3.8.

Learners with Emotional or Behavioral Disorders

Students with emotional or behavioral disorders represent an extremely heterogeneous group of learners. These individuals often exhibit a wide range of behaviors encompassing not only acting out and aggressive behaviors, but also such debilitating disorders as schizophrenia, depression, anxiety, and conduct disorders. Despite this

| Table 3.7 | Observable Expressive and Receptive Language Disorders |

Expressive Language Problems

- Uses incorrect grammar or syntax ("They walk down together the hill," "I go not to school")
- Lacks specificity ("It's over there by the place over there")
- Frequently hesitates ("You know, uhm, I would, uhm, well, er, like a, er, Coke")
- Jumps from topic to topic ("What are feathers? Well, I like to go hunting with my uncle")
- Has limited use of vocabulary
- Has trouble finding the right word to communicate meaning (word finding)
- Uses social language poorly (inability to change communication style to fit specific situations, to repair communication breakdowns, and to maintain the topic during a conversation)
- Is afraid to ask questions, does not know what question to ask, or does not know how to ask a question
- Repeats same information again and again in a conversation
- Has difficulty discussing abstract, temporal, or spatial concepts
- Often does not provide enough information to the listener ("We had a big fight with them," *we* and *them* are not explained)

Receptive Language Problems

- Does not respond to questions appropriately
- Cannot think abstractly or comprehend abstractions as idioms ("mind sharp as a tack," "eyes dancing in the dark")
- Cannot retain information presented verbally
- Has difficulty following oral directions
- Cannot detect breakdowns in communication
- Misses parts of material presented verbally, particularly less concrete words such as articles (*the* book; *a* book) and auxiliary verbs and tense markers (He *was* going; She *is* going)
- Cannot recall sequences of ideas presented orally
- May confuse the sounds of letters that are similar (*b,d; m,n*) or reverse the order of sounds and syllables in words (*was, saw*)
- Has difficulty understanding humor or figurative language
- Has difficulty comprehending concepts showing quantity, function, comparative size, and temporal and spatial relationships
- Has difficulty comprehending compound and complex sentences

Source: Adapted from C. Bos and S. Vaughn, *Strategies for Teaching Students with Learning and Behavioral Problems,* 5th ed. (Needham Heights, MA: Allyn & Bacon, 2002).

| Table 3.8 | Behaviors Resulting in Teacher Referral for Possible Language Impairments in Children |

The following behaviors may indicate that a child in your classroom has a language impairment that is in need of clinical intervention. Please check the appropriate items.

____ Child mispronounces sounds and words.

____ Child omits word endings, such as plural -s and past tense -ed.

____ Child omits small unemphasized words, such as auxiliary verbs or prepositions.

____ Child uses an immature vocabulary, overuses empty words, such as *one* and *thing*, or seems to have difficulty recalling or finding the right word. Child has difficulty comprehending new words and concepts.

____ Child's sentence structure seems immature or overreliant on forms, such as subject-verb-object. It's unoriginal, dull.

____ Child's question and/or negative sentence style is immature.

____ Child has difficulty with one of the following:

____ Verb tensing	____ Articles	____ Auxiliary verbs
____ Pronouns	____ Irreg. verbs	____ Prepositions
____ Word order	____ Irreg. plurals	____ Conjunctions

____ Child has difficulty relating sequential events.

____ Child has difficulty following directions.

____ Child's questions often inaccurate or vague.

____ Child's questions often poorly formed.

____ Child has difficulty answering questions.

____ Child's comments often off topic or inappropriate for the conversation.

____ There are long pauses between a remark and the child's reply or between successive remarks by the child. It's as if the child is searching for a response or is confused.

____ Child appears to be attending to communication but remembers little of what is said.

____ Child has difficulty using language socially for the following purposes:

____ Request needs	____ Pretend/imagine	____ Protest
____ Greet	____ Request information	____ Gain attention
____ Respond/reply	____ Share ideas, feelings	____ Clarify
____ Relate events	____ Entertain	____ Reason

____ Child has difficulty interpreting the following:

| ____ Figurative language | ____ Humor | ____ Body language |
| ____ Emotions | ____ Gestures | |

____ Child does not alter production for different audiences and locations.

____ Child does not seem to consider the affect of language on the listener.

____ Child often has verbal misunderstandings with others.

____ Child has difficulty with reading and writing.

____ Child's language skills seem to be much lower than other areas, such as mechanical, artistic, or social skills.

Source: R. Owens, *Language Disorders: A Functional Approach to Assessment and Intervention,* 4th ed. (Needham Heights, MA: Allyn & Bacon, 2004), p. 355.

heterogeneity, however, they share at least three experiences in common. First, their behaviors are almost always upsetting and troubling to those who teach, live, and work with them. Second, they are often blamed for their disability by those around them, who do not recognize that they are disabled and believe they are capable of changing their behavior if they so desire. Finally, these students encounter ostracism and isolation because of the stigma associated with individuals considered to be **mentally ill**—a generic term used by many professionals outside the field of special education for individuals with emotional or behavioral disorders. In fact, for these students, the reactions of others are often more debilitating than the disability itself.

Defining Emotional or Behavioral Disorders

There is no universally accepted definition of **emotional or behavioral disorders** (Webber & Plotts, 2008). Similarly, the terms we use to describe this population are many and diverse: emotionally disturbed, behaviorally disordered, emotionally conflicted, socially handicapped, personally impaired, socially impaired, and many others. This diversity of definitions and terms is compounded by the marked variability in people's definitions of "normal" behavior. We each view behavior through personal lenses that reflect our own standards, values, and beliefs. What appears to you as abnormal or deviant behavior may appear to another person as within the range of normal human behavior (Rosenberg, Wilson, Maheady, & Sindelar, 2004).

The Individuals with Disabilities Education Improvement Act of 2004 (IDEA), or PL 108-446, uses the term **emotional disturbance** to describe the population referred to in this chapter as individuals with emotional or behavioral disorders. The IDEA definition (*Federal Register,* 2006), modeled after one proposed by Eli Bower (1960) almost 50 years ago, is as follows:

> The term means a condition exhibiting one or more of the following characteristics over a long period of time and to a marked degree that adversely affects a child's educational performance:
> - An inability to learn that cannot be explained by intellectual, sensory, or health factors.
> - An inability to build or maintain satisfactory interpersonal relationships with peers and teachers.
> - Inappropriate types of behavior or feelings under normal circumstances.
> - A general pervasive mood of unhappiness or depression.
> - A tendency to develop physical symptoms or fears associated with personal or school problems.
>
> The term includes schizophrenia. The term does not apply to children who are socially maladjusted, unless it is determined that they have an emotional disturbance.
> (34 C.F.R. § 300.7 [c][4])

Since the passage of Public Law 94-142 in the mid-1970s, only two changes have been made to this definition: (1) Autism, originally included in this category, became a separate disability category in 1990. (2) Prior to 1997, the term used was *serious emotional disturbance.*

Classification of Learners with Emotional or Behavioral Disorders

The term *emotional or behavioral disorder* encompasses a wide range of disorders. To provide greater clarity and specificity, educators and mental health professionals have attempted to classify the many different types of emotional or behavioral disorders.

Although there are no universally accepted systems for classifying persons with emotional or behavioral disorders, two widely used classification schemes are pertinent to the field of education. **Clinically derived classification systems** have been developed by psychiatrists and mental health professionals to describe, using standardized terminology, childhood, adolescent, and adult mental disorders. The most widely used psychiatric, or clinically derived, classification system in the United States is the *Diagnostic and Statistical Manual of Mental Disorders, Fourth Edition, Text Revision* (DSM-IV-TR), which was revised by the American Psychiatric Association in 2000. **Statistically derived classification systems** are developed using sophisticated statistical techniques to analyze the patterns or "dimensions" of behaviors that characterize children and youth with emotional or behavioral disorders.

Clinically Derived Classification Systems

In general, there are no "tests" available to medical professionals to diagnosis emotional or behavioral disorders among children and youth. For many years, psychiatrists and other mental health professionals have relied on clinically derived classification systems, such as the DSM-IV-TR, to assist them in making psychiatric diagnoses. These systems group behaviors into diagnostic categories and provide criteria useful for making diagnoses. Clinically derived systems also include descriptions or symptoms, indicators of severity, prevalence estimates, and information about variations of disorders. To make a diagnosis, psychiatrists and other mental health professionals may observe an individual's behavior over time and across different settings and then compare these behaviors to diagnostic criteria provided in a classification system.

Statistically Derived Classification Systems

Some researchers use sophisticated statistical techniques to establish categories, "dimensions," or patterns of disordered behavior that appear to be common among children and youth with emotional or behavioral disorders.

Two global dimensions that have been consistently identified are **externalizing disorders** and **internalizing disorders** (Furlong, Morrison, & Jimerson, 2004; Gresham & Kern, 2004). Externalizing disorders, sometimes referred to as "undercontrolled" disorders, are characterized by aggressiveness, temper tantrums, acting out, hostile, defiant, and noncompliant behaviors. Externalizing behaviors are disturbing to others and generally result in considerable disruption in the classroom. In contrast, internalizing disorders, sometimes referred to as "overcontrolled" disorders, are characterized by social withdrawal, depression, phobias, excessive shyness, and anxiety. Children and adolescents with internalizing disorders are far less likely to be identified by their teachers and families because they do not create the "chaos" that often characterizes children and youth with externalizing disorder. These internalizing disorders, however, are equally serious; if left untreated, they can lead to a variety of negative long-term outcomes, including suicide (U.S. Department of Education, 2000). In general, males tend to be at more risk for developing externalizing disorders, whereas females appear to be at greater risk for developing internalizing disorders (Webber & Plotts, 2008).

How Many Learners Exhibit Emotional or Behavioral Disorders?

How prevalent are emotional or behavioral disorders among school-age children and youth? The answer to this question is not a simple one; prevalence estimates for this population vary widely. Among the reasons for this variance are conflicting definitions and a lack of consensus on what constitutes acceptable behavior.

The U.S. Department of Education (2008) reports that during the 2006–2007 school year about 459,000 students ages 6–21 were receiving a special education and related services because of an emotional disturbance. This number represents

7.5 percent of the total number of students served in special education, making this the fifth largest disability category for students in this age range. The U.S. Department of Education reports that 0.69 percent of all students in public schools were identified as having emotional or behavioral disorders.

Although less than 1 percent of the school-age population currently receives special education services for emotional or behavioral disorders, some professionals believe that the actual number of individuals in need of services is closer to 3–6 percent of all learners. Boys are significantly more likely to be identified as having emotional or behavioral disorders than girls are (Kauffman & Landrum, 2009).

What Are Some of the Causes of Emotional or Behavioral Disorders?

Although most behavioral disorders have no known cause, the *suspected* factors are typically grouped into two categories—biological and environmental. One important finding in recent years is that biological and environmental factors are often not mutually independent influences in the development of emotional or behavioral disorders; that is, one may dynamically influence or interact with the other. Biological factors are believed to be particularly influential in the etiology of several disorders. Biological influences include genetic, neurological, and biochemical contributions. Emotional or behavioral disorders that most likely have a biological foundation include depression, schizophrenia, child temperament, and obsessive-compulsive disorders among others.

Psychosocial or environmental risk factors include, for example, dysfunctional child-rearing practices, domestic violence, parental mental illness, overcrowding, adverse school experiences, child abuse/neglect, and poverty (Kauffman & Landrum, 2009). Keep in mind that the preceding are only possible causes, not all youngsters who are exposed to adverse environmental conditions develop emotional or behavioral disorders. Finally, allow us to reiterate an earlier point: speculation about possible causes rarely provides useful information needed to craft effective instructional programs.

Selected Learning and Behavioral Characteristics of Learners with Emotional or Behavioral Disorders

Because children and adolescents with emotional or behavioral disorders are an extremely heterogeneous population, the characteristics that they display are highly diverse. There is no one profile of learners with emotional or behavioral disorders. Not every student with emotional or behavioral disorders will exhibit all of the characteristics described here; rather, each student will be unique in terms of both strengths and needs.

Learning Characteristics

Although intellectually students with emotional or behavioral disorders may include individuals who are gifted and those who are mentally retarded, a consistent finding of research has been that pupils with emotional or behavioral disorders typically score in the low-average range on measures of intelligence (Kauffman & Landrum, 2009). Despite about average intellectual ability, many of these pupils evidence academic deficits typically performing two or more years below grade level expectations in reading, math, and spelling (Reid, Gonzalez, Nordness, Trout, & Epstein, 2004). It is not surprising that poor grades, chronic absenteeism, and grade retention are frequent issues for these learners. A particularly alarming statistic, however, is that approximately one-half of the students with emotional or behavioral disorders leave school before graduation—the highest dropout rate among all individuals with disabilities (National Center for Education Statistics, 2007).

peers and adults. On average, these pupils are less socially skilled than their peers.
Some children may be particularly aggressive and hostile toward others, whereas
other individuals may appear withdrawn and socially isolated. Their inappropriate
social skills result in fewer friends. Poor relationships with others will often adversely affect the student's performance in the classroom (Cullinan, 2004; Kauffman
& Landrum, 2009).

Learners with Attention Deficit Hyperactivity Disorder

Attention deficit hyperactivity disorder (ADHD) is frequently misunderstood; it is a
disability plagued by misconceptions and myths. The behavior of individuals with
ADHD is also often misinterpreted, with their actions being seen as indicators of
laziness, a lack of self-control, and even willful misbehavior. Some people even question the legitimacy of this disability, believing that it has only been created to absolve
parents (and teachers) of any responsibility for the child's conduct (Cohen, 2006).

ADHD is believed to affect about 3–5 percent of the school-age population
(American Psychiatric Association, 2000; Barkley, 2006). Despite the relatively high
estimate of prevalence, ADHD is not recognized as a separate disability category
under the current IDEA legislation. However, youngsters who have ADHD may
still be eligible for a special education. In response to the lobbying efforts of parents, professionals, and advocates, in 1991 the U.S. Department of Education issued
a memorandum directed to state departments of education, stating that pupils with
ADHD could receive a special education and related services under the disability
category "other health impaired" (OHI). In fact, the regulations that accompany
IDEA 2004 specifically mention ADHD as a condition that renders an individual eligible for services under the rubric "other health impaired." Children with ADHD are
also eligible for accommodations in general education classrooms under the protections of Section 504 of the Rehabilitation Act of 1973 (PL 93-112).

Defining Attention Deficit Hyperactivity Disorder

Because IDEA does not define ADHD, we use the definition put forth by the American Psychiatric Association (2000), which describes this condition as "a persistent pattern of inattention and/or hyperactive impulsivity that is more frequent and severe than is typically observed in individuals at a comparable level of development" (p. 85). This description, derived from the *Diagnostic and Statistical Manual of Mental Disorders, Fourth Edition, Text Revision,* commonly referred to as DSM-IV-TR, also contains criteria to assist professionals, mainly physicians, in determining whether a child has ADHD. These guidelines are listed in Table 3.9. In examining the table, you may recognize yourself (we are all forgetful at times and occasionally easily distracted); but in individuals with ADHD, it is the chronic nature of the characteristics and their duration that often leads to impaired functioning in activities of daily living.

Table 3.9	Diagnostic Criteria for Attention Deficit Hyperactivity Disorder

Six (or more) of the following symptoms of inattention and/or hyperactivity-impulsivity that have persisted for at least 6 months to a degree that is maladaptive and inconsistent with developmental level:

Inattention
- Often fails to give close attention to details or makes careless mistakes in schoolwork, work, or other activities
- Often has difficulty sustaining attention in tasks or play activities
- Often does not seem to listen when spoken to directly
- Often does not follow through on instructions and fails to finish schoolwork, chores, or duties in the workplace (not due to oppositional behavior or failure to understand instructions)
- Often has difficulty organizing tasks and activities
- Often avoids, dislikes, or is reluctant to engage in tasks that require sustained mental effort (such as schoolwork or homework)
- Often loses things necessary for tasks or activities (e.g., toys, school assignments, pencils, books, or tools)
- Is often easily distracted by extraneous stimuli
- Is often forgetful in daily activities

Hyperactivity
- Often fidgets with hands or feet or squirms in seat
- Often leaves seat in classroom or in other situations in which remaining seated is expected
- Often runs about or climbs excessively in situations in which it is inappropriate (in adolescents or adults, may be limited to subjective feelings of restlessness)
- Often has difficulty playing or engaging in leisure activities quietly
- Is often "on the go" or often acts as if "driven by a motor"
- Often talks excessively

Impulsivity
- Often blurts out answers before questions have been completed
- Often has difficulty awaiting turn
- Often interrupts or intrudes on other (e.g., butts into conversations or games)

Also, some hyperactive-impulsive or inattentive symptoms were present before age 7.

The symptoms must be present in two or more settings (e.g., at school [or work] and at home).

Clear evidence of clinically significant impairment in social, academic, or occupational functioning must be demonstrated.

The symptoms do not occur exclusively during the course of a pervasive developmental disorder, schizophrenia, or other psychotic disorder and are not better accounted for by another mental disorder (e.g., mood disorder, anxiety disorder, dissociative disorder, or a personality disorder).

Source: Adapted from American Psychiatric Association, *Diagnostic and Statistical Manual of Mental Disorders—Text Revision,* 4th ed. (Washington, DC: , 2000), pp. 92–93.

The American Psychiatric Association (2000) definition recognizes three subtypes of ADHD based on the individual's unique profile of symptoms: (1) ADHD, predominantly inattentive type; (2) ADHD, predominantly hyperactive-impulsive type; and (3) ADHD, combined type. The vast majority of individuals with ADHD exhibit the combined type (Barkley, 2006).

How Many Learners Have Attention Deficit Hyperactivity Disorder?

As we noted earlier, ADHD is believed to affect approximately 3–5 percent of the school-age population or an estimated 1.46–2.46 million children (U.S. Department of Education, 2006a). According to Lerner and Kline (2006), ADHD represents one of the most common chronic conditions of childhood. It is obvious that the number of individuals with ADHD continues to grow, most likely because of greater awareness and improved diagnostic procedures.

Recall that ADHD is not one of the thirteen disability categories recognized by the federal government; these pupils may be served, however, under the label "other health impaired." Between the 1996–1997 school year and the 2006–2007 school year, the OHI category saw an increase of more than 438,000 students, or an astonishing 272 percent increase (U.S. Department of Education, 2006b, 2008). Of course, not all of the growth can be attributed to pupils with ADHD. We suspect, however, that individuals with ADHD are largely responsible for the dramatic growth of this category.

The research literature generally suggests that ADHD is more readily identified in males than females. This condition is diagnosed four to nine times more often in boys than in girls (U.S. Department of Education, 2006a). This statistic suggests the possibility of a gender bias in identification and diagnosis: Boys may be overidentified and girls underidentified. We believe that this situation exists because ADHD manifests itself differently in males and females. Boys are more likely to exhibit disruptive, hyperactive behavior, thus being more noticeable to teachers. Girls are more likely to be withdrawn and exhibit inattention; consequently, they are less likely to be identified (Vaughn, Bos, & Schumm, 2007). Though gender bias may explain part of the discrepancy between males and females, scientific evidence points to actual biological differences as the primary contributing factor (Barkley, 2006).

What Are Some of the Causes of Attention Deficit Hyperactivity Disorder?

The precise cause of attention deficit hyperactivity disorder is unknown. To date, no single etiological factor has been discovered, although researchers are exploring several possibilities including neurological foundations, hereditary contributions, and environmental conditions. As scientists learn more about ADHD, it is likely that multiple causes will be identified.

Neurological Dysfunction

Research suggests that neurological dysfunction plays a key role in individuals with ADHD. Anatomical differences and imbalances in brain chemistry are being closely examined as etiological possibilities (Salend & Rohena, 2003; Weyandt, 2005). In recent years, neuroscientists have been able to advance our understanding of the functioning of the human brain—particularly as it relates to individuals with ADHD. Aided by advances in neuroimaging technology, researchers are using scans of the brain such as computerized axial tomography (CAT) and magnetic resonance imaging (MRI) procedures, as well as other techniques, to learn about brain structure and activity. Several regions of the brain appear to consistently exhibit abnormalities in persons with ADHD (Barkley, 2006; Sowell et al., 2003).

Scientists are also exploring the possibility of chemical abnormalities in the brain as a reason for ADHD. Although the neurological basis for ADHD is not fully comprehended, a deficiency or imbalance in one or more of the neurotransmitters (chemicals that transport electrical impulses (messages) from one part of the brain to another) in the brain is suspected. Researchers believe that ADHD results from a deficiency or dysfunction of the neurotransmitter dopamine in the regions of the brain that control activity and attention (Gupta, 2000).

Hereditary Factors

There is strong evidence of the role of heredity in contributing to ADHD. Hereditary factors are believed to account for a large percentage of hyperactive-impulse behavior. Approximately one out of three persons with ADHD also has relatives with this condition (Barkley, 2006). Family studies further reveal that a child who has ADHD is much more likely to have parents who exhibit ADHD (Levy, Hay, & Bennett, 2006). Additionally, researchers investigating monozygotic (identical) and dizygotic (fraternal) twins have consistently found a higher concordance of ADHD in identical twins than in fraternal twins, strongly suggesting a genetic link (Martin, Levy, Picka, & Hay, 2006).

Environmental Factors

Various pre-, peri-, and postnatal traumas are also implicated as contributing to ADHD (Barkley, 2006; Zappitelli, Pinto, & Grizenko, 2001). Examples of environmental factors include maternal smoking and alcohol abuse, lead poisoning, low birth weight, and prematurity. Many of these factors are also suspected as leading to mental retardation and learning disabilities.

Research (Hallahan et al., 2005; National Institute of Mental Health, 2006) has discounted many other environmental explanations. Among the popular myths regarding suspected causes of ADHD, but lacking in scientific support, are too much/too little sugar, food additives/coloring, yeast, fluorescent lighting, bad parenting, and too much television.

For most learners with ADHD the exact cause of their disorder may never fully be explained. Although many teachers (and parents too) may question why a child is ADHD, this question is largely irrelevant because it offers very little in the way of guiding educational planning or suggesting instructional interventions.

Selected Learning and Behavioral Characteristics of Learners with Attention Deficit Hyperactivity Disorder

Characteristics of persons with attention deficit hyperactivity disorder vary considerably. This disorder generally manifests itself early in a child's life. In fact, some precursors have been noted in infancy (Barkley, 2000). It would not be uncommon for behaviors associated with ADHD to be exhibited as early as kindergarten or first grade.

ADHD presents itself in many different ways. In some students, inattention is the primary deficit. These pupils have difficulty concentrating on a specific task; they are forgetful and easily distracted. Students who exhibit hyperactive impulsive disorder are constantly in motion; racing from one activity to another, they have difficulty sitting still or playing quietly. Individuals with a combined type of ADHD manifest aspects of both types. Table 3.10 provides examples of characteristics typical of students with ADHD.

Behavioral Inhibition and Executive Functioning

Contemporary thinking suggests that problems with **behavioral inhibition** are the primary characteristic of persons with ADHD (Barkley, 2006). Behavioral inhibition consists of three elements that affect the ability to (1) withhold a planned response;

Table 3.10	Representative Characteristics of Pupils with Attention Deficit Hyperactivity Disorder	
Inattention	**Hyperactivity**	**Impulsivity**
• Making careless mistakes • Having difficulty sustaining attention • Seeming not to listen • Failing to finish tasks • Having difficulty organizing • Avoiding tasks requiring sustained attention • Losing things • Becoming easily distracted • Being forgetful	• Fidgeting • Being unable to stay seated • Moving excessively (restless) • Having difficulty engaging quietly in leisure activities • Being "on the go" • Talking excessively	• Blurting answers before questions are completed • Having difficulty awaiting turn • Interrupting/intruding upon others

Source: Adapted from M. Wolraich and A. Baumgaertel, "The Practical Aspects of Diagnosing and Managing Children with Attention Deficit Hyperactivity Disorder," *Clinical Pediatrics, 36*(9), 1997, pp. 497–504.

(2) interrupt a response that has already been initiated; and (3) protect an ongoing activity from competing or distracting stimuli (Lawrence et al., 2002). Problems with behavioral inhibition can lead to a variety of difficulties in the classroom. According to Hallahan et al. (2005), students may have trouble, for example, waiting their turn, resisting distractions, delaying immediate gratification, or interrupting a faulty line of thinking.

Barkley (2006) notes that individuals with ADHD also often have difficulty with **executive functions**. Executive functions involve a number of self-directed behaviors, such as self-regulation, working memory, inner speech (talking to one's self), and arousal levels. Impaired executive functioning in children with ADHD affects a wide range of performance. Difficulty following rules or directions, forgetfulness, and a lack of emotional control are just a few of the ways that students are affected.

Social and Emotional Issues

Social problems and emotional difficulties are not uncommon among individuals with ADHD. Children with ADHD often experience difficulty making friends and maintaining appropriate relationships with peers (Chronis, Jones, & Raggi, 2006). Diminished self-confidence, low self-esteem, and feelings of social isolation/rejection are fairly typical in some individuals with ADHD. In some instances, in their attempts to be popular and gain friends, students with ADHD, because of their impaired impulse control, actually wind up aggravating peers and further ostracizing themselves from the very individuals with whom they are attempting to establish relationships.

Persons with ADHD may manifest a wide variety of emotional difficulties. Researchers have found that children with ADHD have coexisting psychiatric disorders at a much higher rate than their peers without ADHD (U.S. Department of Education, 2006a). Some individuals may exhibit aggression and antisocial behaviors; in others, withdrawn behavior, depression, and anxiety disorders are typical (National Institute of Mental Health, 2006).

Comorbidity

Students with ADHD frequently have other academic and behavioral difficulties. Learning disabilities, for example, are very common among individuals with ADHD (Bender, 2008). Pupils who are gifted and talented are also frequently recognized as having ADHD. In an interesting distinction, Silver (1999) observes that a learning disability affects the brain's *ability* to learn, whereas ADHD interferes with a person's *availability* for learning.

Learners with Gifts and Talents

Children and adolescents who are gifted and talented are often portrayed as "geeks," young geniuses but individuals who, although very bright, are physically weak and have limited social skills. Of course, this is an inaccurate and misleading stereotype, but one that, unfortunately, is fairly common. Do you know of someone who is recognized as gifted or talented? How would you characterize this individual?

There are many different meanings to the term *gifted*. It is a concept that is neither easily nor well defined. People often speak of the gifted athlete or musician, when it comes to students, however, children who are **gifted and talented** have abilities and talents that can be demonstrated or have the potential for being developed at exceptional levels. These children have needs that differ in some degree from those of other children.

Defining Giftedness

Because learners with gifts and talents are not recognized as disabled but rather as exceptional students, there is no federal interpretation of giftedness codified in the IDEA legislation. Over the years, however, there have been many different renderings of this term generated by various agencies, associations, and experts in the field.

The first national report on gifted education, known as the Marland Report, offered the following definition, specifying six categories of giftedness (Marland, 1972, p. 10):

> Gifted and talented children are those identified by professionally qualified persons who by virtue of outstanding abilities are capable of high performance. These are children who require differentiated educational programs and/or services beyond those normally provided by the regular school program in order to realize their contribution to self and society.
>
> Children capable of high performance include those with demonstrated achievement and/or potential ability in any of the following areas: (1) general intellectual ability, (2) specific academic aptitude, (3) creative or productive thinking, (4) leadership ability, (5) visual and performing arts, and (6) psychomotor ability.

Many states have essentially adopted this definition, with the exception of psychomotor ability. Although individuals do demonstrate giftedness in psychomotor ability, the category has been removed because the development of athletic ability is generously funded in other ways.

Identifying giftedness and talent in specific categories highlights the need for services to be customized to the individual's area(s) of identified strength(s). Identifying areas of giftedness is essential in order to match services and learning opportunities to need.

Although IDEA is silent when it comes to learners with gifts and talents, other federal legislation speaks to this issue. A federal definition of giftedness was put forth in the Jacob K. Javits Gifted and Talented Students Education Act of 1988 (PL 100-297), which was reauthorized in 2001 as part of the No Child Left Behind Act (PL 107-110). Language in this legislation identifies individuals who are gifted and talented as

> students, children, or youth who give evidence of high achievement capability in areas such as intellectual, creative, artistic, or leadership capacity or in specific academic fields, and who need services or activities not ordinarily provided by the school in order to fully develop those capabilities. (Sec. 9101 (A) (22))

Even though this definition notes that pupils require special services, it does *not* mandate a special education for students who are gifted and talented. It is up to the discretion of each state as to whether or not services are offered. Presently only about 60 percent of the states have legislation mandating services; in the remaining

Jacek Chabraszewski/Fotolia

Services for pupils with gifts and talents are largely determined by state and local educational policy.

states, it is a matter for the local schools (Turnbull, Turnbull, & Wehmeyer, 2007). This represents an important distinction—services for pupils with disabilities are mandated; yet, services for learners with gifts and talents are largely determined by state and local policies.

How Many Learners Are Gifted and Talented?

Educators believe that approximately 3–5 percent of the school-age population is gifted (Clark, 2008). Of course, the number of students identified as gifted or talented depends on the definition of giftedness used by each state. Many pupils exhibit gifts and talents across several areas, and this overlapping results in much higher estimates of who is gifted or talented. Some professionals (Renzulli & Reis, 2003) believe that 10–15 percent of the school-age population can be thought of as gifted. Data from the National Center for Education Statistics (2007) suggests that more than three million pupils are identified as gifted, representing about 6.4 percent of the school-age population. If the Center's figures are accurate, then individuals considered gifted or talented could conceivably constitute the largest group of students with exceptionalities.

What Are Some of the Causes of Giftedness and Talent?

What makes a child gifted and talented? No doubt giftedness results from a combination of genetic makeup and environmental stimulation. No one knows the precise role of genetics or of the environment, but it is clear that both genetic patterns and environmental stimulation play key roles in developing a child's potential to perform at exceptionally high levels. Understanding giftedness necessitates recognizing that the relationship between genes and a stimulating environment is complex. No longer is it acceptable to view intelligence as fixed at birth; rather, potential intelligence is created by a far more complex interplay between nature and nurture (Clark, 2008).

Neuroscience provides evidence of the vital role played by stimulation in increasing a child's capacity to learn. According to Clark (2008), "the development of intelligence is enhanced or inhibited by the interaction between the genetic pattern of an individual and the opportunities provided by the environment throughout the individual's lifespan" (p. 56). The brain changes physically and chemically when stimulated or challenged. Parents and educators, therefore, play significant roles in developing an optimum level of children's capacity to learn at high levels.

Selected Learning and Behavioral Characteristics of Learners with Gifts and Talents

Understanding the characteristics of children and young people who are gifted and talented can help educators and parents recognize behaviors that are indicative of giftedness (see Table 3.11). Many characteristics resemble the characteristics of all children; however, the degree and intensity of the characteristic provide clues that the child may be exceptional. For example, all children are curious, but children who are intellectually gifted and talented may ask so many probing questions that adults think they may be driven to distraction.

Interestingly, the very characteristics identified in Table 3.11 sometimes result in a phenomenon known as the "paradoxical negative effect" (Blackbourn, Patton, & Trainor, 2004). In this situation, behaviors displayed by students with gifts and talents may work to their detriment. For example, high verbal abilities may lead the student to dominate class discussion, self-confidence may be misinterpreted as arrogance, and a dislike for rules and routine may be perceived as a disruptive influence. Figure 3.2 summarizes characteristics of individuals who are gifted or talented on five dimensions typically associated with giftedness.

Summary of Selected Learning and Behavioral Characteristics

Students with high incidence disabilities as well as those with gifts and talents can certainly present a variety of instructional and classroom management challenges to teachers. Some of their unique learning and behavioral needs are presented in

Table 3.11	Representative Characteristics of Students Who Are Intellectually Gifted and Talented*
Academic/Learning Characteristics	
• Ability to reason and think abstractly	• Sees relationships among seemingly unrelated items, facts, and ideas
• Acquires information easily	• Early reader
• Enjoys learning	• Exhibits sustained attention and concentration
• Highly inquisitive	• Excellent memory
• Demonstrates interest in a variety of areas/activities	• Highly verbal
• Generalizes knowledge to novel settings	• Generates elaborate and possibly nontraditional responses to questions
• Intellectually curious	• Good problem-solving skills
• Highly motivated, persistent learner	• Conceptualizes and synthesizes information quickly
Social and Emotional Characteristics	
• Works well independently	• Risk taker
• High energy level	• Critical of self, strives for perfection
• Self-confident	• Concern for justice and idealism
• Exhibits qualities of leadership	• Low social self-concept
• Relates well to older classmates, teachers, and adults	• Intense
• Sensitive and empathetic	• Dislike of routine, rules, and regulations
• Intrinsically motivated	• Likely to have internal locus of control

*Attributes are examples only; not all individuals identified as intellectually gifted will exhibit these features.
Source: Adapted from B. Clark, *Growing Up Gifted*, 7th ed. (Upper Saddle River, NJ: Pearson Education, 2008).

Visual/performing arts
- Outstanding in sense of spatial relationships
- Unusual ability for expressing self feelings, moods, etc., through art, dance, drama, music
- Good motor coordination
- Exhibits creative expression
- Desire for producing "own product" (not content with mere copying)
- Observant

Leadership
- Assumes responsibility
- High expectations for self and others
- Fluent, concise self-expression
- Foresees consequences and implications of decisions
- Good judgment in decision making
- Likes structure
- Well-liked by peers
- Self-confident
- Organized

Creative thinking
- Independent thinker
- Exhibits original thinking in oral and written expression
- Comes up with several solutions to a given problem
- Possesses a sense of humor
- Creates and invents
- Challenged by creative tasks
- Improvises often
- Does not mind being different from the crowd

General intellectual ability
- Formulates abstractions
- Processes information in complex ways
- Observant
- Excited about new ideas
- Enjoys hypothesizing
- Learns rapidly
- Uses a large vocabulary
- Inquisitive
- Self-starter

Specific academic ability
- Good memorization ability
- Advanced comprehension
- Acquires basic-skills knowledge quickly
- Widely read in special-interest area
- High academic success in special-interest area
- Pursues special interests with enthusiasm and vigor

Figure 3.2 Characteristics of Various Areas of Giftedness

Source: Copyrighted material from the National Association for Gifted Children (NAGC). This material may not be reprinted without the permission of NAGC, Washington, DC, (202) 785–4268, www.nagc.org

Table 3.12. It is vitally important, however, that teachers focus on the learner and the similarity of needs rather than their disability label. Instruction should always be based on the individual needs of the student and not a particular category of exceptionality. The maxim that no two pupils are alike, despite sharing the same label, is definitely true.

Table 3.12 Summary of Selected Learning and Behavioral Characteristics of Learners with High Incidence Disabilities and Gifts and Talents

Characteristics	Exceptionality*					
	Mental Retardation	Learning Disabilities	Speech/ Language	Emotional or Behavioral Disorders	ADHD	Gifted and Talented
Cognitive Impairments	X			X		
Academic Deficiencies	X	X		X	X	
Language Disorders	X	X	X	X		
Motivational Deficits	X	X		X		
Memory Problems	X	X				
Social/Emotional Difficulties	X	X	X	X	X	X
Attention Disorders	X	X			X	
Generalization Difficulties	X					
Speech Impairments	X		X			
Motor/Coordination Problems	X	X				
Hyperactivity/Impulsivity	X	X		X	X	X

*Not all learners within the category will exhibit the particular characteristic.

Thematic Summary

- Today's teachers are encountering an increasingly diverse population of students. Many of these individuals are being served in general education classrooms.
- Students with high incidence disabilities and learners with attention deficit hyperactivity disorder often have similar causes for their impairments.
- The etiology of a disability is usually of little instructional relevance.
- In many instances, pupils with high incidence disabilities and those with attention deficit hyperactivity disorder share similar learning and behavioral profiles.
- Effective teachers focus on the individual needs of the learner and not their disability label.
- There is no federal mandate to serve students recognized as gifted and talented. These learners are considered to be exceptional rather than disabled.

Making Connections for Inclusive Teaching

1. As a teacher, what are the benefits of focusing on the needs of your students and not their disability or exceptionality?
2. Why might some professionals believe that the cause of a student's disability is of little educational relevance? Do you think it is important for teachers to know why a learner exhibits special needs?

Learning Activities

1. Make arrangements to visit classrooms serving students with mental retardation. What differences did you observe between elementary and secondary programs? How did the instructional program differ for students with cognitive impairments in comparison to pupils without mental retardation? What pedagogical techniques or teaching strategies did the teachers use? How did the other children relate to their classmates with mental retardation?
2. Obtain a copy of the definition of learning disabilities from your state department of education and compare it with the IDEA definition. In what ways are these definitions similar and dissimilar? Pay particular attention to eligibility criteria. How would you improve your state's definition?

3. Visit an educational setting serving students with speech and language disorders. How was the students' classroom performance affected by their communication difficulty? How were their social interactions with other students and teachers affected? Were any special teaching techniques used or classroom modifications made to enhance their performance? Was therapy given outside of the general education classroom? Was this arrangement positive or negative? How did intervention differ for older children? What was your overall impression of the services provided?

4. Prepare a class presentation on one of the following topics:
   - conduct disorders
   - schizophrenia
   - obsessive-compulsive disorder
   - depression and/or suicide

5. Observe students with ADHD in both elementary and secondary classrooms. Ask their teachers what accommodations they typically provide to these pupils. Discover if there are particular instructional strategies that these educators prefer.

6. Write a statement about your philosophy of learning that could guide your teaching of students with gifts and talents.

Looking at the Standards

The content of the chapter most closely aligns itself with the following standards:

INTASC Standards

- *Student Development*. The teacher understands how children learn and develop, and can provide learning opportunities that support their intellectual, social, and personal development.
- *Diverse Learners*. The teacher understands how students differ in their approaches to learning and creates instructional opportunities that are adapted to diverse learners.

Council for Exceptional Children
Special educators are to have knowledge of the following:

- CC1K5: Issues in definition and identification of individuals with exceptional learning needs, including those from culturally and linguistically diverse backgrounds.
- CC2K1: Typical and atypical human growth and development.
- CC2K2: Educational implications of characteristics of various exceptionalities.
- CC2K5: Similarities and differences of individuals with and without exceptional learning needs.
- GC2K4: Psychological and social-emotional characteristics of individuals with disabilities.
- CC2K6: Similarities and differences among individuals with exceptional learning needs.
- CC3K1: Effects an exceptional condition(s) can have on an individual's life.
- CC3K2: Impact of learner's academic and social abilities, interests, and values, on instruction and career development.
- CC5K1: Demands of learning environments.
- CC5K5: Social skills needed for educational and other environments.

Key Concepts and Terms

high incidence disabilities
attention deficit hyperactivity
    disorder
gifted and talented
adaptive behavior
level of support
etiology
prenatal
perinatal
postnatal
response-to-intervention
speech
language
communication
articulation disorders

voice disorders
phonation
resonance
hypernasality
hyponasality
fluency disorders
phonology
morphology
semantics
syntax
pragmatics
receptive language
expressive language
organic
functional

aphasia
cleft palate
mentally ill
emotional or behavioral
    disorders
emotional disturbance
clinically derived
    classification systems
statistically derived
    classification systems
externalizing disorders
internalizing disorders
behavioral inhibition
executive functions

References

American Psychiatric Association. (2000). *Diagnostic and statistical manual of mental disorders—Text revision* (4th ed.). Washington, DC: Author.

American Speech-Language-Hearing Association. (1993). Definitions of communication disorders and variations. *ASHA, 35* (Suppl. 10), 40–41.

Ariel, A. (1992). *Education of children and adolescents with learning disabilities.* New York: Macmillan.

Barkley, R. (2000). *Taking charge of ADHD: The complete authoritative guide for parents* (Rev. ed.). New York: Guilford.

Barkley, R. (2006). *Attention deficit hyperactivity disorder* (3rd ed.). New York: Guilford.

Beirne-Smith, M., Patton, J., & Kim, S. (2006). *Mental retardation* (7th ed.). Upper Saddle River, NJ: Pearson Education.

Bender, W. (2008). *Learning disabilities: Characteristics, identification, and teaching strategies* (6th ed.). Needham Heights, MA: Allyn & Bacon.

Blackbourn, J., Patton, J., & Trainor, A. (2004). *Exceptional individuals in focus* (7th ed.). Upper Saddle River, NJ: Pearson Education.

Bower, E. M. (1960). *Early identification of emotionally disturbed children in school.* Springfield, IL: Charles C Thomas.

Bradley, R., Danielson, L., & Doolittle, J. (2007). Responsiveness to intervention: 1997–2007. *Teaching Exceptional Children, 39* (5), 8–12.

Bryant, D., Smith, D., & Bryant, B. (2008). *Teaching students with special needs.* Boston: Pearson Education.

Chronis, A., Jones, H., & Raggi, V. (2006). Evidence-based psychological treatments for children and adolescents with attention-deficit/hyperactivity disorder. *Clinical Psychology Review, 26,* 486–502.

Clark, B. (2008). *Growing up gifted: Developing the potential of children at home and at school* (7th ed.). Upper Saddle River, NJ: Pearson Education.

Clements, S. (1966). *Minimal brain dysfunction in children: Terminology and identification* (Public Health Services Publication No. 1415). Washington, DC: U.S. Department of Health, Education, and Welfare.

Cohen, D. (2006). Critiques of the "ADHD" enterprise. In G. Lloyd, J. Snead, & D. Cohen (Eds.), *Critical new perspectives on ADHD* (pp. 12–33). London: Routledge.

Council for Learning Disabilities. (1986). Use of discrepancy formulas in the identification of learning disabled individuals. *Learning Disabilities Quarterly, 9,* 245.

Cruickshank, W. (1972). Some issues facing the field of learning disabilities. *Journal of Learning Disabilities, 5*(5), 380–388.

Cullinan, D. (2004). Classification and definition of emotional and behavioral disorders. In R. Rutherford, M. Quinn, & S. Mathur (Eds.), *Handbook of research in emotional and behavioral disorders* (pp. 32–53). New York: Guilford.

Deiner, P. (1993). *Resources for teaching children with diverse abilities.* Fort Worth, TX: Harcourt Brace Jovanovich.

Denning, C., Chamberlain, J., & Polloway, E. (2000). An evaluation of state guidelines for mental retardation: Focus on definition and classification practices. *Education and Training in Mental Retardation and Developmental Disabilities, 35*(2), 135–144.

Drew, C., & Hardman, M. (2007). *Mental retardation: A life cycle approach* (9th ed.). Upper Saddle River, NJ: Pearson Education.

Federal Register. (2006, July 1). Assistance to states for the education of children with disabilities. *71*(2), 12–14.

Furlong, M., Morrison, G., & Jimerson, S. (2004). Externalizing behaviors of aggression and violence and the school context. In R. Rutherford, M. Quinn, & S. Mathur (Eds.), *Handbook of research in emotional and behavioral disorders* (pp. 243–261). New York: Guilford.

Gargiulo, R. (2009). *Special education in contemporary society* (3rd ed.). Thousand Oaks, CA: Sage.

Gelb, S. (2002). The dignity of humanity is not a scientific construct. *Mental Retardation, 40*(1), 55–56.

Gresham, F., & Kern, L. (2004). Internalizing behavior problems in children and adolescents. In R. Rutherford, M. Quinn, & S. Mathur (Eds.), *Handbook of research in emotional and behavioral disorders* (pp. 262–281). New York: Guilford.

Grossman, H. (1983). *Classification in mental retardation.* Washington, DC: American Association on Mental Deficiency.

Gupta, V. (2000). A closer look at ADD/ADHD. *Exceptional Parent, 30*(8), 74–81.

Hallahan, D., Lloyd, J., Kauffman, J., Weiss, M., & Martinez, E. (2005). *Learning disabilities: Foundations, characteristics, and effective teaching* (3rd ed.). Boston: Pearson Education.

Hammill, D. (1990). On defining learning disabilities: An emerging consensus. *Journal of Learning Disabilities, 23*(2), 74–84.

Kauffman, J., & Landrum, T. (2009). *Characteristics of emotional and behavioral disorders of children and youth* (9th ed.). Upper Saddle River, NJ: Pearson Education.

Lawrence, V., Houghton, S., Tannock, R., Douglas, G., Dunkin, K., & Whiting, K. (2002). ADHD outside the laboratory: Boys' executive function performance on tasks in video-game play and on a visit to the zoo. *Journal of Abnormal Child Psychology, 30*, 447–462.

Lerner, J., & Kline, F. (2006). *Learning disabilities and related disorders* (10th ed.). Boston: Houghton Mifflin.

Levy, F., Hay, D., & Bennett, K. (2006). Genetics of attention deficit hyperactivity disorder: A current review and future prospects. *International Journal of Disability, Development, and Education, 53*, 5–20.

Luckasson, R., Borthwick-Duffy, S., Buntinx, W., Coulter, D., Craig, E., Reeve, A., Schalock, R., Snell, M., Spitalnick, D., Spreat, S., & Tassé, M. (2002). *Mental retardation: Definition, support, and systems of supports* (10th ed.). Washington, DC: American Association on Mental Retardation.

Marland, S. (1972). *Education of the gifted and the talented: Report to the Congress of the United States by the U.S. Commissioner of Education.* Washington, DC: U.S. Government Printing Office.

Martin, N., Levy, F., Picka, J., & Hay, D. (2006). A genetic study of attention deficit hyperactivity, conduct disorder, oppositional defiant disorder, and reading disability: Aetiological overlaps and implications. *International Journal of Disability, Development, and Education, 53*, 21–34.

National Center for Education Statistics. (2007). *Digest of education statistics, 2006.* Washington, DC: U.S. Government Printing Office.

National Dissemination Center for Children with Disabilities. (2004). Fact Sheet 11: *Speech and language disorders.* Washington, DC: Author.

National Institute of Mental Health. (2006). *Attention deficit hyperactivity disorder.* Retrieved March 20, 2008 from http://www.nimh.nih.gov/health/publications/adhd/summary.shtml

Polloway, E., Smith, J., Chamberlain, J., Denning, C., & Smith, T. (1999). Levels of deficits or supports in the classification of mental retardation: Implementation practices. *Education and Training in Mental Retardation and Developmental Disabilities, 34*(2), 200–206.

Reid, R., Gonzalez, J., Nordness, P., Trout, A., & Epstein, M. (2004). A meta-analysis of the academic status of students with emotional/behavioral disturbance. *Journal of Special Education, 38*(3), 130–143.

Renzulli, J., & Reis, S. (2003). The school-wide enrichment model: Developing creative and productive giftedness. In N. Colangelo & G. Davis (Eds.), *Handbook of gifted education* (3rd ed., pp. 184–203). Boston: Allyn & Bacon.

Reynolds, C. (1992). Two key concepts in the diagnosis of learning disabilities and the habilitation of learning. *Learning Disability Quarterly, 15*, 2–12.

Roid, G. (2003). *Stanford-Binet Intelligence Scale—Fifth Edition.* Itasca, IL: Riverside.

Rosenberg, M. S., Wilson, R., Maheady, L., & Sindelar, P. T. (2004). *Educating students with behavior disorders* (3rd ed.). Needham Heights, MA: Allyn & Bacon.

Salend, S., & Rohena, E. (2003). Students with attention deficit disorders: An overview. *Intervention in School and Clinic, 38*, 259–266.

Silver, L. (1999). *Attention-deficit/hyperactivity disorders* (2nd ed.). Washington, DC: American Psychiatric Press.

Smith, T., Polloway, E., Patton, J., & Dowdy, C. (2008). *Teaching students with special needs in inclusive settings* (5th ed.). Boston: Pearson Education.

Sowell, E., Thompson, P., Welcome, S., Henkenius, A., Toga, A., & Peterson, B. (2003). Cortical abnormalities in children and adolescents with attention-deficit hyperactivity disorder. *Lancet, 362*, 1699–1707.

Turnbull, A., Turnbull, R., & Wehmeyer, M. (2007). *Exceptional lives* (5th ed.). Upper Saddle River, NJ: Pearson Education.

U.S. Department of Education. (2000). *Safeguarding our children: An action guide.* Washington, DC: Author.

U.S. Department of Education. (2006a). *Teaching children with attention deficit hyperactivity disorders: Instructional strategies and practices.* Washington, DC: Author.

U.S. Department of Education. (2006b). *Twenty-sixth annual report to Congress on the implementation of the Individuals with Disabilities Education Act, 2004* (Vol. 2). Washington, DC: U.S. Government Printing Office.

U.S. Department of Education. (2008). *IDEA data.* Retrieved March 27, 2008 from https://www.ideadata.org/PartBReport.asp

U.S. Office of Education. (1977, December 29). Assistance to the states for education of handicapped children: Procedures for evaluating specific learning disabilities. *Federal Register, 42* (250), 65082–65085.

Vaughn, R., & Hodges, L. (1973). A statistical survey into a definition of learning disabilities. *Journal of Learning Disabilities,*
6(10), 658–664.

Vaughn, S., Bos, C., & Schumm, J. (2007). *Teaching exceptional,*
diverse, and at-risk students in the general education classroom.
Boston: Allyn & Bacon.

Warren, S. (2000, May-June). Mental retardation: Curse, characteristic, or coin of the realm? *American Association on Mental*
Retardation News and Notes, 13(3), 1, 10–11.

Webber, J., & Plotts, C. (2008). *Emotional and behavioral disorders:*
Theory and practice (5th ed.). Boston: Allyn & Bacon.

Wechsler, D. (2003). *Wechsler Intelligence Scale for Children—*
Fourth Edition. San Antonio, TX: Psychological Corporation.

Weyandt, L. (2005). *The physiological bases of cognitive and beha-*
vioral disorders. Mahwah, NJ: Erlbaum.

Zappitelli, M., Pinto, T., & Grizenko, N. (2001). Pre-, peri-, and
postnatal trauma in subjects with attention-deficit hyperactivity disorder. *Canadian Journal of Psychiatry, 46,* 342–348.

Learners with Autism Spectrum Disorders

Defining Autism Spectrum Disorders

How Many Learners Exhibit Autism Spectrum Disorders?

What Are Some of the Causes of Autism Spectrum Disorders?

Selected Learning and Behavioral Characteristics of Learners with Autism Spectrum Disorders

Learners with Physical Disabilities, Health Disabilities, or Traumatic Brain Injury

Defining Physical Disabilities, Health Disabilities, and Traumatic Brain Injury

Conditions Associated with Physical and Health Disabilities

How Many Learners Have Physical Disabilities, Health Disabilities, or Traumatic Brain Injury?

What Are Some of the Causes of Physical Disabilities, Health Disabilities, and Traumatic Brain Injury?

Selected Learning and Behavioral Characteristics of Learners with Physical Disabilities, Health Disabilities, or Traumatic Brain Injury

Learners Who Are Culturally and Linguistically Diverse

Terminology of Cultural Differences

Bilingual Education: Concepts and Characteristics

Cultural and Linguistic Diversity and Special Education

Learners Who Are at Risk for Failure in School

Defining At Risk

Family Poverty

Homelessness

Child Abuse and Neglect

Summary of Selected Learning and Behavioral Characteristics

In Chapter 3, we examined at the features and characteristics of students with high incidence disabilities, learners with attention deficit hyperactivity disorder as well as individuals viewed as gifted and talented. In this chapter we turn our attention to pupils with **low incidence disabilities**—children and adolescents with sensory impairments, autism spectrum disorders, physical/health disabilities or traumatic brain injury.[1] During the 2006–2007 school year, about one out of every five students (18.7 percent) receiving a special education evidenced a low incidence disability (U.S. Department of Education, 2008), their instructional and behavioral needs can sometimes be especially challenging. Many of these pupils are currently educated in inclusive settings (U.S. Department of Education). General educators, therefore, will play a major role in the educational lives of these children.

Additionally, we will look at two other groups of learners with special educational needs—students considered at risk for a variety of school difficulties due to adverse environmental or situational variables and children who exhibit culturally and linguistically diverse backgrounds. We have included these two groups of pupils because they represent a growing population of individuals whose opportunity to experience academic success is often in jeopardy. Yet, it is important for teachers to focus on the strengths of each individual learner rather than a particular label or designation. Today's classrooms must address the needs of *all* learners. As we noted in the previous chapter, teachers who focus on the similarities and strengths

[1]Content adapted from R. Gargiulo, *Special Education in Contemporary Society*, 3rd ed. (Thousand Oaks, CA: Sage, 2009).

of their pupils are often able to create inclusive learning communities where all students encounter success and acceptance.

Learners with Hearing Impairments

For most people, hearing is an automatic process; an ability frequently taken for granted. The ability to hear allows individuals to gain information about the world around them and themselves. Hearing is also vitally important to the development of speech and language. Unfortunately, for a small number of children, their hearing is compromised. The loss of one's hearing is an invisible or hidden disability; it often goes unrecognized until communication becomes necessary. The greatest impact of a hearing impairment is in the realm of speech and language. It also dramatically affects academic achievement, literacy performance, and the acquisition of appropriate social skills (Kuder, 2008; Pakulski & Kaderavek, 2002).

Hearing impairment is a general term used to describe disordered hearing. We should point out that the use of this term is offensive to some individuals who are deaf and hard of hearing because the word *impairment* implies a deficiency, something in need of repair or correction. Members of the **Deaf community**, however, do not view their hearing loss as disabling or pathological, consequently, they do not need to be "fixed." Rather, they see themselves as simply belonging to a different culture with its own language, traditions, and values. For these persons, sign language is their language of choice with spoken English being an optional second language. Although we acknowledge this viewpoint, the label *hearing impairment* is preferred by the federal government when describing the disability category. We have chosen to be consistent with the terminology used by the U.S. Department of Education.

Defining Hearing Impairments

The term **deaf** is often overused and misunderstood, and maybe applied inappropriately to describe a wide variety of hearing loss. It can be defined as referring to those for whom the sense of hearing is nonfunctional for the ordinary purposes of life. The IDEA definition describes deafness as a "hearing impairment that is so severe that the child is impaired in processing linguistic information through hearing, with or without amplification, that adversely effects a child's educational performance" (34 C.F.R. § 300.7 [c][3]) (*Federal Register*, 2006). Deafness precludes successful processing of linguistic information through audition (the act or sense of hearing), with or without a hearing aid (Kuder, 2008). Essentially, deafness, by its very definition, prevents individuals from understanding speech.

Classification of Learners with Hearing Impairments

Two different methods are often used to classify hearing loss. One way is to classify according to the location or site of the disorder. A **conductive hearing loss** is caused by a blockage or barrier to the transmission of sound through the outer or middle ear. It is referred to as a conductive hearing loss because sound is not transmitted normally through the outer or middle ear. As a result, sounds are often soft or attenuated in some way for the listener, but clearly heard when loud enough. A **sensorineural hearing loss** is typically caused by disorders of the inner ear (cochlea), the auditory nerve that transmits impulses to the brain, or both. In this type of hearing loss, there is not only a loss of hearing sensitivity, but sounds are usually distorted to the listener and speech often is not heard clearly.

The second method of classifying hearing impairment is by degree. Hearing loss can range from mild to profound based on the level of intensity required (measured in **decibels**, or dB) at various frequencies (described in **hertz**, or Hz) to establish hearing threshold.

Decibels are units of sound pressure. Sound pressure is a physical measure that can be precisely determined. It is associated with the psychological sensation of loudness, which is not perceived identically by all persons. In general, as sound pressure in decibels increases, the sensation of loudness increases. Human speech normally ranges between 40 and 60 dB; any sound at 130 dB, such as large electrical turbines (145 dB), can be extremely painful and damaging (Bess & Humes, 2003).

The **frequency** of a particular sound is a measure of the rate at which the sound source vibrates and is measured in hertz (Hz), so named in honor of a German scientist. The frequency of sound can be precisely measured electronically. Pitch is the psychological correlate of frequency and cannot be measured as precisely because it is perceived differently from one person to the next. But in general, as the frequency of sound increases, the listener perceives the sound as having increased in pitch. Most sounds important to human beings fall between 125 and 8,000 Hz, with most human speech concentrated in 500 to 3,000 Hz (Berk, 2006).

This classification system is directly related to an individual's ability to hear and comprehend speech. Professionals (Andrews, Leigh, & Weiner, 2004; Owens, Metz, & Haas, 2003) typically classify the degree of hearing loss as follows:

- mild (26–40 dB loss)
- moderate (41–55 dB loss)
- moderate to severe (56–70 dB loss)
- severe (71–90 dB loss)
- profound (91 dB loss and higher)

Individuals are typically classified as deaf if their hearing loss exceeds 70 dB.

Hearing loss obviously affects the student's educational performance. Table 4.1 portrays the impact of a hearing loss on the learner, its effect on speech and language, as well as instructional/educational implications.

Table 4.1 Impact of Hearing Loss on Students

Degree of Hearing Loss	Possible Psychosocial Impact of Hearing Loss	Effect of Hearing Loss on Speech and Language	Potential Educational Needs and Programs
Mild 26–40 dB	• Barriers begin to build, with negative impact on self-esteem as child is accused of "hearing when he or she wants to," "daydreaming," or "not paying attention." • Child begins to lose ability for selective hearing and has increasing difficulty suppressing background noise, which makes the learning environment stressful. • Child is more fatigued than classmates because of listening effort needed.	• At 30 dB, 25–40% of speech is missed. • The degree of difficulty experienced in school will depend upon the noise level in the classroom, distance from teacher, and the configuration of the hearing loss. • Without amplification, the child with 35–40 dB loss may miss at least 50% of class discussions, especially when voices are faint or the speaker is not in line of vision. • Will miss consonants, especially when a high-frequency hearing loss is present.	• Will benefit from a hearing aid and use of a personal FM or sound field FM system in the classroom. • Needs favorable seating and lighting. • Refer to special education for language evaluation and educational follow-up. • Needs auditory skill building. • May need attention to vocabulary and language development, articulation or speech reading, and/or special support in reading. • May need help with self-esteem. • Teacher inservice required.
Moderate 41–55 dB	• Communication is often significantly affected, and socialization with peers with normal hearing becomes increasingly difficult. • With full-time use of hearing aids/FM systems, child may be judged as a less competent learner. • There is an increasing impact on self-esteem.	• Understands conversational speech at a distance of 3–5 feet (face-to-face) only if structure and vocabulary controlled. • Without amplification, the amount of speech missed can be 50–75% with 40 dB loss and 80–100% with 50 dB loss. • Is likely to have delayed or defective syntax, limited vocabulary, imperfect speech production, and an atonal voice quality.	• Refer to special education for language evaluation and for educational follow-up. • Amplification is essential (hearing aids and FM system). • Special education support may be needed, especially for primary-age children. • Attention to oral language development, reading, and written language. • Auditory skill development and speech therapy usually needed. • Teacher inservice required.

Table 4.1 Impact of Hearing Loss on Students (*Continued*)			
Degree of Hearing Loss	**Possible Psychosocial Impact of Hearing Loss**	**Effect of Hearing Loss on Speech and Language**	**Potential Educational Needs and Programs**
Moderate to severe 56–70 dB	• Full-time use of hearing aids/FM systems may result in child being judged as a less competent learner, resulting in poorer self-concept and diminished social maturity, and contributing to sense of rejection. • Inservice to address these attitudes may be helpful.	• Without amplification, conversation must be very loud to be understood. • A 55 dB loss can cause child to miss up to 100% of speech information. • Will have marked difficulty in school situations requiring verbal communication in both one-to-one and group situations. • Delayed language, syntax, reduced speech intelligibility, and atonal voice quality likely.	• Full-time use of amplification is essential. • Will need resource teacher or special class depending on magnitude of language delay. • May require special help in all language skills, language-based academic subjects, vocabulary, grammar, and pragmatics, as well as reading and writing. • Probably needs assistance to expand experiential language base. • Inservice of general educators required.
Severe 71–90 dB	• Child may prefer other children with hearing impairments as friends and playmates. • This may further isolate the child from the mainstream; however, these peer relationships may foster improved self-concept and a sense of cultural identity.	• Without amplification, may hear loud voices about one foot from ear. • When amplified optimally, children with hearing ability of 90 dB or better should be able to identify environmental sounds and detect all the sounds of speech. • If loss is of a prelingual onset, oral language and speech may not develop spontaneously or will be severely delayed. • If hearing loss is of recent onset, speech is likely to deteriorate with quality becoming atonal.	• May need full-time special aural/oral program with emphasis on all auditory language skills, speech reading, concept development, and speech. • As loss approaches 80–90 dB, may benefit from a total communication approach, especially in the early language learning years. • Individual hearing aid/personal FM system essential. • Need to monitor effectiveness of communication modality. • Participation in regular classes as much as possible. • Inservice of general educators essential.
Profound > 90 dB	• Depending on auditory/oral competence, peer use of sign language, parental attitude, and other factors, child may or may not increasingly prefer association with the Deaf culture.	• Aware of vibrations more than tonal pattern. • Many rely on vision rather than hearing as primary avenue for communication and learning. • Detection of speech sounds dependent upon loss configuration and use of amplification. • Speech and language will not develop spontaneously and are likely to deteriorate rapidly if hearing loss is of recent onset.	• May need special program for children who are deaf, with emphasis on all language skills and academic areas. • Program needs specialized supervision and comprehensive support services. • Early use of amplification likely to help if part of an intensive training program. • May be cochlear implant or vibrotactile aid candidate. • Requires continual appraisal of needs in regard to communication and learning mode. • Part-time in general education classes as much as benefits student.

Source: Adapted from K. Anderson, "Hearing Conservation in the Public Schools Revisited," *Seminars in Hearing, 12*(4), 1991, pp. 361–363.

How Many Learners Are Hearing Impaired?

According to the U.S. Department of Education (2008), approximately 72,600 students between the ages of 6 and 21 were defined as having a hearing impairment and receiving special education services during the 2006–2007 school year. These students represent 1.2 percent of all pupils with disabilities and 0.11 percent of the total school-age population.

What Are Some of the Causes of Hearing Impairment?

Many different factors contribute to a hearing impairment. In over 55 percent of the instances of hearing loss in children, the cause is unknown (Gallaudet Research Institute, 2006). Some of the known reasons may be due to genetic or hereditary factors, representing one of the leading causes of deafness in children (Herer, Knightly, & Steinberg, 2007). Down syndrome is an example of a congenital chromosomal abnormality frequently resulting in hearing loss.

Infections are also a common cause of hearing impairment. Examples include rubella or German measles (one of the chief reasons for hearing loss in children in the 1960s and early 1970s) and **cytomegalovirus** (CMV), a herpes virus, which is the leading cause of sensorineural hearing loss in children (Picard, 2004). Viral infections such as measles and mumps are also associated with hearing impairments.

Otitis media (an infection of the middle ear) is one of the leading causes of mild to moderate conductive hearing loss in children (Gallaudet Research Institute, 2005). It is the most common reason for visits to physicians for children under age 6 (Schirmer, 2001). Fluid accumulation in the middle ear resulting from viral or bacterial factors typically causes a 15–40 dB conductive hearing loss and, if left untreated, can lead to a permanent conductive hearing loss. Otitis media is often treated by administering antibiotics or in some instances, through placement of tubes in the ears.

Low birth weight, prematurity, anoxia, meningitis, head injuries, and the side effects of some antibiotics are examples of additional possible causes of hearing loss in children. The aging process is a frequent contributor to hearing loss in adults.

Noise pollution—repeated exposure to loud noises, is currently receiving a great deal of attention as a cause of hearing loss. Operating heavy equipment or machinery without ear protection, listening to amplified music for extended periods of time, riding a motorcycle, and exposure to jet noise or gunfire are just some of the possibilities leading to a gradual hearing loss. Prolonged exposure to noise in excess of 90 dB is suspected of causing hearing loss, especially in adolescents and adults. Fortunately, hearing loss due to environmental factors is preventable by the wearing of ear protection devices.

Like many other professionals, we believe that knowing the particular cause of a hearing impairment is usually unimportant for teachers, being knowledgeable of the etiology rarely leads to effective instructional interventions. However, educators should be aware of the indicators of possible hearing difficulties. Table 4.2 presents some of the warning signs that teachers should look for.

Table 4.2   Indicators of Possible Hearing Impairment in Children

- Daydreaming or frequently inattentive
- Impaired speech
- Limited vocabulary
- Lethargic—complains of always being tired
- Often turns head to favored side
- Mouth breathing
- Difficulty following verbal commands or directions
- Nonresponsive to environmental sounds
- Complains of earaches, ringing noises in the ear
- Recurring ear infections
- Inappropriate responses to verbal questions
- Tugs or pulls ear(s)
- Excessive volume when listening to audio devices (television, radio, portable music player)
- Imitates or mimics the actions/movements of peers and classmates
- Frequent requests to repeat verbal information
- Difficulty hearing telephone conversation

Selected Learning and Behavioral Characteristics of Learners with Hearing Impairment

Variations in the degree and type of hearing loss, age of onset, and etiology are just some of the variables that result in a heterogeneous group of learners with hearing impairments. Students who experience hearing loss often encounter challenges in the area of academic achievement, speech and language, and social development.

Academic Achievement

Because deafness per se does not limit cognitive abilities (Karchmer & Mitchell, 2005), investigators have found that the distribution of intelligence for individuals with hearing impairments is similar to that of hearing children (Maller, 2005; Simeonsson & Rosenthal, 2001). Findings suggest that intellectual development for people with a hearing impairment is more a function of language development than cognitive ability. Unfortunately, despite their intellectual abilities, pupils who are deaf or have a hearing loss experience considerable difficulty succeeding in an educational system that depends primarily on the spoken word and written language to transmit knowledge. Low achievement is characteristic of students who are deaf (Geers, 2006); they average three to four years below their age-appropriate grade levels. Even students with mild to moderate hearing losses achieve below expectations based on their performance on tests of cognitive abilities (Williams & Finnegan, 2003).

Reading is the academic area most negatively affected for students with a hearing impairment. Any hearing loss, whether mild or profound, appears to have detrimental effects on reading performance. At the time of high school graduation, the typical learner who is deaf reads at approximately a fourth-grade level (Gallaudet Research Institute, 2007).

Speech and Language

Speech and language skills are the areas of development most severely affected for those with a hearing impairment, particularly for children who are born deaf. The majority of deaf children have a very difficult time learning to use speech (McLean, Wolery, & Bailey, 2004). For pupils who experience mild to moderate hearing losses, the effect may be minimal. Even for those children born with a moderate loss, effective communication skills are possible because the voiced sounds of conversational speech remain audible. Thus, in the vast majority of instances, learners who experience a hearing loss are able to use speech as the primary mode for language acquisition.

For students with profound deafness, most loud speech is inaudible, even with the use of the most sophisticated hearing aids. These individuals are unable to receive information through speech unless they have learned to speech read (lip read). Sounds produced by an individual who is deaf are often difficult to understand. Children who are deaf exhibit significant articulation, voice quality, and tone discrimination problems.

Psychosocial Development

Social-emotional development depends, in part, on the ability to communicate with others. Children with hearing impairments often encounter difficulties in developing friendships and other social interactions. These individuals frequently express feeling lonely, isolated, and depressed (Connolly, Rose, & Austen, 2006; Scheetz, 2004). A sense of feeling isolated and a lack of friendships can hinder successful integration in inclusive classrooms (Kluwin, Stinson, & Colarossi, 2002). It is perhaps for this reason that many persons who are deaf have a strong preference for associating with others who are also hearing impaired (Moores, 2001).

Many individuals who are visually impaired lead successful and independent lives.

Scott T. Baxter/PhotoLibrary

Learners with Visual Impairments

Visual impairment is a term that describes people who cannot see well even with correction. Throughout history, *blindness* has been used as a term to mean something is not understood, such as "I was blind to that idea," or the aged person is "old and blind." How many times do we use stereotypes of the blind beggar on the street corner and the blind person groping for mobility in the environment? The stigma associated with loss of vision affects encounters with others, who may assume that the person is dependent on others for everything. Fortunately, in most instances, this assumption is false. Individuals who are blind are often quite capable of leading successful and independent lives. A few persons even achieve significant fame and recognition; two examples are Helen Keller and her teacher, Anne Sullivan, and Mary Ingalls, whose determination and accomplishments were portrayed by her sister, Laura Ingalls Wilder, in the popular television series, *Little House on the Prairie*. Musicians such as Ray Charles, Stevie Wonder, and Andrea Bocelli, have helped to change the image of persons with visual impairments. In the vast number of cases, people who are visually impaired are competent and independent, who only require a few accommodations in their everyday world, such as Braille menus, voice output computers, Braille calendars, or "talking" watches. Many times the only difference between a sighted person and one without sight is the loss of visual acuity.

Defining Visual Impairments

Visual impairment including blindness is defined in the regulations (*Federal Register*, 2006) accompanying the Individuals with Disabilities Education Improvement Act of 2004 (PL 108-446) as an impairment in vision that, even with correction, adversely affects an individual's educational performance. The term includes both partial sight and blindness (34 C.F.R. § 300.7 [c][13]).

Educational services for students with visual impairments are determined by variations of the definition specified in IDEA. This definition encompasses students with a wide range of visual impairments, who may vary significantly in their visual abilities. One student may have no functional vision and must learn through tactile means (Braille); another student may be able to read print with modifications such as enlarged print; still others may use a combination of Braille and print.

Over the years, the term **legally blind** has been used as a federal definition of blindness. This definition involves using a **Snellen chart**, which is a clinical measurement of the true amount of distance vision an individual has under certain conditions. Legal blindness is a visual acuity of 20/200 or less in the better eye with correction or a visual field that is no greater than 20 degrees. In this definition, 20 feet is the distance at which visual acuity is measured. The 200 in this definition indicates the distance (200 feet) a person with normal vision would be able to identify the largest symbol on the eye chart. The second part of the definition refers to field restriction, which involves the amount of vision a person has to view objects peripherally. The legal definition is considered in education, but by itself has little value in planning a functional educational program for students with visual impairments.

Classification of Learners with Visual Impairments

Students with visual impairments are typically classified into three categories on the basis of their ability to use their vision—blind, functionally blind or having low vision.

Individuals identified as **blind** use tactile and auditory abilities as the primary channels of learning. They may have some minimal light or form perception or be totally without sight. Braille or other tactile media are commonly the preferred literacy channel. Orientation and mobility training is required for all students who are blind.

Individuals are considered **functionally blind** when the primary channel of learning is through tactile or auditory means. They may use limited vision to obtain additional information about the environment. These individuals usually use Braille as the **primary literacy medium** (most frequently used method of reading) and require orientation and mobility training.

A person is described as having **low vision** when the visual impairment interferes with the ability to perform daily activities. The primary channel of learning is through visual means with the use of prescription and nonprescription devices. The literacy medium varies with each individual according to the use of the remaining vision and the use of low vision devices. Orientation and mobility training is required for students to learn to use **residual vision** (usable vision).

How Many Learners Are Visually Impaired?

The U.S. Department of Education (2008) reports that approximately 26,000 children, ages 6–21, were receiving services in the 2006–2007 school year because of a visual impairment. These students represent 0.43 percent of all pupils with disabilities and 0.04 percent of the total school-age population. Visual impairments, therefore, is one of the least prevalent disabilities.

What Are Some of the Causes of Visual Impairment?

The eye is a very complicated organ. Damage to any part of the vision mechanism may result in impaired vision. Pre- peri- and postnatal factors are often implicated as causing visual impairments. Fortunately, some but not all, vision disorders can be corrected or minimized thanks in part to medical breakthroughs. Some of the conditions affecting a student's ability to see and process information visually include:

- *Refractive Errors* (an inability of the eye to focus light rays correctly on the retina)
  - Myopia: commonly called nearsightedness, pupil is able to read their textbook but has difficulty seeing the chalkboard
  - Hyperopia: condition opposite of myopia, commonly known as farsightedness, student can see objects at a distance but has difficulty seeing materials close by
  - Astigmatism: an irregularity in the curvature of the cornea resulting in distorted or blurred vision
- *Defects of the Ocular Muscle*
  - Strabismus: an improper alignment or imbalance of the eyes, commonly referred to as crossed eye, left untreated will cause permanent blindness
  - Nystagmus: a rapid, involuntary movement of the eye
- *Disorders of the Cornea, Iris, or Lens*
  - Cataracts: a clouding of the lens of the eye resulting in blurred vision, may be corrected surgically
  - Glaucoma: a build up of fluid pressure in the eye, central and peripheral vision may be permanently impaired
- *Other Conditions*
  - Retinitis pigmentosa: a common hereditary condition, usually causes "tunnel vision" and night blindness prior to total blindness
  - Retinopathy of prematurity: at one time a leading cause of blindness due to excessive concentrations of oxygen given to infants placed in incubators
  - Diabetic retinopathy: damage to blood vessels in proximity of the retina, caused by diabetes
  - Cortical visual impairment: damage or dysfunction in the area of the brain responsible for vision, significant daily variations in visual abilities

Whereas it may be interesting and helpful to know the etiology of a learner's vision difficulty, teachers need to be concerned with the functional result of the impairment and how the student uses their vision in the classroom setting. Educators are often the first professional to become aware of a child's vision problem. Table 4.3 presents possible indicators of vision difficulties in children.

Selected Learning and Behavioral Characteristics of Learners with Visual Impairment

Characteristics of persons with visual impairments are highly variable depending upon the amount of vision loss, the type of impairment, and the age of onset. These three variables often interact uniquely affecting the individual in various areas of functioning and development. Still, a child with a visual impairment is more like their sighted peers than they are different.

Academic Achievement

The intellectual abilities of children and adolescents with visual impairments are, in most instances, similar to those of their sighted peers. There is no reason to suspect that a vision loss results in lower intellectual ability (Hallahan, Kauffman, & Pullen, 2009). Despite this fact, learners with visual impairment often experience significant academic delays. One reason for this finding is their limited opportunity to acquire information visually (Pogrund & Fazzi, 2007). Unlike sighted children, incidental learning obtained from interacting with the environment is severely restricted in children with visual impairments (Liefert, 2003). Conceptual development, therefore, primarily depends on tactile (touch) experiences rather than vision.

Social/Emotional Development

A loss of vision often negatively affects the acquisition of appropriate social skills. For example, when conversing with friends, sighted individuals typically face the person while standing at a socially appropriate distance; children who are blind frequently fail to exhibit these necessary social skills. They are also unaware of the individual's body language and subtle nonverbal social cues. In other instances, students with visual impairments are frequently excluded from group activities such as attending a sporting event. Feelings of isolation and a lack of acceptance are common among many children and adolescents with visual impairments. The lack of opportunity to develop appropriate social skills frequently leads to diminished self-esteem and negatively impacts self-concept (Sacks & Silberman, 2000).

Table 4.3	Indicators of Possible Visual Impairments in Children

- Excessive rubbing of the eye
- Watery and/or itchy eyes
- Extreme sensitivity to light
- Squinting one or both eyes
- Difficulty seeing material from a distance
- Holds objects close to eyes
- Complains of frequent headaches, dizziness
- Excessive blinking
- Tilts head while reading
- Swollen or inflamed eyes
- Poor penmanship; eye-hand coordination difficulties
- Appears clumsy, exhibits awkward movements
- Inward or outward rotation of eyes
- Complains of blurred or double vision

In the Classroom

Orientation and Mobility Tips for the General Educator

- Eliminate unnecessary obstacles; inform student of changes in room arrangement or of any temporary obstacles.
- Keep doors completely closed or completely open to eliminate the possibility of the student's running into a partially open door.
- Allow the student to travel with a companion to frequently used rooms such as the library, school office, restroom, and gym. Discuss routes with turns and landmarks.
- Allow student to move about freely until the room and route are familiar.

- Encourage sighted guide for fire drills, field trips, assemblies, and seating in rooms that ordinarily have no assigned seats.
- Encourage independent travel in the familiar settings at school.

Source: Adapted from R. Craig and C. Howard, "Visual Impairment," in M. Hardman, M. Egan, and D. Landau (Eds.), *What Will We Do in the Morning?* (Dubuque, IA: W. C. Brown, 1981), p. 191.

Finally, some students with visual impairments engage in a variety of repetitive behaviors such as rubbing their eyes, head weaving, hand flapping, and body rocking. These actions are known as **stereotypic behaviors**. These movements, although generally not harmful, do attract unwelcomed and negative attention. If done to an extreme they have the potential for interfering with learning and socialization.

Orientation and Mobility

Orientation is being aware of where you are, where you are going, and the route to get there. Mobility is moving safely and efficiently from place to place. How successful a pupil is at navigating their environment significantly affects their independence as well as their social development.

Mobility skills greatly vary among individuals with visual impairments. This skill typically depends on the severity of the person's impairment, the age of onset, and their spatial ability. Individuals with visual impairments generally use three methods of orientation and mobility: the long cane, human guides, and guide dogs.

Orientation and mobility services for children with visual impairments are currently included in the IDEA definition of related services. Instruction in this area is quite common in the IEP of learners with significant vision loss. The accompanying In the Classroom feature provides suggestions for teachers regarding orientation and mobility.

Learners with Autism Spectrum Disorders

Although many people are familiar with the term autism (derived from the Greek word *autos* meaning "self"), their understanding and perception of individuals with **autism spectrum disorders** (ASD) is often distorted by how they are portrayed in movies and television. For instance, in the 1988 Academy Award winning movie *Rain Man*, an adult with ASD was portrayed as having special mathematical skills that allowed him to beat a blackjack dealer's odds in Las Vegas. You may believe that all individuals with autism spectrum disorders possess these unique abilities. This is a common misperception; only rarely do individuals with ASD (commonly called autistic savants) actually demonstrate these highly developed, but rarely functional skills.

Television shows frequently portray individuals with autism spectrum disorders as locked away in their own world, unable to communicate or to give or receive affection. Often, it is implied that if someone could just break through their autistic isolation, there would be a genius inside. In addition, individuals with autism spectrum disorders are often shown as being aggressive and/or self-injurious. These are all common misconceptions about ASD. Most individuals with autism spectrum disorders learn to speak or communicate with sign language, picture symbols, or via assistive technology. Although their deficits may impair the way they give and receive affection, even the most severely impaired individuals with autism spectrum disorders are often able to demonstrate and accept affection from the significant individuals in their lives. The belief that a genius exists inside each individual with ASD is fueled by the presence by unevenly developed skills; for example, an 8-year-old may be able to solve complex calculus problems but be unable to tell time.

Defining Autism Spectrum Disorders

Our understanding of autism has been an evolving process. Leo Kanner, a psychiatrist at Johns Hopkins Hospital, first identified this condition more than 60 years ago. Kanner (1943/1985) described 11 children with an "inability to relate themselves in an ordinary way to people and situations" (p. 41). Kanner used the term *autistic*, which means "to escape from reality," to characterize this disorder. He also observed that this group of youngsters shared the following unique features among other distinguishing characteristics:

- excellent rote memory
- delays in the acquisition of speech and language (including pronoun reversals, echolalia, mutism, and extreme literalness)
- an obsessive desire for the maintenance of sameness
- bizarre and repetitive physical movements (spinning, rocking)
- resistance to being held or picked up by their parents

Kanner's research helped to distinguish children with autism from those with childhood schizophrenia.

IDEA Definition

Federal law first recognized autism as a discrete disability category with the enactment of PL 101-476 in 1990. Prior to the passage of this legislation, students with autism (the term presently used by the U.S. Department of Education) were generally served under the labels of emotionally disturbed or other health impairments. Under the current regulations (34 C.F.R. § 300.7 [c][1]) autism is defined as a

> developmental disability significantly affecting verbal and nonverbal communication and social interaction, usually evident before age 3, that adversely affects a child's educational performance. Other characteristics often associated with autism are engagement in repetitive activities and stereotyped movements, resistance to environmental change or change in daily routines, and unusual responses to sensory experiences. The term does not apply if a child's educational performance is adversely affected primarily because the child has an emotional disturbance, . . . (Federal Register, 2006, pp. 12–14)

American Psychiatric Association Definition

The current version of the *Diagnostic and Statistical Manual of Mental Disorders* (DSM-IV-TR) (American Psychiatric Association, 2000) classifies autism as one of five discrete childhood disorders falling under the umbrella term, pervasive developmental disorders (PDD). Included in this category are autism, Rett's disorder, childhood disintegrative disorder, Asperger's disorder, and pervasive developmental disorder not otherwise specified. Educators, and most other professionals, use the term autism spectrum disorders instead of PDD when referring to some or all of these five related disorders (Volkmar & Pauls, 2003). The American Psychiatric Association did not recognize autism as a distinct disorder until 1977. The diagnostic criteria for autism appear in Table 4.4.

Table 4.4	Diagnostic Criteria for Autism

(A) A total of six (or more) items from (1), (2), and (3) with at least two from (1) and one each from (2) and (3):

   (1) qualitative impairment in social interaction, as manifested by at least two of the following:

      (a) marked impairment in the use of multiple nonverbal behaviors such as eye-to-eye gaze, facial expression, body postures, and gestures to regulate social interaction

      (b) failure to develop peer relationships appropriate to developmental level

      (c) a lack of spontaneous seeking to share enjoyment, interests, or achievements with other people (e.g., by a lack of showing, bringing, or pointing out objects of interest)

      (d) lack of social or emotional reciprocity

   (2) qualitative impairment in communication as manifested by at least one of the following:

      (a) delay in or total lack of the development of spoken language (not accompanied by an attempt to compensate through alternative modes of communication such as gesture or mime)

      (b) in individuals with adequate speech, marked impairment in the ability to initiate or sustain a conversation with others

      (c) stereotyped and repetitive use of language or idiosyncratic language

      (d) lack of varied, spontaneous make-believe play or social imitative play appropriate to developmental level

   (3) restrictive repetitive and stereotyped patterns of behavior, interests, and activities as manifested by at least one of the following:

      (a) encompassing preoccupation with one or more stereotyped and restricted patterns of interest that is abnormal either in intensity or focus

      (b) apparently inflexible adherence to specific, nonfunctional routines or rituals

      (c) stereotyped and repetitive motor mannerisms (e.g., hand or finger flapping or twisting, or complex whole-body movements)

      (d) persistent preoccupation with parts of objects

(B) Delays or abnormal functioning in at least one of the following areas, with onset prior to age 3 years; (1) social Interaction, (2) language as used in social communication, or symbolic or imaginative play.

(C) The disturbance is not better accounted for by Rett's disorder or childhood disintegrative disorder

Source: American Psychiatric Association, *Diagnostic and Statistical Manual—Text Revision*, 4th ed. (Washington, DC: Author, 2000), p. 75.

How Many Learners Exhibit Autism Spectrum Disorders?

Autism spectrum disorders are the fastest growing developmental disability (Autism Society of America, 2008). The American Psychiatric Association (2000) cites a conservative range of 2–5 cases per 10,000, compared with the Autism Society of America's rate of 1 in every 150 individuals.

Recent statistics compiled by the U.S. government indicate that approximately 224,000 pupils ages 6–21 were identified as having autism in the 2006–2007 school year (U.S. Department of Education, 2008). Individuals with autism represent 3.70 percent of all pupils with disabilities and 0.34 percent of the school-age population. Data about individuals with autism were first reported in the 1991–1992 school year. Since that time, the number of pupils receiving a special education due to autism has increased more than 2100 percent. The factors responsible for this huge increase are not completely clear (Fombonne, 2003).

What Are Some of the Causes of Autism Spectrum Disorders?

The etiology of autism spectrum disorders is complex. Even though investigators do not know the precise cause(s) of ASD, research has implicated neurological, genetic, and environmental factors as possible causal agents. Biomedical research has focused on abnormalities in brain development, structure, and neurochemical functioning (Courchesne, 2004; National Institute of Mental Health, 2008). There is also very strong evidence for a genetic contribution to ASD, although the exact mode of transmission is still hypothesized (Volkmar & Pauls, 2003). Several environmental factors such as food allergies, vitamin deficiencies, and vaccinations, specifically MMR (measles, mumps, and rubella) inoculations were, at one time, suspected of causing autism spectrum disorders. While there is some supportive anecdotal evidence, rigorous scientific investigations have failed to confirm these variables as contributing to ASD.

It is perhaps best to think of autism spectrum disorders as having multiple biological causes. As researchers attempt to unravel the intriguing question of what

Autism spectrum disorders are the fastest growing developmental disability.

causes ASD, we do know that poor or ineffective parenting does *not* cause this disorder as was once commonly believed.

Selected Learning and Behavioral Characteristics of Learners with Autism Spectrum Disorders

Because individuals with autism spectrum disorders present a unique profile of characteristics generalizations are often difficult to make. Despite this fact, there are three defining characteristics typical of learners with ASD: impaired social interaction, impaired communication skills, and repetitive and restrictive behaviors (see Table 4.4 for specific features of each category). In addition to these three primary traits, other characteristics that frequently coexist include the areas summarized in Table 4.5.

Learners with Physical Disabilities, Health Disabilities, or Traumatic Brain Injury

Students who have physical disabilities, health disabilities, or traumatic brain injury constitute one of the most diverse categories of students in special education, because of the wide range of diseases and disorders included in this category. Learners with **physical disabilities** may range from those with severe physical conditions resulting in an inability to talk, walk, point, or make any purposeful movement to those pupils with only some difficulty walking or an unseen skeletal abnormality. Individuals with **health disabilities** may range from those with severe health problems forcing them to stay home to those with a hidden disability, such as a tumor. Students with physical or health disabilities may range in intelligence from profoundly mentally retarded to gifted. Additional sensory impairments,

Table 4.5	**Associated Characteristics of Individuals with Autism Spectrum Disorders**
Intellectual/Academic Functioning	<ul><li>Full range of intellectual abilities possible; however, a significant number of individuals exhibit mental retardation</li><li>Uneven skill development, "splinter skills" are common (unexpectedly high performance in comparison to other domains of functioning)</li><li>Impaired verbal and reasoning skills</li><li>Uneven academic achievement</li><li>Poor reading comprehension</li></ul>
Concentration and Attention	<ul><li>Hyperactivity</li><li>Short attention span</li><li>Impulsivity</li><li>Impaired concentration</li></ul>
Self-Injurious Behaviors	<ul><li>Head banging</li><li>Finger, hand, wrist biting</li><li>Excessive rubbing or scratching</li></ul>
Eating Abnormalities	<ul><li>Diet limited to a few select items</li><li>Ingestion of nonedibles (pica)</li></ul>
Sleep Disorders	<ul><li>Difficulty falling asleep</li><li>Frequent awaking while asleep</li><li>Early morning awakening</li><li>Enuresis (bed-wetting)</li></ul>
Abnormalities of Mood or Affect	<ul><li>Giggling or weeping for no apparent reason</li><li>Depression</li><li>Lack of emotional reaction</li></ul>
Sensory Perception Deficits	<ul><li>High threshold for pain</li><li>Oversensitivity to sounds or touch (tactually defensive)</li><li>Exaggerated responses to lights or colors</li><li>Hypersensitive hearing</li></ul>

Source: Adapted from R. Gargiulo, *Special Education in Contemporary Society*, 3rd ed. (Thousand Oaks, CA: Sage, 2009).

behavioral disorders, or learning disabilities may be present. Individuals with **traumatic brain injury**, which is often due to external trauma, frequently have impaired functioning in one or more areas such as reduced cognitive ability, limited attention, or psychosocial impairment. What places these students together in this section is that they all share aspects of physical or health impairments.

Defining Physical Disabilities, Health Disabilities, and Traumatic Brain Injury

Many learners have various physical or health conditions, but only those with physical or health disabilities that interfere with their educational performance require special education services. According to the regulations (34 C.F.R. § 300.7 [c]) (*Federal Register*, 2006) accompanying the Individuals with Disabilities Education Improvement Act of 2004 (PL 108-446), students with physical impairments may qualify for special education services under three possible categories:

- orthopedic impairments
- multiple disabilities
- traumatic brain injury

Pupils with health disabilities may qualify under the IDEA category of **other health impairments**. The federal definition of orthopedic impairments provides examples of impairments resulting from congenital anomalies (irregularities or defects present at birth), diseases, or other causes (see Table 4.6).

When students have two or more primary disabilities that cannot be accommodated by one special education program, they may be classified as having **multiple**

Table 4.6 Federal Definitions Pertaining to Physical and Health Disabilities

Orthopedic impairment:
- A severe orthopedic impairment that adversely affects a child's educational performance.
- Includes impairments caused by congenital anomaly (e.g., clubfoot, absence of some member), impairments caused by disease (e.g., poliomyelitis, bone tuberculosis), and impairments from other causes (e.g., cerebral palsy, amputations, and fractures or burns that cause contractures).

Multiple disabilities:
- Concomitant impairments (e.g., mental retardation-blindness, mental retardation-orthopedic impairment), the combination of which causes such severe educational needs that they cannot be accommodated in special education programs solely for one of the impairments.
- Term does not include deaf-blindness.

Traumatic brain injury:
- An acquired injury to the brain caused by an external physical force, resulting in total or partial functional disability or psychosocial impairment, or both, that adversely affects educational performance.
- Term applies to open or closed head injuries resulting in impairments in one or more areas, such as cognition; language; memory; attention; reasoning; abstract thinking; judgment; problem solving; sensory, perceptual, and motor abilities; psychosocial behavior; physical functions; information processing; and speech.
- Term does not apply to brain injuries that are congenital or degenerative, or to brain injuries induced by birth trauma.

Other health impairment:
- Having limited strength, vitality, or alertness, including a heightened alertness to environmental stimuli, that results in limited alertness with respect to the education environment that is due to chronic or acute health problems such as asthma, attention deficit disorder or attention deficit hyperactivity disorder, diabetes, epilepsy, a heart condition, hemophilia, lead poisoning, leukemia, nephritis, rheumatic fever, and sickle cell anemia; and adversely affects a child's educational performance

Source: Adapted from *Federal Register* (July 1, 2006), § 300.7[c], *71*(2), pp. 12–14.

disabilities. For example, a child who has a severe physical impairment and is deaf may be classified as having multiple disabilities; this pupil will most likely require services from a teacher certified to teach students with orthopedic impairments and another teacher certified in deaf/hard of hearing. Many possible combinations of disabilities fall under the category of multiple disabilities, but because a physical or health disability is often involved, this category is also addressed in this section.

Children who have an acquired brain injury as a result of external force, such as an automobile accident or a fall may be served under the category of traumatic brain injury. This category does not include individuals who have brain injury that occurred before or during birth or that was acquired as a result of a degenerative disease.

Students with "other health impairments" have limited alertness to the educational environment because of health problems that limit strength, vitality, or alertness. This health impairment may be chronic (persisting over a long period of time) or acute (having a short and usually severe course). The federal definitions in Table 4.6 give examples of health impairments, including asthma, heart conditions, diabetes, and attention deficit hyperactivity disorder. This is only a partial listing of all of the possible conditions that may be included in this disability area.

Conditions Associated with Physical and Health Disabilities

Students with physical and health disabilities exhibit a wide range of conditions. Each impairment has its own unique characteristics, prognoses, and distinguishing attributes. Because of the multitude of physical and health disabilities encountered in today's classroom, we have chosen to discuss only a few representative conditions associated with this label.

Physical Disabilities

Orthopedic Impairments

The IDEA category of orthopedic impairments contains a wide variety of disorders. The following are examples of some of the more common orthopedic impairments found in school-age children.

Cerebral Palsy

Cerebral palsy refers to several nonprogressive disorders of voluntary movement or posture that are caused by malfunction of or damage to the developing brain that occurs before or during birth or within the first few years of life (Beers, Porter, Jones, Kaplan, & Berkwitz, 2006). This disorder is associated with many different etiologies. It is neither contagious nor curable.

Individuals with cerebral palsy have abnormal, involuntary, and/or uncoordinated motor movements. The severity can range from mild to severe. Some mild forms of cerebral palsy may only be noticeable when the person runs and appears to move in an uncoordinated fashion. At the other extreme, individuals with severe forms of cerebral palsy are unable to make the motor movements necessary to walk, sit without support, feed themselves, chew food, pick up an object, or speak.

The four most common types of cerebral palsy are spastic, athetoid, ataxia, and mixed. **Spastic cerebral palsy** is characterized by very tight muscles occurring in one or more muscle groups. This tightness results in stiff, uncoordinated movements. In **athetoid cerebral palsy**, movements are contorted, abnormal, and purposeless. Individuals with **ataxic cerebral palsy**, or ataxia, have poor balance and equilibrium in addition to uncoordinated voluntary movement. **Mixed cerebral palsy** refers to a combination of types, such as spastic and athetoid.

Cerebral palsy is also classified by which limbs (arms and legs) are affected. This classification system is also used for other types of motor disorders and paralysis. Some of the major classifications are **hemiplegia**, in which the left or right side of the body is involved; **diplegia**, in which the legs are more affected than the arms; **paraplegia**, in which only the legs are involved; and **quadriplegia**, in which all four limbs are involved (see Figure 4.1).

Orthopedic impairments represent a wide variety of disorders.

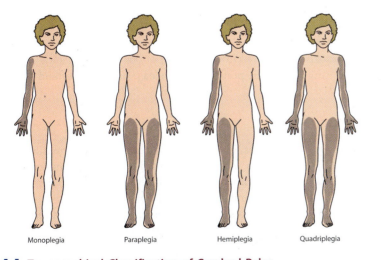

| Monoplegia | Paraplegia | Hemiplegia | Quadriplegia |

Figure 4.1 Topographical Classification of Cerebral Palsy
Source: Adapted from R. Gargiulo, *Special Education in Contemporary Society*, 3rd ed. (Thousand Oaks, CA: Sage, 2009), p. 499.

SPINA BIFIDA

During the first 28 days of pregnancy, special embryo cells form a closed tube that will become the brain and spinal cord. When this process is interrupted and the tube does not completely close, a congenital abnormality known as a neural tube defect occurs. When it occurs in the area of the spinal cord, a condition known as spina bifida (meaning divided into two) results. In the most severe form, myelomeningocele spina bifida, the baby is born with a sac on its back, and the spinal cord pouches out into the sack. The spinal cord does not properly function at the point of the sac and below. Surgery will be performed to remove the sac when the infant is born, but the damage to the spinal cord cannot be reversed (Herring, 2002). However, research is being done to determine if the effects of spina bifida can be decreased by closing the defect with prenatal surgery during the second trimester (Management of Myelomeningocele Study, 2008).

The characteristics of myelomeningocele spina bifida depend on the location of the defect. As with a spinal cord injury, there will be a lack of movement and sensation below the area of injury. Although the defect can occur anywhere along the spinal column, it typically occurs in the lower part of the spinal cord. Usually the student will have difficulty walking, but can do so with braces, crutches, or a walker. Some children will need a wheelchair for long distances, and others may only be able to get about using a wheelchair.

MUSCULAR DYSTROPHY

Muscular dystrophy includes a group of inherited diseases that are characterized by progressive muscle weakness from degeneration of the muscle fiber. When an infant is born with **Duchenne muscular dystrophy**, no disability is apparent at birth. Usually by age 3, leg weakness begins to manifest in some problems walking and running; by age 5, walking may appear abnormal. Between ages 5 and 10, there is further weakness of the legs accompanied by arm weakness. Often around 10–12 years of age, the child can no longer walk and needs a wheelchair. Through the teenage years, muscle weakness continues; the child will no longer be able to maneuver the wheelchair and will need an electric wheelchair. Over time, it will become increasingly difficult to move the arms or keep the head upright. As the muscles used for breathing weaken, most individuals will develop respiratory infections and die in their late teens or early 20s. It is important to remember that only the muscles are deteriorating, not the individual's mind.

There is no cure for muscular dystrophy at this time and currently no effective treatment. The aim of treatment is to try to maintain functioning and help the person walk as long as possible. Physical and occupational therapy are used in an effort to prevent deformity of the legs and arms and may include the use of braces and splints. Medications will be prescribed for a variety of problems, such as respiratory infections, and surgery may be performed to release contractures and prevent early deformity.

Multiple Disabilities

The Individuals with Disabilities Education Improvement Act designation of multiple disabilities refers to individuals with concomitant impairments whose needs cannot be met in a special education program designed solely for one of the impairments. Although there is no single definition, the term does imply two or more disabilities whose combination usually creates an interactional, multiplicative effect rather than just an additive one. Some examples include learners with:

- intellectual disabilities and spina bifida
- deafness and AIDS
- behavior disorders and muscular dystrophy
- cerebral palsy and seizures
- learning disabilities and asthma

Traumatic Brain Injury

Traumatic brain injury first appeared as a discrete disability category with the reauthorization of the Individuals with Disabilities Education Act in 1990 (PL 101-476). It was added in part because of the unique and multiple characteristics associated with this impairment that frequently interfere with learning and functioning.

Traumatic brain injury refers to a temporary or permanent injury to the brain from acquired causes such as accidents, accidental falls, and gunshot wounds to the head; it does not include congenital or degenerative conditions or birth trauma. Most traumatic brain injuries result from car accidents and falls. The effects of the injury will differ depending on the cause.

The consequences of a traumatic brain injury can range from no ill effects to severe disability. Most head injuries are mild, with no abnormalities found on neurological exams, and the person often does not require medical treatment. Even following a mild injury, however, problems such as headache, fatigue, distractibility, memory problems, and perceptual motor slowing can occur and persist for months, years, or permanently. These problems often go undetected until difficulties arise during classroom activities.

Moderate and severe cases of traumatic brain injury typically require hospital stays and rehabilitation services before reentering school. The person with severe traumatic brain injury often enters the hospital in a coma and slowly regains some or most abilities. Typically, motor skills return first and higher-level cognitive skills, such as reasoning and abstract thinking last. Improvement can be a long process, with the most dramatic gains occurring over the first year, but skills continuing to improve over about a five-year period.

Some individuals may fully recover from a traumatic brain injury, whereas others may have permanent disabilities. A traumatic brain injury has the potential for causing life long disabilities across physical, cognitive, social, behavioral, health, and sensory domains.

Health Disabilities

Other Health Impairments

Disabilities that fall under the IDEA category of other health impairments are often divided into two areas: *major health impairments* and *infectious diseases*. Students will *not* typically require special education services unless these conditions are severe. These impairments often result in more absences, fatigue, and decreased stamina.

MAJOR HEALTH IMPAIRMENTS

Many of the disorders under this category can be treated effectively, whereas others have no cure. Some of these impairments may give rise to emergency situations that require immediate attention. One of the more commonly occurring health impairments are seizure disorders.

Seizure Disorders

A seizure is a sudden, temporary change in the normal functioning of the brain's electrical system as a result of excessive, uncontrolled electrical activity in the brain. A seizure may be due to a high fever, ingestion of certain drugs or poisons, certain metabolic disorders, or chemical imbalances. Seizures may also be the result of a prenatal or perinatal brain injury, head trauma, infections such as meningitis, congenital malformations, or unknown causes (Beers et al., 2006). A person has a seizure disorder, also known as **epilepsy**, when the seizures are recurrent. Often the reason for the seizure disorder is unknown.

Seizures are of many different types, depending on where in the brain the abnormal electrical activity occurs. Seizures may be characterized by altered consciousness, motor activity, sensory phenomena, inappropriate behaviors, or some combination of these. Three of the most commonly encountered seizure disorders are absence seizures, complex partial seizures, and tonic-clonic seizures.

An individual who has **absence seizures** (formally known as *petit mal* seizures) will suddenly lose consciousness, stop moving, and stare straight ahead (or the eyes may roll upward). The person will not fall, but will simply stop and appear to be in a trance. If the seizure occurs when the person is talking, the person will stop in mid-sentence and, when the seizure ends, continue the sentence as if nothing has happened. Typically, these seizures do not last more than 30 seconds, but they can occur from dozens to hundreds of times a day. Often the person is not aware of what has happened. When the seizure occurs during a teacher's lecture, the child often doesn't understand why the teacher is suddenly talking about something different. These seizures have been mistaken for daydreaming, but the student cannot be brought out of the seizure by touch or loud voices. Often it is the observant teacher who first detects that something is wrong with the student.

In a **complex partial seizure**, consciousness is impaired and the person usually exhibits a series of motor movements that may appear voluntary but are beyond the person's control. For example, some individuals having a complex partial seizure will appear dazed and engage in purposeless activity such as walking aimlessly, picking up objects, or picking at their clothes. Some individuals may start laughing, gesturing, or repeating a phrase. Whatever the person's particular pattern, the same pattern will usually be repeated with each seizure. In other words, if a child walks in a circle when having a complex partial seizure, then that is what his seizures are expected to look like each time one occurs.

Tonic-clonic seizures (formally known as *grand mal* seizures) are typically what people think of when they hear that a person has a seizure disorder. This is a convulsive seizure in which the person loses consciousness and becomes very stiff (tonic phase). A person who is standing when the seizure occurs will drop to the floor and may sustain injuries from the fall. This stiffness is followed by a jerking (clonic) phase in which the body makes rhythmic jerking motions that gradually decrease. During this phase, saliva may pool in the mouth and bubble at the lips. Breathing may become shallow or irregular. Usually there is a loss of bladder control. These seizures usually last between two and five minutes. After the seizure, the student may be slightly disoriented at first and not realize what has happened. The person is usually exhausted and will often sleep. There are many misconceptions of what to do when this type of seizure occurs. See the In the Classroom feature for information on the steps to take when a tonic-clonic seizure occurs.

In the Classroom

Steps for Teachers to Take When a Tonic-Clonic Seizure Occurs

What to Do

1. Stay calm; note time of onset.
2. Move furniture out of the way to prevent injury.
3. Loosen shirt collar and put something soft under head.
4. Turn student on his or her side to allow saliva to drain out of mouth.
5. If seizure continues more than 5 minutes, or if multiple seizures occur one right after another, or if this is the first seizure, call for an ambulance.
6. If seizure stops but the student is not breathing, give mouth-to-mouth resuscitation (this rarely occurs).

7. After the seizure is over, reassure student.
8. Allow student to rest.

What NOT to Do

1. Do not put anything in the mouth.
2. Do not restrain movements.
3. Do not give liquids immediately after seizure.

Source: R. Gargiulo, *Special Education in Contemporary Society*, 3rd ed. (Thousand Oaks, CA: Sage, 2009), p. 508.

INFECTIOUS DISEASES

Several infectious diseases fall under the heading of other health impairments. Some infectious diseases are readily transmittable (such as tuberculosis); others may pose no threat in the school environment (such as AIDS).

Acquired Immune Deficiency Syndrome (AIDS)

This disease is one of the newest chronic illnesses of childhood. It is caused by the human immunodeficiency virus (HIV) that destroys the immune system, leaving the person vulnerable to serious, opportunistic life-threatening diseases (such as pneumonia). Transmission generally occurs in one of three ways: (1) having sex with an infected partner, (2) sharing contaminated needles during drug use, and (3) passing on the infection from mother to infant. It cannot be acquired through casual contact because it is only transmitted in blood, semen, vaginal secretions, and breast milk (Best & Heller, 2009). Because it is not transmitted in saliva, even sharing toothbrushes or kissing will not transmit the infection.

Some students are born with the infection from an infected mother; adolescents may acquire the infection from sex with an infected partner or by sharing needles during drug use. Children born with the HIV virus may have developmental delays, motor problems, nervous system damage, and additional infections. Adolescents acquiring the disease may also develop life-threatening infections, nervous system abnormalities, and other impairments (such as visual impairments). Treatment consists of a combination of medications that may slow the disease's effect on the immune system. However, the disease is considered terminal in most cases.

Often children with AIDS will not initially need any modifications in the school setting. However, as the disease progresses, they will require some modifications because of fatigue and frequent absences. A supportive attitude should be in place, especially given the social stigma surrounding the disease.

Neither the student with AIDS nor their parents are required to inform school officials of their medical status. Children with AIDS cannot be excluded from attending school. Because of fear, misinformation, and misconceptions about this disease, many school districts have developed specific policies and procedures about the education of individuals with AIDS. Teachers are strongly encouraged to become knowledgeable of their district's policy.

How Many Learners Have Physical Disabilities, Health Disabilities, or Traumatic Brain Injury?

According to statistics from the U.S. Department of Education (2008), over 819,000 students, ages 6–21, received special education services across the categories of multiple disabilities (134,000), orthopedic impairments (62,000), other health impairments (599,500), and traumatic brain injury (24,000) during the 2006–2007 school year. These four groups constitute 13 percent of pupils receiving a special education with a range of 0.4 percent (traumatic brain injury) to 9.8 percent (other health impairments).

What Are Some of the Causes of Physical Disabilities, Health Disabilities, and Traumatic Brain Injury?

The etiology (or cause) of physical and health disabilities varies greatly according to the specific disease or disorder. Some of the more common etiologies resulting in physical and health disabilities are genetic and chromosomal defects, congenital infections, prematurity and complications of pregnancy, and acquired causes. In some cases, certain physical or health disabilities have multiple etiologies, whereas in a few instances the exact cause is unknown.

Several genetic defects are believed to contribute to a range of physical and health disabilities, such as muscular dystrophy, sickle cell anemia, hemophilia, and cystic fibrosis (Heller, Forney, Alberto, Best, & Schwartzman, 2009). Certain congenital infections can result in severe multiple disabilities in the unborn child. These prenatal infections are commonly referred to by the acronym STORCH—syphilis, toxoplasmosis, other, rubella, cytomegalovirus, and herpes. The effects of these infections on the fetus can vary from no adverse effect to severe disabilities or death. A baby who contracts one of these infections during gestation may be born with cerebral palsy, blindness, deafness, mental retardation, and several other abnormalities, including heart defects, kidney defects, and brain abnormalities (Best & Heller, 2009).

Many physical and health disabilities are acquired after birth. These acquired causes include trauma (sports injuries, falls, or car accidents—also leading causes of traumatic brain injury), child abuse, infections, environmental toxins, and disease. The extent of disability will depend on the cause and its severity.

Selected Learning and Behavioral Characteristics of Learners with Physical Disabilities, Health Disabilities, or Traumatic Brain Injury

Students with Physical or Health Disabilities

The specific learning and behavioral characteristics of a student who has a physical or health disability will depend on the specific disease, its severity, and individual factors. Two pupils with identical diagnoses may be quite different in terms of their capabilities. Because of the myriad or conditions associated with students with physical or health disabilities, we have chosen to address the variables affecting learning and behavior in a generalized fashion. Only characteristics associated with traumatic brain injury are presented individually.

Several variables affect school performance for a student with a physical or health disability. These variables can be divided into three major areas: type of disability, functional effects, and psychosocial and environmental factors (see Figure 4.2). Students with physical or health disabilities will typically have one or more problems in each of these major areas, and their interaction can negatively affect the students' school performance.

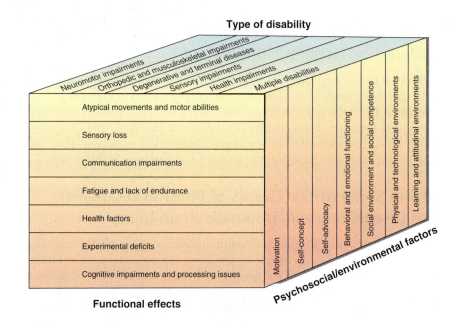

Figure 4.2 Impact of Physical and Health Disabilities on School Performance
Source: K. Heller, P. Forney, P. Alberto, S. Best, & M. Schwartzman, *Understanding Physical, Health, and Multiple Disabilities,* 2nd ed. (Upper Saddle River, NJ: Pearson Education, 2009), p. 19.

Type of Disability

The first major area to affect the student's performance is the type of disability. Students with orthopedic impairments, for example, often have problems accessing materials, whereas pupils with other health impairments are more likely to have problems of endurance and stamina. The severity of the specific disability will also be a factor. The teacher will need to be familiar with the student's specific disability, its severity, and its implications for academic performance.

Functional Effects of the Disability

The second area that affects student performance is the functional effect of the disability on each particular student. As shown in Figure 4.2, this area is divided into seven categories. The student's disability, its severity, and how it affects the particular learner will determine which of these seven categories is a factor in affecting academic performance.

Psychosocial and Environmental Factors

The third major area that can affect school performance consists of seven individual and environmental factors. Each one of these is shaped by the student's personality, reaction to his or her disability, and the reactions of those in the student's environment.

Students with Traumatic Brain Injury

Learners who have a traumatic brain injury exhibit a wide variety of learning and psychosocial characteristics. Physical and sensory changes are also fairly common. The specific impact of the injury is highly individualized and depends upon the age of the student, the severity and location of the insult in addition to the time elapsed since the injury (von Hahan, 2004). Some pupils experience minimal changes; in other instances, the impact on their performance in the classroom is dramatic. Learning and behavioral deficits may persist long after the child has physically recovered. Table 4.7 illustrates some of the characteristics typical of individuals with traumatic brain injury.

Table 4.7	**Characteristics Associated with Traumatic Brain Injury**

Cognitive/Learning

- Long- and short-term memory problems
- Attentional disorders
- Organizational and planning difficulties
- Uneven academic abilities
- Impaired oral and written language
- Problem solving and abnormal reasoning deficits
- Perseveration (continual repetition of an action or thought)

Social/Emotional

- Mood swings
- Depression
- Heightened irritability
- Diminished motivation
- Increased aggressiveness
- Difficulty responding appropriately to social cues
- Decreased impulse control
- Difficulty adapting to changes in routines or schedule

Source: Adapted from J. Hill, *Meeting the Needs of Children with Special Physical and Health Care Needs* (Upper Saddle River, NJ: Prentice Hall, 1999), pp. 259–260. National Dissemination Center for Children with Disabilities, Fact Sheet 18: *Traumatic Brain Injury* (May 2006). Available at http://www.nichcy.org/pubs/factshe/fs18txt.htm

Learners Who Are Culturally and Linguistically Diverse

The United States is an enormously diverse and pluralistic society—an amalgamation of different races, languages, folkways, religious beliefs, traditions, values, and even foods and music. As a nation, we greatly benefit from this cultural mix; is it s defining characteristic of the United States and one of our great strengths. Perhaps nowhere else is this diversity more noticeable than in our schools. What are the implications of the following estimates and projections for our schools and classroom practices?

- By the year 2020, students of color are projected to make up almost half of all school-age youth (Gollnick & Chinn, 2009).
- By the year 2050, the U.S. population is projected to be 53 percent Anglo, 24 percent Latino, 13 percent black, 9 percent Asian, and 1 percent Native American (Chinn, 2002).
- About one in five residents, or approximately 19 percent of the U.S. population over the age of 5, speaks a language other than English at home (U.S. Census Bureau, 2007).
- At the present time, children of color make up the majority of students in several states and many urban areas, including Detroit, Los Angeles, Atlanta, Miami, Baltimore, New York, Chicago, Birmingham, and Houston (Lustig & Koestner, 2006; National Center for Education Statistics, 2007b).
- Despite increasing cultural and linguistic diversity in our schools, almost 90 percent of general and special education teachers are white (Boyer & Mainzer, 2003).

The reasons for these changing demographics are many and varied. They include shifting immigration patterns and varying birthrates among women of various ethnic groups in addition to other factors.

It is abundantly clear that the ethnic make up of the United States is changing. It is equally obvious that this diversity will be reflected in our schools. Classrooms in the coming years will evidence even greater diversity than we find today. Teachers will most likely encounter students whose beliefs and practices vary

Cengage Learning/Wadsworth

Today's classrooms serve an increasingly diverse student population.

significantly in important ways from those of mainstream American pupils. The challenge confronting educators and other professionals is how best to meet the needs of this changing and expanding population of learners.

Terminology of Cultural Differences

Educators and other professionals in the field of education are confronted with a barrage of labels and terms used to describe the education of children from different cultural backgrounds. Sometimes this terminology contributes to inaccurate generalizations, stereotyping, and incorrect assumptions about certain individuals or groups of people. The topic of cultural and linguistic diversity can easily become a source of confusion and controversy. Perhaps it is best to begin our discussion of key terminology by arriving at an understanding of what we mean by culture.

Culture

We define **culture** as the attitudes, values, belief systems, norms, and traditions shared by a particular group of people that collectively form their heritage. A culture is transmitted in various ways from one generation to another. It is typically reflected in language religion, dress, diet, social customs, and other aspects of a particular lifestyle (Gargiulo & Kilgo, 2005). Siccone (1995) points out that culture also includes the way particular groups of people interpret the world. It provides individuals with a frame of reference or perspective for attaching meaning to specific events or situations, such as the value and purpose of education or the birth of a child with a disability.

Multiculturalism

We live in a multicultural society; yet **multiculturalism** is a confusing and sometimes poorly understood concept. In its most basic interpretation, multiculturalism refers to more than one culture. It acknowledges basic commonalities among groups of people while appreciating their differences. Implicit within the concept of multiculturalism is the belief that an individual can function within more than one culture. Multiculturalism also provides us with a foundation for understanding multicultural education.

Multicultural Education

Multicultural education is an ambiguous and somewhat controversial concept. Sleeter and Grant (2006) characterize multicultural education as an umbrella concept involving issues of race, language, social class, and culture as well as disability and gender. Gollnick and Chinn (2009) portray multicultural education as an educational strategy wherein the cultural background of each pupil is valued, viewed positively, and used to develop effective instruction.

Bilingual Education

A term frequently associated with multicultural education is **bilingual education**, an equally controversial and somewhat confusing concept. These two terms, however, are not synonymous. Multicultural education can be infused throughout the curriculum without the benefit of bilingual education. Simply defined, bilingual education is an educational strategy whereby students whose first language is not English are instructed primarily through their native language while developing their competency and proficiency in English. Teachers initially use the language that the child knows best (Baca & Baca, 2004a). Once a satisfactory command of English is achieved, it becomes the medium of instruction.

Bilingual Education: Concepts and Characteristics

As noted previously, approximately one out of five Americans, or almost 20 percent of the population, speaks a language other than English. The U.S. government estimates that there are over 10 million school-age children whose primary language is not English (National Center for Education Statistics, 2007b). Yet controversy and debate continue over how best to meet the needs of these students. In many school districts, bilingual education provides one possible answer. Not everyone, however, agrees with this strategy. Thirty states have enacted legislation or passed constitutional amendments establishing English as the "official" language of their state (Crawford, 2004; U.S. English, 2008) and five states actually prohibit bilingual education in their schools (Baca & Baca, 2004b).

Students whose first language is not English represent a very heterogeneous group of individuals. Their competency in their primary language as well as English may vary greatly. Some of these pupils may be identified as **limited English proficient** (the term incorporated in IDEA 2004); other professionals prefer the label **English Language Learners**. The term limited English proficient refers to a reduced or diminished fluency in reading, writing, or speaking English. Typically, these students are unable to profit fully from instruction provided in English. Limited English proficiency is not a disparaging label. "It does not equate with lack of capacity or an inherent limitation," Winzer and Mazurek (1998) write, "but it is synonymous with the reality of children who speak another language and are not yet adept in English" (p. 51).

The primary purpose of bilingual education is not to teach English or a second language per se; but rather, to provide assistance to students with limited proficiency in English by delivering instruction using the language the pupils know best and then reinforcing this information through English. Bilingual education also promotes cognitive as well as affective development and cultural enrichment (Gollnick & Chinn, 2009). Although it is not explicitly stated, we believe that another principal goal of bilingual education is to provide increased educational opportunities for students whose native language is not English. It is interesting to note that, contrary to popular belief, the original aim of bilingual education was not to advocate bilingualism but rather to promote the acquisition of English language skills. Bilingual education was thought to be the quickest way for a non-English-speaking person to become literate in English (Janzen, 1994).

The research evidence on the effectiveness of bilingual education strongly suggests that bilingual education is the most appropriate approach for working with students with limited proficiency in English. Greater academic gains and improved language skills can be directly attributed to bilingual education (Gollnick & Chinn, 2009). Of course, the key to effective bilingual education is to match the instructional strategy to the specific needs and background of the student. Depending on the child's proficiency in his or her native language and English, different instructional models are used. The In the Classroom feature summarizes some of the approaches typically used with students who are bilingual.

Experts in the field of bilingual education disagree as to which pedagogical strategy is most effective for teaching students who are bilingual. There is general agreement, however, that the more opportunities individuals have to use their newly acquired language skills with classmates, friends, family members, and others, the more proficient they will become. In comparison to classroom settings, the natural environment seems to better facilitate language development.

Cultural and Linguistic Diversity and Special Education

One unfortunate fact in many schools across America is that racial and ethnic minorities as well as culturally and linguistically diverse students are disproportionately placed in programs for learners with disabilities. The disproportionate presence of

In the Classroom

Instructional Options for Students Who Are Bilingual: Approach and Strategies

Transitional Programs

Students are instructed in academic content areas via their native language only until they are sufficiently competent in English, then they transition to all-English classes. Primary goal of this program is to move students as quickly as possible to English-only classes. Many students exit after two to three years of instruction. Most common instructional model; bilingual education legislation favors this approach.

Maintenance (Developmental) Programs

Strong native language emphasis. Incorporates students' cultural heritage into the instruction. Pupils maintain proficiency in first language while receiving instruction in English. A long-term approach with less emphasis on leaving program. Solid academic foundation is stressed.

Enrichment Programs

Typically used with monolingual children, who are introduced to new language and culture.

Immersion Programs

English language is the exclusive medium of instruction; first language and culture are not incorporated. A "sink-or-swim" philosophy.

English as a Second Language (ESL) Programs

Not a true form of bilingual education. Children typically receive instruction in English outside the regular classroom. Goal is to quickly develop English proficiency in bilingual students. Exclusive emphasis on English for teaching and learning; native language not used in instruction. An assimilationist model with multiple variations.

Sheltered English

Students receive instruction in academic subjects exclusively in English; no effort is made to maintain or develop proficiency in first language. English instruction is continually monitored and modified to ensure pupil's comprehension. Simultaneous exposure to English language and subject content matter.

Source: R. Gargiulo, *Special Education in Contemporary Society*, 3rd ed. (Thousand Oaks, CA: Sage, 2009).

pupils from minority groups in special education programs has been a pressing and volatile concern of educators for more than four decades (Blanchett, Mumford, & Beachum, 2005; Skiba et al., 2008). The fact that greater numbers of children from minority groups are placed in special education programs than would be anticipated based on their proportion of the general school population is commonly referred to as **overrepresentation**. At the same time, there is a long-standing pattern of **underrepresentation** (fewer students in a particular category than one might expect based on their numbers in the school population) of African Americans, Native Americans, and Hispanics in programs for children and youth who are gifted and talented (Clark, 2008; Ford, Grantham, & Whiting, 2008). Asian American children and Pacific Islanders are typically underrepresented in special education classes but overrepresented in classes for the gifted and talented (Donovan & Cross, 2002; Ford et al.; U.S. Department of Education, 2008).

The fact that a disproportionate number of students from minority groups are enrolled in special education classrooms is a stinging indictment of the efficacy of the professional practices of special educators and a challenge to the concept of honoring diversity—presumably the cornerstone of our field (Artiles & Trent, 1994). At the heart of the discussion about disproportional representation is the issue of inappropriate placement in special education programs. The primary concern is with false positives—when a pupil from a cultural or linguistic minority is identified as disabled when, in fact, he or she is *not* disabled and is therefore inappropriately placed in a class for students with disabilities. To ignore the gifts and talents of children from diverse backgrounds is equally damaging and denies them the opportunity to reach their full potential (Artiles & Zamora-Durán, 1997). Many complex factors and circumstances influence student placement; however, for those racially and ethnically diverse students who are misclassified and inappropriately placed or denied access to appropriate services, the outcomes are often serious and enduring.

It should be noted that the problem of overrepresentation does not occur across all categories of disabilities. The disproportionate presence of students from minority groups occurs only in those disability categories in which professional judgment and opinion play a role in the decision-making process, such as mild mental retardation and emotional or behavior disorders. Overrepresentation is not a problem in disability areas that have a clear biological basis. For instance, sensory or motor impairments do not yield dramatically different proportions than one would anticipate on the basis of the ethnic composition of the general school population (Skiba et al., 2008; U.S. Department of Education, 2008).

A myriad of explanations have been put forth to explain the problem of over- and underrepresentation of culturally diverse students in some categories of special education. No one explanation fully accounts for this situation. The overrepresentation of children of color is perhaps best understood as a relationship between family socioeconomic status and disability rather than between disability and minority group status per se (Bowe, 2004; Skiba et al., 2006) Individuals from minority groups typically populate urban centers and tend to be poor. Poverty and ethnicity are an inextricably interwoven variable in American society (Donovan & Cross, 2002; MacMillan & Reschly, 1998). Report after report and survey after survey routinely indicate an overrepresentation of minority groups living in poverty. According to the Children's Defense Fund (2007), approximately 13 million children, or nearly one out of every five youngsters, lives in poverty.

Poverty often means limited access to health care (especially prenatal care), poor nutrition, and adverse living conditions. All of these variables increase the probability of a child being at risk for learning and developmental difficulties. Cultural and language differences only exacerbate the student's vulnerability, increasing the likelihood of educational failure and his or her need for special education services (Gargiulo & Kilgo, 2005).

The evidence strongly suggests that socioeconomic status rather than ethnicity is one of the primary reasons that students from racially and ethnically diverse populations encounter persistent academic problems in the public schools (MacMillan & Reschly, 1998). Poverty, however, is not the only culprit contributing to the disproportional representation of minorities in some special education programs. Faulty identification procedures, ineffective prereferral strategies, test bias, limited educational opportunities, and inappropriate assessment techniques may also account for some of the overrepresentation (Skiba et al., 2008).

The over- and underenrollment of racial and ethnic minorities in some special education programs often leads to uneven educational opportunities. The educational experiences of racially, ethnically, and culturally diverse pupils often put them at risk for underachievement and dropping out of school. It is imperative, therefore, that teachers are sensitive to the cultural heritage of each student and attempt to provide educational experiences that are culturally relevant and appropriate. Our instructional practices must be culturally affirming, sensitive, and responsive. Instructional success with children from diverse populations depends largely on the teacher's ability to construct pedagogical bridges that cross over different cultural systems (Gay, 1997). "When instruction and learning are compatible with a child's culture and when minority students' language and culture are incorporated into the school program, more effective learning takes place" (Winzer & Mazurek, 1998, p. vii).

Learners Who Are at Risk for Failure in School

Children with disabilities are not the only group of learners who experience difficulties in school. Some individuals are at risk for school failure as a result of exposure to adverse situations or conditions that negatively affects their learning. The reasons for their lack of success are many and varied and may include such factors as child maltreatment, substance abuse, homelessness, and teen pregnancy. We will shortly explore some of these variables.

Pupils considered at risk represent a very diverse group of learners. These children come from various socioeconomic, linguistic, racial, and ethnic backgrounds. Children of color and youngsters from extremely impoverished environments, however, are at substantially greater risk for developing academic and behavior problems than are other students. The overwhelming majority of these learners are found in general education classrooms.

Before defining the term **at risk**, we must stress the point that exposure to adverse circumstances *may* lead to behavioral difficulties and/or learning delays, but it is not a guarantee that such problems will present themselves. Many students are exposed to a wide range of risks, yet they fail to evidence problems in the classroom. In many instances, children are especially resilient when confronted with difficult life situations.

Defining At Risk

The term at risk is not clearly defined, and it often means different things to different professionals. The term was first used in the mid-1980s with the publication of a report, *A Nation at Risk* (National Commission on Excellence in Education, 1983), which assailed the educational system in the United States for failing to produce graduates prepared to lead our country in the world's marketplace. Many believe that this publication sparked the educational reform movement in America.

Children viewed as at risk are individuals who experience a host of adverse conditions that severely limit or reduce their potential for success in school and later in life. As we mentioned earlier, this is an incredibly heterogeneous group of learners. Some students experience greater vulnerability and have a heightened potential for future problems in school as a result of being exposed to factors identified in Table 4.8. Remember, these indicators do not guarantee that problems will emerge, they only set the stage. Of the variables identified in Table 4.8 we have chosen three that commonly affect a child's performance in school.

Family Poverty

Poverty is one of the most significant factors placing children at risk for school failure. Regrettably, it is a fact of life for many children in the United States. Despite tremendous wealth, the child poverty rate in our country is one of the highest in the developed world (Anne E. Casey Foundation, 2007). Recent statistics indicate that over 13 million children or more than one out of every six youngsters were

Table 4.8	Examples of Common At-Risk Factors

- Family poverty
- Grade retention
- Alcohol and/or drug abuse
- Excessive absenteeism
- Multiple school enrollments within the academic year
- Homelessness
- Exposure to domestic violence
- Chronic parental unemployment
- Victim of abuse or neglect
- Below grade level performance
- English is not child's primary language
- Frequent suspension from school
- Juvenile delinquency—history of arrests
- Parental alcohol and/or drug abuse
- Teen parenthood
- Single parent household
- Mother/father who did not graduate from high school
- Resides in an inner city or rural area

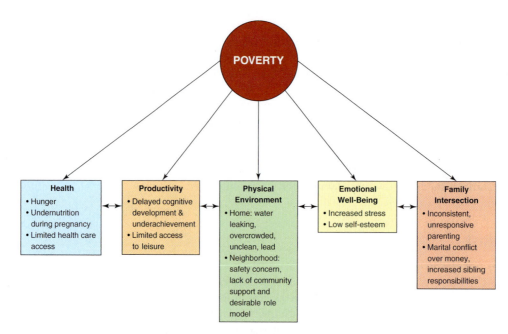

Figure 4.3 Impact of Poverty on Five Dimensions of Family Life
Source: J. Park, A. Turnbull, and H. Turnbull, "Impact of Poverty on Quality of Life in Families of Children with Disabilities," *Exceptional Children, 68*(2), 2002, p. 154.

poor in 2004. This number represents a 12.4 percent increase in the child poverty rate since 2000. Stated another way, there are more children living in poverty today than there were almost four decades ago. Black and Hispanic children are about three times more likely to be poor than white children (Children's Defense Fund, 2005).

Familial poverty is associated with a multitude of perils, many of which place a child at risk for failing in school. These factors, many of which are interrelated, include limited prenatal healthcare, inadequate nutrition, increased childhood illness, greater stress, substandard housing, lack of health insurance, greater likelihood of abuse or neglect, and fewer school supplies and educational materials. According to the Children's Defense Fund (2005), "children who grow up in poverty are more likely to become teen parents and, as adults, to earn less, to be unemployed more frequently, and to raise their own children in poverty" (p. 2). The pervasive and detrimental effects of poverty are illustrated in Figure 4.3.

Finally, a family's socioeconomic level also significantly influences the chances of a student completing high school; and, in turn, employment opportunities (Gollnick & Chinn, 2009). Each day in the United States over 2,200 adolescents drop out of school (Children's Defense Fund, 2007). Whereas children living in poverty are more likely to drop out of school than are their economically advantaged peers, children of color are especially at risk for not completing high school. Recent government statistics indicate that in 2006, 5.8 percent of white adolescents dropped out of school compared with 10.7 percent of black students and 22.1 percent of Hispanic young adults (National Center for Education Statistics, 2007a). Poverty is thus a significant threat to educational achievement and later success in life.

Homelessness[2]

A common problem frequently associated with the deleterious effects of poverty is homelessness. Obviously not all children who are poor are homeless, but the link between homelessness and poverty is substantial. Homelessness is a tragic and

[2]Adapted from R. Gargiulo, "Homeless and Disabled: Rights, Responsibilities, and Recommendations for Serving Young Children with Special Needs," *Early Childhood Education Journal, 33*(5), 2006, pp. 357–362.

growing phenomenon in the United States. Over the years the "face" of homelessness has gradually changed. Two decades ago adult males were the primary group of citizens lacking permanent shelter today, however, families with children are the fastest growing segment of the homeless population (Gargiulo & Kilgo, 2005). Approximately 15 years ago the U.S. Department of Education (1995) estimated that there were slightly more than 740,000 homeless children and youth. Demographers currently suspect that over one million children are homeless each night, including 250,000 preschoolers (Gargiulo & Kilgo). The National Coalition for the Homeless (2007a) believes that 1.35 million children (about 2 percent of all students) will experience homelessness over the course of a year. The average homeless child in the United States is only 6 years old.

Defining Homelessness

In its simplest terms, a homeless child is any youngster who lacks a fixed, regular, and adequate nighttime residence (*CEC Today*, 2003). Codified in federal legislation (Title X, Part C, § 1302 of PL 107-110 [No Child Left Behind Act of 2001]) are some examples of inadequate living arrangements such as individuals and families who reside in abandoned buildings, parks, campgrounds, automobiles, bus/train stations, motels, or emergency/transitional shelters. Essentially, homelessness is a lack of permanent housing resulting from a variety of reasons. (For a portrait of homelessness in contemporary America, see Table 4.9.).

The Origins of Homelessness

The sources of homelessness are many and varied and they are frequently commingled. Some of the commonly identified contributing factors include unemployment, domestic violence, alcohol/drug abuse, abandonment, illiteracy, chronic poverty, natural disasters, mental illness, and the lack of affordable housing (National Coalition for the Homeless, 2007b; U.S. Conference of Mayors, 2007). Surprisingly, "family homelessness is not necessarily a factor of socioeconomic status" (Swick, 2004, p. 117). Some economically advantaged families may also confront a loss of housing. A medical crisis, job termination, or unexpected bills could easily push a family into homelessness.

Consequences of Homelessness

The experience of being homeless is especially destructive for children. Homelessness has been characterized as a breeding ground for disabilities. Researchers believe that approximately 50 percent of students who are homeless exhibit a disability (Taylor, Smiley, & Richards, 2009). Youngsters who are homeless are twice as likely to have a

Table 4.9	Quick Facts About Homelessness in the United States

- 40% of the homeless population are families with children
- 67% of the homeless population are single parent families
- 39% of the homeless population are children
- 12% of children who are homeless are denied access to school
- 42% of homeless children are under the age of five
- 15% of homeless children are enrolled in preschool
- 44% of the homeless population are employed
- 38% of the homeless population do not have a high school diploma
- 55% of homeless individuals do not have medical insurance
- 50% of homeless citizens are African American; 35% White; 12% Hispanic; 2% Native American; and 1% Asian

Source: Adapted from *Key Data Concerning Homeless Persons in America*, National Law Center on Homelessness and Poverty, July 2004; *Homelessness and Poverty in America*, National Law Center on Homelessness and Poverty, retrieved August 31, 2006 from http://www.nlchp.org/

learning disability, four times more likely to have a developmental disability, three times more likely to manifest emotional problems, and twice as likely to repeat a grade than their classmates who are not homeless (National Center on Family Homelessness, 2008). Pupils who are homeless often exhibit inattentiveness, frustration, aggression, and diminished academic achievement—characteristics typical of individuals who frequently qualify for special education services (Myers & Popp, 2003a).

Jackson's (2004) synthesis of the research literature strongly suggests that conditions associated with homelessness substantially increase the risk of a youngster requiring special education services. Children who experience homelessness

> are more likely to suffer from poor nutrition, inadequate healthcare, exposure to health hazards (e.g., lead poisoning), health problems associated with overcrowding, unhygienic living situations, chronic illnesses (e.g., asthma and ear infections), exposure to domestic violence and other types of violence, and severe emotional stress related to extreme poverty and unstable living conditions. (p. 3)

It is important to note, however, that not all pupils who are homeless manifest learning and behavioral difficulties or require a special education. Many children who are homeless are academically successful, exhibit a high degree of resilience, and some students may even be gifted (Myers & Popp, 2003b). (See Table 4.10 for signs commonly associated with homelessness in school age children.)

Child Abuse and Neglect

Child abuse and neglect is an all too common social malady in this country. It is an offense against children that thrives in the shadows of privacy and secrecy and lives by inattention (Bakan, 1971). Each day four children die as a result of abuse or neglect, and approximately 2,400 other youngsters are confirmed victims of abuse and neglect (Children's Defense Fund, 2005, 2007). An estimated 3.6 million children were alleged to have been abused or neglected in 2006. Child abuse and neglect can occur in all families, disregarding racial, religious, ethnic, and socioeconomic boundaries. It equally occurs in urban, suburban, and rural communities. Approximately eight out of ten perpetrators are parents (U.S. Department of Health and Human Services, 2008).

There are four specific types of child maltreatment, although precise interpretations vary according to state statute. Generally speaking,

- **neglect** means failing to provide for the child's basic needs (physical, emotional, educational);
- **physical abuse** means infliction of bodily harm or injury regardless of intent or source of injury;

Table 4.10	**Indicators of Possible Homelessness in Children**

- Absence of school records
- Chronic absenteeism/frequent tardiness
- Inconsistent personal hygiene
- Habitual tiredness in school
- Complaints of hunger—evidence of hoarding food
- Unmet health care needs
- Lack of school supplies
- Inadequate/inappropriate school apparel
- Incomplete homework assignments
- Reluctance or inability to provide address or telephone number
- Unresponsive parent/guardian—notes from school go unsigned
- Unwillingness to go home after school
- History of multiple school enrollments

Note: Indicators may suggest situations other than homelessness such as neglect or abandonment.
Source: CEC Today, "Exceptional and Homeless," 9(6), 2003, p. 7; National Center for Homeless Education, 2008, "Identifying Children and Youth Experiencing Homelessness." Available at http://www.serve.org/nche/ibt/sc_ident.php

- **emotional abuse** refers to maltreatment that attacks the child's self-esteem and emotional development resulting from constant criticism, threats, humiliation, and/or the withholding of affection;
- **sexual abuse** lives in a veil of secrecy and a conspiracy of silence, it is the most underreported form of abuse and may include incest, rape, indecent exposure, and inappropriate fondling in addition to sexual exploitation by prostitution or pornography (American Humane, 2008).

One way of distinguishing between abuse and neglect is to view abuse as an act of *commission* and neglect is an act of *omission*. Abuse implies an active, participatory relationship between an adult caregiver and child victim, whereas neglect is characterized by adult withdrawal, indifference, and nonrecognition of the various needs of the child. Neglect is the most common form of child maltreatment. More than six out of ten child victims are neglected by their parent(s) or other caregivers with approximately 15 percent being physically abused (U.S. Department of Health and Human Services, 2008).

Table 4.11 presents indicators of abuse and neglect. This list is neither exhaustive nor necessarily inclusive. These indicators are only clues; recognition, however, is the first step toward elimination of abuse and neglect. Additionally, teachers must also consider the family's cultural background and values as well as community standards of care. In some instances, the various indicators identified in Table 4.11 are a reflection of unique cultural perspectives and/or a lack of resources, knowledge, and information.

The Etiology of Abuse and Neglect

One question frequently posed by teachers and other professionals is, "Why would a parent abuse their own child?" Unfortunately, there is neither a simple nor concise response. Generally speaking, there is no one condition or single situation that produces an abusive individual. Rather, abusive parents/caregivers are the by-product of a complex interaction of individual psychological characteristics and specific environmental conditions.

Child abuse requires three elements—the perpetrator, the victim, and a precipitating crisis. Although all parents have the potential to be abusive, chronically abusive individuals exhibit particular characteristics and behavior patterns. Likewise, some children are more vulnerable than others; for example, students with disabilities or youngsters who are adopted. Finally, when life circumstances become too stressful for the caregiver, events such as long-term illness, financial problems, divorce, or job-related difficulties can cause the parent to lose control and overreact, frequently resulting child abuse (Ohio Department of Public Welfare, n.d.).

Abusive and neglectful parents typically share several common characteristics. These indicators may be both personal and environmental (Crosson-Tower, 2008). We stress the caveat that the mere presence of one or more descriptors does not mean that parent is abusing his or her child.

- Substance abuse
- Chronic unemployment
- Marital discord
- Geographic and/or social isolation
- Economic hardships
- Child with a disability
- Emotional immaturity
- Poor impulse control
- Low self-esteem
- Absence of appropriate child-rearing practices
- Personal history of abuse or neglect
- Unrealistic behavioral expectations

Table 4.11	**Examples of Physical and Behavioral Indicators of Child Abuse and Neglect**

Physical Abuse

Physical Indicators	**Behavioral Indicators**
• Bruises, welts, cuts • Burn marks • Lacerations and abrasions • Head injuries • Skeletal injuries • Fractures, sprains	• Fearful of physical contact • Overly compliant, passive • Wearing concealing clothing • Unwillingness to go home • Wariness of adults • Behavioral extremes—overly aggressive or very withdrawn • Lacks reasonable explanation for injury • Complains about pain or soreness

Neglect

Physical Indicators	**Behavioral Indicators**
• Poor personal hygiene • Inadequate or inappropriate clothing • Lack of needed medical/dental care • Abandonment • Lack of supervision • Complaints of constant hunger • Excessive school absence and/or tardiness	• Hoarding or stealing of food • Lethargic, falls asleep in school • Irregular school attendance • Rejection by classmates due to offensive body odor • Dirty clothes, wears same attire for several days

Emotional Abuse

Physical Indicators	**Behavioral Indicators**
• Emotional abuse is rarely manifested via physical signs. It is usually associated with other forms of maltreatment. The individual's behavior is often the best clue.	• Lack of positive self-image • Low self-esteem • Depression • Sleep and/or eating disorder • Overly fearful, vigilant • Behavioral extremes—overly compliant/passive or aggressive/demanding • Poor peer relationships • Suicidal ideation • Temper tantrums • Enuresis

Sexual Abuse

Physical Indicators	**Behavioral Indicators**
• Torn, stained, or bloody undergarments • Pain in genital area • Presence of sexually transmitted diseases • Pregnancy • Difficulty with urination • Presence of semen • Difficulty walking or sitting	• Sexually sophisticated/mature • Sexual themes during play • Poor peer relationships • Seductive behavior • Irregular school attendance • Reluctance to participate in physical activities • Infantile behavior • Fear of physical contact • Statements of sexual abuse

Source: Adapted from R. Gargiulo, "Child Abuse and Neglect: An Overview," in R. Goldman and R. Gargiulo (Eds.), *Children at Risk* (Austin, TX: Pro-Ed, 1990), pp. 19–23.

- Lack of emotional support
- Difficulty coping with situational stress
- Inappropriate or excessive discipline
- Emotionally dependent, passive spouse
- High mobility

Table 4.12 Summary of Learning and Behavioral Characteristics of Learners with Low Incidence Disabilities and Special Needs

Characteristics	Disabilities and Special Needs*					
	Hearing Impairment	Visual Impairment	Autism Spectrum Disorders	Physical, Health Disabilities or TBI	Cultural and Linguistic Diversity	At Risk
Cognitive Impairments			X	X		X
Academic Deficiencies	X	X	X	X	X	X
Language Disorders	X		X	X	X	
Motivational Deficits				X		X
Memory Problems				X		
Social/ Emotional Difficulties	X	X	X	X	X	X
Attention Disorders			X	X		X
Speech Impairments	X		X	X		
Mobility Problems		X		X		
Hyperactivity/Impulsivity			X	X		X

*Not all learners within the category will exhibit the particular characteristic.

Reporting Child Abuse and Neglect: The Teacher's Role

Educators and other professionals are legally (and we believe morally) responsible for reporting *suspected* instances child abuse and neglect. Every state has reporting legislation. The purpose of these statutes is to identify and protect children who may be abused or neglected, not to punish the perpetrator. All jurisdictions provide for the legal protection of reporters. Immunity from liability, both civil and criminal, is granted to mandated reporters (teachers and others who act in good faith and without malice). It is vitally important that teacher become familiar with the reporting requirements in their state and their school district's reporting procedures. Whereas a few teachers might be reluctant to "get involved" in the personal lives of their students and their families, failure to report suspicions of abuse and neglect could lead to legal difficulties for the teacher. Fines, misdemeanor charges, and in some instances, charges of negligence are possible. Our primary consideration should be the welfare of our pupils. Perhaps the greatest tragedy, however, is the child who suffers, and possibly dies as a consequence of inaction by a teacher (or other professional).

Summary of Selected Learning and Behavioral Characteristics

The disability categories and special needs reviewed in this chapter represent a tremendously diverse group of learners. Many of these students will present educators with a myriad of instructional and management challenges. Some of these issues are presented in Table 4.12. Yet, as we noted in Chapter 3, teachers need to focus on the strengths of their pupils and similarity of needs rather than their limitations or disability label. Remember, your instructional strategies should always be based on the *individual* requirements of the learner and not their label.

Thematic Summary

- Although students with low incidence disabilities represent only a small percentage of individuals enrolled in special education, their instructional and behavioral needs can sometimes be especially challenging.
- Opportunities to experience academic success are oftentimes limited for learners with culturally and linguistically diverse backgrounds and pupils who are exposed to adverse living situations and conditions.
- In most instances, the cause of a child's disability is of little instructional value.

- Events and circumstances that place a student at risk for success in the classroom are not a guarantee that problems will occur.
- Effective teachers focus on the strengths and individual needs of their students and not how they are categorized or labeled.
- Inclusive learning communities demand that teachers demonstrate acceptance and respect of all learners.

Making Connections for Inclusive Teaching

1. Schools are serving an increasingly heterogeneous population of learners. What would you do to ensure the success of all your students?
2. Should pupils with significant learning, medical, or health needs be served in the general education classroom? Defend your viewpoint.

Learning Activities

1. Observe an inclusive general education classroom that serves students with sensory impairments.
   - What services are available for students with hearing or vision impairments?
   - How did the other students interact with and relate to their classmates with sensory impairments?
   - What types of accommodations did you observe?
   - How was technology used?
   - How did the teacher communicate with their pupils with sensory impairments?
   - What was the role of the special educator? What types of assistance did he or she provide to the learners with sensory impairments and to their teacher?
   - Describe your personal and professional reactions to this experience.
2. Observe a student with autism spectrum disorders in a special education classroom and an inclusive setting. What are the advantages and disadvantages of both settings? What types of educational interventions did you observe? Which type of placement is the most appropriate for pupils with ASD? Defend your position.
3. Contact your state department of education. How does your state define physical disabilities, health disabilities, other health impairments, and traumatic brain injury? What types of special education certification does your state provide? Is specialized training in traumatic brain injury, autism, and physical or health disabilities available in your state?
4. Visit/volunteer at a local shelter serving homeless children and their families. What types of services and supports are available? What is your community doing to meet the needs of individuals who are homeless? How are schools in your area responding to the needs of students without permanent residence?
5. How does your state define child maltreatment? What are the reporting requirements for teachers? Examine a copy of your local school district's policy and procedures manual. How does this document address child abuse and neglect? What should teachers do when confronted with suspected instances of abuse of neglect?

Looking at the Standards

The content of the chapter most closely aligns itself with the following standards:

INTASC Standards

- *Student Development.* The teacher understands how children learn and develop, and can provide learning opportunities that support their intellectual, social, and personal development.
- *Diverse Learners.* The teacher understands how students differ in their approaches to learning and creates instructional opportunities that are adapted to diverse learners.

Council for Exceptional Children

Special educators are to have knowledge of the following:

- CC1K5: Issues in definition and identification of individuals with exceptional learning needs, including those from culturally and linguistically diverse backgrounds.
- CC1K10: Potential impact of differences in values, languages, and customs that can exist between the home and school.
- CC2K1: Typical and atypical human growth and development.
- CC2K2: Educational implications of characteristics of various exceptionalities.
- CC2K3: Characteristics and the effects of the cultural and environmental milieu of the individual with exceptional learning needs and the family.
- CC2K5: Similarities and differences of individuals with and without exceptional learning needs.
- CC2K6: Similarities and differences among individuals with exceptional learning needs.
- GC2K3: Etiologies and medical aspects of conditions affecting individuals with disabilities.
- GC2K4: Psychological and social-emotional characteristics of individuals with disabilities.
- GC2K5: Common etiologies and the impact of sensory disabilities on learning and experience.
- GC2K6: Types and transmission routes of infectious disease.
- CC3K1: Effects an exceptional condition(s) can have on an individual's life.
- CC3K2: Impact of learner's academic and social abilities, interests, and values, on instruction and career development.
- CC3K3: Variations in beliefs, traditions, and values across and within cultures and their effects on relationships among individuals with exceptional learning needs, family, and schooling.
- CC3K4: Cultural perspectives influencing the relationships among families, schools, and communities as related to instruction.
- CC5K1: Demands of learning environments.
- CC5K5: Social skills needed for educational and other environments.
- CC5K7: Strategies for preparing individuals to live harmoniously and productively in a culturally diverse world.
- CC5K8: Ways to create learning environments that allow individuals to retain and appreciate their own and each other's respective language and cultural heritage.
- CC6K2: Characteristics of one's own culture and use of language and the ways in which these can differ from other cultures and uses of language.

Key Concepts and Terms

low incidence disabilities	stereotypic behaviors	absence seizures
hearing impairment	autism spectrum	complex partial seizure
Deaf community	disorders	tonic-clonic seizures
deaf	physical disabilities	culture
conductive hearing loss	health disabilities	multiculturalism
sensorineural hearing loss	traumatic brain injury	multicultural education
decibels	other health impairments	bilingual education
hertz	multiple disabilities	limited English proficient
frequency	spastic cerebral palsy	English Language
cytomegalovirus	athetoid cerebral palsy	Learners
otitis media	ataxic cerebral palsy	overrepresentation
visual impairment	mixed cerebral palsy	underrepresentation
legally blind	hemiplegia	at risk
Snellen chart	diplegia	neglect
blind	paraplegia	physical abuse
functionally blind	quadriplegia	emotional abuse
primary literacy medium	Duchenne muscular	sexual abuse
low vision	dystrophy	
residual vision	epilepsy	

References

American Humane. (2008). *Child abuse and neglect fact sheets.* Retrieved May 1, 2008 from http://www.americanhumane.org/site/PageServer?pagename=pc_facts_info

American Psychiatric Association. (2000). *Diagnostic and statistical manual—text revision* (4th ed.). Washington, DC: Author.

Andrews, J., Leigh, I., & Weiner, M. (2004). *Deaf people: Evolving perspectives from psychology, education, and sociology.* Boston: Allyn & Bacon.

Anne E. Casey Foundation. (2007). *2007 kids count data book.* Baltimore: Author.

Artiles, A., & Trent, S. (1994). Overrepresentation of minority students in special education: A continuing debate. *Journal of Special Education, 27,* 410–437.

Artiles, A., & Zamora-Durán, G. (1997). Disproportionate representation: A contentious and unresolved predicament. In A. Artiles & G. Zamora-Durán (Eds.), *Reducing disproportionate representation of culturally diverse students in special and gifted education* (pp. 1–6). Reston, VA: Council for Exceptional Children.

Autism Society of America. (2008). *What is autism spectrum disorders?* Retrieved April 27, 2008 from http://www.autismsociety.org/site/PageServer?pagename=about_whatis

Baca, L., & Baca, E. (2004a). Bilingualism and bilingual education. In L. Baca & H. Cervantes (Eds.), *The bilingual special education interface* (4th ed., pp. 24–45). Upper Saddle River, NJ: Pearson Education.

Baca, L., & Baca, E. (2004b). Bilingual special education: A judicial perspective. In L. Baca & H. Cervantes (Eds.), *The bilingual special education interface* (4th ed., pp. 76–99). Upper Saddle River, NJ: Pearson Education.

Bakan, D. (1971). *Slaughter of the innocents.* San Francisco: Jossey-Bass.

Beers, M., Porter, R., Jones, T., Kaplan, J., & Berkwitz, M. (2006). *The Merck manual of diagnosis and therapy* (18th ed.). Whitehouse Station, NJ: Merck.

Berk, L. (2006). *Child development* (7th ed.). Boston: Allyn & Bacon.

Bess, F., & Humes, L. (2003). *Audiology: The fundamentals* (3rd ed.). Baltimore: Lippincott Williams & Wilkins.

Best, S., & Heller, K. (2009). Acquired infections and AIDS. In K. Heller, P. Forney, P. Alberto, S. Best, & M. Schwartzman (Eds.), *Understanding physical, health, and multiple disabilities* (2nd ed., pp. 368–386). Upper Saddle River, NJ: Pearson Education.

Blanchett, W., Mumford, V., & Beachum, F. (2005). Urban school failure and disproportionality in a post-Brown era. *Remedial and Special Education, 26*(2), 70–81.

Bowe, F. (2004). *Birth to eight: Early childhood special education* (3rd ed.). Clifton Park, NY: Delmar.

Boyer, L., & Mainzer, R. (2003). Who's teaching students with disabilities? *Teaching Exceptional Children, 35*(6), 8–11.

CEC Today. (2003). Exceptional and homeless, *9*(6), 1–2, 7, 13, 15.

Children's Defense Fund. (2005). *The state of America's children 2005.* Washington, DC: Author.

Children's Defense Fund. (2007). *Annual report 2006.* Washington, DC: Author.

Chinn, P. (2002). *Changing demographics in America.* Nashville, TN: Alliance Project, Vanderbilt University.

Clark, B. (2008). *Growing up gifted* (7th ed.). Upper Saddle River, NJ: Pearson Education.

Connolly, C., Rose, J., & Austen, S. (2006). Identifying and assessing depression in prelingually deaf people: A literature review. *American Annals of the Deaf, 151,* 49–60.

Courchesne, E. (2004). Brain development in autism: Early over-growth followed by premature arrest of growth. *Mental Retardation and Developmental Disabilities, 10,* 106–111.

Crawford, J. (2004). Language legislation in the USA. Cited in L. Baca & H. Cervantes (Eds.), *The bilingual special education interface* (4th ed.). Upper Saddle River, NJ: Pearson Education.

Crosson-Tower, C. (2008). *Understanding child abuse and neglect* (7th ed.). Boston: Pearson Education.

Donovan, S., & Cross, C. (Eds.). (2002). *Minority students in special and gifted education.* Washington, DC: National Research Council.

Federal Register. (2006, July 1). Assistance to states for the education of children with disabilities. *71*(2), 12–14.

Fombonne, E. (2003). The prevalence of autism. *Journal of the American Medical Association, 289*(1), 87–89.

Ford, D., Grantham, T., & Whiting, G. (2008). Culturally and linguistically diverse students in gifted education: Recruitment and retention issues. *Exceptional Children, 74*(3), 289–306.

Gallaudet Research Institute. (2005, December). *Regional and national summary report of data from the 2004–2005 annual survey of deaf and hard of hearing children and youth.* Washington, DC: Gallaudet University.

Gallaudet Research Institute. (2006, December). *Regional and national summary report of data from the 2006–2007 annual survey of deaf and hard of hearing children and youth.* Washington, DC: Gallaudet University.

Gallaudet Research Institute. (2007). *Literacy & deaf students.* Retrieved April 3, 2008 from http://gri.gallaudet.edu/Literacy/

Gargiulo, R., & Kilgo, J. (2005). *Young children with special needs* (2nd ed.). Clifton Park, NY: Delmar.

Gay, G. (1997). Multicultural infusion in teacher education. In A. Morey & M. Kitano (Eds.), *Multicultural course transformation in higher education* (pp. 192–210). Boston: Allyn & Bacon.

Geers, A. (2006). Spoken language in children with cochlear implants. In P. Spencer & M. Marscark (Eds.), *Advances in spoken language development of deaf and hard-of-hearing children* (pp. 244–270). New York: Oxford University Press.

Gollnick, D., & Chinn, P. (2009). *Multicultural education in a pluralistic society* (8th ed.). Upper Saddle River, NJ: Pearson Education.

Hallahan, D., Kauffman, J., & Pullen, P. (2009). *Exceptional learners* (11th ed.). Boston: Pearson Education.

Heller, K., Forney, P., Alberto, P., Best, S., & Schwartzman, M. (2009). *Understanding physical, health, and multiple disabilities* (2nd ed.). Upper Saddle River, NJ: Pearson Education.

Herer, G., Knightly, C., & Steinberg, A. (2007). Hearing: Sounds and silences. In M. Batshaw, L. Pellegrino, & N. Roizen (Eds.), *Children with disabilities* (6th ed., pp. 157–183). Baltimore: Paul H. Brookes.

Herring, J. (2002). *Tachdjian's pediatric orthopaedics* (3rd ed.). Philadelphia: W.B. Saunders.

Jackson, T. (2004). *Homelessness and students with disabilities: Educational rights and challenges.* Alexandria, VA: Project Forum, National Association of State Directors of Special Education.

Janzen, R. (1994). Melting pot or mosaic? *Educational Leadership, 51*(8), 9–11.

Kanner, L. (1943/1985). Autistic disturbance of affective contact. In A. Donnellan (Ed.), *Classic readings in autism* (pp. 11–50). New York: Teachers College Press.

Karchmer, M., & Mitchell, R. (2005). Demographic and achievement characteristics of deaf and hard-of-hearing students. In M. Marschark & P. Spencer (Eds.), *Oxford handbook of deaf studies, language, and education* (pp. 21–37). New York: Oxford University Press.

Kluwin, T., Stinson, M., & Colarossi, G. (2002). Social processes and outcomes of in-school contact between deaf and hearing peers. *Journal of Deaf Studies and Deaf Education, 7*(3), 200–218.

Kuder, S. (2008). *Teaching students with language and communication disabilities* (3rd ed.). Boston: Allyn & Bacon.

Liefert, F. (2003). Introduction to visual impairment. In S. Goodman & S. Wittenstein (Eds.), *Collaborative assessment* (pp. 1–12). New York: American Foundation for the Blind.

Lustig, M., & Koestner, J. (2006). *Intercultural competence: Interpersonal communication across cultures* (5th ed.). Boston: Allyn & Bacon.

MacMillan, D., & Reschly, D. (1998). Overrepresentation of minority students: The case for greater specificity or reconsideration of the variables examined. *Journal of Special Education, 32*(1), 15–24.

Maller, S. (2005). Intellectual assessment of deaf people: A critical review of core concepts and issues. In M. Marschark & P. Spencer (Eds.), *Oxford handbook of deaf studies, language, and education* (pp. 451–463). New York: Oxford University Press.

Management of Myelomeningocele Study. (2008). Overview of management of myelomeningocele. Retrieved April 16, 2008 from http://spinabifidamoms.com/English/overview.html

McLean, M., Wolery, M., & Bailey, D. (2004). *Assessing infants and preschoolers with special needs* (3rd ed.). Upper Saddle River, NJ: Pearson Education.

Moores, D. (2001). *Education the deaf: Psychology, principles, and practices* (5th ed.). Boston: Houghton Mifflin.

Myers, M., & Popp, P. (2003a, Fall). *What educators need to know about homelessness and special education* (Information Brief 7). Retrieved April 28, 2008 from http://web.wm.edu/hope/infobrief/personnel-complete.pdf

Myers, M., & Popp, P. (2003b, Fall). *What families and shelters need to know about homelessness and special education* (Information Brief 8). Retrieved April 28, 2008 from http://web.wm.edu/hope/infobrief/family-complete.pdf

National Center for Education Statistics. (2007a). *Digest of education statistics, 2007.* Washington, DC: U.S. Government Printing Office.

National Center for Education Statistics. (2007b). *The condition of education 2007.* Washington, DC: U.S. Government Printing Office.

National Center on Family Homelessness. (2008). *Homeless children: America's new outcasts.* Retrieved April 29, 2008 from http://www.familyhomelessness.org/pdf/fact_outcasts.pdf

National Coalition for the Homeless. (2007a). *Education of homeless children and youth. Fact sheet 10.* Retrieved May 1, 2008 from http://www.nationalhomeless.org/publications/facts/education.html

National Coalition for the Homeless. (2007b). *Why are people homeless? Fact sheet 1.* Retrieved May 1, 2008 from http://www.nationalhomeless.org/publications/facts/why.pdf

National Commission on Excellence in Education. (1983). *A nation at risk: The imperative for educational reform.* Washington, DC: Author.

National Institute of Mental Health. (2008). *Autism spectrum disorders (pervasive developmental disorders).* Retrieved April 15, 2008 from http://www.nimh.nih.gov/health/publications/autism/complete-publication.shtml

Ohio Department of Public Welfare. (n.d.). *Open the door on child abuse and neglect.* Columbus, OH: Author.

Owens, R., Metz, D., & Haas, A. (2003). *Introduction to communication disorders* (2nd ed.). Boston: Allyn & Bacon.

Pakulski, L., & Kaderavek, J. (2002). Children with minimal hearing loss: Interventions in the classroom. *Intervention in School and Clinic, 38*(2), 96–103.

Picard, M. (2004). Children with permanent hearing loss and associated disabilities. Revisiting current epidemiological data and causes of deafness. *Volta Review, 104*(4), 221–236.

Pogrund, R., & Fazzi, D. (Eds.). (2007). *Early focus: Working with young blind and visually impaired children and their families* (3rd ed.). New York: American Foundation for the Blind.

Sacks, S., & Silberman, R. (2000). Social skills. In M. Holbrook & A. Koenig (Eds.), *Foundations of education: Instructional strategies for teaching children and youths with visual impairments* (2nd ed., Vol. 2, pp. 616–648). New York: American Foundation for the Blind Press.

Scheetz, N. (2004). *Psychological aspects of deafness.* Boston: Allyn & Bacon.

Schirmer, B. (2001). *Psychological, social, and educational dimensions of deafness.* Boston: Allyn & Bacon.

Siccone, F. (1995). *Celebrating diversity: Building self-esteem in today's multicultural classrooms.* Boston: Allyn & Bacon.

Simeonsson, R., & Rosenthal, S. (Eds.). (2001). *Psychological and developmental assessment: Children with disabilities and chronic conditions.* New York: Guilford.

Skiba, R., Simmons, A., Ritter, S., Kohler, K., Henderson, M., & Wu, T. (2006). The context of minority disproportionality: Practitioner perspectives on special education referral. *Teachers College Record, 108*(7), 1424–1459.

Skiba, R., Simmons, A., Ritter, S., Rausch, M., Cuadrado, J., & Chung, C. (2008). Achieving equity in special education: History, status, and current challenges. *Exceptional Children, 74*(3), 244–288.

Sleeter, C., & Grant, C. (2006). *Making choices for multicultural education* (5th ed.). New York: Wiley.

Swick, K. (2004). The dynamics of families who are homeless. *Childhood Education, 80*(3), 116–120.

Taylor, R., Smiley, L., & Richards, S. (2009). *Exceptional students.* New York: McGraw-Hill.

U.S. Census Bureau. (2007). *Statistical abstract of the United States: 2008* (127th ed.). Washington, DC: Author.

U.S. Conference of Mayors. (2007). *Homelessness in America's cities: A 23-city survey.* Washington, DC: Author.

U.S. Department of Education. (1995). *Preliminary guidance for the education of homeless children and youth program, Title VII, Subtitle B.* Washington, DC: Author.

U.S. Department of Education. (2008). *IDEA data.* Retrieved April 1, 2008 from https://www.ideadata.org/PartBReport.asp

U.S. Department of Health and Human Services. (2008). *Child maltreatment 2006.* Retrieved May 1, 2008 from http://www.acf.hhs.gov/programs/cb/pubs/cm06/cm06.pdf

U.S. English. (2008). *About U.S. English.* Retrieved April 19, 2008 from http://www.us-english.org/inc/about/

Volkmar, F., & Pauls, D. (2003). Autism. *The Lancet, 362,* 1133–1141.

von Hahan, L. (2004). Traumatic brain injury: Medical considerations and educational implications. *Exceptional Parent, 33*(11), 40–42.

Williams, C., & Finnegan, M. (2003). From myth to reality: Sound information for teachers about students who are deaf. *Teaching Exceptional Children, 35*(3), 40–45.

Winzer, M., & Mazurek, K. (1998). *Special education in multicultural contexts.* Upper Saddle River, NJ: Prentice Hall.

Cengage Learning/Wadsworth

Collaboration and Cooperative Teaching: Tools for Teaching All Learners

Collaboration
Collaboration Between General and Special Educators
Collaborating with Paraprofessionals
Collaborating with Parents/Families

Collaborative Consultation

Teaming Models
Multidisciplinary Teams
Interdisciplinary Teams
Transdisciplinary Teams

Cooperative Teaching
Cooperative Teaching Options
Research Support
Suggestions for Building Successful Cooperative Teaching Arrangements

Learning Outcomes

After studying this chapter, you should be able to:

- Define the term *collaboration* and identify the purpose and value of collaborative relationships.
- Describe the role and function of paraprofessionals in today's classrooms.
- Explain the benefits of collaborative consultation for the classroom teacher.
- Summarize the characteristics that distinguish multidisciplinary, interdisciplinary, and transdisciplinary educational teams.
- Discuss how cooperative teaching benefits students with and without disabilities.
- Identify six different models of cooperative teaching noting their pedagogical similarities and differences.

Over the years collaboration has become an integral dimension of effective schools. Presently, there is a growing recognition among educators of the importance of and need for working in a cooperative and collaborative fashion with other professionals. Teachers today no longer work in isolation. As we saw in Chapter 2, due to tremendous student diversity, it is increasingly common for educators to work in partnership with professionals from other disciplines. Successfully meeting the needs of learners with special needs requires collaborative relationships and cooperation between and among a wide range of professionals as well as parents.

It is safe to say that as a teacher you will be expected to work with others. In fact, IDEA 2004 requires teaming; participation in a multidisciplinary assessment team and the development of an IEP (individualized education program) team are but two illustrations of mandated collaborative efforts. Participating in a prereferral team (also known as teacher assistance teams or child study teams) is yet another example of how professionals are expected to work together. Collaboration is also reflected in the growing movement toward inclusive instructional practices (Polloway, Patton, & Serna, 2008). Hobbs and Westling (1998) note that successfully "serving students with disabilities in inclusive settings depends greatly on effective collaboration among professionals" (p. 14). One of the cornerstones of this textbook is the necessity for general and special educators functioning as a team when planning and delivering instruction to students with special needs, especially those learners served in inclusive settings. Professional cooperation and partnership are crucial to providing educational services in an effective and integrated fashion (Gargiulo, 2009).

There are several different ways in which general educators might work with other professionals. Opportunities will present themselves as a recipient of consultation, as a member of a service delivery team, or in the many different approaches to cooperative teaching. Prior to exploring these various interactions we wish to first examine some of the many facets of collaboration.

Collaboration

Collaboration frequently means different things to different people. In the present context **collaboration** is viewed as a cooperative partnership or relationship between two or more individuals who are working toward achieving a mutually agreed upon goal. Friend and Cook (2007) characterize collaboration as a style of interaction that professionals choose to use in order to accomplish a common goal. Collaboration is *how* people are working together, it describes the interaction that is taking place rather than *what* the parties are doing. Collaboration may be viewed as an umbrella term for interactions that are built on a common philosophy and goals as well as shared accountability and responsibility coupled with collegiality (Reinhiller, 1996; Wiggins & Damore, 2006).

For collaboration to be effective, however, professionals must exhibit a high degree of cooperation, trust, and mutual respect and must share the decision-making process. Additional key attributes necessary for meaningful collaboration include voluntary participation and parity in the relationship, along with shared goals, accountability, and resources (Friend & Cook, 2007).

Echoing these thoughts Freund and Rich (2005) identify seven core principles of effective collaboration including:

- *Willing participation.* Collaboration will be unsuccessful if mandated; effective collaboration is a voluntary action requiring a positive attitude.
- *Reflection.* Collaborators must be open to self-questioning, self-analysis, and self-evaluation. Individuals engaging in a collaborative process must be "willing to think about the effectiveness of their own practices, accept the suggestions of others, and implement changes that grow from these suggestions" (p. 105).

Collaboration between teachers and other professionals is becoming increasingly common in today's schools.

- *Mutual respect and reciprocity*. Meaningful collaboration is based on the recognition and appreciation of the other person's unique skills and expertise, which serve to strengthen the alliance and result in an equality in the relationship.
- *Clear communication*. Active listening is a key ingredient of effective alliances. Professionals must listen to their colleagues as well as parents with sensitivity and understanding. Individuals seeking to establish meaningful partnerships must focus on the feelings and attitudes that accompany the person's words while also attending to their body language.
- *Shared responsibility for planning and accountability of outcomes*. Shared responsibility does not necessarily mean equal work; it does suggest, however, a parity in the relationship whereby everyone's suggestions and efforts are equally valued. Shared accountability directly flows from shared responsibility and decision making. All stakeholders are accountable for the consequences of their decisions whether or not the outcomes are positive or negative.
- *Common goals*. Individuals can only truly collaborate when they share a mutually agreed upon goal. Sometimes this requires that those involved in the collaborative process set aside personal or professional differences in order to reach a goal that is in the best interest of the pupil.
- *Adequate time*. Without adequate time for meeting, planning, and conferencing attempts at collaboration will frequently fail. Innovative and creative strategies are often necessary when attempting to find time for collaborative activities.

Collaboration Between General and Special Educators

Collaboration between general and special educators is sometimes portrayed as a marriage with benefits and some tension being fairly common. Like a marriage, both parties bring different things into the relationship. Teachers are no different. "Special educators and general educators must strive to acknowledge that they both have specialized skills, but their experiences, values, and knowledge bases are different" (Wood, 2006, p. 31). Yet, despite differences in professional preparation, personal belief systems, and teaching styles the ever mounting demands placed upon educators has made collaboration among teachers imperative. Meeting the needs of an increasingly diverse student population is a potentially overwhelming responsibility, one that can best be accomplished collaboratively (Wiggins & Damore, 2006). Collaborative practices are becoming increasingly valued for the positive effect they can have on student learning in inclusive environments. Administrators as well as teachers consider collaboration as the critical component for success in inclusive settings (Freund & Rich, 2005; Murray, 2004). We should point out, however, that collaboration is not synonymous with inclusion. Collaboration describes the relationship between two or more individuals as they work toward a common goal. "Sometimes that goal is supporting a student with disabilities in a general education classroom. In that instance, collaboration can facilitate inclusion, but the two are *not* [italics added] synonymous" (Spencer, 2005, p. 297). Later in this chapter we will examine cooperative teaching, which is one type of collaborative activity that can facilitate inclusion.

Collaborating with Paraprofessionals

Paraprofessionals, also frequently known as educational or classroom assistants, teachers' aides, and paraeducators (or similar titles) have played a key role in schools for more than 40 years. During this time, their role has gradually evolved from simply providing clerical assistance to one of a vital and valued member of the educational team providing instructional support and assistance to learners with and without disabilities or other special needs in a variety of educational settings. Today, for example, paraprofessionals can be found providing personal care to a preschooler with cerebral palsy or they might be tutoring a fourth grader who is challenged by problems with reading while in other instances a paraprofessional might assist an adolescent in developing appropriate job skills in a community setting (Carroll, 2001; Council for Exceptional Children, 2008).

Who Is the Paraprofessional?

Paraprofessionals are individuals who provide instructional as well as noninstructional support and assistance to pupils (typically those with disabilities) in the general education classroom and/or a special education setting. They work under the direction and supervision of the classroom teacher who retains responsibility for student progress. The U.S. Department of Education (2008) reports that during the 2005–2006 school year over 393,000 paraprofessionals were providing services to children with disabilities.

Qualifications of Paraprofessionals

Generally speaking, most paraprofessionals are females from the local community who do not possess a college degree. In fact, in most instances, the only requirement for employment is a high school diploma or equivalent (Carroll, 2001; Friend & Cook, 2007). Some paraprofessionals, however, have a baccalaureate degree and years of classroom experience. It is interesting that, despite the invaluable assistance provided by paraprofessionals, the most recent revision of the Individuals with Disabilities Education Act (PL 108-446) is silent regarding the qualifications of paraprofessionals. Specific expectations can be found, however, for paraprofessionals who work in Title 1 schools (schools whose pupils experience a high degree of poverty). The No Child Left Behind Act of 2001 (PL 107-110) stipulates that paraprofessionals who provide instructional support must meet specific requirements including an associate's degree (or two years of college) or have preparation such that they can successfully pass a rigorous state developed assessment of skills necessary to assist in instruction in reading, writing, mathematics, and school readiness. While not mandated, several school districts have adopted these requirements regardless of the specific school in which the paraprofessional works.

The Council for Exceptional Children (2008) has identified several personal qualities of paraprofessionals viewed as beneficial including:

- enjoyment of children
- willingness to assist and support the teacher
- dedication to helping students
- flexibility and resourcefulness
- ability to collaborate with teachers and other paraprofessionals

Training of Paraprofessionals

Certification requirements for paraprofessionals are lacking in most states. In fact, the overwhelming majority of paraprofessionals are employed without prior training (Council for Exceptional Children, 2008). IDEA 2004 requires that paraprofessionals receive training in order to assist in providing a special education to learners with disabilities. Yet, states differ substantially in their training requirements. While some states have core competencies and others have mandated training, the most common mechanism is on-the-job training. Much of this training is left to the classroom teacher and other professional staff and/or experienced paraprofessionals (Carroll, 2001; Council for Exceptional Children). School districts typically provide general training via workshops, inservice opportunities, and other professional development activities. The acquisition of specific skills, however, is often necessary if paraprofessionals are to perform their jobs effectively. Focused training with student-specific and context-based information is often provided by teachers in conjunction with related services professionals (Friend & Cook, 2007). Most paraprofessionals will require ongoing professional development and personalized support as the student population they work with changes.

Responsibilities of Paraprofessionals

Paraprofessionals assume a wide range of instructional and noninstructional duties. Their responsibilities will typically vary depending on whether they are working in a general education classroom or a special education setting. Historically speaking, paraprofessionals typically assumed largely clerical responsibilities (collecting field trip money, taking attendance). In some instances, they still fulfill this responsibility; but today, most paraprofessionals work with individual pupils or small groups of students enabling them to be successful in inclusive environments as well as more restrictive placements (Friend & Cook, 2007). Regardless of their specific functions, it is vitally important that paraprofessionals are viewed and treated as a key member of the team. Table 5.1 outlines some of the many duties typically performed by these valuable classroom assistants.

Teachers' Responsibilities

As a teacher the relationship that you enjoy with your paraprofessional will be slightly different from the collaborative partnerships you establish with other professionals. This difference is largely due to your supervisory role. Despite the importance of this function, most educators are reluctant to assume this responsibility (Friend & Cook, 2007). Bowe (2005) recently identified four critical factors necessary for successful teacher/paraprofessional collaboration:

1. teachers need to offer training and direction so paraprofessionals can become skilled in accomplishing their jobs;
2. teachers need to provide ongoing supervision and support;

Table 5.1	Representative Responsibilities of Paraprofessionals

- Performing clerical duties (taking attendance, photocopying, distributing classroom materials, preparing instructional aids, maintaining learning centers)
- Assisting with personal hygiene and health needs of students with disabilities
- Supervising pupils on the playground, cafeteria, or study halls
- Providing instructional support (listening to children read, reviewing or reinforcing a concept or skill, monitoring/charting student behavior, grading assignments, reading test questions)
- Serving as a cultural liaison and/or translator for pupils and families from a culturally and linguistically diverse background
- Facilitating social interactions between and among classmates
- Ensuring student safety during fire drills and similar procedures

Source: Adapted from D. Carroll, "Considering Paraeducator Training, Roles, and Responsibilities," *Teaching Exceptional Children, 34*(2), 2001, pp. 60–64; N. French, "Supervising Paraprofessionals: A Survey of Teacher Practices," *Journal of Special Education, 35*(1), 2001, pp. 41–53.

3. teachers must acknowledge and respect the contributions of the paraprofessionals; and

4. teachers should solicit and value input and feedback from the paraprofessional.

Additional suggestions for establishing meaningful partnerships with paraprofessionals are offered in Table 5.2.

Collaborating with Parents/Families

Many teachers believe that a collaborative partnership with parents is critical to a child's success at school, especially for students with exceptionalities and other special needs. Research, in fact, strongly suggests that meaningful home-school collaboration leads to fewer discipline problems and improved academic performance (Freund & Rich, 2005). Collaboration between teachers and families is also vitally important to the success of inclusion (Bowe, 2005).

Parents represent a valuable resource for professionals; in comparison to teachers and other service providers, parents typically have a greater investment in their children, not only of time but also emotion. Generally, no one else will know the child as well as the parents do; their experiences predate and exceed those of the professional.

Despite counterproductive relationships in the past, today's parents are viewed as collaborators and equal partners with professionals thanks largely to IDEA, which requires that parents participate fully in educational decisions affecting their son or daughter. The enactment of PL 94-142 in 1975 ushered in a new era of parent-professional relationships. The status of parents evolved from that of passive recipients of services and professionals' advice to one of active participation. In many instances, functioning as educational decision makers who are actively involved in the identification, planning, and evaluation process in addition to offering input on educational goals and placement recommendations (Gargiulo, 2009).

Many authorities are recommending that educators expand their thinking and focus on *family* involvement rather than the narrower, restrictive concept of parent participation. In many instances, the stereotypic nuclear family is becoming increasingly rare. Family is a more inclusive term and can include whomever the individuals decide to recognize as a family member (Turnbull, Turnbull, Erwin, & Soodak, 2006). A family constellation might include grandparents, a community leader or tribal elder, an extended family member or anyone who fulfills the role typically associated with being a parent.

The contemporary emphasis on building family-professional partnerships implies that families are full and equal partners with professionals. It also strongly suggests that professionals no longer have power *over* families but rather achieve power *with* families. Families and professionals thus find themselves linked together in a mutually supportive and empowering alliance (Gargiulo, 2009).

Table 5.2	Guidelines for Working Effectively with Paraprofessionals

- Consider the paraprofessional an important member of the instructional team. Be sure to include him or her in team meetings whenever possible.
- Treat the paraprofessional with dignity and respect. Provide support and backup.
- Discuss goals, priorities, and plans with the paraprofessional on a daily basis.
- Avoid interrupting the paraprofessional when he or she is engaged in an activity. Keep interruptions to a minimum.
- Coordinate activities with the paraprofessional so you both accomplish as much as possible.
- Provide as much lead time as you can. Avoid last-minute rush jobs for the paraprofessional.
- Discuss problems and ideas with the paraprofessional. Ask for his or her ideas, suggestions, and opinions.
- If you must leave the classroom temporarily, tell the paraprofessional where you are going, how you can be reached, and when you will return. Adhere to district policies concerning leaving paraprofessionals alone with groups of students.
- Keep the paraprofessional fully informed about what is happening in the school environment. Ask what he or she would like to know about your priorities.
- Expect the best. Include the paraprofessional in staff development opportunities whenever possible.
- If you are one of several teachers with whom a paraprofessional works, be alert for contradictory directions that may be given. Clarify expectations as needed.
- Ask the paraprofessional whether you are using his or her time wisely or somehow hindering his or her performance. Make changes based on the feedback you receive.

Source: Adapted from K. Gerlach, *Strengthening the Partnership: Para-educators and Teachers Working Together* (Seattle, WA: Pacific Training Associates, 1994), p. 18.

Parental Reactions to Disability

The birth of a child with a disability or the identification of an impairment in the early school years can often have a profound impact on a family. How a family, particularly parents, respond to this situation can significantly effect relationships with professionals as well as the overall functioning and dynamics of the family. Emotional reactions are often highly individualized and are frequently mediated by structural, religious, cultural, financial, and other important variables. In some families, the person with a disability is considered to be just another member. In other cases, however, the child with a disability elicits a wide range of emotional responses.

Over the years a number of writers and theorists have adopted a stage theory approach for describing the adjustment process that many parents go through upon learning that their son or daughter has a disability (Anderegg, Vergason, & Smith, 1992; Blacher, 1984; Lambie, 2000). This popular approach suggests that some parents pass through a series of transformative stages in reaction to the news of their child's disability. Anecdotal reports from parents also support this thinking (Holland, 2006).

It is of course, impossible to predict how families, and parents in particular, will respond to a disability. Most stage theory models are constructed around the premise that families experience a grief or mourning cycle much like the developmental stages of reaction to the death of a loved one (Kübler-Ross, 1969). Some models are more elaborate than others, but most identify three distinct stages or phrases of parental reaction.

The early work of Gargiulo (1985) is characteristic of this thinking and is representative of more contemporary models (e.g., Cook, Klein, & Tessier, 2008; Fiedler, Simpson, & Clark, 2007; Smith, Gartin, Murdick, & Hilton, 2006). According to this model (see Figure 5.1), parental reaction to a disability includes three stages and encompasses a wide range of feelings and reactions. It is a generic model because parents of children with different disabilities frequently experience common feelings and react in similar fashion. Reactions differ more in degree than in kind. Gargiulo

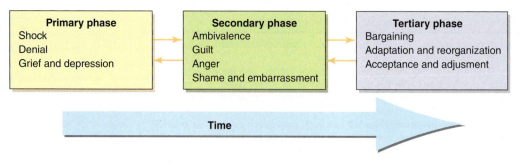

Figure 5.1 A Stage Model of Parental Reaction to Disability
Source: R. Gargiulo, *Working with Parents of Exceptional Children: A Guide for Professionals* (Boston: Houghton Mifflin, 1985), pp. 22–30.

stresses the uniqueness and variability of the response pattern. He also emphasizes flexibility because of each family's unique situation and that feelings and emotions are likely to recur over the family life cycle. The order of parental response is not predictable, nor does movement depend on successful resolution of an earlier feeling. Gargiulo explains,

> It should be noted that not all parents follow a sequential pattern of reaction according to a predetermined timetable. The stages should be viewed as fluid, with parents passing forward and backward as their individual adjustment process allows. Some individuals may never progress beyond hurt and anger, others may not experience denial; still others accept and adjust rather quickly to their child's abilities and disabilities. Also both parents do not necessarily move through these stages together. Each parent will react in his or her own unique way. (p. 21)

Gargiulo (1985) and more recently, Berry and Hardman (1998), believe that the reactions and feelings experienced by some parents are legitimate, automatic, understandable, and perfectly normal. Parents have a right to exhibit these emotions and to express their feelings. They are natural and necessary for adjustment. They do not represent reflections of pathology or maladjustment. Still, these emotions have the potential for significantly affecting collaborative partnerships with professionals. It is crucial, therefore, that educators respect and understand these responses while providing the appropriate support needed to establish meaningful alliances with parents. We fully agree with Salend's (2008) recommendation that teachers can further assist families "by being honest with them, showing genuine care and compassion, being empathetic rather than sympathetic, and encouraging them to obtain supportive services" (p. 185).

Working with Culturally and Linguistically Diverse Families

As we discovered in Chapter 4, teachers are working with a growing population of pupils who are culturally and linguistically diverse, of which a disproportionate number are enrolled in special education programs. Effective teachers are sensitive to the needs of these children as well as the needs of their parents and extended family members. If the cultural and linguistic heritage of the parents is not respected, then the development of optimal relationships will likely be undermined (Voltz, 1995).

Many of the strategies and programs, however, that are designed to solicit parental involvement have been devised primarily to serve middle- and upper-income English-speaking families from the macroculture (Kalyanpur & Harry, 1999; Salend & Taylor, 1993). Thus, it is highly probable that some families from culturally and linguistically diverse backgrounds will fail to appreciate and respond to strategies designed to support home-school partnerships and enhance their role in the educational process.

Some of the roadblocks or obstacles that may impede the full and meaningful involvement of caregivers from outside the mainstream American culture include the parents' limited English proficiency, their previous negative experiences with schools, an unfamiliarity with their rights and responsibilities, and a deference to teachers and other professionals as the decision makers ("teacher knows best") (Parette & Petch-Hogan, 2000; Voltz, 1998). Establishing meaningful collaborative relationships with families from culturally and linguistically diverse backgrounds also requires that professionals respect the family's interpretation of the disability and its origin; their child-rearing beliefs, medical practices, and traditions; the family's structure and decision-making style; and their religious views and preferred manner of communication (Gargiulo & Kilgo, 2005). The best intentions of teachers can easily be misinterpreted if they fail to consider the family's value system and cultural traditions. For example, an Hispanic American family may be uncomfortable with and reluctant to agree to a recommendation that they consider placement in a group home for their adult daughter with mental retardation. To the transition specialist, this may appear to be a perfectly reasonable and appropriate suggestion. However, unlike Anglo-Americans, who generally emphasize accomplishment, independence, and self-reliance, Hispanic Americans are more likely to value interdependence, cooperation, and familial cohesiveness. Because of these differences in values and beliefs, this recommendation will likely be inappropriate for this particular family.

It is very important that teachers exhibit cultural sensitivity when working with families with a cultural or linguistic heritage different from their own. **Cultural sensitivity** implies an awareness of, respect for, and appreciation of the many factors that influence and shape the values, priorities, and perspectives of both individuals and families (Dennis & Giangreco, 1996). Educators need to be knowledgeable about different values, social customs, and traditions so that they can respond effectively to the needs of all their pupils while concurrently building partnerships with the students' families. By becoming informed about and sensitive to cultural differences, teachers are in a position to empower parents and create equitable relationships (Sileo, Sileo, & Prater, 1996). We offer the following note of caution, however: Building effective alliances with families from different cultural groups demands that professionals refrain from generalizing about families. Although similarities

Cengage Learning/Wadsworth

Teachers must exhibit cultural sensitivity when working with families from culturally and linguistically diverse backgrounds.

In the Classroom

Recommendations for Building Culturally Sensitive Relationships

- Share information using the family's desired language and preferred means of communication—written notes, e-mails, telephone calls, informal meetings, or even audiotapes.
- Always strive to provide written communication in parent's native language.
- When appropriate, recognize that extended family members often play a key role in a child's educational development. Give deference to key decision makers in the family.
- Use culturally competent and trained interpreters who are not only familiar with the language but also knowledgeable about educational issues, terminology, and the special education process.
- Seek cultural informants from the local community who can assist teachers in understanding culturally relevant variables such as nonverbal communication patterns, child-rearing strategies, gender roles, academic expectations, medical practices, and specific folkways that might affect the family's relationships with professionals.
- Attend social events and other functions held in the local community.
- With the help of other parents or volunteers, develop a survival vocabulary of key words and phrases in the family's native language.

- Learn the correct pronunciation of your student's first name and the family's last name.
- Address parents and other caregivers as "Mr.," "Ms.," or "Mrs.," rather than using first names. Formality and respect are essential, especially when speaking with older members of the family.
- When arranging meetings, be sensitive to possible barriers such as time conflicts, transportation difficulties, and child-care issues.
- Conduct meetings, if necessary, in family-friendly settings such as a local community center, library, or house of worship.
- Invite community volunteers to serve as cultural liaisons between the school and the pupil's family.
- Encourage parents and other family members to visit your classroom and become involved in school activities and functions. Assess parent's willingness to share their cultural heritage with your students.

Source: Adapted from R. Gargiulo, *Special Education in Contemporary Society,* 3rd ed. (Thousand Oaks, CA: Sage, 2009).

may exist among families, such as a shared heritage or common language, assuming that a family will behave in a certain way simply because of membership in a particular group often leads to stereotyping, which only hinders the development of meaningful home-school partnerships. Remember, just as each student is unique, so is each family. Although families are influenced by their cultural background, they should not be defined by it.

See the In the Classroom feature for suggestions on creating meaningful relationships with families from culturally and linguistically diverse backgrounds.

Collaborative Consultation

Collaborative consultation has a rich history and is widely regarded as an effective school-based practice for providing support and assistance to both general and special educators. It is also a strategy that is often used to facilitate the successful inclusion of pupils with disabilities and other special needs (Dover, 2005; Lamar-Dukes & Dukes, 2005).

Collaborative consultation is a voluntary, focused, and shared problem-solving process in which one individual offers expertise and assistance to another. Idol, Nevin, and Paolucci-Whitcomb (1994) consider collaborative consultation to be "an interactive process that enables groups of people with diverse expertise to generate creative solutions to mutually defined problems" (p. 1). The intent of this process is to modify teaching tactics and/or the learning environment in order to accommodate the learning, social, or behavioral needs of an individual learner. Instructional planning and responsibility thus becomes a *shared* duty among various professionals. Collaborative consultation is much more than just joint planning and problem solving; it is the relationship between people, often from different professional backgrounds, that makes the process possible. To be effective collaborative consultation necessitates shared responsibility, resources, and accountability coupled with a willingness to appreciate one another's viewpoints, vocabulary, and values. Essentially, it is a commitment to the belief that "two heads are better than one" (McCormick, Loeb, & Schiefelbusch, 2003).

Assistance to the classroom teacher can come from several different resources. A vision specialist for example may provide suggestions on how to use a new piece of technology needed by a student who is visually impaired; while a school psychologist or behavior management specialist may offer suggestions for dealing with the aggressive, acting-out behaviors of a middle school student with emotional problems. In some instances, parents may be able to offer teachers unique and useful insights and information about their son or daughter. Hourcade and Bauwens (2003) refer to this type of aid as **indirect consultation**. In other instance, services are rendered directly to the student by professionals other than the classroom teacher. In this situation, specific areas of weakness or deficit are the target of remediation. Interventions are increasingly being provided by related services personnel in the general education classroom. The general educator also typically receives instructional guidance on how to carry out the remediation efforts in the absence of the service provider.

We should also point out that collaborative consultation is equally valuable for special educators. The diverse needs of pupils with disabilities frequently require that special education teachers seek programming suggestions and other types of assistance from colleagues and related services personnel. It should be obvious that no one discipline or professional possesses all of the answers. The complex demands of today's inclusive classroom dictate that professionals work together in a cooperative fashion.

A successful collaborative consultation experience typically involves a number of basic steps. While the sequence is not rigid and not every step will occur during a given contact, the following six steps, as identified by Friend and Cook (2007), provide a framework for effective and focused problem solving.

- **entry**—the physical and psychological beginning of a series of interactions and the establishment of trust and respect;
- **problem identification**—the establishment of a goal for the interaction;
- **planning**—the decision about how to reach the intended goal;
- **intervention**—carrying out the planned interventions;
- **evaluation**—the determination of intervention success; and
- **exit**—the termination of the consulting relationship. (p. 92)

Figure 5.2 illustrates a collaborative consultation planning document that may be used to record the decisions made by the team.

According to Pugach and Johnson (2002), consultative services are an appropriate and beneficial strategy, a means whereby all school personnel can collaboratively interact as part of their commitment to serving *all* children. Furthermore, a truly collaborative culture promotes a heightened sense of shared responsibility for the success of all students (Walther-Thomas, Korinek, McLaughlin, & Williams, 2000). Meaningful collaborative consultation necessitates mutual support, respect, flexibility, and a sharing of expertise. No one professional should consider him- or herself more of an expert than others. Each of the parties involved, including parents, can learn and benefit from the others' expertise. Basic guidelines for a successful collaborative consultation relationship are identified in Table 5.3.

Teaming Models

Today very few educators work in isolation. In fact, many teachers find themselves engaged in some sort of collaborative relationship almost on a daily basis. Being part of a team, even if it only involves one or two other individuals, has been part of the fabric of special education service delivery for more than three decades.

Student_____   Grade_____   Teacher(s)_____
                                                                    _____
                                                                    _____

Meeting Date _____

Team Members Present
                    _____   _____
                    _____   _____
                    _____   _____

Student's Strengths and Interests
_____
_____

Concerns about Student's Learning/Behavior
_____
_____

Problem Statement
_____
_____

Brainstorming Suggestions
_____
_____

Idea(s) Selected
_____
_____

Implementation
        How/What?
                _____

        When?
                _____

        Who?
                _____

Timeline for Implementation
_____
_____

Evaluation of Intervention
        Outcomes:
                _____

        Follow up Date(s)
                _____

        Future Plans:
                _____

Figure 5.2 **Collaborative Consultation Planning Form**
Source: Adapted from D. Appl, C. Troha, and J. Rowell, "Reflections of a First-Year Team: The Growth of a Collaborative Partnership," *Teaching Exceptional Children, 33*(3), 2001, p. 6.

Evaluating, planning, and delivering services to students with special needs typically involves a team approach. The three most common models identified in the professional literature are multidisciplinary, interdisciplinary, and transdisciplinary teams (McDonnell, Hardman, & McDonnell, 2003; McGoningel, Woodruff, & Roszmann-Millican, 1994). Although these teams may share a common goal, how they accomplish their tasks varies tremendously.

Multidisciplinary Teams

The concept of a **multidisciplinary** team was originally mandated in PL 94-142 and was recently reiterated in the 2004 reauthorization of IDEA (PL 108-446). This approach utilizes the expertise of professionals from several disciplines (for example, physical therapist, speech-language pathologist, occupational therapist), each of whom usually performs his or her assessments, interventions, and other tasks independent of the others. Individuals contribute according to their own

Table 5.3	Recommendations for Effective Collaborative Consultation

- Behave in ways showing respect for and trust of one another's opinions, skills, and abilities.
- Share ownership of the problem as well as the proposed solutions.
- Learn from one another by regularly exchanging roles (shifting from expert to recipient and vice versa).
- Use active listening and responding techniques (such as clarification, paraphrasing, and acknowledging feelings) to facilitate communication.
- Give credit for each other's ideas and provide immediate positive feedback for one another when mutually agreed-on goals are achieved.
- Avoid professional jargon.
- Be available for one another.

Source: Adapted from L. McCormick, D. Loeb, and R. Schiefelbusch, *Supporting Children with Communication Difficulties in Inclusive Settings*, 2nd ed. (Boston: Allyn & Bacon, 2003), p. 181.

specialty area with little regard for the actions of other professionals. There is a high degree of professional autonomy and minimal integration. A team exists only in the sense that each person shares a common goal. There is very little coordination or collaboration across discipline areas. Friend and Cook (2007) characterize this model as a patchwork quilt whereby different, and sometimes contrasting information, are integrated but not necessarily with a unified outcomes.

Parents of children with disabilities typically meet with each team member individually. They are generally passive recipients of information about their son or daughter. Because information flows to them from several sources, some parents have difficulty synthesizing all of the data and recommendations from the various experts. Gargiulo and Kilgo (2005) do not consider the multidisciplinary team to be especially "family friendly."

Interdisciplinary Teams

The **interdisciplinary** team evolved from dissatisfaction with the fragmented services and lack of communication typically associated with the multidisciplinary team model (McCormick et al., 2003). With this model of teaming, team members perform their evaluations independently, but program development and instructional recommendations are the result of information sharing and joint planning. Significant cooperation among the team members leads to an integrated plan of services and holistic view of student's strengths and needs. Greater communication, coordination, and collaboration are the distinctive trademarks of this model. Direct services such as physical therapy, however, are usually provided in isolation from one another. Families typically meet with the entire team or its representative; in many cases, a special educator performs this role.

Transdisciplinary Teams

The **transdisciplinary** approach to providing services builds upon the strengths of the interdisciplinary model. In this model, team members are committed to working collaboratively across individual discipline lines. The transdisciplinary model is further distinguished by two additional and related features: role sharing and a primary interventionist. Professionals from various disciplines conduct their initial evaluations and assessments, but they relinquish their role (role release) as service providers by teaching their skills to other team members, one of whom will serve as the primary interventionist. This person is regarded as the team leader. For many children and adolescents with special needs, this role is usually filled by an educator. This individual relies heavily on the support and consultation provided by his or her professional peers. Discipline-specific interventions are still available, although they occur less frequently.

"The primary purpose of this approach," according to Bruder (1994), "is to pool and integrate the expertise of team members so that more efficient and comprehensive assessment and intervention services may be provided" (p. 61). The aim of the

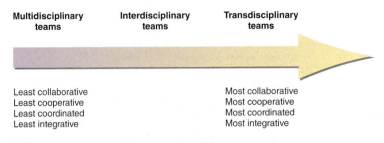

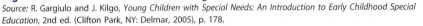

| Multidisciplinary teams | Interdisciplinary teams | Transdisciplinary teams |

Least collaborative
Least cooperative
Least coordinated
Least integrative

Most collaborative
Most cooperative
Most coordinated
Most integrative

Figure 5.3 Characteristics of Teaming Models
Source: R. Gargiulo and J. Kilgo, *Young Children with Special Needs: An Introduction to Early Childhood Special Education,* 2nd ed. (Clifton Park, NY: Delmar, 2005), p. 178.

transdisciplinary model is to avoid compartmentalization and fragmentation of services. It attempts to provide a more coordinated and unified approach to assessment and service delivery. Members of a transdisciplinary team see parents as full-fledged members of the group with a strong voice in the team's recommendations and decisions.

Figure 5.3 illustrates some of the characteristics of each team model as viewed by Gargiulo and Kilgo (2005), and Table 5.4 summarizes key components of service delivery across each of our three models of collaborative teaming.

Cooperative Teaching

Cooperative teaching, or co-teaching as it is sometimes called, represents a logical extension of collaborative efforts between educators. Cooperative teaching is built on the same principles as any other successful collaborative relationship (Freund & Rich, 2005). It is becoming an increasingly common service delivery approach for expanding instructional options for learners with disabilities, providing access to the general education curriculum, and enhancing the performance and participation

Table 5.4	Key Components of Collaborative Teams		
Component	**Multidisciplinary**	**Interdisciplinary**	**Transdisciplinary**
Philosophy of Team Interaction	Team members recognize the importance of contributions from several disciplines.	Team members are willing and able to share responsibility for services among disciplines.	Team members commit to teach, learn, and work across disciplinary boundaries to plan and provide integrated services.
Family's Role	Generally, families meet with team members separately by discipline.	The family may or may not be considered a team member. Families may work with the whole team or team representatives.	Families are always members of the team and determine their own team roles.
Lines of Communication	Lines of communication are typically informal. Members may not think of themselves as part of a team.	The team meets regularly for case conferences, consultations, etc.	The team meets regularly to share information and to teach and learn across disciplines (for consultations, team building, etc.).
Assessment Process	Team members conduct separate assessments by disciplines.	Team members conduct assessments by discipline and share results.	The team participates in an arena assessment, observing and recording across disciplines.
Program Development	Team members develop separate plans for intervention within their own discipline.	Goals are developed by discipline and shared with the rest of the team to form a single service plan.	Staff and family develop plan together based on family concerns, priorities, and resources.
Program Implementation	Team members implement their plan separately by discipline.	Team members implement parts of the plan for which their disciplines are responsible.	Team members share responsibility and are accountable for how the plan is implemented by one person, with the family.

Source: Adapted from C. Garland, J. McGonigel, A. Frank, and D. Buck, *The Transdisciplinary Model of Service Delivery* (Lightfoot, VA: Child Development Resources, 1989) and G. Woodruff and C. Hanson, *Project KAI Training Packet* (Funded by the U.S. Department of Education, Office of Special Education Programs, Handicapped Children's Early Education Program, 1987).

of students with special needs in the general education classroom (Walsh & Jones, 2004; Zigmond & Magiera, 2001).

Cooperative teaching is also a popular approach for achieving inclusion; in fact, it was suggested as one of the first "mainstreaming strategies" (Bauwens & Hourcade, 1991). Cooperative teaching within an inclusive environment is currently considered "best practice"— one way of effectively meeting the diverse needs of pupils with disabilities (Spencer, 2005). Cooperative teaching, according to Walther-Thomas et al. (2000), "enriches learning opportunities for all students by targeting students with unique learning needs and many peers who struggle in school but fail to qualify for extra help" (p. 184). With this strategy general education teachers and special educators work together in a collaborative and cooperative manner; with each professional sharing in the planning and delivery of instruction to a heterogeneous group of students. Hourcade and Bauwens (2003), define cooperative teaching as

> direct collaboration in which a general educator and one or more support service providers voluntarily agree to work together in a co-active and coordinated fashion in the general education classroom. These educators, who possess distinct and complementary sets of skills, share roles, resources, and responsibilities in a sustained effort while working toward the common goal of school success for all students. (p. 41)

Likewise, Friend and Cook (2007) see cooperative teaching as a special form of teaming, a service delivery option whereby substantive instruction is jointly provided by one or more professionals to a diverse group of learners within the general education classroom.

As we have just seen, cooperative teaching is a service delivery approach based on collaboration. It is an instructional model that fosters shared responsibility for coordinating and delivering instruction to a group of children with unique learning needs. Effective cooperative teachers share responsibility for planning, delivering, monitoring, and evaluating instruction; they also share authority and prestige in the classroom. These educators also believe that *all* pupils in the classroom are their students (Walther-Thomas et al., 2000). Cooperative teachers talk about "our goals for the year," "our classroom," "the lessons we planned." Essentially, cooperative teaching is about a true partnership and parity in the instructional process. This alliance allows teachers to "respond effectively to the varied needs of their students, lower the student-teacher ratio, and expands the professional expertise that can be directed to those needs" (Friend & Cook, 2007, p. 117).

Cooperative Teaching Options

The aim of cooperative teaching is to create options for learning and to provide support to *all* learners in the general education classroom by combining the content expertise of the general educator with the instructional accommodation talents of the special educator (Murawski & Dieker, 2004; Wilson & Michaels, 2006). Cooperative teaching can be implemented in several different ways, there are multiple versions of this instructional strategy. These arrangements, as identified by Friend and Cook (2007), typically occur for set periods of time each day or only on certain days of the week. Some of the more common instructional models for cooperative teaching are depicted in Figure 5.4. The particular strategy chosen often depends on the needs and characteristics of the pupils, curricular demands, amount of professional experience, and teacher preference, as well as such practical matters as the amount of space available. Many educators use a variety of arrangements depending upon their specific circumstances.

One Teach, One Observe

In this version of cooperative teaching one teacher presents the instruction to the entire class while the second educator circulates gathering information (data) on a specific pupil, a small group of students, or targeted behaviors across the whole

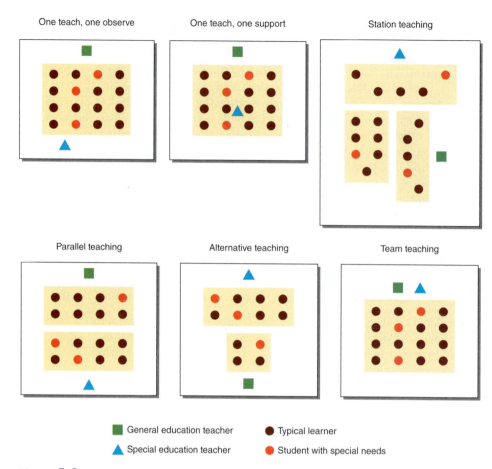

Figure **5.4** Cooperative Teaching Arrangements
Source: Adapted from M. Friend and L. Cook, *Interactions: Collaboration Skills for School Professionals*, 5th ed. (Boston: Pearson Education, 2007), p. 121.

class such as productive use of free time. Although this model requires a minimal amount of joint planning, it is very important that teachers periodically exchange roles to avoid one professional from being perceived by students, and possibly parents, as the "assistant teacher."

One Teach, One Support

Both individuals are present, but one teacher takes the instructional lead while the other quietly provides support and assistance to the students. It is important that one professional (usually the special educator) is not always expected to function as the assistant; rotating roles can help to alleviate this potential problem. It is also recommended that this model be used sparingly, or as one of several approaches, in order to avoid students from becoming overly dependent on additional assistance as well as jeopardizing the credibility of one of the teachers.

Station Teaching

In this type of cooperative teaching, the lesson is divided into two or more segments and presented in different locations in the classroom. One teacher presents one portion of the lesson while the other teacher provides a different portion. Then the groups rotate, and the teachers repeat their information to new groups of pupils. Depending on the class, a third station can be established where students work independently or with a learning buddy to review material. Station teaching has been shown to be effective at all grade levels and it affords both teachers the opportunity to instruct all of the pupils, albeit on different content.

Will Hart/PhotoEdit

Cooperative teaching within an inclusive learning environment is currently considered "best practice."

Parallel Teaching

This instructional arrangement lowers the teacher/pupil ratio. Instruction is planned jointly but is delivered by each teacher to one-half of a heterogeneous group of learners. Coordination of efforts is crucial. This format lends itself to drill-and-practice activities rather than initial instruction or projects that require close teacher supervision. As with station teaching, noise and activity levels may pose problems.

Alternative Teaching

Some students benefit from small group instruction; alternative teaching meets that need. With this model, one teacher provides instruction to a heterogeneous group of learners while the other teacher interacts with a small group of pupils. Although commonly used for remediation purposes, alternative teaching is equally appropriate for enrichment as well as for preteaching activities and in-depth study. Teachers need to be cautious, however, that children with disabilities are not exclusively and routinely assigned to the small group; all members of the class should participate periodically in the functions of the smaller group.

Team Teaching

In this type of cooperative teaching, which is the most collaborative of our six models, both teachers equally share the instructional activities for the entire class. Each teacher, for example, may take turns leading a discussion about the causes of World War II, or one teacher may talk about multiplication of fractions while the co-teacher gives several examples illustrating this concept. Students view each teacher, therefore, as having equal status. This form of cooperative teaching, sometimes called interactive teaching (Walther-Thomas et al., 2000), requires a significant amount of professional trust and a high level of commitment. Compatibility of teaching styles is another key component for successful teaming.

Advantages and disadvantages of cooperative teaching options are summarized in Table 5.5. Strategies for implementing cooperative teaching, regardless of the specific approach used, are offered in the accompanying In the Classroom feature.

Table 5.5	Advantages and Disadvantages of Representative Cooperative Teaching Arrangements	
Instructional Model	**Advantages**	**Disadvantages**
Team Teaching (Whole Class)	• Provides systematic observation/data collection • Promotes role/content sharing • Facilitates individual assistance • Models appropriate academic, social, and help-seeking behaviors • Teaches question asking • Provides clarification (e.g., concepts, rules, vocabulary)	• May be job sharing, not learning enriching • Requires considerable planning • Requires modeling and role-playing skills • Becomes easy to "typecast" specialist with this role
Station Teaching (Small Group)	• Provides active learning format • Increase small-group attention • Encourages cooperation and independence • Allows strategic grouping • Increases response rate	• Requires considerable planning and preparation • Increase noise level • Requires group and independent work skills • Is difficult to monitor
Parallel Teaching (Small Group)	• Provides effective review format • Encourages student responses • Reduces pupil/teacher ratio for group instruction or review	• Hard to achieve equal depth of content coverage • May be difficult to coordinate • Requires monitoring of partner pacing • Increases noise level • Encourages some teacher-student competition
Alternative Teaching (Large Group, Small Group)	• Facilitates enrichment opportunities • Offers absent students "catch up" times • Keeps individuals and class on pace • Offers time to develop missing skills	• May select same low-achieving students for help • Creates segregated learning environments • Is difficult to coordinate • May single out students

Source: Adapted from C. Walther-Thomas, L. Korinek, V. McLaughlin, and B. Williams, *Collaboration for Inclusive Education* (Needham Heights, MA: Allyn & Bacon, 2000), p. 190.

Research Support

To date, most of the research literature on cooperative teaching has been more prescriptive than analytical; that is, descriptions and explanations of the process of cooperative teaching rather than evidence of its effectiveness on student accomplishment (Bowe, 2005; Murawski, 2006). Yet, in a large meta-analysis investigation of cooperative teaching research, Murawski and Swanson (2001) concluded that the data are suggestive of positive student outcomes (improved grades, test scores). Likewise, a more recent review of cooperative teaching research in inclusive settings also found positive outcomes across academic and social domains for pupils in both elementary and secondary classrooms (Scruggs, Mastropieri, & McDuffie, 2007). We believe, however, as others do (Friend & Hurley-Chamberlain, 2006), that additional research is needed in order to substantiate the effectiveness of this service delivery approach.

Suggestions for Building Successful Cooperative Teaching Arrangements

Cooperative teaching should not be viewed as a panacea for meeting the multiple challenges frequently encountered when serving students with disabilities and other special needs in general education classrooms; it is, however, one mechanism for facilitating successful inclusion. If cooperative teaching is to be successful, teachers need to openly address potential obstacles or barriers such as classroom responsibilities, work load issues, discipline strategies, and grading criteria in addition to finding sufficient time for joint planning. Friend and Cook (2007) also recommend that teachers engaged in cooperative teaching address the following seven topics, which are designed to clarify roles and responsibilities while strengthening their partnership. The questions posed in Table 5.6 should be addressed prior to beginning a cooperative teaching venture and routinely throughout the experience.

In the Classroom

Tips for a Successful Cooperative Teaching Experience

1. **Planning is the key**. It is important that you make time to plan lessons and discuss exactly how you will work together throughout your cooperative teaching experience. Some teachers set aside one lunch period each week for this purpose, whereas others meet biweekly after school. In some schools, specific planning periods are built into the teachers' schedules.

2. **Discuss your views on teaching and learning with your partner**. What are your goals for students for the lessons you are teaching? Do you expect all students to master all of them? Experienced cooperative teachers agree that to be effective, the teachers should share basic beliefs about instruction.

3. **Attend to details**. When another professional is teaching with you, you'll need to clarify classroom rules and procedures, such as
   - Class routines for leaving the room, using free time, turning in assignments
   - Discipline matters
   - The division of such chores as grading student work or making bulletin boards
   - Pet peeves, such as gum chewing

4. **Prepare parents**. A few parents may wonder what a co-taught classroom means for their children. Does this mean you'll be teaching less material? Will expectations for behavior be lower? Does the special education teacher work with all children? The answers to these questions should be *no, no,* and *yes.* Explain to parents that having two teachers in the classroom gives *every* child the opportunity to receive more attention than before.

5. **Make the special education teacher feel welcome in your classroom**. Clear a place in the room for your colleague's personal items, and be sure to prominently display his or her name. Also, plan how you will introduce your teaching partner to the students. Many cooperative teachers describe the special educator as a teacher who helps students learn how to learn.

6. **Avoid the "paraprofessional trap."** The most common compliant about cooperative teaching is that the special education teacher simply becomes a classroom helper. This soon becomes boring for the special educator. More importantly, it is a very limited use of their expertise and talents. Having two teachers in a classroom opens up instructional opportunities that you may never have had before; the excitement of cooperative teaching comes from taking advantage of this situation.

7. **When disagreements occur, talk them out**. To have disagreements in a cooperative teaching relationship is normal. What is important is to raise your concerns while they are still minor and to recognize that both of you may have to compromise in order to resolve them.

8. **Go slowly**. If you begin your cooperative teaching experience with approaches that require less reliance on each other, you will then have a chance to learn each other's teaching styles and preferences. As you comfort level increases, you can experiment with more complex cooperative teaching arrangements. Above all else, periodically stop to discuss with your partner what is working and what needs revision.

Source: Adapted from M. Friend and L. Cook, "The New Mainstreaming," *Instructor, 101*(7), 1992, p. 34.

Table 5.6	Issues Important to Creating a Successful Cooperative Teaching Partnership
Topic	**Questions**
Philosophy and beliefs	• What are our overriding philosophies about the roles of teachers and teaching and about students and learning? • How do our instructional beliefs affect our instructional practice?
Parity signals	• How will we convey to students and others (e.g., teachers, parents) that we are equals in the classroom? • How can we ensure a sense of parity in the planning and delivery of instruction?
Classroom routines	• What are the instructional routines for the classroom (e.g., how previous lessons are reviewed, what strategies are used to encourage student involvement)? • What are the organizational routines for the classroom (e.g., are students allowed to go to their lockers during class; what should students do if they complete independent work before classmates)?
Discipline	• What is acceptable and unacceptable student behavior? • Who is to intervene at what point in students' behavior? • What are the rewards and consequences used in the classroom?
Feedback	• What is the best way to give each other feedback? When? • How will we ensure that both positive and negative issues are raised?
Noise	• What noise level are we comfortable with in the classroom?
Pet peeves	• What aspects of teaching and classroom life does each of us feel strongly about? • How can we identify our pet peeves so as to avoid them?

Source: M. Friend and L. Cook, *Interactions: Collaboration Skills for School Professionals*, 5th ed. (Boston: Pearson Education, 2007), p. 131.

To ensure that cooperative teaching is efficient and effective, Reinhiller (1996) recommends that teachers also consider the following five questions:

- Why do we want to co-teach?
- How will we know whether our goals are being met?
- How will we communicate and document the collaboration?
- How will we share responsibility for the instruction of all students?
- How will we gain support from others? (p. 46)

Keefe, Moore, and Duff (2004) offer the following guidelines for creating and maintaining a successful cooperative teaching experience:

- *Know yourself*—recognize your strengths and weaknesses; acknowledge preconceived notions about teaching in an inclusive setting.
- *Know your partner*—foster a friendship; accept each other's idiosyncrasies; appreciate differences in teaching styles.
- *Know your students*—discover the students' interests, listen to their dreams; embrace acceptance.
- *Know your "stuff"*—share information and responsibility; jointly create IEPs; be knowledgeable about classroom routines.

Like Murawski and Dieker (2004), we believe that in the final analysis the key question that teachers must answer is, "Is what we are doing good for our students and good for us?"

See Table 5.7 for a national award-winning teacher's recommendations for facilitating a successful cooperative teaching experience. We conclude our discussion of cooperative teaching by offering the following personal perspective (see the Teacher Voices feature) on the challenges and opportunities that are possible when working in a collaborative fashion in an inclusive classroom.

Table 5.7	Recommendations for Successful Cooperative Teaching: A Special Educator's Perspective
When working with children with disabilities:	**When working with general education teachers:**
• When you construct your plan, think about how you can make it visual, auditory, tactile, and kinesthetic. You'll have a better chance of meeting different learning styles. • Think about what is the most important thing all students need to learn and then think about how you can break the task into smaller parts for some students and make it more challenging for students who are ready to move ahead. • Be keenly aware of student strengths, and plan to find a way for each student to be successful academically every day. • Working with a peer/buddy is often a helpful strategy. • Mix up your groups now and then. A student may need a different group for reading than for math. Try not to "label" anyone. • Children with disabilities (many children actually) need very clear, precise directions. Pair auditory with visual directions if possible. Students with more severe impairments may need to see objects. • It may be helpful to only give one direction at a time. This doesn't mean the pace has to be slow. In fact, a fast pace is often quite effective. Using signals (for getting attention, transitions, for example) can also be very helpful. • Be consistent. • Notice students being "good"—offer verbal praise or perhaps a small positive note. • Have high expectations for *all* children.	• Find teachers who welcome your students and whom you enjoy working with if possible. It is helpful to find co-teachers who have different strengths so you can complement each other. • Faithfully plan ahead with these teachers—at least a week ahead. • Be willing to do more than your share at first if necessary to get a solid footing for the year. It will pay off. • Keep communication open and frequent. Use positive language with each other as much as possible. Brainstorm solutions to challenges together, and try different solutions. • Document the work you do with students. Help with assessment as much as possible. • Attend open houses, parent conferences, and other similar meetings so the parents view you as part of the classroom community. • Look for the good in the teacher(s) and students, and tell them when you see a "best practice." • If you don't know the answer to something, ask. If you don't know some of the content very well, study. Find out who does something well, and observe him/her if it is a skill you need to work on. • When you say you will do something, be sure you follow through.

Source: D. Metcalf, H. B. Sugg Elementary School, Farmville, NC. The Council for Exceptional Children (CEC) 2004 Clarissa Hug Teacher of the Year.

Teacher Voices

One Teacher's View of Collaboration and Inclusion

I am a career-long special educator. For the past twenty-plus years of my teaching career, I have watched as trends, strategies, methodologies, and philosophical beliefs have come and gone in our quest to educate students with special needs.

Inclusive Education Experience

As a new and inexperienced teacher, I found myself in a self-contained classroom with students with special needs in a small room in a remote area of the school with very little contact with students or other teachers from the general education classroom. Our chances for interaction occurred for only short periods each day in the lunchroom or gym. As my experience and courage grew, I was able to talk a few teachers into allowing students from my class the opportunity to join in the "mainstream" for certain academic or social occasions. Later I participated in a school program that offered support and services to students with special needs in the general education classroom. To be quite honest, I was very happy to have the opportunity to teach in an inclusive setting. It was a welcome change from my early years of teaching.

Working in an inclusive classroom is a challenging but rewarding experience. I like to believe that if a visitor came to the door of our inclusive classroom, the students with special needs would be invisible. The visitor would see students engaged in small group instruction with one teacher, working in center groups as the other teacher actively moves around the room, or an individual student working silently at a desk. The visitor would see a general education classroom with students actively engaged in learning, not a class with students with special needs receiving separate instruction. I have seen many students with special needs in the general education class make significant progress academically and socially as an accepted member of a classroom learning community. When looking at placing a student with special needs, we realized we should ask ourselves, "Can the student receive all of his or her instruction in the classroom with supports?" We discovered that for the large majority of students, the answer was yes. With that question in mind, our decisions for the student with special needs became easier. Making accommodations and modifications within the general classroom setting becomes easier when both the special education and general education teachers are making them together.

Strategies for Inclusive Classrooms

Needless to say, inclusive practice is not an easy concept to put into place. It takes time, effort, administrative support, and collaboration between teachers. I found that every new school year brought new students with different needs. Our inclusive strategies had to change each year to accommodate the needs of our students. One common problem our staff experienced was in scheduling, but we have gotten creative with some of our solutions. One year we used half-day substitutes for the general education teachers once every two weeks to allow joint planning time and collaboration. The most successful solution we used was to divide staff so that every grade level had an inclusion specialist providing support for that grade level exclusively. That inclusion specialist joined that team and had common planning time with each teacher at least one time per two-week period. We used the area classes such as music, art, and counseling to accomplish this.

Successful Collaboration

Collaboration between professionals is one of the key steps in creating successful inclusive practices. Many teachers had never experienced having another adult in their classroom. We solved this problem by making the choice to participate in an inclusive classroom a voluntary one. Also, we found some applications that have led to effective collaborative partnerships. These include:

- Focus on a shared need.
- Identify problem areas.
- Share problem solving and design of solutions.
- Share planning.
- Share evaluation of the outcome.

Successful collaborative teams usually embrace the belief that everyone in the school is responsible for the education of *all* the students—those with special needs and their nondisabled peers.

Working with Parents and Families

Parents are a vital part of the collaborative team. They know their child better than anyone else. Parents, therefore, have a responsibility to share their knowledge of the child's specific needs with the team. Parents also often need to be encouraged to share their goals and vision for their son or daughter. Meaningful parental involvement and honest, open communication between team members and the parents are very helpful in creating a successful partnership.

Suggestions for Making Inclusion and Collaboration Work

It has been my experience that for inclusive strategies and practices to be successful, collaborative teams must have a shared focus. Administrators, general and special education teachers, service providers, paraprofessionals, and parents must all be involved. Communication and flexibility are a must. The team must show a sense of shared ownership. The team needs to use phrases such as "our class" and "our students." Team effort, shared individual strengths, shared beliefs, and dependability make team collaboration successful. Collaboration is the main support of successful inclusive strategies and practices. The desired outcome of meeting the needs of *all* students can be realized with inclusion.

Linda L. Brady
Early Childhood Special Educator
Jefferson County (Alabama) Board of Education

Thematic Summary

- Teachers today no longer work in isolation. The demands placed upon educators by an increasingly diverse student population require that teachers work in partnership with other professionals as well as parents.
- We view collaboration as a cooperative relationship between two or more individuals who are committed to working toward a mutually agreed upon goal.
- Collaboration between general education teachers and special educators is vital for creating inclusive learning communities.
- It is increasingly common to find paraprofessionals providing instructional as well as noninstructional support to students with and without disabilities or special needs.
- Creating partnerships with parents/families is crucial to a learner's success at school; especially for children with exceptionalities.

- Collaborative consultation is one way in which the classroom teacher can receive direct assistance from other professionals. This process involves not only the sharing of expertise but the sharing of responsibility and accountability as well.
- The three most common types of educational teams are the multidisciplinary, interdisciplinary, and transdisciplinary service delivery models.
- Cooperative teaching, or co-teaching, as it is sometimes called, is a popular strategy for achieving inclusion. It is a special type of teaming in which a general educator and a special educator jointly deliver instruction to a diverse group of learners in the general education classroom.

Making Connections for Inclusive Teaching

1. What do you see as the advantages and disadvantages of establishing partnerships between general educators and special education teachers? What role does collaboration play in the inclusion process?
2. Think about the unique features of multi-, inter-, and transdisciplinary teams. Which model is most efficient and effective in a school setting? Why?
3. What are your personal feelings about cooperative teaching as a service delivery model? Is this an instructional approach that you wish to experience? How prepared are you to engage in co-teaching relationships? What concerns, if any, do you have about working in this type of setting?

Learning Activities

1. Develop a list of activities that you would incorporate in your classroom to meaningfully involve family members of children who are culturally or linguistically diverse.
2. "Shadow" a paraprofessional for a day. What types of pupils did he or she work with? In what types of classroom settings did they perform their duties? Maintain a list of this individual's roles and responsibilities. Learn about his or her professional background. What type of training or preparation did they receive and who provided this experience? Compare your findings with those of your classmates.
3. Interview several teachers and other school professionals about their experiences with collaborative consultation. With whom do they frequently collaborate? Do they view this process as beneficial? How often do they engage in collaborative consultation? What do these teachers see as the advantages and disadvantages of this type of relationship?
4. Visit schools in your area that engage in cooperative teaching. What form of cooperative teaching did you see? How do the teachers feel about this form of teaming? What do they see as the advantages and disadvantages of cooperative teaching? Would you like to teach in a co-teaching arrangement? Why or why not?

Looking at the Standards

The content of the chapter most closely aligns itself with the following standards:

INTASC Standards

- *Student Development.* The teacher understands how children learn and develop, and can provide learning opportunities that support their intellectual, social, and personal development.

- *Diverse Learners*. The teacher understands how students differ in their approaches to learning and creates instructional opportunities that are adapted to diverse learners.
- *Multiple Instructional Resources*. The teacher understands and uses a variety of instructional strategies to encourage students' development of critical thinking, problem solving, and performance skills.

Council for Exceptional Children

Special educators are to have knowledge of the following:

- CC10K1: Models and strategies of consultation and collaboration.
- CC10K2: Roles of individuals with exceptional learning needs, families, and school and community personnel in planning of an individualized program.
- CC10K4: Culturally responsive factors that promote effective communication and collaboration with individuals with exceptional learning needs, families, school personnel, and community members.
- CC7K5: Roles and responsibilities of the paraeducators related to instruction, intervention, and direct service.
- GC4K3: Advantages and limitations of instructional strategies and practices for teaching individuals with disabilities.
- GC10K4: Co-planning and co-teaching methods to strengthen content acquisition of individuals with disabilities.

Key Concepts and Terms

collaboration	collaborative consultation	interdisciplinary
paraprofessionals	indirect consultation	transdisciplinary
cultural sensitivity	multidisciplinary	cooperative teaching

References

Anderegg, M., Vergason, G., & Smith, M. (1992). A visual representation of the grief cycle for use by teachers with families of children with disabilities. *Remedial and Special Education, 13*(2), 17–23.

Bauwens, J., & Hourcade, J. (1991). Making co-teaching a mainstreaming strategy. *Preventing School Failure, 35*(1), 19–24.

Berry, J., & Hardman, M. (1998). *Lifespan perspectives on the family and disability.* Needham Heights, MA: Allyn & Bacon.

Blacher, J. (1984). A dynamic perspective on the impact of a severely handicapped child on the family. In J. Blacher (Ed.), *Severely handicapped children and their families* (pp. 3–50). Orlando, FL: Academic Press.

Bowe, F. (2005). *Making inclusion work.* Upper Saddle River, NJ: Pearson Education.

Bruder, M. (1994). Working with members of other disciplines: Collaboration for success. In M. Wolery & J. Wilbers (Eds.), *Including children with special needs in early childhood programs* (pp. 45–70). Washington, DC: National Association for the Education of Young Children.

Carroll, D. (2001). Considering paraeducators training, roles, and responsibilities. *Teaching Exceptional Children, 34*(2), 60–64.

Cook, R., Klein, M., & Tessier, A. (2008). *Adapting early childhood curricula for children in inclusive settings* (7th ed.). Upper Saddle River, NJ: Pearson Education.

Council for Exceptional Children. (2008). *Paraeducators.* Retrieved May 7, 2008 from http://www.cec.sped.org/AM/Template .cfm?Section=Job_Profiles&Template=/CM/ContentDisplay .cfm&ContentID=2086

Dennis, R., & Giangreco, M. (1996). Creating conversation: Reflections on cultural sensitivity in family interviewing. *Exceptional Children, 63*(1), 103–116.

Dover, W. (2005). Consult and support students with special needs in inclusive classrooms. *Intervention in School and Clinic, 41*(1), 32–35.

Fiedler, C., Simpson, R., & Clark, D. (2007). *Parents and families of children with disabilities.* Upper Saddle River, NJ: Pearson Education.

Freund, L., & Rich, R. (2005). *Teaching students with learning problems in the inclusive classroom.* Upper Saddle River, NJ: Pearson Education.

Friend, M., & Cook, L. (2007). *Interactions: Collaboration skills for school professionals* (5th ed.). Needham Heights, MA: Allyn & Bacon.

Friend, M., & Hurley-Chamberlain, D. (2006). *Is co-teaching effective?* Retrieved May 18, 2008 from http://www.cec.sped.org/AM/PrinterTemplate.cfm?Section=Home&TEMPLATE=/CM/ContentDisplay.cfm&CONTENTID=7504

Gargiulo, R. (1985). *Working with parents of exceptional children.* Boston: Houghton Mifflin.

Gargiulo, R. (2009). *Special education in contemporary society* (3rd ed.). Thousand Oaks, CA: Sage.

Gargiulo, R., & Kilgo, J. (2005). *Young children with special needs* (2nd ed.). Clifton Park, NY: Delmar.

Hobbs, T., & Westling, D. (1998). Promoting successful inclusion through collaborative problem solving. *Teaching Exceptional Children, 31*(1), 12–19.

Holland, K. (2006). Understanding the parent of the special needs child. *Exceptional Parent, 36*(8), 60–62.

Hourcade, J., & Bauwens, J. (2003). *Cooperative teaching: Rebuilding and sharing the schoolhouse* (2nd ed.). Austin, TX: Pro-Ed.

Idol, L., Nevin, A., & Paolucci-Whitcomb, P. (1994). *Collaborative consultation* (2nd ed.). Austin, TX: Pro-Ed.

Kalyanpur, M., & Harry, B. (1999). *Culture in special education.* Baltimore: Paul H. Brookes.

Keefe, E., Moore, V., & Duff, F. (2004). The four "knows" of collaborative teaching. *Teaching Exceptional Children, 36*(5), 36–41.

Kübler-Ross, E. (1969). *On death and dying.* New York: Macmillan.

Lamar-Dukes, P., & Dukes, C. (2005). Consider the roles and responsibilities of the inclusion support teacher. *Intervention in School and Clinic, 41*(1), 55–61.

Lambie, R. (2000). *Family systems within educational context* (2nd ed.). Denver: Love.

McCormick, L., Loeb, D., & Schiefelbusch, R. (2003). *Supporting children with communication difficulties in inclusive settings* (2nd ed.). Boston: Allyn & Bacon.

McDonnell, J., Hardman, M., & McDonnell, A. (2003). *Introduction to persons with moderate and severe disabilities* (2nd ed.). Needham Heights, MA: Allyn & Bacon.

McGoningel, M., Woodruff, C., & Roszmann-Millican, M. (1994). The transdisciplinary team: A model for family-centered early intervention. In L. Johnson, R. Gallagher, M. LaMontagne, J. Jordan, J. Gallagher, P. Hutinger, & M. Karnes (Eds.), *Meeting early intervention challenges* (pp. 95–131). Baltimore: Paul H. Brookes.

Murawski, W. (2006). Student outcomes in co-taught secondary English classes: How can we improve? *Reading and Writing Quarterly, 22*(3), 227–247.

Murawski, W., & Dieker, L. (2004). Tips and strategies for co-teaching at the secondary level. *Teaching Exceptional Children, 36*(5), 52–58.

Murawski, W., & Swanson, H. (2001). A meta-analysis of co-teaching research: Where are the data? *Remedial and Special Education, 22*(5), 258–267.

Murray, C. (2004). Clarifying collaborative roles in urban high schools: General educators perspectives. *Teaching Exceptional Children, 36*(5), 44–51.

Parette, H., & Petch-Hogan, B. (2000). Approaching families: Facilitating culturally/linguistically diverse family involvement. *Teaching Exceptional Children, 33*(2), 4–10.

Polloway, E., Patton, J., & Serna, L. (2008). *Strategies for teaching learners with special needs* (9th ed.). Upper Saddle River, NJ: Pearson Education.

Pugach, M., & Johnson, L. (2002). *Collaborative practitioners, collaborative schools* (2nd ed.). Denver: Love.

Reinhiller, N. (1996). Co-teaching: New variations on a not-so-new practice. *Teacher Education and Special Education, 19*(1), 34–48.

Salend, S. (2008). *Creating inclusive classrooms* (6th ed.). Upper Saddle River, NJ: Pearson Education.

Salend, S., & Taylor, L. (1993). Working with families: A cross-cultural perspective. *Remedial and Special Education, 14*(5), 25–32, 39.

Scruggs, T., Mastropieri, M., & McDuffie, K. (2007). Co-teaching in inclusive classrooms: A metasynthesis of qualitative research. *Exceptional Children, 73*(4), 392–416.

Sileo, T., Sileo, A., & Prater, M. (1996). Parent and professional partnership in special education. *Intervention in School and Clinic, 31*(3), 145–153.

Smith, T., Gartin, B., Murdick, N., & Hilton, A. (2006). *Families and children with special needs.* Upper Saddle River, NJ: Pearson Education.

Spencer, S. (2005). Lynne Cook and June Downing: The practicalities of collaboration in special education service delivery. *Intervention in School and Clinic, 40*(5), 296–300.

Turnbull, A., Turnbull, H., Erwin, E., & Soodak, L. (2006). *Families, professionals, and exceptionality* (5th ed.). Upper Saddle River, NJ: Pearson Education.

U.S. Department of Education. (2008). *IDEA data.* Retrieved May 12, 2008 from http://www.ideadata.org/PartBReport.asp

Voltz, D. (1995). Learning and cultural diversities in general and special education classes: Frameworks for success. *Multiple Voices for Ethnically Diverse Exceptional Learners, 1*(1), 1–11.

Voltz, D. (1998). Cultural diversity and special education teacher preparation: Critical issues confronting the field. *Teacher Education and Special Education, 21*(1), 63–70.

Walsh, J., & Jones, B. (2004). New models of cooperative teaching. *Teaching Exceptional Children, 36*(5), 14–20.

Walther-Thomas, C., Korinek, L., McLaughlin, V., & Williams, B. (2000). *Collaboration for inclusive education.* Needham Heights, MA: Allyn & Bacon.

Wiggins, K., & Damore, S. (2006). "Survivors" or "friends"? A framework for assessing effective collaboration. *Teaching Exceptional Children, 38*(5), 49–56.

Wilson, G., & Michaels, C. (2006). General and special education students' perceptions of co-teaching: Implications for secondary-level literacy instruction. *Reading and Writing Quarterly, 22*(3), 205–225.

Wood, J. (2006). *Teaching students in inclusive settings* (5th ed.). Upper Saddle River, NJ: Pearson Education.

Zigmond, N., & Magiera, L. (2001). Current pratice alerts: A focus on co-teaching: Use with caution. *Alerts, 6*, 1–4.

Assistive Technology: Key to Accessing the General Education Curriculum
Academic Outcomes
Learner Needs and Preferences
Differentiated Instruction and Assistive Technology
Function over Disability

A Framework for Selecting Assistive Technology
The Student
The Environment(s)
The Task(s)
The Tool(s)

Active Learning through Innovative Technology

Social Software Tools

Visual and Media Literacy Tools

Opportunities through Technology

Imagine yourself in your classroom with the learning tools of the future. Typical textbook lectures are replaced by interactive journeys through virtual learning environments and microworlds. Visualize your students learning about Newton's Laws of Motion in a 3-D immersive environment where they experience each law firsthand as they apply different forces on an object and explore the outcomes (Zoning in on Physics, 2001). Imagine your students completing challenging learning tasks, things they thought they could never do. Imagine a lesson on meiosis and mitosis where the Internet and multimedia software encourages students to go beyond basic understanding to explore and develop critical-thinking skills about nuclear division through real-world application (CELLS alive!, 2006).

Go ahead; take a look inside, move around the classroom. Instead of student desks, you see learning pods, where three to four students can collaborate and engage in teamwork. Seated within the pods are personal computers that are connected to the classroom network. Teaching activities and teacher and student notes can be seen on each team member's monitor. Instead of seeing students with their heads down on their desks because they are bored, you see students involved in hands-on projects and creative problem solving. Students with diverse abilities, needs, and experiences are exploring and using a variety of assistive technologies such as text-to-speech software, word prediction software, screen magnification software, and/or mind-mapping software to accomplish academic tasks necessary for educational achievement. Imagine a classroom of youngsters using laptops, instant text messaging, and personal digital assistants (PDAs) to collect data and research the topic at hand.

Imagine your teacher duties such as taking attendance being eliminated due to an automated computer log-on screen with biometric software initiated at each student's pod. (Wikipedia defines **biometrics**—ancient Greek: bios = "life," metron = "measure"—as the study of automated methods for uniquely recognizing humans based on one or more intrinsic physical or behavioral traits. Examples of physical characteristics include fingerprints, eye retinas and irises, facial patterns, and hand measurements.)

Imagine self-monitored electronic student portfolios created simply by taking current work at the end of the day and displaying in appropriate categories or files electronically. Imagine grades being given by a computer that has artificial intelligence and can determine the actual percentage of effort a student applied to a particular teamwork assignment. For some, this could mean completing an electronic research project, or inventing a new product; for others this could be communicating simple sentences through the use of an augmentative communication device to express current feelings and ideas essential to being a contributing team member. Imagine student performance data collected and the ability to adjust the curriculum to meet the educational needs of all students. Imagine yourself as a 21st-century educator.

As 21st-century educators, we must accept the fact that in order to prepare our students to be successful in a technology-infused global economy, it is imperative to incorporate and effectively use technology as a tool for teaching and learning (Brooks-Young, 2006). Interestingly enough, the tools described above actually exist and are infused in some of today's classrooms.

Digital Native or Digital Immigrant?

Are you under 30 years of age? Have you ever seen any of the following items? (a) a telephone with a rotary dial; (b) 5¼-inch floppy computer disk; (c) an eight-track tape; or (d) a record player? Can you remember a time in society without cell phones or scanning cash registers (Brooks-Young, 2006)? If you answered yes to only the first question above, you are most likely a digital native.

Digital natives spend their entire lives surrounded by technology such as computer, videogames, DVD players, digital cameras, cell phones, and other tools and gadgets of the digital age (Prensky, 2001). Digital natives prefer to process information through pictures, sounds, and video before reading text. They want instant gratification and instant rewards or feedback. They prefer to multitask and process information from multiple sources. Digital natives believe that learning should be relevant, instantly useful, and fun. Brooks-Young (2006) shares that it is typical for digital natives to be doing several things at once, such as watching television, reviewing a website, taking notes, and instant messaging friends. Prensky states "Our students today are all 'native speakers' of the digital language of computers, video games and the Internet" (p. 1).

In contrast, **digital immigrants** are typically over the age of 30. They have experienced a childhood without cell phones, personal computers, and the Information Highway. Although they were not born into the digital world, at some point they begin to become fascinated by and embrace different aspects of new technology (Prensky, 2001). Digital immigrants tend to be linear in their approach to learning and prefer to complete one task before going onto another. They prefer slow and controlled amounts of information from limited resources. They read text before looking at pictures or exploring sounds and video. They learn to use technology similar to learning a new language after childhood. They learn new technology in reference to their previous learning. As a result they often complete familiar tasks faster but tend to ignore how to complete such tasks in new ways thus not using technology to its fullest potential (Brooks-Young, 2006). Prensky shares many examples of the differences between digital natives and digital immigrants. He shares that digital immigrants tend to keep an "accent." He illustrates the digital immigrant accent with such examples as printing out your e-mail, printing out a document in order to read and edit it (rather than just editing on the screen), and phoning someone and asking them if they got the e-mail you sent.

Are you a digital native or a digital immigrant? Why does it matter? Whether you are a digital native or a digital immigrant, your comfort level and use of technology is essential to the classroom. Research has documented that one of the impediments to technology use in our schools is the fact that most of the teachers in classrooms today did not grow up as technology users themselves (Brooks-Young, 2006). Prensky (2001) cautions us to take a closer look at the impact of digital immigrant instructors teaching a population (digital natives) that speaks a new language. Digital immigrants can no longer assume that their students can and will

Cengage Learning/Wadsworth

High-tech classroom environments can foster active learning and collaboration to meet the needs of students with diverse abilities.

learn the same as they did. Today's learners are different. Prensky states, "Our students have changed radically. Today's students are no longer the people our educational system was designed to teach" (p. 1). Future educators will have to take a closer look and gain insight to the impact of technology on thinking and learning in order for students to achieve. Digital natives who become educators will have to take the lead in redesigning curriculum and infusing technology into learning activities as effective learning tools. They have the insight and firsthand experience needed to communicate in the language and learning style of their students.

Technology Myths and Facts

Technology has been in the classroom for over 25 years. Throughout these years, technology has been incorporated into learning and teaching activities with varying degrees of success. Computers have proved to be valuable in supporting teaching, learning, and professional development. Although technology has been around for over two decades; myths about the magic of technology still persist (Caldwell, 1981; Woronov, 1994). Here are some computer myths and facts that you might find interesting.

Myth #1: Computers dehumanize the learning process. This myth began in the early 1980s and is still lingering today. People believe that computers will remove the human element from learning. Computers will eliminate the need for humans to process information. Although, in today's society where calculators and touch-screen cash registers play a vital role, there is still a need for a person to interact with the technology in order to perform basic functions or for any means of learning to take place. This leads us to Myth #2.

Myth #2: Computers will replace teachers. Not so fast here. Computer-assisted instruction provides students with a very systematic means in approaching new learning and practicing new skills in multiple ways or formats. For example, phonics can be practiced through a variety of word games or drill-and-practice activities (e.g., Earobics software, Wordmaker software, Simon Sounds it Out software, and interactive websites such as PawPark3 http://www.cogcon.com/gamegoo/games/pawpark3/pawpark3.html). It is important to realize that the skills being practiced through computer-assisted instruction must first be taught. Another use of technology is to provide an avenue for an inductive approach to inquiry or problem solving into the content or subject matter. In this case, the teacher must facilitate students through the mental processes that they must employ in order to be successful problem solvers. Let's take a closer look at problem solving in our next myth.

Myth #3: Computers build "thinking" and "problem-solving skills." Woronov (1994) shares that the jury is still out on trying to determine if there are cognitive benefits in the use of computers, multimedia, or "edutainment" (computer games with nominally educational content). Researchers are still discovering what kinds of cognitive benefits that technology may bring and effective ways to measure or determine such learning outcomes.

Myth #4: Computers and technological resources such as the Internet will narrow inequities in U.S. education. Just depends. Over 97 percent of kindergarteners have access to a computer at school and home. The National Education Technology Plan (U.S. Department of Education, 2004) documents that over the past decade, 99 percent of our schools have been connected to the Internet with a 5:1 student-to-computer ratio. Yet how are these computers being implemented at school? Previous investigations reveal that students in poorer school districts or in lower academic tracks were often only exposed to drill-and-practice work on the computers, while "brighter" students were using computers for other academic tasks such as problem solving and inquiry (Woronov, 1994). If this is the case, then the inequities will continue to exist. One thing is for sure, students are mastering the wonders of the Internet at home and not in our schools (U.S. Department of Education). As future educators you are the teachers who are going to change the way we use technology for teaching and learning.

Myth #5: Kids love computers, so they must be learning. Just by being engaged in computer activity doesn't mean students are learning anything important from them (Woronov, 1994). In an interview, educational technologist, Seymour Papert shares, "It's one thing for a child to play a computer game; it's another thing altogether for a child to build his or her own game. And this, according to Papert, is where the computer's true power as an educational medium lies—in the ability to facilitate and extend children's awesome natural ability and drive to construct, hypothesize, explore, experiment, evaluate, draw conclusions—in short to learn—all by themselves" (Schwartz, 1999, p. 1). It is this very drive that technology and future educators need to encourage learning through inquiry and exploration of true interests and passions.

Although many computer myths exist, it is equally important to become familiar with the findings found through two decades of scientific investigations of the impact of computers in the classroom. Research-based evidence (U.S. Department of Education, 2004) reveals some interesting facts about computers and our schools:

- **Fact #1—The largest group of new users of the Internet from 2000–2002 were 2- to 5-year-olds**.
- **Fact #2—Only a few schools are slowly embracing technology to redesign curricula and organizational structures**. In other words, few schools are actually changing what and how they teach and learn through technology.
- **Fact #3—Lack of technology training for teachers is documented as a major barrier in the use of technology in our schools**.
- **Fact #4—Computers and new standards**. Nearly 50 million students attend today's elementary, middle, and high schools in America. These students represent the largest and most diverse student body (30% minority) in history. Technology is providing an efficient mechanism to collect and

synthesize student academic performance data in relation to racial and ethnic groups. Such data reveals alarming gaps in achievement among students. It is reported that in the fourth grade, only 41 percent of Whites, 38 percent of Asians, 13 percent of African Americans, 15 percent of Hispanics, and 16 percent of Native Americans are reading at grade level. Similar findings have been found in the area of mathematics.

New educational standards provide higher expectations of student learning outcomes. State standardized testing is used to validate learning achievement. In addition to academic standards, all but three states (Minnesota, Mississippi, and South Dakota) include technology standards for students in order for them to be better prepared for the 21st century (Ringstaff & Kelley, 2002). Interestingly, only four states—Arizona, New York, North Carolina, and Utah—actually test students on the state technology standards (Ringstaff & Kelley). Innovative software provides school districts with the tools needed to monitor student performance in comparison to factors such curriculum, resources, and student demographics. This is often referred to as data mining.

- **Fact #5—Computers can increase student performance on standardized tests**. Computer-assisted instruction and drill-and-practice software can significantly improve students' scores on standardized achievement tests. Findings from over 500 individual studies of computer-based instruction showed significant gains on achievement tests. In addition, it was found that computers reduced the amount of time required for students to learn basic skills (Ringstaff & Kelley, 2002).

- **Fact #6—Technology can increase student motivation and improve self-concept**. Over 300 research studies found technology to have a positive effect on student attitudes toward learning, self-confidence, self-esteem, school attendance, and dropout rates. Technology also had a positive impact on student's independence and feelings of responsibility for their own learning (Ringstaff & Kelley, 2002).

- **Fact #7—Inclusion of students with disabilities**. One of the most powerful uses of technology in education is to individualize instruction for students with disabilities (Ringstaff & Kelley, 2002). Technology has enabled students with a wide range of disabilities to participate fully in the general education curriculum and develop skills previously considered beyond expectations (Woronov, 1994).

Technology for People with Disabilities

In this chapter, you will be learning about the laws that mandate the use of technology for individuals with disabilities; definition and examples of assistive technology, the role of assistive technology in accessing the educational curriculum, and other innovative learning tools. Up to this point, only computer technology and its impact in the classroom has been introduced. To gain a better understanding and appreciation of how technology has improved lives of those with disabilities, it might be helpful to take a glance back in time.

Historically, major technological breakthroughs for individuals with disabilities were a result of innovative research and development in the military and through medical advancements. Since the early 1800s, technology has been used to address the unique needs of people with disabilities. Here are a few examples excerpted from the research of A. E. Blackhurst (2005):

- In 1803 the use of raised dots for military messages known as *night writing* was used by soldiers to communicate after dark. This paved the way for the development of Braille code in 1834 by Louis Braille. Braille is accepted throughout the world as the fundamental form of written communication for individuals with blindness, and it remains basically as Louis Braille invented it (Brunson, 2005).

- In 1863, a socket with a suction cup was developed to attach lower-limb prosthesis.
- In 1892, the Braille typewriter was developed. In the early 1900s the first electrical amplifying device for people with hearing impairments was invented.
- In 1926, the first audiometer was developed to identify hearing impairments.
- In 1945, improvements in prosthetic limbs were made to meet the needs of wounded World War II veterans.
- In 1966, the laser cane was developed for use by people who are blind.
- In 1957, the Russians launched a satellite called Sputnik, which provided a driving force for U.S. military to investigate and develop a transit system of satellites later to be used for the Global Positioning System (GPS).
- In 1967, the atomic clock technology was refined and made available. Through a series of such military research involving satellites and atomic time, GPS was created in 1993 for military use.
- In 1996, the White House had made available a modified GPS to be used by anyone. Blind people and others achieve independent mobility through the availability and responsiveness of Braille, audio, and visual navigation provided by today's GPS. Many new automobiles have GPS built into the dash to provide just-in-time directional assistance.

Medical advances have enabled individuals with disabilities to live productive lives in their own homes and communities. The 20th century brought remarkable medical and technological advancements (Blackhurst, 2005). From 1914 with the development of the low-tech Simplex Hearing tube that was used to collect and funnel sound to facilitate hearing to the high-tech Cochlear implant approved in 1984.

Cengage Learning/Wadsworth

Student performance on standardized achievement tests can increase with computer-assisted instruction, skill drill, and test-taking practice.

Other advancements include laser surgery for the treatment of visual loss, ventilators to aid in breathing, feeding tubes for those who cannot take food orally and the use of microchips to regain movement and use of paralyzed muscles (Blackhurst, 2005). These are just as few examples of how technology has the potential for improving the quality of life for individuals with disabilities.

The Definition of Assistive Technology

The definition of an assistive technology device has been defined throughout legislative mandates. The Assistive Technology Act of 2004 (PL 108-364) defines an **assistive technology device** as "any item, piece of equipment or product system, whether acquired commercially off the shelf, modified, or customized, that is used to increase, maintain, or improve functional capabilities of individuals with disabilities." This definition has also been used in the Individuals with Disabilities Education Improvement Act of 2004 (IDEA) (PL 108-446) and the Americans with Disabilities Act (ADA) (PL 101-336). Within the legislation is also the definition of **assistive technology services**, which is defined as "any service that directly assists an individual with a disability in the selection, acquisition, or use of an assistive technology device" (Assistive Technology Act of 2004 [PL 108-364]).

It is important to realize that the potential range of assistive technology devices and services are incredibly broad and should be taken in careful consideration for each individual (Behrmann, 1998). Assistive technology isn't a one-size-fits-all concept. Classroom teachers must carefully look at the individual strengths and needs of each student and what technology would be needed to access the curriculum and achieve successful academic outcomes.

Examples of Assistive Technology

Assistive technology (AT) can support all types of learners. Generally speaking, it has two fundamental purposes: (1) It can enhance an individual's strength so that his or her abilities counterbalance the effort of any disabilities, and (2) it can provide an alternate mode of performing a task so that disabilities are compensated for or bypassed entirely (Lewis, 1998). For example, Tomeshia is a 5th-grade student identified as having dyslexia. She has very strong auditory skills and relies on them for learning new information. In order to complete a major research paper, the use of a text-to-speech software program that highlights the word as it is being read can build on such auditory strengths to achieve the academic task. If Tomeshia wanted to eliminate or bypass her text challenge altogether, she could get information and research her topic through podcasts, MP3s, and other audio resources.

AT is not a luxury; it is a necessity for individuals with disabilities to achieve everyday tasks to reach their dreams and aspirations.

Assistive technology can be subdivided into the following common areas:

1. Communication aids
2. Daily living aids
3. Ergonomic aids
4. Environmental aids
5. Sensory aids
6. Mobility and transportation aids
7. Seating and positioning aids
8. Sports, recreation, and leisure aids
9. Computer access aids
10. Education and learning aids

Let's take a closer look at each (see Table 6.1).

Table 6.1   Ten Common Areas of Assistive Technologies

Assistive Technology Area	Examples	
Ten Common Areas of Assistive Technologies and Examples		
1. Communication	• Picture communication boards • Single message switches	• Multiple message output devices • Communications software
2. Daily Living	• Picture schedules • Dressing stick, zipper pull, button hook	• Adapted bathing aids • Adapted cooking and eating utensils
3. Ergonomic	• Adjustable tables • Wrist/arm supports	• Adapted furniture • Adjustable lighting
4. Environmental	• Switch-operated appliances • Automatic doors	• Adapted doorknobs • Swimming pool lifts
5. Sensory	• Personal amplification system • Braille transcription	• Screen magnifiers • Audiobooks
6. Mobility and Transportation	• Standing and walking devices • Scooters	• Wheelchairs • Transfer aids
7. Seating and Positioning	• Support cushions or braces • Chairlifts	• Seat wedges • Standing tables
8. Sports, Recreation, and Leisure	• Modified sports equipment • Adapted video games	• Video descriptions and captioning • Modified cameras
9. Computer Access	• Screen readers • Eye-gaze systems	• Alternative and adaptive mice and keyboards • Voice recognition software, and on-screen keyboards
10. Education and Learning	• Graphic organizers • Word prediction software	• Personal digital assistants (PDAs) • Talking calculators

Communication Aids

Communication aids are designed to assist individuals in language and communication tasks. Such tasks might involve initiating a conversation with your friends, communicating your needs and wants to those around you, or talking on the telephone, or exchanging information at school and social events. Communication among teachers and students is an intrinsic component of learning (Ball, Bilyeu, Prentice, & Beukelman, 2005). Think for a moment about your classroom and having a student that cannot communicate his/her needs or respond to your class questions. How would you teach and assess this student? How would you provide the student with the strategies and assistive technology tools that could make this possible? When students are unable to communicate needs through traditional modalities such as speech, listening, reading and writing then communication aids can provide necessary support (Ball et al.). Examples of communication devices range from selecting choices from a picture communication board, single message switches, communication templates/software, and multiple message output devices.

Daily Living Aids

Daily living aids include a wide variety of devices that increases participation in daily activities such as cooking, bathing, personal hygiene, dressing, and toilet aids. Completing or not completing such tasks can have a positive or negative impact on the classroom. Surprisingly enough, an important role of any classroom teacher is to ensure that their students' daily living needs are being met. Although you may not have an academic unit on personal hygiene in your content area curriculum, you may find your role is to model and monitor appropriate hygiene and dress for your students. Many students need guidance and assistance in this area. If a student's basic daily living needs are not being met then the student enters the classroom with the inability to focus on the academic tasks at hand. One advantage is to be aware of daily living aids to advocate students to practice personal hygiene skills.

Daily living aids may include a picture schedule of hygiene tasks to be used as a reminder what should be complete in the morning, a shower bench, long-handled hairbrush, adapted bathing aids, dressing stick, zipper pull, easy-grip eating utensils, adapted plates, and cups.

Ergonomic Aids

Ergonomic aids assist us in completing everyday repetitive tasks without causing undue stress to parts of our bodies. Often at work or in the classroom, our work-stations can cause injury due to repetitive job/learning tasks. Take a closer look at your own work area. Do you have a comfortable adjustable chair? Is your computer monitor at the appropriate height? Are you looking down on your computer screen rather than looking up with a bent neck? As we design learning areas in the class-room we need to keep ergonomics in mind. We need to provide the appropriate tools that allow us and our students to complete tasks in a comfortable and efficient manner. Such aids include adjustable-height work tables, adapted furniture, wrist/arm supports, back supports, and adjustable lighting.

Environmental Aids

"All school buildings today are required to be accessible for individuals with physical disabilities or mobility challenges. Accessibility doesn't stop at the front door of the school building" (George, Schaff, & Jeffs, 2005, p. 373). As a classroom teacher, it is your responsibility to create a classroom community in which all students are active participants and engaged in learning. You will need to pay particular attention to your classroom physical surroundings. Are work areas, activity areas, and materials accessible to all students? Can a student with limited use of their hands access the stapler or your classroom resource library? Environmental aids reduce or eliminate physical barriers for individuals with disabilities. Such aids may include the use of environmental control units that allow students to turn small appliances on or off with their voice or a single switch, switch-operated scissors, lowered counters or work space, adapted doorknobs on cabinets, well-planned activity centers, or labora-tories with adapted furniture. Often you will find literacy-rich classroom environ-ments that label items within the environment with both a picture and text to display its purpose or use to the students. Other environmental aids you may see in schools include wheelchair lifts, swimming pool lifts, elevators, and automatic doors.

Sensory Aids

Students with sensory disabilities such as those who are blind, visually impaired, deaf, hearing impaired, or have difficulty with the sense of touch may benefit from the use of sensory aids and instructional accommodations to make learning materials and the learning environment more accessible. Providing materials in different for-mats can minimize access challenges. This can be accomplished by taking printed material and recording it onto audiotapes or taking text and printing it from a Braille output device. In return, providing access to information in an audio format for stu-dents with hearing impairments or deafness can be accomplished by converting the same information into a text-based format. Sensory aids in the classroom might include items such as personal amplification systems, hearing aids, assistive listening devices, Braille transcription and translation devices, screen magnifiers, large-print books, audiobooks, and closed-circuit television for magnifying class documents.

Mobility and Transportation Aids

Mobility and transportation aids provide a means for which students with disabilities can gain independence when moving within their classrooms and the school environ-ment as a whole. Barrier-free environments work well for everyone. Everyone can benefit from aisles that are at least 35½ inches wide between student desks, with shelving, coat hooks, and lockers at reachable levels. Mobility and transportation aids enable independence and self-confidence through the use of such aids as standing and walking devices, scooters, wheelchairs, stair lifts, and transfer aids. As you begin to think about student mobility and traffic patterns in your future classroom take the time to plan out activity or designated learning areas so that every student can maneuver safely and efficiently. Make sure items are within all the students' reach and can be removed safely off a shelf independently without the risk of the shelving unit tipping over and hurting a student.

Seating and Positioning Aids

Seating and positioning aids assist students with mobility impairments or other disabilities by providing greater body stability, posture, and needed support. Such aids include adapted seating, support cushions or wedges, braces, chairlifts, standing tables, and wheelchair modifications. Occupational and physical therapists work closely with individual students and often consult with classroom teachers to make sure seating and positioning needs are being met. On a daily basis, you should observe your students seating and positioning needs and communicate any signs of being uncomfortable, irritable, or restless. Be sure to initiate and keep open communication with the therapists working with the students in your classroom.

Sports, Recreation, and Leisure Aids

Sports, recreation, and leisure activities are essential elements to enjoying a quality life. Such activities are embedded within the school environment through special interest groups, clubs, and sports. We meet new friends, develop social skills and competencies, and spend time with others who have similar likes and interests. Extracurricular activities empower students to make their own decisions, voice their own opinions, gain experiences, and build leadership skills that are beneficial in everyday life. Through personal encouragement and the use of adapted sports, recreation, and leisure aids students with disabilities can become involved in their school environment through extracurricular activities. Such aids include modified sports equipment, audio descriptions and captioning for movies, adapted video games, modified skis, rackets, musical instruments, adapted spinners and game pieces, and modified cameras to name just a few. If you are involved in coaching or sponsoring an extracurricular activity (e.g., drama club, chess club, computer club), encourage all students to take advantage of the great opportunity to get involved. In most cases minimal adaptations or modifications are usually needed in order to ensure a student to become successful.

Computer Access Aids

With more and more emphasis placed on computer use in our schools and in society; computer access is essential for today's learners to flourish and become successful. Computer hardware and software access aids enable individuals with disabilities to access, interact, and productively use a computer at school or work. These include screen readers, alternative and adaptive mice, adapted keyboards, key guards, head-operated pointing devices, eye-gaze systems, switch access, voice-recognition software, and on-screen keyboards. Video examples of computer access are available at AssistiveWare (http://www.assistiveware.com/videos.php).

Education and Learning Aids

When purchasing classroom software, investigate the software's ability to be modified to meet the specific needs of the end user. For example, can time limitations be removed? Can the access method be changed (touch screen, switch, or mouse

Student with low vision can access class materials using a computer with a screen magnifier in an inclusive setting.

access)? Can background colors and font colors be changed? Is text described in a sound narrative or video? Are videos or verbal instructions displayed through text? All of these features can make a software program more accessible for students with disabilities and should be considered when selecting and purchasing software for your classroom.

Assistive Technology: Key to Accessing the General Education Curriculum

Educational/learning technologies are used to teach students essential skills needed in the content areas. Such skills include matching, associations, reasoning, decision making, and problem solving. In addition, students must also possess good reading and writing skills, organizational skills, math skills, verbal, and listening skills in order to be successful in the classroom. Educational and learning aids include picture cards, highlighters, flashcards, text-to-speech software, audiobooks, Internet resources, raised lined paper, graphic organizers, personal reminder systems, personal digital assistants, and many, many more devices and software. The remainder of this chapter will focus on the use of assistive technology and innovative technology in the classroom, specifically focusing on educational/learning tools and strategies.

Academic Outcomes

The primary purpose of assistive technology is to maximize an individual's ability in completing a task by minimizing barriers and unleashing potential to achieve desired outcomes. There are three basic categories of assistive technology: (1) no-tech, (2) low-tech, and (3) high-tech. No-tech is simply that; no technology is involved in finding a solution in completing a task or achieving the desired outcomes. For example, no-tech solutions for writing may include using such things as using highlighters, index cards, rulers, prompts, or cues. No-tech also involves strategies such as extended time, and chunking the information or task into

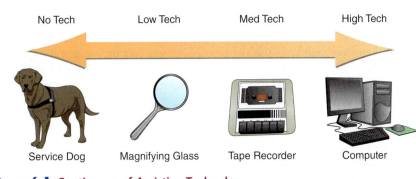

No Tech   Low Tech   Med Tech   High Tech

Service Dog   Magnifying Glass   Tape Recorder   Computer

Figure 6.1 Continuum of Assistive Technology
Source: Cindy L. George, Kellar Institute for Human DisAbilities, George Mason University.

manageable components. Low-technology solutions involves simple technologies such as slanted writing board, adapted pencil grip, specialized lined paper, step-by-step picture reminders, tape recorder, and/or printed labels with essential vocabulary. A high-tech solution typically involves the computer or has its own computer components. Specialized software and advanced hardware devices fall into this category. High-tech solutions for writing might include voice recognition software, modified keyboards, talking word processors, talking dictionary, word prediction, graphic organizers, and/or a web-based visual thesaurus.

When considering assistive technology, one must keep in mind that the simpler the better in reaching a technology solution. No-tech solutions should be tried first and moving progressively along the continuum to high-technology solutions, if needed (see Figure 6.1).

Ultimately, one finds the best technology that matches the user preferences and enables the student to complete successfully the task at hand. For example, if a student has difficulty remembering to do his/her homework, several assistive technology solutions could be tried. Starting first with no-tech solutions, such as sticky notes on the outside of the textbook cueing the student that there is homework for the night; placing textbooks for classes in which he or she has homework right into the backpack to avoid getting lost in the bottom of the school locker. If that doesn't seem to work, other low-tech solutions might be tried such as an assignment notebook requiring the student or classroom teacher to sign if there is homework, or a picture-chart as a reminder where the student checks off necessary steps before leaving the school building each day, one of those steps being to make sure they have their homework. High-tech solutions might involve a class website that provides homework information, telephone assignment hotline, handheld personal recorder or reminder system; leaving a voice message on the home telephone or cell phone to oneself as a reminder to do homework tonight; electronic organizers such as personal digital assistants (PDAs); and/or software programs for the PDA that provides just in time visual and auditory reminders.

Learner Needs and Preferences

As a classroom teacher, you will be providing guidance and support in the area of assistive technology and encouraging students in trying different ways to approach the task. The ultimate factor in determining the best technology solution is to involve the student in the decision making process. Let's say that another way. Here is an example, of how important the student (end user) must have input in considering and selecting assistive technology:

Eyeglasses are a form of assistive technology, right? They enable a person to do things (in this case see clearly) they otherwise could not do. Let's say that you have gone to the optometrist and you were told that you needed glasses or new glasses (if you already wear glasses). So the time comes when you must purchase some glasses and you enter the store. As you walk up to the counter the clerk shares with you that you are number

32 and that your glasses will be right up. You are thinking, "Wait a minute. I haven't order any glasses or even picked any glasses out. In fact, I want contacts." The clerk replies, "Oh, I am sorry but since you are number 32, you only have one style of glasses that is right for you." She hands you a pair of glasses with very large round frames. You are so embarrassed. You leave the story angry and upset. What do you think the chances are that you will ever wear those glasses?

In order for assistive technology to be successfully used in the classroom, it must match the learning needs and preferences of the individual using the technology. You can advise and assist the student in exploring no-tech, low-tech, and high-tech solutions in order to be successful in your classroom. Ideally, the student ultimately chooses the final technology solution needed to achieve the desired outcome and determines his or her level of satisfaction with the assistive technology software, device or service.

It is important to understand that on a daily basis, teachers are naturally offering solutions to their students to achieve success in their classroom. Quite often teachers naturally suggest no-tech solutions to problem-solve or complete a task because they are at hand or easily obtainable. For example, if a student is struggling with new vocabulary words in a chapter of the textbook; the teacher may prompt the student to isolate the word and write the word on an index card to flip through and practice at a later time.

Classroom teachers are constantly looking at academic learning tasks, goals, and student outcomes. In addition, teachers need to be aware of technology available to assist their students in completing a particular function or task. It is essential that you become familiar with common no-tech, low-tech, and high-tech solutions for your students. AT consideration for an individual with a disability is a team decision. As a general education classroom teacher you are an essential team member. The individualized education program team (consisting of a general education teacher, special educator, exceptional student director, AT specialist, guidance counselor, family members, school administrator, and in some instances the student) carefully examines the need and consideration for AT. Quite often other students in your classroom can benefit from such technology.

Differentiated Instruction and Assistive Technology

As a classroom teacher you will need to design and create your learning environments and activities so that all your students can become successful learners. Be aware of the classroom environment, learning activities, student expectations, learning outcomes, teaching pace, interactions with students, and learning tools and supports that are needed for academic success.

Differentiated instructional strategies provide teachers with a means of offering additional supports and individualization during regular instruction. The use of differentiated instruction can open the door to classroom content, making it more accessible to diverse learners (Castellani & Jeffs, 2004). Assistive technology enhances differentiated instructional strategies and can provide the learner with necessary learning supports. For example, students who struggle with reading and writing often find it difficult to learn new content through text.

Typically, when starting a new chapter in a textbook, students are asked to read the chapter and answer comprehension questions. Struggling readers and writers often display behaviors such as laying their heads down, staring off into space that indicate that they are uninterested, or lack the motivation in learning the topic at hand. In reality, the new content seems impossible for your struggling students to decode or make meaningful. So, why should they bother? In your classroom, assistive technology can provide struggling readers and writers with a different way in approaching the academic task. Suggesting no-tech, low-tech, and high-tech ways of approaching the reading or writing task can provide needed learning tools and assistance in accessing your curriculum. As you continue through the chapters in this textbook, no-tech, low-tech, and high-tech examples will be provided for reading, writing, math, organization, study skills, and more. When considering different technologies it is important to enable your students to look carefully at their own strengths, abilities, learning preferences, and domains in comparison to the required learning task and expected learning outcome.

Function over Disability

When looking at specific learning tools and assistive technology devices and services necessary to ensure learning success for the students in your classroom, remember to focus on the functional learning outcome rather than technology for a specific disability. For example, a common tool that has been proven helpful in the reading and writing process is text-to speech software. This software reads text on the computer screen aloud to the student, thus allowing the student to interface with information on the Internet, word processor, and other text documents in electronic format. This same assistive technology may be useful for students with learning disabilities, physical disabilities, students who are blind, or students with attention deficit hyperactivity disorder. Technology should *not* be disability specific. Rather, teachers should assist students in making decisions about which tools to use, based on the learning task at hand and student strengths rather than on disability or deficits.

A Framework for Selecting Assistive Technology

The key to consideration and selection of AT for academic success is to look carefully at the **s**tudent, **e**nvironment, **t**ask, and **t**ools; this is commonly referred to as the SETT Framework (Zabala, 2002). This framework provides an organizational tool for educational teams (including the student) to collaboratively communicate and look carefully at technology considerations for student success. In addition, team members must have an opportunity to share multiple perspectives, pertinent information, and knowledge.

Guiding questions under each area provides an opportunity for the educational team to discuss, research and reach a consensus for viable AT solutions. Such guiding questions may include (but are not limited to) the following:

The Student

- What is the functional area of concern?
- What does the student need to be able to do that is difficult or impossible to do independently at this time?
- What are the preferred learning domains (visual, auditory, tactile), preferences, strengths, and current abilities of the student?
- What motivates the student?
- What are the special needs or consideration for the student to complete the task at hand?

The Environment(s)

- Where will the required task take place? Examine closely the physical and instructional arrangement of the learning environment.
- What available support exists for the student and the teacher/staff?
- What materials and equipment are commonly found in the environment and used by others?
- What technological, physical, and instructional challenges hinder access to the curriculum or learning task?
- What attitudes and expectations exist in the learning environment?

- What natural supports or items exist that provides assistance as needed? Natural supports may include peer tutoring or a friend that can take and share notes.

The Task(s)

- What specific task(s) can the student perform in the environment(s) that enables progress toward academic goals and objectives?
- What specific tasks are required for active involvement in the identified environments? Break down the challenging task(s) into smaller more approachable parts. Identify strategies, tools, and technologies that can be used to complete different aspects of the task.

The Tool(s)

After the student, environment, and task have been closely examined, then it is important to identify viable tools needed to assist the student in completing the task at hand. In the SETT Framework, tools include technology, devices, and strategies that maybe needed to assist the student in succeeding. Look carefully at current tools available and match these tools to the student's strengths and learning preferences. Without such tools, can the student reach reasonable progress toward educational goals and objectives? If the answer is no, then the tools are essential and should be considered (Zabala, 2002).

Figure 6.2 offers an analogy for the SETT Framework. Think about the student as the shopper for technology. The student pushes the cart through the store looking over the products/choices available for academic success. On the shopping list, learner attributes, abilities, motivation, and preferences are noted. This list represents the student's assessment. The student comes to three aisles and will need to make choices from each one. The first aisle stocks environmental items. Choices include various physical arrangements, furniture, labs, and workstations. Attitudes and expectations are also on these shelves.

The next aisle stocks "ask" items for areas such as reading, writing, math, problem solving, study skills, and more. These shelves hold "how-to" products, such as note-taking methods, graphic organizers, and study skills, reading, and math strategies.

The third aisle holds tools such as word prediction programs, text-to-speech products, and manipulatives. These rows are stocked with items like calculators, globes, GPS systems, magnetic letters, keyboards, and computers.

Note all the people stocking the shelves. These figures represent the collaborative team in a school working with the student to provide what he or she needs. These people try to help the student shopper match what is on the shopping list to what is in stock. If they don't have it, they will try to find a way to order it or at least to find the closest match. The main idea of the analogy is that it takes everyone working together to set up the best learning situation possible for the student based on his or her learning strengths and needs.

Active Learning through Innovative Technology

Careful planning and designing of the learning environment and necessary learning tools are essential for student success. Even with such planning and attention to details some students will need technology to make learning accessible or possible, as discussed earlier in this chapter. In addition to providing access, technology can be the catalyst for actively engaging students in the learning process. Technology provides students with an environment that encourages collaboration, problem solving, role playing, and the development of critical thinking skills. It can take abstract concepts and make them visual, concrete, and meaningful. Technology

Figure 6.2 Shopping for Technology
Source: John Metcalf, original contribution.

provides a multiple means of how a student can approach, engage, and complete the learning task. In our multimediated world, learners seek out multimedia learning formats. Take a minute and think about all the multimedia and information you are exposed to in a single day. Such might include radio, television, newspapers, magazines, billboards, text messaging, phone messages while being placed on hold, and even baseball caps. Thoman and Jolls (2003) emphasize that students of the 21st century will need to "critically interpret powerful images of multimedia culture and express themselves in multimedia forms" (p. 4).

Innovative technologies that are currently being used in the learning process within today's classrooms include social software tools (e.g., interactive whiteboards, blogs, wikis, and text messaging) and visual and media literacy tools (concept maps, info murals, cartoons, digital storytelling, graphing calculators, geospatial technologies, personal digital assistants, and the use of MP3 files or podcasting). Such technology enables students to acquire new knowledge through authentic learning experiences.

Social Software Tools

Interactive whiteboards are becoming increasingly popular in the classroom. They involve a large electronic touch-sensitive board connected to a computer and a projection system or plasma panel display. The touch screen capability eliminates the need for a mouse and/or keyboard. Interactive whiteboards impact learning by

Courtesy of Stan Vonog

Students acquire new knowledge as they engage in authentic learning using an interactive whiteboard.

increasing engagement and motivation. This learning tool enables a classroom of learners to physically interact and manipulate learning objects, to share and collaborate on ideas, and to engage in active discussion. Interactive whiteboards support the principles of Universal Design for Learning by providing a flexible learning environment. Students of all ability levels are eager to take part in the projected activity.

Blogs provide students with the opportunity to create a personal web-based writing space. Such space can be very motivating because students have an anytime, anywhere writing platform that publishes their research, opinions, artwork, etc. Additionally motivating is the fact that there is an audience (possibly the world if released as a public blog) that is able to read and react to their digital print. It is estimated today that there are over 27 million blogs. Within the classroom, blogs can provide an opportunity for collaboration and peer mentoring and can be an active place to house student productivity and academic artifacts.

Wiki technology is a web-based tool that enables multiple users to work together on the same document or content. It provides an easy-to-use interface where each user can add, remove, or edit content in a seamless manner. Wikipedia is a popular wiki application. It is an encyclopedia that is collaboratively written and edited by its users. In Wikipedia, thousands of changes or updates are made each hour. Wikis can be very powerful in the classroom by allowing students in your class to approach a topic and participate in an online collaborative creation. Students are able to engage in the evolution of a project by writing, editing, and practicing online skills needed for job opportunities in the future.

It is important to emphasize that any web-based tool requires careful monitoring of student use. Critics of blogs and wikis point out those tools can be strictly opinion or have no factual content. Although this is possible, blogs and wikis provide an avenue for students to learn how to create and interact in an ethical manner with others. Students learn through authentic projects how to find information, evaluate information resources, and apply information to real life situations. Such skills are essential for the workplace in the 21st century.

Text messaging or instant messaging provides students with just-in-time learning resources, information or mentoring. In our instant gratification, "24 hours/ 7 days a week" society, we have seen the resourceful use of text messaging or instant messaging in our libraries, technical/product support, and *ask an expert* online. This just-in-time media can provide students with a go anywhere/learn anywhere tool. In the United States, over 200,000 children (ages 5–9) and seven million children (ages 10–14) carry cell phones (Dodds & Manson, 2005). Students are text messaging and quizzing one another, one question at a time, in a trivia-type format on important information needed for tests and projects preparation. Mobile phones are becoming useful tools that allow learning to go beyond the walls of the traditional classroom. More information on mobile learning research can be found at http://www.m-learn ing.org/knowledge-centre/m-learning-research.htm. Although, many schools struggle with mobile telephones in the classroom, others are embracing the technology and setting policies that enable teachers to model and facilitate responsible use and etiquette. Some teachers are providing extension activities outside of the school day that provide students with opportunities to use their cell phones to engage in information sharing, research, and mobile technology tools (such as cameras, dictionaries, and Internet access). Most often students on their own integrate this technology to their academic advantage.

Visual and Media Literacy Tools

Concept maps, webbing, mind mapping, visual cognitive maps, and graphic organizers are visual tools that enable learners to take a concept and analyze it into visual components. They are often used in text books and class lecture notes to provide students with visual roadmaps on a specific topic or concept. When students create their own concept or visual map they select graphics, animations, and background colors to represent and organize information. Through such selection and organization students begin to construct personal meaning and connection of new information to already learned knowledge.

Info murals, **graphic novels**, and **digital storytelling** all provide an alternative means to traditional text-based literacy or informational tools. In 1998, Robert Horn introduced the concept of visual language and its relevance to our culture. He shares that visual language is all around us. It consists of the integration of words, images, and shapes that result in various media formats such as paper documents, computer screens, projected media, idea sketches, and info murals. Current research demonstrates that the integration of verbal and visual elements is more effective than text separated from visual elements and can increase communication and learning (Horn, 1998).

Info murals represent information in large, often bigger-than-life-size visuals displaying many different types of messages. Students immediately scan the mural surface for familiar objects and then move to objects of interest. Color, size, and texture of objects add dimension to integrated messages. One example of an info mural in today's schools is one that represents character education at Waverly Public Elementary School in Bowmanville, Ontario, Canada. Larger-than-life objects lead the students down the right path to building good character (see Figure 6.3). Archways leading to each of the different hallways have a message to remind students of positive ways to build character.

Graphic novels are similar to comic books except they are longer in length and often have a complex story, one that is often associated with a novel. Often while reading traditional books, struggling readers cannot visualize what they are reading and therefore become lost in the text. Using pop culture and the media of graphic novels enables diverse learners to learn essential reading, writing, and interpretation skills. Graphic novels also enable students to become knowledgeable consumers of ideas and information (Frey & Fisher, 2004). Graphic novels are available in both

Figure 6.3 Example of Info Mural

Source: Info Mural "Building Character," Waverly Public School, Bowmanville, Ontario, Canada.

Table 6.2	Popular Graphic Novels

Moby Dick by Will Eisner
Manga Shakespeare: Romeo and Juliet by Richard Appignanesi
Tenth Muse: Odyssey by Darren Davis
Pedro and Me by Judd Winick
The Tale of One Bad Rat by Bryan Talbot
The Adventures of Tintin (Vol. 1) by Leslie Lonsdale Cooper and Michael Turner
The Collected Alison Dare: Little Miss Adventure by J. Torres and J. Bone
The Adventure of Jimmy Neutron Boy Genius Tinkering with Destiny by John Davis
Pinky and Stinky by James Kochalka
Akira by Otomo Katsuhiro
The Civil War by Mark Millar
Doctor Who: The Flood by Scott Gray and Gareth Roberts
The Smartest Kid on Earth by Jimmy Corrigan and Chris Ware
Patrick Henry: Liberty or Death by Jason Glaser
The Boston Tea Party by Matt Doeden
Amelia Earhart Legendary Aviator by James Anderson
The Apollo 13 Mission by Donald Lemke
The Attack on Pearl Harbor by Jane Sutcliff

paperback and electronic format. Table 6.2 contains a listing of popular graphic novels in paperback form. An example of an electronic graphic novel can be found at http://www.nbc.com/Heroes/novels/.

Digital storytelling combines the art of telling stories with a variety of multimedia tools. Photos, soundtracks, drawings, animation and web publishing are used to communicate and express personal reflection. In the classroom, digital storytelling is effective in introducing, new material and guiding students to research and transform their thoughts and feelings on a specific topic. This powerful learning medium allows the student to be in control of the content and to plan and create interesting stories. A written script transforms into a digitized product. Digital storytelling appeals to diverse learning styles and at the same time builds essential writing and communication skills. For a wonderful digital story example please visit http://www.wmich.edu/pt3/ds/look.html.

Graphing calculators have been in the classroom over 20 years. Generation after generation have been impressed with the technology and how it continues to change and become more robust. Pictorial representation provides students an opportunity to view information in multiple perspectives. Uses of graphing calculators are expanding into other content areas such as science, social studies, and economics. The capability to display information in multiple representations enhances students' learning and understanding. Careful analysis and the ease of changing data representations allow students to engage in higher-order things skills.

Geospatial technologies include geographic information system (GIS), Global Positioning System (GPS), and remote sensing (RS) tools. We are beginning to see the importance of these tools in our everyday lives. Global and local imagery tools are extremely helpful in making decisions and analyzing the impact of decisions before they are actually being made. School systems are using these tools to analyze building sites, bus routes, and possible rezoning needs.

Such technology is increasingly a part of lessons in geography, environmental science, biological science, Earth science, economics, and mathematical studies in our classrooms today. The National Research Council report (2006), *Learning to Think Spatially: GIS as a Support System in the K-12 Curriculum*, points to the importance of spatial thinking and learning across subject areas to prepare our students with skills and learning strategies needed in their everyday lives (available online at http://www.nap.edu/catalog/11019.html#toc). Eschool News Online provides wonderful resources in exploring background literature, created lessons, and training for teachers who are interested in getting started with geospatial technologies. For information on getting started with geospatial technologies see http://www.esri.com/industries/k-12/education/thinking_spatially.html.

Geocaching (http://www.geocaching.com/) is a popular adventure activity that involves the use of GPS to locate hidden or planted treasures (referred to as "cache"). Over 40,000 individuals and organizations set up caches all over the world and share the locations of these caches on the Internet. GPS users then begin the hunt by using the location coordinates needed to find the caches. The appeal to this adventure is that appears surprisingly easy but this is a deception. The hunt then becomes a challenge enticing the player to continue. The reward in finding the cache is the cache itself. Players are required to make a log entry and leave something for the next visitor.

Personal digital assistant (PDA) is a generic term that often refers to a small mobile handheld device that provides the integration of tools and applications for such tasks as information storage, the Internet, and managing and organizing personal information. In the K-12 classroom PDAs are implemented for science experiments, photography, writing, organizing school or class schedules, composing music, reviewing lectures, and comparing class notes. Roschelle and Pea (2002) compiled the benefits of this affordable technology. These include (a) portability and ease of use; (b) wide variety of educational application; (c) promotes autonomous learning and student organization; and (d) supports collaboration, communication and inquiry-based instruction.

PDAs run standard productivity applications such as Word and Excel in addition to specialty software such as GPS software and probeware. Probeware involves the use of probes and sensors connected to the PDA to collect and display elements such as temperature, light, motion, and sound levels.

Podcasting is a term resulting from the Apple Computer Corporation's iPod. The iPod is a portable digital audio player that allows the user to download digital audio files (most commonly in MP3 format). Today there are many different kinds of MP3 players and podcasting has gone beyond the single Apple Computer device. Podcasting is enabling education to become portable thus promoting that learning should occur anywhere and anytime. The simple, easy-to-use, affordable technology used for podcasting allows the classroom teacher and his/her students to record academic content, field observations, interviews, and reflections. Podcasting allows the dissemination of audio files through an RSS (Really Simple Syndication) feed. Such a feed notifies subscribers that a new podcast is available and then is downloaded directly into a computer or MP3 player.

Classroom teachers are discovering the power of the spoken word. Podcasts support different learners and learning styles (e.g., auditory learners and English language learners) and provide multiple means of representing course content. The Educational Podcast Network (visit http://epnweb.org/) provides a collection of podcast topics that might be of interest in one location. This site provides useful resources on individual and class projects, in addition to subject specific podcasts and ideas.

Teachers are engaging their students in academic activities by using podcasting for interviewing others, engaging in storytelling, sharing audiobook reviews, creating tutorials and instructions, summarizing key content, giving directions, sharing information, and providing feedback. Implementing podcasts into the classroom brings pop culture into education. Students are already familiar with such technology-based entertainment systems and embrace technology in the learning process.

Opportunities through Technology

Technology is providing opportunities for realizing potential in the world and outer space as we know them. Through advancements in technology individuals can begin to exceed expectations in achieving personal and professional goals. Take, for example, Dr. Stephen Hawking, a famous physicist, who at the age of 21 was diagnosed with a debilitating disease called amyotrophic lateral sclerosis (ALS), commonly referred to as "Lou Gehrig's Disease." In April 2007, Dr. Hawking had the opportunity to experience a zero gravity flight in preparation to go into space in 2009 (video available at http://www.msnbc.msn.com/id/18334489/). For the first time in over 40 years Dr. Hawking experienced movement and motion without the confines of a wheelchair. His work as a great physicist and this flight into zero gravity would not have been possible without the advancements of technology. Steven Hawking has depended on the use of a communication device and other technologies in college and in his professional career to share his knowledge, ideas, and ways of thinking. What if he had never had such technologies or opportunities? (For more information visit his homepage http://www.hawking.org.uk/.)

As you are faced with the challenge of meeting the educational needs of tomorrow's diverse learners, celebrate their innovative thinking and ways of learning and embrace resulting classroom challenges through the implementation of technology. Students who struggle in traditional classroom learning often excel in learning through computers and technology. As a classroom teacher you must continually identify and build on students' strengths to release their learning potential.

On the surface such a challenge may seem impossible, but it is important to build a repository for identifying and acquiring tools, strategies, resources, and training for technology. Many state agencies and local communities have assistive technology lending libraries or programs, where classroom teachers can borrow, learn, and try a variety of technologies without the school having to purchase them. If teachers can identify and articulate their students' or classroom needs there are many community resources and vendor partnership programs available for obtaining needed technologies. Websites like http://www.donorschose.com and http://www.agiftforteaching.org/ provide an opportunity for teachers to advocate for innovative teaching tools that schools could not otherwise provide.

Assistive technology, specifically targeted by law for students with disabilities, in reality could benefit many learners in your classroom to reach their learning potential. Will you be the teacher who opens new doors and guides your students in discovering new learning paths, or will you settle in saying, *"This is just the best I can do with the given situation"*?

Remember, technology is essential in designing new learning environments and solutions in the 21st century. Technology is continually changing and today's computing will look very different five years from now. Imagine computers that no longer need a mouse and keyboard to input information. Despite the many changes that are coming with future technologies, it is the teachers that embrace technology in their own lives that make technology integration into the learning process and classrooms happen.

Imagine, at the end of the school day, with the slightest touch to a icon on the computer control panel you send home 32 daily progress reports and homework reminders. You sit back and watch, as Juanita, the last of your students to go home, logs out of her learning pod, places her thumb on the fingerprint scanner, and says, "Time to go," only made possible by a voice implant box that connects her mental thoughts directly to a speech output device.

Thematic Summary

- Whether digital native or digital immigrant, teacher comfort level in using technology is essential to technology integration in the classroom.
- Educators of tomorrow must look closely and gain insight to the impact of technology on thinking and learning for student achievement.
- Assistive technology is not a luxury; it is a necessity for individuals with disabilities to achieve everyday tasks to reach their dreams and aspirations.

- There are 10 common areas of assistive technology:
  - Communication
  - Daily living
  - Ergonomics
  - Environmental
  - Sensory
  - Mobility and transportation
  - Seating and positioning
  - Recreation and leisure
  - Computer access
  - Education and learning
- Assistive technology isn't a one-size-fits-all concept. Teachers must carefully look at the individual strengths and needs of each student and what technology would be needed to access the curriculum and achieve successful outcomes.
- SETT Framework is used in consideration and selection of assistive technology.
- Social software and visual and media tools provide students with the means to acquire new knowledge through authentic learning experiences.
- Innovative technologies are critical for learning in the 21st century

Making Connections for Inclusive Teaching

1. Keep a running list of technology that you use in a given day. Look carefully at the list and reflect on what life would be like without those technologies.
2. Are you or any family member an assistive technology user? Do you wear glasses? Use a rolling backpack? Use a personal calendar or PDA? Think of other assistive technologies that you use every day.
3. After reading this chapter, can you list other myths or misconceptions about technology?
4. For one week, keep a close look at the media you access for news and new developments in assistive technology.
5. What innovative technology have you used or seen integrated into the classroom to increase student participation and academic outcomes?
6. On the Internet, find a video of a person using assistive technology.

Learning Activities

1. Make a table of assistive technologies and innovative tools that you have used personally and would like to use in your teaching.
2. Visit a classroom where technology is being used. Interview the teacher to gather ideas and different strategies for infusing technology into the classroom.
3. Outline a curriculum unit you plan to use. List possible no-tech, low-tech, and high-tech tools to assist student learning.
4. Create a podcast, participate in geocaching, or design an info mural or digital story to share with your class.
5. Evaluate a popular software program used in your current content area (e.g., The Human Body) and look closely for accessible features:
   - Can time limitations be removed?
   - Can the access method (touch screen, switch, or mouse access) be changed?
   - Can background colors and font colors be changed?
   - Is text described in a sound narrative or video?
   - Are videos or verbal instructions displayed through text?

6. Explore and research 10 assistive technologies that could be useful for struggling readers in your classroom.
7. Create an electronic toolbox, blog, or wiki that lists web resources, and innovative technology tools for your content area.
8. Write or revise your teaching philosophy to include the role of technology integration and meeting the needs of diverse learners.
9. Develop an innovative tool artifact (e.g., mind map, digital story, graphing calculator, or PDA activity) to demonstrate your technology skills as a 21st-century educator and include it in your professional portfolio.

Looking at the Standards

The content of this chapter most closely aligns itself with the following standards:

INTASC Standards

- *Diverse Learners.* The teacher understands how students differ in their approaches to learning and creates instructional opportunities that are adapted to diverse learners.
- *Communication and Technology.* The teacher uses knowledge of effective verbal, nonverbal, and media communication techniques to foster active inquiry, collaboration, and supportive interaction in the classroom.

Council for Exceptional Children

Special educators are to have knowledge of the following:

- GC1K3: Historical foundations, classic studies, major contributors, major legislation, and current issues related to knowledge and practice.
- CC4S3: Select, adapt, and use instructional strategies and materials according to characteristics of the individual with exceptional learning needs.
- GC4S7: Use appropriate adaptations and technology for all individuals with disabilities.
- GC5K2: Adaptation of the physical environment to provide optimal learning opportunities for individuals with disabilities.
- CC7S9: Incorporate and implement instructional and assistive technology into the educational program.
- GC7S4: Select, design, and use technology, materials, and resources required to educate individuals whose disabilities interfere with communication.
- GC7SS: Interpret sensory, mobility, reflex, and perceptual information to create or adapt appropriate learning plans.

Key Concepts and Terms

biometrics	interactive whiteboards	digital storytelling
digital natives	blogs	graphing calculators
digital immigrants	wiki	geospatial technologies
assistive technology device	text messaging	personal digital assistant
assistive technology services	concept maps	podcasting
	info murals	
	graphic novels	

References

Ball, L. J., Bilyeu, D. V., Prentice, C., & Beukelman, D. R. (2005). Augmentative and alternative communication: Infusing communication in an academic setting. In D. Edyburn, K. Higgins, & R. Boone (Eds.), *Handbook of special education technology research and practice* (pp. 423–451). Whitefish Bay, WI: Knowledge by Design.

Behrmann, M. (1998). Assistive technology for young children in special education. In C. Dede (Ed.), *Learning with technology* (pp. 73–93). Alexandria, VA: Association for Supervision and Curriculum Development.

Blackhurst, A. E. (2005). Historical perspectives about technology applications for people with disabilities. In D. Edyburn, K. Higgins, & R. Boone (Eds.), *Handbook of special education technology research and practice* (pp. 3–29). Whitefish Bay, WI: Knowledge by Design.

Brooks-Young, S. (2006). *Critical technology: Issues for school leaders.* Thousand Oaks, CA: Corwin Press.

Brunson, M. (2005). *A brief history of Braille.* Retrieved June 23, 2007 from http://www.acb.org/resources/braille-history.html

Caldwell, R. M. (1981). Computers and curriculum: Promises and problems. *Proceedings of the National Conference on Technology and Education, 1*–14.

Castellani, J., & Jeffs, T. (2004). Using technology to provide access to the general education curriculum—techniques to try. *Technology in Action, 3,* 1–8.

CELLS alive! (2006). Retrieved May 18, 2008 from http://www.cellsalive.com/mitosis.htm

Dodds, R., & Manson, C. Y. (2005). Cell phones and PDA's hit k-6. *Education Digest: Essential Readings Condensed for Quick Review, 70,* 52–53.

Frey, N., & Fisher, D. (2004). Using graphic novels, anime, and the internet in an urban high school. *English Journal, 93*(3), 19–25.

George, C. L., Schaff, J. I., & Jeffs, T. L. (2005). Physical access in today's schools: Empowerment through assistive technology. In D. Edyburn, K. Higgins, & R. Boone (Eds.), *Handbook of special education technology research and practice* (pp. 355–377). Whitefish Bay, WI: Knowledge by Design.

Horn, R. E. (1998). *Visual language: Global communication for the 21st century.* Bainbridge Island, WA: MacroVU, Inc.

Lewis, R. B. (1998). Assistive technology and learning disabilities: Today's realities and tomorrow's promises. *Journal of Learning Disabilities, 31,* 16–26, 54.

National Research Council. (2006). *Learning to think spatially: GIS as a support system in the k-12 curriculum.* Retrieved June 23, 2007 from http://www.nap.edu/catalog/11019.html#toc

Prensky, M. (2001). *Digital natives, digital immigrants.* Retrieved June 23, 2007 from http://www.marcprensky.com/writing/default.asp

Ringstaff, C., & Kelly, L. (2002). *The learning return on our educational technology investment: A review of findings from research.* Retrieved June 23, 2007 from http://rtecexchange.edgateway.net/learningreturn.pdf

Roschelle, J., & Pea, R. (2002). A walk on the WILD side: How wireless handhelds may change computer-supported collaborative learning. *International Journal of Cognition and Technology, 1*(1), 145–168.

Schwartz, D. (1999). *Ghost in the machines: Seymour Papert on how computers fundamentally change the way kids learn.* Retrieved June 23, 2007 from http://www.papert.org/articles/GhostInTheMachine.html

Thoman, E., & Jolls, T. (2003). *Literacy for the 21st century: An overview and orientation guide to media literacy education.* Retrieved June 23, 2007 from www.medialit.org

U.S. Department of Education, Office of Educational Technology. (2004). *Toward a new golden age in American education: How the internet, the law and today's students are revolutionizing expectations.* Retrieved June 23, 2007 from http://www.ed.gov/about/offices/list/os/technology/plan/2004/plan.pdf

Woronov, T. (1994). Myths about the magic of technology in schools. *Education Digest, 60*(4), 12–15.

Zabala, J. (2002). *A brief introduction to the SETT framework.* Retrieved June 23, 2007 from http://sweb.uky.edu/~jszaba0/SETTUPDATE.PDF

Zoning in on Physics. (2001). Retrieved May 18, 2008 from http://ziop.gmu.edu/index.html

Imagine going to a fast-food restaurant and not being able to read the menu because of a reading disability, language difference, or vision problem. What if you can't speak to place your order? What if you are dieting and there are no low-fat options? What if every item on the menu has meat and you are a vegetarian? Perhaps you have three very active children with you and there is no play area. Fortunately, fast-food restaurants have used the principles of universal design to make their environments and meals more accessible. These changes were planned with the consumer in mind, and the "designers" considered the wide array of their wants and needs. Portions were adjusted for children, and prices were adjusted for "seniors." There are super sizes for the hungriest eaters and "light" offerings for dieters. Play areas are available for children with seats for the parents. Menus display pictures of the food choices and are numbered. Value meals make it possible to order a complete meal with the point of a finger or the response of a number. Some menus can be read aloud and many are offered in Spanish and Braille. Designers monitor trends and current issues and periodically change menus accordingly. For example, menus in our country changed with the popularity of the "no-carb" or "low-carb" diets. Many restaurants highlighted the items that were low in carbohydrates and adjusted other entrees to fit the requirements without totally revamping the entire menu. Unlike our fast-food restaurants, many classrooms in America today limit the full participation of many students who learn differently by heavily depending on one mode to plan, deliver, engage, and assess learning. When schools limit the way a subject is taught/learned and the number of diverse learners increases, it is important to see what we can do differently.

You have already learned that recent legislation and the school reform movement are requiring schools to ensure that each student has access to and accountability for progress in the general curriculum. The statistics presented in Chapter 1 clearly show that the number of students in our country with special needs, different racial/ethnic representations, limited knowledge and use of the English language, and impoverished home environments is growing. Additionally, the National Center for Learning Disabilities reports that 38.7 percent of high school students with learning disabilities drop out of school compared with 11 percent of the general population (Wendorf, 2006). With this increasingly diverse student population, high dropout rates, and the movement toward making our schools as inclusive as possible, it makes sense to design curriculum and learning environments up front that will be flexible enough to stretch and bend as schools reach out to meet the needs of each learner. In fact, it is critical.

In this chapter, we will take a closer look at **Universal Design for Learning (UDL)** for such a framework. As introduced in Chapter 1, you will recall that UDL is a learning approach that designs curricular materials and activities that have the flexibility to match learner strengths and needs so they can reach their learning goals. It considers the different abilities of the learner "to see, hear, speak, move, read, write, comprehend English, attend, organize, engage, and remember" (Orkwis, 2003, p. 1).

In the last decade, considerable research in special education has been devoted to the notion of constructing the universally designed classroom that can benefit all learners. A considerable amount of the material you will read in this chapter references work done at the Center for Applied Special Technology (CAST) and related work published through the Council for Exceptional Children. Researchers at CAST have been developing guidelines and tools to support physical access to electronic curricula and media since 1984. In addition, the National Center on Accessing the General Curriculum (NCAC), funded by the U.S. Department of Education, Office of Special Education Programs, was established in 2001. This group provides reports and information on teacher practices, curriculum enhancements, and policy issues about access to the general curriculum and Universal Design for Learning. Before we go any further, let's step back and trace the development of the concept of universal design.

The Concept of Universal Design

Background in Architecture

As discussed in Chapter 1, the Americans with Disabilities Act (ADA) (PL 101-336) was established in 1990 to ensure people with disabilities would not be discriminated against in public or private sectors. Throughout the years, progress was made. In the early 1990s, many schools and public buildings were "retrofitted" to meet the requirements of the ADA (Pisha & Coyne, 2001). Existing structures were remodeled to meet the needs of people with physical and sensory disabilities. For example, water fountains were lowered, doorways were widened to allow access for wheelchairs, hand rails were added to bathroom stalls, ramps were added to entrances, and street curbs were cut for wheelchairs. Signs in buildings were labeled in Braille. Schools were full of sawdust, and construction workers—working around students, faculty, and staff in the middle of their studies—were in a frenzy to meet the new requirements of the law.

The term **universal design** originally comes to us from the field of architectural studies at the Center for Universal Design in Raleigh, North Carolina (Center for Universal Design, 1997). Ron Mace, an architect who happened to have a physical impairment, created this term to advocate the following inclusive philosophy: "Universal design seeks to encourage products that are more usable by everyone. It is a design built for the environment and consumer products for a very broad definition of user" (Mace, 1998, p. 1).

Mace's passion for universal design led him to a lifelong career in working with architects and educating those around him about the importance of planning for accessibility in the initial design of buildings rather than modifying or adapting existing structures (Bremer, Clapper, Hitchcock, Hall, & Kachgal, 2002). Mace advocated that if an accessible design is created and established up front, time and money would be saved in the long run, and people with disabilities would benefit.

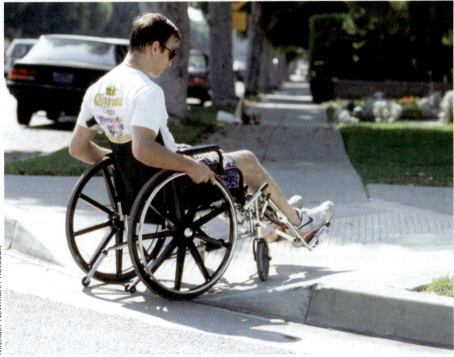

Michael Newman/PhotoEdit

Curb cuts help students with special physical needs access buildings, sidewalks, and other public spaces.

The Seven Principles of Universal Design

The field of architecture has subsequently shown us how creative, innovative think-ers design buildings that make our lives easier, more comfortable, and more stream-lined based on the following principles of universal design as described in Table 7.1.

Mace envisioned environments and products that would be accessible to a diverse group of people (not just people in wheelchairs or people with sensory dis-orders). Spaces and products would adapt to changes with relative ease and minor adjustments. Product and equipment would be easily understood, and people who speak other languages or have difficulty perceiving/understanding information would have the clearest directions possible in a format they could best receive. Safety is essential, as is reducing the amount of physical effort. The design doesn't create any new hazard. Size and space of environments in relation to human needs are also kept in mind.

Universal Design Applications in Society

These seven principles can easily be seen applied in our everyday lives. It is not sur-prising that these guidelines end up benefiting many more people than those the ADA first targeted. In fact, it is likely that all of us benefit.

For example, when you woke up this morning, perhaps a vibrating alarm or a digital clock with enlarged numbers rang or played music to get you moving. Your lamp came on with a touch of a finger. You turned on the television by remote con-trol to check the weather, sent a text message to a friend by cell phone, checked your assignments/appointments on your PDA or computer, downloaded your e-mail, and went to the gym for an early morning workout. At the gym, you watched the news via closed-captioned television while you worked out, at the same time listening to music on your MP3 player. Both hands were free to get a full-body workout.

So many products on the market today reflect the idea of universal design. Car manufacturers, for example, responded to the idea of universal design by designing multiple options for access into vans by people in wheelchairs, traffic engineers put beeps in the traffic light signals for people with visual impairments, and car seat manufacturers adapted their products to be sure all children could ride as safely as possible. Manuals that come with appliances and technology devices are often accompanied by directions in a variety of languages, and they often have pictures

---

Table 7.1   The Seven Principles of Universal Design

Principle One: Equitable Use: The design is useful and marketable to people with diverse abilities.

Principle Two: Flexibility in Use: The design accommodates a wide range of individual preferences and abilities.

Principle Three: Simple and Intuitive Use: Use of the design is easy to understand, regardless of the user's experience, knowledge, language skills, or current concentration level.

Principle Four: Perceptible Information: The design communicates necessary information effectively to the user, regardless of ambient conditions or the user's sensory abilities.

Principle Five: Tolerance for Error: The design minimizes hazards and the adverse conse-quences of accidental or unintended actions.

Principle Six: Low Physical Effort: The design can be used efficiently and comfortably and with a minimum of fatigue.

Principle Seven: Size and Space for Approach and Use: Appropriate size and space is pro-vided for approach, reach, manipulation, and use regardless of user's body size, posture, or mobility.

Source: From *The Principles of Universal Design* (Version 2.0). (Raleigh: North Carolina State University, Center for Uni-versal Design, 1997).

showing each step. It is not unusual in some parts of the United States to see signs in Spanish as well as English.

A working mother with three school-aged children may plan her day using her PDA, color coding each child's schedule along with her own. She might have a basket or bin for each child's school materials by the door, a step stool by the counter so the shortest child can get his own cereal. The car will have a variety of car seats and booster seats for their travel to school.

The principles of universal design appear everywhere today. Popular TV shows like "Designing Spaces" and "House Doctor" and magazines such as "Real Simple" take all the clutter out of a living space and arrange what is left to make it as functional, comfortable, and aesthetic as possible to the user. The occupant considers what is most important to keep and gets rid of the extraneous things. Writers and manufacturers offer systems for making clothing selections and food preparation easier through organization and easy access, with the hope of safely freeing us up so we may have more quality time to spend on the things that really matter to us in this fast-paced society.

Implications for Today's Classrooms

How can today's schools/classrooms embrace the principles of universal design to make learning more accessible? How can we better accommodate students who have a wide range of intelligences and abilities? How can we be more efficient with the limited time and space we have? How can we minimize adverse consequences that may be the result of curricula and environments that don't fit? With the demands on teachers and learners in schools today, how can we move away from classrooms that are heavily print based (textbooks, workbooks, and worksheets), which leave far too many students without access to the curriculum? How can we work smarter through curricular design with what we already know from what research tells us? Keep the seven principles of universal design in mind as we explore ways to plan up front for each and every learner in our classrooms. If we take a closer look at universal design and apply it to today's schools, and if we view diversity as a positive element that embraces a school, then we might find some answers in the process.

The Development of Universal Design for Learning

Just as Ron Mace worked to find ways to make the physical accessibility of public buildings a greater reality, current educational reforms are challenging school systems in similar ways to make the general curriculum accessible to all learners. School systems, therefore, may benefit from looking at teaching and learning in today's schools in the same way that Mace looked at making buildings accessible.

As mentioned earlier, Universal Design for Learning (UDL) has been presented as a framework for teaching, learning, assessment, and curriculum. Even though many researchers focus on studying and implementing more digital media because of its flexibility in the learning design, the implications for this approach are much broader (Rose & Meyer, 2002). Teachers look at what the student *can* do and are no longer limited to a single student characteristic. Universal Design for Learning encourages educators to design curriculum, learning environments, and assessments that are "smart from the start" (Pisha & Coyne, 2001). If the comprehensive plan for teaching and learning is initially designed with the diverse learner in mind, opportunities to impact student learning increase.

Researchers have taken the principles of universal design and applied them to increase access to and improve learning in schools. These design principles benefit many students with a variety of needs within the learning environment. For example, the curb cuts in sidewalks help not only those students/teachers who use wheelchairs, but also those who wheel book bags/computers into buildings. Recorded books designed for the blind have benefited many other students who have difficulty reading or simply paying attention to what is read. Recorded material also allows students to listen to required "reading" while in their cars, biking, or walking. Pens with soft grips originally designed for people with fine motor difficulty are becoming commonplace in office supply stores because they are more comfortable for everyone to use.

Brain-Based Research: Recognition, Strategic, Affective Systems

Universal Design for Learning reflects and supports many of the findings in brain-based research, work from cognitive-social theorists, educational psychologists, and educational researchers. Brain-based research, studies on multiple intelligences, learning styles, and differentiated instruction, tell us that there are no "regular" students. We all learn in different ways and may perform differently in different environments. No one strategy fits all learners. Some students who are learning disabled in a general print-based classroom, for example, might not be disabled in a visual-auditory-based environment (Rose & Meyer, 2002). Once words are on paper, options are limited. Universal Design for Learning researchers suggest that digital formats increase our options for access. For example, print in digital format becomes flexible. It can be changed in size and color. It can be hyperlinked to definitions, pronounced, and translated into another language. It can be paired with pictures or sign language. If necessary, it can be read aloud to keep up with comprehension and problem-solving tasks. In addition, students who access print easily will likely find that school environments with a variety of learning choices make their experiences more meaningful and motivating. We will talk more about these options in future chapters.

Based on research done by neurologists, CAST has suggested a three-part framework for how the brain works. It works through (1) recognition, (2) strategic, and (3) affective systems (Cytowic, 1996; Meyer & Rose, 2000). These systems represent three separate areas of the brain in terms of spatiality and function. They are, however, interconnected in the learning process. They also tell us that each one of us has a unique way of using these systems, just as we each have a unique set of fingerprints and our own DNA.

The **recognition system** identifies patterns in the brain. If we visualize the brain as a file cabinet (Figure 7.1), its ability to store information is seemingly unlimited. However, it first needs to be able to gather and receive the information through a sensory channel before it can file it. Initially, the learner needs to gather and name things that will be going into these file folders. Interaction occurs as the learner looks for ways to receive and interpret information. This involves attention, memory, and perception (Vygotsky, 1978). If we can identify the sensory system (sight, sound, touch, movement) that initially works best for each learner, that may help us tailor the student's educational program more effectively from the start. Positron emission tomography (PET) scans, a type of nuclear medicine imaging, offer exciting future possibilities for understanding how a student learns by enabling medical professionals to link task activity to a specific area of the brain. For example, a learner who has difficulty with visual processing (which occurs in the occipital lobe) may best receive his/her information through sound/speech (temporal lobe) (Sousa, 2001). Knowing this, teachers can think about presenting lessons that allow for flexible accessibility. The recognition system is referred to as the "what" of learning (CAST, 1998).

Strategic systems are located in the frontal lobes in the anterior half of the brain (Fuster, 1997). The learner uses these systems to construct his/her own meaning to information that is received and to sort and classify it. If we think about the file cabinet analogy, the learner begins to get organized with his/her thinking by describing, summarizing, reporting, expressing, and retelling as he/she puts labels on the folders and begins to fill them up. Eventually the learner identifies patterns and makes connections between information that is received and perceived by sequencing, comparing, showing, and investigating. The learner is processing his/her experience, accepting new encounters, and fitting them into his/her existing filing system. An educational term that describes this process is **metacognition**, which means thinking about your thinking. In the classroom, students demonstrate the use of strategic systems when they write paragraphs, give a speech, participate in a debate, or solve algebra problems. On the basketball court, players tap on these strategic systems as they dribble, pass, and shoot basketballs. When students develop strong metacognitive abilities, they can plan and organize better, make more-accurate predictions, solve problems, perform tasks more efficiently, and achieve more independence because they can identify and articulate their own abilities and limitations (Swanson, 1996). These strategic networks are referred to as the "how" of learning (CAST, 1998).

Finally, in the third part of the framework, the **affective systems** look at the engagement or social interaction of the learner. These systems can be found in the limbic system of the brain, located above the brainstem (Sousa, 2006). Sousa refers to this as the *emotional* system and describes this area of the brain as responsible for long-term memory, making connections between emotions, cognitive learning, and memory. Brain research suggests that the learner's emotional system drives attention, and attention drives meaning and memory. The development of the affective systems in learners will be influenced by emotional reactions to experiences (Cytowic, 1996; Meyer & Rose, 2000). Therefore, engagement must occur to make learning meaningful and to internalize it. The social, cultural, and historical context in which learning occurs for each student is complex (Pisha & Coyne, 2001; Vygotsky, 1978). Learner interest and feedback from teachers, peers, and significant others can impact this system. Learner engagement increases when the task is active, interesting, and paired with both positive and corrective feedback. On the flip side, if learners find presentations boring, delivered in a language that can't be understood or in print that can't be decoded, and if there is little, no, or mostly negative feedback, many of these learners will disengage and become frustrated over time. If learners can remember what is permanently stored in their "file cabinets," chances are they will find learning more enjoyable and exciting. They "cut-and-paste" information/experiences they can retrieve easily and transfer them to new experiences/learning. Engagement and motivation are increased. The affective dimension of learning is referred to as the "why" of learning (CAST, 1998).

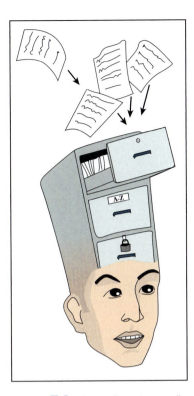

Figure 7.1 The "Filing System" of the Brain
Source: John Metcalf.

Cognitive-Social Learning Theories

As we take a closer look at who the learners are and how we can make our schools more accessible for all of them, it is helpful to take a brief look back at some of the cognitive and social sciences theorists who have offered us time-tested ways of looking at teaching and learning. The work of Russian psychologist Lev Vygotsky, for example, appears to support CAST's framework for the three brain systems just described (Vygotsky, 1978). In addition to the framework, he suggested, through his research, that each learner has a **zone of proximal development** (ZPD). He defines this zone as the area or difference between a person's actual independent level of learning/problem solving and his/her potential level of development of higher-level learning/problem solving. This higher level of learning can eventually be achieved to independence through the guidance of an adult or through peer collaboration (Vygotsky, 1986). Simply stated, the skilled teacher or capable peers must find this optimal place to guide and teach the learner that is not too hard or too easy, but just right. Supports will be provided that will eventually fade away as the learner progresses. When students are engaged in meaningful and challenging work within this zone, motivation tends to increase.

It may also be helpful to revisit Swiss developmental psychologist Jean Piaget's cognitive theory as we think about *all* learners. Piaget, sometimes referred to as "The Father of Child Psychology," suggested that learners move through four stages as they develop intelligence as shown in Table 7.2 (Atherton, 2005). In the *sensorimotor* stage, he explains, using sensory and motor activities to receive information is important. In the early years, a typical child usually begins repeating, naming, and recalling objects and people in the environment. This aligns well with the recognition system of Universal Design for Learning. In the *preoperational* stage, learning is still concrete, but language develops and decisions begin to be made by perceptions. In the third stage, *concrete operational*, the learner continues to make connections and organize thinking through the manipulation of physical objects. Learners begin to reason as they see differences and sequences. In the final stage, *formal operational*, the learner answers "what-if" questions. An individual might have to make a decision in this stage of whether to accept new information and change to a new system or accommodate the existing system. Even though Piaget suggested age stages, he measured the highest level of intellectual functioning by what stage a child was in and not by chronological age (Ginsburg & Opper, 1988). Piaget's child centered approach also acknowledged the importance of social interactions in a child's development (Atherton, 2005).

The work of educational psychologist Benjamin Bloom also helps set the stage for an introduction to the concept of Universal Design for Learning. Bloom worked with colleagues to identify six categories of thinking within the cognitive domain that were typically used in school settings for assessment (Bloom, 1956). Bloom reflected extensively about how people think and how the learning/thinking process could be improved. Fifty years later, educators and many other professionals refer back to his original work. It has also been extended and revised over the years. It is helpful to step back and think about the original framework as referenced in Table 7.3. This framework can be very useful as you observe teachers and formulate your own questions, write lesson objectives, and contemplate types of activities and responses that you will ask of students. It is important that different levels/categories of thinking are purposefully and frequently infused into one's practice. In 1956, Bloom found that 95 percent of test questions students encountered were lower-level questions such as those beginning with the words *who, what, when,* and *where*. Questions that demanded learners to express *why* and *how* answers were limited. Bloom's contemplative thinking gave us a tremendous vehicle for improving our practices even today.

Bloom's system has been revised over the years to align it more closely with current research (Anderson & Krathwohl, 2001) and to allow for more flexibility

Table 7.2	Piaget's Stages of Development	
Stage	**Approximate Age**	**Description**
Sensorimotor	0–2 yrs	• Awareness of self (bodies) and environment and discovery of relationships between the two through seeing, touching, sucking, feeling, using their senses and motor activities • Realization that an object can be moved by hand (causality) and of object permanence (it's still there even if hidden)
Preoperational	2–7 yrs	• Preschool years • Language starts to represent objects; egocentric, concrete, lacks concept of conservation • Decisions are dominated by perceptions and may center only on one dimension of an event and ignore important details
Concrete Operational	7–11 yrs	• Begins to organize thoughts in terms of actual physical objects • Beginning to sequence objects, see differences, and understand conservation (concrete) and reversibility; beginning of logical reasoning
Formal Operational	11–12 yrs through adult	• Some people never reach it • Abstract thinking and understanding of form or construction of math problems • Able to reason, argue, accomplish tasks, and answer "what-if" questions

Table 7.3	Bloom's Taxonomy of Educational Objectives	
Level of Question with Definition	**Examples of Verbs Associated with Levels**	**Example of Learner Skills/Student Roles**
1. Remember Students absorb and recall or recognize specific information from long-term memory.	Choosing, collecting, defining, describing, examining, identifying, labeling, listing, locating, matching, memorizing, naming, quoting, recalling, recognizing, recording, showing, tabulating, telling	• Observing/receiving of information • Remembering information • Seeing the big picture or ideas of the content • Working toward mastery of subject matter
2. Understand Students understand the information. They construct meaning from it.	Associating, classifying, comparing, differentiating, discussing, distinguishing, estimating, explaining, exemplifying, inferring, interpreting, observing, outlining, paraphrasing, predicting, reporting, researching, summarizing	• Actively participating • Translating/explaining information given • Providing examples • Demonstrating (showing and telling)
3. Apply Students use concepts, methods, principles, and theories learned in new situations.	Adapting, applying, calculating, changing, choosing, computing, constructing, demonstrating, dramatizing, employing, experimenting, illustrating, implementing, interpreting, making, manipulating, operating, painting, practicing, preparing, producing, scheduling, recording, sketching, solving, teaching, using, writing	• Actively participating • Constructing • Using information • Demonstrating use of knowledge (methods, concepts, skills, theories) in new situations • Solving problems with this information
4. Analyze Students break information down into steps or parts (elements).	Arranging, attributing, categorizing, comparing, connecting, contrasting, deducing, diagramming, discovering, dissecting, dividing, examining, experimenting, explaining, grouping, inferring, inspecting, interpreting, ordering, organizing, questioning, probing, relating, selecting, separating, sorting, surveying, testing	• Actively participating • Seeing patterns • Organizing and planning (listing, outlining, graphing) • Recognizing hidden meanings • Identifying components • Discussing and reporting findings
5. Evaluate Students judge or assess the value of ideas, materials, and methods using standards and criteria.	Arguing, appraising, assessing, checking, choosing, concluding, convincing, critiquing, debating, deciding, deducing, defending, discriminating, estimating, explaining, grading, judging, justifying, measuring, probing, ranking, recommending, rejecting, selecting, supporting, telling why, using criteria, valuing	• Actively participating • Assessing value of theories, presentations • Making choices based on reasoned argument • Recognizing subjectivity
6. Create Students combine parts to construct a whole as they create new meaning or structure from their knowledge.	Acting, assembling, combining, compiling, composing, constructing, creating, designing, developing, hypothesizing, imagining, inferring, integrating, inventing, modifying, planning, preparing, producing, organizing, rearranging, revising, role playing, substituting, formulating, preparing, generalizing, writing	• Actively participating • Generalizing from given facts • Comparing and contrasting • Relating knowledge from several areas • Predicting, drawing conclusions

Sources: Adapted from C. A. Lutz, *Roles, Process Verbs and Products from Bloom's Taxonomy of the Cognitive Domain* (Juneau: Alaska Department of Education and Early Development's Curriculum Frameworks Project, September 1991), available at http://www.eed.state.ak.us/TLS/FRAMEWORKS/sstudies/part3a1.htm; adapted from L. W. Anderson and D. R. Krathwohl (Eds.), *A Taxonomy for Learning, Teaching, and Assessing: A Revision of Bloom's Taxonomy of Educational Objectives* (New York: Longman, 2001).

between levels. The wording is useful in writing lesson objectives because the levels are named using measurable verbs. In the first level, students need to absorb and recall facts from the long-term memory and then construct meaning from the facts in the second level. The third level, *apply*, has the learner directly practicing and showing what is learned. Next, *analysis* causes the learner to think about why things are done the way they are. *Create* represents the highest level of thinking.

Piaget's stages of development align fairly closely with Bloom's categorization system and also offer us a tool for assessment and planning. Part of Piaget's theory, however, may be debatable as to whether or not a learner can skip a step/stage. Sometimes, if students have been working on a skill for a long time (sometimes years), it may be necessary to bypass a step and offer an alternative so the student can develop skills that are needed for life. For example, if a student is significantly below grade level with computational skills and has received extensive, prolonged remediation with few or very small gains, then it might be best to let him/her work with a calculator so a different set of skills/concepts (that are based on computation skills) can be developed. Most students, for example, will need to know how sales tax is computed and added to products they buy so they can determine if they have enough money. If the computation is allowed on a calculator, the concept of what sales tax is and how it works can be applied. Students can become better consumers.

The same way of thinking can be applied in reading. In a rather extreme example, think about a student who has difficulty naming alphabet letters even though he/she can visualize them (usually with a picture) and produce and segment the sounds. If intensive remediation over time has been tried and progress is slow, it may make sense to go ahead and move forward with another set of reading skills. It will be important, for example, to keep the student's vocabulary and reading comprehension skills progressing while working on the letter naming. Extra time spent drilling letter names can perhaps be done using a software drill-and-practice program or extra practice with a reading interventionist. Meanwhile, choral reading, audio books, and other text-to-speech technologies (or some other similar type of adaptations) are examples of useful tools that can help a student along the way to keep up with and develop other needed reading/language arts skills. Other learning pathways must be available to extend thinking and help the learner progress while very basic interventions are also being made.

Remember to be flexible when working between "stages" as you apply Bloom's taxonomy in planning for and assessing learning. In a universally designed learning environment, *all* learners will need to work through and respond to different levels of questions and skills. These levels do not necessarily need to progress sequentially from lowest to highest. Everyone benefits from work at different thinking levels. Think about how young children create their own versions of stories or construct inventively with blocks. They don't necessarily have the all the basic knowledge and haven't progressed through all the steps, and yet they "play" at a high level of thinking. Remember that learners at *all* stages of development have the ability to solve problems. It might take some students longer and they may need more direct instruction, demonstration teaching, modeling, and scaffolding, but everyone can make gains. Learning is more interesting and motivating to each one of us when we are challenged in our thinking no matter who we are.

Cengage Learning/Wadsworth

Reading along with audiobooks can help students access content while developing language and decoding skills.

Cognitive psychologist Jerome Bruner looked at the structure of teaching and learning as a process more than sequencing through developmental stages (Bruner, 1960). He considered environmental factors that impact growth such as social, political, language, and other cultural influences. He suggested that children can explore difficult subjects and be active problem solvers if teaching is strategic. If students are actively interested in materials, they can be problem solvers. Bruner is credited with the idea of a **spiral curriculum** (Smith, 2002b). A spiral curriculum provides the basic ideas of a subject that students revisit frequently and use as a springboard for more-advanced learning.

Multiple Intelligences and Learning Preferences

Howard Gardner, a researcher and psychologist who studied with Bruner, also expanded the concepts of cognitive development suggested by Piaget. He provided evidence that a child may be at very different stages of development at any given time. For example, a student might be struggling in math class and yet be a star on the baseball team. The learner likely has a higher level of maturation/development in bodily/kinesthetic relationships than in number sense development. Knowledge at any one particular developmental stage does not necessarily mean that every area of the brain is functioning at the same level. Gardner doesn't see intelligence as a single number determined by an IQ test, but rather suggests that people have **multiple intelligences**. Over many years, he has identified at least eight intelligence areas (Gardner, 1993; Smith, 2002a). Each area exists as a distinct entity even though they may be somewhat related and interactive. These areas are described in Table 7.4. Examples of some gifted individuals who personify each category are included. You will likely note that some people have attributes that suggest more than one area of intelligence.

Table 7.4	Gardner's List of Multiple Intelligences		
	Intelligence Area	**Description**	**Examples**
	Verbal/linguistic	A sensitivity to the meaning and order of words	Maya Angelou, Ernest Hemingway, Martin Luther King, Jr.
	Logical/mathematical	Ability in mathematics and other complex logical systems	Albert Einstein, Stephen Hawking
	Musical/rhythmic	The ability to understand and create music	Ludwig von Beethoven, Ella Fitzgerald, Itzhak Perlman
	Bodily/kinesthetic	The ability to use one's body in a skilled way, for self-expression or toward a goal	Mikhail Baryshnikov, Michael Jordan, Nadia Comenici
	Visual/spatial	The ability to "think in pictures," to perceive the visual world accurately, and to recreate (or alter) it in the mind or on paper	Michelangelo, Pablo Picasso, Frank Lloyd Wright, Temple Grandin
	Interpersonal	An ability to perceive and understand other individuals' moods, desires, and motivations	Madeleine Albright, Nelson Mandela, Carl Rogers
	Intrapersonal	An understanding of one's own emotions	Sigmund Freud, Mother Theresa
	Naturalist	The ability to recognize and classify plants, minerals, and animals, including rocks and grass and all variety of flora and fauna	John Audobon, Rachel Carson, Charles Darwin

Source: Adapted from M. K. Smith, *Howard Gardner and Multiple Intelligences* (2002), available at http://www.infed.org/thinkers/gardner.htm

Gardner adds that the degree to which an intelligence area is developed is not only due to genetics, but also to social, cultural, and environmental factors. To develop fully, a person must have access to needed materials and be encouraged and supported in his/her environment (Smith, 2002a).

Jeff Hawkins, a researcher in artificial intelligence and the inventor of the Palm-Pilot, suggests human intelligence is measured by a person's ability to remember and predict patterns in the world (Hawkins & Blakeslee, 2004). The brain receives patterns through experiences including language, mathematics, social situations, and the properties of objects. Intelligence is measured by the brain's ability to receive patterns, store/remember them, and then combine them to make predictions (Sousa, 2006). This is what we do when we solve problems. This is what takes us to the top levels of thinking suggested by Piaget and Bloom. Perhaps if we think of the big idea of intelligence as one's ability to problem-solve through such connections, we can see more clearly how every student has the ability to learn. Some students, for example, put a great deal of energy into figuring out how *not* to do the work! How can we rechannel that "problem-solving" energy in a positive way?

Implications for Teaching and Learning

According to Sousa (2001) and Jensen (1998), prolific writers on brain-based educational research, teachers must instruct with the brain in mind. No one strategy can fit all learners. Jensen suggests that the actual "biology" of learners is different today than it was 30 years ago partly because of environmental factors. For example, there are more additives in foods today and greater exposure to drugs and medication. There are more single-parent households and fewer resources for many families. Children tend to get less motor stimulation in the early years as they spend more time indoors in front of television screens and playing video games and less time playing outside on swings, bicycles, and playgrounds because of heightened safety concerns. Children may also spend considerably more time strapped into car seats and seatbelts than they did in years past, once again restricting movement. These environmental influences may also be helpful to consider as one thinks about how to work most successfully in today's schools.

Studies conducted in the mid-1990s estimated that the sensory preferences of the students in the United States in grades 3–12 were as follows: Visual: 48 percent; Auditory: 19 percent; and Kinesthetic-Tactile: 35 percent (Sousa, 1997; Swanson, 1995). More-recent studies, however, suggest that as many as 90 percent of today's learners likely prefer the visual mode (Holt & Kysilka, 2006; Jensen, 1998). These findings suggest that the percentage of learners with visual preferences has nearly doubled in the last 10 years. In addition, clinical psychiatry studies at Harvard University are showing that movement is critical to help the brain produce chemicals that make them stronger and healthier, suggesting that increased physical activity can positively impact growth in reading, writing, mathematics, and thinking abilities (Ratey, 2001).

Teaching to and through sensory preferences is also referred to as a **learning preferences** approach. Just as Gardner contends we have stronger areas of intelligences, students typically have different strengths in the visual, auditory, tactile, and kinesthetic areas as well. Few documented studies on the effectiveness of teaching to learning preferences exist, although most researchers believe they can be helpful in an informal way (Burns, Johnson, & Gable, 1998). Use learning preferences information as another possible tool for your toolbox. Perhaps the most helpful thing about this way of thinking is that it makes you consider different ways you can present and receive information to and from your students in the classroom.

The learning preferences model in Table 7.5 may be helpful in planning your teaching for diverse learners. It presents four general approaches to learning: (1) visual/verbal, (2) tactile/kinesthetic, (3) visual/nonverbal, and (4) auditory/verbal. This model is particularly helpful when thinking about learners who don't

Cengage Learning/Wadsworth

Students of all ages learn through active "hands-on" activity with teacher facilitation.

Table 7.5	Learning Preferences	
Type of Learner	**Learning Characteristics**	**Learning Tools**
Visual/ Verbal	• Prefers receiving visual information paired with print • Visualizes information to be learned • Likes to study in quiet room	• Lecture with overhead • Textbooks • Class notes • Outlines
Tactile/ Kinesthetic	• Prefers "hands-on" learning • Active, learns through physical movement	• Demonstration teaching • Field experiences
Visual/ Nonverbal	• Prefers information presented visually • May be artistic • Tends to prefer a quiet room rather than study groups • Uses visual pictures to remember	• Visual aids (video, maps, charts, diagrams, pictures, film)
Auditory/ Verbal	• Prefers listening to a lecture • Learns best through interaction with others—exchanging ideas • Uses what is heard to remember and may repeat information out loud	• Group discussion • Audiotapes

Source: Adapted from S. Winebrenner, *Teaching Kids with Learning Difficulties in the Regular Classroom* (Minneapolis, MN: Free Spirit Publishing, 1996).

quite fit the traditional educational patterns we were raised with. An example of someone who has visual/nonverbal characteristics is Dr. Temple Grandin, a gifted animal scientist with autism who designs livestock-handling facilities. In her book, *Thinking in Pictures: My Life with Autism*, she tells us:

> Words are like a second language to me. I translate both spoken and written words into full-color movies, complete with sound, which run like a VCR tape in my head. When somebody speaks to me, his words are instantly translated into pictures . . . in my job . . . visual thinking is a tremendous advantage. (It) has enabled me to build entire systems in my imagination. (p. 3)

Therefore, it might be helpful to take note of learning preferences and approaches that might work when we encounter learners who baffle us. Once again, learners will likely "fit" into more than one category so look for the category that best represents the learner in general as you consider the possibilities. Remember, too, that by exposing *all* learners to different approaches, new ways of discovering and learning information are made available to them. A rich array of teaching and learning benefits everyone.

Some proponents of using learning preferences as assessment and teaching tools suggest that auditory/verbal learners tend to be analytical and logical thinkers who do their best work in a step-by-step, sequential fashion and that the other three categories of learners tend to think more globally. Global learners may be more intuitive and random. They may work backwards from whole to parts and may learn most favorably through open-ended tasks. They enjoy creating new ideas (Winebrenner, 1996). With Universal Design for Learning, all learning preferences are considered when planning instruction.

If assessed learner strengths and needs are used to plan and implement instruction and methods and if materials and learning tools are a "good fit," teachers likely have a better chance of impacting student achievement. If each learner, in turn, learns to identify his/her best ways to learn and then advocates for himself/herself by sharing this information with future teachers, he/she will be even more empowered and will likely take more control of his or her own learning. For all these reasons, when looking at accessibility options in UDL classrooms in subsequent chapters, we will consider cognitive-social theories, Bloom's taxonomy, learning preferences, multiple intelligences, and behavioral, medical, and environmental factors.

Just as learners need to know their best way of learning, teachers need to know their own best teaching preferences. We will talk more in future chapters about ways to work collaboratively on teams so there are a variety of options for students and teachers. If we have a limited amount of time and opportunity to make a difference, we need this information up front. By matching student learning preferences to flexible instructional practices that offer multiple formats for successful participation by all, we can maximize the time spent together in our schools.

Three Essential Qualities of UDL: Representation, Engagement, and Expression

Taking what we know from universal design, brain research, cognitive-social learning theories, and learning preferences/multiple intelligences studies can further help us understand the idea of Universal Design for Learning for application in today's schools. Universal Design for Learning suggests schools offer an array of flexible options up front to diverse groups of learners so that each student has an equal opportunity to learn from the start. There are three essential qualities of Universal Design for Learning that must be considered when designing curriculum to meet the needs of all learners. They are (1) multiple means of representation, (2) multiple means of engagement, and (3) multiple means of expression (see Figure 7.2). These three essential qualities for UDL were presented by developers at the Center for Applied Special Technology (Rose & Meyer, 2002). As mentioned earlier, much of their work has focused on using digital formats because of their great flexibility. However, as you continue reading, you will see that there are many other possible formats, representing a continuum of technology, including "low-tech" options as well.

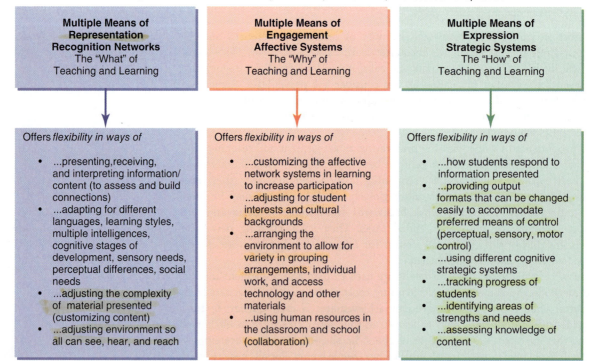

Essential Question: What do curriculum, instruction, environment, and assessment provide?

Multiple Means of Representation **Recognition Networks** The "What" of Teaching and Learning	**Multiple Means of Engagement** **Affective Systems** The "Why" of Teaching and Learning	**Multiple Means of Expression** **Strategic Systems** The "How" of Teaching and Learning
Offers *flexibility in ways of* • ...presenting, receiving, and interpreting information/content (to assess and build connections) • ...adapting for different languages, learning styles, multiple intelligences, cognitive stages of development, sensory needs, perceptual differences, social needs • ...adjusting the complexity of material presented (customizing content) • ...adjusting environment so all can see, hear, and reach	Offers *flexibility in ways of* • ...customizing the affective network systems in learning to increase participation • ...adjusting for student interests and cultural backgrounds • ...arranging the environment to allow for variety in grouping arrangements, individual work, and access technology and other materials • ...using human resources in the classroom and school (collaboration)	Offers *flexibility in ways of* • ...how students respond to information presented • ...providing output formats that can be changed easily to accommodate preferred means of control (perceptual, sensory, motor control) • ...using different cognitive strategic systems • ...tracking progress of students • ...identifying areas of strengths and needs • ...assessing knowledge of content

Figure 7.2 Three Essential Qualities of Universal Design for Learning—The 3 M's of UDL

Source: Adapted from R. Orkwis, *Universally Designed Instruction* (Arlington, VA: Council for Exceptional Children, 2003) (ERIC Document Reproduction Service No. ED468709).

Multiple Means of Representation

The first quality of UDL is **multiple means of representation**. Students are provided with a variety of ways to receive and interpret information. Think about your own college courses and perhaps classrooms you work in. Many students benefit more from a lecture when it includes a visual presentation (overhead projector or PowerPoint presentations, for example) accompanied by an outline. Other students might simply record a lecture or get a copy of a classmate's notes so they can concentrate on the presentation. Some students benefit from accessing the text or lecture through tapes, eBooks, or other recordings. Digital text can be read aloud or translated, and it can be linked to definitions, files, and related web resources. Some students may live too far away to come to campus and work online instead, with the presentations offered digitally along with a discussion board, chat rooms, or video conferencing. Some instructors may use video clips to provide examples of the material they are teaching, whereas others may provide a demonstration.

By offering different ways of presenting information, not only can we reduce physical barriers to learning, but also sensory, perceptual, and other learning "roadblocks" students may have. Students can choose their own best way to receive and identify sensory data and, as the neuroscientists and theorists suggest, find a pattern, and make connections. If your plan is flexible, you can move relatively smoothly between options and detect a pattern. If you are blind, the path is more restricted and finding a pattern from sensory input becomes more challenging, but is still possible if Braille and/or auditory input is offered.

Meyer and Rose (1998) tell us that some learners do better when they receive information through multiple modalities (bimodal—visual and auditory, for example). Nolet and McLaughlin (2005) suggest using redundancy (parallel systems). That is, present the same information in different formats. The science concept presented in a lecture, for example, could also be presented on tape or CD in Spanish for the native Spanish speaker, paired with a video clip and/or perhaps a "hands-on" demonstration. Table 7.6 suggests different ways material might be best received

Universal Design for Learning in the Classroom

Multiple Means of Representation (Elementary)

UDL means presenting information to students in different ways because students each have different ways of learning . . . Don't we all? For example, I am very visual and hands-on, while my daughter is auditory. When she was having trouble learning the multiplication facts in 4th grade, I would tell her to close her eyes and envision a black chalkboard with the problem and answer written boldly in a bright color. "Mom," she would cry. "When I close my eyes, it's dark!" She was so frustrated, and so was I! I found a recording of the multiplication facts sung to a jazzy set of melodies. She listened to them repeatedly in her room, singing along

happily, and within a week she had the facts memorized!

Carol Dinsdale, NBCT
Mount Vernon Elementary
St. Petersburg, FL
Council for Exceptional Children, Clarissa Hug Teacher of the Year 2005

Example of Multiple Means of Representation (Secondary)

It does not matter if the number is large or small, there are strategies you can implement regularly to help all students in your classroom. Start with planning. Where do you want your students to go and how will you know when they get there? What activities will assist their understanding of your

content? Plan to include modeling and demonstration before you ever move the students into guided practice. Do not transition out of guided practice until you have assessed that they are ready to move to independent practice. If you are lecturing, have "talking points" on the projector or overhead for students to see as you are sharing content. Use, but do not overuse, PowerPoint to aid in your presentations. If needed, print out your lecture notes for students who need help in processing and keeping up with the pace of the lesson.

Libby Jackson Ortmann, NBCT
Curriculum Resource Teacher
Alice Drive Middle School
Sumter School District 17
Sumter, SC

Will Hart/PhotoEdit

Use multiple methods of presentation to communicate concepts in different formats to maximize meaningful learning.

when presented through different learning modes. Affective ways of presenting material are also included. The more modalities incorporated in classroom presentations up front, the greater the chances that students will be engaged. Using multiple methods also varies repetition for those who need lots of extra practice. Technology enhances the work because it can add images and sound to illustrate a concept. This list is by no means exhaustive, and some methods can fit under more than one category.

Sometimes if we look at a more extreme example, we can glean even more insight. Think back, for example, to Helen Keller and her teacher, Anne Sullivan, in the early years. Anne would finger spell words into Helen's hand during their daily lessons. Anne didn't know what this meant at first but she enjoyed this game of "shapes" until the novelty wore off. One day, Helen got tired of it and ran outside before her lesson was over. A frustrated Anne followed her, and they came to a water pump. You may be familiar with what happened next:

> She (Anne) began to bang the pump handle up and down, and soon a stream of water poured from its lip. She grabbed Helen's hand and stuck it under the icy flow, and in the same instant began to spell W–A–T–E–R into the wet palm. Helen went rigid and pulled wildly toward freedom. But Annie [Anne] held on. W–A–T–E–R . . . W–A–T–E–R . . . Suddenly Helen stopped struggling . . . she felt the word burn down

Table 7.6	Multiple Ways to Present Lesson Content			
Auditory	**Visual**	**Tactile/Kinesthetic**	**Affective**	**Technology Options**
• Lecturing • Presenting information orally through a character • Singing • Reading aloud	• Reading articles, books • Watching video clips or a slide show • Showing on a poster, chart, graph, or slide • Watching a play • Using sign language • Providing an advanced organizer	• Taking a field trip • Demonstrating (e.g., drawing, sculpting, constructing, playing a game) • Watching a dance • Using sign language/ gestures • Using Braille	• Presenting to large or small groups • One-on-one presentations or tutorials • Cross-age tutoring • Role playing • Connecting to student interest areas	• Overhead projector • Electronic whiteboard • Books on tape • Video/DVD • TV/VCR (closed caption) • Podcasts • Online tutorials • YouTube

through her hand and into her brain . . . a light flooded her face . . . Life came rushing in on Helen. (Davidson, 1965, pp. 125–126)

Each one of us looks at the world a little differently depending on how we are physically "wired," whether it is due to biological, environmental, or cultural factors. Like Anne Sullivan and Helen Keller, having flexibility in representation can offer multiple ways a student can receive information and make learning come alive.

Multiple Means of Engagement

Even if our schools are physically accessible and equipped with accessible curricular materials, it doesn't mean students will learn. A classroom might have lots of high-tech equipment such as computers, electronic whiteboards, and tools with digital capabilities, but it will only be as effective as the thought and planning that goes into its use. In a classroom where books are accessible on tape, in digital formats, in different languages, and in Braille, there are still students who will read or hear the words, but do not know the meaning. Many learners can read or listen to a whole page of text or sit through a presentation and recall nothing about it. This leads to a second essential quality of UDL, **multiple means of engagement**, in the quest to remove curricular barriers.

Engagement can be increased first by knowing the students. By looking over previous assessments, using interest and learning preference/multiple intelligence inventories, and talking with students, parents, and other teachers who work or have worked with your learners, you can gather important information that will help engage and motivate students. When student interests are matched to learning activities that foster independence, motivation typically increases. Spending time identifying student interest areas, strengths, needs, backgrounds, and learning preferences provides valuable information to teachers. In return, teachers can offer a variety of visual, auditory, tactile, and kinesthetic materials, including technology and activities that increase engagement options. This practice ultimately increases the chances of involving all learners. It is time up front that is well spent. For

 Universal Design for Learning in the Classroom

Multiple Means of Engagement (Elementary)

UDL means engaging my students because I must "sell them" on the relevance of the lesson to their lives. What does it mean to them? Why do they need this skill or knowledge? I must make sure my lessons have something that appeals to everyone at their developmental and interest level. I can find out what they like with interest surveys and just by talking and listening to them. I use materials they are interested in. For example, my class loves animals, especially reptiles. *We have woven animal research, writing, oral presentations, and much more into our integrated units this year.*

Applying a UDL framework maximizes participation by offering choice for response.

If you have one child at a time coming up to the board, you've lost the other 20! Each child must be involved every step of the way. Provide individual whiteboards so the other 20 can do the problem at their seats. Create teams and make it a competition.

Carol Dinsdale, NBCT
Mount Vernon Elementary
St. Petersburg, FL
Council for Exceptional Children, Clarissa Hug
Teacher of the Year 2005

Multiple Means of Engagement (Secondary)

Include activities that are engaging and have the students up and moving to experience the content. Illustrations, role-plays, scenarios, discussion, group work, and sharing are all possibilities in a diverse classroom with students having mixed abilities. Laptops in the classroom with daily lessons for each student will greatly assist instruction. Students love electronic communication, so why not send academic prompts via e-mail or class web pages so they can "chat" with their teacher about difficult lessons or share successes with their homework. When possible, use podcasts of interesting stories to connect with your lessons. Have them listen at home or in class.

Libby Jackson Ortmann, NBCT
Curriculum Resource Teacher
Alice Drive Middle School
Sumter School District 17
Sumter, SC

example, teachers can identify what "hooks" to use in working with students. If a student is into basketball, for example, the teacher might want to infuse some video clips and basketball statistics in a math lesson. Adding digital formats to what teachers do makes learning interactive and generally increases engagement.

Even when students have access to curricular materials, the teacher still must consider the process of teaching, learning, monitoring progress, and giving feedback. This is why it is critical for teachers to identify each student's zone of proximal development (ZPD) as described earlier and facilitate the engagement of learning at this level. Some students will need more supported instruction than others, and some will need more feedback and praise so they can engage and move ahead. For others, changes in the environment might be needed. Table 7.7 offers some examples of ways to increase student participation.

In the field of special education, there are many research-based strategies that facilitate the process of strategic learning that may also benefit the learning process of other students. The University of Kansas Center for Research on Learning has developed the Strategic Instruction Model (SIM), for example, to guide secondary students with learning disabilities through instruction. These learning strategies typically include visual organizers, sequenced steps, and strategy prompts. Marzano et al. (1992) describe an "abstract strategy" that helps students understand the essence of a genre at a higher level. There are many effective multisensory strategies as well. We will talk more about effective research-based strategies that increase engagement for diverse learners in upcoming chapters.

As discussed earlier, most students want and need to work with others, particularly their peers. They need that interaction to make learning meaningful (Vygotsky, 1986). It can be challenging as well as motivating. You may recall that this is the affective brain system—the "why" of learning (CAST, 1998). As educators, we know that students learn a great deal from each other. A learner, for example, might understand the language of a peer better than the language of the teacher. The peer might explain what has been presented in his or her own words to the learner. A student who speaks a different language will likely benefit from working with a peer who speaks both English and that student's native language. As you will see in the next chapters, the principles of Universal Design for Learning support offering different ways to work with others.

Multiple Means of Expression

A third quality of UDL is **multiple means of expression**. This quality accommodates the strategic and motor system as suggested by the field of neuroscience and the cognitive-social theorists mentioned earlier by reflecting on what different ways

Table 7.7	Examples of Multiple Ways to Engage Students			
Auditory	**Visual**	**Tactile/Kinesthetic**	**Affective**	**Technology Options**
• Listening to text read aloud	• Using a dictionary	• Using a Braille dictionary	• Working in areas of student interest	• Talking dictionary
• Listening to and retelling directions	• Highlighting key points	• Touching words on a word wall	• Working with a partner who can help with definitions	• Recording on tape or iPods
• Asking and answering questions	• Outlining steps to solving a problem	• Using manipulatives	• Working alone or in cooperative groups	• Word processing
• Debating	• Completing a graphic organizer	• Building a model	• Discussion groups/book clubs	• Talking calculators
• Discussing	• Designing a poster	• Using response cards	• Seminar participation	• Creating spreadsheets
• Giving verbal prompts	• Illustrating/taking pictures	• Using a game format	• Giving feedback	• Creating a video
• Talking through steps	• Drawing		• Praising	• Video conferencing
			• Changing work environment	• Blogging, text messaging

PhotoSpin

Diverse students can benefit from social interaction to make learning meaningful.

students may respond using the information they have received. Some students have no idea of how to begin to respond at all without direction. Others will blurt out answers or begin writing without organizing their thinking first. Some students will require more wait time and will need to rehearse their answers. Others have motor impairments and may need electronic communication devices. Some simply do not have the words at all and need a visual communication system. Writing with a pencil or pen is uncomfortable for some students with fine motor challenges. Forming the letters, making reversals, and misspelling words are all barriers to expression for others. Having access to a word processor, spell checker, or a method of dictation can make access to expression much easier.

Students with social/emotional issues, including extreme shyness or anxiety, may have difficulty responding orally in class. A gifted, prolific writer may contribute to an electronic discussion board, but never speak in a large group due to shyness. Some students express themselves best through pictures, actions, or presentations. For others, it might be through an eye gaze or a pointer. Some learners simply need some extra processing time (wait time) before offering a response. Building multiple means of expression into the initial learning design may help reduce these kinds of barriers.

By offering alternative approaches to responding to information received, learners can think about their thinking (metacognition) and organize it (Pisha & Coyne, 2001). Such an approach to response can also increase self-regulation, which should, in turn, help students take ownership of their learning because they know how to get information in and out of those "file folders" in their brains. They build stronger connections that create and improve ways for them to think about what has been taken in and respond to it. When students feel empowered by their learning, they tend to feel better about school.

Table 7.8 offers suggestions for multiple ways students might express themselves. Some of these examples for response can fit in multiple columns. This is by no means a complete list, but it does illustrate how a teacher can be thinking about learners in terms of learning preferences and multiple intelligences.

If schools offer more choices in the way of expression, some people worry that such creative mediums of expression may lower work standards; however, in reality, they can promote high-quality work. Students working using their learning

Universal Design for Learning in the Classroom

Multiple Means of Response (Elementary)

UDL lends itself to performance assessment of class activities and other projects. Some examples include: participating in science experiments, creating a puppet as the main character of a familiar story who retells the story from that character's point of view, or placing students correctly on human timelines when acting as a famous person in history like George Washington or Martin Luther King, Jr.

As long as standards are being met, guidelines are followed, and achievement is increasing, let them have some choice! I believe we've been a high achieving school because our students are involved learners!

Carol Dinsdale, NBCT
Mount Vernon Elementary
St. Petersburg, FL
Council for Exceptional Children, Clarissa Hug
Teacher of the Year 2005

Multiple Means of Response (Secondary)

Offer students choices for assessments. Some students need writing, others may need oral presentations, while still others need more product-oriented assessments. Be sure to include self-reflection so students are able to check for self-knowledge. Allow students to revise, revisit, and refine their work. As the teacher, give plenty of feedback and allow

students to revise based on the feedback. Create electronic folders and files for students and showcase their work on your class web pages to celebrate their accomplishments.

Remember, all students in your class are important and have different learning styles and abilities. Offering variety, planning for understanding, and making assessment meaningful will make all the difference in the world.

Libby Jackson Ortmann, NBCT
Curriculum Resource Teacher
Alice Drive Middle School
Sumter School District 17
Sumter, SC

---

preferences and areas of strength (often involving technology tools) are more likely to be engaged in their learning because it is interesting and meaningful. When they experience success, they are more likely to find pride in their work, want to learn more, and stay in school. They may even gain enough confidence to take more risks in learning that takes place outside of their comfort zones.

In summary, not all curriculum today is interesting or accessible to students. Typically, students at risk for disengaging or dropping out of school receive little feedback or encouragement inside and/or outside of school. They may not feel valued or respected. Their learning preferences may not match that of the teacher or the lesson.

Students may become disengaged when they cannot make connections between their lives/experiences and the curriculum. They may feel disconnected from their peers. If this happens long enough, students lose their desire to work (Meyer & Rose, 2000). Students often drop out because they lose motivation and shut down. When you come to school every day and fail to experience success day after day, attendance becomes painful. Universal Design for Learning allows for different levels of support (as needed) and an array of options to work toward a common learning goal.

Table 7.8   Multiple Ways Students Can Express Themselves

Auditory	Visual	Tactile/Kinesthetic	Affective	Technology Options
• Oral report	• Visual demonstration using a chart, graph	• Demonstration of an experiment	• Group presentation or response	• A recorded tape/CD/DVD
• Speech/debate	• Written report	• Dance	• Drama/play production	• Multimedia productions
• Song/rap	• Drawing/poster	• Written report	• Role play demonstration	• Podcast
• Storytelling	• Portfolio	• Pointing or gazing at answers		• Electronic book production
• Interview	• Journal/diary	• Filling in a bubble sheet/worksheet		• Photographic essay
	• Mural	• Puppet show		• Word-processed report
				• Electronic assessment
				• WebQuest creation

By offering multiple means of expression, students can produce high-quality work using their areas of strength.

UDL and Differentiated Instruction

Universal Design for Learning implementation supports **differentiated instruction** and vice versa (Hall, Strangman, & Meyer, 2008). Differentiated instruction is an instructional process that offers teachers flexibility in ways to teach students from diverse backgrounds in today's classrooms. Like UDL, it first considers the strengths and needs of individual, diverse learners within a classroom setting. Preassessment is used to determine prior knowledge, learning abilities, interests, and talents so that instructional time can be maximized for each learner. In differentiated instruction, the teacher meets the student at the place just above the student level of mastery, the zone of proximal development, and assists that student in moving forward. It also considers ideas about learning preferences, multiple intelligences, and Bloom's taxonomy.

The three basic components of differentiated instruction are *content, process*, and *product*. Based on individual student preassessments, the teacher plans what *content* to teach, how he/she will deliver the instruction, and how students will *process* the content/skills to be learned. The *product* has flexible requirements and expectations so that each student's learning can be assessed as accurately as possible for that student. Different approaches to teaching and learning are considered as curriculum is adjusted accordingly (Tomlinson, 2001). Table 7.9 briefly compares UDL and differentiated instruction.

Table 7.9	Comparing the Elements of UDL and Differentiated Instruction
UDL	**Differentiated Instruction**
Multiple Means of **Representation**	**Content**—What the teacher plans to teach
Multiple Means of **Engagement**	**Process**—Why the teacher chooses a particular method, strategy, or approach to teach content/skills to a given set of learners
Multiple Means of **Expression**	**Product**—How students respond to information presented and how the students will be assessed

You will see in future chapters how the elements of differentiated instruction consistently support the principles of UDL in creating flexible teaching and learning environments. Curricular planning based on individual assessment, flexibility in instructional delivery/process, and accessibility to materials can help more students reach their learning goals. All students are challenged to show progress, and effort is made to remove learning barriers.

The Benefits of Flexible Options

We have talked about what Universal Design for Learning is. Let's briefly consider what it is not. First, it is not "one-size-fits-all." If you ever purchased "one-size-fits-all" clothing, it was likely too large, too small, or not tailored to fit your body. Your individual style and uniqueness was likely hidden by a garment designed for the masses. The production was more economical and less complicated to produce, but, in the long run, there were still some people who couldn't wear it at all and many others who found it fit poorly. Along the same lines, Universal Design for Learning does not advocate "watering down" the curriculum or finding one specific topic in the content that everyone can learn in the same way. Students are still held to high standards through Universal Design for Learning, but there are simply more ways to get there. In fact, Universal Design for Learning allows students with a wide range of abilities equal access to the whole curriculum.

The process of Universal Design for Learning is like shopping for clothes in a store that employs a tailor. The tailor is armed up front with the materials needed to custom fit each patron's clothing. Universal Design for Learning is an instructional source that offers flexibility to maximize the number of learners who receive, engage in, and respond to skills and objectives being taught in any given course of study. For example, Universal Design for Learning is more than just playing an audio tape along with a book. The way in which learners engage themselves in a text and respond to it must also be considered for an adaptation to be effective. The adaptation may involve incorporating a suitable cognitive and/or organizational strategy to fully access the text (Schumaker & Deshler, 1984). The aim of Universal Design for Learning is to "level the playing field" so every learner has a chance to learn successfully. Curriculum that has "built-in" adaptations up front increases the chance that each student will find a meaningful way to access the subject matter (Orkwis, 2003).

School reform in America is demanding that schools revamp their ways of doing things. As teachers, we know how difficult it is to be in a room for approximately seven hours a day with sometimes 30 or more diverse learners at a time with limited planning time. It is time consuming to prepare a variety of presentations and to implement and organize a variety of assessments. Universal Design for Learning provides the teacher with a framework in which to implement standards-based reform for *all* learners in their classrooms (Voltz, Sims, Nelson, & Bivens, 2005). When schools advocate for curriculum planning that is designed "up front," infusing today's technologies, perhaps we would not need to adapt so much, saving on time spent creating and offering "add-on" and other alternative formats to students (O'Bannon & Puckett, 2007). Offering multiple means of representation, engagement, and expression just might result in the empowerment and inclusion of more students. How can we rethink the way we deliver instruction and how students access and respond, using today's technologies, to make learning come alive for most, if not all, of them?

Remember, Universal Design for Learning is for all students—not just for students who learn differently. As mentioned earlier, even though many of our technologies and strategies may have been designed originally for diverse learners, the results have benefited countless others. Just as closed-caption television was designed to give people with hearing loss access to television, many more people ended up benefiting from it as they worked out at the gym or caught the news or ball game at a noisy eatery.

Universal Design for Learning also benefits the learner with extraordinary abilities (Orkwis, 2003). Imagine you have someone like Albert Einstein in your class. Einstein acknowledged that he had some problems in school in the early years and found learning in some subject areas difficult. He found rote memorization tasks overwhelming and was punished for asking too many questions (Bucky, 1992). How would he fare in a "one-size-fits-all" classroom? It is not unusual for a gifted learner to become the "class clown" or even drop out of school because he/she isn't being challenged. What if your classroom offered opportunities to research topics of interest, create original works using multiple pathways, or to ponder the "deep" questions? As a former gifted third-grade student with ADHD and a learning disability in written expression recently related, when teachers started asking him to formulate his own questions and not just recall facts, learning became meaningful to him. He also stated that 10 minutes of lecture was about all students could take in at a time without a break. When teachers stop and have students discuss what was heard with a partner, they can absorb more information. This young man later became the editor of his high school newspaper. Computer technologies became his writing and organizational tools. Imagine the engagement of electronic newsletters and podcasts for today's learners.

Universal Design for Learning, in theory, has the potential to produce a more-inclusionary school environment. More students can work together toward similar goals and objectives in a variety of ways. Individual strengths are emphasized and developed. Each person in the group can contribute through his or her strength to make learning multidimensional and exciting. Teachers focus on how to fit instruction to different learners instead of relying on just one format. Maybe fewer students would need to be pulled out for work in remedial programs that are sometimes disconnected from the overall goals and objectives of the curriculum.

Universal Design for Learning may cost more in the beginning—particularly to provide the technology resources in the schools that it advocates. However, the money saved by reducing remedial programs, add-on supplements to teacher's guides, and the costs society bears when students are suspended and drop out *may* make up for the cost of implementing UDL. Think also of the time teachers can save preparing alternate materials. Universal Design for Learning helps teachers with the organization of assessments as well. Today's teachers can quickly enter student assessment data and retrieve computer printouts that show areas of progress and areas of need. The assessment chapter is devoted to this topic. Overall, teachers typically have more time to spend interacting with students by applying Universal Design for Learning principles.

The use of Universal Design for Learning increases compliance with mandates from the Americans with Disabilities Act (ADA), Individuals with Disabilities Education Improvement Act (IDEA) of 2004, and No Child Left Behind (NCLB). By removing barriers of access to the general curriculum and providing supports to address the needs of diverse learners (including learners with linguistic or cultural challenges as well as students who are gifted and talented and those with disabilities), more students will hopefully be motivated to work together toward meaningful goals. Once a student experiences frequent success at the right learning level with appropriate methods and tools, motivation typically increases.

Schools that have implemented Universal Design for Learning have reported many positive changes:

- Students have increased academic progress, motivation, and literacy scores on state tests.
- The classroom focus has changed to giving student access to the curriculum.
- Teachers are more satisfied in their work and believe that they have the skills necessary to teach all students (Delaware Department of Education, 2004, p. 9).

Gone are the days of teaching facts and the notion that what is presented will be what is learned. Today's teachers must focus on what the student can and will learn. If flexible individual pathways to learning are built into the plan, flexibility increases. Less "retrofitting" of curriculum, instruction, assessment, and environments in schools will be needed. Universal Design for Learning has great potential to make our schools better and eventually more "usable, elegant, and economical" (Pisha & Coyne, 2001). Future chapters will show how technology tools can increase flexible options for learners.

Thematic Summary

- The term universal design was coined in the field of architecture in response to the vision of an architect with a physical disability. The Americans with Disabilities Act (ADA) paved the way for widespread implementation.
- Universal Design for Learning (UDL) evolved from universal design principles. It has been found to benefit learners with a diverse set of needs.
- UDL researchers describe three processes in the brain that are connected to the learning. First, information is gathered through the senses (the recognition system). Then it is organized and cross-referenced using strategic systems. The affective system drives the emotional/social side of learning, which can move learning into the long-term memory.
- The three essential qualities of UDL are multiple means of representation, multiple means of expression, and multiple means of engagement. If teachers/schools provide flexibility in terms of these qualities, learners can be empowered.
- By revisiting the work of cognitive-social theorists, thoughts and findings about how people learn support Universal Design for Learning principles. Revisiting work done with learning styles, multiple intelligences, and Bloom's taxonomy will be helpful to design and implement UDL environments.
- UDL and differentiated instruction share common elements.

Making Connections for Inclusive Teaching

1. Where do you see other examples of universal design in your own experiences? Do these examples benefit only people with special needs or do the benefits extend to others? Explain.
2. Do you think understanding the basic processes of the brain can influence a teacher's approach to instructional delivery and student learning? Defend your viewpoint.
3. How can understanding the theories of researchers such as Vygotsky, Piaget, Bruner, Bloom, and Gardner offer today's teachers important insights? How do the ideas of these five theorists (and perhaps others you are familiar with) impact student learning in today's classrooms?
4. Do you agree or disagree with Piaget's theory that a learner must be successful at one stage of learning before progressing to the next stage? Defend your answer.
5. Explain how implementing the three essential qualities of Universal Design for Learning might impact teaching and learning in today's classrooms.
6. What examples of differentiated instruction have you observed in your own educational experience?

Learning Activities

1. Tour a public building in your area and record all the features you observe that reflect universal design. What principles of universal design can you apply to each of your observations?

2. Interview someone who is working in a public school building now and also prior to 1990. What architectural features changed in the school(s)? How did this change occur? How has it changed access for students and perhaps also professionals who work there? What else does this person feel needs to be in place in schools of the future?

3. Poll three general education teachers. Ask each to give an example of how he/she differentiates instruction for learners in the classroom. Describe, analyze, and discuss their responses.

4. Observe a child younger than 13 while he/she participates in either a structured or unstructured activity. What does the evidence you collect tell you about how this child learns? Using one or more models of learning presented in this chapter, explain what systems of the brain he/she appears to be using. Depending on the activity, what other learner skills/strengths do you informally see? Include a brief description of the child and the observational setting with your response.

5. Observe a general education teacher and script all the questions the teacher asks during one lesson. Analyze and reflect on the types of questions asked according to Bloom's taxonomy. Report your findings.

6. Think about your own learning. Using the three essential qualities of Universal Design for Learning, what modes of representation, expression, and engagement have worked best for you? Provide at least one personal example for each quality.

Looking at the Standards

The content of this chapter most closely aligns itself with the following standards:

INTASC Standards

- *Student Development*. The teacher understands how children learn and develop and can provide learning opportunities that support their intellectual, social, and personal development.
- *Diverse Learners*. The teacher understands how students differ in their approaches to learning and creates instructional opportunities that are adapted to diverse learners.

Council for Exceptional Children

Council for Exceptional Children
The voice and vision of special education

Special educators are to have knowledge of the following:

- GC1K3: Historical foundations, classic studies, major contributors, major legislation, and current issues related to knowledge and practice.
- CC2K1: Typical and atypical human growth and development.
- CC3K5: Differing ways of learning of individuals with exceptional learning needs, including those from culturally diverse backgrounds, and strategies for addressing these differences.

- GC5K1: Barriers to accessibility and acceptance of individuals with disabilities.
- GC5K2: Adaptation of the physical environment to provide optimal learning opportunities for individuals with disabilities.

Key Concepts and Terms

Universal Design for
  Learning (UDL)
universal design
recognition system
strategic systems
metacognition
affective systems

zone of proximal
  development
spiral curriculum
multiple intelligences
learning preferences
multiple means
  of representation

multiple means of
  engagement
multiple means of
  expression
differentiated instruction

References

Anderson, L. W., & Krathwohl, D. R. (Eds.). (2001). A taxonomy for learning, teaching, and assessing: A revision of Bloom's taxonomy of educational objectives. New York: Longman.

Atherton, J. (2005). *Learning and teaching: Piaget's developmental theory.* Retrieved March 12, 2008, from http://www .learningandteaching.info/learning/piaget.htm

Bloom, B. (1956). *Taxonomy of educational objectives, handbook 1: Cognitive domain.* New York: Longman.

Bremer, C., Clapper, A., Hitchcock, C., Hall, T., & Kachgal, M. (2002). *Universal design: A strategy to support students' access to the general education curriculum* (National Center on Secondary Education and Transition Information Brief, 1(3)). Retrieved March 28, 2008, from http://www.ncset.org/ publications/viewdesc.asp?id=707

Bruner, J. (1960). *The process of education.* Cambridge, MA: Harvard University Press.

Bucky, P. (1992). *The private Albert Einstein.* Kansas City, MO: Andrews and McMeel.

Burns, D., Johnson, S., & Gable, R. (1998). Can we generalize about the learning style characteristics of high academic achievers? *Roeper Review, 20*(4), 276–282.

Cass, M., Cates, D., Smith, M., & Jackson, C. (2003). Effects of manipulative instruction on solving area and perimeter problems by students with learning disabilities. *Learning Disabilities Research & Practice, 18,* 112–120.

Center for Applied Special Technology. (1998). *What is universal design for learning?* Wakefield, MA: Author. Retrieved March 28, 2008, from http://www.cast.org/research/udl/index.html

Center for Universal Design. (1997). *What is universal design?* Center for Universal Design, North Carolina State University. Retrieved July 5, 2006, from www.design.ncsu.edu/cud/

Cytowic, R. E. (1996). *The neurological side of neuropsychology.* Cambridge, MA: MIT Press.

Davidson, M. (1965). *Helen Keller's teacher.* New York: Scholastic.

Delaware Department of Education. (2004). *Universal design for learning: Reaching all, teaching all.* Retrieved March 28, 2008, from http://www.doe.state.de.us/files/pdf/ de_udlpaper.pdf

Fuster, J. (1997). *The prefrontal cortex: Anatomy, physiology, and neuropsychology of the frontal lobe.* New York: Lippincott.

Gardner, H. (1993). *Frames of mind: The theory of multiple intelligences* (2nd ed.). New York: Basic Books.

Ginsburg, H., & Opper, S. (1988). *Piaget's theory of intellectual development* (3rd ed.). New York: Prentice Hall.

Grandin, T. (2006). *Thinking in pictures: My life with autism* (2nd ed.). New York: Vintage Books.

Hall, T., Strangman, N., & Meyer, A. (2008). *Differentiated instruction and implications for UDL implementation.* Retrieved February 29, 2008, from http://www.cast.org/publications/ ncac/ncac_diffinstructudl.html

Hawkins, J., & Blakeslee, S. (2004). *On intelligence.* New York: Times Books.

Holt, L., & Kysilka, M. (2006). *Instructional patterns: Strategies for maximizing student learning.* Thousand Oaks, CA: Sage.

Jensen, E. (1998). *Teaching with the brain in mind.* Alexandria, VA: Association for Supervision and Curriculum Development.

Mace, R. (1998). *A perspective on universal design.* Retrieved March 28, 2008, from http://www.adaptenv.org/adp/profiles/ 1_mace.php

Marzano, R., Pickering, D., Arredondo, D., Blackburn, G., Brandt, R., & Moffett, C. (1992). *Dimensions of learning.* Alexandria, VA: Association for Supervision and Curriculum Development.

Meyer, A., & Rose, D. H. (1998). *Learning to read in the computer age.* Cambridge, MA: Brookline Books.

Meyer, A., & Rose, D. H. (2000). Universal design for individual differences. *Educational Leadership, 58*(3), 39–43.

Nolet, V., & McLaughlin, M. (2005). *Accessing the general curriculum: Including students with disabilities in standards-based reform* (2nd ed.). Thousand Oaks, CA: Corwin Press.

O'Bannon, B., & Puckett, K. (2007). *Preparing to use technology: A practical guide to curriculum integration.* Boston: Pearson Education.

Orkwis, R. (2003). *Universally designed instruction.* Arlington, VA: Council for Exceptional Children. (ERIC Document Reproduction Service No. ED475386)

Pisha, B., & Coyne, P. (2001). Smart from the start: The promise of universal design for learning. *Remedial and Special Education, 22*(4), 197–203.

Ratey, J. (2001). *User's guide to the brain.* New York: Pantheon Books.

Rose, D., & Meyer, A. (2002). *Teaching every student in the digital age: Universal design for learning.* Alexandria, VA: Association for Supervision and Curriculum Development.

Schumaker, J. B., & Deshler, D. (1984). An integrated system for providing content to learning disabled adolescents using an audio-taped format. In W. M. Cruickshank & J. M. Kliebhan (Eds.), *Early adolescence to early adulthood* (Vol. 5, pp. 79–107). Syracuse, NY: Syracuse University Press.

Smith, M. K. (2002a). *Howard Gardner and multiple intelligences.* Retrieved March 28, 2008, from http://www.infed.org/thinkers/gardner.htm

Smith, M. K. (2002b). *Jerome S. Bruner and the process of education.* Retrieved March 28, 2008, from http://www.infed.org/thinkers/bruner.htm

Sousa, D. A. (1997). *Sensory preferences of New Jersey students, grades 3 to 12.* Unpublished data, Seton Hall University, South Orange, NJ.

Sousa, D. A. (2001). *How the special needs brain learns.* Thousand Oaks, CA: Corwin Press.

Sousa, D. A. (2006). *How the brain learns* (3rd ed.). Thousand Oaks, CA: Corwin Press.

Swanson, H. (1996). Informational processing: An introduction. In D. Reid, W. Hresko, & H. Swanson (Eds.), *Cognitive approaches to learning disabilities* (pp. 251–286). Austin, TX: Pro-Ed.

Swanson, L. J. (1995). *Learning styles: A review of the literature.* Claremont, CA: Claremont Graduate University. (ERIC Document Reproduction Service No. ED387067)

Tomlinson, C. (2001). *How to differentiate instruction in mixed-ability classrooms* (2nd ed.) Alexandria, VA: Association for Supervision and Curriculum Development.

Voltz, D., Sims, M. J., Nelson, B., & Bivens, C. (2005). M^2ECCA: A framework for inclusion in the context of standards-based reform. *Teaching Exceptional Children, 37*(5), 14–19.

Vygotsky, L. S. (1978). *Mind in society.* Cambridge, MA: Harvard University Press.

Vygotsky, L. S. (1986). *Thought and language* (A. Kozulin, Trans.). Cambridge, MA: MIT Press.

Wendorf, J. (2006). *Children with LD need your help!* New York: National Center for Learning Disabilities.

Winebrenner, S. (1996). *Teaching kids with learning difficulties in the regular classroom.* Minneapolis, MN: Free Spirit Publishing.

Assessing and Evaluating Learner Progress

Contributed by Jennifer Williams

The Importance of Classroom Assessment
    Large-Scale Assessments
    Ongoing Assessment
    UDL Applied to Assessment

Effective Classroom Assessment Approaches
    Approaches to Initial Assessment that Increase Learner Engagement
    Review of School Records
    Formal and Informal Assessment
    Apply Inventories
    Working Collaboratively
    Interpreting Standardized Tests
    Interpreting Behavior Rating Scales
    Positive Behavior Supports
    Functional Behavior Assessments

Assessment Organization
    Planning for Ongoing Assessment
    Formative Assessments

Learning Outcomes

After studying this chapter, you should be able to:

- Identify effective classroom assessment approaches.
- Distinguish between formative and summative assessments.
- Distinguish between informal and formal assessments.
- Describe the importance of classroom assessment.
- Explain methods for planning and organizing ongoing assessment.
- Identify high-tech and low-tech materials and assessment options.
- Summarize methods for incorporating multiple means of representation, engagement, and expression in assessment.

Summative Assessments
Organizational Systems for Assessments

Recording Assessments
Probes
Curriculum-Based Measurement
Rubrics

Methods for Ongoing Assessment
High-Tech and Low-Tech Materials
Computerized Assessments

Multiple Means of Engagement in Assessment
Fostering Motivation
Providing Student Feedback

Multiple Means of Representation in Assessment
High-Tech and Low-Tech Options
Presenting Testing Accommodations

Student Expression in Assessment
High-Tech and Low-Tech Options
Multimedia Projects
Portfolios

Final Thoughts

Just as knowing what you have on hand is important in planning your grocery or clothing shopping needs, the same thing is true for assessment. A clothing inventory as the seasons change can help you see the gaps in your wardrobe. It can also help you put irresistible "bargains" in perspective. A $110 blouse at $40 is no bargain if you haven't anything to wear with it.

The task before teachers is so enormous that we have to be very skillful "shoppers" of materials, resources, and methods. You must first decide strategies/materials/methods that would pay the biggest dividend for your students and concentrate your largest efforts there. Assessment is what tells you where to begin and, paired with standards and scope/sequence charts, where to go next. Realize that assessment does take time but it is definitely worth it in savings.

The Importance of Classroom Assessment

Assessments are administered for various reasons. The purposes of assessment can range from evaluating the performance of individual students and student learning to evaluating and comparing the performance of teachers, schools, and local education agencies (LEAs). As a teacher, you will be using assessment techniques to identify the strengths and needs of your students, set goals for student learning, monitor student progress, and inform your instruction.

Large-Scale Assessments

Many states use **large-scale assessments** to make high-stakes educational decisions such as graduation or promotion. In the last decade, there has been a growing increase in large-scale assessments to document teacher, school, and school system accountability of student progress and performance. In 2002, President Bush signed the **No Child Left Behind Act** (NCLB) (PL 107-110), which focuses on increased accountability for states, school districts, and schools, more flexibility for states and LEAs in the use of federal education dollars, greater choice in schools for parents and students attending low performing schools, and an emphasis on educationally proven materials. The NCLB Act mandates that there are statewide accountability systems in the form of annual assessments that are based on state standards in reading and math for grades 3–8. Student progress is broken down into adequate yearly progress (AYP) for the subgroups of poverty, race, ethnicity, disability, and limited English proficiency to ensure that no group is left behind.

Due to the strong emphasis on large-scale assessments, they need to be valid and should accurately measure student performance. Safeguards should be in place to ensure that these assessments are appropriate for all groups of students and learners with various needs. For the administration of valid, large-scale assessments, students need to access to the supports they are currently using in their daily learning and in the classroom to demonstrate their knowledge and understanding (Dolan & Hall, 2001). Later in the chapter we will discuss various examples of testing accommodations and suggestions for incorporating technology based accommodations to create accurate assessments.

Ongoing Assessment

Although large-scale assessment is an important accountability factor in meeting the needs of all students, we must remember it is only one piece of the puzzle or big picture when determining the strengths and needs of our students. The increased accountability is good for our students, but the large-scale assessments do not always document progress on specific skills. For example, a student may not demonstrate significant growth on a fourth grade large-scale reading assessment when reading on the second grade level, yet she may have increased in reading by more than one grade level that year based on your ongoing informal assessment measures. For that reason, it is important for us to ensure that student assessment is ongoing and continuously integrated into our instruction. Additional assessment information must be collected!

Ongoing assessment allows us to plan specifically for the needs of our students throughout the year and helps to inform us if our instruction has been effective or

Cengage Learning/Wadsworth

Large-scale assessments are used to document student progress and growth in today's schools.

if it needs to be adjusted. Additionally, ongoing assessment gives us a vehicle to share student progress with other teachers, parents, and even the students themselves. In terms of engaging students in their learning, it is critical for students to know where they are so they can set appropriate goals for learning and to be able to chart their progress to enhance motivation.

UDL Applied to Assessment

As discussed in Chapter 7, Universal Design for Learning provides a framework for teaching, learning, assessment, and curriculum development and maximizes instructional opportunities. In Chapter 7, much emphasis was placed on the three essential qualities of Universal Design for Learning: representation, expression, and engagement. As will be demonstrated throughout this chapter, each of these qualities can be applied to the area of assessment. Once again, if we design our assessments with the diverse learner in mind, the time invested will be well worth it since we will know the exact areas to target our instruction for maximum learning to occur. Assessment provides information that allows you to develop and deliver effective instruction that will empower your students as learners.

Effective Classroom Assessment Approaches

Approaches to Initial Assessment That Increase Learner Engagement

In order to engage students in your instruction, you will need to learn all that you can about your students' present level of performance including their strengths and learning preferences. A great deal of assessment information can be located in a student's school record or confidential folder, but other helpful information from interest, learning styles, and multiple intelligences inventories will need to be collected by you.

Review of School Records

A wealth of information is located in a student's school record. This is the first place you will want to start to identify the strengths and needs of your students. Here you may find some existing information from **norm-referenced tests** (a student performance as compared to that of his or her peers), **criterion-referenced tests** (student performance compared to a particular level of mastery), and individual informal assessment measures such as running records, benchmarks, and academic profiles that help paint the "educational portrait" of a student's abilities. For a student with learning differences, there may be additional information from student-assistance teams or school-based intervention assistance teams regarding prereferral, referral, formal and informal assessments, functional behavior assessments, and individualized educational programs as described in Chapter 2 and Table 2.1.

Formal and Informal Assessment

Norm-referenced measures can be divided into two general categories: **formal assessment** and **informal assessment**. Using formal assessment, comparisons can be made by comparing your student's performance to the performance of a nationally representative sample of students of the same age or grade. In formal assessment, there are procedures for standardized testing, and all administrators follow the same script and procedures for presenting the testing materials and information. In formal assessment, results are used for primarily eligibility decisions to determine if the student's performance is significantly different enough from the norm group to warrant special education support services. On the other hand, informal assessment compares your student's performance to some criterion. Reading level in your school's reading series, number of words that students recognize on a word list, types of math addition problems that students can complete, and spelling errors are all examples of informal assessments with a criterion. In informal assessment, the procedures are more flexible, and an administrator can probe, prompt, or question students to obtain additional information about how the student is completing the task. Informal assessment is used primarily to make instructional decisions. You can determine how the student performs a task, what they can and can't do, and identify entry-level skills and instructional needs.

Even though formal assessment information is extremely helpful in identifying the academic skill areas where areas of need may exist, it may not provide quite enough information to plan educational interventions. We need much more information about a student's specific skills. Informal assessment methods enable us to narrow our search even further to pinpoint specific skills that a child needs to develop in order to be successful.

Additional information regarding your students can be gathered through close communication with parents, former teachers, related service providers, and special educators. Prior to the beginning of the school year, it may be beneficial to arrange a time to talk with teachers from previous years to discuss any prior assessment results. The additional pieces provided by those who have previously worked closely with your students can assist in forming a complete picture of the students with which you are working.

Applying Inventories

To continue to build the "educational portrait" of your students' abilities, you can apply a variety of inventories. Interest inventories can assist in developing instruction to motivate your learners, learning styles inventories can help you determine the learning modalities of your students, and multiple intelligence inventories can help you identify specific areas of strength in your students.

Interest Inventories

Information obtained from **interest inventories** can give you a greater understanding of the specific interests of your students to assist in planning instruction that motivates your learners. Teacher-created or commercial-interest inventories address a variety of topics such as reading, career choices, and hobbies, and are a terrific means to learn more about your students to engage them in learning. For example, if you discover that one of your students has a particular interest in learning about animals, you can integrate that content into your assessments and instruction to foster motivation. Reading is often one area that teachers wish to target student interests. Figure 8.1 displays an example of a reading interest inventory that can be filled out by your students or completed orally in an interview format for those needing a different means of presentation.

Learning Styles Inventories

We mention in Chapter 7 that learning styles information can be used as another possible "tool" for your "toolbox." Just as Table 7.5 (see page 191) is helpful in planning your teaching for diverse learners, it is also helpful in planning assessments that meet the learning styles of your students. There are several **learning styles inventories** that can help you gather information on the modalities (visual, auditory, kinesthetic, etc.) by which your students may better receive and present information. To maximize learning for your students, it is important to build on the strengths of your students by matching your instruction to their learning styles. Furthermore, knowing

Reading Interest Survey

1. Do you like to read?

   _____

2. How much time do you spend reading?

   _____

3. What are some of the books you have read lately?

   _____

4. Do you have a library card? How often do you use it?

   _____

5. Do you ever get books from the school library?

   _____

6. About how many books do you own?

   _____

7. What are some books you would like to own?

   _____

8. Put a check mark next to the kind of reading you like best/topics you might like to read about

☐ history	☐ travel	☐ play
☐ sports	☐ science fiction	☐ adventure
☐ romance	☐ detective stories	☐ war stories
☐ poetry	☐ car stories	☐ novels
☐ biography	☐ supernatural stories	☐ astrology
☐ humor	☐ folktale	☐ how-to
☐ mysteries	☐ art	☐ westerns

9. Do you like to read the newspaper?

   _____

10. If "yes," place a check next to the part of the newspaper listed below you like to read.

☐ Advertisements	☐ Entertainment	☐ Columnists
☐ Headlines	☐ Comic Strips	☐ Political
☐ Current Events	☐ Sports	☐ Editorials
☐ Others: (please list)		

11. What are your favorite television programs?

    _____

12. How much time do you spend watching television?

    _____

13. What is your favorite magazine?

    _____

14. Do you have a hobby? If so, what is it?

    _____

15. What are the two best movies you have ever seen?

    _____

16. Who are your favorite entertainers and/or movie stars?

    _____

17. When you were little, did you enjoy having someone read aloud to you?

    _____

18. List topics, subjects, etc. that you might like to read about:

    _____

19. What does you the word "reading" mean to you?

    _____

20. Say anything else that you would like to say about reading:

    _____

Figure 8.1 Reading Interest Inventory

Source: D. Hildebrandt, "But There's Nothing Good to Read (in the Library Media Center)," *Media Spectrum: The Journal for Library Media Specialists in Michigan, 28*(3), 2001, pp. 34–37.

your students' preferences for learning will allow you to develop assessments that tap into their learning so they can successfully express what they have learned. For example, if a student displays a strength in the auditory modality, you will want to create assessments that are auditory in nature. When students are taught with approaches that match their learning preferences, they demonstrate higher achievement scores (Dunn, 1990). According to Dunn, "Students are not failing because of the curriculum. Student can learn almost any subject matter when they are taught with methods and approaches responsive to their learning style strengths" (p. 16).

There are several learning styles inventories that address not only identifying learning modalities but also preferences for learning such as group work or individual learning to help in planning for delivery of your instruction. Three of the most widely used learning style inventories are the Dunn, Dunn, and Price (1985) Learning Style Inventory (LSI), the Kolb Learning Style Inventory (Kolb, 1984), and Fleming's VARK (visual, aural, read/write, kinesthetic) Questionnaire (Fleming, 2001). Figure 8.2 provides a sample page of questions from the VARK Questionnaire.

Multiple Intelligence Inventories

In Chapter 7, we introduced the concept of **multiple intelligences** and eight intelligence areas as defined by Howard Gardner (1993). To learn more about the intelligence areas of our students, we can administer a multiple intelligences inventory. Through these inventories we can identify intelligence areas of our students to help us teach to their strengths. In an action research study with foreign language and

How Do I Learn Best?

1. You are helping someone who wants to go to your airport, town centre or railway station. You would:
    a. Go with her.
    b. Tell her the directions.
    c. Write down the directions (without a map).
    d. Draw, or give her a map.

2. You are not sure whether a word should be spelled 'dependent' or 'dependant'. You would:
    a. See the words in your mind and choose by the way they look.
    b. Think about how each word sounds and choose one.
    c. Find it in a dictionary.
    d. Write both words on paper and choose one.

3. You are planning a holiday for a group. You want some feedback from them about the plan. You would:
    a. Describe some of the highlights.
    b. Use a map or website to show them the places.
    c. Give them a copy of the printed itinerary.
    d. Phone, text, or email them.

4. You are going to cook something as a special treat for your family. You would:
    a. Cook something you know without the need for instructions.
    b. Ask friends for suggestions.
    c. Look through the cookbook for ideas from the pictures.
    d. Use a cookbook where you know there is a good recipe.

5. A group of tourists want to learn about the parks or wildlife reserves in your area. You would:
    a. Talk about, or arrange a talk for them about parks or wildlife reserves.
    b. Show them internet pictures, photographs or picture books.
    c. Take them to a park or wildlife reserve and walk with them.
    d. Give them a book or pamphlets about the parks or wildlife reserves.

Figure 8.2 Sample Questions from the VARK Questionnaire
Source: Copyright Version 7.0 (2006) held by Neil D. Fleming, Christchurch, New Zealand and Charles C. Bonwell, Green Mountain Falls, CO 80819.

second language classes, teachers used the multiple intelligences theory to inform instructional strategies, shape curriculum, and develop alternative assessments (Haley, 2004). According to Haley, the students in the experimental group receiving instruction based on the multiple intelligences theory academically out performed those students in the control group. Additionally, most students expressed positive feelings, attitudes, and enthusiasm toward learning due to the flexibility and choice provided using the multiple intelligences theory.

As a teacher, you can plan for assessment and use assessment instruments that support the principles of the multiple intelligences theory to measure your students' skills and progress. Assessments based on the multiple intelligences theory allow students to connect and apply what they have learned in a manner that fits their learning style. For example, a student who displays strengths in the bodily/kinesthetic area may not do well on a world history essay test, yet he/she may be able to kinesthetically reenact a major historical event to demonstrate mastery of content. Armstrong (1994) developed an assessment checklist (see Figure 8.3) based on Gardner's theory of multiple intelligences that can be used as an additional tool for gathering information on your students.

Name of Student: _____

Check items that apply:

Linguistic Intelligence

☐ writes better than average for age

☐ spins tall tales or tells jokes and stories

☐ has a good memory for names, places, dates, or trivia

☐ enjoys word games

☐ enjoys reading books

☐ spells words accurately (or if preschool, does developmental spelling that is advanced for age)

☐ appreciates nonsense rhymes, puns, tongue twisters

☐ enjoys listening to the spoken word (stories, commentary on the radio, talking books)

☐ has a good vocabulary for age

☐ communicates to others in a highly verbal way

Logical-Mathematical Intelligence

☐ asks a lot of questions about how things work

☐ enjoys working or playing with numbers

☐ enjoys math class (or if preschool, enjoys counting and doing other things with numbers)

☐ finds math and computer games interesting (or if no exposure to computers, enjoys other math or science games)

☐ enjoys playing chess, checkers, or other strategy games

☐ enjoys working on logic puzzles or brainteasers (or if preschool, enjoys hearing logical nonsense)

☐ enjoys putting things in categories, hierarchies, or other logical patterns

☐ likes to do experiments in science class or in free play

☐ shows interest in science-related subjects

☐ does well on Piagetian-type assessments of logical thinking

Spatial Intelligence

☐ reports clear visual images

☐ reads maps, charts, and diagrams more easily than text (or if preschool, enjoys looking at more than text)

☐ daydreams a lot

☐ enjoys art activities

☐ good at drawings

☐ likes to view movies, slides, or other visual presentations

☐ enjoys doing puzzles, mazes, or similar visual activities

☐ builds interesting three-dimensional constructions (e.g., LEGO buildings)

☐ gets more out of pictures than words while reading

☐ doodles on workbooks, worksheets, or other materials

Bodily-Kinesthetic Intelligence

☐ excels in one or more sports (or if preschool, shows physical prowess advanced for age)

☐ moves, twitches, taps, or fidgets while seated for a long time in one spot

☐ cleverly mimics other people's gestures or mannerisms

Figure 8.3 Armstrong's Checklist for Assessing Students' Multiple Intelligences

Source: Adapted from T. Armstrong, *Multiple Intelligences in the Classroom* (Alexandria, VA: Association for Supervision and Curriculum Development, 1994).

- ☐ loves to take things apart and put them back together again
- ☐ puts his/her hands all over something he/she's just seen
- ☐ enjoys running, jumping, wrestling, or similar activities (or if older, will show these interests in a more "restrained" way, e.g., running to class, jumping over a chair)
- ☐ shows skill in a craft (e.g., woodworking, sewing, mechanics) or good fine-motor coordination in other ways
- ☐ has a dramatic way of expressing herself/himself
- ☐ reports different physical sensations while thinking or working
- ☐ enjoys working with clay or other tactile experiences (e.g., fingerpainting)

Musical Intelligence

- ☐ tells you when music sounds off-key or disturbing in some other way
- ☐ remembers melodies of songs
- ☐ has a good singing voice
- ☐ plays a musical instrument or sings in a choir or other group (or if preschool, enjoys playing percussion instruments and/or singing in a group)
- ☐ has a rhythmic way of speaking and/or moving
- ☐ unconsciously hums to himself/herself
- ☐ taps rhythmically on the table or desk as he/she works
- ☐ sensitive to environmental noises (e.g., rain on the roof)
- ☐ responds favorably when a piece of music is put on
- ☐ sings songs that he/she has learned outside of the classroom

Interpersonal Intelligence

- ☐ enjoys socializing with peers
- ☐ seems to be a natural leader
- ☐ gives advice to friends who have problems
- ☐ seems to be street smart
- ☐ belongs to clubs, committees, organizations, or informal peer groups
- ☐ enjoys informally teaching other kids
- ☐ likes to play games with other kids
- ☐ has two or more close friends
- ☐ has a good sense of empathy or concern for others
- ☐ others seek out his/her company

Intrapersonal Intelligence

- ☐ displays a sense of independence or a strong will
- ☐ has a realistic sense of his/her abilities and weaknesses
- ☐ does well when left alone to play or study
- ☐ marches to the beat of a different drummer in his/her style of living and learning
- ☐ has an interest or hobby that he/she doesn't talk much about
- ☐ has a good sense of self-direction
- ☐ prefers working alone to working with others
- ☐ accurately expresses how he/she is feeling
- ☐ is able to learn from his/her failures and successes in life
- ☐ has good self-esteem

Naturalist Intelligence

- ☐ talks a lot about favorite pets, or preferred spots in nature, during class sharing
- ☐ likes field trips in nature, to the zoo, or to a natural history museum
- ☐ shows sensitivity to natural formations (e.g., while walking outside with the class, will notice mountains, clouds; or if in an urban environment, may show this ability in sensitivity to popular culture "formations" such as sneakers or automobile styles)
- ☐ likes to water and tend to the plants in the classroom
- ☐ likes to hang around the gerbil cage, the aquarium, or the terrarium in class
- ☐ gets excited when studying about ecology, nature, plants, or animals
- ☐ speaks out in class for the rights of animals, or the preservation of planet Earth
- ☐ enjoys doing nature projects, such as bird watching, butterfly or insect collections, tree study, or raising animals
- ☐ brings to school bugs, flowers, leaves, or other natural things to share with classmates or teachers
- ☐ does well in topics at school that involve living systems (e.g., biological topics in science, environmental issues in social studies)

Figure 8.3 Armstrong's Checklist for Assessing Students' Multiple Intelligences (Continued)

Building an MI Assessment Profile

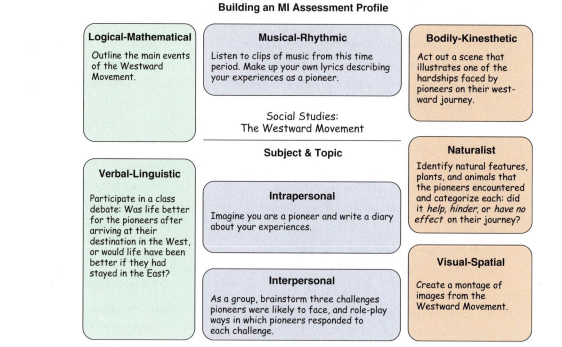

Figure 8.4 Sample Multiple Intelligence Assessment Profile
Source: Performance Learning Systems, Inc., Assessing Through Multiple Intelligences. *Performance Learning Plus, 35,* 1997, retrieved from http://www.plsweb.com/resources/newsletters/enews_archives/35/2004/03/16/

Once you have identified the intelligence areas of your students, you can tailor your assessments to tap into their individual strengths and needs. Figure 8.4 displays an example of a completed assessment profile which is a helpful tool in planning assessments in a variety of formats prior to instruction.

Similar to Gardner's theory, Mel Levine's All Kinds of Minds approach, emphasizes the power in celebrating students' strengths. Levine's approach focuses on identifying students' hidden assets to work on specific areas of weakness. For example, a student might use her expressive language abilities to learn a concept in math by dictating an explanation of the math concept into a tape recorder to put it into her own language in order to comprehend and understand it (Levine & Scherer, 2006). Levine also stresses the value of using content affinities (an area of content a student is drawn toward) such as sports, animals, or the ocean to teach important skills in reading, writing, or math. Through Levine's approach, students work on their weaknesses while continuing to build in their strengths.

Working Collaboratively

As you are in the process of getting to know your students, you will have the opportunity to work collaboratively with other individuals to effectively assess and gather assessment information on your students. You will have the opportunity to communicate effectively with other teachers, administrators, parents, special educators, and related service providers within your school. You may find yourself working collaboratively with special educators to create IEP progress reports to document student progress toward IEP goals. A school psychologist may be an excellent resource to help you understand what psychological evaluations and standardized testing results tell you about your students. A veteran teacher within your school may be a strong resource for assistance with interpreting high stakes testing results or routine assessments administered districtwide. You might also work collaboratively with student problem-solving teams such as student support teams, teacher assistance teams, or child study teams to assist students with special learning needs. It

By working collaboratively, student assessments can be analyzed and used for problem solving by all stakeholders in a school community.

is your job to seek out those individuals in your school who effectively assess students to make arrangement to talk with them or observe them.

Interpreting Standardized Tests

As a classroom teacher of students with various learning needs, you may have the opportunity to participate in an IEP meeting where evaluation results are interpreted, eligibility decision are made, and IEPs are developed. The psychological testing and norm-referenced tests discussed can give you some useful information on your students' learning strengths and areas of need.

First, it is necessary to understand the distinction among intelligence, achievement, and adaptive behavior. As a general categorization of these areas, you can think of intelligence as the cognitive processing abilities a student brings to a task (auditory perception, visual perception, motor, memory, language, reasoning, etc.). The student uses these abilities to learn and the efficiency of these processing systems affects a student's ability and rate of learning. Although we can't see these processes directly, we can infer them from behaviors the student demonstrates on a test (e.g., when a student can identify which item is "bigger" we can assume he has visual perception and discrimination as well as the concept of size). Achievement refers to the child's application of this ability to basic skill acquisition in a classroom setting; what he/she has learned (e.g., he can read a sentence, add two-digit numbers, spell "works," recall factual information). Finally, adaptive behavior is the application of this ability in the student's environment (home, school, community) and how well he/she adjusts to and functions in the world around them. These three areas (intelligence, achievement, and adaptive behavior) can be compared to determine the functioning level of the student.

The assessment process is frequently a search for answers about why a child is having difficulty with specific academic, behavioral, or social skills. The assessment team members often feel like detectives who are searching for clues. They may start with a broad general picture of the child using IQ scores, general achievement data, and behavior information. Based on this information, they begin to narrow their search by gathering confirming data or exploring an area of need in more depth to determine what specific subskill may be contributing to a student's difficulty.

Web Resources

For more information on possible causes of high or low *Wechsler Intelligence Scale for Children— Fourth Edition* (WISC-IV) subtest scores, check this text's companion website. Using this information can help you identify processing strengths and select areas for further informal assessment.

Interpreting Behavior Rating Scales

Often, in order to gather assessment information on a student, various behavior rating scales are used. Adaptive behavior rating scales can provide specific information on a student's independent functioning, communication, daily living, and social skills. Numerous rating scales exist that are sometimes completed by parents and teachers or even by the students themselves to specifically identify difficulties with attention, impulsivity, behavior, anxiety, social skills, etc. These items can help you learn more about the nonacademic or intellectual needs of your students that can be taken into consideration when planning your instruction.

Positive Behavior Supports

To emphasize proactive strategies to support student behavior that is appropriate and classroom environments that are positive, **positive behavior supports** can be implemented at the schoolwide, classroom, and individual student level. These supports focus on teaching positive social behaviors that are implemented by all individuals involved in the student's life (e.g., teachers, parents, community members). Several key components of effective positive behavioral support systems are described below.

Functional Behavior Assessments

A **functional behavior assessment** is a problem-solving process where the circumstances that occur around a particular behavior are examined to identify the purpose of the behavior that occurs. Once factors associated with the occurrence of a behavior are isolated, the assessment team can recommend interventions, techniques, and strategies to assist in supporting student behavior through a **behavior intervention plan**. The behavioral intervention plan is based on knowledge of "why" certain behaviors might occur and what might be done to address them. As a teacher, you can gather as much information up front from these assessments to plan for instructional techniques for student success (e.g., compatible peer tutors, use of a paraprofessional in the classroom, providing a "time-away" space in the classroom).

As you can see, there are many formal and informal effective techniques for collecting assessment information on your students to help you plan accordingly. The documentation and assessment results you collect on your students are an integral part of planning for effective instruction that will ensure the success of your students.

Assessment Organization

When organizing your assessments, it is necessary to plan ahead. Efficient food and clothing consumers typically keep a running list or inventory of what is needed and what will soon be needed. The list is flexible enough that is can be adjusted as needed. If you don't plan ahead, you become more haphazard in your teaching and just throw anything into your shopping cart that catches your fancy. Planning ahead saves you time in the long run, and it maximizes your instructional time.

If you are able to use assessment to plan at least weeks ahead, you will know which materials/resources you will need to collect to have on hand. You might in fact have the big ideas for most of the school year mapped out and that will help you even more.

Planning for Ongoing Assessment

You can organize your assessments into the types of assessment you plan to conduct—when and how often. You will be planning a combination of **formative assessments** (those that are ongoing during your instruction and a certain period of time) and **summative assessments** (those that occur at the end of a program or at the end of the year). You can also organize the implementation of certain assessments required by your district. Through this organization you can carefully plan how your student data is going to be collected and how student progress will be recorded and monitored.

Formative Assessments

Formative assessments can be incorporated into your classroom and linked to your instruction in a variety of ways. Classroom activities, journal, observations, quizzes, teacher-made tests, question answer sessions, and assignments that allow students to demonstrate what they have learned are all examples of formative assessments. However, do remember that not all assessments are paper/pencil driven. There are numerous ways you can assess your students' learning embracing the essential qualities of Universal Design for Learning: representation, expression, and engagement. Specific assessment techniques using UDL are presented later in the chapter.

Summative Assessments

Summative assessments can help you evaluate a student's performance as well as your instruction. Most often we think of end-of-year high stakes testing and packaged cumulative assessments that may accompany adopted textbook/educational programs as summative assessments. However, other examples may include unit tests, cumulative student projects, final student performances, and portfolios.

Organizational Systems for Assessment

Regardless of the forms of assessment you use, your organization should be simple enough that you can find systems that will make assessment fit comfortably into your day/week. Remember, you don't need to assess everything! Your assessment can be as simple and low tech as having a notebook or folder system or you may choose to use one of the technology assessment tools displayed in the WWW Resources box. You can also let your students help out in the assessment process through self-assessment techniques and peer-assessment. This is an excellent way

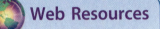

Web Resources

Go to the text's companion website (**http://www.academic.cengage.com/education/Gargiulo**) for access to the following web-based assessment tools: InteGrade Pro (an electronic gradebook system), Grade Connect, Engrade, and Thinkwave (a free online grade management system).

Monkey Business/Fotolia

Summative assessments can include project presentations or performances.

for your students to take ownership of their learning. Students and peers can assess a variety of assessment products through reflections, checklists, and rubrics.

Recording Assessments

Regardless of which assessment organization system you use, it is important that assessments are recorded often and are ongoing to document the progress of your students. You can use probes to collect student data, rubrics to evaluate work samples, and computerized programs to monitor student progress.

Probes

Probes are frequent and repeated measures that allow for instructional planning. Probes allow us to collect information to drive our instruction by determining which strategies we need to select for our students. Probes can be teacher created or may be part of a commercial educational program.

Curriculum-Based Measurement

Curriculum-based measurement (CBM) is one type of assessment that uses repeated probes to directly measure a student's progress in reading, math, writing, and spelling with results documented in a systematic and reliable format (Deno, Fuchs, Marston, & Shin, 2001). According to Howell and Nolet (1999), CBM is a set of specific measurement methods for assessing student progress over time and for identifying students in need of additional instructional support or further diagnostic testing. CBM allows you to:

- Monitor progress toward IEP goals
- Document gains in basic skills
- Adjust instruction
- Predict performance on state assessment
- Assist in eligibility/placement decisions
- Determine the effectiveness of programs
- Identifying those students at risk

To implement CBM, you can easily identify the curriculum goals you expect students to master and develop the necessary probes. Individual probes may include brief reading passages, word identification lists, short spelling lists, or samples of math computation problems from the curriculum. Using these probes, you would assess your students' progress one to two times a week and record the scores on a graph that can be used to make instructional decisions. Since CBM can be implemented on a regular, repeating basis, you can determine if your instructional approaches are effective or if changes in the delivery and content of your instruction need to be made. Figure 8.5 displays sample graphs for charting math and reading accuracy. CBM is a perfect opportunity for students and teachers to discuss daily and long-term learning goals and visually graph progress. CBM allows students to participate in goal setting for learning resulting in a potential increase in academic performance (Deno et al., 2001). Additional examples of CBM will follow in this text when discussing assessment techniques for various content areas. Example probes and tools for charting progress can also be found at http://www.interventioncentral.org/htmdocs/interventions/cbmwarehouse.php.

Rubrics

Rubrics are student or teacher created scoring systems that are used as evaluation tools of a performance based product. **Analytic rubrics** are used to assign points for responses on an assessment or work sample based on specific predetermined

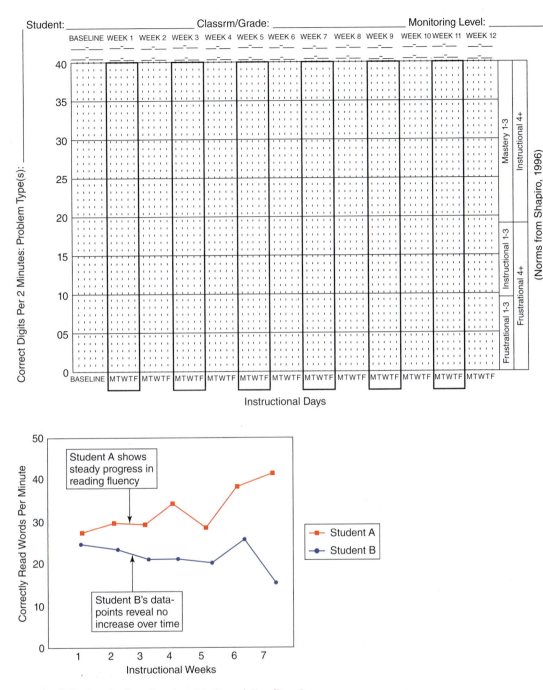

Student: _____   Classrm/Grade: _____   Monitoring Level: _____

Instructional Days

Figure **8.5** **Graphs for Charting Math and Reading Accuracy**
Source: Jim Wright, available at http://www.interventioncentral.org

criteria. Those points are then added to determine and overall score indicating a level of performance. **Holistic rubrics** are used to determine the quality of a student's response and rely more on the product or performance rather than the actual process. Examples of analytic and holistic rubrics will be shared later in the text as they specifically relate to reading, math, and written expression. According to Finson and Ormsbee (1998), rubrics can accurately reflect student achievement in the general education setting and can be used objectively to access the learning of students with learning and behavior difficulties.

Students can also use rubrics as a means of self-assessment. When students create their own evaluation tools such as rubrics and contracts, it promotes

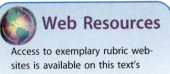

Web Resources

Access to exemplary rubric websites is available on this text's companion website, **http://www.academic.cengage.com/education/Gargiulo**.

empowerment and self-confidence (Ogle, 1994). An advantage of rubrics is that they are flexible and can be adapted to varying assessment situations. The WWW Resources box includes a few excellent website resources on rubrics.

Methods for Ongoing Assessment

We probably all know teachers who collect every teaching material perhaps because someone gave it to them (retiring teachers love to do this), the publisher offered a special, and/or it was on sale and looked interesting. Collections of this nature can become overwhelming and make it difficult to sort and determine what is really important to have in the learning environment. It is rather like spending hours clipping store coupons and filing them only to discover the items you buy this way don't really fit with the meals you make or the coupons end up expiring before you get around to using them. As tempting as it is, try to clear your plate and determine what materials/resources/methods are needed according to your assessments. You might be surprised in your school/district that many of these materials are already accessible to you or you can request them. On the other hand, there are certain "staples" you will need that are fine to stock up on, such as different kinds of writing instruments, paper, and fidgets.

Think back to the previous chapter on Universal Design for Learning. Effective assessment procedures can help you choose high-quality *materials, media,* and *methods* that are flexible in nature just as your instruction to meet the needs of your learners and build on their strengths. Some additional materials that you will have on hand to work with are your curriculum standards and the curriculum which you will need to analyze to determine exactly what you need to teach your students. From this material, you can pull out the "big ideas" on what the curriculum and standards say we need to teach. Using those big ideas, you can create assessments that will document student progress and specifically link to the standards and curriculum goals.

In addition to curriculum goals, you will most likely have assessment resources and materials that are part of the adopted curriculum within your school or district such as running records, writing profiles, or material that accompany textbooks. Prepackaged materials often offer an array of assessment protocols and devices, but keep in mind that it is your job as an effective teacher to administer or modify those assessments in a manner that meets the individual needs of your learners.

High-Tech and Low-Tech Materials

Administering or modifying assessments to meet the individual needs of your learners can be done with the help of high- and low-tech assistive technology materials. Some of your students may benefit from the use of digital voice recorders, color-coded response cards, switches, communication boards, pointers, highlighting tape, talking calculators, magnifying devices, portable word processors, and text-to-speech software while participating in various assessment activities.

Computerized Assessments

Some materials you might want to consider to use in your classroom are computerized assessments. There are a variety of web-based assessment technologies that provide extra practice, monitor student progress, and record assessment results. Students often find these programs motivating as they can monitor their own progress, and teachers enjoy the benefit of programming these supplemental assessments to address individual learning levels. Go to the text's companion website for more information about computerized assessment programs.

Now that you know your learners assessment preferences and have a good idea of your materials and resources on hand, it is time to plan for what you specifically need to teach your students. At this point, you will take the curriculum standards and standard course of study objectives and analyze them. You will need to determine the skills and knowledge that your students have already acquired through assessment prior to instruction. Assessment tools will help you determine exactly "what" you need to teach to build on existing skills or what needs to be taught to fill in any existing gaps. Once you have identified the "what" you will need to determine "how" you are going to instruct and assess your students. As you plan your instruction, you will need to integrate assessment techniques provide for multiple means of engagement, multiples means of representation, and multiple means of presentation.

Multiple Means of Engagement in Assessment

If you integrate ongoing assessment into your daily instruction, it becomes a normal part of learning rather than an isolated event. As an isolated event, assessment can sometimes affect student engagement leading to anxiety and decreased student motivation. Integrated assessment allows your students to be engaged resulting in reduced anxiety and increased motivation for accurate assessment results.

Fostering Motivation

There are numerous ways to increase and foster student motivation when it comes to assessment. First of all, providing students with choices of various assessment formats can be powerful. If students can choose an assessment format that maximizes their strengths and learning modalities, they are likely to do better and in turn become engaged in their learning. Furthermore, providing a choice in terms of content within a particular assessment allows students to focus assessment on personal interests to make learning relevant and meaningful. For example, if a task or activity is intended to assess reading comprehension of a nonfiction, informational passage, a student can choose to read on a topic of interest, whether it be a passage about volcanoes or perhaps space exploration.

In addition, students need to take ownership of their learning and share what they have learned with others to increase motivation. The assessment activities you plan within your instruction should incorporate opportunities for setting personal goals, create an environment in which each student can share, and provide opportunities for student collaboration. Most importantly, as a teacher you should always model your enthusiasm for learning to foster motivation!

Providing Student Feedback

Providing feedback on student performance on an ongoing basis can increase student engagement and help students develop a sense of self-efficacy. Students need feedback that is individualized, specific, and most importantly, given in a format that is accessible. For example, you may provide student feedback in a verbal form through the use of a digitized recorder instead of written comments on paper. Also, the use of self-monitoring by students to chart their own learning progress and peer feedback can be important tools in enhancing engagement.

The difficulty level of material included in assessments is another factor which can affect student engagement and motivation. Providing students with individualized assessment activities on their appropriate instructional level and ongoing assessments based on your instruction can lead to reduce anxiety regarding assessment. Oftentimes, the content of high-stakes testing cannot be modified; however, the presentation format can be flexible resulting in reduced text anxiety. Additionally, specific strategies can be introduced and taught to your students that address text anxiety.

Student feedback can increase engagement and self-efficacy. Consider recording comments when face-to-face interaction isn't possible.

Multiple Means of Representation in Assessment

To engage students in their learning, you will need to carefully consider the presentation format of your assessment instruments. For example, everyone has a preference when it comes to shopping. Some people like to shop online, some prefer a group, some enjoy bargain shopping, some have a personal shopper, and some think shopping is fun. Just as there are multiple forms of shopping, there are multiple forms of presentation for the assessment that you plan. Now that you know "what" you need to assess with your students, the next step is to determine and "how" you will plan and present those assessments to your students. To embrace

Universal Design for Learning in the Classroom

Multiple Means of Assessment—Elementary Example

Multiple means of assessing student understanding is important. Sometimes, I check for understanding simply by asking questions. In a lesson comparing same/different within a larger unit about communities, for example, I might ask: "Who can tell me which state is the largest and which is the smallest?" I do this at various times. For example, when students are lined up and ready to go outside or to P.E. class, I may ask a few questions related to the lesson.

Often I begin our lessons with a few questions to help my students think about what they have already learned. I make mental notes to myself,* noting which students responded and how. Later, this information is recorded in a notebook. During these question and answer moments, I am able to see if

students are recalling factual information, if there are any errors in their thinking, and where we need to review.

My students enjoy sharing their knowledge with others. My class has pen pals from a school in Michigan. I have suggested that students share what they have learned with their pen pals by writing about it in their weekly letters. From their letters, I can determine how well students understand the information we have covered. Some are able to write without their journals, while others refer to the pages of their writing journals for information. Their letters become another way to evaluate their understanding.

Toward the end of the year, when more information has been accumulated, my students use this information to create travel

posters about Alaska. Sitka is a town heavily frequented by tourists, and we put our posters on display in stores throughout town.

Barbara Renoux
K-2 multiage classroom
Baranof Elementary School
Sitka, Alaska

*Write these on a sticky note and place in writing portfolio or lesson plan book later. "E-pals" can be motivating too!

Source: Adapted from Digital Edge Learning Interchange, *Postcards to Learning*. Retrieved May 9, 2008 from http://edcommunity.apple.com/ali/story.php?itemID=460

Universal Design for Learning in the Classroom

Multiple Means of Assessment—Middle School Example

By offering my students a mix of verbal, non-verbal, or written responses, I get a better idea of where they are with their learning. Sometimes we use pinch cards, response cards, or individual whiteboards that the students can hold up after they have solved a problem. With a quick glance of the room, I can see which students are ready to move ahead and which ones may need extra practice. Using a computer response system, students can click in a multiple-choice response and I can quickly scan the computer screen for the same kind of information. My students find working problems on the board or overhead projector or on individual white boards very engaging. This also gives me an opportunity to see exactly where skill strengths and deficits are. My students are also motivated by computer testing and review games such as "Jeopardy." Having computer templates for Jeopardy-type games has saved me a lot of preparation time. I just change the questions to match the lesson/unit objectives.

Laura Jones
Master Teacher, Math
G. R. Whitfield School
Grimesland, NC

the principles of UDL, your assessments should be presented in multiple formats. Your assessments may take on alternate formats in the form of written products, visual products, and performance products that incorporate the principles of UDL. Oftentimes, teachers provide assessments in the very same format for all students within their class. Unfortunately, this approach does not always tap into the knowledge of our students who need a different means of presentation. For example, a student who struggles with reading and writing may do poorly on a written science test even if he has mastered the content knowledge. A performance-based assessment or an assessment delivered in an alternate format through oral representation may better represent his knowledge and skills. As you can see, you will need to offer multiple, flexible assessment options to your students, as no one format will target the diversity of your learners to demonstrate their understanding.

High-Tech and Low-Tech Options

As you consider the presentation of your assessment, you will encounter many high- and low-tech options. We have already discussed the high-tech option of computerized assessments. In addition, some other high-tech options in presentation are assessments created using PowerPoint, podcasts, digital media, and other software. Examples of high-tech assessment presentations could be using a text-to-speech software program to read a quiz or even using a PowerPoint with enlarged print, audio files, and graphics to create a student assessment. Low-tech presentation examples may include assessments offered in paper-pencil formats, print formats, and verbal assessments such as a test or activity read aloud.

Presenting Testing Accommodations

Currently, there are many testing accommodations that are offered to students participating in assessment, such as marking in the book, read aloud, and large print. However, due to the often limited effectiveness of these accommodations, we need to move beyond retrofitting accommodations into incorporating technology-based accommodations to create accurate assessments that allow for optimum student success. Table 8.1 presents some ideas for technology-based approaches to providing testing accommodations.

Student Expression in Assessment

Not only do we need to look at how we present and organize our assessment, but we should closely examine the various formats we allow for student expression in assessments. Commonly, as an accommodation, teachers may allow students to

Table 8.1	Technology-Based Approaches to Providing Testing Accommodations	
UDL Principles	**Standard Accommodations/ Administration**	**Technology-Based Accommodations**
Multiple Means of Representation	Read aloud on math sections for a student with a learning disability in reading	• Audio text • Talking word processors • Represent math questions both in word problems and graphically
Multiple Means of Expression	Scribe to record responses for a student with a physical disability	• Single switches • Alternative pointing devices • Speech-to-text
Multiple Means of Engagement	Read a passage to measure reading comprehension skills	• Allow a choice of topic based on interest

Source: Adapted from R. P. Dolan and T. E. Hall, "Universal Design for Learning: Implications for Large Scale Assessment," *IDA Perspectives, 27*(4), 2001, pp. 22–25.

orally express their responses to pencil/paper assessment or provide extended time. However, these minor adjustments still may not provide accessibility. Many students require assessments that go beyond routine modifications. To reach diverse learners and maximize information gained from assessment, alternative choices in terms of expression format can be provided to our students.

High-Tech and Low-Tech Options

As in representation of assessment, there are many high- and low-tech options for student expression in assessment. For example, in addition to offering a multiple choice test to demonstrate comprehension of a passage read, a teacher may offer a low-tech option such as providing a drawing or skit to demonstrate understanding and comprehension or a medium-tech option such as a timeline or photo essay. As a high-tech option, a teacher may provide the opportunity for students to create an electronic portfolio or a multimedia project to show understanding. Table 8.2 displays low-tech and high-tech options for your students.

Universal Design for Learning in the Classroom

Multiple Means of Assessment—Secondary Example

Before beginning a new ecology unit for my high school biology students, I assessed their existing levels of prior knowledge to help me plan their instruction more effectively. This assessment provided an understanding of where I needed to begin, of what content needed to be more thoroughly covered, and what content could be eliminated due to existing competence. At the beginning of this instructional sequence, my students participated in the Internet WebQuest for pond ecology terms. I required them to write definitions in their own words and to share their definitions with the class. This provided an informal method to assess the initial knowledge levels of my students.

Throughout the instructional sequence, I continually assessed student thinking and understanding informally through questioning and through discussions. These discussions allowed me to scrutinize individual student misconceptions and to realign them. I gave a couple of short quizzes (multiple choice, true/false, short answer) that afforded me insight into their ongoing progress. I formally evaluated the laboratory investigation, report, and presentation through the use of a scoring rubric that assessed the level of achievement for specific criteria. I established these requirements prior to the investigation and discussed them with the students so they could understand my expectations. At the conclusion of the unit, the students took an authentic assessment exam which contained several environmental scenarios and inquiries. They were asked to point out discrepancies or experimental errors in the design and/or the interpretation of the results of ecological

investigations similar to those they had conducted. It is important to utilize many forms of assessment at many points throughout a unit. This approach helps to minimize test anxiety that occurs when a large portion of a grading period comes from a single test grade. My quizzes and rubrics for assessments are available in both PDF format and as Microsoft Word documents so they can be easily adapted as needed for learners.

Susie Stevens, NBCT
Biology Teacher, Latta High School
Ada, OK

Source: Adapted from Digital Edge Learning Interchange, *Probing Ponds*. Retrieved May 10, 2008 from http://newali.apple.com/ali_sites/deli/exhibits/1000723/Assessment.html

Table 8.2	**Low-Tech and High-Tech Student Expression Formats**	
Area of Difficulty	**Low-Tech Options**	**High-Tech Options**
Cognitive/Academic	Demonstration, matching, choosing/pointing	Electronic portfolio, multimedia project
Hyperactivity	Mark in book, oral responses, tape-recorded responses, demonstrations, experiments, how-to sessions	Digitized recording of performance, movies, digital portfolios
Motor	Switch responses, scribe, dictation, oral presentations, speeches, interviews	Audio recordings, podcasts, radio broadcasts, MP3 recordings, use of voice recognition software
Memory/Generalization	Write a song, rap, or poem, use manipulatives, construct a game	Produce a play, record a song
Speech	Write letters, short stories, narrative essays, newsletters, newspapers; create models, diagrams, scrapbooks, collages	Create blogs, e-journals, online discussions, Power-Points, slide shows
Language	Create posters, pictures, cartoons, illustrations, models, diagrams, exhibits, dioramas	Use software to create graphic organizers, illustrations, posters
Motivation	Demonstrate understanding through role playing, skits, real-world problem solving, music, drama, creative play, dance	Design WebQuests, webpages, video broadcasts, virtual tours

Multimedia Projects

Students can use scanned pictures, Internet websites, digitized video clips, and software such as Microsoft PowerPoint to represent what they have learned in multiple formats. Elder-Hinshaw, Manset-Williamson, Nelson, and Dunn (2006) created a step-by-step procedure and rubric to create and evaluate a **multimedia inquiry project** and support reading comprehension skills across the curriculum. See Figures 8.6 and 8.7, as well as Table 8.3.

Dunn et al. (2006) used introductory sessions to provide instruction with media and storyboarding steps. Inquiry sessions allowed students to develop questions and organization using the POSE strategy. Next, student participated in resource sessions to gather information, storyboard sessions to organize information, and PowerPoint

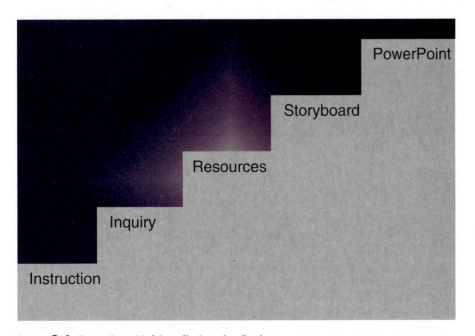

Figure 8.6 Steps in a Multimedia Inquiry Project
Source: R. Elder-Hinshaw, G. Manset-Williamson, J. Nelson, and M. Dunn, "Engaging Older Students with Reading Disabilities: Multimedia Inquiry Projects Supported by Reading Assistive Technology," *Teaching Exceptional Children, 39*(1), 2006, p. 8.

Predict what information you will find out about your topic.

Lives in Scotland

Like a dinosaur

Hides from people

What are some of your questions?

Is it real?

What does it eat?

Where does it live?

Organize your thoughts.

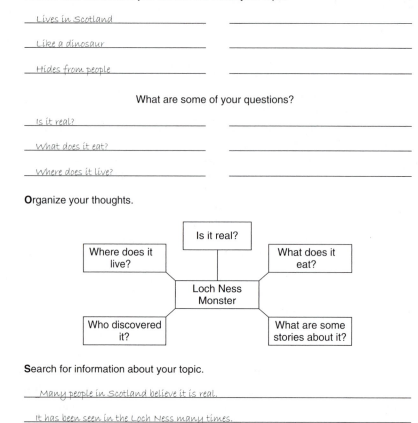

Search for information about your topic.

Many people in Scotland believe it is real.

It has been seen in the Loch Ness many times.

Evaluate your results. What will you keep? What will you leave out?

Figure 8.7 POSE Strategy

Source: R. Elder-Hinshaw, G. Manset-Williamson, J. Nelson, and M. Dunn, "Engaging Older Students with Reading Disabilities: Multimedia Inquiry Projects Supported by Reading Assistive Technology," *Teaching Exceptional Children,* 39(1), 2006, p. 9.

sessions to present information. This multimedia method engaged students with their reading, led students to apply reading comprehension strategies, and fostered student motivation. Multimedia inquiry projects embrace the principles of UDL by providing accessibility, flexibility, and multiple forms of presentation and representation which is beneficial to all students with and without disabilities (Dunn et al.).

Portfolios

Portfolios are an excellent way to document success in performance-based assessments or alternative assessments. Portfolios are a collection of student work over a specific period of time. To incorporate UDL principles, portfolios can be represented in an electronic format. Portfolios may be a collection of writing samples, pictures, drawings, video clips, and PowerPoint presentations displayed through multiple means of representation to demonstrate mastery of skills or objectives. To develop a portfolio, students self-select artifacts to allow for student ownership. Once selected, students and teachers can compare artifacts to document growth. It is important to include all drafts, rubrics, and checklists within the portfolio to demonstrate ongoing growth.

Portfolios represent authentic and alternative learning experiences and provide a vehicle for reflection, goal setting, and self-assessment (Boerum, 2000). According to

Table 8.3	Multimedia PowerPoint Inquiry Project Rubric			
Category	**4**	**3**	**2**	**1**
Inquiry process	Student/tutor dyad followed all required steps of the project (POSE, research, read, summarize, choose graphics, storyboard, create PowerPoint).	Student/tutor dyad followed all required steps of the project (POSE, research, read, summarize, choose graphics, storyboard, create PowerPoint) with one prompt from researcher.	Student/tutor dyad followed all required steps of the project (POSE, research, read, summarize, choose graphics, storyboard, create PowerPoint) with many prompts from researchers.	Student/tutor dyad followed few of required steps of the project (POSE, research, read, summarize, choose graphics, storyboard, create PowerPoint).
Focus on research question	The entire PowerPoint is related to the research question and allows the reader to understand much more about the topic.	Most of the PowerPoint is related to the research question. The PowerPoint wanders off at one point, but the reader can still learn something about the topic.	Some of the PowerPoint is related to the research question, but a reader does not learn much about the topic.	Little attempt has been made to relate the PowerPoint to the research question.
Organization	The PowerPoint is very well organized. Each idea or slide is arranged in a logical sequence with an identifiable text structure and clear transitions.	The PowerPoint is very well organized. Most ideas or slides are arranged in a logical sequence with an identifiable text structure and clear transitions. One idea or slide may seem out of place. Clear transitions are used.	The PowerPoint is a little hard to follow. The transitions are sometimes not clear and text structure is often not identifiable.	Ideas and slides seem to be randomly arranged.
Graphics and sound	Graphics and/or sound add to the reader's understanding of research topic.	Graphics and/or sound add to the reader's understanding of the research topic, except for one slide.	Some of graphics and/or sound add to some of the reader's understanding of the research topic.	None of the graphics and/or sound adds to the reader's understanding of the research topic.

Source: R. Elder-Hinshaw, G. Manset-Williamson, J. Nelson, and M. Dunn, "Engaging Older Students with Reading Disabilities: Multimedia Inquiry Projects Supported by Reading Assistive Technology," *Teaching Exceptional Children, 39*(1), 2006, p. 10.

Boerum, students with learning disabilities participating in performance-based activities and assessments, clarified their strengths and needs as learners to set goals for improvement. The use of portfolios increased student motivation and desire to learn resulting in improved student performance. Boerum identified five areas of learning to reflect student progress. Students collected drafts, final copies, media products, rubrics, checklists, and reflections to compile a portfolio that represented two pieces (a best piece and comparison piece) to show growth as a researcher, reader/writer, oral presenter, creative thinker, and problem. See Figure 8.8 for an example of Boerum's portfolio design format.

In addition, informal assessment measures can be used to analyze your student portfolios to develop appropriate instruction and assist in determining appropriate goals for your students. Portfolios are an excellent way for both teachers and students to be collaboratively engaged to monitor progress (Boerum, 2000).

Portfolios are an excellent tool to use in combination with student-led conferences. Students are able to establish connections to their learning within and outside of school as well as assume responsibility as learners (Conderman, Ikan, & Hatcher, 2000). Additionally, student-led conferences with portfolios enhance student-parent-teacher communication, focus on strengths and progress, and demonstrate growth toward curriculum goals and objectives in the inclusive, general education setting. Steps for using portfolios in student-led conferences include:

1. Inform
2. Educate, Model, and Teach
3. Set Goals
4. Practice
5. Implement
6. Evaluate (Conderman et al., 2000)

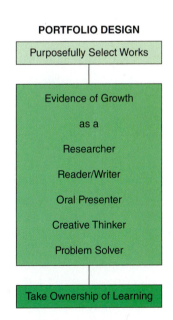

Figure 8.8 Portfolio Design
Source: L. Boerum, "Developing Portfolios with Learning Disabled Students," *Reading & Writing Quarterly, 16*(3), 2006, p. 214.

Final Thoughts

Now that you have pulled all the clothes out of your closet, tried them on, and have decided to put back only those items you really use and like after assessing your needs and style. You have a large pile of clothes to give away. You realize you are very good at selecting colors that work for you, but all of your pants are either too short or just don't fit right. You only have one pair to put back in the closet. What are you going to do to improve this need? It's time to research "pants" and find out how you can get it right. Your strategies might include researching clothing sizing/fitting online, visiting a specialty store or alterations expert and getting first-hand advice, or getting a friend to help.

This same analogy can be applied to teaching. You have assessed student needs and now you need to "shop" for the best strategies to meet these needs. Remember to keep the strengths of the students in mind so they can feel successful and look for ways to showcase these strengths while you work diligently on improving needs. The next chapter will give you many "shopping" tips!

Thematic Summary

- Large-scale assessments are used to collect, compare, and analyze performances of teachers, schools, and school systems. In our country today, the stakes for these assessments are high.
- Teachers use ongoing, formative assessment to identify student strengths and needs, set goals, monitor student growth, and inform/guide instruction. Curriculum-based assessment is an example of this. It uses probes and frequent charting of progress to chart growth.
- Summative assessments can be large scale or they can be the culminating assessment of a student project or unit of study. Scoring systems such as rubrics can be created and used by teachers and students to determine the level of a performance.
- By reviewing school records, formal and informal assessments, and talking/collaborating with parents, former teachers, school psychologists, and related service professionals, teachers can learn important information about student strengths, needs, and learning preferences.
- Using learning style and multiple intelligences inventories can help you discover how your students learn best. This will help you in your lesson planning.
- Ongoing collaboration with parents, teachers, administrators, school psychologists, and other related service professionals is important for problem solving.
- Applying UDL principles to assessment using high- and low-technology tools and programs fosters accessibility/participation for *all* students.
- Authentic and alternative assessments such as portfolio building and student-led conferences can be powerful ways to communicate student strengths, needs, and progress for *all* learners.

Making Connections for Inclusive Teaching

1. What is your opinion of large-scale assessments? Do you think they are more important, less important, or just as important as other types of assessments? Defend your viewpoint.
2. How do you (or would you) use both formal and informal assessments in your classroom? Give some examples of each.

3. What are the benefits of working collaboratively with other professionals in your school? Who are some of the individuals you would seek out to work with, and what would you hope they would help you achieve?
4. Review the examples of various technology-assessment tools. Choose one and explain how you would use it in regards to assessing your students.
5. Of the computerized assessments listed, which ones are used in your school and how are they used?
6. In your opinion, what is the biggest challenge in using multiple means of representation in assessment? How can you overcome this challenge and tailor your assessment practices to meet the needs of all your students?

Learning Activities

1. Think about your own experiences with assessment. Which kinds have worked best for you and why? On the other hand, describe a negative experience you have had with assessment. Provide at least one personal example of an effective and an ineffective type of assessment.
2. Design an interest inventory that you would like to use with your students.
3. Review the various type of rubrics. Design one that you would use in your classroom.
4. Interview veteran teachers about their methods of assessment. What types of assessment do they choose to use and what types are they required to use? How has this changed, for better and for worse, over the years?
5. Observe several different classrooms during periods in which they will be performing assessments. What types of assessment do you see being used? Do you feel they are being used effectively? If some types are more effective than others, what makes these more effective? What could the teacher do to improve his or her types and methods of assessment?

Looking at the Standards

The content of this chapter most closely aligns itself with the following standards:

INTASC Standards

- *Assessment.* The teacher understands and uses formal and informal assessment strategies to evaluate and ensure the continuous intellectual, social, and physical development of the learner.

Council for Exceptional Children

Special educators are to have knowledge of the following:

- CC8K1: Basic terminology used in assessment.
- CC8S1: Gather relevant background information.
- CC8S3: Use technology to conduct assessments.
- CC855: Interpret information from formal and informal assessments.
- CC8S8: Evaluate instruction and monitor progress of individuals with exceptional learning needs.
- GC8S3: Select, adapt, and modify assessments to accommodate the unique abilities and needs of individuals with disabilities.

Key Concepts and Terms

large-scale assessments
No Child Left Behind Act
norm-referenced tests
criterion-referenced tests
formal assessment
informal assessment
interest inventories
learning styles inventories
multiple intelligences

positive behavior supports
functional behavior
    assessment
behavior intervention
    plan
formative assessments
summative assessments
probes

curriculum-based
    measurement
rubrics
analytic rubrics
holistic rubrics
multimedia inquiry
    project
portfolios

References

Armstrong, T. (1994). *Multiple intelligences in the classroom.* Alexandria, VA: Association for Supervision and Curriculum Development.

Boerum, L. J. (2000). Developing portfolios with learning disabled students. *Reading & Writing Quarterly, 16*(3), 211–238.

Conderman, G., Ikan, P. A., & Hatcher, R. E. (2000). Student-led conferences in inclusive settings. *Intervention in School & Clinic, 36*(1), 22–27.

Deno, S. L., Fuchs, L. S., Marston, D., & Shin, J. (2001). Using curriculum-based measurement to establish growth standards for students with learning disabilities. *School Psychology Review, 30*(4), 507–524.

Dolan, R. P., & Hall, T. E. (2001). Universal design for learning: Implications for large scale assessment. *IDA Perspectives, 27*(4), 22–25.

Dunn, R. (1990). Rita Dunn answers questions on learning styles. *Educational Leadership, 48*(2), 15–19.

Dunn, R., Dunn, K., & Price, G. (1985). *Manual: Learning style inventory.* Lawrence, KS: Price Systems.

Elder-Hinshaw, R., Manset-Williamson, G., Nelson, J., & Dunn, M. (2006). Engaging older students with reading disabilities: Multimedia inquiry projects supported by reading assistive technology. *Teaching Exceptional Children, 39*(1), 6–11.

Finson, K. D., & Ormsbee, C. K. (1998). Rubrics and their use in inclusive science. *Intervention in School and Clinic, 34*(2), 79–89.

Fleming, N. D. (2001). *Teaching and learning styles, VARK strategies.* Christchurch, New Zealand. Retrieved October 8, 2008 from http://www.vark-learn.com/english/index.asp

Gardner, H. (1993). *Frames of mind: The theory of multiple intelligences.* New York: Basic Books.

Haley, M. H. (2004). Learner-centered instruction and the theory of multiple intelligences with second language learners. *Teachers College Record, 106*(1), 163–180.

Howell, K. W., & Nolet, V. (1999). *Curriculum-based evaluation: Teaching and decision making* (3rd ed.). Belmont, CA: Wadsworth.

Kolb, D. A. (1984). *Experiential learning: Experience as the source of learning and development.* Englewood Cliffs, NJ: Prentice Hall.

Levine, M., & Scherer, M. (2006). Celebrate strengths, nurture affinities: A conversation with Mel Levine. *Educational Leadership, 64*(1), 8–15.

Ogle, D. (1994). Assessments: Helping our students see their learning. *Teaching Pre K-8, 25*(2), 100–101.

Sean Nel/istockphoto.com

Selecting Instructional Interventions for Teaching All Learners

Considering Stages of Learning in Intervention Selection

Acquisition Stage
Proficiency
Maintenance
Generalization
Adaptation

Using Curricular Design Principles in Intervention Selection

Begin with Big Ideas
Activate Prior Knowledge
Integrate Learning Goals
Use Conspicuous Strategies
Apply Mediated Scaffolding
Provide Purposeful and Cumulative Review

Learning Outcomes

After studying this chapter, you should be able to:

- Identify student learning stages and provide examples of teacher behavior and intervention selection that is appropriate for learners at each stage.
- Tell why setting goals and implementing interventions around a "big idea" is critical to all learners.
- Explain what anchored instruction is and how related general strategic practices empower *all* learners.
- Describe high- and low-tech applications of general strategic practices.
- Describe various interventions or techniques that can be used according to student learning domains and provide classroom examples for each.
- Apply the principles of UDL in intervention selection.

Outcomes *(continued)*

- Match learner characteristics and learning styles in intervention selection.
- Tell why all learners need to be challenged to problem-solve at every level of learning.

Considering Specific Learning Domains in General Intervention Selection

Cognitive/Generalization

Giftedness

Language/Speech

Memory

Study Skills, Organization, and Test Taking

Attention Disorders/Hyperactivity/Impulsivity

Social/Emotional/Motivational Challenges

Physical/Motor/Sensory Challenges

Using Classroom Websites and Other Web Tools

You can really understand a lot about UDL teaching, interventions, and techniques by spending time in today's health clubs. In an aerobics class such as Step or Body Pump, for example, there are people who learn the steps/movements quickly and those who really need the steps broken down with many repetitions to learn. Typically, the fast learners are in the front of the class. Those who struggle or are new to the "language" of the program are usually in the back unless they are strong self-advocates who position themselves close to the instructor. To accommodate the participants in the back, there are video monitors and speakers so everyone has access to instructions in multiple ways. Members with low vision might even have a friend or coach to talk them though the movements.

Instructors demonstrate each movement and enthusiastically talk participants through each step using sound systems. They prepare and cue exercisers for transitions between movements to keep the pace, maximize the allotted time, and keep people from making rapid changes that might cause injury. Music is added to keep the rhythm and break the boredom. Fast music is played to accelerate movement and slower music is offered to relax. These organized classes with direct instruction are great for people who need to work in groups to stay motivated.

There are a variety of cardio- and body-strengthening machines and tools for those who prefer working alone or with a friend. On the machines or nearby walls, posted laminated cards with visual directions paired with pictures show how to use each one.

Personal trainers are available to provide one-on-one training. They use their assessments to design individualized fitness programs with self-monitoring systems based on the identified strengths and needs of the consumer. Together you can set a goal to lose 20 pounds or train to run a marathon. Trainers can provide task analysis, direct instruction, observation with feedback, and continual encouragement.

Most health clubs or gyms are designed to offer the necessary tools and information to the user, regardless of his or her sensory abilities. It is easy to access the "curriculum" of exercise when many options for representation, engagement, and expression exist. To find the club or gym to best fit your needs, you shop around and compare quality of staff and equipment, diversity in offerings, hours of operation, appearance, location, and price. You check to see if access to print and electronic schedules is available in advance so you can plan your workout time. You want a gym that is welcoming and designed to meet your needs.

Joining a health club or gym, of course, is just one exercise option. Many people prefer to walk, run, bike, swim, or play a sport without joining a gym. Other people have equipment at home or access a nearby park. There are lots of self-help books, plans, and DVDs/videos available for home use. How do you select the right interventions to reach your fitness goals?

The students in your classroom are, in many ways, like people in the gym. As in the weight room, some need heavy weights to push themselves to a higher level;

others find lifting lighter weights meets their needs for strengthening and toning. Some people push themselves to run farther/faster; others find walking on a tread-mill the right personal challenge. Many standards and curricular goals are predeter-mined, yet some students will need adjustments because of their special talents and needs. It will be important for you to know what is expected of you and your learners as well as your learners' strengths and needs to select appropriate practices. As in exercise, an overarching goal for *all* is to increase performance levels. People will achieve their personal objectives and goals in different ways and at different rates.

Unlike the above analogy, students don't typically get to choose what school, class-room, or class they go to before college. They typically don't get to choose the method of representation, engagement, or expression that is used. This chapter will show you many proven techniques and some tools you might use to increase these options for all students applying the principles of UDL in a very general way. It is designed to help you reach the diverse learners in your classroom by considering learning stages, cur-ricular design principles, and specific learning domains. Not surprisingly, you will likely find that many of these practices and tools work for *all* students.

Considering Stages of Learning in Intervention Selection

As we begin to discuss various instructional practices and interventions, it will be important to consider student learning stages. Learning stages have been frequently presented in the literature and have been valued in designing and implementing effective instruction (Alberto & Troutman, 2003; Mercer & Mercer, 2005; Rivera & Smith, 1997). Intervention selection will depend, to a degree, on each individual's stage of learning. Material that is completely new and challenging to one learner at the beginning or acquisition stage might be repetitive and easy to another stu-dent. Teachers have to adjust for these differences in the way they teach. Just like at the health club, students learn at different rates; some need more practice than others, and some perceive and process information in different ways. Some students will need a lot of direct instruction, whereas others may do better when the envir-onment is set up for them to explore problem-solving tasks through independent learning. Most people need a combination of both. In addition, some people pro-gress better when working alone; others are critically dependent on the direct inter-action with another person. Assessment linked to learning goals, as discussed pre-viously, will be critical to strategy/intervention selection. You will also want to link appropriate interventions and techniques to specific learner needs and interests at a given time to maximize teaching and learning.

Consider the following five stages of learning, as well as the suggestions for teacher interventions. These methods may be useful at different stages as well and are not restricted to a particular level of learning. More interventions will be offered as the text progresses. The practices and techniques suggested are appropriate for students of all ages—from those learning to tie a pair of shoes to those learning cal-culus. They will simply need to be applied in an age-appropriate manner. The goal of this section is to provide a general foundation for the content sections that follow.

Acquisition Stage

In the **acquisition stage of learning**, assessment scores may range from 0 to 80%. All, most, or some of the skills need to be learned. In the very beginning, this might be compared to someone's first attempt to ever ride a bicycle, ski, or hit a baseball. Demonstration teaching and modeling with many concrete examples are necessary for most diverse learners at this level. As Piaget suggested and some current research supports, diverse learners may need to progress sequentially from the

Cengage Learning/Wadsworth

Working with manipulatives helps students of all ages in the acquisition stage of learning.

concrete to the pictorial to the abstract stages of learning (Miller, Harris, Strawser, Jones, & Mercer, 1998; Witzel, Mercer, & Miller, 2003).

Once students have some idea of the skill or concept being taught, they can move ahead by participating in discrimination exercises that compare and contrast attributes within skill area(s). Teachers can pair some nonexamples with previous examples to strengthen meaning and memory. Just as in a Body Step class, participants need to know the correct way to step on a riser and the incorrect way. In English class, differentiating between present and future tense verbs might be the exercise.

Multiple practice activities with many opportunities to respond help all learners (McTighe & O'Connor, 2005). Correct errors quickly and give specific feedback (Konold, Miller, & Konold, 2004). Show students how to improve and build in positive reinforcement as a reward for accuracy as you continue with direct instruction.

Proficiency

In the next stage of learning, **proficiency**, teachers strive for automaticity. Students increase their speed and maintain the desired rate of accuracy as they become fluent with the skill being taught. Students in this stage will benefit greatly from modeling and goal setting (Mercer & Mercer, 2005). Try to pair them with models they find attractive and who are masters at the targeted skill. Students at this stage may need a reason for increasing their rate of accuracy because they may be satisfied with their success so far. A lot of positive reinforcement will likely be needed here. Self-management strategies may also be helpful to get students to push it to the limit. This stage might be compared to that last stretch of a marathon. The runner has done well until the last couple of miles and wants to quit. It is most likely that these runners have things they say to themselves or visualizations they pull from their heads to make it through those last grueling miles.

Maintenance

The third stage of learning is **maintenance**. This next stage of learning is particularly difficult for many diverse learners. Maintenance requires memory because practice alone is not enough. Some things seem to stay with us forever once we learn them (like swimming, running, riding a bike) but other things need periodic review for retention. Once you teach a skill, it will be important to go back and cumulatively review it from time to time. Diverse learners may also need to overlearn a task or skill in order to take it to the next step. There are also specific memory strategies we will discuss later in this chapter that can help with retention. Social reinforcement and continued self-management will also be important here. For example, if you have a running group or club, you might be more inclined to continue to keep your running skills up. Just as we plan our days/weeks to include exercising our bodies, learners (particularly those who struggle) must learn to set up their own practice and review times. Homework can help with this if students can develop, implement, and stick with a system. They will likely need help developing this routine.

Generalization

Remember that consistently linking learning to real-life situations and building on prior knowledge will help greatly with retention. This leads to the fourth learning stage, which is **generalization**—also referred to as **transfer of learning**. In generalization, the skills a student learns in one situation are applied to different ones. The time of day and the setting may be different but the skill is the same or similar (Stokes & Baer, 1977). For example, a student might successfully compute mathematically at school but not be able to check change received after making a purchase at the store. Socially, a student may greet others appropriately at school but not in the larger community.

Many students with learning difficulties don't generalize learning and must be systematically taught (Mercer & Mercer, 2005). Social skills that are learned in the classroom can be purposefully be applied and practiced in the cafeteria and at sporting events. Field trips (including virtual ones) may provide other opportunities to practice skill sets in different settings and times of day. Some researchers also suggest that other learning stages must be in place to obtain generalization (Alberto & Troutman, 2003). To help students generalize, teachers can provide rationales for learning skills and provide activities that actually use the skill sets in different places and times. Teachers who plan collaboratively with interdisciplinary approaches can structure opportunities to generalize within their units of instruction. Communication with parents and/or other significant adults in a student's life on social and academic skills being taught can also assist with this transfer.

Adaptation

The fifth and highest level of learning is **adaptation**. In this stage, students independently make discoveries. They categorize, make decisions, see relationships/analogies, analyze, estimate, compare/contrast, show flexibility, and identify items that are irrelevant. Students may work in individual or small groups on exploratory activities of interest and reflect on their work. As mentioned earlier, UDL research suggests to us that *all* students can discover on their own and problem-solve at all levels of learning—at least to some extent. It also suggests that all learners need these types of challenges at least some of the time so they can progress and be motivated. Some students just need different levels of support and accommodations. Most people, for example, if given the opportunity, make food choices on their own. Even struggling learners at early stages can often compare things like hot/cold, sweet/sour, and hard/soft on their own. Socially, *all* students can choose whether or not to participate on their own.

Table 9.1 summarizes the stages of learning and examples of instructional practices suggested so far in this chapter. To promote adaptations for *all* learners,

Table 9.1	Stages of Learning and Instructional Practices
Stages of Learning	**Examples of Effective Instructional Practices**
Acquisition Initial: 0–25% Advanced: 65–80% Aim for 90–100%	• Modeling/demonstrating • Directly teaching with concrete materials • Providing examples and nonexamples • Practicing with corrective feedback
Proficiency Students are fluent with what is learned with a high rate of accuracy.	• Setting goals • Applying self-management techniques • Pairing with peer model • Providing positive reinforcement
Maintenance Students retain what is learned accurately at a high rate.	• Reviewing periodically • Adding social reinforcement • Doing homework consistently
Generalization Students transfer or expand knowledge to new settings or responses.	• Planning collaboratively • Integrating units of study • Communicating with families • Changing settings (field trips, home, social settings)
Adaptation Students expand or extend their knowledge.	• Participating in exploratory activities • Choosing activities that involve constructing relationships and/or making analogies • Investigating real-life problems • Reflecting on learning

Source: Stages of Learning adapted from D. D. Smith, *Teaching the Learning Disabled* (Englewood Cliffs, NJ: Prentice Hall), p. 68.

additional strategies and techniques that support UDL are presented later in the chapter. We will begin with *adaptation* as the end in mind.

Using Curricular Design Principles in Intervention Selection

Some teachers tend to rely on textbooks as they plan a unit of study. A textbook, however, like a computer, is just one of many tools you have as a resource. When beginning to design the learning process and environment for your classroom with UDL in mind, it can be helpful to focus on six curricular design principles (Coyne, Kame'enui, & Carnine, 2007). These principles have been adopted by the National Center to Improve the Tools of Educators (NCITE) as classroom research suggests the six curricular design principles work especially well with learners with diverse needs (Burke, Hagan, & Grossen, 1998). The principles of curricular design are used as a guide throughout the remainder of the text. Each principle will be discussed in terms of universal methods/strategies that tend to work for a diverse set of learners. The strategies and methods that are highlighted were chosen with the qualities of UDL in mind. Examples are offered that have high- and low-tech applications.

Begin with Big Ideas

The first step in curricular planning is thinking through **big ideas**. Students who struggle with learning typically have a hard time seeing the big picture and separating the key concepts in a unit of study from less-important details. Using core content area concepts/principles across a broad range of experiences and topics, teachers can define big ideas that can help everyone make sense out of the many goals and objectives that are required in teaching and learning in a unit. The brain will make important connections when content/principles, standards, learning goals, learning strategies, and assessment measures from both academic and nonacademic areas are integrated. Big ideas can actually help students learn more with less by providing them a way to summarize concepts learned and problem-solve. An example of a big idea in science, for example, might be *form and function*. This can be applied to a study on how plants grow, evolve, and adapt to their environments. The same idea can later link similar principles in a study of simple machines—how they are formed, how they work, and how they have been adapted over time. Objectives from reading/language arts, math, social studies, and other disciplines can easily be integrated with this approach.

Centering instruction around big ideas offers a vehicle for all learners to access the menu of objectives at all stages of learning. If access is planned up front, *all* learners can be working at the *adaptation* stage of learning at least part of the time because *all* learners have the ability to use their cognitive skills to solve problems (Marzano & Arredondo, 1986). By using big ideas, teachers can ensure that problem solving is at the heart of lessons and that thinking skills are purposefully taught in lessons designed around it. Having big ideas clear in the beginning helps ensure this most critical phase of thinking and learning is not unintentionally overlooked.

Activate Prior Knowledge

To improve the acquisition of new knowledge, prior learning needs to either be primed or bypassed. Diverse learners may not automatically remember information or strategies previously taught. The teacher must first assess background knowledge and determine skill levels. If there is an academic, social, or physical "roadblock," the teacher must consider what background information and skills must be taught, prompted, or bypassed to get the learner ready to work on a difficult task or part of a task.

Table 9.2 KWL Chart		
What I Know (K)	**What I Want to Know (W)**	**What I Learned (L)**

Source: Adapted from D. Ogle in A. Palincsar, D. Ogle, B. Jones, and E. Carr (Eds.), *Teaching Reading as Thinking*, Teleconference Resource Guide (Alexandria, VA: Association for Supervision and Curriculum Development, 1986), pp. 11–17.

Techniques that might help with this priming include brainstorming, cueing, questioning, telling a story, and creating semantic webs. These tools need to focus on what is important and help the most when used before a learning experience (Marzano, Pickering, & Pollock, 2001). A **KWL chart** is one example of a tool that helps learners focus on what is important. When beginning a unit or lesson, activate prior learning by finding out what students already know (K) about the subject. Lead students in goal setting by facilitating discussion about what (W) they want to learn. At the end of the lesson or unit, help students construct meaning using what they learned (L) (Fitzharris & Hay, 2001) using higher-order thinking skills. Try to create a visual organizer using the KWL framework (see Table 9.2) when preparing to teach new learning concepts.

Assessment linked to learning goals allows teachers to continually prime students' background knowledge and move forward. One doesn't work as effectively without the other. It tells the teachers when to back up, what's next, and when a student(s) needs to move ahead.

Integrate Learning Goals

Strategic integration of learning goals blends the new ideas with the old and purposefully assists with the transfer of knowledge from one setting/area to another. Within a subject such as reading, for example, if learners have learned to hear sounds in words and associate letters and sounds, they can purposely be moved toward word recognition (Coyne et al., 2007).

UDL lessons suggest the application of **authentic learning** to infuse such goal integration. In authentic learning, isolated topics are incorporated into the real world and connected. This way, students can understand and visualize what they are learning so that it is meaningful. This makes culture an integral part of the school assignments so that it is even more accessible by diverse learners. Students can be directed to use inquiry as they construct and share meaning in their work to produce knowledge (Siegel et al., 2000). Passive learners can become active and creative learners. Authentic learning provides for social interaction and can foster conversations between learners (Newman & Wehlage, 1993). It lends itself to the use of a wide range of technology tools from high-tech to low-tech. Students, for example, can be asked to design and create their own books, electronic newsletters, music, plays, and to produce their own films based on experiences they have had. The creation of the product is the "hook" and the process of that design is more exciting than simply reading a newsletter, listening to a song, or watching a movie. If situations are created in which students are in charge of their own learning, there will likely be more engagement and excitement about the process.

One authentic learning approach that applies UDL principles around big ideas is **anchored instruction**. Anchored instruction offers the student real-life problem-solving situations as he/she works through a shared experience and perspective through an *anchor* such as a realistic narrative story or case study. Learning activities are designed around an anchor to draw in and challenge the learner to explore,

Field experiences are an example of authentic learning.

manipulate a situation, and eventually solve a problem. The teacher provides the structure and serves as facilitator; the students are the investigators. Other subject areas can be incorporated so learners can make more connections to other disciplines (Crews, Biswas, Goldman, & Bransford, 1997). Seven guiding principles of anchored instruction can be seen in Table 9.3.

Table 9.3	The Seven Guiding Principles of Anchored Instruction
Principle 1	• Choose an appropriate anchor based on goals, learner interests, and age levels. • Connect any video used directly to educational goals and the anchor.
Principle 2	• Develop shared teacher and student expertise around an anchor. • Use teacher "think alouds" to lead students in taking more control. Show enthusiasm so students can realize the ongoing nature of the learning process.
Principle 3	• Add more than one anchor if needed to integrate additional objectives in a meaningful way so that all students can relate according to their interests and needs.
Principle 4	• Model and support students as needed while exposing them to critical thinking. • Have students apply knowledge immediately so they learn to use it as a tool. • Model the transfer of learning during the process.
Principle 5	• Tie the anchor to the curricular goals through teacher self-talk. • Empower students as learners as they model this.
Principle 6	• Merge the anchor with traditional literacy-based experiences (reading, writing, oral language) to strengthen literacy skills and continually engage students.
Principle 7	• Let students explore the possibilities and take advantage of opportunities to "dig deeper." Let them become the experts in certain areas and learn from each other. • Set up programs from the start to link multiple objectives from the curriculum as you work "smarter" in your classroom.

Sources: Adapted from K. McLarty, J. Goodman, V. Risko, C. Kinzer, N. Vye, D. Rowe, et al., *Implementing Anchored Instruction: Guiding Principles for Curriculum Development.* Paper presented at the 39th annual meeting of the National Reading Conference, Austin, TX (1989) (ERIC Document Reproduction Service No. ED315736); M. Love, "Multimodality of Learning through Anchored Instruction," *Journal of Adolescent & Adult Literacy, 48*(4), 2004, p. 302.

Jamie Wilson/Big Stock Photo

In a "high-tech" setting, an initial presentation can be made through an anchor in an interactive videodisc program to set up the problem (Kearsley, 1994–2008). In one example from Vanderbilt University, students are asked to find a missing person by solving algebraic equations. In a "low-tech" setting, someone from the school community can provide a dramatic representation of a period being studied as an actor or narrator poses a question. If the study is weather, someone could play the part of a meteorologist to present the problem. Regardless of the presentation format, a problem is concretely presented and students work cooperatively to solve this problem from a shared perspective. Sometimes learners can choose or create their own endings. This type of instruction offers all learners access to the full range or hierarchy of thinking skills.

When student interests are considered and incorporated into anchored instruction, motivation increases. Teachers can use it to imbed background knowledge that some learners may need. Other benefits of anchored instruction include its flexible pacing of instruction, grouping options, opportunities for individualized work, and an increased understanding of the problem-solving process. As with all other instructional practices and techniques, always be sure instruction connects to learning goals.

Another similar teaching tool for strategically integrating learning goals is a **ClassAct Portal**. A ClassAct Portal takes authentic learning to an active, multi-faceted level using a flexible web-based focus on a single topic from either a traditional curricular area (mathematics or biology, for example), a wider range of areas (such as world events), or from instructor and/or student interest (pets or cartooning, for example) (March, 2005).

In a ClassAct Portal, teachers and students are encouraged to select a topic they are passionate about to increase engagement. The goal is to become immersed in the topic (March, 2006). Once immersed, the topic can be linked to goals and objectives. Interdisciplinary relationships between concept and skill areas can be established. An example of a ClassAct Portal is Child Slave Labor News located at http://ihscslnews.org/ (March, 2005). Teachers and students can begin to build a ClassAct Portal by using online blogs, preferably in personal web space to allow for flexibility if photo galleries and other graphics are added. These can be linked directly to lesson plans.

Cengage Learning/Wadsworth

Students can work individually or in groups to conduct investigations and problem-solve using web-based ClassAct Portals or WebQuests.

The next step is to gather a "hotlist" of links on the chosen topic and have the students critique and annotate them. Students can send thank-you notes to the people who have the most interesting sites. They can also keep up with the latest news and postings on the topics. Think of the website as the kitchen refrigerator on which you showcase great work. Work formats can be audio podcasts, drawings, movies, and/or written text. Discussion blogs and/or pen pal/e-pal exchanges can be used for interaction with people beyond the classroom, making this truly authentic learning (March, 2005).

Though not as comprehensive as anchored learning or a ClassAct Portal, the use of **WebQuests** can also provide multiple means of representation, engagement, and expression in learning units. A WebQuest is an inquiry-based activity that gathers information for learners on a topic from the Internet (Dodge, 1997). Teachers and students can use ready-made WebQuests or design their own to support learning goals and objectives. The tasks within provide support for all levels of learning and thinking so that all learners can access information. Students may also work with another person, teacher, or small group. Those who need greater challenges, given the topic and learning goals, may find creating a WebQuest for others in class invigorating.

If high-tech is not available, a similar model might be the development and use of scavenger hunts. Reference information can be selected from print and nonprint sources. Activities would lead to purposeful investigation of these references to solve presented problems or requests.

These big-idea examples have strategically integrated learning goals. Thematic teaching helps students build bigger ideas and transfer their thinking. There are times when it is appropriate to teach factual information in a content area or subsets of skills in isolation; however, train yourself to "cross file" or "hyperlink" this learning to something else. Remember how the brain seeks to make connections. These connections build toward higher-level thinking skills and foster generalization. If learning is constructed so that it builds on and transfers to what the learner already knows, he or she can develop stronger thinking skills. Just as at the gym, you likely wouldn't work on just your arms or your abs at the expense of working other body parts. You might use isolated exercises to help you become a better

Universal Design for Learning in the Classroom

Transform physical space at school to promote authentic learning for high- to low-tech settings. Rooms or sections of rooms can become rain forests, bat caves, international restaurants, or settings for plays and novels. Here's an example of a larger-than-life ear canal designed to meet science objectives on sound:

My colleagues and I have always enjoyed designing experiences that foster more academic, physical, and social collaboration for all students. One year, our grade level was working on science objectives related to sound and, at the same time, trying to increase the diversity sensitivity in our school. We collaborated with the art teacher to construct a giant ear canal. Students sculpted a huge outer ear and eardrum complete with bones representing the hammer, anvil, and stirrup. These were suspended in the hallway outside the door to the art room. We hung black cloth parallel to the wall. All classes were invited to have a tour of our "Earie Canal." Our students, many with learning differences, were the tour guides, wearing lab coats and carrying flashlights. They led their classmates through the ear canal, explaining how sound travels, and took them into the large art room, which was filled with learning stations. Students rotated through and learned sign language, built model ear canals with clay, heard the story of Helen Keller, used TDY machines and other assistive technology devices (supplied by the local phone company), and received tips on how to communicate with classmates with hearing impairments from the itinerant teacher for students with hearing impairments. This was followed by a whole-school celebration in the cafeteria with a sign language song-and-dance group from the nearby university. Many of the students who participated in this particular event told us many years later that this was one of the most memorable things they ever did in school.

Using authentic learning, the strengths of individual students can be tapped to allow for participation by everyone. Artists, illustrators, researchers, speakers, tour guides, writers, musicians, dancers, and many other roles will need to be filled.

Debbie Metcalf, NBCT
Clarissa Hug Teacher of the Year 2004
Interventionist
Pitt County Schools
Greenville, NC

racquetball player or to tone up the abdominals but these would be combined with an overall fitness plan to make you perform and feel better all over. In future chapters, we will show you how to plan units and lessons with UDL applications in mind.

Use Conspicuous Strategies

Once you know your learners, have your big ideas, and have your basic unit plan with the strategic integration of learning goals in mind, you will want to consider what **conspicuous strategies** you apply within it. Conspicuous strategies are clear, concise, explicit steps that are used to present and learn content. Their use reflects another principle in curricular design that can be applied to facilitate the learning of all students.

Research suggests that *all* students, including students with learning challenges at all levels, benefit from direct instruction of interventions/strategies that match the concepts being taught (Rosenshine & Meister, 1992; Traver, 1992). A **learning strategies approach** is an instructional approach that emphasizes both the attainment of observable skills and behaviors as well as cognitive strategies that go beyond specific content areas. Students are taught how to learn purposefully and efficiently so they can eventually recall material. Scholars at the University of Kansas Center for Research on Learning have developed a working model for directly teaching specific learning strategies (Deshler, Ellis, & Lenz, 1996; Lenz, Ellis, & Scanlon, 1996). Extensive training is offered for teachers to apply the strategies in this particular model.

For the general purposes of this chapter, conspicuous strategies and related methods will be defined as explicit, sequenced, instructional steps or frameworks that help many students reach their goals. Examples of useful, research-based general methods and techniques are presented here and their applications in more-specific content areas will be shown in Part III of this text. Keep in mind there are many conspicuous strategies available and that the ones presented are just some of the basic "tools" for your toolbox (see Figure 9.1). Also keep in mind that it is usually best to only teach a few strategies at a time so students learn them thoroughly and generalize their use.

Forward and backward chaining are strategies that have been shown to be effective for students with cognitive challenges in learning and recalling the steps or sequence of a task or set of data (Batra & Batra, 2005). In forward chaining, the first step in a task is learned through direct instruction. Assistance is provided until the student reaches mastery. Success is positively reinforced. Upon mastery, the student moves to the next step. The student can build a knowledge base as data is acquired that will hopefully trigger inference.

In backward chaining, the last step is taught first. The advantage here is that the student can see the whole product/performance from the beginning. This can serve as a reinforcer as the student goes back and learns the steps. The student can see the connections. For tasks that require many steps, this may help motivate students to reach their goals (Macfarlane, 1998; Wehman & Kregel, 2004).

Content enhancements are interventions that help students understand major concepts, ideas, and vocabulary in a manner that is conductive to knowledge acquisition, organization, and retrieval (Bulgren, 2006; Lenz, Deshler, & Kissam, 2004). Their purpose is not to "water down" material but rather to provide visual structures that enhance the learning of students as they work to understand important concepts, ideas, and vocabulary (Boudah, Lenz, Bulgren, Schumaker, & Deshler, 2000). They include tools such as graphic organizers, semantic maps, advance organizers (agendas), study guides, content diagrams, and guided notes. These structures can help learners who are at the knowledge-acquisition stage to organize and recall material. Content enhancements can also be helpful in making connections between concepts, seeing relationships, making links to prior learning, and fostering

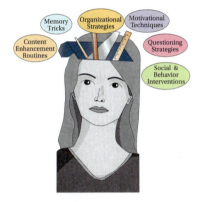

Figure 9.1 Toolbox for Learning
Source: John Metcalf.

higher-level thinking. Many different content enhancements will be modeled in the content chapters of this text.

Low-tech applications might include creating Thinking Maps on chart paper. Similar software such as Inspiration/Kidspiration can be loaded on computers. A student's graphic organizer can be converted into an outline with the click of a mouse. Picture symbols can be used as well as print.

Instruction with **mnemonic devices** is a research-based memory-enhancing technique that can help students recall facts and see relationships between units of information. These devices offer students a tool for encoding and storing information that is needed to meet larger learning goals. Its effectiveness has been demonstrated with many students in the general curriculum, including those with high-incidence disabilities (Levin, 1993; Mastropieri & Scruggs, 1998). Factual knowledge of vocabulary is critical for success with high-stakes testing and for successful performance in content area classes (Hess & Brigham, 2000; Scruggs & Mastropieri, 1992).

There are several different types of devices used in mnemonic instruction. One type, **keyword mnemonics**, combines abstract vocabulary that needs to be learned with words that sound similar and are already known. For example, if a student is learning the meaning of the word "barrister," he/she might picture a bear speaking to a lawyer or perhaps even carrying a briefcase (Mastropieri & Scruggs, 1990).

A **mnemonic letter strategy** uses the first letters of a word or phrase to be remembered in acronyms or acrostics. An *acrostic* takes the first letter in a series of items to be recalled and assigns each letter to a word, forming an entire sentence. For example, the sentence "**E**very **g**ood **b**oy **d**oes **f**ine," helps many of us remember the order of the lines on a treble clef staff (e,g,b,d,f). An *acronym* takes the first letters of the words to be recalled to form another word that can aid memory. For example, the acrostic "HOMES" is helpful in learning the names of the Great Lakes (Huron, Ontario, etc.).

Students often enjoy creating their own mnemonic devices to remember material that is difficult to recall. A mnemonic-building strategy called IT FITS guides students in their own strategy creation:

IT FITS
- **I**dentify the term.
- **T**ell the definition of the term.
- **F**ind a keyword.
- **I**magine the definition doing something with the keyword.
- **T**hink about the definition doing something with the keyword.
- **S**tudy what you imagined until you know the definition.

(King-Sears, Mercer, & Sindelar, 1992)

A helpful website that has many mnemonic tools in a variety of academic areas, including reading, math, organization, study skills, test-tasking skills, note taking, and advanced thinking skills for students, teachers, and parents can be found at James Madison University's *The Learning Toolbox* website (http://coe.jmu.edu/learningToolbox/index.html).

Match-to-sample is another intervention useful with learners who are at the very earliest levels of acquisition of a skill (Rivera & Smith, 1997). The learner looks for the object, picture, letter, number, or word that is the same as the one presented. There might be a poster or template nearby for quick reference to the correct answer. Some students may need to keep a template or device in his/her work space to see models of letter and number formations, correct spellings of commonly missed words, times tables, or mathematical formulas so that focus can be on the problem-solving process that follows rather than on the skill itself. The goal would be to fade out this assistance, but for some learners it can be continued for use as a support if it helps them learn a skill or concept.

For students with greater cognitive challenges, matching objects and pictures while pairing them with language can be effective. Augmentative communication devices and language boards can be helpful for this. When the student becomes proficient, the matching fades (Rivera & Smith, 1997).

Using **flow lists** with words and/or pictures to make connections is another effective strategy to use with diverse learners, including students who are learning English. Vocabulary is organized in units or topics to help students increase their language comprehension. Words are typically presented in alphabetical order unless there is a natural order to the words (months of the year or numbers, for example). Words can be grouped by category within a topic. In a unit on climate and weather, for example, one list may contain adjectives that describe weather and another list may describe different clothing to be worn in different weather conditions. The lists enable learners to build vocabulary while making connections. Many free, premade vocabulary lists can be found on the web at Skyline English (http://www.skyline-english.com) and at Vocabulary.com (http://www.vocabulary.com).

Research-based **questioning strategies** can also help maximize student learning (Bell, 2002; Bond, 2007; Conderman & Morin, 2002). Try to incorporate questions into your lessons from the start. Refer back to Bloom's taxonomy in Chapter 7 for a moment. Remember you will want to have some very basic questions (who, what, when, where) to help students recall basic facts, develop vocabulary comprehension, and acquire new knowledge as well as higher-level questions that ask the student to connect with the author and connect to prior learning and real-life experiences. Try to have a variety of questions from all levels so all learners can be engaged because they are challenged and can learn from each other. Table 9.4 shows an example of leveled questions that could follow a reading selection about Helen Keller and Anne Sullivan.

There are many researched-based questioning interventions available to teachers (QAR, for example) that will be shown in the content chapters. You may also want to explore the **Socratic questioning** method as a guide in developing thinking skills and insights about a complex topic. In this method, students respond to readings by discussing and building upon each other's ideas. The teacher facilitates the discussion by guiding the students to higher-level thinking through a series of steps (Wilen, 1991).

Another tool for your box is the **Think Aloud** technique. Using Think Aloud, the teacher explicitly models procedures or steps by speaking while verbalizing his or her own thinking process (Wilhelm, 2001). This is particularly helpful in understanding text, print, and language in general. Thinking-aloud modeling helps students become skillful at comprehension (Israel & Massey, 2005). Teachers talk out loud about things they see, do, and feel while they are reading, speaking, performing, or demonstrating a task. A teacher may, for example, talk about what he or she did when coming to an unknown word in the text. Perhaps using the context, including any pictures, charts, or diagrams might work to figure it out. Roots of unknown words may be dissected and sounded out loud. Other visual clues might be offered orally to show how similar looking words might provide other clues. Unknown words are given meaning.

To foster comprehension, a teacher might orally summarize what he/she thinks the author is saying and show how meaning can be inferred. In math, a teacher may talk through a computation method while demonstrating the problem. The teacher might talk about *why* a certain operation was chosen. Perhaps a mnemonic device

Table 9.4	Levels of Questioning—Story of Helen Keller
1. Knowledge	Who are the main characters in the story?
2. Comprehension	Why did Anne Sullivan come to Tuscaloosa?
3. Application	What is an example of noncompliant behavior?
4. Analysis	Why was Helen so angry?
5. Synthesis	How does the inability to communicate in conventional ways affect quality of life?
6. Evaluation	Was Anne Sullivan an effective teacher for Helen? Why or why not?

was referenced and spoken aloud as the problem was solved. If students can become aware of their thinking process, they can eventually monitor their own comprehension. A Think Aloud can also be helpful when modeling a social skill (greeting a friend, for example). After the teacher models a think aloud, the students can be encouraged to engage in this manner while working with peers or teachers. As with all conspicuous strategies, the teacher supports student efforts until independence is achieved.

Just as at the health club, when new routines are being taught and learned, the instructor or personal trainer will talk participants through the steps. He/she may tell why something is important and think aloud about a good way to visually remember a routine. He/she may talk about how the routine can be modified while demonstrating it. This idea of providing support to move students toward independence, leads us to **mediated scaffolding**, the third principle in the curricular design framework.

Apply Mediated Scaffolding

"Mediated scaffolding refers to the personal guidance, assistance, and support that a teacher, peer, materials, or task provides a learner" (Simmons & Kame'enui, 1996). Mediated scaffolding helps students to bridge the gap between their current level of performance and the intended goal of independent performance (Rosenshine & Meister, 1992). It may be intense in the beginning but needs to fade systematically as the learner acquires the skill/concept being taught. Scaffolded instruction has been compared to the experience we all have of learning to ride a bicycle. Parents/caregivers provide training wheels or hold the bike seat for the child and gradually let go. You will likely find that most diverse learners need a great deal of systematic scaffolding. Some need it for a very long time. Other learners need very little and, once again, that is why your curriculum needs to be flexible. Levels of intensity will depend also on learning goals and the difficulty of the task. If supports and examples are built into technology, print, and other resources, it is easier for teachers to access materials for students. Students can work at their own pace more efficiently and easily.

The term *direct instruction* (di) has been used so far to refer to general teaching procedures. When the first letters of both words are capitalized, **Direct Instruction** (DI) refers to a specific teaching approach that offers a variety of research-based practices aimed at helping learners achieve academic content at high rates. It emphasizes instruction through sequenced tasks to teach the learner skills directly and efficiently, and procedures that take into account research on learning. DI offers a correction procedure—the teacher models the correct answer, leads the student response, and then tests the student for a correct response. Students learn quickly from their mistakes by immediately receiving feedback in a systematic way (Engelmann & Carnine, 1991). Concepts are defined with a wide range of examples that have rule relationships and are interconnected. Teaching and learning is not left up to chance. DI is typically used to teach at the acquisition level of learning and students develop mastery at each step. Modeling and explicit procedures fade as the student becomes more proficient with the skill. Lessons are typically fast paced and often use a signal to guide instruction. Often there are group responses that help with engagement along with lots of opportunities for practice and cumulative review. Research on DI has shown that it enables students to make significant gains in academic work (Adams & Engelmann, 1996; Becker, 1992; Forness, Kavale, Blum, & Lloyd, 1997). DI works particularly well in teaching mathematical computation and procedures, reading decoding, map skills, foreign language vocabulary, science, and social science facts and concepts. It is not as effective in teaching less-structured areas such as composition, reading comprehension, and literature analysis (Rosenshine, 1986).

Computer software and interactive websites can assist with the drill and practice parts of direct instruction when matched to curricular objectives. They often include feedback for correct responses and extra practice and explanations for incorrect responses. Some tutorial software may assist in presenting new information and concepts in a sequential way. Both types of software may include branching to higher or lower alternate paths of learning, depending on learner responses. These programs must first be reviewed to match learning levels and learning styles. Examples should be provided with multiple opportunities for practice (Conway, 1997).

It is interesting to note that textbooks in Japan offer far more examples with solutions and strategies to solve problems than American textbooks do. Diverse learners need these multiple strategic examples (Mayer, Sims, & Tajika, 1995). Look for materials that provide such supports when you have opportunities to evaluate published curriculum.

In **guided discovery learning**, learners construct knowledge through problem solving to arrive at their own conclusions. This approach can help all students become more independent and critical in their thinking. It supports strategy instruction and cooperative learning. It fosters a community in which teachers and students learn from each other (Rosenberg, O'Shea, & O'Shea, 2006). This method/process already works well for many learners who are self-starters and need to learn at their own pace. It also works for students who prefer working alone or with a peer. The big-idea frameworks that foster UDL are set up for this kind of guided discovery learning. The effective teacher will find a way to incorporate direct instruction as needed for specific skills in the classroom within these overarching guided discovery frameworks.

Modeling is a term used frequently by special educators, particularly when you implement academic, social, and language interventions. Modeling is teaching by demonstrating the skill to be taught to one or more observers. The observer(s) are asked to imitate the skill that they witnessed. Pairing the model with verbal and/or written directions and pictures or a diagram helps some learners. Video self-monitoring of the correct performance of an academic or social skill can also be effective (Buggey, 2005; Hitchcock, Dowrick, & Prater, 2003; Parsons, 2006). Modeling is probably the most natural of all the teaching techniques humans have. We modeled our parents growing up when brushing our teeth, cooking a meal, and washing dishes. It is important to model slowly and carefully, ensuring the observers understand each step. You might stop to ask clarifying questions and have observers repeat what they are seeing after modeling each step.

When using modeling with groups or individuals, be sure that observers are at the same level of skill in the academic or nonacademic area you are modeling. Students who have mastered the skill need to move ahead. Modeling works well whether you are teaching a specific learning strategy or organizing a notebook.

Chunking is a way of organizing material into manageable parts. Take the big idea and have supporting material organized so that it can be presented and accessed as needed. Most learners can grasp smaller parts of the "whole" versus having it all presented at once. According to the "chunking principle," typical learners can retain from five to nine separate units of information (Horn, 1990). As material becomes more complex, the number of units presented at a time needs to be reduced.

Teachers can apply the chunking technique to a lecture presentation by breaking sections apart and having students summarize the main idea with a partner before proceeding to the next section. Students may even engage in an activity related to a chunk of information. A high-tech example of chunking is the use of "web links" that connect to examples and provide additional information that can be accessed on the web to increase background knowledge or for further in-depth study.

Current research strongly suggests the effectiveness of **self-monitoring strategies** for improving both academic and behavioral performance in school (McConnell, 1999). Students are guided to observe a certain behavior and then directed to keep track of this behavior while working using cues. A student may, for example, ask himself/herself, "Am I working?" at certain timed intervals and then record the response on a card and chart the progress. Timed intervals might be cued visually by having the teacher hold up a card or make a signal. Auditory cues using the teacher's voice or a sound tone may be offered. Some teachers use prerecorded

Bob Daemmrich/PhotoEdit

A teacher models calculator use on an interactive whiteboard.

taped sounds the student hears through headphones. A physical cue such as a tap on the shoulder can also be effective. Cue choice will depend on learner preference. Some high-tech tactile approaches use devices that elicit electronic vibrations at preset intervals. Some of these devices look like pagers and can clip on a belt (Amato-Zech, Hoff, & Doepke, 2006). Research also suggests adult feedback increases the effectiveness of self-monitoring strategies (Freeman & Dexter-Mazza, 2004). Student conferencing may also be incorporated.

Another practice, **task analysis**, takes a target behavior or skill and breaks it down into sequenced steps. This allows the teacher to determine the exact point at which the student is experiencing difficulty with a skill. The teacher can then develop instructional sequences for the next steps. If you have ever taught a child to tie his or her shoes, you have likely applied task analysis. When you learn a new routine in an exercise class, an effective instructor will break down the steps to see what parts need more or less direct instruction, repetition, and/or modeling. Perhaps a different style of presentation altogether may be needed.

Shaping is a behavioral technique that is used to take a close approximation of the desired skill and move it to skill mastery. The reinforcement is given frequently at first for most attempts (successful or not) and gradually fades until it is only given for the desired skill performance level. For example, you might be good at surfing and swimming but you want to try your hand at wind surfing. You have an affinity for water sports but you can't seem to get the hang of it, so you take lessons. Using a shaping procedure, the instructor would first applaud you for being in the water with the board and sail. Then he or she would have you walk on the board first without worrying about the sail. Next you are shown how to check for wind direction and how to set your sail correctly. In the next step, you learn the feet position and how to stand up by bending your knees and not your waist. How you work the mast and ropes/lines is next. Finally, you move into a squatting position as you sail perpendicular to the wind.

Shaping can be used with or without modeling, depending on the learner. Some learners can figure the skill out with specific auditory output, reading directions, and following a series of pictures. The reinforcers would need to be included if these adaptations are made.

The same technique can be applied to a skill such as keyboarding. At first, you might accept the "hunt-and-peck" method while students familiarize themselves with the keyboard, but then you move toward proper keyboarding using demonstration/ modeling, posters, templates, software programs, and perhaps memory strategies to help students learn proper keyboarding. You will encourage students greatly in the beginning and then gradually saving the reinforcement only for correct keyboarding as students become more successful.

Cues and prompts can also help with mediated scaffolding. Cues or prompts can be applied in teacher presentations as well as for student responses (Salend, 2001). Language, visual, and physical cues will be discussed here.

Language cues can offer help with context. Some students have difficulty auditorily and/or visually retrieving words. Examples may include having students fill in the blank or finish a sentence (The man was going to the _____), offering a rhyming word (this word rhymes with _____), providing the opposite word, or providing the initial sound. Sometimes speaking through a sequence or chain of steps or visual models will assist the learner in arriving at the correct response (What comes next, before, after . . .) (Thompson & Taymans, 1994).

Visual cues can be picture cues (pairing word with picture) as in a rebus story. Picture cues can also help with reversals (drawing a bat and a ball to remember the directionality of the letter "b", for example), making your lips shape the beginning sound of a word. Words for vocabulary comprehension might be paired with pictures that trigger the memory. Students might have pictures, symbols, or words on cards that they hold up to answer a question. Sometimes difficult parts of words or problems can be color coded. In some early reading programs, for example, the vowels are all one color and consonants another. With older students, perhaps root words or parts of sentences may be coded and sorted by color. Pointing to pictures, objects, and words are other examples of visual cueing.

Visually framing key information (e.g., a word, sentence, paragraph, picture) can also help students focus on material to be learned. In a low-tech world, index cards can be used. They can be cut in the shape of a word, line, or passage. With high-tech, many computer programs allow one to adjust how much information is presented on a screen at once. Highlighters can also be used in both high- and low-tech environments to focus on keywords and information.

Physical cues might include gestures or the acting out of a word or concept. Touching, pointing, or tapping may also help in physically cueing students. Having signals for transitions, attention, or procedures are other examples.

Peer tutoring can be another powerful learning approach. Enlisting others in your classroom or school can assist greatly with teaching and learning. Other students are often very good at explaining something in "student" language. In this systematic approach, a student who is at the mastery level of learning a skill (or higher) is paired with a learner (tutee) in the acquisition stage. The student explains the process/skill in his/her own words and provides multiple practice opportunities. Be careful to not always pair your top learners with the struggling ones (at least not all the time). The average learner often makes the best tutor with students working at a lower level. Pairing high/average achieving students can also be effective. The tutor often benefits from deeper learning in the role of "teacher," so look for peer tutoring systems that trade tutor and tutee roles.

The ideal peer tutor needs to have a complex set of skills. The tutor needs to have a strong grasp of the content knowledge, knowledge of the rules/procedures, and a clear understanding of the task (Mastropieri & Scruggs, 1993). In addition, this person needs to be an attractive role model to the tutee and know how to interact positively in different situations (Kauffman, Mostert, Trent, & Hallahan, 2006). Time invested in training peer tutors with these potential skills can be time very well spent.

Direct instruction, modeling, task analysis, shaping, cueing/prompting, and peer tutoring are all examples of mediated scaffolding that all teachers can use to help most students learn new skills. They will particularly assist teachers in moving learners in the concrete stages toward the abstract. Hopefully, supports can fade. If not, adaptations can be made so each learner can show progress in academic and social growth.

Cengage Learning/Wadsworth

Peer tutoring can be a powerful teaching and learning tool.

Provide Purposeful and Cumulative Review

One critical design principle teachers sometimes inadvertently leave out is the **judicious review** of learning. Most students need multiple review opportunities to reinforce the critical building blocks of information in both academic and non-academic areas to increase understanding. However, the saying "practice makes perfect" is not a reliable standard to ensure successful learning. Simple repetition of information alone will not ensure efficient learning (Dempster, 1991). These reviews can be done in a variety of formats to increase understanding and to keep review motivational. If material learned is reviewed with many kinds of different examples, there are also more opportunities for students to generalize or transfer what is learned in new contexts (Grossen, Romance, & Vitale, 1994).

Dixon, Carnine, and Kame'enui (1996) identified four critical dimensions of judicious review. The review must be:

1. Sufficient to enable a student to perform the task without hesitation.
2. Distributed over time.
3. Cumulative with information integrated into more-complex tasks.
4. Varied, to illustrate the wide application of a student's understanding of the information.

Teachers need to select information for review, purposefully schedule the reviews, and create activities that extend student understanding of skills, concepts, and strategies. One intervention that fosters judicious review is **spaced repetitions** (Dempster, 1991). In spaced repetitions, a learner is frequently asked to recall a learning experience or academic information on different days. The time spent in repeated repetition recall is fairly short but it is distributed over time. Lengthier, "one-shot" reviews have not be shown to be as effective. For *all* students, particularly students who struggle, building a system for cumulative review into your schedule is critical (Simmons & Kame'enui, 1996). It can enhance memory and generalization skills if material is reviewed, applied, and practiced in a variety of ways. It can also positively impact the related goal of fluency (Coyne et al., 2007). Judicious review is built into many research-based direct instruction programs that will be referenced in the content chapters. Game formats are great for periodic and cumulative review. They can take away or reduce some of the boredom of repeated review. These can be high- or low-tech. Spin-offs of television game shows often work well (*Jeopardy!* or *Who Wants to Be a Millionaire*, for example). Computerized multimedia software can be used to create games or they can be purchased premade. Games on boards and file folders also work well.

Response cards can be effective tools for quick reviews in large or small groups because all students can be engaged simultaneously by holding up their answers to questions posed by the teacher. Research also suggests their use helps learners remember more information after a time delay (Cristle, & Schuster, 2003; Heward et al., 1996). Low-tech response cards can be made by placing information to be learned (vocabulary words, for example) on index cards, signs, or other items that students hold up to answer questions posed by the teacher. Cards can also be made for true/false, numbered, or lettered responses. Reuseable response cards can also be easily made by laminating heavy paper or using small dry erase boards.

Classroom response systems are high-tech versions of response cards. Students enter their numbered or lettered responses with a handheld device that can be viewed immediately by the teacher on a computer screen. The teacher can survey individual answers in a group for quick assessment. These systems can also increase student participation. Students who are proficient with a topic and need a challenge could create game formats that use response systems for other students to use for review.

Remember homework can also foster judicious review. It may need to be adapted, however, for some students for length and purpose. Be sure goals and directions are

Lettered response cards can increase engagement when reviewing using a multiple-choice test format.

clear and vary the way students may respond. Encourage the use of homework planners or other clear assignment sheets. Provide study guides that highlight key concepts and vocabulary. Coordinate with other teachers to make sure the student isn't being bombarded with homework on certain nights. A homework buddy or club may be helpful as well as an online class website with homework assignments posted.

Olympic runners are extreme examples of products of judicious review. Most runners begin running short distances with a focus on skill development. They systematically and gradually increase their skills with countless repetitions. They study nutrition, clothing, footwear, and body alignment to improve performance. Some increase the complexity of the task by adding swimming and biking to perform in triathlons. Judicious review requires perseverance and determination on the part of all involved. We all know how easy it is to stop doing things that push us to the next level.

Table 9.5 summarizes the six principles of curricular design with strategies and techniques that were offered as examples in this section of the chapter. Note that challenges for learners who are working at an accelerated pace have also been brainstormed and included by the authors. Use this table as a reference tool when you explore planning using Universal Design for Learning principles in the next chapter.

Table 9.5	**Six Principles of Curricular Design with Examples of UDL Applications**		
Principle	**Explanation**	**Suggested Practices**	**Examples of UDL Applications**
Big Ideas	• Starting place • Core concept/principles in a content area that help the learners acquire knowledge across a broad range of experiences • Sets up the thinking pattern	• Use graphic organizers and other planning tools • Plan for anchored instruction **Challenge:** Plan with as many team members as possible.	**High-Tech:** Use a computer graphing/drawing program or table to map core unit/lesson principles/goals; hyperlink lesson features that connect **Low-Tech:** Graphic organizer/planner or chart paper to brainstorm and map out core unit/lesson principles/goals; color code connections
Strategic Integration	• Integrate learning goals • Blend new ideas with what is already known • Build toward bigger ideas • Plan how and when to transfer thinking • Foster making connections across disciplines/settings	• Thematic teaching units • Systematic instruction • Infusing authentic learning • Anchored instruction in real life problem solving • Cooperative learning • Flexible grouping **Challenge:** Some students may build ClassAct portals for the next unit or solve a real-life problem related to learning objectives.	**High-Tech:** Computer mapping software with hyperlinks to lesson features that connect; find or design WebQuests and ClassAct Portals; virtual field trips, blogs, wikis, podcasts, e-pals **Low-Tech:** Graphic organizers for unit organizing; color code connections between lessons; set up field trips; resource links within culture/community; take picture "walks"; pen pals
Primed Background Knowledge	• Activate prior knowledge • Assessment/evaluation of prior learning to determine if prerequisite skills are in place or if student(s) need adaptations to improve acquisition of new knowledge. • Focus and review to prepare student to work on difficult task	• Brainstorming • Cueing • Questioning • Graphic organizers (KWL chart, for example) **Challenge:** Use assessment to differentiate learning tasks.	**High-Tech:** Provide interactive DVD/video clips/websites to access background knowledge in accessible language; highlight important features through a PowerPoint slideshow; allow students to view these at other times **Low-Tech:** Lecture, read a story or news article that summarizes critical background knowledge; provide students with print and nonprint materials to gain background knowledge using accessible language
Conspicuous Strategies	• Explicit modeling of problem-solving steps • Consider how content is presented. • Specific techniques that help learners make progress toward a goal	• Learning Strategies approach • Direct instruction (DI) • Modeling/direction instruction (di) of: • Forward and backward chaining • Content enhancement routines	**High-Tech:** Graphic organizer software, strategy supports (including questions, vocabulary lists) embedded in digital text, lists on PDA, links to models and procedures, video self-modeling,

Table 9.5	Six Principles of Curricular Design with Examples of UDL Applications (Continued)		
Principle	**Explanation**	**Suggested Practices**	**Examples of UDL Applications**
	• May decrease as students build a wide base of facts and information	• Matching • Mnemonic devices • Word lists • Questioning strategies • Think Aloud **Challenge:** Students build mnemonic strategies for unit and create memory games; increase Socratic questioning; offer more complex graphic organizers.	"Concentration"-type electronic memory games, audio recording of steps in task/mnemonic **Low-Tech:** Advance organizers, visual maps, posters, index cards on a ring to reinforce strategies presented for learning vocabulary, formulas, key information, sticky notes for lists, number lines, reference charts
Mediated Scaffolding	• Support, guidance, assistance that fades as learners move toward independence • Some students will need less than others	• Direct instruction • Guided discovery learning • Modeling • Chunking strategies • Task analysis • Shaping • Cueing and prompting • Peer tutoring • Self-monitoring **Challenge:** Students who are proficient are trained as peer tutors for others; Allow time to work on independent projects or work in learning clusters.	**High-Tech:** Video or audio recording of direct instruction and directions for repeated reference; drill and practice computer software, digital text with read aloud and embedded strategic supports; adjusting amount of text that appears on computer screen, highlighting features; pagers **Low-Tech:** Checklists; cue cards with words and/or pictures; visual framing of material; peer/mentor trained to cue/prompt; provide visual/auditory/physical signals for prompts (timer, touching, pointing, tapping)
Judicious Review	• Review is purposeful and cumulative • Multiple opportunities to review to increase retention • Draws upon prior learning	• Spaced repetitions • Game formats • Response cards • Practice quizzes • Study guide review • Homework **Challenge:** Students create an electronic review game.	**High-Tech:** Computer programs with built-in spaced repetitions; game formats; classroom response systems; Web-based assessment software linked to objectives; class website with study guides and homework posted **Low-Tech:** Gameboards, index cards, study guides; planner with review schedules

Source: Adapted from M. Coyne, E. Kame'enui, and D. Carnine, *Effective Teaching Strategies that Accommodate Diverse Learners,* 3rd ed. (Upper Saddle River, NJ: Pearson Education, 2007).

Considering Specific Learning Domains in General Intervention Selection

Many of the strategies and techniques presented so far address the cognitive and academic side of learning. As a general rule, try to find materials that are easy to understand regardless of the students' background knowledge, concentration level, and language skills. Many publishers and vendors today offer a variety of adaptations. Manipulatives, CDs, and leveled reading texts, for example, can be ordered with many programs. In this next part of the chapter, general instructional strategies that may be useful for students with challenges in other domains will be offered. The following techniques will focus more on learning characteristics and preferences. Depending on your learners, you can infuse them into your total instruction as needed. You will find that techniques that tend to work in one domain may also be helpful in another. These suggestions are just some of the many ideas available. Remember that speech/language specialists, physical and occupational specialists, and other professionals can help identity interventions.

Cognitive/Generalization

In addition to all the techniques presented so far, remember that "hands-on" activities typically work well in teaching students with cognitive impairments. When teaching a new skill, try to work with concrete materials/manipulatives as much as possible. Try to activate many learning preferences. When teaching addition, for example, begin with something the student can touch and move (beans, counters, pennies, for example) for demonstration and practice. When a student masters the skill using manipulatives, move to the pictorial representation (tally marks, drawings). Use samples of finished products as models. With practice and judicious review, most students should eventually move to the abstract.

Group students heterogeneously when possible to foster peer interactions and peer-tutoring situations. Remember to focus on student strengths and reinforce positive efforts and gains, no matter how small. Incorporate conspicuous strategies and scaffolding techniques as well to foster success.

Utilize discussion groups, **reciprocal teaching**, and questioning. In reciprocal teaching, students model a teacher-student dialogue with each other using teacher-provided prompts. Typically this technique is used for reading comprehension. A story is read, summarized, and future outcomes are predicted (Lederer, 2000; Palincsar & Klenk, 1991). If a student uses an assistive technology device, make sure the student has a way to respond and that vocabulary is updated in content areas being studied.

Set up opportunities for generalization in your school and community when possible. For example, if you are working with money and time in the classroom, ask cafeteria workers to reinforce a specific skill when the student pays for food. If you are working on content in biology, perhaps students could work on multimedia presentations during computer lab sessions. Perhaps literature linked to the topic can be integrated.

Giftedness

Curriculum compacting is an instructional procedure that has been effective with students who need a greater challenge (Renzulli & Reis, 2008). In this procedure, goals and objectives are first determined and student knowledge about them pre-assessed. Time spent working on the goals can be reduced depending on the prior knowledge of the student(s). Individual students or **cluster grouping** of students with similar interests/needs work on the same big idea but the curriculum is differentiated. These students will go into greater depth as they develop more-complex products. Some allowance for choice of theme and content may also be important

Cengage Learning/Wadsworth

Cluster grouping of students helps differentiate learning for students with similar interests and/or needs.

for engagement. These groupings can go across grade levels. Learning must be accelerated to accommodate the intensity and focus they have. These cluster groupings have been shown to also benefit lower achieving students (Gentry & Owen, 1999; Kulik, 1992). Differentiated instruction serves all students and its principles will be considered in future chapters in planning a flexible curriculum.

Apprenticeships, mentorships, and internships might also be considered for some of these students who have a high degree of interest in a subject. These arrangements can also be helpful for students who are disengaged in the formal classroom (Renzulli & Reis, 2008). Participation in after-school and weekend enrichment programs in the community that interest the student may also be considered.

As with all students, teachers must be knowledgeable about the cultural and ethnic differences, traditions, and histories of their students and display positive attitudes toward diversity. Current studies on gifted students who are culturally diverse suggest that their social coping strategies may keep them from entering gifted programs (Henfield, Moore, & Wood, 2008). Cultural sensitivity toward understanding peer pressure and student fears of ridicule is important.

Language/Speech

Remember that the way you give directions is important for many students with language and related processing challenges. Most students of all ages do their best with clear, concise, specific directions, particularly during the acquisition stage of learning. It is helpful to only give and receive one direction at a time with learners who need to develop language skills. Have students repeat directions to enhance understanding. Pair verbal directions with print and pictures, symbols, gestures, or objects when necessary. Scale down the words you use as much as possible or at least be very conscious about word choice to be certain language is understood. A student with auditory processing or attending difficulty, for example, may only remember the last chunk of information or last direction given and forget the first part.

Many students will need extra **wait time** to process a response. Wait time is the thinking time allowed after a teacher poses a question. Research suggests most learners need about three to five seconds to process questioning (Rowe, 1987; Stahl, 1994) but learners who struggle with language will usually need more time. They must receive, comprehend, and retrieve information previously remembered. Then they must find the words for the answer and consider how it will be received.

Communicating about a response with a partner before actually responding using the **Think-Pair-Share** (Lyman, 1981) technique allows for this critical processing time. Using the Think-Pair-Share strategy, teachers can pair students with language difficulty with someone more verbal or perhaps with a translator. This gives students a chance to find their words and usually produce a better quality answer. Another variation can be simply having students summarize chunks of information that have been presented with a partner during natural breaks in lectures or demonstrations. You might also consider posing a question/problem and having students write or draw their answers on dry erase boards or paper. Whichever technique is used, have a cue for students to respond after a reasonable amount of time.

Preteaching vocabulary prior to introducing a new unit is also helpful for many students who struggle with word pronunciation and meaning. Visualizing and rehearsing vocabulary and key concepts can help. Modeling an appropriate response can also be effective. Verbally rehearsing responses can help students increase student engagement in both large and small group interactions. Teachers might even present some questions ahead of time to these students that will come up in class so the student can practice possible responses.

Remember that any visual or physical representations you can provide should enhance learning for those who struggle with language. Making physical models, drawing pictures, using graphic organizers, and incorporating kinesthetic activities will likely help with vocabulary development and comprehension.

Assistive technology devices that may be helpful for some students include communication books/boards with pictures/words/objects and electronic dictionaries with pronunciation devices. Step-by-step switch devices and other audio recordings can assist with verbal rehearsal and following directions.

Memory

In addition to mnenomics and chunking, as mentioned earlier, memory aids such as planners, notebooks, cards, and prompts can be helpful for students who struggle with recall. Again, visualization techniques and associations can help. Have the student picture what he/she is going to express before doing so. For certainly skills, redundancy and additional practice can help. Increasing one's attention can also improve recall.

Use backward chaining to review and learn a series of pictures, words, and/or numbers. Show and say the entire list. Cover up the last picture, word, or number, and say the entire list again. Continue this procedure, covering up one more item to be learned at a time but speaking (or signing) the whole list. An example of this might be learning the order of the planets.

Study Skills, Organization, and Test Taking

Providing schedules and calendars with print/pictures/objects helps many students. Encourage students to keep an assignment notebook. This may be color coded to match content areas to be studied. Folders and textbook covers can be color coded to match as well. Some parents and students find it helpful to have an extra set of textbooks at home. Self-monitoring checklists for doing work, including homework and studying, help organize learners. Notes on student desks may also be effective. A "map" of where materials are placed in a desk can also help students stay organized.

Post homework and, when necessary, materials needed for a project in a prominent, consistent place. Allow time for recording it. A buddy can be assigned to assist with this recording task. Many schools have home/school notebooks or planners. If yours doesn't, you can create your own system. Teachers and parents can record notes back and forth as needed. Ask special educators, parents, or other adults in your school to assist with gathering materials and helping implement projects. Teaching cannot take place in isolation. A high-tech solution to some of this is the creation and use of a class website. Homework and notes can be posted by the teacher and families/guardians can check as well as ask questions online.

Teaching note-taking skills and keeping a consistent format will help many students. Outlines/agendas that can be used for guided notes provided by the teacher can be extremely helpful for more students. Teaching note-taking strategies can also benefit many students. Having students number or bullet main points also helps. An example of a strategic note-taking form is provided in Figure 9.2 (Boyle, 2001). Another system, Cornell notes (Fisher, Frey, & Williams, 2002), instructs students to draw a vertical line about two inches from the left side of the page. The student writes keywords and main concepts here. On the right side, details about these keywords and main points are added. Main ideas are summarized at the bottom of the page.

Teachers can assist students in using these note-taking tools by emphasizing the key points in their presentations. A similar outline that is projected or posted can be physically and verbally referenced. Using transitional words such as "first," "second," and "next," and highlighting keywords and main points will help students as well. Stopping periodically to review and summarize notes can also be helpful.

On tests, students may benefit from strategy instruction for pacing and timing themselves even if they have the extended time adaptations. They may need help in learning how to approach and analyze test directions and questions. Taking time to teach a test-taking strategy such as FLEAS (see Figure 9.3) can be helpful for many students. *The Learning Toolbox* at http://coe.jmu.edu/learningtoolbox/index.html has many more strategies for test taking.

Fill in this portion before the lecture begins.

What is today's topic? _____

Describe what you know about the topic.

As the instructor lectures, use these pages to take notes of the lecture.

Today's topic? _____

Name three to seven main points with details of today's topic as they are being discussed.

1. _____

2. _____

3. _____

Summary — Quickly describe how the ideas are related.

_____

Name three to seven *new* main points with details as they are being discussed.

1. _____

2. _____

3. _____

New Vocabulary or Terms:

Summary — Quickly describe how the ideas are related.

_____

Name three to seven *new* main points with details as they are being discussed..

1. _____

2. _____

3. _____

4. _____

5. _____

6. _____

7. _____

New Vocabulary or Terms:

Summary — Quickly describe how the ideas are related.

_____

At End of Lecture

Write five main points of the lecture and describe each point

1. _____

2 _____

3. _____

4. _____

5. _____

Figure 9.2 **Strategic Note-Taking Form**
Source: Adapted from J. R. Boyle, "Enhancing the Note-Taking Skills of Students with Mild Disabilities," *Intervention in School and Clinic, 36,* 2001, pp. 221–224.

First read the directions and put them in your own words. Ask for clarification if that is allowed. Use the context to figure out words you don't understand.

Look over the test. Divide the total amount of time by the numbers of questions so you can see how much time you can spend on each question. Also, questions that are worth more points may need to be given more time.

Easiest questions are done first.

Answer questions that are worth more points if you have to choose.

Skip a question if you are spending too much time on it, put a mark by it and try to come back to it later.

Figure 9.3 FLEAS Strategy for Timed Tests
Source: Adapted from James Madison University, *The Learning Toolbox*, retrieved June 23, 2008, from http://coe.jmu .edu/LearningToolbox/fleas.html

Technology tools that assist with study skills and organization might include devices such as tape recorders, PDAs or MP3 players. Lectures can be recorded and listened to multiple times. PowerPoint presentations can also be downloaded and revisited as many times as needed. Electronic folders on desktop or laptop computers can be used to categorize information within different subject areas. Electronic highlighters can emphasize key words and terms in notes or documents.

Attention Disorders/Hyperactivity/Impulsivity

For students with attention disorders, state rules and procedures promptly and consistently. These students need a structured environment that has a consistent routine with some built-in flexibility. It is often helpful to have the student in close proximity to the teacher. Help may be needed with organization skills. Students will benefit from outlines and organizers in presentations and in task completion. Try alternating high- and low-interest tasks and allow frequent breaks. Allow trips to the pencil sharpener or stapler. Above all, be enthusiastic!

A physically active student may benefit from standing or kneeling by his/her desk or workstation if it doesn't bother others. Provide work areas that are free of distractions. This may mean increasing the distance between work spaces.

Students with ADHD generally need time to think and plan before beginning assignments. Allow wait time and stress accuracy more than speed regarding assignment completion. Have the student verbalize the task before starting the work. Allow subvocalization during work. Try to ignore calling-out and talking-out-of-turn behaviors and praise positive behaviors. Increase the immediacy of rewards and consequences as needed. Encourage students to self-monitor their behavior. More ideas to help students with ADHD will be presented in subsequent chapters.

Social/Emotional/Motivational Challenges

As with all students, be sure to set high yet realistic and appropriate expectations and goals with students who have social, emotional, and/or motivational challenges. Help them understand why it is important to learn a concept or skill. These students usually need to experience a high rate of success. Some students will be afraid to try a task. They may have tried before and failed at least once. Others are fearful of the unknown. Some have no control over events in their personal lives and this might be the only way feel they have any control. Be sure each student feels comfortable and safe in the environment and that the classroom climate is respectful. Be careful not to place students under too much pressure for time and competition.

Although some of these learners may wish to work alone, **cooperative learning** is an instructional method that allows learners to work together toward a common goal in small groups or teams. Group members are responsible for each other's learning as well as their own. The beauty of cooperative learning is that learners with different strengths and needs can complement each other's skills. If set up purposefully, students' self-esteem can increase (Slavin, 1991). Students can learn from each other as they share and combine their best efforts to solve a problem or create a project/performance.

Sometimes working with just one peer who has mastered a skill can help a student who is still working on proficiency. The language and social reinforcement of a peer is sometimes just what is needed to get to the next step. You will need to think about which peers would be best suited to work together. Remember that the peer who is teaching will likely need some initial mentoring guidance from the teacher. Keep in mind, too, that some learners will need a lot of practice with feedback and others will need much less.

To increase motivation, have students work with you to set realistic goals. Encourage self-regulation and self-monitoring. Remember that having rubrics that show clear steps working toward a goal help with this. Many students also respond well to point systems that are tied into intrinsic or extrinsic rewards. Offer frequent, positive reinforcement for small steps of progress along the way. As a general rule, praise in public and correct privately. Hold high expectations for goals, monitor progress, and celebrate achievement. Experiencing success is a great motivator.

Continue to get to know your students and take note of their learning preferences. Incorporate activities that have visual, auditory, tactile, and kinesthetic components as much as possible to keep them motivated. Talk with parents and other community people to see what kinds of possible rewards and or projects might be available for the student to transfer both academic and nonacademic knowledge in other settings.

Some students will need to receive direct instruction in social skills and will benefit from rehearsing social interactions and using social stories. These techniques and more will be addressed in future chapters. Strategies for students with more-challenging behaviors will specifically be discussed in Chapter 14.

Physical/Motor/Sensory Challenges

Some students may need physical guidance. For example, a student learning to write or press a switch may need someone's hand over or under his/her hand in the beginning. A student with low vision may need someone's arm to hold or maybe even the lead of a service dog when exploring a new environment. For students with fine-motor challenges, scissors may need to be adapted, pencil grips added, and enlarged keyboards, monitors, and touch screens provided. A scribe or recording device may be needed for expression.

Be sure to select/adjust materials and resources that minimize accidental mistakes. Some students with physical disabilities, for example, might need more time to log into a computer, press a switch, or enter other information electronically and get cut off in the process if the speed isn't adjusted.

Make certain learning areas and materials are accessible. Use hook-and-loop fasteners to stabilize items or to place them within reach. Be sure the student is positioned comfortably. Table height, lighting, and seating all must be considered for student comfort.

If projects are required that are physically intensive, you may want to allow an alternative such as computer-generated drawing, a research paper, or a lab demonstration/explanation with downloaded pictures. These students will likely need training in the technology use as well as organizational strategies for production.

Students with low vision will rely more on auditory and tactile output. If you are writing words on a whiteboard, for example, say them aloud. Try using enlarged black print on a yellow background, positioned at eye level for visual reading. There are also recorded/audio textbooks and large-print materials available from the Library for the Blind and Recording for the Blind and Dyslexic. Having a peer tutor or buddy who can narrate or explain visuals used in presentations helps. Try to arrange seating so that students with visual impairments aren't facing windows to reduce problems with glare.

There are specialists in school systems that can help with adaptations such as converting text to Braille, scanning, and enlarging text. Copy machines can also magnify text. Try not to clutter the page. Many students with low vision are successfully using laptop computers with magnification, screen readers, and voice output tools.

Students with hearing impairments may benefit from the use of auditory trainers, visual cueing systems, and having print (pictures/sign language/words) paired with auditory presentations. Seating near the speaker for listening or speech reading is important. Provide a buddy to make sure directions and concepts are understood. The buddy may also help provide examples. Use videos and software that are closed captioned. Directions should be short and specific. Speak clearly and reduce your own movement. Always face the student when you are talking so he/she can see your lips and facial expressions.

For students with other sensory sensitivities, you may provide headphones to lower stimulation, approach a student from the front, allow water bottles, minimize auditory/visual distractions, and alternate pleasurable activities with difficult ones. Students who are sensitive to fluorescent lighting may be allowed to wear a baseball cap, or you can try to arrange to have more natural lighting available. Remember that your speech/language, physical, and occupational therapists can be very helpful in many of these areas.

Table 9.6 summarizes many of the research-based interventions highlighted in the learner domain section of this chapter. It also offers related technology applications that support UDL principles. Keep in mind this has been a very general overview of what interventions are possible. Additional study is recommended for interventions that you may choose to use.

Table 9.6   Instructional and Related Practices Categorized by Learning Domains

Learning Domain	Instructional Practice Ideas	UDL Application Examples
Cognitive/ Generalization	• Use concrete objects/visuals • Provide models • Strategically group students • Scaffold instruction • Apply skills learned in different settings	**High-Tech:** Virtual manipulatives/electronic images, multimedia presentations (with fading feature), virtual field trips **Low-Tech:** Lab materials, manipulatives, posters, charts
Giftedness	• Compact Curriculum • Cluster students • Differentiate instruction • Accelerate learning	**High-Tech:** Create podcasts, WebQuests; computer research **Low-Tech:** Research projects with print and nonprint resources; prepare print materials (perhaps quiz reviews) for other students
Language/Speech	• Provide clear, concise directions • Pair verbal with visual/print/gesture/object • Offer wait time • Use Think-Pair-Share • Visualize/rehearse	**High-Tech:** Recording/listening/output devices, electronic or Internet dictionary/images, step-by-step switches **Low-Tech:** Communication book, dictionary, dry erase board, partner work
Memory	• Use mnemonics • Chunk information • Visualize/associate • Employ redundancy • Use backward chaining	**High-Tech:** Audio/video recording for repeated listening, clip art added to words/concepts to be recalled **Low-Tech:** Mnemonics on index cards, posters; rehearsing with peer
Study Skills/ Organization/ Test Taking	• Use note-taking strategies • Apply time management • Manage materials • Develop test-taking strategies	**High-Tech:** Schedules on computer/PDAs, electronic note taking, electronic test review software **Low-Tech:** Calendars/planners/agendas, color-coded notebooks/ folders, index study cards for strategies, review sheets for tests

Table 9.6	Instructional and Related Practices Categorized by Learning Domains (Continued)	
Learning Domain	**Instructional Practice Ideas**	**UDL Application Examples**
ADHD/Impulsivity	• State rules/procedures consistently • Have a structured, consistent schedule/routine • Alternate high-/low-interest tasks • Incorporate movement/build in stretch breaks • Reduce distractions	**High-Tech:** Add pictures, animations, color, music to presentations; use interactive computer programs for engagement **Low-Tech:** Hand fidgets, ball chairs
Social/Emotional/ Motivational	• Set goals, monitor progress • Increase VAKT activities • Provide high rates of success • Use cooperative learning • Teach social skills • Use positive reinforcement	**High-Tech:** Videos of social stories/motivational tapes; graphing of individual progress; e-mail/social networking tools for mentoring **Low-Tech:** Books with social skills incorporated; paper/pencil graphs of individual progress
Physical/Motor/ Sensory	• Vary writing, pointing tools • Adjust lighting/ seating/positioning • Peer tutor or buddy • Reduce glare • Physical, visual/auditory cueing	**High-Tech:** Physical control devices to turn on technologies; enlarged keyboards/monitors; enlarged font; touch screens; closed-caption video **Low-Tech:** Pencil grips, box under feet to position; cushions/wedges; headphones

Note: These suggestions may work in more than one domain and may not work for all learners.

Using Classroom Websites and Other Web Tools

As you can see, electronic possibilities are one of the most important resources we have to increase access for all students. Educational publishers are including technology tools, including web resources, as part of the curriculum to keep up with the times. You read about many new technologies in Chapter 6 that were referenced in the text and intervention tables in this chapter. Remember that it is always important to evaluate published materials and any websites you use carefully. Look for basic design principles and links to learning goals. In addition, always check websites for safety. Be knowledgeable about your school district's acceptable use policy for using student names and images on websites. If you provide interactive Internet formats, use open source software that allows you to be the site administrator so you can see and monitor student postings, control who else has access to the program, and control postings of articles (March, 2005). These spaces should be guarded with a password entry.

Designing a class website can be an excellent way to keep students and families informed. It can also help you stay organized by including and categorizing items such as daily agendas, calendars, schedules, homework and project assignments, study guides, and other strategies or interventions provided in class for easy access by all. Some predesigned teacher websites are available for free or at low cost (see the companion website for examples). Best practices for selecting and designing websites and other electronic materials include:

- Using high-contrast backgrounds and text (black or blue on white, for example).
- Using enlarged font and sans serif fonts (such as Verdana, Arial, and Geneva) for text for simplicity and clarity.
- Using boldface rather than italics because italics are hard to read.
- Using digitized text.
- Making liberal use of chunking (short paragraphs, different levels of subheads, bullet and block paragraphs strategically).
- Providing captions for all graphics and images.
- Offering descriptions of what is viewed. Using ALT tags with graphics to provide a description. Include scripts of audio files that can narrate the text when possible.
- Helping learners focus on important information.

- Changing color of font (on PDAs, for example).
- Avoiding the use of frames (screen readers go from left to right across the full screen; having two frames side by side limits accessibility).
- Having text read aloud (all or part).
- Asking volunteers or using high-speed scanners to record printed material that can be read and stored on a server to be used by whole school district (ERIC/OSEP, 1999).

Thematic Summary

- By identifying learning stages and appropriate interventions for each stage, teachers can make more-informed decisions in selecting instructional practices.
- Intervention practices for teaching and learning are useful in reaching both academic and nonacademic learning goals.
- Using the principles of curricular design to inform teaching strategy/ technique selection can help teachers maximize instructional time.
- Anchored instruction allows teachers flexible use of strategies while implementing "big ideas."
- Most conspicuous strategies benefit all learners but some will need more them more than others. Mediated scaffolding benefits most learners at various times and in various settings.
- Interventions can have high- and low-tech applications.
- Considering learning domains and preferences can positively impact the selection of strategies and teaching techniques.
- All learners need to be challenged at every level.
- Technology tools hold promise for greater access by all.

Making Connections for Inclusive Teaching

1. Give an example of a situation in which a student may need to bypass a learning step that cannot be mastered after a reasonable amount of time in order to move ahead. What adaptation(s) might you make?
2. A teacher on your hall says, "Johnny is so disruptive in my class. I don't have time to prepare extra materials to teach to his learning style. If I did, I know he would be more engaged." What strategies might you offer this teacher?
3. What are some examples of authentic learning? Do you think teachers should try to incorporate more of this into their teaching? Why or why not?
4. Give an example of a conspicuous strategy that has helped you in school. Explain how it worked and why it was effective.
5. What technologies do you use for organizing and accessing your academic work?

Learning Activities

1. Design a toolbox using index cards or an electronic table in which to file/ collect strategies and techniques to help diverse learners. Use the three essential qualities of UDL (multiple means of representation, multiple means of expression, and multiple means of engagement) as headings for sections or columns. Place at least five strategies or techniques in each section or column. Describe each and provide an example.
2. Technology is making a big difference in accessing learning for all students. Locate, read, and summarize a recent educational journal article to find out how schools can protect the safety of students as they work with different technologies, including the World Wide Web. Offer your opinion in closing.
3. You have been asked to present to your grade-level team a short overview of interventions and teaching techniques that might be helpful for students

with mild autism in a general classroom. At least one team member serves a student who has difficulty following rules and procedures. Whenever there is a change in schedule, the student becomes agitated. His language is sometimes inappropriate, and he has difficulty interacting with his peers. Although he reads and writes just below grade level, he finds the task of writing physically fatiguing. Comprehending what is read and solving math word problems are difficult for him. The student prefers a visual/nonverbal learning style. What kinds of instructional practices and related techniques might you suggest? List five or more. Choose and indicate the approximate grade level. Include low- and high-tech ideas.

Looking at the Standards

The content of this chapter most closely aligns itself with the following standards:

INTASC Standards

- *Diverse Learners*. The teacher understands how students differ in their approaches to learning and creates instructional opportunities that are adapted to diverse learners.
- *Multiple Instructional Resources*. The teacher understands and uses a variety of instructional strategies to encourage student development of critical thinking, problem solving, and performance skills.
- *Communication and Technology*. The teacher uses knowledge of effective verbal, nonverbal, and media communication techniques to foster active inquiry, collaboration, and supportive interaction in the classroom.

Council for Exceptional Children

Special educators are to have knowledge of the following:

- CC4S1: Use strategies to facilitate integration into various settings.
- GC4K2: Strategies to prepare for and take tests.
- GC7S2: Select and use specialized instructional strategies appropriate to the abilities and needs of the individual.
- CC4S4: Use strategies to facilitate maintenance and generalization of skills across learning environments.
- GC4S1: Use research-supported methods for academic and nonacademic instruction of individuals with disabilities.
- GC4S2: Use strategies from multiple theoretical approaches for individuals with disabilities.
- GC4S3: Teach learning strategies and study skills to acquire academic content.
- GC4S10: Identify and teach basic structures and relationships within and across curricula.
- GC4S11: Use instructional methods to strengthen and compensate for deficits in perception, comprehension, memory, and retrieval.
- GC4S13: Identify and teach essential concepts, vocabulary, and content across the general curriculum.

Key Concepts and Terms

acquisition stage of
   learning
proficiency
maintenance
generalization
transfer of learning
adaptation
big ideas
KWL chart
strategic integration
authentic learning
anchored instruction
ClassAct Portal
WebQuests
conspicuous strategies
learning strategies
   approach

forward and backward
   chaining
content enhancements
mnemonic devices
keyword mnemonics
mnemonic letter strategy
match-to-sample
flow lists
questioning strategies
socratic questioning
Think Aloud
mediated scaffolding
Direct Instruction
guided discovery learning
modeling
chunking
self-monitoring
   strategies

task analysis
shaping
cues and prompts
peer tutoring
judicious review
spaced repetitions
response cards
classroom response
   systems
reciprocal teaching
curriculum compacting
cluster grouping
wait time
Think-Pair-Share
preteaching vocabulary
cooperative learning

References

Adams, G. L. & Engelmann, S. (1996). *Research on direct instruction: 25 years beyond DISTAR.* Seattle, WA: Educational Achievement Systems.

Alberto, P. A., & Troutman, A. C. (2003). *Applied behavior analysis for teachers* (6th ed.). Upper Saddle River, NJ: Merrill/ Prentice Hall.

Amato-Zech, N., Hoff, K., & Doepke, K. (2006). Increasing on-task behavior in the classroom: Extension of self-monitoring strategies. *Psychology in the Schools, 43*(2), 211–221.

Batra, M., & Batra, V. (2005). Comparison between forward chaining and backward chaining techniques in children with mental retardation. *The Indian Journal of Occupational Therapy, 47*(3), 57–63.

Becker, W. C. (1992). Direct instruction: A twenty year review. In R. P. West and L. A. Hamerlynck (Eds.), *Designs for excellence in education: The legacy of B. F. Skinner* (pp. 71–112). Longmont, CO: Sopris West.

Bell, L. I. (2002). Strategies that close the gap. *Educational Leadership, 60*(4), 32–34.

Bond, N. (2007). 12 questioning strategies that minimize classroom management problems. *Kappa Delta Pi Record, 44*(1), 18–21.

Boudah, D. J., Lenz, B. K., Bulgren, J. A., Schumaker, J. B., & Deshler, D. D. (2000). Don't water down! Enhance content learning through the advanced unit organizer content routine. *Teaching Exceptional Children, 32*(3), 48–56.

Boyle, J. (2001). Enhancing the note-taking skills of students with mild disabilities. *Intervention in School and Clinic, 36,* 221–224.

Buggey, T. (2005). Video self-modeling applications with students with autism spectrum disorder in a small private school setting. *Focus on Autism and other Developmental Disabilities, 20,* 52–63.

Bulgren, J. A. (2006). Integrated content enhancement routines: Responding to the needs of adolescents with disabilities in rigorous inclusive secondary content classes. *Teaching Exceptional Children, 38*(6), 54–58.

Burke, M., Hagan, S., & Grossen, B. (1998). What curricular designs and strategies accommodate diverse learners? *Teaching Exceptional Children, 31*(2), 34–38.

Conderman, G., & Morin, J. (2002). Successful instruction for all students. *Kappa Delta Pi Record, 38*(4), 170–173.

Conway, J. (1997). *Educational technology's effect on models of instruction.* Retrieved June 23, 2008, from http://copland .udel.edu/~jconway/EDST666.htm

Coyne, M., Kame'enui, E., & Carnine, D. (2007). *Effective teaching strategies that accommodate diverse learners* (3rd ed.). Upper Saddle River, NJ: Pearson Education.

Crews, T., Biswas, G., Goldman, S., & Bransford, J. (1997). *Anchored interactive learning environments.* Retrieved June 23, 2008, from http://www.vuse.vanderbilt.edu/~biswas/ Research/ile/papers/postscript/advplay.pdf

Cristle, C. A., & Schuster, J. W. (2003). The effects of using response cards on student participation, academic achievement, and on-task behavior during whole-class, math instruction. *Journal of Behavioral Education, 12*(3), 147–165.

Dempster, F. (1991). Synthesis of research on reviews and tests. *Journal of Educational Leadership, 48*(7), 71–76.

Deshler, D., Ellis, E., & Lenz, B. (1996). *Teaching adolescents with learning disabilities: Strategies and methods* (2nd ed.). Denver, CO: Love.

Dixon, R., Carnine, D. W., & Kame'enui, E. J. (1996). *Curriculum guidelines for diverse learners* (Monograph). Eugene: University of Oregon, National Center to Improve the Tools of Educators.

Dodge, B. (1997). *Some thoughts about webquests.* Retrieved June 23, 2008, from http://webquest.sdsu.edu/about_webquests.html

Engelmann, S., & Carnine, D. (1991). *Theory of instruction: Principles and practices.* Eugene, OR: ADI Press.

ERIC/OSEP. (1999, Fall). Universal design: Ensuring access to the general education curriculum. *Research Connections in Special Education, 5.* Reston, VA: The Council for Exceptional Children. (ERIC Document Reproduction Service No. ED433666)

Fisher, D., Frey, N., & Williams, D. (2002). Seven literacy strategies that work. *Reading and Writing in the Content Areas, 60*(3), 70–73.

Fitzharris, L. H., & Hay, G. H. (2001). Working collaboratively to support struggling readers in the inclusive classroom. *Reading and Writing Quarterly: Overcoming Learning Difficulties, 17,* 175–180.

Forness, S., Kavale, K., Blum, I., & Lloyd, J. (1997). Mega-analysis of meta-analysis. *Teaching Exceptional Children, 29*(6), 4–9.

Freeman, K. A., & Dexter-Mazza, E. (2004). Using self-monitoring with an adolescent with disruptive classroom behavior. *Behavior Modification, 28*(3), 402–419.

Gentry, M., & Owen, S. (1999). An investigation of the effects of total school flexible cluster grouping on identification, achievement, and classroom practices. *Gifted Child Quarterly, 43*(4), 224–242.

Grossen, B., Romance, N., & Vitale, M. (1994). Science: Educational tools for diverse learners. *School Psychology Review, 23*(3), 442–468.

Henfield, M. S., Moore, J. L., & Wood, C. (2008). Inside and outside gifted education programming: Hidden challenges for African American students. *Exceptional Children, 74*(4), 433–450.

Hess, F., & Brigham, F. J. (2000). The promises and pitfalls of high stakes testing. *American School Board Journal, 187*(1), 26–29.

Heward, W. L., Gardner, R., Cavanaugh, R. A., Courson, F. H., Grossi, T. A., & Barbetta, P. M. (1996). Everyone participates in this class: Using response cards to increase active student response. *Teaching Exceptional Children, 28*(2), 4–10.

Hitchcock, C., Dowrick, P. W., & Prater, M. A. (2003). Video self-modeling intervention in school-based settings: A review. *Remedial and Special Education, 24,* 36–45, 56.

Horn, R. (1990). Mapping hypertext: The analysis, organization, and display of knowledge for the next generation of on-line text and graphics. Lexington, KY: Lexington Institute.

Israel, S. E., & Massey, D. (2005). Metacognitive think-alouds: Using a gradual release model with middle school students. In S. E. Israel, C. C. Block, K. L. Bauserman, & K. Kinnucan-Welsch (Eds.), Metacognition in literacy learning: Theory, assessment, instruction, and professional development (pp. 183–198). Mahwah, NJ: Lawrence Erlbaum.

James Madison University. (n.d.). *The learning toolbox.* Retrieved June 22, 2008, from http://coe.jmu.edu/Learningtoolbox/index.html

Kauffman, J., Mostert, M., Trent, S., & Hallahan, D. (2006). *Managing classroom behavior* (3rd ed.). Boston: Allyn & Bacon.

Kearsley, G. (1994–2008). *Explorations in learning & instruction: Theory into practice database.* Retrieved June 23, 2008, from http://www.gwu.edu/~tip/

King-Sears, M. E., Mercer, C. D., & Sindelar, P. T. (1992). Toward independence with keyword mnemonics: A strategy for science vocabulary instruction. *Remedial and Special Education, 13,* 22–33.

Konold, K. E., Miller, S. P., & Konold, K. B. (2004). Using teacher feedback to enhance student learning. *Teaching Exceptional Children, 36*(6), 64–69.

Kulik, J. A. (1992). *An analysis of the research on ability grouping: Historical and contemporary perspective* (Research Monograph No. 9204). Storrs: National Research Center on the Gifted and Talented, University of Connecticut.

Lederer, J. (2000). Implementing reciprocal teaching in the classroom. *Journal of Learning Disabilities, 33,* 91–106.

Lenz, B. K., Deshler, D. D., & Kissam, B. R. (2004). *Teaching content to all: Evidence-based inclusive practices in middle and secondary schools.* Boston: Allyn & Bacon.

Lenz, B. K., Ellis, E. S., & Scanlon, D. (1996). *Teaching learning strategies to adolescents and adults with learning disabilities.* Austin, TX: Pro-Ed.

Levin, J. R. (1993). Mnemonic strategies and classroom learning: A twenty-year report card. *The Elementary School Journal, 94*(2), 235–244.

Lyman, F. (1981). The responsive classroom discussion. In A. S. Anderson (Ed.), *Mainstreaming digest* (pp. 109–113). College Park: University of Maryland College of Education.

Macfarlane, C. (1998). Assessment: The key to appropriate curriculum and instruction. In A. Hilton & R. Ringlaben (Eds.), *Best and promising practices in developmental disabilities* (pp. 35–60). Austin, TX: Pro-Ed.

March, T. (2005). The New WWW: Whatever, whenever, wherever. *Educational Leadership, 63*(4), 14–19.

March, T. (2006). *Why ClassAct Portals? An introduction.* Retrieved June 23, 2008, from http://tommarch.com/writings/why_portals.php

Marzano, R., & Arredondo, D. (1986). Restructuring schools through the teaching of thinking skills. *Educational Leadership, 43*(8), 20–26.

Marzano, R., Pickering, D., & Pollock, J. (2001). *Classroom instruction that works: Research-based strategies for increasing student achievement.* Alexandria, VA: Association for Supervision and Curriculum Development.

Mastropieri, M. A., & Scruggs, T. E. (1990). *Teaching students ways to remember: Strategies for learning mnemonically.* Cambridge, MA: Brookline Books.

Mastropieri, M., & Scruggs, T. (1993). *A practical guide for teaching science to students with special needs in inclusive settings.* Austin, TX: Pro-Ed.

Mastropieri, M. A., & Scruggs, T. E. (1998). Enhancing school success with mnemonic strategies. *Intervention in School and Clinic, 33*(4), 201–208.

Mayer, R., Sims, V., & Tajika, H. (1995). A comparison of how textbooks teach mathematical problem solving in Japan and the United States. *American Educational Research Journal, 32*(2), 443–460.

McConnell, M. E. (1999). Self-monitoring, cueing, recording, and managing. *Teaching Exceptional Children, 32*(2), 14.

McThighe, J., & O'Connor, K. (2005). Seven practices for effective learning. *Educational Leadership, 63*(3), 10–17.

Mercer, C. D., & Mercer, A. R. (2005). *Teaching students with learning problems.* Upper Saddle River, NJ: Pearson Education.

Miller, S. P., Harris, C., Strawser, S., Jones, W. P., and Mercer, C. D. (1998). Teaching multiplication to second graders in inclusive settings. *Focus on Learning Problems in Mathematics, 20,* 50–70.

Newman, F. M., & Wehlage, G. G. (1993). Five standards of authentic instruction. *Educational Leadership, 50*(7), 8–12.

Palincsar, A., & Klenk, L. (1991). Dialogues promoting reading comprehension. In B. Means, C. Chelemer, & M. S. Knapp (Eds.), *Teaching advanced skills to at-risk students* (pp. 112–140). San Francisco, CA: Jossey-Bass.

Parsons, L. D. (2006). Using video to teach social skills to secondary students with autism. *Teaching Exceptional Children, 39*(2), 32–38.

Renzulli, J., & Reis, S. (2008). *Enriching curriculum for all students* (2nd ed.). Thousand Oaks, CA: Corwin Press, pp. 76–77.

Rivera, D., & Smith, D. (1997). *Teaching students with learning and behavior problems* (3rd ed.). Boston, MA: Allyn & Bacon.

Rosenberg, M., O'Shea, L., & O'Shea, D. (2006). *Student teacher to master teacher: A practical guide for educating students with special needs* (4th ed.). Upper Saddle River, NJ: Pearson Education.

Rosenshine, B. (1986). Synthesis of research on explicit teaching. *Educational Leadership, 43*(7), 60–69.

Rosenshine, B., & Meister, C. (1992). The use of scaffolds for teaching higher-level cognitive strategies. *Educational Leadership, 49*(7), 26–33.

Rowe, M. B. (1987). Wait time: Slowing down may be a way of speeding up. *American Educator, 11,* 38–43.

Salend, S. J. (2001). *Creating inclusive classrooms: Effective and reflective practices.* Upper Saddle River, NJ: Pearson Education.

Scruggs, T. E., & Mastropieri, M. A. (1992). Classroom applications of mnemonic instruction: Acquisition, maintenance, and generalization. *Exceptional Children, 58,* 219–229.

Siegel, M., Derry, S. J., Kim, J., Steinkeuhler, C. A., Street, J., Canty, N., et al. (2000). Promoting teachers' flexible use of the learning sciences through case-based problem solving on the WWW: A theoretical design approach. In B. Fishman & S. O'Connor-Divelbiss (Eds.), *Proceedings of the Fourth International Conference of the Learning Sciences* (pp. 273–279). Mahwah, NJ: Erlbaum.

Simmons, D., & Kame'enui, E. (1996). A focus on curriculum design: When children fail. *Focus on Exceptional Children, 28*(7), 1–16.

Slavin, R. (1991). Synthesis of research on cooperative learning. *Educational Leadership, 48*(5), 71–82.

Stahl, R. J. (1994). *Using "think-time" and "wait-time" skillfully in the classroom* (Report No. OERI-RR99002014). Bloomington, IN: ERIC Clearinghouse for Social Studies/Social Science Education. (ERIC Document Reproduction Service No. ED370885)

Stokes, T. F., & Baer, D. M. (1977). An implicit technology of generalization. *Journal of Applied Behavior Analysis, 10,* 349–367.

Thompson, K., & Taymans, J. (1994). Development of a reading strategies program: Bridging the gaps among decoding, literature, and thinking skills. *Intervention in School and Clinic, 30*(1), 21.

Traver, S. (1992). Direct instruction. In W. Stainback & S. Stainback (Eds.), *Controversial issues confronting special education: Divergent perspectives* (2nd ed., pp. 143–165). Boston: Allyn & Bacon.

Wehman, P., & Kregel, J. (Eds.) (2004). *Functional curriculum for elementary, middle, and secondary age students with special needs* (2nd ed.). Austin, TX: Pro-Ed.

Wilen, W. W. (1991). *Questioning skills for teachers* (3rd ed.). Washington, DC: National Education Association.

Wilhelm, J. (2001). Think-alouds: Boost reading comprehension. *Instructor, 111*(4), 26–28.

Witzel, B. S., Mercer, C. D., & Miller, M. D. (2003). Teaching algebra to students with learning difficulties: An investigation of an explicit instruction model. *Learning Disabilities: Research and Practice, 18*(2), 121–131.

Designing Learning that Works for All Students

Four Components of Universally Designed Curriculum

Designing Academic Learning for Access

    Goals

    Materials and Resources

    Methods

    Assessment

    The UDL Lesson Plan

Designing Physical Learning Environments

    Physical Environment Considerations

    ACCESS Physical Environment

Designing Social Learning Environments

    ACCESS Social Environments

    PBS and UDL

Adaptations that Support Universally Designed Learning Environments

    Accommodations

    Modifications

Learning Outcomes

After studying this chapter, you should be able to:

- Describe the three basic elements that must be considered when planning Universally Designed Learning environments—academic, physical, and social.
- Identify and explain the four essential UDL curricular components to use in planning and constructing accessible academic learning.
- Take a traditional lesson plan and expand it to increase its use with diverse learners by applying Universal Design for Learning and differentiated instruction principles.
- Compare and contrast the terms accommodations and modifications when discussing adaptations.
- List and explain the principles for access to the physical and social environments that need to be considered in planning Universally Designed Learning.

Outcomes *(continued)*
● Identify benefits of collaboration and co-teaching in universally designed learning environments and the impact on the roles of professionals and others in school communities.

Collaboration in Planning Universally Designed Learning Environments

Collaborative Planning and Teaching
Collaborative Problem Solving

Imagine you are planning a road trip. Where are you going and why? How will you plan your routes? What if there are detours? How much time do you have? How many miles do you need to drive each day to reach your destination on time? How will you know if you are making progress or not? Where will you spend the nights?

Once you have made your plan, your thoughts turn to your vehicle. Is it in good shape? If not, what needs to be done to get it ready and minimize hazards along the way? When will you stop to check on fuel and tires?

You also likely think about the social side of the trip and subsequent adaptations you might have to make unless you are traveling alone. If you have traveling companions, how will you choose them? If you have children, how will you adapt the trip to meet their needs? What if one of your passengers is elderly? What if someone uses a wheelchair? If you take a pet, how will that work? If you travel into a different country, how will you adapt to the language/culture?

The curriculum in a school is the "road map" for teaching. It is the tool we use to initially design academic learning. Like the road trip, we need to know our destination and we need to plan ahead to determine the best way to get there. The design, however, does not stop there. The physical and social aspects of school must also be considered. Material and physical resources will likely be limited. Teachers will face some detours with students who learn differently or have varied academic, linguistic, physical, and social/emotional needs.

Despite limitations, if we take inventory of the adaptations, materials, and the resources we do have control over at the beginning of the trip, we can plan ahead and avoid many of the potholes on the roads we travel. For example, we can have our car or van serviced before we go, check to see that there is a good spare tire, and secure current maps through travel clubs, interactive online map directories, or a Global Positioning System (GPS) receiver. We can plan our daily itinerary by phone or online, making reservations for campsites or rooms that are easily accessible at motels or hotels for each night. If applicable, we can find out which places take pets ahead of time. The car can be packed with a cell phone, snacks, books, video games, CD players, MP3 players, and/or DVDs for entertaining both adult passengers and children. An electronic language translator can be packed to use when entering a different country. Electronic device chargers may also be included. The more planning done up front and the more technologies integrated, the more likely the trip will be smooth, comfortable, and enjoyable. The possibility of arriving at the destination safely, in good spirits, and in a timely manner increases.

This chapter will focus on applying the principles of Universal Design for Learning (UDL) in curricular and environmental planning. It considers designing learning for all students by considering the relationship between three critical elements—*academic*, *physical*, and *social*. It also looks at the roles of professional collaboration that play such an important part in structuring schools for success. An overarching premise in the planning will be on technology integration from the start—from high tech to low tech—to maximize student access to the curriculum.

Four Components of Universally Designed Curriculum

The dictionary defines **curriculum** as "(1) the courses offered by an educational institution, and (2) a set of courses constituting an area of specialization" (*Merriam-Webster's Collegiate Dictionary*, 1994). In practical terms, curriculum can be thought of as a set of learning opportunities (or road trips) for students with varied destinations. Once the students and the standards/curricular goals they must meet are known, teachers can begin to map out the educational plan for them. The researchers at the Center for Applied Special Technology (CAST) (Hitchcock, Meyer, Rose, & Jackson, 2002), offer four components to consider up front as teachers strive to maximize curriculum accessibility for a group of diverse learners. These components are based on the three essential qualities of Universal Design for Learning (UDL) described in Chapter 8 (multiple means of representation, multiple means of expression, and multiple means of engagement). They are: (1) **goals**, (2) **materials and resources**, (3) **methods**, and (4) **assessment**. In this chapter, we will first take a look at how these components might be applied to *academic* needs. The design of the *physical* and *social* classroom needs will be considered next. These frameworks will all impact the effectiveness of meeting curricular demands and, ultimately, student learning.

Designing Academic Learning for Access
Goals

Once assigned to a class, teachers must determine the academic goals for the given set of students based on the information provided by the school district. What are the demands of the curriculum? Teachers will initially consider goals, objectives, and benchmarks that are typically provided by state departments of public instruction and/or local school districts, along with pacing guides. National discipline specific and professional organizations may also have standards that you and/or your class may be measured against. Student assessment information from the previous school year(s) will be reviewed. This may include any individualized education program (IEP) goals, 504 plans, adaptations, and/or other special programming documents.

Next, teachers look at the range of topics/content areas to be covered and assessed in the coming weeks, months, and school year. This can be overwhelming but it is critical in the development of unit and lesson plans. To make it manageable and clear, teachers can initially map out the main goals as the standards are dissected—by digging deeply at the start, the broad range of goals and objectives to focus on must be clearly identified. Remember these are the **big ideas** introduced in Chapter 9—the core concepts/principles in the content areas that help learners acquire knowledge across a broad range of experiences (Coyne, Kame'enui, & Carnine, 2007). Establishing clear goals based on the standards is a critical first step. Just as on the road trip, the driver identifies the destination before planning the routes.

Teachers can further increase access or approachability to the general curriculum by focusing on the way goals and objectives are initially written from these big ideas (Rose, Meyer, & Hitchcock, 2005). This can be done by writing objectives with verbs that offer the greatest amount flexibility in terms of representation, engagement, and expression. For example, if an objective in language arts is "*to write* an essay on . . . ," some learners with language and writing difficulties are denied access from the start. However, if the goal is reworded to say "*to express* ideas about . . . ," all students can participate. (See Table 10.1.) Another example might be changing an objective such as "*to write* a book report on a biography" to "*to summarize* a biography using print, media, and/or technology resources." These objectives are still observable and measurable—just more accessible. Additional examples are provided in Table 10.2. In summary, once it is determined what all students in a classroom must learn and be able to do, think about how goals and objectives can be constructed to make it possible for all learners to be involved and work toward them. Try to identify the content first, and then decide how it will be achieved. If goals are too narrow, some students get left out. By initially writing clear, accessible goals and objectives, fewer adaptations typically need to be made for students along the way.

Table 10.1	Writing Goals and Objectives that Increase Access
Goals/Objectives that LIMIT Access: Instead of	**Goals/Objectives that ALLOW Access: Try**
"The student will write . . ."	"The student will express . . ."
	"The student will generate . . ."
"The student will read . . ."	"The student will receive information from a variety of sources . . ."
"The student will spell . . ."	"The student will select . . ."
"The student will compute . . ."	"The student will solve . . ."
"The student will define . . ."	"The student will show . . ."

Next, the basic questions are developed to frame units and lessons. These **essential questions** are at the heart of the unit and its lessons. These questions reflect the big ideas and are the same for *all* learners and not differentiated. Table 10.2 offers an example of how teachers might map out and align goals that come to them from different sources in a math unit on charting numbers and modeling/analyzing data. Essential questions can be brainstormed immediately following this alignment process.

Once accessible goals/objectives and essential questions are determined, teachers must also look specifically at the needs of the students in terms of extra support and challenge/enrichment. Specific student strengths and needs must be considered as teachers think about ways to scaffold, challenge, and/or enrich instruction. What are possible barriers to learning? Attention to individualized needs can by given by integrating them right away into the big ideas you develop for the whole group of students. The diverse learner is still exposed to the big ideas while his or her individualized areas of skill are also being addressed.

Teachers also need to consider what textbook and/or other content sources will be used, available technology supports, and kinds of activities/groupings that would lend themselves to lessons that offer flexibility in representation, engagement, and expression. Figure 10.1 offers a preplanning template that can help organize the brainstorming process before planning units and lessons when applying a UDL approach. This chapter will offer additional planning ideas and tools to incorporate into this planning template as it progresses.

Table 10.2	Fourth-Grade Example of Goal/Standard Alignment with Essential Questions: Big Ideas: Charting Numbers and Modeling/Analyzing Data

National Standard	State Standard Example	Broad IEP Goals (Where Applicable)	Unit Goals and Essential Questions for All Students
5.4 Accessing and Investigating Data	**Competency Goal 4:** The learner will understand and use graphs, probability, and data analysis. **Objectives: 4.01**—Collect, organize, analyze, and display data (including line graphs and bar graphs to solve problems. **4.02**—Describe the distribution of data using median, range and mode. **4.03**—Solve problems by comparing two sets of related data. **4.04**—Design experiments and list all possible outcomes and probabilities for an event.	**Modified Example:** The student will receive, discuss, and answer questions pertaining to a bar graph (4.01 and 4.04) **Extension Example:** (Mastery of 4th-grade objectives plus 5th grade): **4.01**—Collect, organize, analyze, and display data (including stem-and-leaf plots) to solve problems. **4.02**—Compare and contrast different representations of the same data; discuss the effectiveness of each representation.	**Probability/Statistics Unit Goal:** To collect, analyze, and make sense of real-world data. **Sample Essential Questions:** • What is a bar graph? • How does a bar graph compare to other types of graphs? • How is a bar graph constructed?

Sources: Adapted from National Council for Teachers of Mathematics, *Principles and Standards for School Mathematics* (2000), retrieved April 4, 2008, from http://www.nctm.org/standards/; North Carolina Department of Public Instruction, *Mathematics: North Carolina Standard Course of Study and Grade Level Competencies* (2003), retrieved April 4, 2008, from http://www.ncpublicschools.org/curriculum/mathematics/scos/

Preplanning Guide for Universally Designed Instruction

Teacher: _____ Grade Level: _____ Period: _____ Subject: _____ Topic: _____ Text: _____ # of Students: _____	**Students Needing Extra Supports** Adaptations/Modifications: (add student initials): _____ _____ IEPs _____ BIPs _____ Section 504 _____ Language _____ Other needs/challenges: _____ _____	**Students Needing Enrichment Extensions** (add student initials): _____ _____ Notes: _____ _____ _____ _____

Source(s) for digital/scaffolded text for this unit: _____

_____

Computer lab needs/schedule: _____

_____

Other Resources needed: _____

_____

Grouping Students: Large group: _____
Small group: _____
Individual: _____

Brainstorming Activities		
Multiple Means of Representation	**Multiple Means of Engagement**	**Multiple Means of Expression**
• Provide multiple examples (and nonexamples) • Present information in multiple media/formats • Provide support for limited background knowledge (tutors, interpreters, classroom resources)	• Offer choices within content (choice of poem; story selection within a genre to be studied) • Offer choice of tool(s) • Offer adjustable tiers of challenge • Offer reward choices • Offer choice of learning context (e.g., work in study carrel, group, use headphones)	• Provide flexible models • Offer opportunities to practice with supports • Provide ongoing, specific feedback • Provide flexible opportunities to demonstrate skill • Provide novel problems to solve

Figure 10.1 Planning Universally Designed Instruction
Source: Adapted from P. Hubbard, *Reducing Barriers to Learning Through a Universally Designed Classroom,* poster session presented at the 2008 Council for Exceptional Children's Annual Convention and Expo, Boston, MA (2008, April).

A **pyramid planning** graphic organizer can assist teachers when designing instruction that adapts to individual strengths and needs. Originally developed by Schumm, Vaughn, and Leavell (1994), pyramid planning provides a framework that helps develop the big ideas for a diverse group of learners in a classroom striving to apply differentiated instruction as well as Universal Design for Learning principles (see Figure 10.2). The most important concepts *all* students should learn are placed at the base of the pyramid. More direct instruction, practice, and repetition will likely occur here. The middle section indicates what *most* of the students will learn as they extend their thinking and gather additional information about the concept. At the top, place information that is more complex, detailed, or incidental to the major learning goals that will be important for *some* learners. At each section, brainstorm possible technology tools and materials that might be useful. All

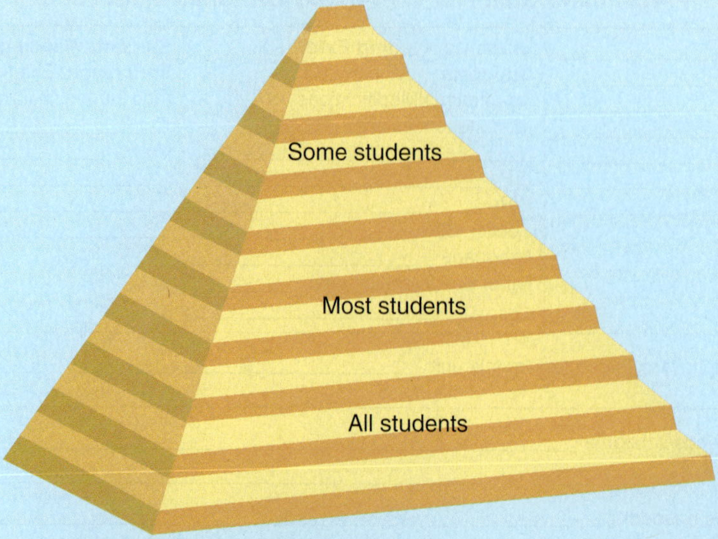

PYRAMID PLANNING	SUGGESTED TECHNOLOGY TOOLS
What SOME Students will learn:	
• To collect data independently and create a bar graph with appropriate scaling.	• Excel spreadsheet • Interactive graphing website • Poster/yardstick/markers • Paper/ruler/pencil
What MOST Students will learn:	
• To describe the purpose of a bar graph. • To create a complete bar graph given only data.	• Excel spreadsheet • Interactive graphing website • Poster/yardstick/markers • Grid paper/ruler/pencil
What All Students should learn (Goal):	
• To identify a bar graph in isolation and when compared to other types of graphs. • To create a bar graph given the appropriate information, including graph labels.	• Interactive graphing website • Poster/yardstick/markers • Grid paper/ruler/pencil • Sticky notes • Real objects • Premade graph labels

Figure 10.2 Pyramid Planning for Differentiating UDL Instruction
Source: Adapted from T. Jeffs, *Accessing the General Curriculum Through Assistive Technology: Yes We Can!* (NC-CEC 2006) (Greenville, NC: East Carolina University), modified from information available at http://www.schoolinfosystem.org/community/larry/PA20060206McQPlanningPyramid.pdf

students have access to all parts of the pyramid. Instruction will just need to be tailored to fit different learner needs. Having clearly defined objectives that work for teaching and learning is the goal.

Here are some questions to ask in pyramid planning:

1. What is the skill or concept to be taught?
2. What are the prerequisite skills for this skill or concept?
3. What does it take for students to master this skill or concept?
4. What are extensions and applications of the skill or concept?

Teachers might benefit from sketching out this pyramid graphic near the top their lesson plans and get in a pattern of asking themselves these four questions each time they plan.

Next, the **strategic integration** of goals can be considered collaboratively and mapped out by a group of teachers. Learners, including those with diverse needs, benefit from knowledge acquired across disciplines that is strategically integrated in a meaningful way if they are to develop higher-level thinking skills (Coyne, Kame'enui, & Carnine, 2007). In science, for example, students may look at patterns of change over time in a study of weather or life cycles. This goal could coordinate well with similar math "big ideas" of measurement and data analysis. Social studies goals, too, may be further aligned when studying changes in communities over time. The impact of changing weather patterns on communities might also be considered. Related vocabulary, literature, and other print/media resources could be infused into language arts courses. Teachers should always be on the lookout for ways that learning goals can connect to "big ideas." Mapping out the keywords and concepts in standards across the K–12 disciplines and grade levels helps give teachers an overall sense of where students are going and where they have been. Learners will be at different places on this map. Some will just be learning to "drive," and others will need to accelerate their learning speed in your classroom. Standards can be used as compass points.

Effective teachers are always on the lookout for ways to connect goals to those in other disciplines. Keeping this in mind up front increases flexibility and options for students as they travel through the school year. The organizer shown in Figure 10.3 may be useful for this kind of brainstorming. This organizer also considers community resources, cultural aspects, and diverse learning preferences as teachers map out goals. These topics will be discussed more in depth when we talk about social environments later in this chapter. Student motivation can be increased significantly by linking learning to student backgrounds and prior knowledge. Planning a culminating activity to bring all the learning activities together also adds motivation and showcases student learning in a celebratory way. The completion of a unit, like a road trip, can offer the same feeling of excitement a traveler gets when reaching his or her destination. A completed model of this organizer can be found in Chapter 13.

A final thought on academic goals: Just as teachers strive to connect goals within themes/units, connections need to be purposefully made between units as

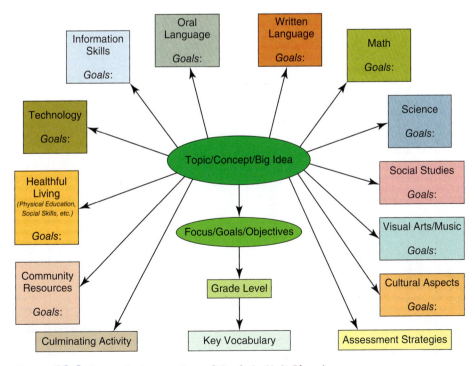

Figure 10.3 Strategic Integration of Goals in Unit Planning

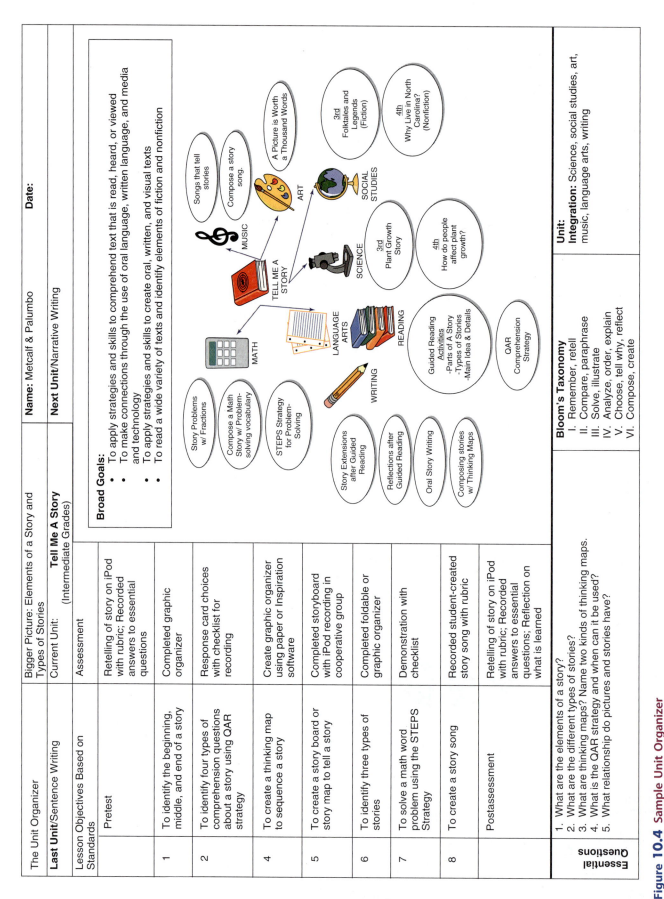

Figure 10.4 Sample Unit Organizer

Source: Adapted from B. K. Lenz, J. A. Bulgren, J. A. Schumaker, D. D. Deshler, & D. A. Boudah, *The Content Enhancement Series: The Unit Organizer Routine* (Lawrence, KS: Edge Enterprises, 1994).

• **Study Guides:** Completed Foldables, Thinking Maps, advance organizers	**UDL components: Multiple Means of Recognition**—Read alouds, lectures, songs character presents, guided reading, digital texts, advance organizer, demonstration, overhead, interactive whiteboard, video clips, charts, podcasts **Multiple Means of Engagement**—Listening, questioning, discussing, talking through steps, outlining steps, using graphic organizers, illustrating, taking pictures, singing, using response cards, using cooperative grouping, recording on iPods, creating podcasts **Multiple Means of Expression**—Songs, oral retelling, visual demonstration, pointing to answers, recorded story/song, completed graphic organizer, worksheet/bubble sheet
• **Resources:** Trade books, eBooks, graphic organizers, foldables, worksheets, iPods, Inspiration software, musical instruments	• **Culminating Activity:** Sharing of stories/story songs with another class(es), families • **Multiple Intelligence:** Verbal-Linguistic, Logical-Mathematical, Visual-Spatial, Interpersonal, Musical/Rhythmic • **Learning Modalities** Hands-on practice, manipulatives, visual posters/models, auditory songs
Tier III Tier II Tier I	What **some** students will learn: Compose/produce a multimedia presentation or podcasts of class stories. What **most** students will learn: Choose graphic organizers that match needed thinking process for given story problems. Work on extending story extensions. What **all** students will learn: All students will retell a story, identify story elements, identify different types of stories, name two or more types of graphic organizers, explain a questioning strategy and tell when it is used, and show the relationship between stories and pictures. All students will reflect on what is learned.

Figure 10.4 Sample Unit Organizer (Continued)

well. Learners need see how to take what is learned in a previous unit into a new one. They also need to see how what they are doing connects to what's coming. This awareness will help the teacher prepare learners who need extra cumulative review, preteaching, adaptations, and curriculum extensions for academic transitions. Keeping both long- and short-term goals in the forefront can make a big difference in everything that follows. Figure 10.4 offers an example of how a unit organizer might be structured to consider many of the features we have discussed so far. Even though it is a representation of a unit planned for intermediate elementary students, the concept behind it can be expanded for primary or secondary learners. This unit map includes a sampling of activities and learning objectives that might be included but is by no means complete. This map considers many of the elements of planning we have considered so far. Creating a flexible computer template to plan units can simplify this large task. Adding picture symbols helps teachers see disciplinary connections. Color coding the font for UDL elements can also be helpful.

As you learned in Chapter 1, we are living in a time of standards-driven reform. With No Child Left Behind (NCLB) legislation and IDEA revisions, schools are being held to higher achievement levels than ever before. Today's teacher must consider both content and achievement standards. **Content standards** help teachers define what knowledge and skills need to be taught in a subject. **Achievement standards** dictate what will be measured (what will be tested) and the level of mastery—along with the "how" and the "when." In essence, standards drive curriculum, so it is critical to look carefully at providing multiple, flexible methods and materials that will support understanding the content. Remember that a single teaching method (a lecture, for example) may not work for all learners and a single material source (a textbook, for example) may not cover all the necessary content standards, so you likely have to pull from a variety of resources. In addition, a single source may not be accessible to all learners. Screen readers, closed captioning, large print, talking calculators, or interpreters, for example, may be needed depending on student needs. It is also important to note that not all content standards are linked to achievement standards (Nolet & McLaughlin, 2005); be sure you know which ones do connect so you can make your instructional time really count.

By targeting the content standards that are linked to achievement standards, students will likely show growth in school. If this isn't done, simply providing a rich learning environment by itself without a specific purpose will not move students to the next level of learning that is required. Teachers can get sidetracked by trying to squeeze in their own favorite topics and activities that may not fit in well. This is not to say lessons can't be enjoyable. However, if the topics are not on the curricular road map and students spend instructional time taking detours by engaging in these other topics without a specific, clearly defined purpose, they will most likely not push themselves to the level of problem solving needed in the content area they are being assessed in and will come to a "dead end." Another risk that comes from a lack of clearly defined goals is that the curriculum may become fractured. Teachers may end up teaching splinter skills that really don't link in content or achievement. They may "retrofit" as they discover they have missed teaching a critical concept or miss teaching it altogether. Remember the power of helping learners make connections from Chapter 7 that help the brain organize and categorize its "file folders." The brain is searching for patterns—not clutter—to build networks.

Even though all students will not have the same level of skill or ability, *all* students *can* participate, learn from and with each other, and be held to high individual expectations and standards as they work together to comprehend the big ideas. Having accurate assessments will be critical in driving instruction. If too much school time is spent taking out and "fixing" certain students and then trying to "catch them up" to their peers later, some students will never catch up. Universal Design for Learning sets up the road map so that all students can reach the final destination on the big "road trip" but they just might get there in different ways and with a variety of adaptations.

Collaborative planning from the start maximizes student access to the curriculum.

Materials and Resources

Once goals are determined, materials and resources need to be considered in a Universal Design for Learning framework. Typically, teachers are given hard copy textbooks for their courses but textbooks are only one part of curricular materials and resources. If there is access to digital media and technology tools, there will be greater opportunities for flexibility in presentation, engagement, and learner expression. In fact, efforts to provide access to these tools up front may have a large payoff. They are also manageable in terms of storage, which also makes them additionally attractive for classroom use (Rose et al., 2005). Some school districts provide teachers with access to educational streaming video sources. Many educational publishers are working hard to offer different materials and resources up front including items such as leveled texts (same content but different reading levels), extension activities for diverse learners, materials in different languages, and CDs that read the print materials (including digitized video) aloud to supplement text. Most have links to a variety of network resources as well. Remember that one single textbook or CD will likely not address every single goal and objective. The extra resources can fill in the "holes." Having and using varied tools also lets teachers customize individual learner's options because no single method works for all. There are many free or inexpensive computer downloads you can access that help greatly with adaptations. In addition, many digital books can be accessed free online. These are referenced in the literacy chapter.

In essence, many support tools are now provided by the software industry, web browsers, accessibility utility programs for computer operating systems, publishing companies, and others. Many of these technologies have been developed year by year by teachers, parents, and students to meet individual needs but have ended up helping many more people. Some general categories and examples of academic materials and resources that are categorized this way are offered in Table 10.3. Survey your classroom, school, and community and brainstorm possibilities. The more variety you have, the more interesting and accessible your lessons become. Most teachers should have access to many low-tech devices. It is also quite common to see computers and other technology in classrooms today. Many new teachers have been raised with technology and will likely use it if it's conveniently available. It is

Table 10.3	Academic Materials and Resources
Low-Tech	**High-Tech**
• Manipulatives (e.g., math, science kits)	• Computer simulation • Video demonstration
• Books in print, including textbooks, encyclopedias • Tape recorder, CD player with recorded books, lectures	• Computer Internet connection to access books and other reading materials, WebQuests • Scanning and reading text
• Print/CD dictionary, encyclopedia, thesaurus • Handheld spelling checkers	• Online dictionaries, encyclopedias • Software programs with spell check • Reading pens
• Pencils, paper	• Speech-to-text computer capability • Word processing
• Musical instruments • CDs	• Music downloads, MP3 players • Electronic keyboard
• Maps, charts, posters	• Maps, charts online/software • PowerPoint presentations
• Field trip/guest speaker • Video/DVD	• Virtual field trip • Video conference
• Pictures, symbols on cards • Computer-produced pictures, symbols • Single switches	• Keyboards, pointer with symbols connected to computer
• Art paper, charcoal pencils, paint	• Draw-and-paint computer program • Computer-animation program
• Number lines, flash cards • Calculators	• Talking calculators • Computerized calculating feature
• Materials to make content-related games (e.g., markers, game boards, dice) • CD game	• Interactive content-related game on Internet

advisable to start out simply and add a new technology tool or program one step at a time. Consequently, the "higher-tech" classroom may take some time to develop. Technology tools will be discussed in greater detail throughout the rest of the text.

If resources are scarce, look for local, state, and federal grant sources. Many communities have educational foundation grants. Some businesses and civic organizations will also consider school requests in writing for specific materials or tools. Parent teacher organizations can also be good contacts. Websites such as http://www.donorschoose.com provide teachers with many resources. Sometimes just identifying your needs and asking is all that it takes.

Methods

The third curricular component of Universal Design for Learning is methods. Once the compass is set toward the defined goals/big ideas and materials/resources are considered, the teacher must plan curricular methods that are flexible and diverse to provide a variety of learning experiences with extensions and supports to meet the demands of all students in the class. Providing models, examples, nonexamples, and multiple opportunities to practice with appropriate supports is characteristic of a UDL approach. Think back to the multiple intelligences and learning preferences information in Chapter 8. Figure 10.5 suggests the range of possible strengths and interests any given group of learners in one space may have. If a variety of visual, auditory, tactile, and kinesthetic activities are built into at least some of the instructional time, the chances of engaging all learners increases. Effective teachers plan activities that build on their learners' areas of strengths while also working on areas of need.

To activate the recognition networks of diverse learners, presentations of content material must be varied. Thinking as high tech as possible is a good way to begin, simply because the higher the technology, the greater the potential to reach

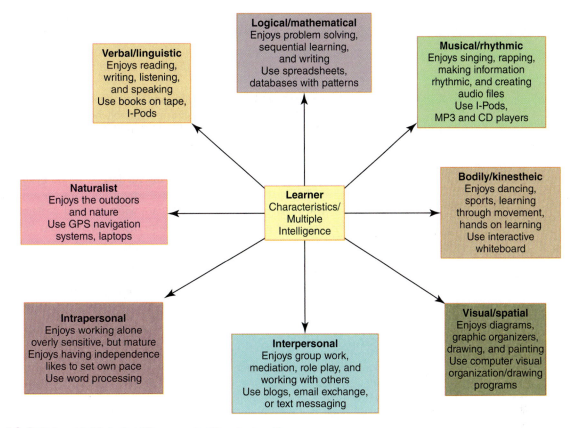

Figure 10.5 Using Multiple Intelligences to Plan Instruction

a broader cross section of diverse learners. Can content material be presented through multimedia? Can oral presentations be paired with visuals (e.g., Power-Point, text projected on a screen)? Perhaps digitized text with text-to-speech and/or different display features can be available. Videos, online simulations, electronic whiteboard activities, and translated text are other technology options. If these materials aren't available, then move on to low-tech options.

Provide a graphic organizer or outline to accompany an oral presentation that can later be used as a study guide. Write keywords on a note card, the overhead, or on a chart and add visual examples with definitions. The challenge is to present the content to a wide range of learners in multiple ways without compromising the learning goal (Hitchcock et al., 2002). Keep in mind that print and the spoken word are not necessarily accessible to all. Expand thinking to see the possibilities rather than viewing this as an overwhelming task. The more examples of a concept/idea that can be presented in different ways, the chances students have of grasping concepts and skills increase. Through the examples, the brain will be searching for those defining features of patterns and will begin to differentiate them. Think about how driving feels when you come to a new place. At first, the routes feel strange and foreign; however, after several practice runs, the brain begins to detect the patterns of a street system and, eventually the driver's internal navigation system becomes more automatic.

To activate the different strategic networks of a diverse student population, there must also be flexible and varied response options. High-tech responses may include creating multimedia presentations, designing WebQuests, generating and analyzing a spreadsheet, or word processing an essay. Low-tech options might include response choices as matching, pointing, answering multiple choice or short answer questions, or building a model.

In planning methodology, offer diverse pathways to activate affective learner networks through flexible, multiple ways to engage students in learning. High-tech options might include using interactive software programs, computerized games with immediate feedback, or a WebQuest. Low-tech options might include using self-checking materials, interacting directly with a teacher or peer, or working through content using a graphic organizer that uses text or pictures. Some students with behavioral needs may need an extrinsic reward system to remain engaged. Contracts or point systems might be incorporated to meet their needs (Jackson, Harper, & Jackson, 2001).

Once goals and objectives, learner needs, and activities for multiple means of representation, expression, and engagement are established, they can easily be aligned in a simple table format. Color coding the multiple means may be helpful when first attempting this task. Once again, technology tools makes these tasks easier for teachers as well as students. Table 10.4 offers a preplanning example of such an organizational tool applied to a primary unit of instruction on dental health.

Be sure to periodically refer back to individual education plans for any academic adaptations that will need to be made. Collaborate with involved parents and specialists for more ideas. For example, a student who has low vision may benefit from an enlarged font on a customized background color. For the student who can't decode, books on tape may be recommended. For the nonfluent reader, choral or duet reading might be a support while he/she builds fluency. For a student who is learning English, words may need translation. For a student with autism, the classroom may need to include more visual structures (i.e., pictures, symbols).

Assessment

Assessment is the fourth component in accessing the general curriculum through Universal Design for Learning. As shown in Chapter 9, academic assessment is a large part of today's learning environment as we move toward more inclusive school communities and accountability for all students. The IDEA 2004 and NCLB place great emphasis on assessment.

Assessment must continually be directly linked to learning goals to measure learning progress. It must be ongoing and accurate in order to reach the goal (Hitchcock et al., 2002). Like the driver on the road trip, teachers must stop periodically to check the map/plan, adapt for any detours/individual needs, refuel, and check the equipment/materials in order to reach the final destination (goal).

Table 10.4	Linking Multiple Means to Objectives: Healthful Living		
	Multiple Means of Representation	**Multiple Means of Engagement**	**Multiple Means of Expression**
Standards/Objectives:			
1.01—Describe influences on health, e.g., food, rest, exercise, hygiene/cleanliness.	• Discussion/KWL • Questioning • Video clip • Use manipulatives and multisensory demonstrations • Read aloud	• Use manipulatives	Allow oral presentation and/or physical demonstration, writing, drawing
3.08—Brush teeth daily and do not share toothbrush.	• Read aloud • Discussion • Questioning • Use pictures and visuals	• Role playing • Use manipulatives	Allow oral presentation and/or physical demonstration (perform desired skills); may be videotaped
Lesson Objectives:			
The students will identify the parts of the mouth correctly on the mouth model with four out of four attempts.	• Use picture and visuals • Discussion • Questioning	• Cooperative learning • Manipulatives	Oral, physical, writing, drawing, models, and manipulatives
The students will identify correctly four healthy snacks out of an assortment on four out of four occasions.	• Use multiple senses and manipulatives • Discussion • Questioning	• Cooperative learning • Manipulatives	Models, manipulatives, physical, oral, writing, drawing

Source: Jennifer Palumbo, Special Educator and North Carolina Teaching Fellow, Brier Creek Elementary School, Raleigh, North Carolina.

Traditionally, assessments have not been accessible to all students in the general curriculum. The outcome of the assessment is usually written to a specific content goal and doesn't make adjustments for difficulties that students might have in areas such as decoding, visual acuity, attention, writing, motivation, or cultural background (Thompson, Johnstone, & Thurlow, 2002). Even commonly used testing accommodations just scratch the surface (Rose et al., 2005). Extra time, for example, doesn't help the student who cannot begin to organize his/her thoughts to respond to a writing prompt. When students can't decode print well, they can't pass the entire reading test even though their comprehension skills may be much higher.

Remember that effective assessment helps each teacher find the appropriate instructional level for each student. It looks at the child as a whole and involves many formal and informal methods. Teachers assess children multiple times each day as they continually check for understanding and determine if it is time to move ahead or if extra time needs to be spent developing a concept. Proper assessment maximizes time for teaching and learning.

A helpful way to see this important connection is to take unit and lesson plan organizers and insert a column next to the learning goals/objectives for assessment. This will remind the teacher that assessment is directly linked to learning goals and is ongoing. Assessment is the evidence (product) that proves students achieved or did not achieve the learning goals. Table 10.5 illustrates this simple yet effective practice.

Refer back to Chapter 8 for various types of assessment formats. Remember that both the product and the process can be considered in assessment. If you are using a process as assessment, be sure to have some type of checklist or rubric available for data assessment.

Table 10.5	Linking Assessment to Learning Goals/Objectives
Learning Goals/Objectives:	**Assessment Link**
To identify core vocabulary	Match definition with word through print, pictures, verbal response, or pointing
To increase reading fluency	Running record, graph of timed passage reading
To explain cause/effect of . . .	Completed graphic organizer with written or verbal explanation

The UDL Lesson Plan

The next step in academic planning is to actually design the lesson itself. A regular lesson plan can be tailored to address diverse learner needs. Table 10.6 shows how the elements of a typical lesson plan can be aligned with a UDL approach. First, the lesson objective and assessment are stated and linked. Next, lesson elements are aligned with procedures. Possible barriers to student learning are added and paired with flexible methods. Materials to increase access and engagement are mapped out. Color coding according to UDL elements helps the teacher see that each is addressed. The WWW Resources box lists websites with examples of UDL lesson plans and additional tips for building effective lessons using this approach.

Just as on the road trip, as you periodically assess your timing, maps, and gauges, you can likely avoid rush-hour traffic, decrease your chances of getting lost, and not run out of gas! You can get where you're going on time and maybe even have some time to spare.

Designing Physical Learning Environments

Considerable time has been spent in this chapter planning for accessible academic learning. The rest of the chapter will focus on two other important elements that must also be considered in the initial planning—physical and social aspects. Just

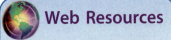

Web Resources

To link to UDL planning websites and more, go to this text's companion site, **http://www.academic.cengage.com/education/Gargiulo.**

Table 10.6	Lesson Planning Elements with UDL Components

Lesson Objective (Goal): Aligned with Standard Course of Study

Lesson Assessment: Directly linked to lesson objective; must be observable/measurable

Lesson Element	UDL Procedure & Materials	Possible Barriers to Learning	UDL Methods
Anticipatory Set • Introduction • Student "hook" • Activate prior knowledge	**Focus & Review** • Statement of Objective/Agenda • Provide advance organizer (outline, graphic organizer) • Set up thinking pattern *Materials:* pencil/paper, overhead, chart paper, video clip, objects, pictures, books, Internet links to background material, PowerPoint, SmartBoard	If a student: • calls out or is disruptive • has attention or motivational challenges • lacks background knowledge • has organizational challenges • needs greater academic challenge	• Use a focus & behavior expectations chart • Write objective on chalkboard or chart • Provide background materials • Provide outline, directions, procedures • Provide plan and materials for self-study (extension)
Teacher Input • Direct instruction • Presentation of content accurately and clearly • Ask relevant questions	• Introduce the problem for the lesson and give the students a "work order" for the lesson • Provide examples and nonexamples • Introduce/review essential vocabulary • Allow time to brainstorm individually • Share with a partner • Share with whole group *Materials:* overhead, PowerPoint, dry erase board, record using iPods, electronic translation, personal interpreter, communication board, electronic dictionaries	• has language challenge • needs to hear directions/steps repeatedly • has low vision • has hearing impairment • needs social interaction	• Interpret reading/translation available as needed/critical vocabulary is on word cards and defined • Provide recorded or hard copy set of directions/steps if needed • Enlarge font • Seat student near teacher • Plan for peer interaction
Guided Practice • Activity must be relevant to objective • Activities must be observable	• Define student roles and responsibilities • Provide directions for activity/task and implement together • Provide choices within activities • Teacher monitors closely • Teacher provides feedback *Materials:* chalkboard, dry erase boards, manipulatives, pencil/paper, computer, SmartBoard, interactive technology program	• can't attend or remember • gives up easily • prefers tactile/kinesthetic learning modality • student masters objective easily	• Provide visual/audio recorded activity directions for easy, frequent reference • Provide frequent feedback • Build in hands-on and movement opportunities • Build in extension activities
Independent Practice • Involves everyone • Relevant, directly related to lesson • Observable • Students work on products	• Cooperative learning or individual activities • Activity centers • Product can be in-class or for homework (or both) • Refer to individual assessment method *Materials:* paper/pencil, chart paper/markers, manipulatives, word processor, oral discussion, PowerPoint, spell checkers, tape recorders, iPods, drawing tools	• has difficulty working in group or with certain other students • has difficulty writing or spelling • has difficulty transitioning • needs concrete representation • needs immediate feedback to stay on task • continues to need help with organization	• Allow students to work alone • Group students, post roles on chart/computer • Pair students with different strengths/needs to complement each other • Give a transitional signal/cue/timer before shifting to a new activity or lesson part • Provide manipulatives, multisensory activities to make product • Provide self-checking materials • Student completes task checklist
Closure/Evaluation • Did students meet the lesson objective? • What adaptations need to be made for next time?	• What did students learn? • May share products • Questioning with checklist *Materials:* PowerPoint, projector, SmartBoard, display materials	• needs behavior plan	• Checked behavior or task focus/organization card • Oral discussion • Completed products with assessment tool

as on the road trip, the destination is determined and the itinerary with its routes, detours, and travel schedule is initially planned. This alone, however, is not enough. Attention must also be given to ensuring the vehicle and other equipment is ready. Planning for the social needs of the travelers is also important.

Schools that embrace the UDL philosophy will likely strive for clearly defined, orderly space that can be accessed by all. Imagine the ideal classroom. This classroom welcomes students with open and adaptable space, flexible furnishings, organized materials, and lots of natural light. Individualized heating and cooling controls are in every room (Rydeem, 1999). Chairs, desks, bookcases, windows, and doors are sized properly, safe, and flexible. Traffic patterns run smoothly, work areas are balanced so they don't get too crowded, and teachers can see students at all times. Students know where to find and return materials. Physical arrangements are flexible enough so that furniture can easily be rearranged for direct instruction, group work, independent work, floor work, and other types of activity. Teachers and students can access technologies with the click of a switch. All students have an individual space at a table or desk and a cubicle, bin, or a locker for personal items. All students have easy access to low- and high-tech materials for presentation, engagement, and response. Just as with academic planning, if you consider the strengths and needs of the learners in the design of your physical space, the payoffs can be great.

Physical Environment Considerations

We know, however, that teachers do not always walk into ideal spaces. Teachers need to assess spaces for teaching and learning and decide what they can and cannot change while determining strengths and needs of the physical setting. Keep in mind that administrators and school leaders may have long-term plans for building and technology improvements, so it is important to stay in communication with the administration or school improvement team about plans that may physically alter the environment.

Just as students come in all different sizes and shapes, they also come with various physical and sensory needs—some have glasses, hearing aids, or cochlear implants. Others may be dealing with attention deficit, asthma, motor, or other challenges. A basic design of the physical setting maximized to meet learner needs can be drawn out on paper or on the computer. It might also be helpful to take everything out of the space and thoughtfully replace only what is needed according to form and function. Physically trying out some of the seats and viewing the positioning of boards and screens from a student's perspective is also helpful. Just as units change throughout the year, physical arrangements can be reassessed and adjusted as needed.

Revisiting the basic principles of universal design in architecture can help assess the classroom setting using the **ACCESS** strategy presented in Figure 10.6. A short discussion of these elements follows with suggestions.

First of all, classroom design needs to be *applicable* to every learner. Having age-appropriate materials available that promote learning in units being taught (e.g., concrete objects, lab materials, props, pictures) will not only help lessons come alive but will also widen the opportunities students in the class have to participate. Having centers, study areas, and labs are just some examples of ways to set up applicable materials. Some teachers set a room or part of a room up around unit themes—a room can become a rain forest, a Greek theatre, or a restaurant in Spain. Rotate and store materials as units change for variety. On a related note, using video, multimedia, and/or virtual simulations, almost any environment can be created electronically to connect a unit to the real world. Center instruction in the real world around the student.

Keeping materials out that will be used frequently and storing the rest will not only help reduce clutter but will also help keep up the teaching pace because time is not lost looking for things.

Plants, flowers, and water in the classroom can also be visual/tactile assets. Fish tanks and small water fountains (designed for relaxation) can provide a calming

Applicable—Is the classroom design useful to everyone? Do all students have the same opportunities to access learning? Is it learner centered and matched to learner needs?

Capability—Is the design flexible? Does it offer choices? Does it easily change to meet the needs of learners with a variety of learning styles, sensory demands, and prerequisite skills? Does it minimize the physical effort needed to access learning?

Clarity—Are the materials/tools simple enough that all learners can understand how they function regardless of student's language skills, sensory needs, and background knowledge? Is needed information straightforward and predictable?

Expression—Does the room design communicate needed information to all users regardless of the conditions of the space or the sensory needs of the student?

Safety—Are there any hazards even with accidental use or movement?

Size and Space—Is furniture/material in proportion and approachable to users? Are materials/technologies within reach of all students and can they be manipulated?

Figure 10.6 ACCESS to the Physical Environment

environment. Some researchers contend that humans need this connection to nature to fully develop mental well-being (Flannery, 2005). Plants, water, and animals can all also offer lessons in patience and observation. Perhaps these universal elements can help center and connect diverse learners because all people can all relate to them.

Next, classroom design must be *capable* of changing as needed. Having special physical and sensory supports in place for students who need them can ease their discomfort when coming into a new situation and also saves time that otherwise might be spent "retrofitting" the room design/arrangement. For example, having different types of available seating and cushions can help. Some students with

Cengage Learning/Wadsworth

Comfortable environments can increase engagement and motivation for students of all ages.

Universal Design for Learning in the Classroom

Establishing a physical learning environment that responds to students' individual strengths, needs, and learning styles is essential. Without such an environment, the students are not prepared to attend to instruction and/or retain information. A goal of Universal Design for Learning is to remove barriers to learning. Therefore, having a classroom learning environment that optimizes student attention, increases focus to the tasks at hand, and allows students to feel safe and comfortable in their surroundings, is one way to eliminate barriers to learning before instruction even begins. Just as UDL emphasizes the need to utilize multiple approaches to meet the needs of diverse learners, learning climates should be established with multiple components that are designed to address the varied strengths, needs, and learning styles of the students. With UDL in mind, I developed F.O.C.U.S., "Fine-tuning of Concentration Utilizing Senses," and my portable teaching unit at Richard L. Sanders School in Pinellas County, Florida went from "pit to palace." I designed F.O.C.U.S. to use saturation of the senses by distracting students' senses in a positive manner, thereby allowing students to concentrate on instruction. As a teacher of students with severe emotional disturbances (SED), I know it was important to prepare my learning environment to be as calming as possible, while at the same time creating an environment that promotes attention to instruction. Therefore I focus on multisensory means of implementing this ideal learning environment. For the sense of sight, I utilize: calming colors of blues and greens wherever possible; natural light versus fluorescent lighting; furniture arrangement that is pleasing to the eye (e.g. round tables instead of numerous small, square desks), and a fish aquarium. For the sense of smell, I use: fresh flowers and aroma therapy scents of grapefruit and lavender (since these scents do not typically affect students' allergies). For the sense of taste, I have mints for the students. For the sense of touch: I provide hand fidgets for the students (i.e. stress balls, weight grips, and putty) and comfortable seating options for the students (i.e. sitting on balls instead of chairs, and having bean bag chairs and alternative seating in the independent reading areas). For the sense of hearing: I play unfamiliar classical music with nature sounds at a low level in the background; and have water fountains that bubble with falling water sounds. It is important to note that all of my classroom learning environment items were either donated by local community businesses or obtained with grant funds. The results of this classroom learning environment have proved to be most effective. Prior to having this classroom set-up (i.e. having a "typical" classroom layout with standard desks set in rows), I had numerous office referrals for behavior disruptions on a weekly basis. However, from the onset of this UDL approach to my classroom learning environment my behavior referrals to the office dropped to almost being non-existent! In addition, 95% of my students demonstrated significant academic improvement, and over 1/3 of my students increased their academic performance by more than two grade levels in one school year.

Dr. Karen S. Voytecki
Clarissa Hug Teacher of the Year 2001
Assistant Professor of Special Education
East Carolina University

sensory difficulties and/or ADHD report that sitting on a rubber seat or ball chair (after learning the proper sitting form) helps them to better focus on their work (Voytecki, Smith-Canter, & Floyd, 2006). Collaboration with an occupational therapist can help with this.

Students with kinesthetic needs may benefit from standing up and/or moving while working. Allowances for movement to different types of seating in the room (e.g., mats, bean bag chairs, stools, cushioned chairs) may help make students more comfortable and break up tasks, likely increasing learning motivation. Offer choices, when possible, that minimize the physical effort needed by students to access learning (unless, of course, the goal is to increase physical effort). Having an enlarged keyboard-to-computer touch screen, for example, can reduce fatigue for a student with motor difficulties.

Seating arrangements that can be easily repositioned also increase flexibility in accommodating diverse learners. There may be times when you need desks in a more traditional setup in rows, particularly when you are introducing new material (Carbonne, 2001). At other times, small groupings of desks or tables will work well for collaborative student work or for students needing more-specific direct instruction and guided practice. Spaces for tutoring and assessment also need to be considered. Quiet spaces for students to work alone may be needed.

In settings for any age, a U-shaped or circle-style arrangement of desks, tables, and chairs increases teacher and student access to every learner. This arrangement also works well for small group direct instruction. Research suggests that rounded corners and circular arrangements often work best for diverse learners because they are inviting, calming, and stress reducing (Rogers, 2001).

Web Resources

For more information on models of classroom seating and room arrangement, go to this text's companion website, **http://www .academic.cengage.com/ education/Gargiulo.**

Remember that ample space is needed for students in wheelchairs, for students doing specialized academic work (from learning centers to labs), and for technology users. To offer even greater flexibility, a basket of clipboards, small whiteboards, and/or portable keyboards are handy for students who want to work away from a desk or even outside.

Consider *clarity* in classroom design next. All learners should be able to use the equipment in a room or at least understand how it is used. It might be that switches or computer keys are color coded or labeled. Simple instruction lists (pictorial, written, or audio) may be provided with a learning tool or piece of equipment. Just as an automobile manual includes numbered steps and pictures, so might classroom equipment. For some students, enlarged keyboards help them see and hit the keys more accurately. Putting a star sticker on the "Enter" key might help a younger students just learning to use a computer.

Planning for maintaining a clean, clear environment can help students who are visually sensitive to focus on what is important in lesson activities. An awareness of lighting and glare reduction is needed. Some students find florescent lighting distracting and perform better when natural light and lamps are an option.

Attention to noise levels is equally important to maximize focusing for students with auditory sensitivity. Providing earphones for students who need to hear recorded text and/or directions can help reduce noise. Having a way of amplifying sounds with a small microphone can also be helpful in focusing attention to a speaker. Sometimes music is helpful in calming students and faster music can liven the pace. Some students, however, may not benefit from background music. Teachers must know their learners.

Next, classrooms designed with the student in mind *express* the needed information to all users. Using graphics with large lettering, high-contrast colors, user-friendly fonts (and even possibly Braille and/or sign language) in the classroom for orientation, directions, timetables, and other information can help many learners access class information. Post these on computers, walls, and/or the board. If this information is initially created on the computer, it is easier to adapt for language, style, size, color, and more. In addition, if a student with a language, physical, or

Cengage Learning/Wadsworth

Providing earphones with technology allows students to work with different materials at an adjustable pace while keeping classroom noise manageable.

sensory need comes along, the file can be opened and adjusted. Having audio directions on tape, iPods, or MP3 players and visual direction on cards, slides, or videotape can also help. Universal adaptations made for students with physical and sensory needs will likely help many more students in the classroom access learning.

Using color coding to organize equipment, materials, and areas in the room can be helpful for diverse learners. Materials can be color coded by subject, by use, and/ or by days or weeks. Part of the room can be color coded and matching color of dots used for transitions.

If you have a choice, using calming colors such as green and blue can help communicate a sense of tranquility in a room and help students stay focused. If painting is not an option, these colors can be used on dividers, portable screens, study carrels, or any fabric/paper used to cover walls or windows. Certain colors tend to reduce eyestrain and increase the amount and quality of work done. Monotone environments tend to be more stressful, promoting anxiety and irritability (Kennedy, 2005).

Younger children often perform better with the more-stimulating colors (red, yellow, orange), and older students tend to respond better with blues and greens (Kennedy, 2005). Knowing your students and their preferences can help you determine their emotional and physiological needs.

Providing physical models up front of notebooks, completed projects, and other products students will work on is very helpful. Allow students to see what a successful product might look like. Again, adding simple directions in multiple formats will help students who need to see or hear the directions more than once.

Classroom design must consider *safety*. Anticipate any possible hazards to students with accidental use or movement. Crowded, cluttered, unstable space may cause materials and equipment to get knocked over. Survey your space to make sure electrical cords are tucked away to avoid tripping and that outlets are not overloaded. Avoid sharp corners and rough wood that may splinter. Be sure any rugs are secured to avoid tripping. During science lab, provide safety glasses as needed.

Space for security drills is also important, where the group can safely congregate away from doors and windows in case of such an emergency.

Size and space are the final considerations in the ACCESS mnemonic for the physical environment. Seats need to be the right size and ergonomically correct, allowing for correct positioning of arms and feet during tasks that require upright seating. Supports for positioning feet at the correct angle can help some learners. All materials/technologies need to be within the learner's reach. Tables, desks, chairs, and workstations can be adjusted in height to save time and effort down the road. If possible, having a desk or two with a tilted or flip top might help a student with a specific writing need to position his/her work.

Note where the electrical outlets and network connections are in your classroom. Whether you use an overhead projector or electronic whiteboard, you need to be near electrical outlets and to allow for adequate distance for display. Technologies for student use, such as earphones, will also need similar access to plugs and other connections. Battery chargers may need to be close by.

Provide adults who help in the classroom clearly defined working spaces with appropriately sized furniture, if possible, to foster respect, inclusiveness, and a collaborative spirit.

Table 10.7 offers an overview of possible low- and high-tech ideas for physical and equipment resources one might consider in creating a UDL classroom. Although it may sometimes be overlooked in classrooms, assessment of the physical environment may offer valuable teaching and learning solutions. Things like flickering lights, tables that wobble, too much noise, too little noise, and visual clutter can interfere with learning.

Just as on the road trip, travelers feel better when the car is washed and things are neatly packed and can be found easily. Maps, itineraries, and CDs are organized, and cell phone battery chargers are in the console. Car seats/booster seats allow small

Table 10.7	Examples of Physical Materials/Resources in a UDL Classroom
Low Tech	**High Tech**
• Alternative seating (bean bags, cushions, pillows) • Adjustable seating, ball chair • Box for foot rest • Desks, tables that can move • Adjustable desks, tables, kidney-shaped tables	• Ergonomic chairs, motorized wheelchairs • Tables/work spaces designed to maximize space and flexibility (with built-in technologies)
• Natural light • Lamps • Blinds on windows, fans	• Skylights • Temperature control in room • Energy-efficient windows, electric shading devices, electric lighting that dims as natural light increases
• Whiteboard(s)/Chalkboards	• Overhead projector • Electronic whiteboards
• Posters with large print, essential print/visuals • Earplugs • Volume-control switches • Pencil grips/variety of writing tools/highlighters • Different color paper to help with contrast • Colored overlays for reading • Clipboards	• Large font on posted material • Scanned/magnified documents • Headphones • Microphones, amplification • Electronic highlighting feature on a computer screen • Changing background color on computer or PDA screen • Portable keyboards, portable tape recorder • iPod
• Plants, water	• Aquarium with electric filter, motorized waterfall

children to look out windows. Seats recline when passengers need to rest. Pockets on the back of the front seat can make toys, books, and even DVDs accessible for entertainment. Having extra oil, a jack, and a spare tire can save a lot of headaches.

So far our journey has taken us through planning the academic and physical designs of teaching and learning. Our last design destination will be the social/affective element of UDL. This element is as important as the academic and physical ones. It may be argued that it is the most critical.

Designing Social Learning Environments

When you are taking a road trip, you usually know who your traveling companions are. You may know their strengths, needs, likes, and differences. If not, you will soon find out! If you are traveling with children, you know you will definitely need to preplan to keep them occupied and in relatively good spirits by having some ground rules and materials. Even travel with a spouse or good friend requires some prior planning to coordinate the packing, driving schedule, food and rest breaks, and types of entertainment (e.g., music, games, books). It requires skill in keeping exchanges about directions, speed, and other topics level headed, especially when people get tired and road conditions worsen. You also know that your own enthusiasm and positive outlook throughout the trip will be important to its overall success. Always keep the destination of the trip in mind. Chart progress toward the goal to keep the motivation up.

How a teacher sets up the social environment in a classroom is also critical to reaching goals. Even if a teacher has the best lesson plans, ideal physical arrangements, and the most up-to-date technology, he/she will not succeed without effective classroom management and positive community-building skills. The social environment will need specific attention. All students will need to feel safe, valued, and respected. A teacher's enthusiasm for learning and caring attitude will influence everything he or she does. Students will need to feel free to take learning risks without a fear of failure or ridicule.

As you will recall from Chapter 7, once learners construct knowledge and concepts from the content, it is often the social side of learning that takes many students to higher levels of thinking. By setting goals, connecting to student interests, providing multiple ways students can use their strengths, and ensuring accessibility, a passion for learning may be sparked. The collaboration, interactivity, and assessment with feedback that UDL advocates can also increase engagement as teachers and students view each other in their areas of strength and see the value in unique individual contributions.

ACCESS to the Social Environment

The mnemonic ACCESS has once again been adapted to show how UDL components can assist the teacher in designing a positive classroom social environment that can work for almost all learners (see Figure 10.7).

First of all, the social environment must be *applicable* or useful to all learners for access from the start. By knowing the learner, instructional space can reflect student interests and culture through displays, discussions, and materials. Learners can access a needed language translation or other communication/learning tool to receive content and social information. Students of all races and gender generally like to have specific class and school responsibilities to maintain a sense of belonging. These can be assigned on a rotating basis. Provide role models and mentors as needed to help foster equity and to make every learner in your classroom feel valued and included (Salend, 2008). These models might be peers or other adults in the school community. Remember that for some students, the school and class environment may provide the most stable, consistent, and positive part of a day.

Applicable—Is the social environment useful and accessible to everyone? Is it learner centered? Does it appreciate and celebrate student differences?

Capability—Is the social design flexible? Does it easily change to meet the needs of learners with a variety of learning preferences and needs? Does it offer choices? Can the pace be adjusted?

Clarity—Is it simple enough that all learners can understand how it functions regardless of their language, experience, and background knowledge? Are the rules and procedures communicated clearly?

Expression—Does the social plan communicate needed information to all users regardless of his/her needs? Does everyone know what to do? Is it welcoming, inclusive, and enthusiastic? Are high expectations communicated to all learners? Is feedback specific and ongoing? Is purposeful communication between students as well as students and teachers planned?

Safety—Is the environment a safe place to take risks? Is there tolerance for error? Is sarcasm avoided? Are Internet social networks safe?

Size and Space for approach—Is the class and/or group size manageable? Are there plans for transitions? Is there flexible grouping of students?

Figure 10.7 ACCESS to the Social Environment

Mentors can give individual students needed academic and social/emotional support.

Integrating technology tools increases the usefulness and accessibility of a UDL environment. For example, Bauer and Ulrich (2002) found that personal digital assistants (PDAs) increased participation for students with disabilities in an inclusive sixth-grade classroom. Students downloaded spelling checkers and dictionaries to help them with their work. They received study guides, outlines, and class notes sent from the teacher. They "beamed" classmates to share work and homework, fostering collaboration. Students recorded points on their personal behavior plans in addition to recording their grades and keeping track of assignments.

To access social environments, the *capacity* to change and adjust must be built into a structure for all learners. Socializing is difficult for many learners with and without disabilities. Some students need help generating and sustaining conversations. Other students may not know when to stop talking and listen. Some have difficulty reading body language. Some are dealing with bullying. Some need to work at a different pace. As we prepare our future workforce, effective social skills will be critical to everyone's success.

Offering choices can work for students who need a feeling of control in their learning or have limited options for acquiring information, processing it, and producing results. Because UDL has built-in choice options, students can choose, for example, between working the math problems out on the board or on a computer software program. The same objective is met but there is a choice in the methods of engagement and response.

Grouping students in different ways is also important. Plans need to build in flexible student grouping arrangements so they have multiple opportunities to interact and learn from each other. Groups need to change up depending on the purpose. Sometimes, for example, students may be grouped based on a specific skill in math or reading that needs extra practice. Other times, groups may be constructed heterogeneously to solve an authentic learning problem related to a big idea in a content area. Adding a technology component into group work (video- and computer-based) expands opportunities for accessibility and can increase motivation. Remember that each student brings his/her own skill sets to the group. Try to spread out the "leaders" so they are not always in the same group. Ensure that the environment allows for such flexible grouping.

Cengage Learning/Wadsworth

The next step using the ACCESS mnemonic is *clarity*. Beginning teachers often report that classroom management is the most difficult challenge they face (Martin, 2004). Students with diverse needs may present social challenges that differ from the "norm." Try to remember that these students may learn differently and often need to be directly taught social skills. Many of them really don't know what "appropriate" behavior is. However, if expectations are high and rules, procedures, directions, and schedules are simple, clear, and consistent, most students can function cooperatively in the school community. The rules (usually three to five), procedures, and routines will need to be modeled and rehearsed often, especially when first presented. Keep them simple and practice them in all the school settings that apply to help with transfer and generalization. Just as in academic instruction, the social skills instruction will need to be structured and scaffolded for some students. Time spent up front doing this will pay off the whole year.

Plan to catch students modeling correct behaviors and praise them verbally and visually. Perhaps record positive behaviors on a card or chart. A word of caution: Some learners do not like to be praised in front of others. When this is the case, a positive sticky note on the desk, a private verbal comment, or a nonverbal chart entry may be effective. Again, time invested up front learning what works for your students will be worth it.

To access the social environment, the plan must attend to the *expression* of needed information to all users regardless of learner needs. Just as with academics, begin by communicating the overall social goal. All learners want to know what they are working for, why it is important for them, and how they will arrive at the goal. Keep the overall objective and the lesson objective up front and clear. Having the objectives visually displayed and referred to at the start of each lesson sets the stage for success. It may also be helpful to incorporate a social skills condition into the daily objective. For example, "Today we will work *in teams* to compare and contrast ecosystems."

All teachers want a high rate of student success. Research shows that the rate of success with students increases when they understand material that is presented and are then asked to engage in work at just the right difficulty level (Mercer & Mercer, 2005). Feedback received in a timely manner can also move them forward. Offer activities with which students can be successful and then take it up a notch. Helping students chart their own progress and set goals is also motivating. Goal setting and self-monitoring will be addressed in more detail in future chapters.

Using a few carefully chosen words for rules and directions can help a student who struggles with language, language processing, or attention. Having too many words can be a barrier for a student challenged this way. Pair the written rules with visuals when possible. Adding pictures and gestures for students who struggle with language can provide access. Other students who simply process information better visually will benefit from pairing the visual with the auditory. Bulleted lists and numbered rules and steps for procedures aid comprehension. Providing time to restate or show that directions are understood with a group or peer can also be helpful.

Disney Teacher of the Year, Ron Clark, describes *The Essential 55* procedures that helped him shape an unruly class of fifth graders in a New York City inner-city school into a model class (Clark, 2003). One example he gives is having students thank the people by name who serve them in the school—such as the cafeteria workers. This not only helps the student develop appropriate social skills but also tends to increase the number of positive responses that students receive from multiple adults within the school community.

Technology can be used to record rules, procedures, schedules, and routines and played back as needed. Software programs can be installed that offer simulations of different learning/social situations, and students can choose options and see consequences of their choices. Consider making videotapes or DVDs of classroom rules, procedures, and routines with students and have them available for viewing as needed. Let students have some control of the social "road map" so they can learn how to drive and navigate their own learning.

A lot of this information needs to be communicated to parents/families. Different folder/notebook systems can work for this. Having a class website works even better if everyone has access to a computer. Posting daily (and long-term) objectives, procedures, and homework assignments in consistent places keeps the communication flowing.

Planning for *safety* in the learning environment is another step in accessing the social side of learning. The environment must be a safe place to take risks without fear of ridicule, sarcasm, or teasing. A sense of humor can serve a teacher well, but avoid sarcasm. Some students will take it literally and personally. This may cause them to retreat socially and not take future risks.

Some students arrive at school hungry and tired; others are already angry or upset by something that happened at home or on the bus. If students are initially greeted at the door, a teacher can usually tell right away if a student has had a difficult morning/day and can run interference, thus preventing a negative outcome (Wong & Wong, 1998). Providing some quiet time away may also help a student regain some control. Remember that providing personal space for belongings and work is also important.

Mistakes should be viewed as opportunities to grow and learn. When students make academic or social mistakes, offer specific, corrective feedback. If there are multiple errors, choose the most critical skill or concept to target (Kauffman, Mostert, Trent, & Pullen, 2006). Let the student know what behavior/skill that will be. If it is a behavior, sometimes the learner isn't even aware that what he/she is doing is disruptive to learning. Effective teachers are student behavior coaches and encouragers.

Once again, the power of technology, including the Internet, connects our students with the outside world. It can provide real-life examples help learners working at the concrete level. Care, however, must be taken to monitor work on Internet sites. Schools will generally block questionable sites but the teacher must still watch. With careful choosing, teachers can also access virtual stories and simulations that teach students what to do in social situations. Multimedia and innovative software abound that make learning come alive through presentations given by a diverse set of people and through animation.

Students may also benefit from using dialogue journals, e-mail, or blogs with peers, teachers, or mentors. Research suggests such journaling provides an outlet for students with emotional/behavioral needs to express themselves with a caring adult. The adult can offer support and influence social skills and behaviors. It can strengthen the teacher-student relationship. Sometimes it provides the adult attention that a learner needs (Regan, 2003; Tobin, 1998). Once again, make sure social networking sites accessed are safe, appropriate language is used, and professionalism is evident.

The final step in accessing the social learning environment considers *size* and *space*. Sometimes something as simple as changing a seat can make a difference. For example, if a student who is off task is placed in a spot you can monitor easily, negative behaviors may decrease. Strategically grouping a student who is reading two grade levels below his/her peers may help him/her avoid being ridiculed. Have the student sit near a student or students who can compliment his/her skills. Paired with a reader, perhaps he/she can assist, in turn, with the illustrations or the oral responses. Consider the personality types of students who are paired together and model how to respond to negative behaviors as you work together to turn them into positives. Remember that using books on tape, eBooks, or digitized text with a text-to-speech feature on the computer are other options you have to reduce frustration some students have with print.

Some students will need space to be alone and/or work quietly at different times. Some students will not want to participate in group work. Be flexible enough to at least compromise and allow some alone time. Using screens, partitions, or furniture to visually block off some quiet working spaces can help as long as students can be viewed.

Think, too, about planning for transitions within and between activities and spaces. Changing space can be difficult for some diverse learners. Provide some

Table 10.8	Suggestions for Transition Cues
Transition Cues for Elementary Students	**Transition Cues for All Students**
• Color-coded cards matched to centers • Line up by name (alphabetically) • Line up by color of clothing • Song • Cards with pictures or symbols of destination printed on them • Verbal cues given by other students (prearranged) • Line up by gender • Find names at destinations • Puppet prompt • Line up by birth month	• Bell/buzzer/timer/musical cue • Signal/gesture • Verbal cue • Lights blink • Dismiss by tables or rows • Color-coded folders or cards • Timetable on desk/planner/check-off schedule • Answer a flash card question and line up • List of names/pictures on chart or board (individual or groups) • Use transition words such as *first, second, next, last*

Source: Adapted from S. Rosenkoetter and S. Fowler, "Teaching Mainstreamed Children to Manage Daily Transitions," *Teaching Exceptional Children, 19*(1), 1986, pp. 20–23.

advanced warning ("In five minutes, we will be packing up"). Using timers or other signals for cues might also be helpful. Table 10.8 offers some suggested transition cues. Planning for transitions can also save valuable instructional time.

Technology can help with "space" needs. If you don't have space to set up the backdrop you want for an ocean unit, for example, you can take a virtual field trip to a beach or aquarium. If your space doesn't enough area for discussion, an electronic discussion board or chat room can be created. This may also allow students to work with other students and/or mentors in other spaces who are working in an advanced curriculum or in another language. Some examples of technology materials and resources that may enhance the affective side of learning can be found in Table 10.9.

Table 10.9	Technology Tools to Increase Access to Social Environments
Low Tech	**High Tech**
• Talking with others, letter writing • Rules, procedures, schedules posted on a chart and/or in a planner • Reflective journals • Role play of desired behavior • Posted positive slogans • Index cards for charting behavior • Class meetings • Group projects	• Telephones, e-mail, video conferencing, e-Pals, social networking websites (check for safety) • Recorded rules, procedures, schedules on an iPod, PDA, or DVD • Electronic journals, e-mail, or blogs • Video, DVD, virtual simulation of desired behavior • Posted electronic posters • Excel spreadsheet for charting behavior • E-mails, blogs, online discussion groups • Group PowerPoint, multimedia presentations

Positive Behavior Support (PBS) and UDL

In schools that embrace the principles of UDL, there is an emphasis on building community in a whole school from the start. Students are part of the decision-making process, procedures model equity, and all learners have a voice (Curry, 2003). Just as differentiated instruction principles fit comfortably with UDL principles, so does **positive behavior support** (PBS). PBS is a proactive, preventative approach to behavior with a growing research base. It identifies and supports effective, systematic schoolwide practices for desirable behavior up front. Everyone teaches, models, and demonstrates desired behaviors in a clear and consistent fashion. As a school, students are acknowledged and rewarded for appropriate behavior. Behavior errors are viewed as learning opportunities. They are identified, targeted, and corrected (Scott & Martinek, 2006). Data is collected and analyzed to guide decision making (e.g., time on task, number of office referrals, time and place). As positive behavior increases, academic achievement can improve significantly (Lassen, Steele, & Sailor, 2006).

In recent years, research in the field of behavioral studies has supported PBS (Sugai & Horner, 2005). PBS communicates high positive expectations and rewards those efforts from the start. With supportive administration, faculty, staff, and families in PBS schools use the same language and training in communicating behavioral expectations to students schoolwide. Parent collaboration and volunteerism at school are encouraged. Specific strategies and methods that further support PBS are presented in Chapter 14. These strategies will be particularly helpful for students who need more-intense interventions to be successful learners.

Using Adaptations to Support Universally Designed Learning Environments

Adaptations in instruction and assessment allow learning environments to become almost seamlessly functional to all students thanks to flexible, usable, and accessible learning tools. The space is learner centered, collaborative, and interactive. The curriculum is constructivist—it builds step by step. Because these flexible options are needed to make UDL work, it is important for teachers to be aware of the difference between the two types of adaptations—accommodations and modifications.

Accommodations

In Chapter 2 you learned about accommodation plans for students with special needs and were provided examples. Remember, an **accommodation** is "a service or support that is provided to help a student fully access the subject matter and instruction" (Nolet & McLaughlin, 2005, p. 84). This service/support allows the student to work on grade-level content with the same achievement expectations as everyone else. Accommodations are often physical or sensory in nature. Some obvious examples might be a student who has low vision and needs enlarged font and magnification devices to access print; a learner who is deaf might need a sign language interpreter. Less-obvious examples might be a student with auditory processing difficulties who needs visual frameworks or a student with ADHD who needs special seating, small group work, and extra opportunities to move. Teachers who provide multiple, flexible ways to present material, engage students, and allow for a variety of student responses will have many accommodations naturally built in to their lessons for a wide range of learners from the start. A word of caution: Be careful to not "give away" main points of lessons when you accommodate learning so that it is still challenging for all students, thus preserving access to learning (Hitchcock et al., 2002). We have a term in the field of special education called **learned helplessness**. Learned helplessness occurs when students depend on adults, peers, or material supports more than is necessary (Lerner, 2006). The overuse of personal aides and other assistance sometimes unintentionally promotes this in classrooms. Just the minimal amount of scaffolding to enable each student to push himself/herself to the next level of learning and become more independent is needed.

Accommodations are also found on plans for students who have "Section 504" plans. As discussed in Chapter 1, students with these accommodation plans have identified disabilities but are generally successful in the general curriculum when accommodations are made. These students can typically remain in the regular classroom setting without special education intervention.

Modifications

Modifications differ from accommodations because a modification actually *changes* the subject matter that is presented or alters the performance level by reducing the content to be learned. Modified curriculum changes the difficulty level of what is taught. For example, in a unit on communities, most students will be expected to compare and contrast two different geographical places. Most students will be expected to describe workers in both communities and explain how they are similar and different. A student with a modified curriculum and performance level might be asked to identify pictures of workers in his/her own community and give a short description of each. Modified curriculum generally keeps the theme/topic, but does change the curricular goals/objectives for that student. Therefore, it must be a team decision when it is used. However, sometimes the content as well as the expectation for the student are quite different compared to the larger group. For example, a student may be working on basic sight words and/or reading an unrelated book with a lower readability level while most of the class is reading independently on grade level or higher. Be careful not to modify more than is needed. Even when the content is the same, reducing the number of problems given for an assignment can also alter a performance outcome if it means the student doesn't have the chance to thoroughly work on a critical skill that he/she will be tested on later (Nolet & McLaughlin, 2005). Be careful that when you reduce the number of problems to be completed the ones chosen cover the scope of the objective.

Figure 10.8 offers a template to use as you think about adaptations that might be needed. As you reflect on the elements, consider academic, physical, and social environments as well as goals.

Modifications can take place in the regular classroom setting unless a student's individualized education program states otherwise. The impact of interacting with one's peers and having positive role models is typically found in the regular education classroom. In most cases, it is the natural setting for socialization. We are preparing all students to live and work independently in communities when they finish school. What better place to learn how to live and work together than in learning environments that embrace diversity?

Lesson Element:	Ideas:
Lesson Presentation—How can it best reach the learner? (Think: VAKT + Technology)	
Learner Engagement—How can the learner be active in the learning process? (Think VAKT + Technology)	
Learner Response—How can the learner tell or show you that he/she understands? (Think VAKT + Technology)	
Time—Is extra time needed for learning?	
Difficulty—What skill levels, conceptual levels, and processes are involved in the learning?	
Support Level—How much is needed?	
Size/Amount of Work—What is length of assignment, is performance or demonstration realistic?	
Format of Materials—Font, graphics, tapes	
Degree of Participation—How much can be expected and is realistic?	
Modified Goals (changes the curriculum)	
Substitute Curriculum	

(VAKT = Visual, Auditory, Tactile, Kinesthetic)

Figure 10.8 Making Adaptations

Collaboration in Planning Universally Designed Environments

On a road-trip, two or more drivers can lessen fatigue; one person can help navigate and assist while the other one drives. If there is car trouble or a detour appears, there can be collaborative problem solving. An extra pair of eyes can watch for potential hazards such as reckless drivers or deer on the road. If there is more than one driver, the price of gas can be split! Generally speaking, in many situations, having two or more people working together is better than one.

Collaborative Planning and Teaching

As discussed in Chapter 5, collaborative planning is critical to the success of learning environments that support UDL. You will likely plan regularly with your grade level or department. Once you have determined the "big idea," it is helpful to also plan with a co-teacher, assistant, and/or other adult. If you are fortunate enough to have a co-teacher, try to meet at least a week ahead of time to share objectives and brainstorm plans and co-teaching arrangements. Purposely planned co-teaching is an instructional strategy that helps many diverse students accomplish their goals. Include any other "players" in this meeting. If you are not co-teaching, it is still critical to exchange information about shared students. Even a "stand up" or cyberspace meeting to share objectives, observations, strategies, tips, needs, and successes can help a great deal. It is hard to teach in isolation. What is taught in a resource room, for example, needs to be part of the "big picture," so that when a student leaves or returns to the regular classroom, he/she doesn't feel singled out or experience fragmented learning.

Setting aside time at least weekly for collaboration allows regular and special educators to determine if students are fully engaged in similar goals and at the right learning level. Teachers can decide if extra supports are needed or if perhaps there is too much support and the learner needs to be moved toward more independence. Assessments can be analyzed consistently and adaptations can be made and adjusted as needed. Accommodations and modifications can be reviewed to ensure they are in place and working (Voltz, Sims, Nelson, & Bivens, 2005). Figure 10.9 offers a simple planning template that might be used as a guide to begin weekly planning (Dieker, 2006). Even though the general and special educator have certain areas they are ultimately responsible for, there needs to be dual ownership in planning with co-teaching. Both teachers will need to consider big ideas, goals, lesson activities, assessments, and adaptations that will be needed. Both will also want to consider what instructional methods, materials, and supports will be needed—peer tutoring, cooperative learning, and using technology, for example. Sharing the workload and ideas can increase the effectiveness of teaching and learning. Dual ownership and commitment are critical for success—from planning to assessment.

In collaborative planning, once the objectives are identified and lessons/activities are brainstormed using the UDL framework, the tasks can be delegated. Remember to tap into those human resources in your community in addition to the faculty/staff who might be able to contribute. Once you start delegating the identified tasks, ask for specific help and you will find the work isn't as overwhelming. An added bonus is that you end up building a caring community. More "players" will have roles, be invested in learning, and take ownership. Be sure to thank the people who work with you. Letters from teachers and students are often the best forms of appreciation.

Collaborative Problem Solving

Another benefit of working in collaboration is that when a cognitive, academic, physical, or social/behavioral difficulty is presenting a road block, having several adults who are familiar with a student problem-solve collaboratively can be very helpful.

Subject _____   Class Hour _____

Target Students: _____   _____

_____   _____

Students with Special Needs:

_____   _____

_____   _____

General Educator Planning Focus	Special Educator Planning Focus
Big Ideas/Goals	Co-Teaching Structure
Lesson Activities	Adaptations
Assessment	Instructional Support Needed

Team Notes: _____

_____

_____

Figure 10.9 Sample Planning Template for Collaborative Planning
Source: Adapted from L. Dieker, *Co-Teaching Lesson Plan Book* (Port Chester, NY: National Professional Resources, Inc., 2006).

Perhaps one adult can observe the student in the class and collect informal data that the team can use to brainstorm solutions. Again, the beauty of a team is that more ideas are typically generated. Once the target behavior/need is identified, solutions can be brainstormed and tried out.

Teaching can be an isolated activity and, if a teacher is too close to a problem, frustration can set in and cloud judgment. By collaborating with different adults in the school/community, student supports can be developed in many places. It might be that a student needs more attention and a mentor can be provided. Sometimes another teacher relates to a child having difficulty and time spent in that teacher's classroom might be arranged. Not surprisingly, asking parents, other family members, and guardians (usually the people who know their child best of all) to help with solutions can be the best course of action.

In conclusion, collaboration in planning academic, physical, and social environments is key to implementing the principles of UDL. By providing the supports students need to learn, a clear focus on the standards, high expectations, and multiple means of representation, expression, and engagement, *all* students can maximize their learning potential. Just as travelers can maximize their chances of a safe arrival, so can teachers. Both can have satisfied "traveling companions" who are ready and eager to explore the next part of the journey.

Thematic Summary

- There are three important elements to considering in planning UDL envir-onments: academic, physical, and social.

- UDL offers four components to consider in designing curriculum to meet the needs of all learners: (1) goals, (2) materials and resources, (3) methods, and (4) assessment.
- The physical environment of a UDL learning environment is purposeful and considers elements of universal design as well as motor/sensory needs and the comfort of students.
- The UDL school social environment encourages a positive classroom climate with rules, procedures, and routines that maximize engaged learning time.
- Successful UDL implementation should reduce the need for extensive behavior management.
- Accommodations and modifications help many students access the curriculum but the terms are different. Modifications alter the curriculum; accommodations do not.
- Collaboration is key to the success of UDL environments.

Making Connections for Inclusive Teaching

1. Why is beginning your planning with a standards-based focus and determining accessible goals so important?
2. Explain and defend the following statement: Assessment drives instruction.
3. Think about some of the materials and resources you might find in a UDL environment. Why is technology an overarching element? Support your answer.
4. Compare and contrast elements of differentiated instruction, positive behavior support, and Universal Design for Learning.
5. Some researchers feel collaborative planning and problem solving will be key to the success of UDL. Do you agree or disagree? Defend your position.

Learning Activities

1. Take the Standard Course of Study from your state and pull out the keywords from the goals/objectives in one subject area you are preparing to teach. Design a matrix for the entire K-12 strand for that subject. How can having this information at a glance assist you in planning? How might you describe the K-12 set of goals in terms of progression?
2. Take a lesson plan you have created or accessed and fill out the pyramid planning sheet in Figure 10.2 to differentiate instruction. Then, brainstorm ways you can apply the three elements of UDL (multiple means of representation, engagement, and expression) to the overall lesson. Write a brief reflection on the process.
3. Research technologies that can be used to increase access to the academic, physical, or social environment. Include one or more technology for each area. Describe each tool and tell how each can help students with diverse needs. Evaluate each tool using the ACCESS mnemonic.
4. As you prepare for the a new school year and read reports about your students, you see that some are from single-family homes, one is homeless, one has a visual impairment, and one student's family recently escaped a war-torn country and speaks no English. Another student has a supportive family but has low motivation along with a history of not completing much work. List five or more adaptations you will have in place up front to foster a welcoming, equitable environment for your class. Use Figures 10.1

and 10.8 (Making Adaptations) as guides. You may choose the subject and the grade level.

5. Review the OSEP Technical Assistance Center website on Positive Behavioral Interventions and Supports at: http://www.pbis.org/schoolwide .htm#PositiveSocialBehavior. Summarize why it is important to focus on teaching positive social behaviors and list the components of a comprehensive schoolwide system of PBS.

Looking at the Standards

The content of this chapter most closely aligns itself with the following standards:

INTASC Standards

- *Diverse Learners*. The teacher understands how students differ in their approaches to learning and creates instructional opportunities that are adapted to diverse learners.
- *Planning*. The teacher plans instruction based upon knowledge of subject matter, students, the community, and curriculum goals.
- *School and Community Involvement*. The teacher fosters relationships with school colleagues, parents, and agencies in the larger community to support students' learning and well-being.

Council for Exceptional Children

Special educators are to have knowledge of the following:

- GC4S10: Identify and teach basic structures and relationships within and across curricula.
- CC7K1: Theories and research that form the basis of curriculum development and instructional practice.
- CC7K3: National, state or provincial, and local curricula standards.
- CC5K1: Demands of learning environments.
- CC5K5: Social skills needed for educational and other environments.
- CC5S1: Create a safe, equitable, positive, and supportive learning environment in which diversities are valued.
- CC5S4: Design learning environments that encourage active participation in individual and group activities.
- CC7S8: Develop and select instructional content, resources, and strategies that respond to cultural, linguistic, and gender differences.
- GC5S6: Establish a consistent classroom routine for individuals with disabilities.

Key Concepts and Terms

curriculum	essential questions	positive behavior support
goals	pyramid planning	adaptations
materials and resources	strategic integration	accommodation
methods	content standards	learned helplessness
assessment	achievement standards	modifications
big ideas	ACCESS	

References

Bauer, A. M., & Ulrich, M. (2002). "I've got a Palm in my pocket": Using handheld computers in an inclusive classroom. *Teaching Exceptional Children, 35*(2), 18–22.

Carbonne, E. (2001). Arranging the classroom with an eye (and ear) for students with ADHD. *Teaching Exceptional Children, 34*(2), 72–81.

Clark, R. (2003). *The essential 55*. New York: Hyperion Books.

Coyne, M., Kame'enui, E., & Carnine, D. (2007). *Effective teaching strategies that accommodate diverse learners* (3rd ed.). Upper Saddle River, NJ: Pearson Education.

Curry, C. (2003). *Strategies to improve access to the general curriculum*. Retrieved October 19, 2006, from http://www.k8accesscenter.org/documents/InstructionalMethodsand Practices_3-16.doc

Dieker, L. (2006). *Co-teaching lesson plan book*. Port Chester, NY: National Professional Resources.

Flannery, M. (2005). Jellyfish on the ceiling and deer in the den: The biology of interior decoration. *Leonardo, 39*(5), 239–244.

Hitchcock, C., Meyer, A., Rose, D., & Jackson, R. (2002). Providing new access to the general curriculum: Universal design for learning. *Teaching Exceptional Children, 35*(2), 8–17.

Jackson, R., Harper, K., & Jackson, J. (2001). *Effective teaching practices and the barriers limiting their use in accessing the curriculum: A review of recent literature*. Wakefield, MA: Center for Applied Special Technology. Retrieved October 10, 2008, from http://www.cast.org/publications/ncac/ncac_effectivetp.html

Kauffman, J., Mostert, M., Trent, S., & Pullen, P. (2006). *Managing classroom behavior: A reflective case-based approach*. Boston: Pearson Education.

Kennedy, M. (2005). Classroom colors. *American School & University, 77*(10), 48, 50, 52.

Lassen, S. R., Steele, M., & Sailor, W. (2006). The relationship of school-wide positive behavior support to academic achievement in an urban middle school. *Psychology in the Schools, 43*(6), 701–712.

Lerner, J. (2006). *Learning disabilities and related disorders: Characteristics and teaching strategies*. Boston: Houghton Mifflin.

Martin, S. (2004). Finding balance: Impact of classroom management conceptions on developing teacher practice. *Teaching & Teacher Education, 20*(5), 405–422. Retrieved November 14, 2006, from the Academic Search Premier database.

Mercer, C. D., & Mercer, A. R. (2005). *Teaching students with learning problems*. Upper Saddle River, NJ: Pearson Education.

Merriam-Webster's Collegiate Dictionary (10th ed.) (1994). Springfield, MA: Merriam-Webster.

Nolet, V., & McLaughlin, M. (2005). *Accessing the general curriculum: Including students with disabilities in standards-based reform* (2nd ed.). Thousand Oaks, CA: Corwin Press.

Regan, K. (2003). Using dialogue journals in the classroom: Forming relationships with students with emotional disturbance. *Teaching Exceptional Children, 36*(2), 36–41.

Rogers, C. (2001). CEC's Clarissa Hug teacher of the year is stimulating her students to learn. *Teaching Exceptional Children, 34*(1), 86–87.

Rose, D., Meyer, A., & Hitchcock, C. (2005). *The universally designed classroom: Accessible curriculum and digital technologies*. Cambridge, MA: Harvard Education Press.

Rydeen, J. (1999). Universal design. *American School & University*. Retrieved August 26, 2006, from http://www.asumag.com/mag/university_universal_design/index.html

Salend, S. (2008). *Creating inclusive classrooms: Effective and reflective practices*. Upper Saddle River, NJ: Pearson Education.

Schumm, J., Vaughn, S., & Leavell, A. (1994). Planning pyramid: A framework for planning for diverse student needs during content area instruction. *The Reading Teacher, 47*, 608–615.

Scott, T., & Martinek, G. (2006). Coaching positive behavior support in school settings: Tactics and data-based decision-making. *Journal of Positive Behavior Interventions, 8*(3), 165–173.

Sugai, G., & Horner, R. H. (2005). School-wide positive behavior supports: Achieving and sustaining effective learning environments for all students. In W. H. Heward (Ed.), *Focus on behavior analysis in education: Achievements, challenges, and opportunities* (pp. 90–102). Upper Saddle River, NJ: Pearson Education.

Thompson, S. J., Johnstone, C. J., & Thurlow, M. L. (2002). Universal design applied to large scale assessments (Synthesis Report 44). Minneapolis: University of Minnesota, National Center on Educational Outcomes. Retrieved July 17, 2006, from http://education.umn.edu/NCEO/OnlinePubs/Synthesis44.html

Tobin, L. (1998). *What do you do with a child like this? Inside the lives of troubled children*. Duluth, MN: Whole Person Associates.

Voltz, D., Sims, M., Nelson, B., & Bivens, C. (2005). M²ECCA: A framework for inclusion in the context of standards-based reform. *Teaching Exceptional Children, 37*(5), 14–19.

Voytecki, K., Smith-Canter, L., & Floyd, K. (2006, March). *Empowering the environment for emergent literacy*. Paper presented at the NC-CEC State Conference, Wilmington, NC.

Wong, H., & Wong, R. (1998). *The first days of school*. Mountain View, CA: Harry K. Wong Publications.

Creating Literacy-Rich Environments for All Learners

Goals: Literacy Instruction Big Ideas

Phonemic Awareness, Phonics, and Word Recognition

Fluency with Text

Vocabulary

Comprehension

Writing/Spelling/Handwriting

Literacy Assessment

Formal Assessments

Reading Interest Inventories

Informal Assessments

Ongoing Assessments

Methods, Materials, and Resources that Promote Literacy for All Learners

Fostering Phonemic Awareness, Phonics, and Word Recognition

Increasing Fluency with Text

Learning Outcomes

After reading this chapter, you will be able to:

- Articulate the big ideas of reading and writing instruction.
- Explain why literacy assessment is important and how it can be used.
- Develop a personal definition of "authentic literacy" and provide an argument for why it needs to be developed across the disciplines.
- Define the five elements of reading and give examples of how UDL can be applied to each one.
- Apply UDL principles and strategies to a "typical" lesson plan.
- Discuss how teachers can find the balance between reading to learn and learning to read.
- Explain four different ways UDL can be applied to reading in the content areas to adapt text for struggling readers.

Outcomes *(continued)*

- List possible AT and other technology-based learning tools and resources that facilitate access to the spoken or printed word or symbol.

Developing Vocabulary

Building Comprehension

Assisting with Writing/Spelling/Handwriting

Applying UDL to Reading in the Content Areas

Eliminate the Reading Requirement Entirely

Modify the Reading Level of the Text

Adapt the Format of the Text/Print Material

Adapt the Presentation of the Text

Other Possible Barriers to Reading

Vision

Social Emotional

ADHD and Motivational

Academically Gifted

Fostering Literacy Collaboration

During your third-period language arts class, you are just about to begin your lesson. The plan is set, the materials are ready, and the students are arriving. As Sam walks in the door, you wonder how he will do with today's activity. You have been collaborating with a science teacher and found a great article on the ozone layer that should bring the lesson alive for the students, and you plan to use it as a springboard for discussion as you work on cause and effect. But, will Sam be able to read it? You know that although he brings a great wealth of background knowledge, he reads well below grade level. For this reason, he often struggles with print material presented in class. You are not using the book today, but how will you help him get through the written material in the article so he can be successful?

Does that sound familiar? The above scenario may be a familiar one in classrooms that have students with diverse learning needs. For a variety of reasons, students may struggle with text and other print material from which they are expected to gain information in the classroom and at home.

Some students, for functional purposes, are considered nonreaders. It is safe to assume that they will not be able to access information from written text. However, this does not mean that all of these students are not capable of the thought processes and learning expected in today's classrooms. For example, a student with an identified learning disability or one who is learning English as a second language may be reading below grade level, yet is served in the general classroom for most of the school day. These students are expected to make gains in content area courses in the general curriculum. Often, they spend so much time and mental energy decoding the text, that fluency and comprehension are often lost.

Students with learning difficulties may have specific differences in how they access and process information. For example, a student with visual processing difficulties may have extreme difficulties tracking and reading large amounts of text. Reading charts and graphs may also be problematic. In addition, some students with disabilities may be able to decode text and pull some information from the reading, but they do not have the metacognitive skills to organize this process. They may have a difficult time finding the main ideas and key components of the readings. Tasks such as sequencing and paraphrasing can also be troublesome.

Gifted students may need access to information that supplements and expands the targeted objectives. They may also struggle with one or more of the learning processes at the same time. For example, a **twice exceptional** student may have exceptionally high creativity and critical thinking skills, but struggle with below average reading and/or spelling skills. Processing deficits may cause the student to work and respond slowly (Nielsen & Higgens, 2005). It is important to remember that *all* students will face challenges with reading and writing at different points in the learning process. We all encounter unfamiliar words. Most of us, too, have read something and wondered afterward what it was about.

As teachers working with students who struggle with reading and language, we are often working to maintain a delicate, but important, balance. It is important, on one hand, to help students progress with their reading skills (teach them how to read). This may occur through special education, other targeted intervention programs, or guided reading activities in the classroom. On the other hand, each student's teachers will need to adapt materials for classes in which reading is not the objective for instruction. This is critical in order for the reading difficulty not to get in the way of each student's ability to learn the concepts/content of the class.

Research suggests that approximately 10 million students in our country are poor readers (Fletcher & Lyon, 1998). About 20 percent of elementary students have reading disabilities that are significant. In 2002, a national reading assessment suggested that 39 percent of our nation's fourth graders read below the basic grade-level expectations and 69 percent were below proficiency standards (National Center for Education Statistics, 2003). For students who are African American, Hispanic, or nonnative English speakers and students living in poverty, the percentage rises to 60–70 percent (American Federation of Teachers, 1999). The importance of early intervention for students with reading difficulties cannot be understated. As students get older, and the focus shifts from *learning to read* to one of *reading to learn,* curriculum demands and other factors make it more and more difficult to help students make significant reading ability gains. Longitudinal data have revealed that of students who have identified reading disabilities in third grade, 74 percent of those students still have reading difficulties in ninth grade (Francis, Shaywitz, Steubing, Shaywitz, & Fletcher, 1994; Shaywitz, Escobar, Shaywitz, Fletcher, & Makuch, 1992). This does not mean that all students cannot make progress with reading ability in later years or that individualized reading instruction should not be provided for these students. However, reading difficulties can interfere with a student's ability to gain meaning from textbooks and other materials that are often beyond his/her independent reading level.

Students who struggle with reading are at risk for school failure.

If these struggling readers don't get the right kinds of support and instruction, this can result in a lack of motivation and behavior problems (Marchand-Martella, Martella, Oriob, & Ebey, 2000). You will likely see these students as passive learners who come to school with no plan to learn and who are masters at **learned help-lessness**. This means they rely on others to structure tasks for them so they can just "get by." They are a product of this history of failure and have little belief in their own abilities. It is everyone's job to break the cycle. However, as students become successful readers and users of print and language, many negative behaviors tend to decrease because the whole world opens up to them.

This chapter is designed to take a look at both sides of the scale. How do we teach reading skills and, at the same time, serve the objective for a specific lesson? How do we maintain high expectations for a student while not allowing the reading difficulties to hinder student progress (i.e., become a handicap)? We will look at the big ideas in literary instruction, some reading assessments, and a sampling of research-based methods, interventions, and adaptations applying UDL principles to promote the development of the reading process along with the understanding of the concept/content being taught.

Goals: Literacy Instruction Big Ideas

Developing literacy skills is a challenge for many learners because it is complex. Language skills directly impact reading, writing, and oral expression. Children come to school with a diverse set of background experiences, including language. This language base will directly impact their ability to take in, process, and respond to print/

symbols meaningfully. As you know, some live in print-rich environments, and others do not.

Some students have neurological challenges. Functional brain imaging shows that three distinct parts of the brain are involved in the reading process alone. Word analysis and articulation take place in the front part of the brain (Broca's area). In the parietotemporal region, in the back of the brain, more word analysis occurs. The occipitotemporal region, also in the back of the brain, is linked to fluency and word formation. Studies of brain imaging in subjects with severe reading disabilities show a breakdown in the circuit between these different areas. The frontal area is often overactive while the back areas are underactive. Students often rely on the spoken language in the front to compensate.

Think, too, about all the phonetic and structural rules there are in teaching students to access and produce our written and spoken language, and yet there are so many exceptions! There are also so many idioms, dialects, and words with multiple meanings. On top of that, the amount of teaching material available to educators on the market today claiming to foster literacy development can be overwhelming.

To get the most out of reading instruction, strive for **balanced literacy** by combining direct instruction in phonics and word study (Fitzgerald, 1999) with opportunities to interact meaningfully with literature, writing, and language. Not surprisingly, proficient readers typically spend more time reading and interacting with print (Rasinski & Padak, 2000) than those who struggle. Literacy improvements at all levels have been shown in classrooms that teach the same content and objectives to all students using differentiated instruction. When this is paired with collaborative partnerships with reading specialists, teachers of English as a second language, special educators, peers, family members, and/or others, the results have been positive for schools with high poverty, minority, and special education populations (Hawkins, 2007). Teaching literacy is truly a "family affair."

Today's learners need excellent literacy instruction across the disciplines. They need **authentic literacy**—the ability to read, write, and think effectively. These components cannot be separated. Proponents of authentic literacy instruction believe that if we teach reading and writing through deep, purposeful reading with interactive text at an early age, the number of literate society members will increase. Literacy opens doors. Begin with higher-level questions that all students can relate to in their lives. Offer a variety of ways to connect new learning to a wide range of learner interests and preferences. Thoughtful interactions with language/words on a daily basis increases literary development. Aim for depth over breadth and offer choice (Schmoker, 2007) to maintain engagement.

The National Reading Panel (2000) has selected the following basic elements of reading instruction to develop effective readers: phonological awareness, phonics (alphabetic principle), fluency, vocabulary, and comprehension. This panel of reading scholars, assigned by the U.S. Congress, has researched thousands of studies focused on reading for K-12 students. These elements will serve as the "big ideas" for teaching literacy to today's diverse learners for this chapter. Consider these principles to guide your selections of reading programs and materials in your teaching.

Phonemic Awareness, Phonics, and Word Recognition

Regardless of what type of instruction is used, many children learn to read by first grade. However, many other students need direct instruction to progress. Research strongly supports the practice of utilizing **phonemic awareness** and **phonics** instruction in the primary grades with initial beginning readers results in successful outcomes in reading acquisition for most students (Bursuck, Smith, Munk, Damer, Mehlig, & Perry, 2004; Groff, 2001). Phonemic awareness focuses on hearing and using sounds. It includes reading books aloud together, singing songs, and chanting rhymes. These activities are critical to early literacy preparation (Adams, 1990). Phonics focuses on applying the **alphabetic principle** (linking sounds to letters/

symbols and patterns) to both known and unknown words in reading and spelling. When taught explicitly and systematically to young students, phonics can strengthen word decoding and formation skills (McCandliss, Beck, Sandak, & Perfetti, 2003). When learners can decode words instantly and effortlessly, reading fluency increases (Speece & Ritchey, 2005). This instruction can be effective regardless of the socioeconomic status of the student (Lyon, 2003).

The systematic instruction of phonemic awareness and the alphabetic principle have been shown to benefit English language learners. A large study done in a Canadian school district reported success implementing such an approach with kindergarten through second grade English language learners, representing 33 different language groups (Lesaux & Siegel, 2003). In another study with first-grade native Spanish-speaking students struggling with reading, all were given intensive, systematic instruction in Spanish phonological sounds. All were able to generalize their phonological skills to English and thus improve their reading skills in both Spanish and English. The coding system in each language was found to be similar (Leafstedt & Gerber, 2005).

Some multisensory, research-based direct instruction reading methods developed in the 1970s continue to be effective today for students with persistent reading disabilities. These programs focus on the structure of language in a highly organized, systematic way, with frequent assessment to ensure mastery. They also focus on rules that guide reading and spelling. Students of all ages are taught by activating the visual, auditory, tactile, and kinesthetic senses and require abundant drill, practice, and repetition (Gillingham & Stillman, 1970; Orton, 1976). Further study related to this methodology can be helpful in providing intensive reading interventions.

Older students who struggle with reading typically have extreme phonological deficits. However, although research with these students is limited, it suggests that remediation in phonemic awareness and phonics can still help them become better readers regardless of age (Greenberg, Fredrick, Hughes, & Bunting, 2002). Bhat, Griffin, and Sindelar (2003) found similar positive results sustained over an extended time period. It will be important, however, to keep instruction age appropriate and interesting. It is also important that phonemic awareness and phonics instruction doesn't become an isolated or dreaded task totally disconnected from the *reading to learn* experiences required of older students.

Fluency with Text

Children who have difficulty reading must have practice developing **fluency**. Fluent readers decode words/symbols rapidly, effortlessly, and automatically (Hook & Jones, 2004). When students are fluent readers, they are better able to predict unknown words they encounter and to comprehend what is read (Nes Ferrara, 2005). Fluency comes with many observations and lots of practice. Students need to have multiple opportunities to read and reread text/print at their current level. Readings should reinforce the words they are learning in passages with few unknown words in order to develop automaticity. Choppy reading interferes with comprehension. Fluent readers can grasp print material in larger units and phrases for more-efficient reading (Chard, Vaughn, & Tyler, 2002; Chard & Osborn, 1999).

The technological nature of our society demands a literate workforce. Fluent reading with comprehension is critical for success. Fluent reading builds the automaticity readers need to quickly and accurately access print so they can focus on what it means and process it with their background knowledge. Reading with expression is also a component in fluency development (Adams, 1990).

Vocabulary

An extensive reading **vocabulary** is needed for reading achievement and comprehension. Using words in context is as critical as simply being able to define what a word means. Think of all the English words with multiple meanings. The same word can be used as a noun or a verb depending upon the context ("I *dish* out the cake on a *dish*"). Our language has many idioms ("Hit the road"), homophones (sea/see), and homonyms (aero/arrow). These variations can be confusing for many native English speakers—not to mention students who are trying to learn English.

Diverse learners, particularly second language learners, typically learn the social vocabulary of a new language before the academic vocabulary. In fact, learners of a second language may need about three years to develop effective academic language (Collier & Thomas, 1989). These students tend to thrive in classrooms with teachers who provide rich, meaningful lessons that support language growth. Such classrooms give them opportunities to work with their peers to discuss concepts and offer "hands-on" projects that help them further interact with ideas discussed in class (Short & Echevarria, 2004). Keep in mind, too, that native English speakers may also have different dialects or cultural language at home. They need to learn the language of school. They may also need to know when it is appropriate to use one language set over another.

Young students will generally come to school with a large oral language base. Each student typically has about 6,000 words he or she can say and understand by listening. Their reading vocabularies, however, are much lower. The gap typically closes as the student matures and learns to read efficiently. The typical high school student, for example, knows about 45,000 words (Stahl, 2004).

Comprehension

The National Reading Panel (2000) identifies reading comprehension as the fifth element of reading instruction. For the purposes of this text in its UDL approach, both reading and listening comprehension will be considered since both have to do with the interaction of the reader/listener with the material presented. Comprehension is the active involvement of the participant in making connections with the text/language. The learner's background knowledge and experiences, level of interest, knowledge of the language (including vocabulary) and its structure, and the way information is received, processed, and organized will impact how effective comprehension is (Chard & Osborn, 1999). Because comprehension requires thinking skills, it follows that the more quickly, smoothly, and accurately a student receives and processes the information, the better the comprehension. Even though some students with reading difficulties may be able to decode the written word, they can still have difficulty understanding the vocabulary, language structure, and/or thinking strategies used to process and organize the written pages of print materials that many good readers understand automatically. Once again, specific and explicit instruction is needed to make them more-effective readers.

Writing/Spelling/Handwriting

Today's early literacy instruction connects reading and writing from the start. It might seem surprising to you, but for some students, writing is actually easier than reading. This is because students write from what they know. When you read or hear another author's words or voice, more processing is involved. You have to internalize the language, try to connect an experience or thought to it, and think again about how to respond. Diverse learners, once again, may struggle just to decode the language.

Most learners will need instruction in the writing process and will benefit from the use of graphic organizers, outlines, and writing strategies. Some may even need another language or symbol system—pictures, signs, objects, Braille dots, or other codes—to express their ideas.

Spelling is problematic for many learners, partly because of the inconsistent patterns within our language. In addition to this, new words are formed in the media

Cengage Learning/Wadsworth

Graphic organizers and outlines can help diverse learners develop writing skills.

every day. Some students can't hold the word in the working memory long enough to "file" it. In reading, context cues, word shapes (configurations), phonics, and structure can be used to figure out an unknown word; however, there often is no such frame of reference in spelling a word that does not directly correspond to its sounds. A good reader can be a poor speller. Sometimes knowing how a word feels is what is needed.

Handwriting is another important life skill for written expression that can be difficult for some diverse learners. Handwriting may take the form of manuscript, cursive, or keyboarding. Being able to visually perceive a letter/word, remember it, and then express it back through a coordinated motor task can be a struggle for even the brightest learners. Difficulty with handwriting can hinder note taking, studying, and assignment completion. For many of those who have great difficulty writing by hand, computer keyboarding has been a particular blessing. Word processing, however, takes a lot of instruction and practice to become a viable substitute for handwriting.

Literacy Assessment

Formal Assessments

Chapter 8 included information about formal, comprehensive standardized tests that have literacy components. There are many assessments, both formal and informal, that focus on the literacy component. Formal assessments can be quite time-intensive and may require specialized training to administer, but they can identify starting points in instruction and pinpoint areas of strength and need. Examples of formal literacy assessment instruments include:

- Woodcock Reading Mastery Tests—Revised (Woodcock, 1998)
- Gray Oral Reading Test (GORT-4) (Wiederholt & Bryant, 2003)
- Brigance Comprehensive Inventory of Basic Skills—Revised (Brigance, 1999)
- Dynamic Indicators of Basic Early Literacy Skills (DIBELS) (Good & Kaminski, 2002)
- Comprehensive Test of Nonverbal Intelligence (CTONI) (Hammill, Pearson, & Wiederholt, 1996)

Ideally, students can be individually assessed so they may be grouped according to instructional needs and, to some extent, interests. There are so many reading assessments available that choosing one can be overwhelming. Since this is a book focusing on UDL, let's look at some other kinds of literacy assessments that might be helpful with *all* learners when taking a balanced literacy approach.

Reading Interest Inventories

Remember that it will be important to know what your students think about reading. Ideally, a Reading Interest Survey (refer back to Figure 8.1 in Chapter 8) can be administered in a small group or individually. This information will help you select texts and other print/media materials that will likely engage your learners.

The Burke Reading Inventory (1987) also has some additional questions that can provide even greater insights as to how a student sees himself/herself as a reader. See Figure 11.1 for some student questions from this inventory with some additional questions for writing. It can also be helpful to ask the student to name or describe any strategies he/she uses for remembering information that is read and for answering questions.

Using an inventory to informally assess comprehension can also be helpful. This can help generalist and content area teachers know what types of strategies their students may or may not have. Figure 11.2 shows an adaptation of such a tool (Hahn, 1984; Paris & Meyers, 1981). Five items on this questionnaire—2, 3, 4, 6, and 10—indicate positive reading strategies. Items 1, 5, 7, 8, and 9 show negative

Web Resources

For more information about informal literacy assessment resources, check this text's companion website, **www.academic .cengage.com/education/ Gargiulo**.

1. What do you do when you come to a word you don't know?
2. What friends of yours are good readers? What do they do?
3. What does your teacher do when he/she comes to a word they don't know?
4. If a friend is having problems reading, what would you tell him/her to do?
5. How did you learn to read?
6. Are you a good reader?
7. What can help you become a better reader?

These same questions could be adapted for writing. Thinking about today's learner, perhaps the following questions might be added as you create your own survey:

8. Who helps you with reading outside of school?
9. What language(s) are spoken in your home?
10. What kind of reading materials are in your home?
11. What technologies help you with reading?
12. What technologies help you with writing?
13. Do you use spell checkers?
14. What is the best way for you to take in and express information (book, movie, DVD, CD, writing, word processing, speaking)?

Figure 11.1 **Burke Reading Inventory Sample Questions**
Source: Adapted from C. Burke, "Burke Reading Interview," in Y. Goodman, D. Watson, & C. Burke (Eds.), *Reading Miscue Inventory: Alternative Procedures* (New York: Richard C. Owen Publishers, 1987).

procedures or strategies. Students who indicate that positive strategies do not help them may benefit from direct reading strategy/procedure instruction. This chapter will offer some reading comprehension strategies and a section on adapting text for reading in the content area.

Does it help you understand a text selection (or a story) if you:

1. Think about something else while you are reading?
   ____always   ____almost always   ____almost never   ____never

2. Write it down in your own words?
   ____always   ____almost always   ____almost never   ____never

3. Underline important parts of the selection?
   ____always   ____almost always   ____almost never   ____never

4. Ask yourself questions about the ideas in the selection?
   ____always   ____almost always   ____almost never   ____never

5. Write down every single word in the selection?
   ____always   ____almost always   ____almost never   ____never

6. Check through the selection to see if you remember all of it?
   ____always   ____almost always   ____almost never   ____never

7. Skip the parts you don't understand in the selection?
   ____always   ____almost always   ____almost never   ____never

8. Read the selection as fast as you can?
   ____always   ____almost always   ____almost never   ____never

9. Say every word over and over?
   ____always   ____almost always   ____almost never   ____never

10. Ask questions about parts of the selection that you don't understand?
    ____always   ____almost always   ____almost never   ____never

Figure 11.2 **Questionnaire for Reading Comprehension**
Source: A. Hahn, "Assessing and Extending Comprehension: Monitoring Strategies in the Classroom," *Reading Horizons, 24,* 1984, pp. 225–230.

You may need to adapt inventories/assessments for students who cannot tell you the answers in writing, in English, or in words at all. Students may need to choose from a menu of options, point to an answer, or supply answers orally (i.e., using a digital voice recorder). You may even need to interview a family member, caregiver, mentor, or last year's teacher for this information. Ideally, each student would have a literacy portfolio, preferably electronic, to pass along updated, authentic assessments each year with examples of reading, language, and written expression products that can be used to measure progress.

Informal Assessments

Authentic, informal assessments can provide valuable insights about how a student approaches the reading process and experiences breakdowns. Perhaps, even more importantly, they can show teachers what kinds of things students like to read and how they best respond. As a simple rule of thumb, if a student struggles to decode more than five words on a page, the book is likely too difficult to read. That's one of the simplest informal measures!

The San Diego State Quick Assessment is another simple, useful tool for a quick screening of word recognition skills and will provide a starting place. It may be particularly useful if you have a large group of students and want to see who might need a closer look. Some teachers also find basic **Dolch sight word** lists are helpful for assessing word recognition skills. This list of 220 frequently used sight words was first compiled in 1948 (Dolch) and has been continually updated and used with students who need extra practice. See the WWW Resource box for links to these resources as well as examples of other informal assessments.

An **informal reading inventory** (IRI) is another type of a reading assessment you can do quickly. It provides general reading skill levels, clues to types of errors made, and a general comprehension level. It also looks at some behavioral considerations. The IRI measures three types of reading levels:

1. Independent (recognizing 98 percent of the words and answering comprehension questions with 90–100 percent accuracy)
2. Instructional (recognizing 95 percent of the words and answering comprehension questions with 75 percent accuracy)
3. Frustration (recognizing less than 90 percent of the words and answering comprehension questions with less than 70 percent accuracy) (Johnson, Kress, & Pikulski, 1987)

Some informal reading inventories are available commercially, or you can create your own.

A spelling inventory that is also simple to use was created by Francine Johnston (Bear, Invernizzi, Templeton, & Johnston, 2004). Using this tool, spelling errors can quickly be analyzed to see where the breakdowns are in dictated words. Figure 11.3 offers one example of a student score sheet. The teacher checks off word parts that are spelled correctly and adds them up using a point system. It's a quick way to see how to target skill instruction. This spelling assessment is also offered in Spanish.

When you are totally perplexed by a student's challenges, consider looking into language assessments. A speech/language, ELL, and/or assistive technology specialist can be extremely helpful here. These professionals are usually willing to observe, assess, and demonstrate helpful language practices in the classroom. Possible areas of breakdowns may be in phonological awareness, vocabulary knowledge/comprehension, listening comprehension, sentence understanding, and/or critical listening. Many students need practice formulating and producing language sounds and sentences. Some simply need to build language from experience. Informal observations of a student in a real environment are, again, often the most telling.

Students need continual opportunities to use their language in discussions, group work, speaking, and explaining. Provide good models, teach in context, and

Web Resources

For more information on informal literacy assessments and creating your own informal reading inventories (IRI), go to this text's companion website, **www.academic.cengage.com/education/Gargiulo**. Also access the companion website for Six Strategies for Spelling, Assistive Technology Supports for Accessing Text, and High Interest/Low Vocabulary Reading Materials.

Name of Child _____ Teacher _____ Grade _____ Date _____ Total Pts _____

Dictated word	Short vowel	Blend/digraph	Long vowels	Other vowels	Complex consonants	Inflection	Syllable juncture	Unaccented syllable	Suffix	Correct	Word Totals
1. speck	e	sp			ck						
2. switch	i	sw			tch						
3. throat			oa		thr						
4. nurse				ur							
5. scrape											
6. charge											
7. phone			o-e								
8. smudge											
9. point											
10. squirt											
11. drawing						-ing					
12. trapped						-pped					
13. waving						-ving					
14. powerful				ow				-er	-ful		
15. battle							tt	-tle			
Feature Totals											**Total Pts:**

Figure 11.3 Example of Elementary Spelling Inventory Score Sheet
Source: Adapted from D. Bear, M. Invernizzi, S. Templeton, & F. Johnston, *Words Their Way: Word Study for Phonics, Vocabulary, and Spelling Instruction* 3rd ed. (Upper Saddle River, NJ: Pearson Education, 2004), p. 313.

role play. Use student interests to get them talking! Almost all students have a favorite movie, game, song, sport, or hobby.

Ongoing Assessments

Collaboration with others in the school(s) may also be needed to rewrite tests for student accessibility. Language/directions may need to be reworded, passages shortened, time extended, and alternate means for response considered. Co-teaching partnerships may be considered for assessment. While one teacher takes the lead in classroom instruction, the other can assess, observe, and collect data on individual students.

Remember to implement curriculum-based measurement. On weekly quizzes or tests, have students record their own progress in targeted skills areas on a simple graph. This not only helps you monitor progress, but can also be quite motivating for the students.

Methods, Materials, and Resources that Promote Literacy for All Learners

It would be impossible to even begin to present all the methods and strategies that exist for teaching reading, writing, spelling, and handwriting in one chapter. However, some helpful interventions will be used as examples to show how teachers can adapt what they already have. High- and low-tech resources will also be provided. Remember to keep balanced literacy in mind as you adapt. For example, elementary programs might include a mix of teacher read-alouds, guided reading, self-selected reading, teacher-selected reading, home reading, vocabulary building, and writing. Secondary programs may include wide, focused reading geared to universal themes rather than to individual books (Fisher & Ivey, 2007). All students do not need to read the same novel in English class, for example. Look for universal themes/ideas and have a menu of choices available to guide instruction (Fisher & Ivey).

Fostering Phonemic Awareness, Phonics, and Word Recognition

To promote phonemic awareness, rhymes, songs, poems, and sound games can engage young students as they are directed to identify sounds and patterns. Older students can also benefit from listening to poetry, songs, chants, raps, and rhyming forms of language with similar guidance to sound and patterns.

To promote phonics and word recognition, some students may benefit from direct phonics instruction and the preteaching of vocabulary before a unit or lesson begins. If collaborative teaching is in place, one professional could work with a small group on new words before the whole class is introduced to them. Young students can stretch out sounds by pretending to pull a rubber band or by moving an object from left to right for each sound. Students of all ages who struggle can tap out the sound progression on their fingers. Tracing the word or writing it in the sky as it is sounded out is also helpful. The more senses you engage, the more chances a student has to receive the information.

Looking for word patterns by sorting words can also help. This can be as basic as sorting words according to a letter sound or as complex as sorting vocabulary words by their Greek or Latin origins. By categorizing words, the student can organize those literacy file folders in the brain. When students encounter an unknown word, they can refer to stored word associations that are structured similarly to figure them out (Bear et al., 2004). Students can also be taught to use context and visual clues to uncover word meanings.

For younger children, using magnetic letters or letter tiles can engage more senses. For everyone, flash or note cards with visual cues or color coding for patterns

Multiple Ways to Increase Phonemic Awareness, Phonics, and Word Recognition	Examples
Representation	• Presenting sounds/sound pictures or other symbols or objects • Tapping out sounds; words presented orally with flash cards and with visual and/or physical cues • Preteaching vocabulary, increasing repetition as needed, providing lots of real-life examples
Engagement	• Read-along methods (e.g., choral reading) that repeat sounds/words, songs, tapping sounds/clapping syllables, rhyming, chants • Tracing letters/words in sand or salt tray, with crayon, or in the sky; moving letter tiles • Playing word and rhyming games • Tapping sound segments and tracking lip movement
Expression	• Completed word webs or other graphic organizers • Acting out a word/sound, matching sounds/letters/words to pictures or symbols/signs • Creating visual cards, posters, and student dictionaries for sounds/words

may be helpful. Older students may benefit from word games that have letter tiles or cubes to manipulate. Computer software programs can offer extra practice/repetition with letter/sound/word sorting and writing stories using word banks. Student writing is read back in many of these programs, providing immediate auditory feedback. Computer reading, writing, and spelling programs are also available in different languages; some have picture dictionaries, word banks, and sign language.

Older students have also benefited from the **Word Identification Strategy** (DISSECT) developed by researchers at the University of Kansas Center for Research on Learning (Lenz, Schumaker, Deshler, & Beals, 1984). Research studies with middle- and high-school students who were two or more grade levels below in word decoding have consistently demonstrated improvement in word identification after students received direct instruction in this strategy (Bremer, Clapper, & Deshler, 2002). This strategy uses prefixes, suffixes, and word stems. Three syllabication rules are applied to the stems.

Increasing Fluency with Text

Repeated oral readings can help increase fluency. The same passage is read and reread several times until the preset criteria for speed and accuracy are achieved (Mercer, Campbell, Miller, Mercer, & Lane, 2000). Researchers suggest practicing a passage this way 10 minutes a day for 3–5 days (Chard et al., 2002). Immediate teacher feedback and guidance is offered. Passages should be at the students' independent reading level (read with 95% accuracy), be of interest to students, and have many common or overlapping words (Dowhower, 1987; Rashotte & Torgesen, 1985). Fluency can be practiced with a teacher, peer, tape recording, or with computer assistance.

Preteaching vocabulary also helps students develop fluency (Chard & Osborn, 1999). Having multiple opportunities to hear text read aloud by teachers, peers, family members, mentors, and on tapes/CDs helps also.

Research in fluency with students with emotional/behavior disorders suggests that working with a person who can provide immediate corrective feedback and reinforcement is most effective (Al Otaiba & Rivera, 2006). When paired with a peer tutor or partner, a higher-ability reader is paired with a lower-ability reader.

Cengage Learning/Wadsworth

Echo reading can help develop reading fluency.

In one technique called **echo reading**, one partner reads a sentence, phrase, or word, and the other person repeats it as he/she tracks the print. An adaptation of this strategy is for each person to read every other word. This can offer variety and, surprisingly, can also help with fluency. Keep in mind that, depending on the student, a first-grade student who struggles may only be able to add two words a week. An older student who has become dependent on learning by sight may only be able to add one word a week (Deno, Fuchs, Marston, & Shinn, 2001). Having multiple, flexible methods and increased intensity (smaller group or individual instruction) may be needed.

Whisper-phones (sometimes called phonics phones) are low-tech handheld devices that can help students hear the speech sounds (phonemes) in the words they say. Students "whisper read" speech sounds/words/passages into the "phone" and hear their own voices back immediately. Some students find this immediate auditory feedback helps them increase their reading fluency. It also helps some students stay on task. Most of the phones have parts that can turn and be used with a reading partner as well. Whisper phones can be hand made out of 3.5-inch piece of PVC pipe with a PVC elbow at each end. They can also be purchased commercially.

Whisper-phone.

Developing Vocabulary

Two "big ideas" to foster vocabulary development are offered by Baker, Simmons, and Kame'enui (1998). The first is to match the depth of the word knowledge with instructional goals to determine what level of word knowledge is needed and then determine teaching techniques. Evaluate how important the word is in everyday use by the student and in academic use. Assess to find out what the student already knows about the word. This way you can determine what strategies for teaching are needed. The second "big idea" is to systematically teach how to find out unknown word meaning by using the context, learning tools (dictionaries), and word structural analysis (root word, prefixes, suffixes). As you know, some words require deeper investigation than others. Ideally, this systematic teaching of vocabulary is eventually internalized, leading the student toward independence.

When teaching vocabulary that connects to units and real life, graphic organizers, such as **word maps**, are a tool that can be very helpful to aid comprehension. Word maps allow the learner to analyze a word through its definition, a synonym, an antonym, a mnemonic (students construct a memory sentence and a mind picture), and the situation(s) in which it might be used. These can be used with print or nonprint activities. Some students may need more pictures and symbols that can be drawn or accessed through software programs. Older and advanced students could be given an extra section tracing the origin of the word. Some students could provide additional antonyms and synonyms. Figure 11.4 provides an example of a word map.

Multiple Ways to Increase Fluency	Examples
Representation	• Direct instruction • Modeling/demonstration of techniques • Point to words/phrases as they are read
Engagement	• Repeated reading, read along with teacher or peer, choral reading, echo reading, reading scripts (such as in Reader's Theater) • Students chart own progress and work toward reinforcements • Create a Reader's Theater Video or rehearse and record a song or play • Use leveled text for readability
Expression	• Sharing of progress reports using CBM • Student performance of Reader's Theater • Final production of video or recorded reading/play

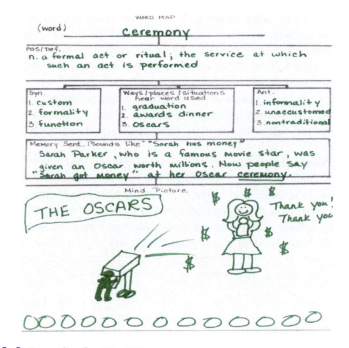

Figure 11.4 Example of a Word Map
Source: Courtesy of S. Thomson.

A **reading pen** is a high-tech tool that can help develop vocabulary. It is a handheld device that allows the reader to scan the unknown words or lines of text. The word(s) and definition(s) is/are shown on a LCD screen and pronounced out loud. Extra features may include Spanish translations, speakers, and headphones.

Another helpful high-tech tool is an **electronic** (or "talking") **dictionary**. This portable handheld device serves as a spell check and will also pronounce and define words typed into it. If used for spelling, the student must be able to type in at least the beginning part of the word to access a menu of possible spelling choices. These choices can be read aloud to help him/her select the desired word. Definitions are also read aloud when the word is selected. Some models allow personal vocabulary storage and have handwriting guides, homophone guides, and word games. Dictionaries, thesauruses, and spell checkers are free online tools that can be used with available text-to-speech features to read both the words and definitions. Some computer programs also have this capability, enabling any text on the screen to be read aloud.

Other useful vocabulary-building tools, such as keywords, mnemonics, and list-making features were mentioned in Chapter 9. Remember to use words that are essential for school, real life, and the interdisciplinary units being taught. Choose critical words that are central or key to the concepts in your unit of study rather than using them just because they appear in bold face print or in a list in the text. Remember, *less is more.* Vocabulary words taught in the context in which they are used repeatedly and that are built on throughout the year have the best chance of being retained. Adding multisensory learning components can help students with diverse learning needs. Offering extended word lists helps students who are ready to expand their vocabularies. The days of memorizing countless flash card definitions—only to forget them after the test—may be a practice of the past.

Building Comprehension

There are many helpful interventions for building comprehension. Three will be discussed briefly here, and many more can be found in the Learning Toolbox at the James Madison University Special Education Program's website: http://coe.jmu

Multiple Ways to Increase Vocabulary	Examples
Representation	• Preteach vocabulary in context, using objects, visuals, keywords, and/or signs paired with related word • Use direct instruction/modeling of vocabulary comprehension strategies, including graphic organizers • Teach dictionary skills • Demonstrate and provide computer sound components that give definition when word is highlighted/clicked • Model software programs that hyperlink words ("click for more information"), repeats, replays, provides hints or cues to information/knowledge • Use analogies that tap into prior knowledge
Engagement	• Practice strategies, using word webs/maps, including words of student interests • Make/practice with flash cards; make flow lists • Discuss, question, play word games with peer(s) • Use songs/lyrics with focused vocabulary • Use interactive software targeting key vocabulary • Listen to tapes/CDs/other recordings • Type, cut, paste, illustrate words in response journal; add sign language • Use puppets for conversations with vocabulary
Expression	• Point, choose, match, read, select words with definitions • Answer questions orally or in writing about vocabulary • Use multiple-choice response assessment • Completed graphic organizers (e.g., word maps) • Explain/teach a strategy to another student (observed by teacher)

.edu/Learningtoolbox/ as well as in many researched texts and journal articles. The interventions themselves help *all* learners and, when multisensory elements are added, their effectiveness is often increased. Remember that graphic organizers are excellent tools for scaffolding comprehension for all learners. They will be discussed more in depth in the UDL section that follows in this chapter.

Thinking aloud can be a powerful intervention tool for fostering comprehension. Purposefully say what you are thinking about as you come to an unknown word, passage, or other trouble spot. Let students "see" how you figure out word or text meaning. As described in Chapter 9, thinking aloud can help students make predictions before reading, form visual images through descriptions, link to prior learning, share analogies (by looking for words such as "like a"), or verbalize a confusing point. Use it for modeling new vocabulary and strategies presented. Thinking aloud can be used to provide examples and nonexamples. Students can also use it as an intervention to monitor their own comprehension.

Another helpful intervention for diverse learners is **paraphrasing**. Have students read or listen to a chunk of material and then summarize or paraphrase it using their own words. The letters RAP are a mnemonic strategy to help learners remember how to use this intervention (Schumaker, Denton, & Deshler, 1984):

- **R**ead a paragraph or a selection of the material you are working on.
  - Do not read long sections because you may not be able to understand the material if you don't break it up into smaller parts.
- **A**sk yourself what the main ideas are.
  - Try to find the sentence or sentences that give the most important ideas in the section you read.
- **P**ut the main ideas in your own words.
  - Paraphrasing is when you put material that you read into your own words.
  - When you paraphrase the main ideas, make sure you try to think of other words to say the same thing as in the book.

Now, look at Figure 11.5 and see how a strategy can be turned into a rap, making it even more accessible to diverse learners. It provides lots of repetition as well as multisensory options by adding a beat, sound effects, and movement, thus increasing

Rap a paragraph (Rap, Rap)
Rap a paragraph (Rap, Rap)

First you take a paragraph
And you read it
You read it (repeat)

Rap a paragraph (Rap, Rap)
Rap a paragraph (Rap, Rap)

Then you ask yourself
The main idea
Idea (repeat)

Rap a paragraph (Rap, Rap)
Rap a paragraph (Rap, Rap)

Then you put the ideas
In your words
In your words (repeat)

Rap a paragraph (Rap, Rap)
Rap a paragraph (Rap, Rap)

Figure 11.5 "RAP" a Paragraph

student engagement. The rap can be downloaded to an MP3 player for many future repetitions!

Another reading comprehension strategy, **Question Answer Response** (QAR), helps students analyze questions before responding. The premise is that there are four types of questions encountered in reading. The first types of questions are concrete, "Right There" questions. The answers are in the text. Next are "Think & Search"—the answers are in several places in the material. These questions help the reader/listener summarize and find the main idea(s). Next, "Author and Me" questions move the learner to higher thinking levels as they are asked to predict or infer what the author means after giving information. The fourth type of question is "On My Own." These questions offer the opportunity for the reader to connect prior knowledge and his/her own experiences to self, the text, and the world. For these last two types of questions, the answers are not in the book.

To make the QAR strategy multisensory, a poster can be created and posted in the room to help visual learners commit it to memory (see Figure 11.6). Then students may create a "foldable" as they activate their tactile senses. **Foldables** are 3-D, interactive graphic organizers that students can create to organize information and use as a study guide (Zike, 2005). Students write the main parts of the strategy on the outside flaps and describe and give examples in the space under the flaps. Not only does this help students organize the information, but it can also serve as a study guide. They can be hole-punched for the students' notebooks. Figure 11.7 shows an example of a foldable for the QAR strategy.

As a cumulative activity, the teacher or students might write a song about the strategy and add hand movements or sign language to it for the visual/auditory/tactile/kinesthetic learner (see Figure 11.8). The song or rap can be recorded and possibly digitized. A copy can be sent home to share with parents and to provide extra practice. Be certain permissions for recording are on file.

Creating multisensory interventions fosters comprehension for a diverse set of learners. You probably already know many interventions similar to QAR from other courses and teaching experiences. What you need to do now is adapt them to engage more senses. Students of all ages may enjoy creating some of these adaptations for

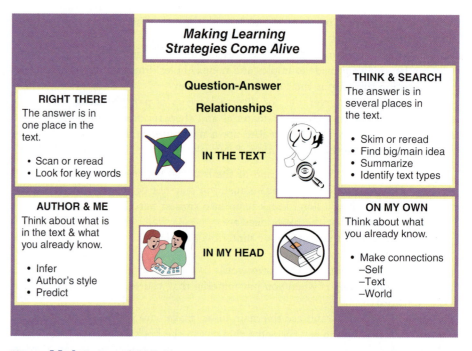

Figure 11.6 Poster of QAR Strategy

Source: Adapted from T. Raphael & K. Au, "QAR: Enhancing Comprehension and Test Taking Across Grades and Content Areas," *Reading Teacher, 59*(3), 2005, pp. 206–221.

Multiple Ways to Increase Comprehension	Examples
Representation	• Use anchored learning • Use graphic organizers, outlines • Model strategies (paraphrasing, think aloud)
Engagement	• Using songs, graphic organizers, questioning (at all levels—more interpretive than factual), reciprocal teaching, text structure analysis • Use the "Say Something" strategy (make a comment or ask a question about what has just been read/presented) • Use word processing programs/alternate recording systems for response journals and to summarize and react to stories/presentations • Create eBooks, artwork on the topic
Expression	• Written products • Student-created eBooks • Art work, role play, performing a dance/acting out a play that reflects comprehension

Figure 11.7 Example of a "Foldable" for QAR Strategy
Source: Adapted from T. Raphael & K. Au, "QAR: Enhancing Comprehension and Test Taking Across Grades and Content Areas," *Reading Teacher, 59*(3), 2005, pp. 206–221.

other interventions and procedures. As we continue to move more purposefully toward UDL, think back to the power of anchored learning in Chapter 10. Try to provide an anchor up front for each unit. As we move into writing strategies, you might even consider having students create a character at the beginning of the school year or incorporate a real character from history, science, sports, or other interest areas into daily activities. Students can write to this character through journaling (written, oral, or signed) about their experiences as they travel through a year's worth of units and lesson plans.

Assisting with Writing/Spelling/Handwriting

Many of our diverse learners lack experiences upon which to write. If possible, provide field trips, videos, sports clips, and virtual experiences. Talk with students about these and other experiences they have frequently to anchor the learning.

QAR Strategy Song

To the tune of "Wheels on the Bus"

All our students are question pros, question pros, question pros.
All our students are question pros, and we love to read!

We have learned to use a questioning tip, questioning tip, questioning tip.
We have learned to use a questioning tip, to help understand.

The first type of question is called "Right There," called "Right There," called "Right There."
For the "Right There" question, you look in the book, and the answers are in the text.

The second type of question is "Think and Search, Think and Search, Think and Search."
For the "Think and Search" question, you look in the passage and think about what you've read.

The third type of question is "Author and You, Author and You, Author and You."
For the "Author and You" question, you connect with the author, but the answers are not in the text.

The fourth type of question is "On My Own, On My Own, On My Own."
For the "On My Own" question, I use what I know, but the answers are not in the text.

Figure 11.8 Primary Song for QAR Strategy
Source: Adapted from T. Raphael & K. Au, "QAR: Enhancing Comprehension and Test Taking Across Grades and Content Areas," *Reading Teacher, 59*(3), 2005, pp. 206–221.

Once you have identified common experiences to respond to, use graphic organizers to organize thinking for subsequent student expression. These can include webs, timelines, diagrams, matrices, or maps. Remember, graphic organizers help explain concepts and can help show relationships between them. Symbols, pictures, and/or objects can be used in their creation in addition to words. You and your students can create your own or choose from the hundreds that are available. Be sure to match the purpose of the organizer you choose with the process you are trying to teach.

Provide multiple opportunities to engage students in extensive forms of expression based on assessment of your learners, and know their strengths and needs. Have writing folders, graphic organizers, different types of paper, tape recorders, specialized and portable keyboards, electronic dictionaries, or other similar tools for expression readily available. Incorporate some self-selected topics not only to activate prior knowledge, but also to provide choice. Construct and implement heterogeneous student writing groups, creating the roles of writers, authors, facilitators, illustrators, and editors. Be sure you model and think aloud as you prepare students to work in these groups.

Many students with cognitive and organizational needs will also benefit from direct instruction in learning the nuts and bolts of basic elements of the writing process:

1. Prewrite (brainstorming thoughts and facts)
2. Write a rough draft (sometimes writing more than one)
3. Revise (looking for ways to improve the writing/product—expand, rearrange, add, and subtract words/sentences/ideas)
4. Edit (looking for spelling/grammar errors)
5. Publish your work

Students will also benefit from working in context to identify and expand their expressive vocabularies through activities such as listing transitional and descriptive words to use in writing and learning how to combine sentences. Students with cognitive and/or physical challenges may need to have partial structures provided. Using a **cloze procedure**, for example, some students may benefit from filling in blanks to supply missing information (Lerner, 2006). Words are deleted from a passage, and the student must construct meaning from the text to fill them in. With older students a similar procedure uses a premade outline or summary of a presentation. Certain words are substituted with blank lines, and the student fills them in as the presentation occurs. This is called a **slot outline**. A completed slot outline can be a study guide.

Students may also write/express words/thoughts on cards or sentence strips and then arrange them together. These procedures may also be used for reading. Software programs/tools are available that allow students to create stories with word and/or picture banks that can be set up ahead of time. Words and sentences can be read back with text help features. Symbols and pictures may be substituted or attached in some programs. Some programs allow for language translations.

There are many research-based strategies available for improving writing that require direct instruction. The Center for Research on Learning at the University of Kansas has been researching writing strategies for over twenty-five years. These strategies typically target students in the upper elementary through high school years, but lend themselves to some earlier levels as well. One example is The **Sentence Writing Strategy** (PENS). Students begin with direct instruction in forming simple sentences with subjects and verbs, progressing systematically to compound and then complex sentences (Schumaker & Sheldon, 1985).

Figure 11.9 shows a snapshot of a typical lesson plan recently used in middle school with students writing research questions. Many of the practices presented so far are highlighted in this plan. Parts of the lesson were color-coded to show UDL applications. Additional possible high- and low-tech UDL applications follow the lesson plan in Figure 11.10 to illustrate the flexibility of UDL applications. Also included is the pyramid planning sketch with some ideas about differentiation

Lesson Objective(s):	*The student will construct at least three research questions to be used to guide information gathering for an informational summary.*
Assessment(s):	*graphic organizer with student questions—completed as pairs*
State Standards Correlation: 7th grade English/Language Arts 2.02 (use multiple sources of print/nonprint); 4.02 (evaluate sources); 6.01 (apply conventions of grammar/language)		

Instructor: S. Williams
Subject: Writing   Grade: 7th

Preplanning Activities: Laminate organizers (or just gather dry erase boards); get DaVinci book

Lesson Element	Procedures	Time	What is the teacher doing?	What are the students doing?	Materials
Lesson Setup & Lesson Opening	• Write homework in planner • Set up expectations for peer work • Distribute webs from yesterday—brainstormed questions about topic • Objective: By the end of today you will have three research questions established to guide your research for the informational summary. Look in notes about Big 6 research steps. Today we'll be able to check off the last part of step 1.	5 min.	• Giving directions • Talking about the objective	• Writing homework assignment • Listening	• None • Students need writing notebooks
Lesson Body	Teacher Input • With "Writer Lenses" look through Informational summary about DaVinci and note the headings. Say that these originated as a "research questions." • Alert students to the fact that I've gone through the questions they brainstormed yesterday and highlighted them with different colors. The questions that are highlighted with the same color seemed to be related to each other in some way. • Model the process of grouping the specific/related questions into one larger (more global) one—more appropriate to guide research. Show my organizer from yesterday about teachers that has also been highlighted. Think aloud about how they are the same. Complete transparency of web for selecting research questions. Model two of the three possible questions. Guided Practice • Using laminated organizers and dry erase markers. Students individually use laminated organizers to develop a suggestion for a research question for the third and fourth set. Hold them up and show me. Choose one student to come write his/hers on the overhead after checking all for appropriateness.	20 min.	• Distributing text • Modeling • Thinking aloud • Questioning students for input in 2nd example • Monitoring and circulating to offer help	• Listening • Responding to teacher questions • Writing on dry erase board	• Writer lenses • DaVinci book • Dry erase boards or laminated organizer • Overhead of organizer
Extended Practice	Pairs of students use their questions to complete the first level of the organizer for their own writing topics.	10 min.	Circulating	Working with partners to write questions	Webs from yesterday organizers
Lesson Closing	Ask students to summarize what they learned about writing research questions today. As a group—check off the 2nd part of step 1.	5 min.	Questioning	Answering questions, checking notes	Student notebooks

UDL Applications Key: Representation; Engagement; Expression

Figure 11.9 Lesson Plan
Source: Lesson plan contributed by S. Williams, East Carolina University teacher, former middle school teacher in Harnett County Schools and Pitt County Schools, NC.

Possible UDL Applications for Extension	
Representation	<u>Low-Tech</u>: List objectives/agenda on board/poster <u>High-Tech</u>: List objectives/agenda through electronic document and projector
Engagement	<u>Low-Tech</u>: Writer's lenses made from paper, DaVinci book, dry erase boards, laminated organizer, student notebooks <u>High-Tech</u>: Using a camera as a writer's lens, DaVinci electronic book, word processing program on computer, Smartboard/projector
Expression	<u>Low-Tech</u>: Verbal responses, paper and pencil organizer, dry erase boards, student notebooks <u>High-Tech</u>: Computer-generated organizer, Smartboard, student-created PowerPoint with questions

Tier III: A few students will conduct independent research in the media center using the DaVinci book and other related sources to answer the research questions they developed and refined after conferencing with the teacher prior to class.

Tier II: Some students will write four to five research questions

Tier I: All students will write three research questions

Possible Learner Barriers:	Possible Solutions:
Some students can't remember directions	Have directions for Big 6 research steps recorded on an MP3 player or iPod
One student has a visual impairment	Change the background to yellow with black letters and use enlarged print or font
Some students lack background knowledge related to DaVinci	Have print materials, a WebQuest, video clips, or other resources available for students to gain background knowledge. Post these to your class web page if possible for study outside of class.
Some students have difficulty writing and/or spelling	Pair students with stronger writers/spellers; allow use of electronic spell checkers/dictionaries, computers, portable keyboards; provide word banks

Figure 11.10 UDL and Differentiation Applications for Writing Lesson Plan

for tiers as described in Chapter 10. The "Possible Barriers with Solutions Box" at the bottom of the figure is paired with possible solutions.

For students with poor handwriting and motor control, portable keyboards can give them access to better written expression. These can be used at desks, in more comfortable places, or even outside. Notes can be taken, data collected, and reports written that can easily be downloaded to another computer later. Some of these keyboards have spell check and word prediction software. Students with motor

Multiple Ways to Increase Writing/ Spelling/Handwriting	
Representation	• Model/demonstrate writing mechanics (up/down) • Provide examples and nonexamples • Model with electronic whiteboards, word prediction software, electronic dictionaries, reading pens
Engagement	• Use a variety of writing tools (including pencil grips) and writing surfaces/keyboarding/word processing/tablet PC • Choose pictures, letters, words/phrases to use in personal writing "bank" or dictionary; computer graphics/clip art; sort by patterns • Practice spelling strategies, write letters in the sky, paint words with water and brush
Expression	• Written product, poster, journal entries • Provide rubric and checkbox to edit writing • Oral presentation, song, student-led conference, tape

challenges may also benefit from receiving copies of another student's notes, a hard copy of the teacher's presentation outline, and/or recording the lecture.

For students who struggle with spelling, familiarize yourself with the work of Grace Fernald (1971). Even though her work was developed almost forty years ago, her methodology still works. In her method, the student says the word, spells it, and traces it with one finger. For kinesthetic/tactile learners, variations might include writing the word with one finger in a salt tray or with other sensory material. Sometimes it helps to activate larger muscles by spelling in the air ("sky writing") or tracing words on a student's back. Younger students may benefit from clapping while spelling; older students may prefer to tap out syllables unobtrusively on their fingers. For visual students, add a picture. For visual and tactile learners, draw lines under each syllable or frame parts of words with paper slides or fingers. For auditory students, add a mnemonic or jingle. Have all kinds of dictionaries available. Technologies such as word prediction software and spell checkers are helpful.

Sometimes students who struggle with writing have physical and/or perceptual challenges. These students may need more work with large muscle development. Floor games, manipulatives, index cards, and word boxes may help. Offering a variety of writing tools, including pencil/pen grips, may be helpful. Copying from the board typically needs to be limited, substituting instead written hard copies or other visual displays. Learning technologies may include word processors, text-to-speech technologies, preprogrammable switches, and tape recorders.

Applying UDL to Reading in the Content Areas

This section of the chapter may be most useful for students who struggle with reading and writing for various reasons and yet need to gain and process content information for their academic and cognitive growth. Accelerated students may assist with the creation of units/lessons that increase accessibility to extend and apply their problem-solving skills. Accelerated students may also access text at higher readability levels. This section is organized into four parts: (1) eliminating the reading requirement entirely, (2) modifying the reading level, (3) adapting the format, and (4) adapting the presentation of text/print.

Eliminate the Reading Requirement Entirely

As mentioned earlier, *reading to learn* is simply not an option for some students. It becomes necessary to have all important material and information presented aloud to these learners. Their listening comprehension and cognitive abilities may very well be high, and once they hear the material, they can participate in discussions and be held to the lesson performance expectation/standard. The following are examples of strategies for presenting text material aloud.

First, begin the lesson with a video clip or other multimedia **anchor** to provide background information, activate prior knowledge, and increase engagement. Next, prepare questions for discussion ahead of time. Include more higher- than lower-level questions, and provide more interpretive than factual questions as well.

The next step is to find the text or other readings in a prerecorded format (CD, cassette, eBook, scanned text) and let the student listen to it read aloud. For text that is not prerecorded, have it recorded or use computer reading programs. Remember that scanned text can be read electronically. If it is possible to scan the text—or access it in digital format, technologies are available that will "read the text" to the student. Software that offers text-to-speech feedback can be found on the companion website. These programs "read" the text on the computer screen to the student. This could be used for anything from reading test questions to reading a novel.

If there is plenty of time before the text will be required, the services of Recording for the Blind and Dyslexic can be used. For quicker turnaround, text can be read into a tape recorder by the teacher, parent volunteer, a peer, or someone off-site. Think creatively! There may be many people who would like to be a school "volunteer," but cannot make it to the school building or during school hours (e.g., church or community members who are at work during the school day or homebound adults—those who cannot physically come to the school but can sit and read/record text). Another idea is to find an associated video that accurately portrays the content of the text. If so, the student may be allowed to watch the video.

For text that has not been prerecorded, and you need it *today*, it may be necessary to have it "read aloud" to the student in class. This can be done in several ways. The teacher can simply read the text to the entire group. Or, as an individual modification, the teacher or a peer can read it to the specific student during a designated part of class.

Modify the Reading Level of the Text

At times, a student's reading level may be two or more levels below the level of the print material. For these students, it may be desirable to take advantage of the reading skills they have (and further develop them) by requiring that they read the same or similar content that has been written in a modified format. This middle-level intervention is not as intrusive as eliminating all reading requirements, but still supports the needs of the student.

Some novels and other literature have been rewritten at a lower reading level. Advantages of this approach are (1) it holds the student accountable for the reading, (2) the student independently reads the material and meets the class goals, and (3) self-esteem and motivation can increase for the student who is able to read age-appropriate text at his/her reading level.

If an assignment involves a choice of books, high-interest/low-reading-level books may be added to the selection list for struggling readers. These books offer topics that would be of interest to older students presented in text written at lower reading levels. Some publishers are now offering texts/books with the same titles and content, but written at different readability levels.

You might also incorporate interactive student-to-student interventions such as Peer-Assisted Learning Strategies (PALS). With this strategy, students alternate tutoring each other as they read aloud, listen, and provide feedback. PALS has been effective in increasing the literacy skills of students who struggle with reading when used in diverse general education classrooms, including students who have learning differences (Saenz, Fuchs, & Fuchs, 2005). It can be used with various subject areas and grade levels.

Reciprocal teaching is another interactive method that can be used by teachers and students to help diverse learners comprehend text (Palinscar & Brown, 1986). This intervention uses text material for dialogue between the teacher and one or more students. Participants take turns being the "teacher." The dialogue is based on the following:

1. Reading and retelling text at the appropriate reading level
2. Shrinking/paraphrasing paragraphs (reading a chunk and then summarizing or saying something about what was read)
3. Prediction relay (predicting, summarizing after reading, checking)

For textbooks or other pieces of literature that have not been professionally modified to a lower reading level, this can be done in-house. This will take some planning ahead and possibly creativity. For example, the teacher can write a summary of the text for older students or rewrite the text for younger students. Students and teachers may create electronic books (eBooks) using programs such as PowerPoint. The books can incorporate focus vocabulary and spelling words. Adding color, animation, and sound increases engagement. Again, individual or cooperative groups of volunteers may help create these books. Once adapted books and summaries are made, they can be kept as resources for future use.

Figure 11.11 shows the **Fry readability index**. You can use this index to determine the general reading level of print material. After you determine readability, find a basic word list, such as the Dolch basic word list, at the student's reading level, along with word lists below that level, and use them to adapt the text. Informal or basic skills assessments also typically have lists of common grade level words.

When rewriting or summarizing print material, you may again want to enlist the assistance of classroom peers. Have students who have strengths in reading and organization read ahead and summarize upcoming print material that will be used in class. This rewritten and/or summarized material can then be proofread by the teacher and provided as a resource to students with reading difficulties. School volunteers can also be a valuable resource with this task. However the revised presentations and/or summaries are acquired, everyone will have the content in hand.

Adapt the Format of the Text/Print Material

For some students, the difficulty is not so much reading the text, but gaining the most important information from what they read. You may encounter this feeling yourself reading some of the college textbooks you are using. This is especially problematic for (but not exclusive to) higher-level textbooks. If this is happening, you might consider presenting the same key ideas and information in an outline format as a supplement or even substitute for the text. This will make the organization of the text very clear for the student.

Another idea is to present the same information in the form of a graphic organizer. There are several different graphic organizer formats that would be appropriate. For example, if your school uses *Thinking Maps,* you can select one of these organizers with which your students will already be familiar. Otherwise, use an organizer you have that is best suited for the material in the text. Software such as *Inspiration* can convert graphic organizers to outline format with one button click. This offers much versatility to the teacher and the student.

Consider using "sticky notes" in the text to clarify key terms, provide definitions, insert questions to prompt/facilitate comprehension, etc. This can be done electronically with software such as *Kurzweil* or manually with sticky notes.

Adapt the Presentation of the Text

At times very powerful adaptations may be very simple to implement based on the specific learning needs of the student. Some examples of simple changes to the way text is presented that may make a dramatic difference in student performance are offered in this section.

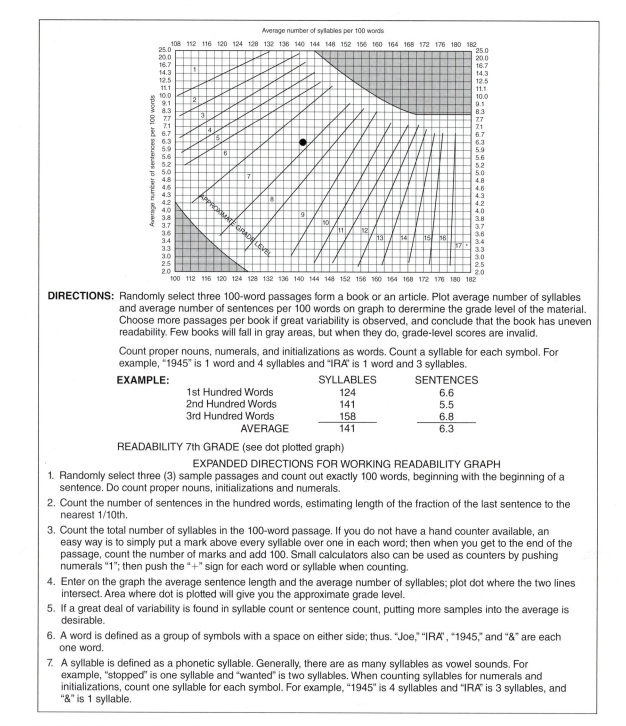

DIRECTIONS: Randomly select three 100-word passages form a book or an article. Plot average number of syllables and average number of sentences per 100 words on graph to derermine the grade level of the material. Choose more passages per book if great variability is observed, and conclude that the book has uneven readability. Few books will fall in gray areas, but when they do, grade-level scores are invalid.

Count proper nouns, numerals, and initializations as words. Count a syllable for each symbol. For example, "1945" is 1 word and 4 syllables and "IRA" is 1 word and 3 syllables.

EXAMPLE:		SYLLABLES	SENTENCES
	1st Hundred Words	124	6.6
	2nd Hundred Words	141	5.5
	3rd Hundred Words	158	6.8
	AVERAGE	141	6.3

READABILITY 7th GRADE (see dot plotted graph)

EXPANDED DIRECTIONS FOR WORKING READABILITY GRAPH

1. Randomly select three (3) sample passages and count out exactly 100 words, beginning with the beginning of a sentence. Do count proper nouns, initializations and numerals.

2. Count the number of sentences in the hundred words, estimating length of the fraction of the last sentence to the nearest 1/10th.

3. Count the total number of syllables in the 100-word passage. If you do not have a hand counter available, an easy way is to simply put a mark above every syllable over one in each word; then when you get to the end of the passage, count the number of marks and add 100. Small calculators also can be used as counters by pushing numerals "1"; then push the "+" sign for each word or syllable when counting.

4. Enter on the graph the average sentence length and the average number of syllables; plot dot where the two lines intersect. Area where dot is plotted will give you the approximate grade level.

5. If a great deal of variability is found in syllable count or sentence count, putting more samples into the average is desirable.

6. A word is defined as a group of symbols with a space on either side; thus "Joe," "IRA", "1945," and "&" are each one word.

7. A syllable is defined as a phonetic syllable. Generally, there are as many syllables as vowel sounds. For example, "stopped" is one syllable and "wanted" is two syllables. When counting syllables for numerals and initializations, count one syllable for each symbol. For example, "1945" is 4 syllables and "IRA" is 3 syllables, and "&" is 1 syllable.

Figure 11.11 The Fry Readability Index
Source: E. Fry, *Elementary Reading Instruction* (New York: McGraw-Hill, 1977), p. 217.

Some students are only able to focus on small units of print/text at a time. Additionally, graphics and extra information on a page may be distracting. Text/print can be **framed** or **masked** using a card or paper to focus attention on the specific text a student is reading. For students focusing on decoding, frames may be cut to focus on words. Sometimes using something as simple as an index card or a cut paper slide to place over or under words, sentences, or paragraphs is helpful.

Using **color overlays** over print is another technique you might try even though it has met with mixed results in the research literature. Some students with visual perception challenges indicate that the use of color overlays helps them focus on words and sentences. Color preferences are diverse, so the choice is individualized.

Another simple strategy for helping students with visual perception difficulties as well as attention challenges is to enlarge the font and/or increase the contrast. By doing this you may also reduce some of the fatigue associated with the reading process. The students themselves are likely the best resource for finding the right size and/or color combination.

Finally, think about eliminating clutter and reducing the quantity of text presented on a page. When selecting text and preparing reading materials/texts, it may be beneficial to reduce the amount of extraneous information (figures, graphics, photos, text) that are on a page. Additionally, reading material may be divided in such a way that the division between major ideas or tasks is clear. A reduction in the amount of text on a page may cause the student to feel much less overwhelmed with the reading task.

Other Possible Barriers to Reading

In this chapter, we have looked at UDL applications in language arts through literacy components and adaptations. Considerable emphasis has been placed on cognitive/academic, language, sensory, and motor domains. There are additional considerations about needs concerning vision, social or emotional state, attention, and giftedness to address as we near closure on this topic.

Vision

As obvious as it seems, sometimes a student needs and even has glasses, but isn't wearing them for various reasons. Likely, the vision problem has been diagnosed at an earlier age, but there might be a communication breakdown about their use from year to year in spite of vision exams and record keeping. Sometimes students are reluctant to tell teachers they should be wearing glasses. Sometimes glasses tend to get misplaced at home. Perhaps an extra pair of glasses could be secured to keep at school.

Access to portable keyboards helps some diverse learners with written expression.

Social Emotional

Remember that students with *social* or *emotional* needs will usually do best when offered choice. They may want to work alone or with a peer. You might identify a universal theme for a reading/interdisciplinary assignment and offer a variety of content material within that theme. Try to find a way to connect student interests to the theme. If possible, try to find books/presentations that also incorporate social skills and show how people handle difficult situations that might parallel their own lives. These students often respond well to poetry and social stories that connect to their interests. Studies of characters in books, novels, and other media using cause-effect charts may also serve dual purposes. An older student may enjoy discussing the underlying motives and moods relating to the development of a character in a novel.

Remember the importance of rehearsing rules and roles when moving these students into group work. They will need consistency practicing routines and procedures. However, with such adaptations, these students may ultimately do very well with debates, role plays, poetry readings, art work, songs, and/or plays. Journal responses (written, taped, or digitized) can also be therapeutic for engagement and response.

ADHD and Motivational

Students with ADHD and motivational challenges may respond best to literacy instruction when it is presented using audio/visual materials. Watching and creating personal or small group PowerPoint presentations and eBooks can be highly engaging. Sometimes these students make excellent media assistants! Reading materials of interest may extend to comic books, trade books, newspaper articles, blogs, and more.

Remember to build in opportunities for movement into lessons. You might consider varying seating/other positioning when students are reading and writing and providing frequent breaks. Remember to check the lighting for glares and use as much natural lighting as possible. Using interactive whiteboards, portable keyboards, GPS systems, and other technology that allows for movement in their day can also help. Sometimes simply asking a student how he/she can do their work best is helpful as well!

Academically Gifted

Remember to consider curriculum compacting for these students. For example, if the curricular area is poetry, the student and teacher(s) may decide that a poetry book will be created representing 10 different genres composed by the student. This collaboration may include other teachers involved in the student's learning so that content can be connected. The rest of the class may be working on fewer poems/genres. Format and presentation style of the poetry book could also be part of the project description. An assessment rubric can be created up front for the project. Responsibilities regarding class discussions and other contributions need to be decided ahead of time along with differentiated assignments.

Fostering Literacy Collaboration

As you have seen in this chapter, literacy instruction is broad, complex, and one size definitely does not fit all. It will be important to establish and maintain collaborative partnerships to be most effective. In courses outside of English/Language Arts, all teachers will be working to circumvent reading difficulties to promote learning of other content. Collaboration with the reading specialist can be invaluable in making strategy choices and in sharing words/skills being worked on so they can be reinforced and integrated in other settings for generalization. Similarly, teachers of high school curriculum assistance programs may be using a particular strategy to teach decoding of multisyllabic words to students with learning disabilities. If content-area teachers know and are able to use the same terminology when speaking with their students ("Can you RAP this paragraph?" for example), reading progress may be enhanced. Communicating the same information to any after school tutoring assistance or help at home further strengthens the connection.

Schools may benefit from exploring scheduling possibilities not only to foster collaboration and planning, but to also make a larger impact on literacy instruction. At the middle school level, for example, a school might structure double blocks of English/Language Arts and differentiate instruction. Depending on the student needs, perhaps a reading specialist, special educator, specialist for English language learners, or a trained volunteer could be paired with a teacher in one block to assist students who are still working on prerequisite skills. These same students would still receive the regular content instruction in the other block. In the ideal world, there would be more than one teacher, professional, and/or volunteer working together in all classrooms. This arrangement offers more opportunities to teach students in smaller groups, which can increase engagement and the amount of critical, prompt feedback that students need to correct any conceptual and procedural errors from the start. Research studies are showing significant student gains with approaches such as these in schools with high minority, poverty, and special education numbers (Hawkins, 2007).

Thematic Summary

- Students come to classrooms today with a wide range of reading and writing ability. Regardless of reading/writing proficiency, all students are expected to learn the basic concepts presented.
- There are five big ideas in reading: phonemic awareness, alphabetic principles, fluency with text, vocabulary, and comprehension.
- Both informal and formal assessments of reading and writing inform instruction.
- Students who struggle with reading and writing need direct instruction in specific reading skills at their working levels as well as scaffolded reading/writing assistance that will let them access the concepts being taught at a given time. Teachers need to find the balance between learning to read and reading to learn.
- Applying the principles of UDL through learning domains can help teachers and students teach/learn through student strengths and needs.
- Students who are gifted may need curriculum compacting. Some may be "twice exceptional" and need a combination of adaptations.
- There are many programs and strategies available to help students with reading and writing. Teachers need to keep the big ideas in mind as they select programs. They also need to look for ways to make learning strategies multisensory.
- Teachers can assist struggling readers in accessing text in four basic ways.
- Assistive technology and innovative learning tools are significantly helping diverse learners access print/language.
- Collaborative partnerships within school communities can help diverse students make significant gains in literacy.

Making Connections for Inclusive Teaching

1. Teachers must find a balance between learning to read and reading to learn. Do you agree or disagree with this statement? Defend your viewpoint.
2. Why do you think teaching literacy skills is so complex? Give two or more real-life examples.
3. Explain why assessment is so critical in the planning and implementation of teaching literacy in reading, spelling, and writing.
4. Does thinking about the "big ideas" in literacy help you think about how you will approach teaching the subject? What might be some advantages? Do you see any disadvantages?
5. Explain how applying the principles of UDL to reading and writing instruction might benefit *all* students.

Learning Activities

1. Administer the Burke Reading Inventory (Figure 11.1) and the Reading Comprehension Questionnaire (Figure 11.2) reading interest survey to two students at the grade level of your choice. Summarize your findings and suggest next steps for these readers.
2. Develop an informal observation checklist for literacy you could use in your grade level/school to determine students' literacy strengths and needs.
3. Using a lesson plan you already have, color code the different ways literacy methods and materials are represented, engaged in, and expressed. Use the UDL Application key in Figure 11.9 as a guide.

4. Take a literacy activity you are planning to use in your classroom. Indicate how you will adapt it for a student with cognitive challenges, for a student who has ADHD, and for a student who is gifted.

5. Use a readability index to estimate the level of two or more textbooks used in your grade level/school. Discuss your findings. How might you adjust them for students who struggle accessing text?

6. Make a list of low- and high-tech tools you currently are familiar with. State how each can help you foster literacy with your students, regardless of age or grade level.

7. Briefly research and try out one of the technology tools mentioned in this chapter that you are not familiar with. Describe the outcome. Learners with what strengths/needs might benefit the most from using this tool?

Looking at the Standards

INTASC Standards

- *Content Pedagogy.* The teacher understands the central concepts, tools of inquiry, and structures of the discipline he or she teaches and can create learning experiences that make these aspects of subject matter meaningful for students.
- *Multiple Instructional Resources.* The teacher understands and uses a variety of instructional strategies to encourage students' development of critical thinking, problem solving, and performance skills.
- *Motivation and Management.* The teacher uses an understanding of individual and group motivation and behavior to create a learning environment that encourages positive social interaction, active engagement in learning, and self-motivation.
- *Communication and Technology.* The teacher uses knowledge of effective verbal, nonverbal, and media communication techniques to foster active inquiry, collaboration, and supportive interaction in the classroom.

Council for Exceptional Children

Council for Exceptional Children

Special educators are to have knowledge of the following:

- CC4S3: Select, adapt, and use instructional strategies and materials according to characteristics of the individual with exceptional learning needs.
- GC4S1: Use research-supported methods for academic and nonacademic instruction of individuals with disabilities.
- GC4S4: Use reading methods appropriate to individuals with disabilities.
- GC4S7: Use appropriate adaptations and technology for all individuals with disabilities.
- GC4S16: Implement systematic instruction to teach accuracy, fluency, and comprehension in content area reading and written language.
- GC4S12: Use responses and errors to guide instructional decisions and provide feedback to learners.
- GC6S1: Enhance vocabulary development.
- GC6S2: Teach strategies for spelling accuracy and generalization.

Key Concepts and Terms

twice exceptional
learned helplessness
balanced literacy
authentic literacy
phonemic awareness
phonics
alphabetic principle
fluency
vocabulary
Dolch sight word
informal reading inventory

Word Identification
   Strategy
echo reading
whisper-phones
word maps
reading pen
electronic dictionary
thinking aloud
paraphrasing
RAP
Question-Answer-Response
foldables

cloze procedure
slot outline
The Sentence Writing
   Strategy
anchor
Peer-Assisted Learning
   Strategies
reciprocal teaching
Fry readability index
framed or masked text
color overlays

References

Adams, M. (1990). *Beginning to read: Thinking and learning about print*. Cambridge, MA: MIT Press.

Al Otaiba, S., & Rivera, M. (2006). Individualizing guided oral reading fluency instruction for students with emotional and behavioral disorders. *Intervention in School and Clinic, 41*(3), 144–149.

American Federation of Teachers. (1999). *Teaching reading is rocket science: What expert teachers of reading should know and be able to do*. Washington, DC: American Federation of Teachers.

Baker, S. K., Simmons, D. C., & Kame'enui, E. J. (1998). Vocabulary acquisition: Research bases. In D. C. Simmons & E. J. Kame'enui (Eds.), *What reading research tells us about children with diverse learning needs*. Mahwah, NJ: Lawrence Erlbaum, 183–218.

Bear, D., Invernizzi, M., Templeton, S., & Johnston, F. (2004). *Words their way: Word study for phonics, vocabulary, and spelling instruction* (3rd ed.). Upper Saddle River, NJ: Pearson Education.

Bhat, P., Griffin, C. C., & Sindelar, P. T. (2003). Phonological awareness instruction for middle school students with learning disabilities. *Learning Disabilities Quarterly, 26*, 73–87.

Bremer, C. D., Clapper, A. T., & Deshler, D. D. (2002). Improving word identification skills using Strategic Instruction Model (SIM) strategies. *Research to Practice Brief: Improving Secondary Education and Transition Services through Research, 1*(4), 1–6.

Brigance, A. H. (1999). *Brigance comprehensive inventory of basic skills* (Rev. ed.). North Billerica, MA: Curriculum Associates.

Burke, C. (1987). Burke Reading Inventory. In Y. Goodman, D. Watson, & C. Burke (Eds.), *Reading miscue inventory: Alternative procedures*. New York: Richard C. Owen Publishers.

Bursuck, W. D., Smith, T., Munk, D., Damer, M., Mehlig, L., & Perry, J. (2004). Evaluating the impact of a prevention-based model of reading on children who are at risk. *Remedial and Special Education, 25*(5), 303–313.

Chard, D., & Osborn, J. (1999). Phonics and word recognition instruction in early reading programs: Guidelines for accessibility. *Learning Disabilities Research & Practice, 14*(2), 107–117.

Chard, D., Vaughn, S., & Tyler, B. (2002). A synthesis of research on effective interventions for building reading fluency with elementary students with learning disabilities. *Journal of Learning Disabilities, 35*(5), 386–406.

Collier, V., & Thomas, W. (1989). How quickly can immigrants become proficient in school English? *Journal of Educational Issues of Language Minority Students, 5*, 26–38.

Deno, S., Fuchs, L., Marston, D., & Shinn, J. (2001). Using curriculum-based measurement to establish growth standards for students with learning disabilities. *School Psychology Review, 30*(4), 389–406.

Dolch, E. W. (1948). *Problems in reading*. Champaign, IL: The Garrard Press.

Dowhower, S. (1987). Effects of repeated reading on second grade transitional readers' fluency and comprehension. *Reading Research Quarterly, 22*(4), 389–406.

Fernald, G. (1971). *Remedial techniques in basic school subjects*. New York: McGraw-Hill.

Fisher, D., & Ivey, G. (2007). Farewell to a farewell to arms: Deemphasizing the whole-class novel. *Phi Delta Kappan, 88*(7), 494–497.

Fitzgerald, J. (1999). What is this thing called "balance"? *The Reading Teacher, 53*(2), 100–107.

Fletcher, J. M., & Lyon, G. R. (1998). Reading: A research-based approach. In W. M. Evers (Ed.) *What's gone wrong in America's classrooms* (pp. 49–90). Stanford, CA: Hoover Institution Press.

Francis, D. J., Shaywitz, S. E., Steubing, K. K., Shaywitz, B. A., & Fletcher, J. M. (1994). Measurement of change: Assessing behavior over time and within a developmental context. In G. R. Lyon (Ed.), *Frames of reference for the assessment of learning disabilities: New views on measurement issues* (pp. 29–58). Baltimore: Paul H. Brookes.

Gillingham, A., & Stillman, B. (1970). *Remedial training for children with specific difficulty in reading, spelling, and penmanship*. Cambridge, MA: Educators Publishing Service.

Good, R. H., & Kaminski, R. A. (Eds.). (2002). *Dynamic indicators of basic early literacy skills* (6th ed.). Eugene, OR: Institute for the Development of Education Achievement.

Greenberg, D., Fredrick, L. D., Hughes, T. A., & Bunting, C. J. (2002). Implementation issues in a reading program for low reading adults. *Journal of Adolescent & Adult Literacy*, 45(7), pp. 626–632.

Groff, P. (2001). Teaching phonics: Letter-to-phoneme, phoneme-to-letter, or both? *Reading & Writing Quarterly*, 17, 291–306.

Hahn, A. (1984). Assessing and extending comprehension: Monitoring strategies in the classroom. *Reading Horizons*, 24, 225–230.

Hammill, D. D., Pearson, N. A., & Wiederholt, J. L. (1996). *Comprehensive test of nonverbal intelligence*. Austin, TX: Pro-Ed.

Hawkins, V. (2007). Narrowing gaps for special-needs students. *Educational Leadership*, 64(5), 61–63.

Hook, P., & Jones, S. (2004). The importance of automaticity and fluency for efficient reading comprehension. *Perspectives: International Dyslexia Association*, 2(2), 16–21.

Johnson, M., Kress, K., & Pikulski, J. (1987). *Informal reading inventories*. Newark, DE: International Reading Association.

Leafstedt, J. M., & Gerber, M. M. (2005). Crossover of phonological processing skills. *Remedial and Special Education*, 26(4), 226–235.

Lenz, B., Schumaker, J., Deshler, D., & Beals, V. (1984*). The word identification strategy: Instructor's manual*. Lawrence: University of Kansas Institute for Research in Learning Disabilities.

Lerner, J. (2006). *Learning disabilities and related disorders: Characteristics and teaching strategies*. Boston, MA: Houghton Mifflin.

Lesaux, N., & Siegel, L. (2003). The development of reading in children who speak English as a second language. *Developmental Psychology*, 39(6), 1005–1019.

Lyon, R. (2003). Reading disabilities: Why do some children have difficulties learning to read? What can be done about it? *Perspectives, The International Dyslexia Association*, 29(2), 17–19.

Marchand-Martella, N., Martella, R. C., Oriob, M., & Ebey, T. (2000). Conducting action research in a rural high school setting using peers as corrective reading instructors for students with disabilities. *Rural Special Education Quarterly*, 19(2), 20–30.

McCandliss, B., Beck, I., Sandak, R., & Perfetti, C. (2003). Focusing attention on decoding for children with poor reading skills: Design and preliminary tests of the word building intervention. *Scientific Studies of Reading*, 7(1), 75–104.

Mercer, C., Campbell, K., Miller, M., Mercer, K., & Lane, H. (2000). Effects of a reading fluency intervention for middle schoolers with specific learning disabilities. *Learning Disabilities Research & Practice*, 15(4), 179–189.

National Center for Education Statistics. (2003). *The nation's report card: Reading highlights 2003*. Retrieved October 2008, from http://nces.ed.gov/pubsearch/pubsinfo.asp?pubid=2004452.

National Reading Panel. (2000). *Teaching children to read: An evidenced-based assessment of the scientific research literature on reading and implications for reading instruction*. Washington, DC: National Institute of Child Health and Human Development. Retrieved June 28, 2008, from http://www.nichd.nih.gov/publications/nrp/upload/smallbook_pdf.pdf

Nes Ferrara, S. L. (2005). Reading fluency and self-efficacy: A case study. *International Journal of Disability, Development and Education*, 52, 215–231.

Nielson, M., & Higgins, L. (2005). The eye of the storm: Programs and services for twice-exceptional learners. *Teaching Exceptional Children*, 38(1), 8–15.

Orton, J. (1976). *A guide to teaching phonics*. Cambridge, MA: Educators Publishing Services.

Palinscar, A. S., & Brown, A. L. (1986). Interactive teaching to promote independent learning from text. *The Reading Teacher*, 39(2), 771–777.

Paris, S. G., & Meyers, M. (1981). Comprehension monitoring, memory, and study strategies of good and poor readers. *Journal of Reading Behavior*, 13(1), 5–22.

Rashotte, C., & Torgesen, J. (1985). Repeated reading and reading fluency in learning disabled children. *Reading Research Quarterly*, 20, 180–188.

Rasinski, T., & Padak, N. (2000). *Effective reading strategies: Teaching students who find reading difficult* (2nd ed.). Upper Saddle River, NJ: Prentice Hall.

Saenz, L. M., Fuchs, L. S., & Fuchs, D. (2005). Peer-assisted learning strategies for English language learners with learning disabilities. *Exceptional Children*, 71, 231–247.

Schmoker, M. (2007). Radically redefining literacy instruction: An immense opportunity. *Phi Delta Kappan*, 88(7), 448–493.

Shaywitz, S. E., Escobar, M. D., Shaywitz, B. A., Fletcher, J. M., & Makuch, R. (1992). Evidence that dyslexia may represent the lower tail of a normal distribution of reading ability. *New England Journal of Medicine*, 326, 145–150.

Short, D., & Echevarria, J. (2004). Teacher skills to support English language learners. *Educational Leadership*, 62(4), 8–13.

Schumaker, J., Denton, P., & Deshler, D. (1984). *The paraphrasing strategy*. Lawrence: The University of Kansas.

Schumaker, J., & Sheldon, J. (1985). *The sentence writing strategy*. Lawrence: The University of Kansas.

Speece, D. L., & Ritchey, K. D. (2005). A longitudinal study of the development of oral reading fluency in young children at risk for reading failure. *Journal of Learning Disabilities*, 38(5), 387–399.

Stahl, S. (2004). Scaly? audacious? debris? salubrious? Vocabulary learning and the child with learning disabilities. *Perspectives (International Dyslexia Association)*, 30(1), 5–12.

Wiederholt, J. L., & Bryant, B. R. (2003). *Gray Oral Reading Tests* (4th ed.). Austin, TX: Pro-Ed.

Woodcock, R. W. (1998). *Woodcock reading mastery tests—revised*. Circle Pines, MN: American Guidance Service.

Zike, D. (2005). *Dinah Zike's teaching mathematics with foldables*. New York: Glencoe McGraw-Hill.

Cengage Learning/Wadsworth

Developing an Understanding of Mathematics in All Learners

Establish Learning Goals: Big Ideas in Mathematics Instruction
Problem Solving
Mathematic Communication
Numbers and Operations
Algebra
Geometry and Spatial Sense
Measurement
Data Analysis and Probability

Assessment of Mathematics
Formal Assessment
Informal Assessment

Methods, Materials, and Resources that Promote Mathematics for All Learners
Problem Solving
Communication of Mathematic Ideas

Learning Outcomes
After reading this chapter, you will be able to:

- Articulate the big ideas of mathematics instruction.
- Describe some of the challenges that face diverse learners in mathematics.
- Explain why mathematics assessment is important and how it can be used.
- Give examples of how the elements of UDL can be applied in each of the seven major categories of mathematics instruction.
- Take a "typical" lesson plan for mathematics and show how it can be extended and how it can be adapted for learners who are still working on prerequisite skills.
- Discuss the benefits of collaborative partnerships in the teaching of mathematics.
- List possible AT and other technology-based learning tools that can offer access to work in mathematics.

Numbers and Operations
Algebra
Geometry and Spatial Sense
Measurement
Data Analysis and Probability

Fostering Collaboration in Mathematics Instruction

Your third-block pre-Algebra class opens with a warm-up exercise problem. You have cho-sen a practical problem that you think the students can relate to. The problem exercises students on finding square roots using the Pythagorean formula that you presented yes-terday. At the end of yesterday's instruction, many students excitedly stated they knew this material after working out problems on dry erase boards and worksheets. However, with a quick check of homework and this warm-up activity, you can tell that only about half of the class really seems to understand it. You were planning to move ahead today but feel like you need to spend some more time on this so students have a solid foundation.

How can you present this lesson and engage students in a different way to maximize learning for these students? How will you challenge the students who are ready to move ahead? Think about how you might answer these questions as you read this chapter.

Each one of us can likely think of students who believe they are not good at mathematics even though they can solve problems in real-life situations. Some-times this may simply be a perception on their part caused by a negative prior experience with mathematics, most likely in school. It is estimated that between 5 and 10 percent of all elementary students struggle with learning mathematics (Kroesbergen & Van Luit, 2003). Between 5 and 8 percent of all children have spe-cific disabilities in math (Fuchs & Fuchs, 2003; Geary, 2004).

In addition, a recent study done by the researchers at the Human Resources Research Organization (Diaz, Le, & Wise, 2006) compared 12th-grade test scores from 2005 monitored by the National Assessment of Educational Progress in the United States (National Assessment of Educational Progress, 2005) to 2000 and 1996 scores. Their analysis revealed that, in spite of some gains in certain areas, 39 percent of high school seniors in the sample still lacked a basic understanding in math. This percentage is higher than in previous years—steadily increasing upward from 31 percent in 1996. Analysis also showed a large gap in achievement by race and ethnicity (Mervis, 2007). Considering the dropout rate mentioned in Chapter 8 (11% of the general population and almost 39% of students with learning disabilities), reforms are warranted.

In the 21st century, higher levels of technical and mathematical skills are demanded of people whether or not they go to college. Just think about the ways we receive and send messages/news today, how we pay bills online, and how we apply for employment. The impact of technology is felt at school, at home, at work, and in the community. We must continually push ourselves to learn and use it.

Our country has seen a shift in mathematics education, largely due to standards-based mathematics reform through the Goals 2000: Educate America Act of 1994, the National Council of the Teachers of Mathematics' (NCTM) *Principles and Stan-dards for School Mathematics* (National Council of Teachers of Mathematics, 2000), and through the No Child Left Behind Act of 2001 (PL 107-110). NCLB legislation addresses the most current legislation regarding math standards. The emphasis on procedural/rule-driven knowledge, although still important, has shifted to the devel-opment of math literacy and conceptual knowledge (Goldman & Hasselbring, 1997; Xin, Jitendra, & Deatline-Buchman, 2005). Teaching students to be critical thinkers and problem solvers is taking priority.

Establish Learning Goals: Big Ideas in Mathematics Instruction

In this section, we will briefly identify and describe seven topics from the National Council of Teachers of Mathematics 2000 standards that help form the big ideas in mathematics instruction today. Some of the challenges each presents to students who learn differently will also be described. This is simply an overview, and more detail can be accessed by visiting the National Council of Teachers of Mathematics website. Keep in mind that these standards address learners from prekindergarten through 12th grade and the focus is on a broad spectrum of understanding, knowledge, and skills. The standards build on one another.

Building on a strong foundation is important for success in math even though we know some skills may need compensation along the way for some students who learn differently. Some students may not have the general prerequisite skills in spatial learning, body image, visual-motor skills, visual-perception, language, direction and time concepts, and memory abilities that are needed to be successful in all of these mathematical areas.

Problem Solving

All students must be able to understand and investigate math problems. In fact, **problem solving** has become the top priority for math curriculum (National Council of Teachers of Mathematics, 2000) in both general and special education (Cawley & Foley, 2001). Problem solving requires confidence, risk taking, and a willingness to learn from one's mistakes. One must be able to make predictions, reason, and evaluate in the quest to resolve an unfamiliar situation. One must be able to sequence and see patterns. Problem solvers must have useful inner language that may take the form of words, pictures, and/or symbols. One might talk oneself through problem-solving steps or perhaps draw out or visualize words, pictures, and/or symbols.

Young students are typically more open to taking risks in math problem solving than older ones, so it is, once again, best to design instruction and space for this learning from the start. As teachers we have a lot of influence in modeling a positive "can-do" attitude toward problem solving. As students get older, risk-taking skills in mathematics tend to subside. If the concepts still evade them, frustration and *learned helplessness* can easily take over.

Problem solving is often the most challenging task in mathematics for students who experience math difficulties, as often evidenced in the execution of word problems. For example, you may know a student who can add or subtract fairly well; however, when the skills need to be applied in a real-life problem, considerable scaffolding and direct instruction need to be provided. Students with cognitive challenges often have difficulty with the generalization and transfer of skills and concepts. Students with ADHD appear to have the most difficulty with problem solving and calculation. They need to focus on the big picture and gain a deeper understanding rather than focusing on less-relevant stimuli (Lucangeli & Cabrele, 2006). When you really think about it, key mathematical concepts are ultimately learned through problem solving and conducting investigations rather than when taught in isolation. As stated in the previous chapter, students today need to be critical thinkers. Once they access information, they need to analyze, evaluate, and arrive at a plan, product, or "next step." Therefore teaching math through authentic, anchored learning will better lend itself to fostering generalization of concepts and skill application.

It will be important to remember that there is no single "best" way to organize and "do" mathematics (Van de Walle, 2004). It sounds like an invitation to the application of UDL, doesn't it?

Students in the 21st century must be proficient with technology.

Cengage Learning/Wadsworth

Mathematic Communication

In **mathematic communication**, one must be able to associate English words with symbols to develop **math literacy**. The word *is*, for example, can also mean "equal to" and is represented by the symbol "=". × in multiplication is called "*times*." It is also an alphabet letter that stands for a variable in algebra. Think about how difficult this can be for a student who struggles with language and/or cognition. If you think about how you can teach a math concept to a nonverbal student, it might help you come up with some very creative ways to teach diverse learners. For example, if you are using the word *backwards* with young students, you might actually want to walk backwards with the students and have everyone count backwards together simultaneously. Later on they will need to understand that *backwards* means different things on horizontal and vertical number lines but at least they will have some frame of reference for the word.

Math vocabulary will need to be directly taught to many diverse learners. A student may know an operation but not know what to call it. Students with challenges in mathematics often have difficulty early on with positional and directional words as well (on/off, left/right, over/under, in/out, for example). These students may also have difficulty with subtle differences in language/semantics. For example, if the time is 3:45, it can be stated several different ways: *three forty-five, forty-five minutes after three, a quarter to four*, or *fifteen minutes to four*. Another example is the use of the word *quarter*. Think about how minutes convert to *quarter* hours and how *quarters* are also used in money. The mathematical relationship makes sense if you understand fractions but the words can be confusing.

In a study with English language learners conducted in England and Wales (with predominately Asian children of Indian, Pakistani, and Bangladeshi origins), it was found that lower performances on math assessments by second-language learners was usually due to a lack of exposure to mathematical words and phrases rather than to the lack of mathematical skill (Hargreaves, 1997). The authors suggest giving mathematical language attention early to these learners to accelerate math performance. They also noted that native English-speaking children must also have the same exposure to early math vocabulary to be successful. If they are deprived of it, their math performance tends to suffer as well. An encouraging note is that Asian-origin students in England tend to have mathematical skills commensurate with their native speaking counterparts at age 16 (Philips & Birrell, 1994). This may imply that math deficits can be overcome with time, given extra effort in learning the language and related math skills.

Remember, too, that culture refers not only to what is visible (i.e., music, art, dress) but also what is often less visible—language and dialect, nonverbal communication, behavior styles, thought patterns, social preferences, methods of reasoning, and different ways of looking at the world (Malloy & Malloy, 1998).

Numbers and Operations

Early number learning is critical for subsequent success in math. Early on, students must learn things like how to match objects, recognize groups of objects, count, name the number that comes *after* and *before*, write numbers in sequence, and establish one-to-one correspondence. They progress to ordering numbers (using number lines, arranging by size and length) and arranging them in patterns according to various rules (such as qualitative differences) and using them in operations. Many diverse learners need an infusion of "hands-on," multisensory math materials and tools into the instruction. They need to see, hold, and move objects to grasp these skills/concepts. Fortunately, most math kits today include lots of manipulatives that make math skills/concepts come alive for students.

Many teachers have done quite well instructing students in operation skills such as addition, subtraction, multiplication, and division. They need to be sure students

Cengage Learning/Wadsworth

Students of all ages need to engage multiple senses as they explore math skills and concepts.

also see how math skills are connected and how they work together. Multiplication, for example, is a faster way to add. The answers in both subtraction and division get smaller. Having such knowledge as a base helps students make reasonable predictions and estimations later on. Students also need a strong knowledge of the base-10 system (place value). They need to know, for example, that *32* represents three tens and two ones and that it also can be factored into 16 × 2, or two sets of 16. As they progress in school, they will need to develop skills in math areas such as proportional reasoning, fractions, decimals, ratios, rates, and percentages.

For students with perceptual challenges, working from right to left to solve column-form calculations can be a real challenge. In reading, we are trained to read from left to right so a shift in directionality can be overwhelming. Students may also have difficulty keeping their places on a worksheet, using a number line, and/or lining up the computational problems in math. Some may get lost in the steps of a process. Mathematical **algorithms** can help students who are challenged with these kinds of problems. Algorithms are steps used to solve math computation problems. Examples will be presented in this chapter.

Computation fluency needs to develop alongside number sense. However, some students who struggle with memory and retrieval, perceptual, and/or other academic/cognitive challenges, may need adaptations. An overload of working memory, for example, appears to affect the cognitive process of calculation in students with ADHD (Lucangeli & Cabrele, 2006). All students need to learn how to calculate accurately and efficiently—whether mentally or by using a calculator, math tables, or a math **algorithm**. They need to learn what works best for them in a given situation. As teachers, we can also empower them by continually linking skill instruction to the big ideas.

Algebra

Algebra is math that shows a functional relationship between two or more variables. Using algebraic symbols (including letters), graphs, tables, and equations, students learn to represent and analyze mathematical situations to see these relationships between numbers. Success in algebra requires students to understand properties of numbers, see patterns, identify symbols, understand the related language, and use their reasoning abilities. You can see right away the challenge for students who think only concretely about math and who may not understand the language of math. Students who are challenged with directionality will also need extra help.

With a problem-solving emphasis in math, algebraic thinking is now evidenced at all grade levels, even if formal terminology isn't used. It will be important to keep building a foundation beginning at an early age, using manipulatives, infusing the language, and connecting it across mathematics and other disciplines as much as possible. Strong skills in algebra are necessary to develop higher-level mathematics skills that are needed in today's workplace.

Geometry and Spatial Sense

Geometry has its own set of language, terms, and symbols to answer questions about sizes, shapes, angles, lines, and points of figures. It also has words for their relationships (*symmetry*, *congruence*, *similarity*, *Cartesian coordinates*, *parallelism*, and *perpendicularity*). Words that refer to position and motion in space (*near to*, *next to*, *horizontal*, *vertical*, *slide*, *flip*, *turn*, *rotate*, *transform*) and words that refer to theories and formulas (*Pythagorean theorem*) are all important. Once again, students with low verbal abilities or a lack of experience with the language may need extra adaptations. Students who are cognitively and/or spatially challenged may also need extra support. Students who have visual spatial strength or "intelligence" will likely do well in geometry and need extended learning activities.

Literacy in geometry is similar to that in reading. Students are asked to describe, compare, predict, analyze, categorize, and investigate problems using lengths, angles, areas, and volumes as they develop their understanding of geometry. As in other mathematical fields, units that are interdisciplinary and anchored in real life will provide broader access to the curriculum and should help more students gain proficiency.

Measurement

Measurement is a basic life skill that is needed to determine the approximate magnitude of object attributes. From cooking, telling time, determining the outside temperature, charting a road trip, and doing laundry to building homes, schools, and space shuttles, a solid foundation in measurement is important. The language of measurement shares vocabulary words with other math areas and also adds on additional words/symbols, such as volume, inches, meters, weight, perimeter area, velocity, and density. Students will need to learn the attributes of the objects that are represented by words/symbols so they can understand and work with them effectively. Students also need to learn that sometimes measurement can be nonstandard, that sometimes it's best to estimate, and that there are times when measurement needs to be precise. They need to learn what tools and methods to choose and how they work. Students in this increasingly global world are not only required to learn how to convert different U.S. customary measurements (e.g., inches to feet to yards, ounces to cups to quarts), but also how to convert measurements in metric and other systems.

Immersion in "hands-on" activities while using the words/symbols/pictures can help students with language acquisition, especially students with language challenges and those who are learning English as a second language. Students with physical challenges may need adaptations to be able to actually use measurement tools. Students with learning disabilities sometimes have great difficulty measuring time and direction. Generally speaking, most students will need concrete experiences and at least some direct instruction to build a strong foundation in measurement. More ideas for applying UDL principles to measurement will follow in this chapter.

Data Analysis and Probability

Data analysis and probability ask the learner to form his or her own questions that can be answered through data collected about one's self and one's surroundings. Data analysis and probability helps us predict the likelihood of future events happening (vocabulary needed may include words like *certain* and *impossible*). A young person might want to find out the likelihood of catching certain kinds of fish in certain ponds; a biologist might want to investigate what is happening to the honeybee population. Concrete objects, pictures, and symbols can be used to create and display data on graphs. Skills in naming, sorting/classifying, and organizing are needed.

Learners will choose the best way to show/display the data collected for the needed function. They will add words such as *variable, median, mode, scatterplots*, and *statistics*. As they become more sophisticated, it is hoped that they will realize that they will need to think about variables in their data samples to make the best predictions and evaluate outcomes. It is the ultimate goal that questions, once answered, will generate new questions and foster lifelong learning. It is important for us as teachers to show students how we use data analysis and probability in our everyday lives so it doesn't seem so abstract. How many of us feared statistics until we realized that they are a part of everyday life?

Assessment of Mathematics

Just as in reading, it will be helpful first to determine a student's working level in mathematics. Once again, there are formal and informal techniques/instruments available. A mixture of assessment tools should offer valuable information as to what the student knows and how he or she learns math best. Formal tests include group standardized survey tests, diagnostic math tests, and individually administered achievement tests that are norm referenced. Informal assessments may include tools or measures such as informal inventories/interviews, observations, error analysis, and curriculum-based assessment. A combination of instruments will help guide the planning and instruction for each student. Knowing what each type of test offers will help you use your time wisely in choosing the right assessment tools.

Decide what types of assessments are available at your school and add your own informal ones so that each student's assessment can be ongoing. Remember that in UDL, assessment is directly linked to learning goals.

Formal Assessment

Achievement tests, diagnostic assessments, and criterion-referenced instruments that can be useful for math assessment include:

- California Achievement Tests, 6th ed. (CAT/6), which includes comprehensive mathematics for K-12;
- Woodcock-Johnson III Tests of Achievement (Woodcock, McGrew, & Mather, 2001), which assesses calculation, math fluency, applied problem solving; and
- Comprehensive Mathematical Abilities Test (Hresko, Schlieve, Herron, Swain, & Sherbenou, 2002), which assesses calculations, mathematical reasoning, and practical applications for grades 2–12.

Achievement tests are typically wider in scope than the diagnostic tests. Diagnostic tests focus more specifically on math skill areas and help determine strengths and needs within the math domain. A criterion-referenced test is helpful for further pinpointing specific skills within a math category.

Web Resources

For more examples of formal assessments for mathematics, including group standardized assessments, individual achievement tests, diagnostic mathematics tests, and criterion references tests, check out this text's companion website, **www .academic.cengage.com/ education/Gargiulo**.

Informal Assessment

Interestingly, the term *assessment* has a Latin root, *assidere*, which means "to sit beside." Remember that careful observation, interviewing, questioning, and other types of informal math assessments give you insights and keys to learning that you likely won't get from formal or group testing. Another great thing about informal assessments is that they are so closely tied to teaching.

Interest inventories, math interviews, error analyses, portfolio assessments, and curriculum-based assessments (CBAs) are just some examples of informal assessments that can be used for math. Figure 12.1 is an example of an interest inventory that can be used for mathematics and adapted for the needs/ages of the students. This information will be helpful in setting up a responsive environment.

If the student is nonverbal or a recent English language learner, you might ask the questions to a parent or teacher who knows the student. You could even use response cards (yes/no, happy/sad faces) and have students draw a picture for the answers that require more than a yes/no response.

It is important to note that many learners have **math anxiety**. Perhaps you or someone you know also suffers from it. It can block initial learning, make transferring of math concepts difficult, and hinder demonstration of skills and concepts on homework and assessments. This emotion-based reaction to math (or other subjects) can hinder the working memory (Cavanagh, 2007). Research is suggesting that using group work in math can help reduce this anxiety. Having peer models and social support can help those who feel helpless in math. When math problems are presented using real-life situations, discussed in a group, and translated using common language, numbers, and pictures/visualizations, students can experience success (Ruffins, 2007). Discussing incorrect answers and eliminating unnecessary competition and time pressures can help as well. Access this text's companion website for an example of an informal self-assessment for math anxiety.

Applying **error analysis** can also be helpful in the informal assessment of mathematics. Give students a few problems at their working level and see how they approach and solve them. If time permits, ask them to talk through their steps. This way, you can see where any breakdowns may occur. For example, in math computation, you might see students working from left to right or not lining up their numbers. Some students have difficulty with place value or with a step or two in a process. Some examples of these types of errors can be seen in Figure 12.2.

Math Interest Inventory

Please answer the following questions.

- Do you like math?

- Do you think math is important? Why or why not?

- What do you like best about math?

- What don't you like about math?

- How do you usually feel when it is time for math at school?

- What math do you use outside of school?

- How could math be made more interesting?

- Do you ever experience math anxiety? Explain.

Figure 12.1 Informal Math Interest Inventory Example

Source: Adapted from C. Mercer and A. Mercer, *Teaching Students with Learning Problems*, 7th ed. (Upper Saddle River, NJ: Pearson Education, 2005), p. 425.

Using curriculum-based measures and assessments (CBM/CBA) with students can be motivating and instructionally effective in math. Students often enjoy charting their own growth, for example, in learning the multiplication tables on paper graphs or on computerized assessment programs. Some mathematics software comes with ready-made curriculum assessments that align with programs and standards; some also include diagnostic and placement tests.

A relatively new term in education, **progress monitoring**, refers not only to the assessment of student progress but also to the effectiveness of instruction. This term really combines the meanings of the terms CBA and CBM. It can be used with a whole class or with individual students. Students are regularly assessed (usually weekly or monthly), and instruction is adjusted as needed. Progress monitoring accelerates learning because students are receiving more-appropriate instruction. It reminds us to use research-based practices and to be flexible in terms of assessment and instructional representation, engagement, and expression.

A cutting-edge technology tool that is helpful for this type of assessment is the wireless **classroom performance system** (CPS). CPS software runs on your computer. Students each have a numbered response device that corresponds to the software. Assessment questions can be projected on a screen or may be read aloud. The students click in their answers from multiple choice responses. A CPS receiver that is connected to the computer by a USB port picks up student responses and delivers them to the CPS software. Data is collected, compiled, and can be displayed on a graph. Group or individual data can be reviewed quickly. The implications for providing students with quick feedback are promising. The group's mastered skills and concepts are easily seen, and areas that need more practice are pinpointed.

Before closing this section, it might be helpful to mention that there are many interesting studies and ideas about gender differences in mathematics. Some studies suggest teachers may give boys more general attention in math. Others suggest boys prefer to use spatial representations and memory to solve math problems whereas girls prefer math strategies paired with manipulatives. There also may be more male role models in math and science careers, although this does appear to be changing. The notion/stereotype that girls can't do math appears to be fading, although it is still voiced. Perhaps it is simply helpful to keep such perceptions/attitudes in mind as we assess our own ability to provide equity in instruction.

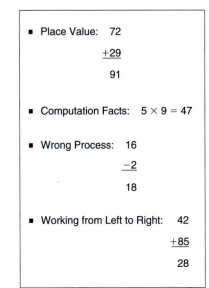

- Place Value: 72
                 +29
                  91

- Computation Facts: 5 × 9 = 47

- Wrong Process: 16
                   −2
                   18

- Working from Left to Right: 42
                               +85
                                28

Figure 12.2 Common Math Errors

Methods, Materials, and Resources that Promote Mathematics for All Learners

In mathematics, as in other areas, you will want to focus on introducing topics with concrete/manipulative materials. The research suggests that there are three instructional stages to consider when teaching for mathematical learning—concrete, representational, and abstract (Cass, Cates, Smith, & Jackson, 2003; Witzel, Mercer, & Miller, 2003). Most students, especially students who struggle, often need to begin at (and revisit from time to time) the **concrete** stage. In this stage, hands-on introductions and practice using manipulatives helps many students develop the number and spatial sense that is critical for future work in algebra and geometry. Students of all ages sometimes need to sit on the floor and pull out tools such as beans/counters, grids, and measuring tools to work out math problems—from early addition to statistics. Similar practices can be done at the computer using icons, drawing tools, and paint programs.

Over time and with practice, most students are able to move to the **representational** stage of math. In this stage, representations become formal and symbolic. In early math, for example, tally marks and circles may be used to teach addition. In algebra, letters can represent variables such as unknown numbers. In geometry, perspective drawings can represent the cubes and blocks students manipulated earlier. A word of caution—this is not to say that students cannot be problem solving in

Cengage Learning/Wadsworth

Group work can reduce math anxiety for diverse learners while fostering math language and skill development.

the concrete and representational stages. They just need to see and feel the learning tools/symbols/representations to get there.

The ultimate goal, of course, is to move learners to the **abstract** stage. When students intuitively know and understand the basic principles in mathematics, they are better able to transfer that understanding to real-life problem solving. Students who excel in math will likely move to the abstract stages quite rapidly, whereas others will need a great deal more time, scaffolding, and practice.

We will show you how you can incorporate hands-on, multisensory methods in all the areas of mathematics that are being considered. Keep thinking as you read about how you will adapt this learning for those who don't require much concrete or representational learning. Maybe they will be the peer tutors or the demonstration builders, or maybe they will be led to solve more-complex mathematical problems that can spring from your unit. They may even develop activities using multimedia tools that can help their classmates understand concepts being taught. Enlist these students to be problem solvers.

With learners at all different stages of mathematical learning in your classroom, it will be critical that you continually use assessment information to help students set realistic goals and keep track of their results. The more immediate the feedback, the better. Not only are you working smarter, you are also motivating your students to work toward a personal goal.

Remember, too, how it is important to integrate mathematics into all curricular areas. In a recent study done in Head Start classrooms, teachers who incorporated math-related activities into all parts of the student day had significantly higher student gains in math achievement than classrooms in which only a designated part of the day was set aside for math (Arnold, Fisher, Doctoroff, & Dobbs, 2002).

Once again, the ideas/strategies presented in this chapter are just a few that are used to illustrate how you might adapt instruction. There are many more strategies and techniques. In addition, you and your students can invent your own. For the purposes of this text, our goal is to show you how you can take a strategy/method and make it multisensory. In the following sections, multiple means of representation, engagement, and expression are presented according to the math "big ideas." Each focus area is summarized in table format at the end of each discussion.

Problem Solving

When students are given a problem to solve, it is often given in a real-life context using lots of words and sometimes extra material. Directions need to be clear and understood. As you know, some problems have many parts or steps. Different number operations may be required within the problem and other math concepts may be involved. Students need to be able to discriminate between different operations and use the information as they generalize to solve problems.

It may be helpful to use teacher or student-created story boards in teaching/solving math problems. Objects, pictures, and/or symbols could be used to go through each step/part, providing a visual and even tactile representation. Manipulatives stored in plastic shoeboxes with mats could be used for some students; other students could build storyboards using pictures/drawings in their math notebooks. IPods and drawing/animation software could be use with others to create a storyboard podcast. Students can also create movies of math concepts to use for instruction with other students in the school.

The direct instruction of memory strategies helps many learners retain math processes. An example of a mnemonic strategy that can be helpful when trying to figure out what is required when given a story problem is called RIDE (Mercer & Mercer, 2005):

R—*Remember* the problem correctly.
I—*Identify* the relevant information.
D—*Determine* the operations and unit for expressing the answer.
E—*Enter* the correct numbers, calculate, and check the answer.

When you introduce strategies like this, try to have them visually displayed on posters, charts, or overheads and easily accessible on notes, study guides, and/or a class website so students can quickly refer to them. Perhaps add a catchy phrase, tune, and/or visual. If you live near the ocean, for example, you might add a surfboard and wave and title it "RIDE the Wave to Math Success." You might even play some upbeat music. After practice/repetition with the strategy, you can simply cue the student by saying "RIDE" and/or pointing to the poster when a reminder to apply it is needed.

A similar mnemonic problem-solving strategy is called DRAW (Mercer & Miller, 1992):

Discover the sign
- Scan the problem and find the operation sign (+, −, ×, ÷)
- Circle and say the name of the computation sign.
- Say what the sign means.
Read the problem
- Read the whole problem.
- Say the problem aloud as you read.
Answer, or draw tallies and/or circles, and check your answer.
- Answer the problem if you know how to solve it.
- If you don't know how to solve the problem, draw pictures to solve it.
Write the answer.

You can make this strategy multisensory by putting it to a simple tune such as "Row, Row, Row Your Boat" for younger children but the tune/rhythm could be changed to a rap for older students. Pull out the keywords and plug it into the music/beat. Add gestures for movement. Notice how we have pulled keywords out of the DRAW strategy to make it easier to remember:

The Draw Strategy Song
    Draw, draw, draw your problem and you'll get it right.
    Discover the sign,
    Read the problem,
    Answer it, and
    Write.

Another effective method is to integrate children's literature into math problem-solving lessons. This practice is done frequently at elementary levels but has also been met with success at secondary levels (Franz & Pope, 2005). Children's literature often offers underlying themes that blend in well with complex mathematical thinking and reasoning. The stories are often engaging, and you can choose books that are culturally relevant and responsive as well. When you think about it, children's literature books are anchored in one or more characters and presented in a context students can relate to. The story *The Water Hole* (Base, 2001), for example, lends itself to preteaching mathematic direct and indirect variations and functions, as well as other math concepts. In this book, more and more animals come to a water hole and are decreasing the drinking water supply. The number of animals consuming the water is inversely proportional to the amount of drinking water there is. The animals discuss this real-world problem and brainstorm solutions. Math ideas of scale, factors, and constants of proportionality can be addressed in investigations that follow the introduction of this story. Another advantage to using children's literature is that it also tends to tie into other disciplines (e.g., writing, science, social studies, art, music, drama) quite well, increasing the ability of students to make connections and lend themselves to offering different types of student expressions/assessments in areas of their interests and strengths.

As with all instruction, try to make mathematics instruction as culturally relevant as possible. Tap into the world the students know—their lives, their cultural heritage, and their needs. Remember the power of anchored learning as discussed in earlier chapters. Students may be more successful in math when they see its direct application to solve real-world problems in their lives/communities, as well as connections within its discipline and to other subjects.

Communication of Mathematic Ideas

A recent study of early math skills of children in day care and preschool settings confirmed earlier studies that there tends to be a significant difference in conventional math knowledge of 4-year-olds according to socioeconomic status. This study also suggested that the more "teacher talk" about mathematics that occurs, the greater the overall achievement in math by all students in these early learning stages (Klibanoff, Levine, Huttenlocher, Vasilyeva, & Hedges, 2006). Initial results from a national survey of preschoolers conducted in 2005 suggests that approximately 60 percent of prekindergarten children in the United States receive nonparental or preschool center-based care (National Center for Education Statistics, 2006). This is

Web Resources

For more ideas about setting up environments and accessible tools, materials, and resources in mathematics, including children's literature with math themes, visit the text's companion website, **www.academic.cengage.com/education/Gargiulo**.

Multiple Ways to Increase Problem-Solving Skills	Examples/Ideas
Representation	• Anchoring the learning in real life (e.g., using a character presenting a real-world math problem) • Beginning the lesson with a children's book that relates to the objective • Showing a math video clip that poses a math problem
Engagement	• Working with graphic organizers • Using/creating mnemonics for key math words and concepts • Allowing time for verbal rehearsal and recording of problem-solving steps
Expression	• Written, verbal, or demonstration of problem-solving method and solution • Drawings/posters of problem-solving steps/strategies • Answers collected using response cards, CPS response clickers, other multiple-choice formats

important information to consider because, not surprisingly, early development in math has long-term effects on math achievement—including into the middle and high school years (Braswell et al., 2001). Promoting "best practices" in math early in preschool and at home can really set the stage for future math success.

Thinking and talking aloud can be helpful practices in the development of math vocabulary. It will also be important to critically target needed math vocabulary and, in many cases, preteach it. Once again, try to make math vocabulary visual on posters, word cards, and word walls. Infuse words, pictures, and symbols. Student-created math dictionaries with categorized math vocabulary (words for fractions, for estimation, for thinking, etc.) and math journals can also be helpful tools.

Make math vocabulary a part of every lesson. It is important to pull out the critical vocabulary in your lessons and preteach it to many diverse learners. This vocabulary must be imbedded in the content, modeled, and used frequently. When possible, try to label objects and visual representations with this same vocabulary. The same vocabulary should also be used in your assessments. Students could collect math terms on flash cards with visual representations on the back if needed for self-checking. Cards can be hole-punched and kept on a ring in a desk or notebook for easy reference.

Strive to use correct, universal mathematical terms. For example, when using the term *reciprocal* in teaching fractions, one might say, "We'll *flip* this fraction" so that the numerator becomes the denominator and vice versa. Using the word *flip* to aid comprehension is fine, but be sure to pair the word *reciprocal* with it and use it often. You might also have the word on a card, poster, or label. Some teachers even wear the card!

LINCS (Ellis, 1996) is a research-based strategy to help remember and generate vocabulary for any subject, including math. In this strategy, focus is put on the key elements of the concept. Using visual imagery, keyword mnemonics, and connections to prior learning, students create a study card for each word. The LINCS acronym helps students do the following:

L—List the parts (List the important parts of the definition of a targeted word on a study card.)

I—Imagine a picture (Create an image in your mind and describe it.)

N—Note a reminding word (Think of a word that sounds like all or part of it.)

C—Construct a LINCing story (Create a short story that has the vocabulary word in it as well as its meaning. Adjust your image to go along with the story.)

S—Self-test your memory (Repeat the LINCS steps you created forwards and backwards. When you move backwards, see if you can recall the vocabulary word.)

An example of applying the LINCS strategy to math follows:

Word: Perimeter

Definition: The boundary of a closed plane figure.

List: Measure around a two-dimensional figure, distance around the outside of a polygon, sum of the lengths of all the sides of a polygon (the rim).

Imagine a picture: I see the area around the Grand Canyon in my mind.

Note: Rim. Perimeter has the word "rim" in it. Perimeter measures the *rim* or distance around a polygon.

Construct a linking story: We walked along and measured the entire *rim* of the Grand Canyon. It took a long time and careful stepping to get the *"perimeter"* without falling in!

Self-test: Now I will say my strategy forwards and then backwards.

Word associations can also be used effectively when students can't remember terms and/or their meanings. When learning the words *median* and *mode*, for example, they can be encouraged to think of visually similar words such as *most* for *mode* and *middle* for *median*. In addition to having the same number of letters and several similar letters in both pairs of words, the meanings are also about the same. When students see the term *mode*, they might ask themselves, "What number is used the *most*?"

Once you and your students start thinking this way, lots of memory tricks can be developed. Sometimes the more outrageous and silly they are, the better—as long as they still make sense!

An example of a similar visual organizer that uses definition, facts, characteristics, and examples/nonexamples to aid vocabulary development is the Frayer Model (Marzano, Pickering, & Pollock, 2001). A middle-school example using this model, built around the term *equation*, is presented in Figure 12.3.

Another graphic organizer, a Circle Map from *Thinking Maps* (http://www.thinkingmaps.com/), can also be helpful when brainstorming a math term. Figure 12.4 is a high-school example created when the term *polynomials* was introduced.

Directly teaching math vocabulary will help students as they talk to their teachers and peers about math concepts and operations. It will also promote math fluency and generalization. This preparation should also help students perform better on standardized tests that are linked to the objectives you are teaching.

A study by Cocking and Chipman (1988) found that bilingual students in the study had particular difficulty translating words into mathematical symbols. These researchers suggest holding discussions with students about what works for them in math and what doesn't. It also suggests pairing students with similar abilities to work strategically on specific needed skills.

When a teacher needs to provide more-direct instruction for some students, students who are ready to move ahead can be working on lesson extensions, freeing up the teacher to work with these pairs. This way, all students have opportunities to use and develop their math language. The more the students can explain and reexplain what they are doing in math, the more embedded the language becomes.

Numbers and Operations

TouchMath has been a helpful multisensory tool for some diverse students learning one-to-one correspondence and computing number operations with accuracy and fluency. In TouchMath, students first learn touch points for numerals 1–9. In the introductory stages, concrete objects such as beans, foam dots, pompoms, and pipe

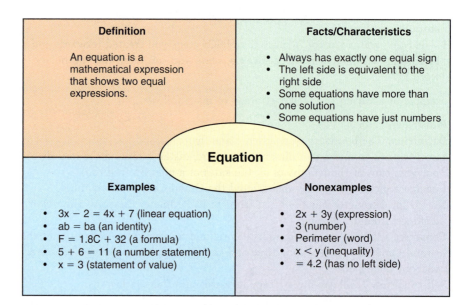

Figure 12.3 Frayer Model Sample (Grades 7–12)
Source: Adapted from Ontario Association for Mathematics Education (2004), *Think Literacy: Mathematics Approaches, Grades 7–12*. Retrieved June 29, 2008, from http://oame.on.ca/main/files/thinklit/FrayerModel.pdf

Circle Map for Vocabulary

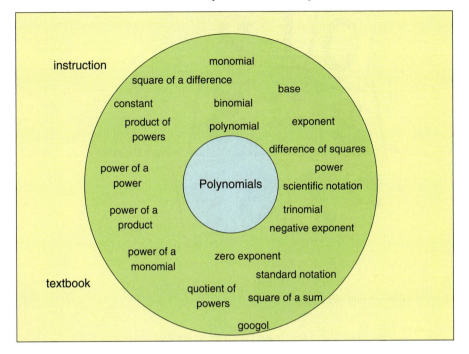

Figure 12.4 Circle Map for Math Vocabulary
Source: M. Metcalf (2004), Ayden Grifton High School, Ayden, NC, using thinking maps with *Inspiration* software.

Multiple Ways to Increase Mathematical Communication	Examples
Representation	• Presenting/pre-teaching vocabulary using cards/graphic organizers with visual symbols or paired with drawings • Providing digital translation, pictures, sign language, as needed • Presenting word problems on video, computer, or tape/CD
Engagement	• Creating math dictionaries • Infusing peer tutoring, thinking aloud, discussions with questioning • Solving/creating word problems with illustrations using role play or computer program
Expression	• Completed math vocabulary graphic organizers (e.g., LINCS, the Frayer Model) • Student-created videos of math functions • Completed posters of math terms

cleaner circles can be placed or glued on the numbers to represent the relationship between the numeral and its value. Students can fade to simply touching the points with a finger or pencil on pre-marked dots and circles. Eventually, most students can work without anything concrete or representational. They might quietly tap with fingers, pencils, or even on their teeth once the touch points are memorized. The goal is to become fluent with the math facts and to eventually commit them to memory. Figure 12.5 provides an example of the touch point models and a very brief sample of basic applications. A free video/DVD and training samples can be accessed at www.touchmath.com.

Web Resources

Visit the companion website for more materials, tools, and web resources for math problem solving, communication, and numbers and operations at **www.academic.cengage.com/education/education/Gargiulo**.

For simple addition:

4   *(Say "4" and then touch the points on the 2 as you count, "5, 6")*
+2

For simple subtraction:

10   *(Say "10" and then count backwards on 3 touch points…"9, 8, 7")*
- 3

For basic multiplication:

4   *(Sequence count by 4 on the three…"4, 8, 12")*
x 3

For complete instructions, go to www.touchmath.com

Figure 12.5 Example of *TouchMath* for Numbers and Computation
Source: Adapted from *TouchMath*. Retrieved June 29, 2008, from http://www.touchmath.com/

Sometimes a multisensory technique needs no extra materials. A method for multiplying by nine, for example, can be used with both hands held in front of the body, palms facing out. Starting at the left pinky finger, count (to the right) the number you are multiplying by and bend down that finger. The number of fingers to the left of the bent finger is the first digit (or number of tens) of the answer. The number of fingers to the right of the bent finger represents the second digit (or ones) of the answer. If you have 3 × 9, for example, the middle finger of your left hand bends down. There are two standing fingers to the left of it, representing 2 tens, and there are seven fingers to the right of it, representing 7 ones. The product is 27.

Paper plates and Circle Maps (from *Thinking Maps*) work well for developing number sense. A number can be placed in the center, and then different ways of arriving at that number can be brainstormed all around it.

For students who have difficulty learning math calculations, remember there are math algorithms that help some students. For example, you might use the **left to**

right subtraction algorithm for students who have difficulty working from right to left and/or regrouping. This algorithm requires the prerequisite skill of place value and asks for minimal or no regrouping. To use this algorithm, look at the following example. Think of the number you are subtracting and think about it as the sum of ones, tens, and hundreds. Expand it to show the parts and then subtract one part of the sum at a time.

Left to Right Subtraction Example:

To find 576–368, expand 368 to 300 + 60 + 8. Next, subtract the parts of the sum one at a time, beginning with the hundreds.

1. Subtract the hundreds:

$$\begin{array}{r} 576 \\ -300 \\ \hline 276 \end{array}$$

2. Subtract the tens:

$$\begin{array}{r} 276 \\ -\ 60 \\ \hline 216 \end{array}$$

3. Subtract the ones:

$$\begin{array}{r} 216 \\ -\ 8 \\ \hline 208 \end{array}$$

(Note: Students can subtract 8 from 16 using TouchMath if regrouping is still a challenge here.)

Another algorithm, the **lattice multiplication** method, is a lifesaver for some students when asked to solve large multiplication problems. Lattice multiplication is visually set up on a grid as shown in Figure 12.6. It breaks the multiplication process down into small, manageable steps. Whenever you can use graphic organizers such as grids to break down steps, learning becomes more manageable for some students. Student and teacher-produced videos illustrating a variety of different math algorithms can be found using a web search, or students can create their own.

Step One: Draw a grid (lattice) that has columns and rows to represent the factors (multiplicand and multipliers) you are multiplying. This grid is set up for the problem 2,314 × 157 so it has four columns and three rows.

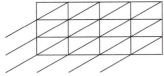

Step Two: Draw a diagonal line from each corner to corner. Extend each line past the grid. ("Corner to corner and out the door.")

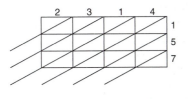

Step Three: Write one factor across the top and the other down the side. Line the digits up with boxes.

Step Four: Multiply each set of numbers and insert answers in the grid. If an answer is less than ten, use a zero as a place holder.

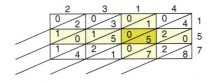

Step Five: Beginning in the lower right-hand corner, add the numbers in each diagonal and write the sum on the extended line ("ride the slide"). If a sum is greater than ten, carry the one to the upper space in the next diagonal to the left. Read the answer by going around the outside of the grid from the upper left to the right (363,298).

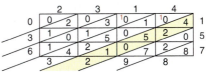

Figure 12.6 Lattice Multiplication Method
Source: Adapted from *Learn NC* (Chapel Hill: University of North Carolina). Retrieved June 29, 2008, from http://www.learnnc.org/lp/pages/4458

These can be downloaded on iPods or computers so that students can review the presentation as many times as needed.

Fractions can be taught with tools such paper folding, cutting and reassembling paper plates, and with children's literature, poetry, and song. A primary example uses the tune "The More We Get Together." Students work in pairs coloring "pies" on paper plates. They divide the pies up according to the number of friends that join them. The song goes like this:

> I baked a cherry pie today
> Just for Allison and me.
> Mike came by and spied the pie
> So now it's pie for three.
> **Refrain:** The more we get together, together, together
> The more we get together, the smaller the piece.

Although some examples are primary, the basic premise is the same for all ages. It's up to you to make them age appropriate!

Figure 12.7 is an example of a lesson plan on equivalent fractions that shows how UDL principles might be applied. The plan has already been designed with diverse learners in mind, and the suggestions simply show its flexibility. They are meant to help you think about possibilities. A planning pyramid for differentiation is also included.

Multiple Ways to Increase Skills with Numbers and Operations	Examples
Representation	• Directly instructing strategies/algorithms • Presenting with manipulatives/visuals/video clips • Infusing computer-based instruction
Engagement	• Working with manipulatives (moved by hand, computer mouse, or keyboard arrow) • Practicing algorithms, using interactive computer programs for skill building and problem solving • Practicing/creating mnemonics, songs, raps for operations
Expression	• Student-produced videos that show operations (students act out/explain) • Student-created posters, written products, demonstrations • Computer or low-tech quizzes (with feedback and scores)

Algebra

Algebra is an abstract concept in mathematics that requires prerequisite skills to be successful. Using all the resources you have, work on specific prerequisite skills students need as efficiently as possible. You may need to preteach definitions/terms you will be using and review needed operational skills. Some students may need to use a calculator for operations as you move forward with the class.

Direct instruction in algebra is critical for many students. Having questions or prompts on a card, worksheet, or some other form of an **advance organizer** can also be helpful as you go through the explanation/process step by step. This organizer may have a place for critical vocabulary and can ask some prerequisite questions about the concept being taught. It can also provide a rationale for the reason the concept is being taught (again, using a real-life example works well). Typically, the organizer can provide a skeleton outline with prompts for the steps/substeps in the concept(s) being taught. This outline might, for example, include a place to draw a picture. When an answer is produced, it might provide the prompt "Does this make sense?"

The STAR strategy (Maccini & Hughes, 2000; Maccini & Ruhl, 2000), similar to the DRAW strategy, works well for older students learning algebra. Figure 12.8 shows how this strategy helps students visualize how to solve an equation. Notice how the concrete, representational and abstract stages are built into it.

Use explicit instructions in self-monitoring. Incorporate "think alouds" to model your own thinking process and encourage students to do the same. Continually ask students to explain or show what they are doing to a peer, another adult, or to you. With guided practice, independent practice, frequent reviews, and corrective and positive feedback, students who struggle with mathematics can increase their ability to reason in algebra.

An example of a thinking map for expressing numbers in scientific notation can be seen in Figure 12.9. This is a flow map that is used for sequencing. Students can visually see the steps in the process. When you number items, use precise wording, and provide models, more students have the opportunity to grasp the concept or skill.

If you are co-teaching, one teacher can orally present the explicit instruction while the other teacher "translates" steps onto a poster, overhead projection, or other means of presentation. Both teachers can model "thinking aloud." This way some students who have difficulty with focusing and note taking can concentrate on the presentation without worrying about writing down information and getting behind.

Figure 12.10 offers an example of another mnemonic strategy, called CAP, for solving equations in algebra by combining like terms, asking questions to isolate the variable, and putting values of the variables in the initial equation (Mercer & Mercer, 2005).

The foundation for algebraic thinking can and should be developed early. Consider manipulatives, such as *Hands-On Equations*, which uses numbered cubes, pawns, and a setup that looks like a balance scale (see Figure 12.11). Students physically represent given equations with these materials and solve them through a series of physical moves. Although, the program is geared for grades 4–8, it has been used successfully with gifted students in second and third grades, and it can also help students at the secondary level develop prerequisite skills. The program itself does not require any algebraic prerequisites. Research using this visual, kinesthetic method has been done with Title I fifth-grade students in west coast inner-city schools with significant results (Barber & Borenson, 2007).

Another way to activate more senses when working on equations is to simply physically underline the focus parts. In a math lesson that uses variables ($3 + 8 + 5 = x + 5$), for example, underlining the steps with a finger and talking aloud through the process helps some students remember. Working at a dry erase board, computer screen, or interactive whiteboard can enhance teaching and learning.

Multiple Ways to Increase Algebra Skills	Examples
Representation	• Directly instructing terms and sequences in algebraic problem solving • Modeling mnemonics/learning strategies • Providing visuals to pair with teaching (e.g., algebra tiles, thinking maps) • Providing advance organizers, outlines • Using video clips with real-life examples
Engagement	• Making posters of strategies • Practicing and creating mnemonics • Folding paper graphic organizers for algebraic terms • Making and solving equations with manipulatives (e.g., algebra tiles, integer blocks, large grids) • Using computer software/interactive web-based algebra programs
Expression	• Student presentations (posters, completed thinking maps, PowerPoint, demonstrations, student-produced videos) • Students answer multiple-choice questions (oral or written) with CPS systems, response cards, or with paper/pencil • Students give oral/written explanations and/or demonstration with manipulatives

Instructor: *A. Evmenova*

Subject: Math   Grade: 3rd

Lesson Objective(s):
The students will express equivalent fractions

Assessment(s): Index card responses

SCS Math Correlation:
1.01-model/describe fraction equivalents

Preplanning Activities: Cut paper squares, prepare fraction game

Lesson Element	Procedures	Time	What is the teacher doing?	What are the students doing?	Materials
Lesson Setup &	• Warm up with timed multiplication drill • Set up expectations for today's work. Tell students we will be playing a game. • Ask if there were any questions about yesterday's homework and write down tonight's homework	5 min.	Giving directions	Writing homework assignment	Math fact folders Planners Math notebooks
Lesson Opening	• Objective: Today you will learn about equivalent fractions. Who can tell me what it means if I say two numbers are equal? They have the same value. So, if I say that two fractions are equivalent, I mean that they are equal or the same.	5 min.	Talking about the objective	Listening, responding to question	
Lesson Body	Teacher Input • "Take this piece of paper and fold it in half just as I am doing. Make sure you are folding it the same way."	15 min.	Modeling fold	Listening	Paper squares for folding, colored pencils, or markers
	• "Now let's color one side (half) of that sheet of paper. If you unfold it now you can see that one half of the paper is colored. Let's name the fraction we have. How many parts do we have? Two. How many are shaded? One. So which fraction is that? 1/2. Excellent"		Thinking aloud	Responding to teacher questions	
	• Now, let's fold the same paper in half again like we did before but this time we'll fold it in half one more time. As you unfold the paper, you can see that not only have you folded the paper in four equal parts but also that half of the paper has the same space shaded. What part of the fraction is shaded this time? (2/4) Very good. Now tell me how 1/2 and 2/4 look. They are absolutely the same. They are equal, so we can say that they are equivalent.		Building in positive statements	Folding paper, coloring	
	• Continue folding the paper into eights and sixteenths. Have students unfold paper and continue to say what all the equivalent fractions are (1/2 = 2/4 = 4/8 = 8/16).				
	• Redirect students to look at the fractions again and ask them to look for a relationship between 1/2 and 2/4 with a partner using Think-Pair-Share. See if they discover the pattern ("If I multiply both parts of 1/2 by 2, I will get 2/4. If I multiply both parts of the fraction 1/2 by 4 I will get 4/8).		Questioning students for input	Talking with partner in Thank-Pair-Share	
	• "This is the rule you need to remember: You can form equivalent fractions by multiplying or dividing the numerator and denominator by the same non-zero number. Write this rule in your math notebook."		Monitoring		
	• "Let's see what that means. What number can you multiply both the numerator and denominator of 3/4 by to get 9/12? (3)"				
	• Ask students to find an equivalent fraction for the fraction 18. Review all the steps multiplying by 2, 3, and so on. Guided Practice • I will use a computer program and the students will tell me what to click after I model the first problem.	10 min.	Running computer program, modeling, and guiding students with questions	Giving answers to problems generated by computer	Computer with projection Encyclopedia of Mathematics: *Fractions* software
Extended Practice	Pairs of students will play a pre-made equivalent fraction card game that is played like "Go Fish." Allow paper/pencil to work out problems.	10 min.	Circulating		Card game Paper/pencil

Figure 12.7 Math Lesson Plan with UDL Applications

Source: Lesson plan adapted for UDL from Anya Evmenova, former teacher, Greene County Schools, NC.

Lesson Closing	5 min.	Ask students to write or draw what equivalent fractions are and how to find an equivalent fraction on an index card. Write their names on the cards, share responses, and turn them in. Homework: Ex. 16–21 p. 199 — you will need to find two equivalent fractions for each problem	Questioning Answering questions Checking notes Writing homework in planner	Index cards
Evaluation				

UDL Key: Representation; Engagement; Expression

Possible UDL Applications for Extension

Representation	Low-Tech: List objectives/agenda on board/poster; use a pizza model as an example of equivalent fractions (connect to real life); act out a real-life problem that needs equivalent fractions to solve (perhaps a cooking simulation). High-Tech: List objectives/agenda through electronic document and projector; show a brief video clip on equivalent fractions in real life (videostreaming).
Engagement	Low-Tech: Have the word *equivalent* on a large card posted where all can see. Tape the actual folded paper right next to it when done and leave it up for future reference; students sing or rap a song about equivalent fractions. High-Tech: Use a PowerPoint slide show to explain/show equivalent fractions; allow students to use calculators with card game. Play an interactive computer game using equivalent fractions during independent practice such as "Fraction Frenzy" at http://www.learningplanet.com or work on equivalent fractions at http://www.studyisland.com
Expression	Low-Tech: Verbal responses; students complete a part-to-whole graphic organizer using equivalent fractions, show different equivalent fractions on dry erase boards, demonstrate understanding in student notebooks. High-Tech: Computer-generated part-to-whole organizer using equivalent fractions, electronic whiteboard demonstration, student-created PowerPoint showing equivalent fractions.

Possible Barriers:	Possible Solution:
Students have difficulty copying from board	Have some preprinted rules cut that students can glue in notebooks.
Some students struggle with language and memory	Have previously learned terms (numerator, denominator) displayed with pictorial representation and/or have on individual index card ring or in personal math dictionary.
Student wants to work alone	Allow student to use self checking fraction equivalent folder game or practice on computer or worksheet.
Student can't write, fold, or draw	This student may record his response on an iPod or tell the teacher orally while others are writing. Work with a peer who can assist with fine motor work.
Student can't sit	Allow student to fold standing up; have student control the mouse during guided practice or have students use premade response cards they keep in their desks; have student help others with folding (perhaps rehearse ahead of time).

Tier III —A few students will solve problems that involve converting fractions that they designed with or provided by the enrichment teacher. These students may also work ahead on objectives on a computer-based program such as Study Island.

Tier II—Some students will solve word problems that are based on the knowledge of equivalent fractions.

Tier I—All students will express two or more equivalent fractions.

Figure 12.7 Math Lesson Plan with UDL Applications (Continued)

1. **S**earch the word problem
    (a) Read the problem carefully
    (b) Ask yourself questions: "What facts do I know?" "What do I need to find?"
    (c) Write down facts.

2. **T**ranslate the words into an equation in picture form
    (a) Choose a variable
    (b) Identify the operation(s)
    (c) Represent the problem with manipulatives (Algebra Lab Gear, for example)—
        Concrete application
        Draw a picture of the representation—Semiconcrete application
        Write an algebraic equation—Abstract application

3. **A**nswer the problem

ADDITION	SUBTRACTION	MULTIPLICATION/ DIVISION
Same Signs: Add numbers and keep signs **Different signs:** Find difference of numbers and keep sign of number farthest from zero	Add opposite of the second term.	**Same signs** + **Different signs** −

4. **R**eview the solution
    (a) Reread the problem
    (b) Ask question, "Does the answer make sense? Why?"
    (c) Check answer

Figure 12.8 The STAR Strategy
Source: J. Gagnon & P. Maccini, "Preparing Students with Disabilities for Algebra," *Teaching Exceptional Children, 34*(1), 2001, p. 10.

Geometry and Spatial Sense

To make geometry concepts meaningful for diverse learners, use concrete objects and video clip representations when possible. Concrete geometric shapes are easy to find—cans for cylinders, balls for spheres, boxes for cubes, and so on. Folding paper to make boxes and other shapes engages students while offering multiple opportunities for developing the language of geometry (*half, vertex, corner, sides*). Students can see and feel what the teacher is describing.

If your school has access to *video streaming*, this can be an excellent way to introduce a math or any other concept. You can access video clips on almost any subject. In a way, it can be like taking a field trip without leaving the school. A fifth-grade math class, for example, might watch a video of other young people taking a trip to a candy factory. The candy is packed in boxes that are different shapes and sizes. Later in the lesson, the students actually construct models of these boxes, give them attributes, and measure them. Many schools subscribe to these types of online, on-demand video streaming sources.

Remember to use gestures, mnemonics, and other tricks for memory. For example, it's easy to position the arms in *parallel* or *perpendicular* positions. Here is a trick for remembering that the number 3.1415926 represents *pi* (retrieved June 29, 2008, from http://mathforum.org/t2t/faq/faq.tricks2.html#errol):

To get the first eight digits of pi, count the number of letters in each word of this phrase: May(3) I(1) have(4) a(1) large(5) container(9) of (2) coffee(6)?

Have students create posters, models, and computer presentations using draw and paint or presentation programs that show the geometric skills or concepts they are working on. Allow them to work alone, with partners, or in small groups according to what you know about your learners.

Technology has been integrated with math for some time and continues to evolve. Calculators, for example, have gradually replaced slide rules. Technology called **dynamic geometry software** (DGS) that uses programs such as Geometer's *Sketchpad* and *Cabri* for teaching and learning have been significantly effective in the development of students' understanding of geometrical concepts (Forsythe, 2007). With Geometer's *Sketchpad*, students can construct objects, figures, and diagrams and see their mathematical properties. By dragging the mouse, for example, a student can change the shape of an object and see how relationships are maintained. Tools like *Sketchpad* allow students to link learning to real life. For example, when teaching the term *slope*, students can take actual digital pictures of rooftops and import them into the program. Students can construct points—one at the top of the roof and one at the eaves—on the grid that overlays the image. They draw a line to connect the points and determine the slope. By using digital images, students can resize images and change the pitch of the roof and see how the mathematical formulas they are using apply. If students do similar activities with accessibility ramps, they may even gain an appreciation for some of the different problems people with disabilities may have. *Sketchpad* can be used in a similar way to teach conic sections, such as hyperbolas (and terms such as *vertex, focus, line of symmetry*), by taking and importing

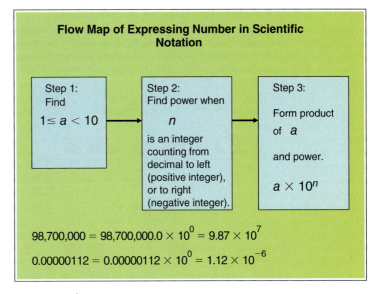

Flow Map of Expressing Number in Scientific Notation

Step 1:
Find
$$1 \le a < 10$$

Step 2:
Find power when
n
is an integer counting from decimal to left (positive integer), or to right (negative integer).

Step 3:
Form product of a
and power.
$$a \times 10^n$$

$$98,700,000 = 98,700,000.0 \times 10^0 = 9.87 \times 10^7$$

$$0.00000112 = 0.00000112 \times 10^0 = 1.12 \times 10^{-6}$$

Figure 12.9 Flow Map of Expressing Numbers in Scientific Notation

Source: M. Metcalf (2004), Ayden-Grifton High School, Ayden, NC.

The CAP Strategy

C—*Combine* like terms. Combine terms on each side of the equation that have the same variable (e.g., 3m + 2m combines to 5m). Combine terms on each side of the equation that do not have a variable (e.g., 15 − 7 combines to 8). Combine terms by doing the computations indicated by the signs (e.g., 6p − 4p combines to 2p + 7 − 13 combines to −6).

A—*Ask* yourself, "How can I isolate the variable?" Remove nonvariable numbers (e.g., +6, −8) by changing them to zero by doing the opposite computation (e.g., −6 removes +6, +8 removes −8). Remove a variable number (e.g., 6s) by changing it to 1 by doing the opposite computation (e.g., 6s becomes s when divided by 6).

P—*Put* the values of the variable in the initial equation, and check to see if the equation is balanced.

Figure 12.10 The CAP Strategy

Source: C. Mercer & A. Mercer, *Teaching Students with Learning Problems,* 7th ed. (Upper Saddle River, NJ: Pearson, 2005), p. 425.

A Sample Problem Using Hands-On Equations

Let's consider the equation 4x + 5 = 2x + 13. The student first represents this equation on the flat laminated balance scale using the game pieces. The blue pawns represent the x's, and the numbered cubes represent the constant. The student is then ready to perform the legal moves in order to simplify and solve the equation. The procedure is illustrated below:

Ex. 4x + 5 = 2x + 13

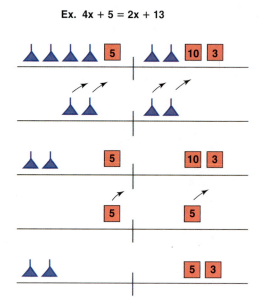

From this we see that **x = 4.** The check, in the **original physical setup**, reveals that 21 = 21.

Note: The above example is taken from Lesson #4 of the program. The three previous lessons help the student to arrive at, and understand, the above solution. Later on in the program, the student will also work with white pawns, which represent the opposite of x, and with green cubes, which represent negative constants.

Figure 12.11 Hands-On Equations Lesson
Source: Hands-On Equations. Retrieved June 29, 2008, from http://www.borenson.com/html/sample.html

digital pictures of drinking fountains and satellite dishes. This lets students graph the modeling equation on the same plane as the picture. Digital images, paired with dynamic geometry software can also be combined with art objectives to locate, for example, vanishing points in perspective art (Sharp, 2007).

By using DGS, Euclidian, transformational, and coordinate geometry truly come to life. Colorful animations clearly show concepts, such as *rotation, dilation,* and *translation,* that are often very difficult for students with academic, cognitive, and perceptual difficulties to grasp. They may be able to connect some of these images to the video games they enjoy, fostering generalization!

Many DGS files can be imported to spreadsheets, word processing programs, and to the Internet. They also often come with presentations, tests, and reports. Some are available in Spanish.

Measurement

You are likely seeing a pattern now in this chapter and can already predict that we will tell you to first approach teaching measurement skills concretely. The earliest nonstandard measurements might be taken with footprints, hands, string, toothpicks, or paper clips. A creative teacher was recently observed having a student measure the school hallway with his plastic wrestling figures! The student had cognitive

Multiple Ways to Increase Geometry Skills and Spatial Sense	Examples
Representation	• Directly instructing/modeling geometric terms and concepts • Video clip/video streaming introduction of geometry concept • Using a children's book to introduce geometry concept • Showing a PowerPoint presentation with questions to present basic geometric terms and concepts
Engagement	• Sorting and classifying solids (real objects); observing and studying properties • Using manipulatives (e.g., tanagrams, geoboards, blocks, spheres) or making posters of geometry terms and concepts • Using dynamic geometry software and interactive websites • Practicing/creating mnemonics for terms and concepts in geometry
Expression	• Constructed word maps for geometry vocabulary • Buildings/drawings that represent 2-D and 3-D models with description • PowerPoint presentations, posters, journal responses, group write-ups reflecting geometric problem solving

and behavioral/oppositional challenges, but the teacher tapped into his interests, and he learned the skill.

Let's look at some more ways measurement concepts come to life. When measuring time and money, try to use real clocks and money (or close reproductions) if possible. When teaching locating points on a grid, consider marking floor tiles or carpet with masking tape. Construct grids that students can actually walk on. Such grids can also be used to solve algebraic problems. The x-axis can be coded one color and the y-axis another.

When teaching measurement conversions, look for activities that engage many senses. The Gallon Man, for example, has students construct a person with a gallon torso, two upper legs and two upper arms (one quart each), and so on (see Figure 12.12). Add a song, rap, or dance to further engage learners. A classroom might even incorporate a behavior management system using a Gallon Man-type framework. Perhaps have the parts on hook-and-loop fasteners or magnets, and

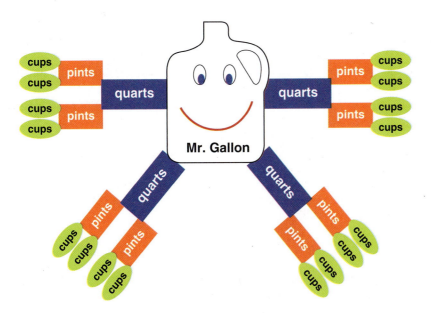

Figure 12.12 The Gallon Man

Source: D. Dees, E. E. Miller School, Greensboro, NC. Retrieved June 29, 2008, from http://www.twogetherexpress.com/gallon%20man2.htm

when you catch the class being "good," add one part to the man. If students complete the whole man, they earn some free time or other reward.

The new **Global Positioning System** (GPS) devices are another exciting technology tool that can help students learn measuring concepts using latitude and longitude. Because measurement of these imaginary lines is a prerequisite skill for using a GPS receiver, you can use the grid made of masking tape on the floor to teach these skills. An extension of this lesson will be highlighted in the Science and Social Studies, Chapter 13.

Adding hand signals, gestures, mnemonics, and other memory tricks can help students remember measurements. When teaching miles at one school, for example, one teacher was observed saying that McDonald's was about one mile from the school. She paired her statement with a sign language "M" and gestured that hand and arm toward the actual restaurant. She had signals for other customary and metric measures as well and would drill the class using them.

Here are some other examples of memory mnemonics to remember how many feet are in a mile and some metric conversions (retrieved June 29, 2008, from http://mathforum.org/t2t/faq/faq.tricks2.html#errol):

To remember how many feet are in a mile: Just say to yourself "5 tomatoes."
There are 5,280 feet in a mile, so you can remember that by saying
5 tomatoes.

5 to mat oes
(5)(2)(8)(0)

A trick for remembering some metric conversions is:

For metric conversions say:

"King Henry Died Monday Drinking Chocolate Milk"

Km   Hm   Dm   M   Dm   Cm   Mm

To convert:

3.75 Hm = _____ Cm

It's 4 jumps to the right from Hm to Cm; simply move the decimal 4 jumps to the right.

3.75 Hm = 37,500 Cm

To convert:

0.59 Dm = _____ Hm

It's 3 jumps to the left from Dm to Hm; simply move the decimal 3 jumps to the left.

0.59 Dm = 0.00059 Hm

Multiple Ways to Increase Measurement Skills	Examples
Representation	• Anchoring measurement skill introduction with video clip, children's book, or real-life problem • Directly instructing and demonstrating with measurement tools (e.g., scales, balances, rulers, meter/yardsticks, thermometers) • Modeling calculator/GPS use for measuring (e.g., distance, velocity, acceleration, motion, temperature, light)
Engagement	• Walking on life-size grids • Measuring with standard and nonstandard tools • Manipulating shapes on *Inspiration* software • Creating a WebQuest on a topic that infuses measurement concept • Creating a GPS scavenger hunt
Expression	• Completed visual organizers (e.g., a tree map for conversions) • Drafting project, map designed to scale • Demonstration of calculator, GPS, or other measurement tool(s) • Math journal entry • Completed measurement-infused WebQuest or PowerPoint presentation

Data Analysis and Probability

Students of all ages can enjoy collecting, organizing, analyzing, and displaying data. Young children typically enjoy sorting colored jelly beans or cereal, for example, on a grid to make a bar graph. The comparisons that follow lend themselves to helpful math communication (*more, less, same*). Data collection easily flows through disciplines—election favorites for social studies, number of books read in English, comparing shoe sizes in math, graphing nutritional contents of products for science, finding the global distribution of earthquakes in geography, graphing running times in track, and so on. Graphing student preferences (movies, TV shows, etc.) can activate the affective domain. Graphs can be made with real objects (such as the jelly beans), sticky notes, or pictures/symbols. Students can plug data into computer programs, and the technology makes graphic displays very easy. With the click of a mouse, students can see the same data displayed as a bar graph, line graph, or pie graph. Remember that students can also graph their own assessments. This can be quite motivational as they try to improve their own performances. A simple bar graph made on grid paper can work quite nicely.

Probability lessons lend themselves quite easily to multisensory learning. Students can connect to activities such as coin tossing and marble drawing when learning probability. Presented in a game format, students usually enjoy predicting the odds of "winning." Setting up the foundations for probability in a multisensory way can pave the way for future applications of probability in advanced areas of study such as genetics.

Another example of remembering data analysis terms in a multisensory way is by creating a song or rap. The concept of calculating mean, median, mode, and range, for example, can be remembered by using a teacher-created product such as the **MMMR Rap**:

The M, The M, The MMMR Rap.
The M, The M, The MMMR Rap.
Now Mode, Mode, I've been told,
is the # that you see the most.

Median, Median, Median, is the man.
The man in the middle, the man in the middle.
Just line up the #'s the best you can
From smallest to largest,
From smallest to largest.
Now Mean, Mean, he is the best.
Of course he is better than all the rest.
Just add, add, add all your #'s,
and when you divide
you won't believe your eyes—
you'll only have one # to your surprise.
Last but not least is our friend the Range—
He isn't the best, but he sure is strange.
You start with the Hiiiggghhhh and subtract
the Loooowwww!!!
You've got the Range and there is no mo'!
The M, The M, The MMMR Rap.
The M, The M, The MMMR Rap.
When you sing it out loud—it's all just a snap! (retrieved August 1, 2007, from http://teachers.net/lessons/posts/2130.html).

After the rap or song is modeled, the students can be guided through it. Multiple practice opportunities can be provided. Students may eventually rap the words in their heads to assist memory when working independently. Be sure to have a visual representation of the poster as a reference from the start. Remember, too, that adding body movements and/or gestures that match the words offers more opportunities to engage students.

By now, you are likely observing patterns in teaching and learning. As cognitive and metacognitive challenges increase, so does the need for concrete representation, direct instruction, scaffolding, and perhaps even some task analysis. Strategy instruction is needed when academic challenges involve memory, visual/auditory processing, and attention. Sometimes this also means more repetitions, more practice, and more examples. Remember, too, that demonstration teaching and modeling are needed to show how the learning can be transferred to other situations.

Multiple Ways to Increase Data Analysis and Probability Skills	Examples
Representation	• Directly instructing/modeling with visuals, spreadsheets, calculators • Demonstrating through a game format • Providing advance organizers/grid paper
Engagement	• Using game formats with coin tossing, drawing marbles, playing cards, dice; making predictions • Creating and conducting surveys • Collecting data and creating graphs, charts and spreadsheets; analyzing, organizing, interpreting and evaluating data; comparing distributions of data; constructing a scatterplot
Expressive	• Student demonstrations • Completed graphs with explanations • Oral or written responses • Calculator or computer displays • Response cards, CRS systems, or pointing system to assess terms and concepts

Fostering Collaboration in Mathematics Instruction

Co-teaching mathematics can work effectively at all levels. At the upper levels, the regular education teacher is typically the math content expert. If a special educator is paired with that teacher for math instruction, the special educator can be debriefed in advance of the concepts being taught and the method. The special educator may suggest an alternate method for representation, engagement, and strategic systems for all or some of the students, depending on the need. He or she may, for example, review a skill with students who need more practice with number operations. Another teacher might be working with gifted students setting up an extra project or training volunteers or other students as tutors/coaches. The regular education teacher might be working on activities other students need in another part of the school space.

Multisensory teaching does take effort and preparation, but many of the higher-tech tools make this easier. The more you plan ahead, the better you will be able to delegate. Students and parents often enjoy helping if they have a specific task (collecting containers for a liquid measurement activity, for example). A student or parent might help you tape out a large grid on a floor, too.

Try to collaborate with art teachers and other community artists to develop math concepts and skills. Many math and art objectives are closely aligned. It is likely that your diverse learners have strengths in art so activate it to build mathematical skill. Working collaboratively, you can imbed the math vocabulary and other objectives right into the art. Provide the resource person with the key terms and concepts you are using ahead of time as he/she prepares to assist you. Art professionals have helped students by showing them how to illustrate their writing using geometric shapes or perspective drawings. They have helped students construct models of animals, people, things, and settings to use in units of study (e.g., endangered species, solar systems, masks, rain forests). These are just a few examples of the kinds of art activities that concretely and meaningfully integrate math principles of measurement, proportionality, spatial sense, and more into the curriculum.

Most music teachers are also pleased to be asked to enhance lessons. The math and music connection activates both hemispheres of the brain. Music, in fact, enhances the abstract reasoning and spatial and temporal conceptualization that is so important for mathematics (Church, 2000). Both disciplines require matching, comparing, and patterning and sequencing skills. In music, pitch, volume, and rhythms are matched and compared. Melodies, rhythms, and lyrics are patterned and sequenced. When you add clapping, hand movements, tapping, and/or dancing, kinesthetic learning is also activated. Physical education teachers are great collaborators, too, if they know what you are working on in advance. They can definitely provide that needed movement. They are often great motivators as well. Be sure to at least ask!

Students may enjoy learning about celebrities who have successfully developed and used their art or musical skill. Artists Pat Buckley Moss and Patricia Polacco, for example, had learning challenges in school yet developed their artistic talents. Both now write children's stories and are great artists and illustrators. Musicians Ray Charles and Stevie Wonder have given us many wonderful songs in spite of visual challenges.

If you have a student who is gifted in math or art and still not challenged in your classroom, perhaps an arrangement could be made for that student to work in a more-advanced math class or be assigned to a math mentor to move ahead.

If you are working with older students, perhaps you can find a teacher to pair up with in a younger grade. Older students can use children's literature books that have math themes and prepare lessons to present to the younger students. They could even create their own books around math objectives for them. What a great way to build up prerequisite skills while helping others in a motivational way!

Thematic Summary

- Many high school seniors lack a fundamental, basic understanding of mathematical concepts. The demands of the 21st century make the need to reverse this trend imperative.
- Using a "big ideas" approach to teaching and learning mathematics may help teachers organize, integrate, and structure studies that will enable them to meet 21st-century mathematical challenges.
- Using a combination of formal and informal assessments in mathematics is important to identifying both group and individual student strengths and needs in mathematics. The information provided by this data must be used to inform, implement, and evaluate ongoing instruction.
- There are seven "big ideas" (learning goals) in mathematics as articulated by NCTM for grades K–12. The skills within and between the various goals build upon one another. Prerequisite skills must be taught, practiced, and reviewed periodically for some diverse students. Some students will also need adaptations to be successful.
- By approaching learning tasks with the UDL principles in mind, teachers ensure recognition, affective, and strategic systems can be activated for *all* learners.
- There are many strategies available for students in mathematics. Applying multisensory techniques can be an effective way to reach diverse learners. Technology tools can help.
- Collaboration between students, teachers, administrators, community members, and other professionals is important in the development and implementation of mathematics instruction.

Making Connections for Inclusive Teaching

1. *All* students can learn the basic principles of mathematics. Do you agree or disagree with this statement? Defend your position.
2. Discuss the mathematical demands you see in our society today. Give some examples from a typical week in your life.
3. Explain how Universal Design for Learning can benefit all students in mathematics. Do you agree or disagree that math teachers today will need to rethink some of their practices?
4. Compare the need for collaborative efforts in mathematical instruction to the collaborative efforts you see in an industry/business that you are familiar with. Share your findings.
5. Do you think the types of collaboration suggested in this chapter are realistic for mathematics instruction? Why is it so difficult for some schools to do this? If more collaboration is needed, what additional supports/resources will need to be in place?

Learning Activities

1. Which of the seven "big ideas" in math are you the strongest in? Which one challenges you the most? Look back over your entire school history and list strategies that have helped you excel and/or compensate in your own mathematics development. Compare and contrast your answers with a classmate.
2. Give the informal math assessment shown in Figure 12.1 to a K–12 student in a school you are working in. Relate what you learned about this student. How might a teacher use this information to create the best learning situation for this student in mathematics?

3. Investigate and construct an annotated list of five or more children's literature books that could be used to develop a math concept. Note the possible math topics each would address and how the books could be used at different grade levels.

4. Create five math vocabulary study cards using either the LINCS strategy or the Frayer Model. Compare them with others in the course and add your favorites to your teaching toolbox.

5. With a partner, create a song or rap that you could use to teach graphing skills or probability.

6. On a math lesson plan you already have, or that you accessed from the Internet, apply the principles of UDL and show how you would differentiate instruction using pyramid planning. Summarize and reflect on your findings.

7. Try out one of the technology tools mentioned in this chapter that you don't know much about. Describe the tool, how you used it, and the outcome.

8. Make a list of environmental factors that can enhance mathematics teaching.

Looking at the Standards

INTASC Standards

- *Content Pedagogy.* The teacher understands the central concepts, tools of inquiry, and structures of the discipline he or she teaches and can create learning experiences that make these aspects of subject matter meaningful for students.
- *Multiple Instructional Resources.* The teacher understands and uses a variety of instructional strategies to encourage students' development of critical thinking, problem solving, and performance skills.
- *Motivation and Management.* The teacher uses an understanding of individual and group motivation and behavior to create a learning environment that encourages positive social interaction, active engagement in learning, and self-motivation.
- *Communication and Technology.* The teacher uses knowledge of effective verbal, nonverbal, and media communication techniques to foster active inquiry, collaboration, and supportive interaction in the classroom.

Council for Exceptional Children

Special educators are to have knowledge of the following:

- CC4S3: Select, adapt, and use instructional strategies and materials according to characteristics of the individual with exceptional learning needs.
- GC4S1: Use research-supported methods for academic and nonacademic instruction of individuals with disabilities.
- GC4K5: Use methods for increasing accuracy and proficiency in math calculations and applications.
- GC4S5: Use methods to teach mathematics appropriate to the individuals with disabilities.
- GC4S7: Use appropriate adaptations and technology for all individuals with disabilities.
- GC4S12: Use responses and errors to guide instructional decisions and provide feedback to learners.

Key Concepts and Terms

problem solving
mathematic
    communication
math literacy
computation fluency
algorithm
algebra
geometry
measurement

data analysis and
    probability
math anxiety
error analysis
progress monitoring
classroom performance
    system
concrete
representational

abstract
TouchMath
left to right subtraction
lattice multiplication
advance organizer
dynamic geometry
    software
Global Positioning System
MMMR Rap

References

Arnold, D., Fisher, P., Doctoroff, G., & Dobbs, J. (2002). Accelerating math development in Head Start classrooms. *Journal of Educational Psychology, 94*(4), 762–771.

Barber, L., & Borenson, H. (2007). *The effect of Hands-On Equations in the learning of algebra by Title I inner city students in the 5th grade.* Retrieved June 29, 2008, from http://www.borenson.com/Validation/HOE5thGradeInnerCityMarch3007.pdf

Base, G. (2001). *The water hole.* New York: Harry Abrams.

Braswell, J. S., Lutkus, A. D., Grigg, W. S., Santapau, S. L., Tay-Lim, B., & Johnson, M. (2001). The nation's report card: Mathematics 2000. Washington, DC: National Center for Education Statistics.

Cass, M., Cates, D., Smith, M., & Jackson, C. (2003). Effects of manipulative instruction: Solving area and perimeter problems by students with learning disabilities. *Learning Disabilities Research & Practice, 18*(2), 112–120.

Cavanagh, S. (2007). Math anxiety confuses the equation for students. *Education Week, 26*(24), 12.

Cawley, J., & Foley, T. (2001). Enhancing the quality of mathematics for students with learning disabilities: Illustrations from subtraction. *Learning Disabilities: A Multidisciplinary Journal, 11*(2), 47–60.

Church, E. (2000). Math & music: The magical connection. *Scholastic Parent & Child 8*(3), 50–54.

Cocking, R., & Chipman, S. (1988). Conceptual issues related to mathematics achievement of language minority children. In R. Cocking & J. Mestre (Eds.), *Linguistic and cultural influences on learning mathematics* (pp. 17–46). Hillsdale, IL: Lawrence Erlbaum.

Diaz, T., Le, H., & Wise, L. (2006). *Twelfth grade math trend estimates.* Retrieved June 29, 2008, from http://new.humrro.org/finalreports/NAEP12mathtrends.pdf

Ellis, E. S. (1996). *LINCS: A starter strategy for vocabulary learning.* Lawrence, KS: Edge Enterprises.

Forsythe, S. (2007). Learning geometry through dynamic geometry software. *Mathematics Teaching, 202,* 31–35.

Franz, D., & Pope, M. (2005). Using children's stories in secondary math. *American Secondary Education, 33*(2), 20–28.

Fuchs, L. S., & Fuchs, D. (2003). Enhancing the mathematical problem solving of students with mathematics disabilities. In H. L. Swanson, K. R. Harris, & S. Graham (Eds.), *Handbook of learning disabilities* (pp. 306–322). New York: Guilford.

Geary, D. C. (2004). Mathematics and LD. *Journal of Learning Disabilities, 37,* 4–15.

Goldman, S. R., & Hasselbring, T. S. (1997). Achieving meaningful mathematics literacy for students with learning disabilities. *Journal of Learning Disabilities, 30,* 198–208.

Hargreaves, E. (1997). Mathematical assessment for children with English as an additional language. *Assessment in Education: Principles, Policy & Practice, 4*(3), 401–412.

Hresko, W. P., Schlieve, P. L., Herron, S. R., Swain, C., & Sherbenou, R. J. (2002). *Comprehensive Mathematical Abilities Test.* Austin, TX: Pro-Ed.

Klibanoff, R., Levine, S., Huttenlocher, J., Vasilyeva, M., & Hedges, L. (2006). Preschool children's mathematical knowledge: The effect of teacher "math talk." *Developmental Psychology, 42*(1), 59–69.

Kroesbergen, H., & Van Luit, J. (2003). Mathematics interventions for children with special education needs: A meta-analysis. *Remedial and Special Education, 24,* 97–114.

Lucangeli, D., & Cabrele, S. (2006). Mathematical difficulties and ADHD. *Exceptionality, 14*(1), 53–62.

Maccini, P., & Hughes, C. (2000). Effects of a problem-solving strategy on the introductory algebra performance of secondary students with learning disabilities. *Learning Disabilities Research & Practice, 15,* 10–21.

Maccini, P., & Ruhl, K. (2000). Effects of a graduated instructional sequence on the algebraic subtraction of integers by secondary students with learning disabilities. *Education & Treatment of Children, 23,* 465–489.

Malloy, C., & Malloy, W. (1998). Issues of culture in mathematics teaching and learning. *The Urban Review, 30*(3), 245–257.

Marzano, R., Pickering, D., & Pollock, J. (2001). *Classroom instruction that works.* Alexandria, VA: Association for Supervision and Curriculum Development.

Mercer, C., & Mercer, A. (2005). *Teaching students with learning problems* (7th ed.). Upper Saddle River, NJ: Pearson Education.

Mercer, C., & Miller, S. (1992). Teaching students with learning problems in math to acquire, understand, and apply basic math facts. *Remedial and Special Education, 13*, 19–35, 61.

Mervis, J. (2007). Math tests don't line up. *Science, 315*, 1484–1485.

National Assessment of Educational Progress. (2005). *The nation's report card.* Retrieved June 30, 2007, from http://nations reportcard.gov/reading_math_grade12_2005/s0301.asp

National Center for Education Statistics. (2006). *Initial results from the 2005 NHES early childhood program participation survey.* Washington, DC: U.S. Government Printing Office. Retrieved June 29, 2008, from http://nces.ed.gov/pubs2006/earlychild/01.asp

National Council of Teachers of Mathematics. (2000). *Principles & standards for school mathematics.* Retrieved June 29, 2008, from http://standards.nctm.org

Philips, C., & Birrell, H. (1994). Number learning of Asian pupils in English primary schools. *Educational Research, 36*, 51–62.

Ruffins, P. (2007). A real fear. *Diverse Issues in Higher Education, 24*(2), 17–19.

Sharp, B. (2007). Making the most of digital imagery. *Mathematics Teacher, 100*(9), 590.

Van de Walle, J. (2004). *Elementary and middle school mathematics: Teaching developmentally.* Boston: Allyn & Bacon.

Witzel, B., Mercer, C., & Miller, M. (2003). Teaching algebra to students with learning difficulties: An investigation of an explicit instructional model. *Learning Disabilities Research & Practice, 18*(2), 121–131.

Woodcock, R. W., McGrew, K. S., & Mather, N. (2001). *Woodcock-Johnson III Tests of Achievement.* Rolling Meadows, IL: Riverside Publishing.

Xin, Y. P., Jitendra, A. K., & Deatline-Buchman, A. (2005) Effects of mathematical word problem-solving instruction on middle school students with learning problems. *Journal of Special Education, 39*(3), 181–192.

Teaching Critical Content in Science and Social Studies to All Learners

Challenges for Diverse Learners in Science and Social Studies

Establishing Learning Goals
    Focusing on Big Ideas in Science
    Focusing on Ideas in Social Studies

Assessing Science and Social Studies Content Areas
    Using Rubrics
    Applying UDL to Science and Social Studies Assessments

Planning Instruction
    Brainstorming with a Graphic Organizer
    Differentiating Instruction
    Identifying Methods, Tools, Materials, and Resources
    Preparing Lessons

Varying Representation in Science and Social Studies Instruction
    Implementing Inquiry-Based Instruction
    Using an Activities-Oriented Approach

Learning Outcomes

After reading this chapter, you will be able to:

- Identify some of the challenges learners have in science and social studies.
- Name the big ideas in science and social studies.
- Be familiar with some assessment tools available for science and social studies.
- Use assessment information to plan differentiated instruction.
- Apply UDL principles in planning science and social studies content area instruction.
- Select varying approaches and strategies that maximize learning in science and social studies for all students.
- Describe environments, materials, technology tools that can help level the playing field in content area instruction.
- Give examples of types of collaboration that can enhance science and social studies instruction for all students.

Providing Field Trips and Community-Based Experiences
Working with Vocabulary and Readability
Applying Memory Strategies

Increasing Engagement in Science and Social Studies
Implementing Cooperative Learning
Involving Peers

Expanding Expression Opportunities in Science and Social Studies
Providing Opportunities to Practice with Support
Offering Flexible Ways to Demonstrate Skill

Making Adaptations
Considering the Social and Physical Environment
Considering the Academic Environment

Fostering Collaboration in Science and Social Studies Instruction
Collaborative Planning
Co-teaching
Building Community Support

Our grades 3–5 team was working on a unit called, "All Systems on Ready!" last summer with a diverse group of learners. After looking at curricular goals and learner assessments, we brainstormed activities that would meet their individual needs. Knowing these learners were into technology, we chose to use maps and Global Positioning System (GPS) receivers to solve authentic science and math problems. First, most of them needed to know what these devices were and how they worked. We knew our school district had a set of hand-held GPS devices that had only been used with gifted learners so far. Why couldn't all learners learn to use them and discover how they can help people? The learners who were familiar with the devices could help us teach others.

The lesson opened with quick skit. One teacher, our anchor, was out hiking and was lost. Mr. Longitude and Mrs. Latitude (acted out by a parent volunteer and another teacher) rescued her using a GPS device. A short PowerPoint presentation and brief video clip quickly followed introducing this navigational tool. A map, globe, and interactive whiteboard were used with student volunteers to show how the satellites worked with the lines of latitude and longitude. This vocabulary had been pretaught and the students could answer introductory questions about them. They were hooked!

We knew we had to make the lesson concrete for most of these learners. So we made a large grid in the hallway outside the classrooms that had a tiled floor. We used red masking tape for the lines of latitude and blue masking tape for longitude. Three satellites were suspended overhead with colored yard attached that could be used to show the signals and plot the waypoints. After a demonstration, students worked in pairs physically walking on the grid to locate their points. They each pulled a card out of buckets—one bucket had degrees of latitude and the other had longitude degrees. They worked together to find their points. Once they found their waypoint, they gently pulled the yarn from the satellites to meet and mark their waypoint. They could see how signal distances lengthened and decreased as they moved across the grid. They could see a route.

The next day, we were ready to move outside. We showed the students how to turn the "pages" on the GPS tools and use the toggle feature—they learned quickly—transferring prior knowledge playing video games! Parents and university students worked with small groups of students as we followed the leader (Mr. Longitude) and marked predesignated points on the soccer field. Each group had a recorder and they took turns using the GPS. The GPS devices were all preset so that students were all led to a "cache" (buried fossils—sharks teeth, arrowheads, rocks) at the end of the activity. The next day each team hid their own numbered cache in a plastic box, marked their corresponding GPS, and then traded with another team. What fun they had finding each other's caches!

The postassessment showed all students learned the basic concepts/vocabulary of the unit and could tell us what a GPS device is and how it is used. All learners were success-ful and can't wait to use them again! Parents were excited, too. As I reflect, I think the teachers learned at least as much as the students!

Science and social studies are subjects that can really draw in all learners. These content areas require us to use active processes to study meaningful real life topics. They offer classrooms great opportunities for full student participation because the topics lend themselves to "hands-on" instruction. Language often improves as we label materials, talk about procedures, engage all the senses, question and interact. Social behavior often improves as well because students are immersed in something they can relate to and are usually interested in. There are many opportunities to work in teams. Sometimes students who struggle can shine in these content areas, particularly when options for accessing the printed and sometimes spoken words are in place. As you explore science and social studies standards and curriculum, the principles of Universal Design for Learning are already evident. When talking about special education, one author recently described the logic of scientific inquiry as "the best trick we know for solving our most pressing problems" (Sasso, 2001, p. 190). Even though he was referring to science as a system of study applied to special education in general, the discipline is naturally motivating, systematic, and lends itself easily to objective observation and curricular integration.

Remember that many students need specialized instruction but that doesn't mean students have to engage in identical tasks. Not all doctors do the same thing in hospitals, and not all lawyers engage in the same activities in a courtroom. They can be in the same place with the same "big idea" even though the content, process, and product might be different (Yinger & Nolen, 2003, p. 389).

The big ideas of both science and social studies are considered together in terms of UDL applications in this chapter. You will notice that science and mathematics principles are often naturally combined in teaching as evidenced in materials and staff development offered by organizations such as *Activities Integrating Mathematics and Science (AIMS)*. The connections often extend to social studies as well. In social studies, students must also learn to question, debate, and explore the world to gain a deeper understanding of systems. Data is collected, organized, and analyzed as we work to understand political, economic, social systems, and more. Hopefully, we use this evidence and these explanations to formulate predictions and plans of action that can improve our world. Try to strategically integrate multiple disciplines as much as you can to help students see these problem-solving patterns. Thus, the material in this chapter is applicable to teachers in *all* content areas. The ways UDL is applied to any topic can, for the most part, be transferred to topics and age groups within other subject areas.

Challenges for Diverse Learners in Science and Social Studies

The foundation for science, as true for most disciplines, is still largely accessed by a textbook (Raisen, 1988, as cited in Parmar & Cawley, 1993). If you have struggling readers, it has been nearly impossible to engage these learners in age appropriate instruction if there is too much reliance on hard copy textbooks and print materials. It may be helpful to refer back to the section in Chapter 11, *Applying UDL to Reading in the Content Areas*, as you plan readings for science and social studies lessons to ensure accessibility of print. It is also important to remember that textbooks do not always cover everything that is needed according to the standards you are charged to teach. An evaluation of middle-school science textbooks by middle-school teachers, university professors of science education, and curriculum specialists revealed these textbooks covered too many topics and didn't help students learn key ideas. Not one textbook received a satisfactory rating (Rosenman, Kesidou, Stern, &

Caldwell, 1999). As you identify resources for your units, keep the curricular goals and objectives close at hand to be sure they match up.

Textbooks in science and social studies tend to be expository texts as well. Expository texts tend to disengage learners who are at risk or have learning problems. A narrative approach in which information is delivered through an anchor (Armbruster & Anderson, 1988) or through a story, on the other hand, increases engagement (Dull & van Garderen, 2005).

The National Council for History Education (2008) tells us that social studies and current issues must be studied not only in the historical context but also in perspective. In social studies there are many debates over the "correctness" of content presented in an expository text by different political, ethnic, religious, and other groups so writers tend to be more neutral and tiptoe around so as not to offend anyone. Using a narrative, different opinions and perspectives can be shown through the eyes of different characters. Intelligent personal and political judgments are critical in making domestic and global decisions today.

When you use a narrative story and supply an anchor (e.g., a character), you give more students a chance to relate. Some people claim we need stories to make connections to the real world (Wilson, 2002). Rural community are often rich in oral story telling traditions. Most students of all ages enjoy and benefit from the use of a story format to get a concept across.

In addition to anchoring instruction and using narratives, there are many other research-based strategies and interventions that help teachers meet the needs of diverse learners in science and social studies. For example, helping students prioritize tasks and providing them with study guides, organizers, graphics, and audio recordings can be effective (Munk, Bruckert, Call, Stoehrmann, & Radandt, 1998). Providing an inclusive, outcome-based environment that considers multiple intelligences, cooperative learning, peer-mediated instruction, and technology infusion has also been suggested (Norman, Caseau, & Stefanich, 1998). By helping students build on prior knowledge, they can explore theories and construct other explanations and ideas (Gallas, 1995). *All* students can increase their problem-solving abilities. The teacher is instrumental in knowing when to provide direct instruction and when to set up a situation/environment for problem solving and facilitating. The effective teacher knows the modalities and strengths to tap for each learner through ongoing assessment.

Michael Newman/PhotoEdit

Anchoring learning through a character or a story helps students connect learning to real life.

Establishing Learning Goals

We are going to briefly review the big ideas in science and social studies instruction in planning and connecting to standards. Remember that standards are the concepts and skills to be taught and assessed. The standards are what *all* students in the general curriculum must access. Applying UDL principles help us make the needed adaptations so all students can make progress in meeting their standards.

Focusing on Big Ideas in Science

The five "big ideas" in science can be found in the National Science Education Standards (National Committee on Science Education Standards and Assessment, 1996). In the standards, they are called, "unifying concepts and processes." These curricular notions make it possible to unify the different parts within the discipline of science. This thought pattern helps develop scientific literacy between subjects such as physics, biology, chemistry, and earth science (Coyne, Kame'enui, & Carnine, 2007).

The first big idea evolves around **systems**, **order**, and **organization**. A system is a whole unit that is made of up parts. These parts are connected and are interdependent. The system is made up in a certain order and this organization is predictable. Systems have a function or plan and they can change. There are many systems in nature. Examples include the human body, space, and weather. When teaching the GPS lesson, we looked at navigational systems—things like maps, signals, movement. We looked at the different parts that made up the whole.

Evidence, **models**, and **explanations** make up the next big idea. Through models (e.g., 3-D structures, sketches, diagrams, video), one can explain how something like using satellite signals to locate a point on a grid works. Using such a model helps one explain the evidence that three or more signals received by a GPS tool will produce specific points of latitude and longitude. Models of plants, the human body, and electrical systems are other examples that help explain evidence.

The third big idea in science evolves around **constancy**, **change**, and **measurement**. Our planet, for example, is a constant but it changes over time and that change can be measured. Other examples might include changes in weather and species of plants and animals. Note that *measurement* in science strategically links to mathematical big ideas.

Evolution and **equilibrium** make up the fourth big idea. The balance among living things, for example, helps them survive and change over time. The topic of global warming might be a study under the "umbrella" of this big idea.

The fifth big science idea is that of **form and function**. The form of a honeybee's wings, for example, affects its ability to fly from flower to flower collecting nectar to make honey (a function). The form of its abdomen with its bright colored pattern warns predators that it also has a weapon (a stinger) to defend itself from harm.

The eight categories of content standards within science are:

- Unifying concepts and processes in science
- Science as inquiry
- Physical science
- Life science
- Earth and space science
- Science and technology
- Science in personal and social perspectives
- History and nature of science

Cengage Learning/Wadsworth

By combining science and technology skills, students can solve authentic problems in our natural world.

Technology and science are closely related, as indicated in the above list. This is important to remember as we continue to think about UDL. What makes science and technology different from each other is in the goal of each. In science, the goal is to understand our natural world (life, earth, for example) and the goal in technology is to make modifications in the world for human needs. When combined, science and technology can help us solve problems. Remember technology gives us all tools to better understand our world (National Research Council (1996).

Focusing on Big Ideas in Social Studies

Just as in science, the breadth of social studies content information is vast. The National Council for the Social Studies (NCSS) defines social studies as "the integrated study of the social sciences and humanities to promote civic competence" (National Council for the Social Studies, 2008). It includes disciplines such as anthropology, archaeology, economics, geography, history, law, philosophy, political science, psychology, religion, and sociology. The 10 thematic strands from the national social studies standards are shown in Table 13.1. The NCSS states that many civic issues are interdisciplinary and must interact with mathematics, natural sciences, and the humanities to be resolved. In other words, if we really want to understand and solve today's civic problems, skills and ideas from all disciplines must work together.

Remember that using big ideas helps to pull out the critical aspects of the content and put them into manageable chunks. Ideas and learning goals can be interconnected to unify concepts and skills within units of study and apply them to real life. "Big ideas" in social studies that might be pulled from these thematic strands after you review curriculum might include problem-solving, decision making, cause and effect, and comparing/contrasting.

Problem-solving includes learning to identify a problem, gathering information, listing and considering options, considering advantages and disadvantages, and evaluating the effectiveness of a solution. From explorers, presidents, soldiers, and lawyers to university students, having effective problem-solving skills is critical for success in life.

Table 13.1	The Ten Thematic Strands from the National Social Studies Standards
Strand	**Definition/Examples**
Culture	The religious, political, racial, social traits/beliefs of a social group of people
Time, Continuity, and Change	Understanding and analyzing the past, its relationship to the present, and implications for the future
People, Places, and Environment	Population distribution; understanding the connection between people and geography
Individual Development and Identity	Understanding that individuals are unique; developing a civic responsibility and integrity in self, in school, in society; understanding rules and laws
Individuals, Groups, and Institutions	Human decisions and consequences, personal and national implications; how institutions respond to human needs
Power, Authority, and Governance	How people create and change structures of power, authority, and governance
Production, Distribution, and Consumption	How people organize for the production, distribution, and consumption of goods and services; movement of people, goods, and ideas
Science, Technology, and Society	How technology has impacted the world; predicting future trends; how society holds onto its beliefs with new technological developments
Global Connections	How countries make decisions about the distribution of economic resources and goods
Civic Ideals and Practices	Students will be informed decision makers as they apply their acquired knowledge about responsible citizenship and human rights based on historical events and perspectives, geographical relationships, economics, political science, and jurisprudence

Source: National Council for the Social Studies, *Curriculum Standards for Social Studies*. Retrieved June 30, 2008, from http://www.socialstudies.org/standards/

Cengage Learning/Wadsworth

Planning around big ideas in social studies helps identify critical content and can unify skills within units of study.

The **decision-making process** is another big idea. Components include identifying a situation that requires a decision, gathering information, identifying options, predicting consequences, and taking action to implement a decision. From world leaders to parents to students of all ages, decision making is critical.

The ability to determine **cause and effect** was and is certainly important for explorers, political and religious leaders, business managers, and many others, including consumers. It is important to know how the development of new ideas and technologies impact people over time. It is also important to understand the consequences of our actions.

By **comparing and contrasting** systems of government, economics, and social systems as well as cultures, geographic regions, and more, we can discover commonalities and better understand their similarities and differences. Understanding the past and the present through the study of history, geography, economics, political science, anthropology and other social studies disciplines helps us make the most of what we have and better prepare ourselves for the future (Kentucky Department of Education, 2005).

The purpose of this brief introduction of big ideas in science and social studies was to help you articulate the larger goals of these disciplines as you make connections with the standards to construct units. If you can link student learning to key ideas, you maximize student learning. Once you have established your goals, assessment is next.

Assessing Science and Social Studies Content Areas

Classroom assessments in science and social studies can take many forms, including, but not limited to, observations of student performance during instructional activities, interviews, formal performance tasks, portfolios, investigative projects, written reports and multiple choice assessments, short-answer tests, and essay examinations. Be sure that the connection between the objective being assessed links clearly to the original learning goal. For example, if a student's ability to obtain and evaluate scientific information is only measured using a short-answer test to identify the sources of high-quality scientific information about toxic waste, we may not know the full extent of the learning that took place. This type of assessment likely requires memorization and tells us what students do and do not know. It will show us achievement that is easily measured. A more-authentic method might be to ask the student to locate the needed information, develop an annotated bibliography on the findings, and provide a judgment about the scientific quality of the information. Such an assessment would tap into multiple student levels of thinking and reasoning. Not only are we assessing achievement but also we are gaining an opportunity to see how our students are learning. The student may also become more fully aware of the need to think "green" and protect the environment using a more-authentic assessment. We must show students how to be ongoing assessors of their own learning (National Research Council, 1996).

Keep in mind that assessment tasks need to be appropriate for the skill level you are assessing when possible. Strive to keep vocabulary and reading skills on the students' grade level or otherwise adapt them for access. Try to keep assessments as free from bias as possible and set them in contexts that students can relate to.

Using Rubrics

Rubrics are great to use in content area instruction, especially with diverse learners and with assessment that goes beyond the multiple choice test. Not only do they allow for some flexibility in process and product, they also communicate the expectation to the student up front. Try to use analytic rather than holistic rubrics to focus on the learning process, thus allowing more learners the opportunity to earn points on the final product (Finson & Ormsbee, 1998). Look back in Chapter 8 if you need a quick review of these types of rubrics. Figures 13.1 and 13.2 are examples of rubrics that could be constructed for use in science and social studies.

Criteria	4	3	2	1
Content: Organization, hypothesis, purpose, analysis, understanding, conclusion	• Ideas are clear and presentation flows. • Critical analysis throughout. • Student's understanding of the scientific process goes above and beyond topic. • Conclusion ties all data together and is clearly stated.	• Evidence of planning, preparation and a format being followed. • Evidence of understanding but analysis is not fully developed. • Conclusion is somewhat confusing.	• Presentation is somewhat planned. • Purpose is general. • Lacks analysis. • Conclusion does not reflect the scientific process.	• Disorganized, confusing, and incomplete. • Purpose is vague. • Low level of understanding. • No conclusion.
Language Use: Appropriate, interesting, clarity	• Language is meaningful, thought provoking, and risk taking.	• Language is effective, appropriate, and specific.	• Language conveys a general message and inconsistencies are evident.	• Language is ineffective, vague, and inappropriate.

Figure 13.1 Sample Rubric for Science

Source: Regina Public Schools and Saskatchewan Learning, (2003), *Best Practices: Pieces of the Puzzle.* Retrieved June 30, 2008, from http://wblrd.sk.ca/~bestpractice/tiered/examples8.html

Dimensions (Categories)	Levels (Criteria)				
	Proficient **4**	**Very Good** **3**	**Acceptable** **2**	**Not Yet** **1**	**Points**
Content	All necessary labels are present and are carefully and accurately placed.	All labels are present and most are accurate.	All but one or two labels are present. Several labels are not accurately placed.	Several labels are not present and many are not accurately or carefully placed.	
Visual Appeal	Map is colorful and neat looking. Labels are clear and easy to read.	Color has been used over most of the map. A few labels are not easy to read.	Color has been used on less than half of the map. Many labels are difficult to read.	Use of color is limited or not at all. Most labels are difficult to read.	
Map Elements	Includes clearly written standard map elements: • title • directional arrow • scale • key • latitude and longitude lines	Includes most standard map elements. Most are accurate and easy to read.	Missing several standard map elements.	Missing most standard map elements.	

Figure 13.2 Sample Social Studies Rubric: A Map Rubric

Source: Regina Public Schools and Saskatchewan Learning, (2003), *Best Practices: Pieces of the Puzzle*. Retrieved June 30, 2008, from http://wblrd.sk.ca/~bestpractice/rubrics/social.html

Applying UDL to Science and Social Studies Assessments

Your computer will be your best friend when creating and accessing alternate assessments for your students (Fernstrom & Goodnite, 2000). On a matching, multiple choice or short answer assessment, for example, you can change the font size as needed. You can reduce the number of items/questions on a page. You might keep one type of test question to a single page (all short answer on one page, for example, and multiple choice on another page). A rule of thumb for multiple choice questions is to have three questions for each concept/idea. Using a computer, you can easily mix up the question and/or answer order to reduce the temptation by some students to copy others. You can also adjust the number of answer choices to fit learner needs.

Using technology, you can have tests read aloud to students. Oral answers can be recorded and listened to later. Students can use technology to create products such as PowerPoint presentations, WebQuests, and annotated bibliographies. Videos, CDs, and podcasts can be made for demonstrations of work done in a laboratory setting. Classroom response systems (CRS), or clickers, as described in Chapter 9, can be used effectively to formatively assess and record responses of whole groups of students quickly as you progress through daily lessons to see what learning is or isn't taking place.

Table 13.2 offers some ideas about types of formative or informal assessments that can be used frequently in science and social studies. Remember that assessment is ongoing and always linked to your objectives. Try to assess the process as well as the achievement so you can make needed adjustments for representation, expression, and engagement.

Table 13.3 shows some summative assessments that might be used in science, social studies, and other content areas. These assessments are typically used once

Table 13.2	Formative Assessment Tools for Science and Social Studies
Formative Assessment Tools	**Description: Student Process and Measuring Achievement**
Short answer, multiple choice, short answer, essay tests (weekly or biweekly)	Define/match/draw: Use pictures/objects when words aren't understood. Have students give examples when possible.
Graphic organizers/diagrams	Products: Students might draw the water cycle using a circle template, fill in a Venn diagram to compare/contrast two economic systems, classify types of animals, create a timeline of the Civil War.
Observations of performance tasks, interviews, skits, demonstrations, investigated projects, oral or written reports/debates, murals, pamphlets, songs, raps, newspaper, photo essay (can be formative or summative)	Checklists, rubrics
CBM monitoring 2–3 times a week	Simple chart or graph; teacher log of progress
Science/social studies notebooks, diaries/journals and/or logs	Allow opportunities to describe as well as to predict, analyze, and reflect
Learning contracts, self-assessment checklists	Checklists for individual students who need more interventions
Technology Tools	
Videos, podcasts, CDs, cameras, tapes of student performances/demonstrations classroom response systems (for oral questions, quick assessments) response cards	

the units of study are completed. They also may be part of benchmark and end-of-grade testing. Be sure you are aware of any students who have testing modifications or accommodations as part of an individual education plan or Section 504 plan. Remember that these types of adaptations should be used consistently throughout the school year with all assessments—not just for summative assessments. Some students may need alternate assessments. For example, some students

Table 13.3	Examples of Summative/Formal Assessments in Science and Social Studies
Formal Science & Social Studies Assessments	**Description**
• Benchmark testing • End of unit • End of grade or course assessments (e.g., teacher, school, district, state, and/or national assessments)	These tend to be multiple choice but may also include other formats such as short answer and essay.
Observations of long-term performance tasks such as: • demonstrations • investigated projects • oral or written reports/debates • murals • pamphlets • newspaper • photo essay Long-term projects can be summative.	Checklists, rubrics Technology tools: iPods, multimedia production tools, computers, GPS systems, PDAs
Portfolio assessment	Work samples: • lab booklet samples/notes • summary of formative evaluation measures • teacher observations and recording, videotapes, audiotapes of oral productions • summaries from the year Technology: Tools for creating electronic portfolios
Electronic assessments: Full Option Science System (FOSS)	Summative and formative assessments that correlate with science standards

Source: Lawrence Hall of Science, University of California at Berkeley, *FOSS Project Site*. Retrieved June 30, 2008, from http://www.lawrencehallofscience.org/foss/components/general/k8sys.html

may need fewer answer choices, language translation, leveled reading, text read aloud, extended time, marking in the booklet, or testing in a separate room. For students with more-significant challenges, curricular goals may be modified and a special educator at your school can assist in planning for assessment.

Planning Instruction

According to Polloway, Patton, and Serna (2005), there are 10 inquiry skills that should be included regularly in science instruction. The first is *observation*. Students must employ their senses to find out/take in information about a topic/subject. Next is *measurement* so they can make observations that are quantitative. Students will need to *classify* things according to similarities and differences and be able to *communicate* their information and ideas to others. They need to *collect*, *organize*, and *graph* data and explain (*infer*) their findings. Then they will be better able to *predict* future events and conditions based on their findings. The ability to *interpret data* (find patterns), will help them *construct hypotheses* (educated guesses) and conduct *experiments* to test these hypotheses.

When teaching science and social studies to all learners, these guiding principles are offered. First, choose themes/topics that have personal relevance to your students and build upon what students already know (Choate, 1997). For example, when planning the unit "All Systems on Ready!" we knew that our students were interested in knowing more about the severe weather in our area. They wanted to know why it was so intense, how meteorologists predicted storms, how satellites worked, and how severe weather is affecting the world. They wanted to know how to keep safe. These were also students who were into video games and computers. Their interest in maps, satellites, and handheld technologies helped us think about using the GPS lesson to meet other necessary learning objectives from the standards.

Brainstorming with a Graphic Organizer

In Chapter 10 we talked about designing integrated units using a visual organizer. An application of this organizer is shown in Figure 13.3. This unit, "All Systems on Ready!" shows you how a team might plan an interdisciplinary unit using a big idea from science as a springboard. Remember to define your goal first and plan the assessment next. Then think about activities and resources that will help students reach those goals (Wiggins & McTighe, 1998; Tomlinson & McTighe, 2006). Brainstorm essential questions ahead of time and explore print, media/technolgy, and other web-based resources.

A quick overview of the organizer shows how content information can be obtained from *information* systems that may include digital texts/print materials, audio/visual, and multimedia materials related to the system being studied. Investigations about how people in different places use systems to find locations of places integrates *social studies*. Problem solving, measurement, data analysis, and other *mathematics* components come into play. *Art* and *music* also have systems that can be integrated. Students can systematically put a band together or mix music. Shapes can be combined to design completed sculptures or drawings. Integrated or **thematic teaching** combines all the individual parts to make a whole unit. This way of brainstorming offers the diverse learner more opportunities to learn through his or her areas of strength and to connect with the real world. Language and reading skills that are so critical for accessibility, can be built up around each content area and connected in a meaningful way (Eichinger & Downing, 2002).

This organizer also has places to brainstorm additional content area goals, key vocabulary, technologies to incorporate, community resources, cultural aspects, assessment strategies, and a culminating activity.

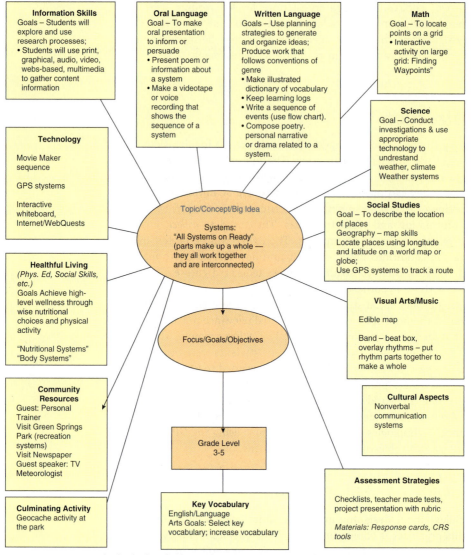

Latitude, longitude, environment, ecosystem, for example

Figure 13.3 Brainstorming with a Graphic Organizer: "Systems" Unit.
Source: Unit topic and organizer used at the Summer Learning Center, East Carolina University, Greenville, NC, 2007.

Differentiating Instruction

Once you have chosen your unit topic, brainstormed objectives/goals and assessments, you are ready to differentiate for the complex (Tomlinson, 2001). Just as in pyramid planning, initially focus on the basic skills that *all* students must learn in Tier I. Some of these students may be working in the low average range and/or may not be motivated or attentive for a variety of reasons. Tier II students are working in the average range, and Tier III students are either working at an advanced level or perhaps working on a modified curricular goal. Students can still have choice within each tier, allowing for learner preferences and interests. Table 13.4 is an example of what a tiered ninth-grade science lesson for data collection and inference might look like.

Preparing and using **essential questions** in preassessment helps in planning differentiated instruction up front as well as for monitoring comprehension during the

Table 13.4	Tiered Instruction for Differentiation

Tier III	**Students will create their own study or experiment**. Most of these students have mastered the experimental process and data collection. Therefore, the real learning and appropriate challenge is the process of planning their own experiment. *This might also be a place a student works on a modified IEP goal.*
Tier II	**Students will attempt a suggested topic to work within**. For example, suggest the group do a behavioral study. One student may study the effects on one's success with vocabulary when being rushed compared to the success of someone not being rushed. Students will see how moods and frustrations play a part in success. Students in this tier are appropriately challenged because they are creating, but you have taken away the weeks of wonder by making a general suggestion for the group.
Tier I	**Use a variety of premade experiments, where the students choose and organize the data collected**. These students often procrastinate, use judgment rather than scientific inferences, and achieve low because of a lack of comfort in the subject or academic skill. When you take away the "wonder" time, you allow these students to move right into achievement.

Source: Adapted from Regina Public Schools and Saskatchewan Learning (2003), *Best Practices: Pieces of the Puzzle.* Retrieved June 30, 2008, from http://wblrd.sk.ca/~bestpractice/tiered/examples4.html

lesson and for postassessment. Referring back to Bloom's taxonomy in Chapter 5, the following questions were developed for the GPS lesson:

- What are the cardinal directions? (remember)
- What is a GPS system and what does it do? (understand)
- What would happen if we tried to use the GPS indoors?" (apply)
- How do you find a waypoint on a grid? (apply)
- How does a GPS system receive its signals? (analyze)
- How precise are the signal locations we received on the trail? (evaluate)
- In what other situation might it be helpful for you to have a GPS tool? (create)

Opening questions showed us that some students already knew about GPS systems. Some had them in the family car. One student had used one before in another class. We also learned that this was the first time some students had ever seen or heard of a GPS. Some did not know cardinal directions or how to use a compass. Others couldn't locate points on a grid. All of these were prerequisite academic skills that needed to be taught.

This preassessment of students through questioning and discussion, paired with additional prior knowledge we had about each student, helped us figure out which tier to start them in. The tiers allow for flexibility of placement but provide a starting place. These kinds of questions and answers can help shape how we think about providing both additional background knowledge and extensions.

Table 13.5 is an example of what the tiered GPS lesson looked like. It is a more detailed version of the pyramid planning figure we have been using in our lesson plan models.

Identifying Methods, Tools, Materials, and Resources

Now it is time to think about teaching methods for concepts and specific skills and to plan purposeful learning extensions for students who need to move on with less direction. Remember that there are times that skills necessary for a task need to be directly taught up front. Just remember some learners will need more direct instruction than will others, so be flexible enough to adjust as needed. All learners will also need some time for exploration and discovery. Be sure your learning environment is respectful of all learner differences and is a safe place to take risks. Remember the students are the "shoppers" and we are stocking the shelves. This will require you to consistently do your homework because you don't want to "run out" of something.

Table 13.5	Tiered Planning Example of GPS Lesson
Tier III	If preassessment determines these students have already mastered this content, they may plan their own related experiment or study. For example, they may be interested in creating and premarking a route on the GPS systems for the other students to try out, creating a WebQuest on navigational systems that other students can benefit from, researching satellites and finding pictures/photos for the class to use as models, or creating a multimedia project to introduce GPS systems to other students in the school. *A student working on an IEP goal in social skills might turn out to be the videographer of the GPS outdoor activity. This can also fit into this tier.*
Tier II	These students will move directly into the grid simulation activity. After we practice it a couple of times as a group, they will each be assigned a buddy from the Tier I group to work with and help with the instruction by "talking aloud" the steps in the process of locating the points of latitude and longitude from the satellite signals on the grid. Students in this group may also choose to work on a WebQuest scavenger hunt activity on navigation systems/maps or work on filling in the names of places on a blank world map using points of latitude and longitude. They may also choose to become involved in satellite construction using picture models that are provided.
Tier I	Students will work on direction words (north, south, each, west) with a teacher assistant and construct/label a compass rose made out of popsicle sticks and practiced a mnemonic for direction words. Then they will practice reading directions on a real compass. They will trace lines of latitude and longitude on a map and grid projected on an electronic whiteboard. During the grid simulation activity, they will be guided through the process with a peer buddy. They will have the same peer buddy when we move to the outdoor activity with the GPS systems. Both students will complete a single data collection worksheet. These students may work on satellite construction when they finish.

Stock your shelves with a variety of methods, tools, materials and other resources. Be familiar with these activities and items that support your objectives.

When planning, be thinking, too, about possible misconceptions your students may have and how you will help them grow in their thinking (Roseman, Kesidou, Stern, & Caldwell, 1999). Your teacher questioning and feedback will need to be timely, specific, and informative to correct some of their incorrect notions. This type of feedback and correction will work as one of many positive behavior supports for the student because it will make each one more successful with the task at hand.

Plan ways to promote positive social interaction with your students. Remember that working with peers is often motivating and productive. Sometimes working outdoors and going on field trips provides opportunities to enjoy conversation and much needed movement. Thematic units make integrating the arts easier, often adding motivation and increasing positive emotions. The arts tap into creativity, add novelty, and provide more opportunities for personal expression. Remember the power of activating the affective system in the brain. Many great decisions are made and problems solved because people are passionate about something! These extra activities are often a great way to draw in other professionals, parents, families, and other community members as well.

For some diverse learners, it will be important to plan in some extrinsic rewards. In the GPS activity discussed earlier, for example, students were led to a buried treasure if they correctly calculated their waypoints. Regional fossils (e.g., arrowheads, sharks' teeth, rocks) were donated by a community member and later buried for a "dig." Using these artifacts as prizes also gave us a chance to revisit some themes and concepts we had worked on in a prior earth science unit that included rocks, minerals, and fossils.

Many of the methods you have read about in this text will be shown in science/ social studies lesson plans that follow. We will look at tools, materials, and resources that can support a variety of methods next.

Technology tools will need to be identified. Having Internet tools and resources listed with annotations in a folder (paper or electronic) is helpful. "Hands-on"

David Cannings-Bushell/istockphoto.com

Field trips extend learning beyond the classroom, and motivate cooperative learning, social interaction, exploration, and discovery.

materials need to organized, labeled, and stored neatly. Easy access will be key. Sometimes there are students or volunteers who enjoy this kind of organizational task. Some schools have central storage areas where shared resources can be kept. It takes time to build up a collection of materials but if you *can identify your needs ahead of time* and let parents and community members know specific items of need, you will be surprised at the response. You may also be able to access small grants for more-expensive items. High-tech devices may cost more initially but tend to offer great flexibility in how they can increase access to information, illustrations, examples, and language for diverse learners.

Having trade books, textbooks, digital texts, library books, magazines, videos, podcasts, web or other resources available that feature experiments and related studies can enhance planning and instruction for all learners. If you have these materials available at different levels of instruction, students who need to extend their learning to a higher or lower level have greater access. In addition, providing a list of resources that students can use to find and select experiments and lessons, can help students who are gifted (Stepanek, 1999) and interested in the subject. Think of textbooks as one reference tool of many. Stay up to date with current events, research, and materials. Examples of the kinds of tools and resources you might need for science and social studies have been brainstormed in Table 13.6. In addition, curriculum, media, and AT specialists are great contacts for additional resources.

Getting started is sometimes the hardest part of planning. Some specific planning tools with examples and additional methods and interventions that can help you will be offered throughout the rest of this chapter.

Preparing Lessons

A science lesson plan will be used as an example during our discussion of lesson preparation. Figure 13.4 (on pages 382–383) is an elementary lesson from the "All Systems on Ready!" unit already described in Figure 13.3. The plan is color coded in the same way lesson plans in previous chapters have been done to show the UDL elements of representation, engagement, and expression (Rose & Meyer, 2002).

Web Resources

For more science and social studies resources that you will definitely want to add to your list, check this text's companion website, **http://www.academic .cengage.com/education/ Gargiulo**.

Table 13.6   Examples of Tools, Materials, Resources for UDL Lessons in Science and Social Studies

Science	Social Studies	Both
• Projecting microscopes	• Fact tables, maps (including relief maps), atlases, illuminating globes	• Computers with extra large screen monitors/projectors
• Big Eye light	• Art materials: e.g., mask making (cultural); quilt making (history)	• Interactive whiteboards
• Magnifying devices	• Multicultural songs/plays/dramas	• Overhead projectors/color transparencies, data projectors (visual paired with auditory)
• Manuals in any needed languages (Braille included)	• Webcams for interviewing	• Internet access/virtual field trips
• Trays with partitions/plastic tubs, different sizes of containers, zipper-lock bags, funnels, scoops (anchor receptacles with hook-and-loop fasteners for students with fine motor problems) for pouring activities	• E-mail, blogs for pen pals, correspondence, other social networking tools (with safety precautions)	• Closed-circuit TVs
• Braille or large print rulers	• Costumes, props	• Portable keyboards for fieldwork
• Hook-and-loop gloves for grasping	• Puppets	• Clear plastic folders, clear photograph cubes to hold directions, vocabulary cards
• GPS devices	• Diaries, journals	• Spell checkers
• Models/aquariums	• Travel brochures	• Recorded lessons
• Magnets	• Storyboards	• Audio supports for ample volume as needed
• Braille or raised-line digital thermometers	• Musical instruments	• Felt boards, magnetic boards, dry erase boards for collecting data
• Measuring wheels for outdoor activities	• Fossils, artifacts	• Newspapers, news channels/websites
• Contact list for human resources such as biologists, geologists, meteorologists	• Contact list for human resources such as reporters, war veterans, politicians, economists	• Computer software/simulation programs
		• Digital cameras, iPods
		• For graphing: stickers, hook-and-loop fasteners, felt or foam dots, rubber stamps with handles (to record data), raised-line graph paper
		• Human resources: art/music/media specialists, parents, community members, museum contacts

Web Resources

For an example of a secondary UDL lesson plan on the New Deal, visit the companion website, **www.academic.cengage.com/education/Gargiulo**.

The objective is paired with assessment at the top of the plan. Standard course of study objectives are also included in this space. Essential questions representing a variety of thinking levels based on lesson objectives are included in the lesson closing, along with vocabulary to be targeted. Following the plan are additional low- and high-tech suggestions, a planning pyramid for differentiating instruction, and a box to brainstorm solutions to possible student barriers. Research-based methods, interventions, strategies and other techniques previously mentioned in Chapters 9, 11, and 12 are included.

In the *preplanning* section of the lesson plan, it is helpful to indicate what you will need in your lesson. The GPS lesson calls for a large grid taped on the floor. Writing this down can remind the teacher to ask a volunteer or possibly students to help set this up the day before. The GPS systems will need to be picked up, props gathered for the skit, and data collection sheets prepared. The fossils will need to be hidden that morning before school. Other typical preplanning activities might include preparing advance organizers/outlines, guided notes, and setting up equipment.

Open and set up the lesson by quickly reviewing the previous lesson and skills to activate prior knowledge. In the GPS lesson, we wanted to teach the students about a GPS and how it works. Remember that it is important to state our lesson objective clearly not only for ourselves but also to motivate our students. If possible, have the objective clearly visible in the room on a board, chart, computer screen, or poster. This establishes the purpose of the lesson up front, helps secure student "buy in," and gets everyone focused.

This is a good place in the lesson to do some quick pre-assessment of what students might know about the day's objective and what they might want to learn. A **KWL chart** (Ogle, 1986) can be used here to discuss and record what students want to know and what they want to learn. This is a simple three-column graphic organizer that helps students engage with the topic. See Figure 13.5 (on page 384) for an example. You might also want to quickly review key vocabulary and focus on one or two keyword(s) for the lesson as you set up the expectations for the day's work.

Throughout the lesson, it can be helpful to project how much time you will need for each part even though you will need to be somewhat flexible with it. Think about what you will be doing and what the students will be doing. Once again, color coding the UDL elements can help you see if you have planned for variety in your presentation and engagement. It might also be helpful to jot down what materials will be needed in each section of the plan. A bulleted checklist of lesson plan steps for you to check off can help with your organization.

Now you are ready to provide the *teacher input* in the *lesson body*. This is your opportunity to provide content with accuracy and clarity. In both sample lesson plans, the teachers begin by presenting a problem. (As you will learn later, this presentation doesn't always have to come at the beginning.) In the GPS lesson, one teacher plays the role of a lost hiker. Another teacher and a volunteer represent "Mr. Longitude" and "Mrs. Latitude," dressed in hiking gear and wearing very large name badges. (An anchor for older students might have been an archaeologist at work or a guest geologist.) Next, a brief PowerPoint presentation (with sound and animation) introduces the GPS system and related vocabulary. A video clip from "Mr. Brain" demonstrating the device is imbedded in the presentation. (This would be an ideal spot to provide a PowerPoint outline for note taking.) An actual GPS tool to show, a satellite model, and a globe will be shown with printed labels attached. The teacher reviews locating points using longitude and latitude on a map grid projected onto an interactive whiteboard. Some students will be involved in the demonstration. The group will be divided in half. One group will go into the hallway to physically practice finding waypoints on the large grid that was taped to the floor. The other group will work individually or in small groups in the classroom on cardinal directions, vocabulary, satellite construction, and research—depending on their individual needs. Then the groups will trade places.

Guided practice follows with activities that are relevant to the objective. Everyone is involved and the teacher(s) monitor. Student work is observable if learning is to take place. In the GPS lesson, some students are finding waypoints. Some students are making visual/tactile word cards, some are creating satellites models, others are researching navigation systems and still others are learning a *mnenomic* as they review the cardinal directions with hand signals (North-East-South-West: **N**ever **E**at **S**hredded **W**heat) and construct a compass rose out of popsicle sticks. The teachers will then take all the students outdoors to demonstrate and practice with the actual GPS devices. Volunteers and students who were proficient with the devices will lead small groups of learners to preset waypoints on the soccer field.

Extended practice is next. In the GPS lesson, teams are given a GPS device, a data collection sheet, and a "cache" (an sealed envelope) to hide. They are asked to mark three waypoints within certain boundaries and hide their cache at the third one. Upon return to the starting place, they trade GPS devices with another team and find their cache. The caches will give them the waypoints to a buried treasure. Teams are reminded that they must work together and complete their data sheets to turn in. The teacher will circulate and ask students to tell or show how to use a GPS. A video camera and iPod will be available to record responses that can be assessed later. Other teachers, volunteers, or students may help collect these assessments.

In the lesson closing, the teacher chooses to end with whole-class discussions using the essential questions. Students will finish filling in their KWL chart (see Figure 13.5 on page 384). All students will share what they learned.

This application of UDL elements to lesson planning in this chapter and other lesson plan examples in previous chapters illustrates the ease and flexibility that UDL provides. The elements of representation, engagement, and expression were applied with ease using a color-coded system. Many similarities in lesson-planning practices are observable through this process even though the authors were in different content areas and were trained at different times in different places. Everyone could infuse low- and high-tech tools, differentiate instruction using the planning pyramid, and brainstorm individual learner barriers and possible solutions. Charts, organizers, and information provided in this text can help with that process. After planning this way a few times, it can become fairly automatic. Keeping this type of

Instructor: _D. Metcalf_
Subject: _Science_
Grade: _3-5th (flexible grouping)_

Lesson Objective(s):
To tell or show how to use a GPS device

Assessment(s):
iPod recording with video or demonstration with teacher checklist

State Standards Correlation:
Science: To identify and use models, maps, and aerial photographs as ways of representing landforms. Math: to solve authentic problems using appropriate technology; review coordinate grids

Preplanning Activities: Prepare taped grid on floor, gather satellite materials, check out GPS systems, prepare data collection sheets, hide fossils

Lesson Element	Procedures	Time	What is the teacher doing?	What are the students doing?	Materials
Lesson Setup & Lesson Opening	• Review what we learned about finding directions on a map yesterday. Check knowledge of coordinate points and vocabulary. • Set up expectations for today's work. Students will be working with a partner and going outside. • State Objective: By the end of this period, each one of you will be able to show someone how to use a GPS system—after practicing with it to find a buried treasure! (hook) • Ask students what they know about GPS systems and their uses. Record on KWL chart.	10 min.	Asking review questions about terms, vocabulary, and concepts Talking and asking questions about the objective Recording student responses on KWL chart	Listening Answering review questions Telling what they know about today's topic	• Posted Map • Globe • Satellite • Vocabulary cards • Objective on board
Lesson Body	Teacher Input • Introduce the problem for today's lesson by presenting students with anchor: 1. Hiker (teacher) is lost, compass is broken, cloudy day 2. Mr. Longitude and Mrs. Latitude come along with a GPS and use their coordinates to help 3. Show "Mr. Brain" video clip on GPS systems 4. Review locating points on a map grid using longitude and latitude on electronic whiteboard. 5. Tell students there are buried treasures (fossils) on the school property we need to find. They will have GPS systems to help them along the way. 6. Move half of students to hallway to show them how to find points on grid on the taped floor tiles using the satellites that are suspended from the ceiling (hang string from each satellite so they can be gathered and way points plotted). Pairs of students will pull cards from buckets indicating degrees of latitude, longitude and mark those points on the grid using the satellites. 7. The rest of the students stay in the classroom and review cardinal directions, vocabulary, and/or work on satellite construction, and/or research according to individual needs. Guided Practice 1. Practice finding waypoints with peer. 2. Trade groups. 3. Give students GPS demonstration. 4. Try GPS outside with partner, using preset waypoints on soccer field to practice. Teachers, interns, volunteers will assist as needed.	15 min.	Presenting skit Making video clip presentation Giving electronic whiteboard demonstration—locating points on map	Listening Finding way points with partner Reviewing directions and vocabulary Building satellites or researching	• Hiking props, word cards to pin to anchors • Computer/projection and internet connection • Electronic whiteboard • Hallway grid and satellites • GPS devices • Preset waypoints on cards
Extended Practice	Teams go outside and mark 3 waypoints (within given boundaries) on their data collection sheet. Hide their "cache." Come back to "start" and trade GPS with another team. Try to find their "cache." Then give teams waypoints for buried treasure.	20 min.	Circulating Checking on #3	Working with partners to plot waypoints, record data, hide cache, find treasure	Clipboards with data collection sheets

Figure **13.4** GPS Lesson Plan

Teams must: 1. Work together to determine waypoints 2. Complete data sheet to turn in 3. Tell, show or record on iPod how to use a GPS *(Note: We ended up doing this the next day because the guided practice took longer than we thought.)*		Answering questions		KWL Chart iPod
Lesson Closing Essential questions boldfaced	Close lesson with a whole class discussion of the following questions. Finish filling in KWL chart (What did you learn?): • What are the cardinal directions? • **What is a GPS system and what does it do?** • What would happen if we tried to use the GPS indoors? • **How do you find a waypoint on a grid?** • How does a GPS system receive its signals? • How precise are the signal locations we received on the trail? • In what other situation might it be helpful for you to have a GPS tool?	10 min.	Questioning Writing keywords for responses on chart Record responses on iPod for assessment	
Vocabulary	**Basic:** GPS, longitude, latitude, grid, navigation system, point, satellite, route, signal waypoint, cache **Extended:** Global Positioning System, equator, Prime Meridian, geocache, waypoint, receiver, altitude, triangulation, and cartography			

Key: Representation   Engagement   Expression

UDL Applications for More Extension

Representation	Low-Tech: Props, word cards, maps, masking tape, index cards, bucket, cardboard satellites, yarn, books, posters
	High-Tech: Video, multimedia presentation, electronic whiteboard, WebQuest, GPS
Engagement	Low-Tech: Clipboard/pencil/paper with questions, written directions for GPS use, peer buddy, satellite construction, "cache" box
	High-Tech: Virtual simulation, create multimedia production, film guided practice, create WebQuest, Internet research
Expression	Low-Tech: Answering questions, written data
	High-Tech: Record using tape recorder or iPods, create podcast, videotape oral presentations; demonstrate using GPS

Planning Pyramid for Differentiated Instruction:

Tier III: *Some* students may build a WebQuest or create a multimedia project that compares and contrasts navigation systems

Tier II: *Most* students will research and build satellite models or complete WebQuest activity on navigation systems.

Tier I: *All* students will tell or show how to use a GPS device

Brainstorm Learner Needs

Possible Barriers:	Possible Solutions:
Some students need more cognitive challenge.	These students might research satellites and possibly build some models; Create a WebQuest on navigation systems (including GPS). Build it around a research question.
One student has low vision.	Pair this student with a student who enjoys talking aloud, describing the activities and surroundings in detail. Choose a student who will watch out for any rocks or pitfalls on the outdoor paths to decrease chances of falling.
A few students cannot remember cardinal directions.	Rehearse mnemonic for North, South, East, West; make a compass rose using popsicle sticks; draw compass rose on index card and keep in pocket; have a signal for traveling N, S, E, and W
One student uses a wheelchair independently.	Be sure outdoor paths are wide and clear enough for him/her to access all areas finding waypoints. Assign a buddy who will allow him/her to move independently.
One student has limited language and prefers to work alone.	Allow this student to document the lesson using a digital camera for later use in a multimedia presentation.

Figure 13.4 GPS Lesson Plan (Continued)

K What Do You Know?	W What Do You Want to Know?	L What Did You Learn?
• We have one in our car. • They help you find your way. • It's easy to get lost.	• What are they? • How do they work? • Can we use them inside? • Can we use them on the golf course?	• You need open outdoor space to use a GPS. • It uses signals from satellites to get the latitude and longitude measurements. • Your parents will always know where you are!

Figure 13.5 Example of KWL Chart for GPS Lesson

template on the computer for planning can help teachers of students of all ages plan more successfully to meet the needs of diverse learners in their classrooms.

Varying Representation in Science and Social Studies Instruction

Implementing Inquiry-Based Instruction

Although we built direct instruction into our lesson plans for specific skills and content delivery from, we also incorporated **inquiry-based instruction**/activities that allow for active participation by students within the structure. In an inquiry-based model, teachers are facilitators in the classroom and much of the work is student directed (National Research Council, 1996; Newby & Higgs, 2005). This is a critical concept in the science reform standards. Students are active learners as teachers facilitate discussions and circulate to offer prompts and guiding questions. Some learners need more-precise instructions than others, some need more help in formulating or choosing questions to investigate than others, and others may need assistance in choosing the materials and tools to use. All students can still be involved in problem-solving, formulate some of their own questions, and think critically.

Science and social studies topics that lend themselves to inquiry-based instruction may include pollution, endangered species, citizenship, nutrition, global warming, and discrimination.

Using an Activities-Oriented Approach

Using an **activities-oriented approach**, teachers plan for engagement at the beginning of the lesson. This approach also uses inquiry and can help learners gain science and social studies knowledge and understanding by relating it to real life (Bargerhuff & Wheatly, 2004; Lynch, Taymans, Watson, Ochsendorf, Pyke, & Szesze, 2007). This can be especially helpful for diverse learners because they can begin the lesson exploring with "hands-on," multisensory materials right away, greatly reducing language and literacy barriers. The activities can be directly related to real life. The teacher can set up the environment for discovery and can add language along the way. The learning objective and preassessment would still drive the instruction. A low-tech example of this approach could be a student creation of a topographical map. The teacher can talk with them about the different landforms and locations of places while they are manipulating art materials. Another example could be using magnets to extract iron out of breakfast cereal to begin a study of nutrition. A high-tech example might be trying out a scientific experiment online at TryScience (http://www.tryscience.org). Students can virtually make a parachute as they learn about gravity or create an oil slick as they explore chemical properties. Offer students opportunities to formulate their own questions and ideas that can be further developed later.

Providing Field Trips and Community-Based Experiences

Field trips and **community-based learning** can really help learning come alive for students who do not have a great deal of background knowledge. Try to visit science and history museums to enhance learning topics (Martin & Seevers, 2003). These types of museums usually have "hands-on" exhibits, visual displays, and self-paced audio tours, along with many artifacts, original documents, and photographs that students can explore. Some museums have traveling tours that will come to schools. Many museums offer teacher training programs (Salend, 2008).

Virtual field trips are accessible to everyone. Students can observe animals up close all over the world. They can board a submarine for ocean exploration or see what it's like to experience extreme weather conditions. Here is an example of technology saving us money!

If possible, plan projects in the community that connect with lesson objectives. A restaurant or grocery store visit can enhance a nutrition unit. Plants and animals can be studied in botanical gardens, zoos, and pet shops. Visiting a recycling center can set the stage for certain environmental topics.

Service learning is a form of community-based instruction for elementary, middle, and secondary students. It is a research-based teaching and learning strategy that integrates learning objectives with meaningful community service. Civic responsibility can be enhanced as students work on needed skills while helping others in the community. Reflective practice is built into instruction. Students learn to systematically think about what they learn and how it will impact their future growth. Project examples may include recycling, tutoring, mentoring, building houses for the homeless, or preparing food for the hungry. They are all based on an identified community need. Many students report that they learn more through service learning than they do in a typical class. Many also become regular community volunteers after high school (refer to the Learning to Serve America website).

Working with Vocabulary and Readability

Remember that time spent up front preteaching and reinforcing *key* vocabulary helps many diverse learners engage more actively in lessons. Put key vocabulary on cards and post it in the room. Place it on daily agendas/organizers. Pair words with objects, pictures, gestures, Braille, and/or signs when possible. Emphasize words purposefully and frequently when using them in context in the lesson. Make word cards using multisensory strategies presented earlier in Chapter 11. Keep cards easily accessible on a ring, list, word wall, and/or a poster. Use words and concepts in low- and high-tech games. Engage peers in preteaching and practicing vocabulary (Munk et al., 1998).

Differentiate vocabulary for diverse learners. In the GPS science lesson, key vocabulary included: *GPS, longitude, latitude, grid, navigation system, point, satellite, route, signal*. It was also important to identify and present extended vocabulary to challenge learners who need more. These words included: *Global Positioning System, equator, Prime Meridian, geocache, waypoint, receiver, altitude, triangulation, and cartography*. All students should have some exposure to the complete set of words but the focus of vocabulary study may be adapted.

The word map technique presented in the Chapter 11 can also be used for the study of science and social studies terms. Another similar learning strategy using the acronym LINCS can be used to help acquire vocabulary (Ellis, 1992). First the student *lists* (L) the critical elements of the word concept. Then he/she *imagines* (I) a picture. A reminding word is then *noted* (N), a mnemonic is *constructed* (C), and the student *self-tests* (*S*). Training in this strategy can be accessed through the University of Kansas Center for Research on Learning (see the companion website for more information).

Refer back to the last section of Chapter 11 when you are adapting reading for the content areas. Remember that there are four ways to adapt text for diverse learners: (1) by eliminating the reading requirement, (2) by modifying the reading level, (3) by adapting the format, and (4) by adapting the presentation. You can also help students prioritize materials by eliminating incidental information and highlighting key information that is necessary for mastery to meet goals. This can be done by scanning and highlighting parts of text or by marking or masking text on a page. Key passages can also be paraphrased and boxed by the original text. Perhaps some of your accelerated students would enjoy helping with this task. Be on the lookout for digital texts that have these features built in.

Applying Memory Strategies

Mnemonic devices such as those presented in Chapter 9 also help students remember science and social studies vocabulary and concepts (Fontana, Scruggs, & Mastropieri, 2007). These can be created using acrostics, acronyms, rhymes, poems, or other visualizations or associations. A rhyme example is "In 1492, Columbus sailed the ocean blue," and a visualization example is seeing Italy in the shape of a "boot." Remember your students may enjoy making up their own examples.

Other sample mnemonics for science and social studies are offered in Table 13.7. **Content enhancements** are helpful for all learners and for especially for diverse learners as they work to understand and organize ideas, concepts, and vocabulary. As you may recall from Chapter 9, content enhancements may include tools such as advance organizers/agendas, outlines, graphic organizers such as Thinking Maps, content diagrams, charts, and study guides. Having these tools in hand as content is presented can greatly help students organize their thinking.

You saw how the KWL chart (Ogle, 1986) was used in the highlighted lessons (refer back to Figure 13.5 for a visual example). A KWL chart can be helpful to use with expository text by activating prior knowledge ("Tell me what you know about _____"), focusing on the learner, and giving a sense of purpose to the materials to be studied. The W (What do you *want* to know?) provides a structure that allows students the opportunity to brainstorm questions. This can give the teacher ideas for connecting to student interests as the lesson is expanded and tailored. If students have difficulty here, ask them what they think they will learn

---

Table 13.7	Sample Mnemonic Devices for Science and Social Studies

SCIENCE:
- To remember the colors in a spectrum is "ROY G. BIV" (Red, Orange, Yellow, Green, Blue, Indigo, Violet).
- A secondary example of a keyword mnemonic is a way to remember the word *euglena*, a single-celled organism that has chlorophyll. The second syllable of *euglena* closely sounds like "green." The organism has green chlorophyll in it (Scruggs & Mastropieri, 1994).
- "Kings Play Chess On Fine Grain Sand" for classifications of living organisms: Kingdom, Phylum, Class, Order, Family, Genus, Species.

SOCIAL STUDIES:
- "HOMES" to remember the Great Lakes in North America: Huron, Ontario, Michigan, Erie, Superior.
- The acronym "FIRE" can represent the countries of the Allied Powers of World War I: **F**rance, **I**taly, **R**ussia, and **E**ngland. (Fontana, Scruggs, & Mastropieri, 2007).
- The first letters in the words of this sentence spell *Geography*: "George's elderly old grandfather rode a pig home yesterday" helps to recall the spelling for the word "geography" (Mastropieri & Scruggs, 1991).

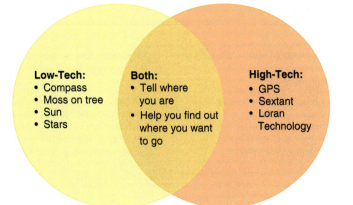

Low-Tech:
• Compass
• Moss on tree
• Sun
• Stars

Both:
• Tell where you are
• Help you find out where you want to go

High-Tech:
• GPS
• Sextant
• Loran Technology

Figure 13.6 Venn Diagram for Comparing/Contrasting Navigational Tools

about the topic. The last column (What did you *learn*?) helps both students and teachers monitor and assess comprehension.

Figure 13.6 shows how a **Venn diagram** can be used for comparing and contrasting content material. On the Venn diagram, you can write what's different in the outside circles and what's the same goes in the part of the circles that overlap. If you want to get away from paper, try placing two hula hoops on the floor to make a Venn diagram and have students place their responses inside the hoops using index cards, sentence strips, or objects. Continue to think of different formats you can use for student engagement and expression.

Figure 13.7 shows yet another organizer we created for the students as they collected their data outdoors for the GPS lesson. This organizer was attached to clipboards. Students worked in teams and one person recorded for the team. Students who had difficulty writing could usually express or show an answer while another student wrote the responses.

Most students are familiar with **story maps** from language arts classes and can transfer that mapping concept to social studies or science work. A social studies map or history frame would consider the setting, characters, plot, action, and outcome/solution of an event, situation, or report (refer to Table 13.8). If used for science, it could be used to write up lab reports (Jones, 2008). The Reading Quest website (http://www.readingquest.org) has many helpful graphic organizers for the content areas that can be downloaded for free.

Low-tech graphic organizers can be created on chart paper with markers, or by folding paper into sections or columns; high-tech ones can be created on the computer using drawing tools or mapping software. Students can have individual organizers or groups can share them. Remember that teachers may need to add objects, pictures, or symbols to help some learners. Make sure they are large enough for students who have fine motor challenges and low vision to manipulate.

GPS Data Collection Sheet

Team Names _____, _____, _____

Mark your waypoints (longitude and latitude):

Waypoint #1 _____

Waypoint #2 _____

Waypoint #3 _____

Draw a picture of the shape you made on your GPS:

What was the last waypoint? _____

Draw a picture of where you ended:

What did you learn?

Figure 13.7 Example of GPS Data Collection Sheet

Table 13.8	Story Map Adaptation for Social Studies and Science	
	Social Studies/History	**Science**
Setting	Time and Place	Time and Conditions
Characters	Key Players	Equipment Used
Problem/Goal	What was the problem/goal? What set events in motion?	Hypothesis
Details	Summarize key events	Steps in experiment
Resolution	How it turned out	Results
Theme (Lesson Learned)	Relevance for today (So What?)	Discuss findings—What do they mean? What was learned about the scientific process?

Source: Adapted from R. Jones, *ReadingQuest: Making Sense in Social Studies*. Retrieved July 1, 2008, from http://www.readingquest.org/strat/storymaps.html

Table 13.9   Representation Ideas for Science and Social Studies

Science Examples	Both	Social Studies Examples
Brainstorm what students know about severe weather on a *Thinking Map* (*Circle Map*)	State objective clearly, review previously learned concepts, check background knowledge (preassess)	Use a KWL chart and/or pretest to assess what students know about a historical event
• May include the steps in the scientific process • Provide data collection sheet • If the topic is earth science, have rocks or other material to be studied	• Provide a advance organizer/agenda/outline • Highlight critical vocabulary, keep visible and accessible (e.g., on sentence strips, posters, monitors), label items • Teach mnemonic strategies to learn vocabulary or steps in a process • Direct students to critical ideas	• Organizer may include a visual of a map depending on topic (of varying complexities) • Provide a "work order" to get ready for press conference or debate • If studying another place/culture, have pictures, objects
• Demonstrate with a lab experiment • Fossil vs. nonfossil	• Incorporate direct instruction, modeling, demonstration when teaching a new skill • Have examples and nonexamples	• Show how to make a timeline on an PDA • Good decision vs. poor decision
What causes some objects to sink and others to float? Apply the scientific process.	Use inquiry-based learning with teacher as facilitator; students work with teacher to design or choose a problem to solve	How did the Underground Railroad affect the lives of the slaves and of those who helped them?
Deliver content through the eyes of a scientist (perhaps Albert Einstein), detective, park ranger, meteorologist, astronaut (e.g., a teacher in space)	• Deliver content with anchor or ClassAct Portal • Use a dramatic account of a real or fictional event, a character from literature or from a news story • Show different perspectives	Deliver content though a historical figure, an anthropologist, an economist, through the eyes of a slave or a soldier in the Civil War
Show video clip/movie of weather, animals/endangered species, environmental issues	Deliver content through video clips, multimedia presentations with comments/narrations	Show video clip/movie of a historical or cultural event, or an exploration
Tour a planetarium, a museum of natural history	Take field trips, including virtual ones or provide a WebQuest	Tour government buildings, a factory, different countries
May include scientific journals, lab reports, news articles and reports, charts, data presentations, textbooks, magazines	Deliver content through print at different readability levels, digital text, audiotapes, podcasts, CDs, multiple texts that support content objectives	May include newspapers, current events, letters, diaries, legislative briefs, speeches, interviews, travelogues, brochures

A few examples of multiple representation tasks that can work when applying UDL principles to science and social studies units are summarized in Table 13.9. There are many more ideas and examples. This framework is simply provided to help you think about the possibilities.

Increasing Engagement in Science and Social Studies

Implementing Cooperative Learning

Models for **cooperative learning** have been described in earlier chapters. However, a model called the **Full Option Science System** (FOSS) was specifically developed at the Lawrence Hall of Science at the University of California at Berkeley (2008), to promote cooperative learning in science activities. Mastropieri and Scruggs (1993) suggest using this model with mixed ability groups. This is a "hands-on" laboratory-based curriculum for grades K-8, although many aspects of it are appropriate for older students. The FOSS model uses discovery learning, cooperative groups, and interdisciplinary activities. It teaches scientific language and use of the related equipment. The *cooperative learning* piece constructs groups of four students. One student is the *reader* and reads all print. Another student is the *recorder* and writes/records/documents all data, observations, predictions, and estimations. The

Cengage Learning/Wadsworth

Students examine seeds in cooperative groups.

getter assembles all the needed materials. The *starter* oversees all work with the materials and makes sure everyone have equal access to using the materials. Remember to give students *choice* in group membership at least some of the time.

Involving Peers

Science and social studies lessons are great places to implement **peer buddies** or **peer tutoring**. In the GPS lesson, for example, students who understood the GPS system were paired with learners who did not. The students with that knowledge were trained as coaches for their partner(s). Research strongly suggests that the student who is the tutor will also increase his/her knowledge and achievement levels as well as the student who is being tutored (Winzer & Mazurek, 1998).

Students can be paired with consideration for physical, cognitive and social needs. Less-verbal students can be matched with more-verbal partners. Students who speak another language may be paired with other bilingual students who have developed greater English language proficiency. A student with a hearing impairment might be paired with a strong note taker during lectures. Clustering students with academic gifts together some of the time offers them opportunities for more-complex dialogue (e.g., book club or through small group research and investigation). It might also be wise to pair a student with a high activity level or strong personality with someone more low keyed.

Some guidelines for using peer tutors might include:

- Having clearly established curricular goals
- Using tutors who have mastered the concept or skill to be taught
- Talking with tutors about kinds of questioning, prompts, feedback, or any special adaptations a student might need
- Having a progress monitoring system
- Limiting the sessions to 30 minutes three times a week (Salend, 2008)

Rehearsal can increase engagement. Practicing responses and expressions ahead of time from something as basic as asking or answering a question to something as complex as rehearsing a dramatic performance helps all students, especially the diverse learner. For example, a student who has limited language can be given a question that will be presented later in class so he/she has time to construct, check, and rehearse the delivery of an answer. The teacher can be sure the student receives that particular question during the lesson. This can boost learner confidence in front of peers, providing additional motivation. If the teacher knows a complex paper-folding activity is coming up (making origami cranes in a study of Hiroshima, for example), the teacher can practice ahead of time with students who are good with tactile and visual motor activities. These students can be the assistants or "experts" during the actual activity. Sometimes these are the students who like to be on the move anyway, and this provides them with a constructive outlet.

Remember, too, that **self-monitoring** is an important part of engagement. Students may need to check off steps toward their learning goal on a card, agenda, or other tangible system. Chapter 14 has additional ideas for students who might need more-intensive self-monitoring systems.

Table 13.10 offers more ideas for increasing engagement in science and social studies lessons and activities for all students. Challenge yourself to think about technology tools that can enhance these activities even more. For example, using a digital camera and iPod to document a lesson about the New Deal would likely increase engagement. Remember that exploring a ClassAct Portal, WebQuest, or taking a virtual field trip can also make lessons inviting.

Table 13.10	**Multiple Means of Engagement**	
Science Examples	**Both**	**Social Studies Examples**
• Why are we having such extreme weather?	• Questioning, interviewing • What do you want to know?	• Why are gas prices so high?
• Do an experiment using the scientific process in the "hands-on" lab or the virtual lab. Use microscopes, measuring tools, etc.	• Offer choices of content and tools (manipulatives) in answering an essential question. Try to match to student interest (from pre-assessment information).	• Which type of economic system would you like to study? How do the parts work together to make a whole? Use money, checkbooks, spreadsheets.
• Label all equipment • Use keywords to remember mineral hardness levels • Create a rap and dance to describe the solar system	• Create notecards for vocabulary/concepts; use songs and raps (highlight, note taking, apply mnemonics)	• Add pictures/symbols to remember terms for landforms and people you are learning in history • Practice a rap to learn states and capitals, the Bill of Rights
• Create poster of types of leaves for biology, create landform models • Analyze scientific data collected	• Create posters, tables, charts, models	• Make campaign posters • Analyze data for charts • Make models of different styles of Greek columns
• Observe and record findings • Draw anatomy/diagram of plant/animal	• Keep a journal (written or audio), write newspaper articles/editorials; draw findings/opinions	• Collect and analyze surveys • Draw political cartoons • Document a school election and interview candidates
• Prepare to demonstrate a science experiment to the group	• Work in cooperative groups (divide up tasks) • Role play • Rehearse group presentations • Set up peer tutoring	• Form a book club; form debate teams; plan a banquet to honor a president (menu planner, speaker, singer)
• Listen to science reports in the news, watch or listen to a debate	• Read, listen to, watch a variety of genre on topic being studied (allow some choice)	• Listen to storytellers, veterans, poets, politicians; read or use text to speech to explore more writings
• Take a WebQuest to outer space	• Work on a WebQuest or scavenger hunt challenge	• Take a scavenger hunt using a GPS receiver
• Create a storyboard that shows the steps in a scientific experiment	• Use digital cameras, iPods to make electronic newsletters or stories	• Create a storyboard for an event in history
• Plan and implement a recycling project	• Participate in service learning project	• Adopt a place in the community to improve—research and plan

Expanding Expression Opportunities in Science and Social Studies

Providing Opportunities to Practice with Support

Diverse learners often need some strategic supports for expression along the way during science and social studies lessons and activities. This is a place your cueing and prompting skills will be important to scaffold learning. Remember to give just the right amount of support—not too little or too much. The following is an example of scaffolding with **structured questioning** from the part of the GPS lesson on locating waypoints on the floor grid for a student (Student A) who struggles with language and cognition. Student A has just pulled a card from the bucket that says 35 degrees N and Student B has selected 80 degrees W. Student B is able to do this task independently and the teacher is coaching Student A. The equator and prime meridian are labeled on the grid. If the student can't say the word, he may point to it. The teacher's questioning, with possible student responses in parentheses, is as follows:

1. Where will you start? (*Say or point to the equator*)
2. Will you walk above the equator or below it? (*Above*)
3. What direction will you walk? (*Say or point to north*)
4. Where do you stop? (*on 35*) Teacher: Yes, 35 degrees north latitude.
5. Do you see your friend (who has located his line)? (*Yes*)
6. What happens when you walk to meet him? (*We bump into each other*) Direct students to walk toward each other on their lines.
7. Are you following the shortest route to meet each other? (*Yes*)
8. Are you walking on a line of latitude or longitude? (*latitude*)
9. What kind of line is your friend walking on? (*longitude*)
10. What do you do now that you've met? (*Pull the yarn down from the three satellites to this spot.*) Students comply.
11. What do we do we call this point that helps us find our way? (*A waypoint*)
12. What are the degrees of latitude and longitude at your waypoint? (*Student may refer to index cards with degrees written on them and confer with partner for response*)

Teachers will need to use cues and prompts to coach students until they are able to master and generalize a skill or concept. Some students may need physical prompts if they have visual, motor, or other difficulties. Some may just need prompts to get started, to stop and check, and to finish. Frequent questioning with feedback can also enhance expression. Refer back to Chapter 9 for more ideas about these techniques.

Students will also need multiple opportunities to practice in different ways. Sometimes an activity used in presentation can be placed in a learning center for extra practice. Sometimes a game format such as "Jeopardy!" or "Who Wants to Be a Millionaire?" can be used in low- or high-tech format (perhaps using CRS devices). There are many software and interactive web-based programs that provide a variety of ways to practice and review in science and social studies skills.

Offering Flexible Ways to Demonstrate Skill

Completed content enhancements can be used to demonstrate student skill and assess comprehension. Sometimes these tools are just what a student who learns visually needs to express himself/herself because they provide the framework for the response. Without it, the student might otherwise just stare at blank paper without a clue where to begin. For some students, they must see the boundaries in the white space to make a connection. Content enhancements also provide structure for students who have difficulty focusing or getting organized for various other reasons. Responses can be written or oral (and tactile if you add objects).

To illustrate the types and quality of responses a content enhancement can help elicit, some additional student responses to the earlier KWL chart example (Figure 13.5) from the students are offered here to the question "What did you learn?":

- "You have to keep it in the sun and get connected to 3 or 4 signals that you get from space . . . from satellites."
- "A Global Positioning System finds your position so you never get lost."
- "With latitude, longitude, satellites, and a GPS, we can find out where we are any place on earth."

These answers helped us monitor the levels of student engagement and critical thinking in the GPS lesson. Be sure *all* students give you some sort of review response. They can be written, oral, recorded (downloaded and saved on iPods or tape recorders), or perhaps demonstrated. Each response is important in formative assessment. Responses help us figure out what kind of adaptations or extensions to make (or not make) in future lessons.

Remember that response cards and CRS technology can be helpful expression tools in science and social studies lessons. In a study of plants, a low-tech response card might be a **pinch card** listing the parts of a plant. When the teacher describes the plant part, the student holds up the card and "pinches" that word (or picture). It can look something like this:

Flower
Leaf
Stem
Root
Seed

As mentioned earlier, science and social students offer many ways for students to express their learning in authentic ways. Learners with visual and tactile preferences may enjoy writing in journals or diaries. They may enjoy creating photo journals, designing game formats, writing stories and poetry. Tactile learners may enjoy building models, conducting experiments, demonstrating a skill, constructing a topographic map, working on a project (e.g., a butterfly garden). Auditory learners may enjoy expression through a debate, interview, radio broadcast, or song/rap creations. All learners will likely enjoy the multisensory nature of creating multimedia products. These products can be used to share with other classes, families, and future students. Table 13.11 has organized these ideas and others in a graphic organizer format for you.

Making Adaptations

Considering the Social and Physical Environment

If you have students with social/behavioral needs, remember the power of having an anchor such as a scientist, explorer, anthropologist, or historic figure of the day to increase engagement in the social/behavioral domain. You might also find such a character narrating a video, digital recording, or podcast. This may be offered as a choice in receiving information. The student may defer control to the anchor. Sometimes this can circumvent a power struggle he or she might be having with the teacher. Try to find anchors who are enthusiastic and interest your students.

As with all subjects, strive to maintain a positive working environment. Be aware of fears your students might have (e.g., of animals, loud noises) and be understanding and encouraging.

The learning environment, particularly in lab work, will need to be safe. Carefully select groups and partners and post any lab rules at the start of class. Consider

Table 13.11	Multiple Means of Expression	
Science Examples	**Both**	**Social Studies Examples**
• Demonstration of a science experiment or write/record findings • Completed mural or flow on water cycle • Scientific journal check • Completed data collection sheet • Present findings of science experiment using multimedia; show presentation created on the dangers of smoking	• Completed graphic organizers (including KWL chart), study guides, worksheets, interviews, oral reports, written reports, journals, experiments • Show student-created PowerPoint presentations, multimedia presentations, WebQuests; present research project or model	• Present radio broadcast of a world event • Hold a press conference and summarize results • Completed journals/diaries • Multimedia presentation that answers a human rights issue question or how an invention impacted a society
Product Examples: • Models, experiment results, demonstration, student-produced multimedia production, research paper, checklists, photo journal with captions, newspaper article, tape recordings • Present report on endangered species • Present model of habitat • Present flower garden designed for school	• Answer essential questions • Check product against rubric • Use a game format to review and express knowledge • Take a quiz • Assess acquisition of target vocabulary	**Product Examples:** Dramatization, explanation, worksheet, illustration, checklist, chart, poster, diagram, sculpture, interview, journal, map, model, performance, presentations, survey, investigation, diary, debate, review, editorial cartoon, machine, invention, video, newspaper, collage, advertisement, plan, song or rap, new game, poem, story

using an activity checklist. Think, too, about including a science safety contract or other type of individual behavior contract during content classes. Be sure to be clear about what is required and what the reward is. Physically, check the heights of tables and chairs. Make sure there are no sharp corners. Prepare work areas for spills. Evaluate tools and materials in terms of safety. If there is potential danger (with mixtures, for instance), make sure there is enough supervision. Be sure everyone can safely move around and access needed lab materials.

Allow for creativity in student examples, hypothesis and procedures (Scruggs & Mastropieri, 1994). Again, offering some choice for engagement and expression helps most students feel they have some control. Sometimes it's as easy as asking, "Would you like to report on your experiment using a PowerPoint presentation or a demonstration?" The same goal is achieved. Chapter 14 will offer you ideas if you need to add individual contracts and rewards in your classroom.

Remember you also may need to guide interaction with hands-on activities and allow for adaptations as needed (Scruggs & Mastropieri, 1994). Some students with low vision may need more-tactile clues. Rubber bands, for example, can mark measurements on rulers. Students who have hearing impairments might need a card with visual and/or written directions. Students with fine motor challenges may need assistance or adaptations for cutting and gluing. Perhaps some materials can be precut or use hook-and-loop fasteners instead of glue. Adapted scissors may be required. Some students may fatigue easily and require more breaks. Other students will need very little or no assistance and will benefit from having the freedom to create a product from "found materials" that after some trial and error, shows they have learned an objective.

Considering the Academic Environment

We have talked a lot in this chapter about how UDL can support the academic learning environment. To summarize, remember to strive for authentic environments, including field trips and community-based experiences. The Internet and virtual world can help make these experiences happen. Try to label objects and pictures that tie into units. Post your objectives daily and have clear outlines of lesson activities for all to access. Post related charts, drawings, and signs for easy reference. Use "teaching" bulletin boards to visually remind students of vocabulary, content presented, and, most importantly, to display their work. This shows that you value it. Use sequenced direction cards or recordings of steps in a process for students to refer back to and guide them through activities. Strive to use more high-tech materials than you did before to increase flexibility and maximize time and material resources. You should be able to increase student expression and engagement by doing this. You will never, however, replace the importance that you as the teacher have in their lives. Your careful planning, assessing, collaboration, activity choices, questioning, feedback, and caring attitude are absolutely critical to their success.

In Chapter 10, we showed you a blank form you might use to when considering adaptations for your lesson plan. Table 13.12 is an example of a completed form. It

Table 13.12	**Making Adaptations**
Lesson Element:	**Ideas:**
Lesson Presentation—How can it best reach the learner? (Think VAKT + Technology)	• More visuals/pictures, fewer words • Provide vocabulary sheet/outline/guided notes • PowerPoint—keep it simple, easy to read, not cluttered or overwhelming; add sound clips, pictures • Be enthusiastic! • Have note packets with spaces for drawing some of the notes
Learner Engagement—How can the learner be active in the learning process? (Think VAKT + Technology)	• Use group work • Use color • Have students write answers to questions during lectures; collect and go over with whole class or just with students who need review • Have something visual/hands on in the lesson
Learner Response—How can the learner tell or show you he/she understands? (Think VAKT + Technology)	• Group similar types of questions on the quiz • Allow a student to write key points and explain orally instead of written report • Allow students to fill in two or three words missing in each sentence in different parts of notes packet • Give options for homework (e.g., create PowerPoint, timeline, poster) • Check notes for accuracy
Time—Is extra time needed for learning?	• May need more time for any summarizing • Independent assignments may need more time • Allow extra time for review and for comprehension
Difficulty—What skill levels, conceptual levels, and processes are involved in the learning?	• Plan ways to scaffold lessons in advance; analyze tasks • Present information in interesting ways to boost comprehension and focus (pictures, movies, Internet)
Support Level—How much is needed (human and material)?	• If independent practice requires homework, some mentoring may need to be built in • Plan for prompts • Have directions/steps recorded for reference • Be available after class or on-line for questions
Size/Amount of Work—What length of assignment, performance, or demonstration is realistic?	• Break down steps; plan for repetition as needed • Let students get up from time to time—even if it is to get supplies • Just have a few procedures
Format of Materials (e.g., font, graphics, tapes)	• Reduce words on a page (including tests) • Print out PowerPoint for students • Watch font and background color—provide contrast for students with visual impairments • Have graphic organizers, models
Degree of Participation—How much can be expected and is realistic?	• Student may work in study carrel part of the time • Student may only complete part of graphic organizer
Modified Goals (remember, these change the curriculum)	Student A will match seeds while the others name, label, and categorize them by attributes.
Substitute Curriculum	Student B will work on a Service Learning Project while the others study for a test on material he has already mastered.

(VAKT = Visual, Auditory, Tactile, Kinesthetic)

takes many of the elements we have shared and discussed and put them into a tool you can use. Many of these suggestions came from beginning teachers.

Fostering Collaboration in Science and Social Studies Instruction

Collaborative Planning

As you can see throughout this chapter, collaboration with other teachers within and across disciplines can make a huge difference on the impact of your teaching. Remember that making connections helps students generalize their knowledge and skills across learning environments. Some schools already have common collaborative planning time set up for all teachers who work with a set of students. If you don't have this, it might be helpful to talk with your grade level or department chair about the possibility. Ultimately, the administrators will need to lead the way. If you have an idea and a plan to share, that may help sell the idea.

Ask the school media specialist for help. He/she can help you locate print and media resources. There are so many resources available that perhaps it would also be helpful to collaborate with other teachers in collecting, organizing, and evaluating software and websites to use with units. Textbook publishers can sometimes help you find adaptations to materials as well. Community libraries and nearby universities are additional helpful resources. Remember the value of collaborating with art, music, and physical education teachers as well.

A word of caution—sometimes in schools, students who need extra or extended work in reading, math, and other areas are pulled out of regular classrooms during science and social studies—at least at the elementary level. This does not always make sense! These are often the subjects these students look forward to the most and are the ones they can successfully participate in.

Co-teaching

Science and social studies topics lend themselves well to the co-teaching models you learned about in Chapter 5. Station teaching might be a good model to start with in science and social studies. First, you have to find at least one other teacher! Then, each teacher chooses a learning objective in his/her area of strength. Students can rotate through the stations or centers and receive instruction in the same goal from each teacher. If the students are grouped in tiers or levels, the teachers can adjust the degree of complexity within each station. Depending upon the nature of the class, there might be one independent group. Let's use a lesson on the water cycle to illustrate this. Using station teaching, one teacher might run an experiment with evaporation/precipitation in one group while another group views and responds to a video clip that shows the water cycle. A third group might be filling in a graphic organizer to learn the cycle.

Students could also be divided into two or more groups (depending on the number of teachers) for parallel teaching. This way each teacher teaches the same content but the teacher-to-student ratio is decreased and students get more "teacher time." Students have more opportunities to be questioned, receive feedback, and respond. If you are incorporating a "hands-on" project such as map making, having a smaller group will also be more manageable. If you have a science experiment, it is easier to control for safe participation.

In team teaching, one teacher could be lecturing or explaining while the other one takes notes for all to see on chart paper or electronically with wall projection. Another example is one teacher in science doing an experiment while the other one explains. This method can also be somewhat conversational if the teachers are comfortable enough with each other. This way the students can see them *thinking aloud*.

Building Community Support

Community resources, including parents, are often good contacts in these content areas so be sure to conduct this assessment early in the school year. Community volunteers may also provide additional and informational cultural links that are needed in units of instruction. For the GPS lesson, for example, a local meteorologist came and spoke to the students. In a previous unit, a geologist shared fossils he had found in a pond near the school and not only talked about physical qualities of the stones/artifacts but also gave the background of the people, animals and plants that lived in the same space long ago. Remember that when you have people from the community assist with presentations it is helpful to give them some of the vocabulary you are using and some specific questions ahead of time, along with the objectives.

Ask students and families to collect and bring pictures and other hands-on materials to class that can be organized in advance to enhance lessons. This practice helps students and families have ownership of the lesson. Working in collaboration can foster a win-win situation for all.

Thematic Summary

- Planning and implementing content area units around big ideas helps teachers identify critical content and guide students in making learning connections.
- There are multiple ways to assess students in science and social studies.
- Differentiating instruction helps teachers address and support a wide range of learner strengths and needs.
- Applying the principles of UDL in content area instruction can foster access to the curriculum for all learners.
- Methods, materials, and innovative technology tools help provide greater access to science and social studies concepts, ideas, and skills for all learners.
- Adaptations in academic, social, and physical environments can foster inclusion.
- Collaboration can enhance content area learning for all students.

Making Connections for Inclusive Teaching

1. Do you agree or disagree with the idea that people need stories to connect to the world around them? Defend your answer.
2. Look back at the "big ideas" and skills in reading, writing, and mathematics. Compare/contrast them with those in science and social studies. Are any of them similar? How? Provide examples.
3. Describe a science or social studies lesson you can remember as a student that had elements of UDL. What makes the thinking behind UDL different today?
4. How do you think today's technologies will change the way students receive, interact with, and respond to information in science and social studies?
5. Do you know someone who needs adaptations to access print in content areas? What kinds of adaptations are made? If you don't know someone, visit your local library and find out how adaptations are made for patrons who have challenges.
6. Do you think technology use in schools will "level the playing field" for students in content areas? Defend your position.

7. Do you think there is more collaboration in science and social studies in the elementary school setting than in the middle and high school settings? Support your opinion.

Learning Activities

1. Think about any strategies you have observed or used in science and social studies to learn vocabulary or concepts. Share them with your classmates and add them to your toolbox.

2. Take a science or social studies activity you or a classmate is planning to use in a classroom. Indicate how you might adapt it for a student with cognitive challenges, for a student who has ADHD, and for a student who is gifted.

3. On a content area lesson plan you or a classmate already have, highlight different ways information is represented in one color, ways students can be engaged in another color, and ways they may respond in a third color.

4. Apply a readability index to a science and a social studies textbook that is used for content area instruction (refer back to Chapter 11 for readability index information). Discuss your findings. How might you adjust reading content textbooks for students who struggle accessing print?

5. Try out one of the high-tech tools or interactive websites mentioned in this chapter or on the companion website. Provide a brief description and your evaluation.

6. Develop a list of possible resources in your community for collaboration in science and social studies instruction.

Looking at the Standards

The content of this chapter most closely aligns itself with the following standards:

INTASC Standards

- *Content Pedagogy.* The teacher understands the central concepts, tools of inquiry, and structures of the discipline he or she teaches and can create learning experiences that make these aspects of subject matter meaningful for students.
- *Multiple Instructional Resources.* The teacher understands and uses a variety of instructional strategies to encourage students' development of critical thinking, problem solving, and performance skills.
- *Motivation and Management.* The teacher uses an understanding of individual and group motivation and behavior to create a learning environment that encourages positive social interaction, active engagement in learning, and self-motivation.
- *Communication and Technology.* The teacher uses knowledge of effective verbal, nonverbal, and media communication techniques to foster active inquiry, collaboration, and supportive interaction in the classroom.

Council for
Exceptional
Children
The voice and vision of special education

Council for Exceptional Children

Special educators are to have knowledge of the following:

- CC4S3: Select, adapt, and use instructional strategies and materials according to characteristics of the individual with exceptional learning needs.
- GC4S1: Use research-supported methods for academic and nonacademic instruction of individuals with disabilities.

- GC4S7: Use appropriate adaptations and technology for all individuals with disabilities.
- GC4K7: Methods for guiding individuals in identifying and organizing critical content.
- CC4S2: Teach individuals to use self-assessment, problem-solving, and other cognitive strategies to meet their needs.
- CC4S4: Use strategies to facilitate maintenance and generalization of skills across learning environments.

Key Concepts and Terms

systems, order, organization, evidence, models, explanations
constancy, change, measurement
evolution, equilibrium
form and function
problem solving
decision-making process
cause and effect
comparing and contrasting

thematic teaching
essential questions
KWL chart
inquiry-based instruction
activities-oriented approach
field trips
community-based learning
service learning
mnemonic devices
content enhancements
Venn diagram

story maps
cooperative learning
Full Option Science System
peer buddies/peer tutoring
rehearsal
self-monitoring
structured questioning
pinch card

References

Armbruster, B., & Anderson, T. (1988). On selecting "considerate content area textbooks." *Remedial and Special Education, 9*(1), 47–52.

Bargerhuff, M. E., & Wheatly, M. (2004). Teach with CLASS: Creating laboratory access for science students with disabilities. *Teacher Education and Special Education, 27*, 313–321.

Choate, J. (1997). *Successful inclusive teaching: Proven ways to detect and correct special needs*. Boston: Allyn & Bacon.

Coyne, M., Kame'enui, E., & Carnine, D. (2007). *Effective teaching strategies that accommodate diverse learners*. Upper Saddle River, NJ: Pearson Education.

Dull, L., & van Garderen, D. (2005). Bringing the story back into history: Teaching social studies to children with learning disabilities. *Preventing School Failure, 49*(3), 27–31.

Eichinger, J., & Downing, J. E. (2002). Instruction in the general education environment. In J. Downing (Ed.), *Including students with severe and multiple disabilities in typical classrooms: Practical strategies for teachers* (2nd ed., pp. 17–36). Baltimore: Paul H. Brookes.

Ellis, E. (1992). *LINCS: A strategy for vocabulary learning*. Lawrence, KS: Edge Enterprises.

Fernstrom, P., & Goodnite, B. (2000). Accommodate student diversity in the general education social studies classroom. *Intervention in School and Clinic, 35*(4), 244–245.

Finson, K., & Ormsbee, C. (1998). Rubrics and their use in inclusive science. *Intervention in School and Clinic, 34*(2), 79–88.

Fontana, J. L., Scruggs, T., & Mastropieri, M. A. (2007). Mnemonic strategy instruction in inclusive secondary social studies classes. *Remedial and Special Education, 28*(6), 345–355.

Gallas, K. (1995). *Talking their way into science: Hearing children's questions and theories, responding with curricula*. New York: Teachers College Press.

Jones, R. (2008). *Frameworks for choosing comprehension strategies*. Retrieved October 28, 2008, from http://www.readingquest.org

Kentucky Department of Education. (2005). *Kentucky High School Assessment Standards draft*. Retrieved June 30, 2008, from http://www.education.ky.gov/users/spalmer/social%20studies%20high%20school%20march%2022.pdf

Lawrence Hall of Science, University of California at Berkeley. (2008). *FOSS project site*. Retrieved June 30, 2008, from http://www.lawrencehallofscience.org/foss/

Lynch, S., Taymans, J., Watson, W. A., Ochsendorf, R. J., Pyke, C., & Szesze, M. J. (2007). Effectiveness of a highly rated science curriculum unit for students with disabilities in general education classrooms. *Exceptional Children, 73*, 202–223.

Martin, S. S., & Seevers, R. L. (2003). A field trip planning guide for early childhood classes. *Preventing School Failure*, *47*, 177–180.

Mastropieri, M., & Scruggs, T. (1993). *A practical guide for teaching science to students with special needs in inclusive settings.* Austin, TX: Pro-Ed.

Munk, D., Bruckert, D., Call, D., Stoehrmann, T., & Radandt, E. (1998). Strategies for enhancing the performance of students with LD in inclusive science classes. *Intervention in School and Clinic*, *34*(2), 73–78.

National Committee on Science Education Standards and Assessment, National Research Council. (1996). *Assessments in science education*. Washington, DC: The National Academies Press.

National Council for History Education. (2008). *About NCHE.* Retrieved June 30, 2008, from http://www.nche.net/

National Council for the Social Studies. (2008). *Curriculum standards for social studies*. Retrieved June 30, 2008, from http://www.socialstudies.org/standards/

National Research Council. (1996). *National science education standards*. Washington, DC: The National Academies Press.

Newby, D. E., & Higgs, P. L. (2005). Using inquiry to teach social studies. *The Charter Schools Research Journal*, *1*(1), 20–31.

Norman, K., Caseau, D., & Stefanich, G. (1998). Teaching students with disabilities in inclusive science classrooms: Survey results. *Science Education*, *82*(2), 127–146.

Ogle, D. M. (1986). K-W-L: A teaching model that develops active reading of expository text. *Reading Teacher*, *39*, 564–570.

Parmar, R., & Cawley, J. (1993). Analysis of science textbook recommendations provided for students with disabilities. *Exceptional Children*, *59*, 518–531.

Polloway, E., Patton, J., & Serna, L. (2005). *Strategies for teaching learners with special needs* (8th ed.). Columbus, OH: Merrill.

Rose, D., & Meyer, A. (2002). *Teaching every student in the digital age: Universal design for learning*. Alexandria, VA: Association for Supervision and Curriculum Development.

Roseman, J. E., Kesidou, S., Stern, L., & Caldwell, A. (1999). Heavy books light on learning: AAAS Project 2061 evaluates middle grades science textbooks. *Science Books & Films*, *35*(6), 243–247.

Salend, S. J. (2008). *Creating inclusive classrooms: Effective and reflective practices* (6th ed.). Upper Saddle River, NJ: Pearson Education.

Sasso, G. (2001). The retreat from inquiry and knowledge in special education. *The Journal of Special Education*, *34*(4), 178–194.

Scruggs, T., & Mastropieri, M. (1994). The construction of scientific knowledge by students with mild disabilities. *The Journal of Special Education*, *28*(3), 307–321.

Stepanek, J. (1999). *The inclusive classroom. Meeting the needs of gifted students: Differentiating mathematics and science instruction*. Portland, OR: Northwest Regional Educational Laboratory.

Tomlinson, C. A. (2001). *How to differentiate instruction in mixed-ability classrooms* (2nd ed.). Alexandria, VA: Association for Supervision and Curriculum Development.

Tomlinson, C. A., & McTighe, J. (2006). *Integrating differentiated instruction and understanding by design*. Alexandra, VA: Association for Supervision and Curriculum Development.

Wiggins, G., & McTighe, J. (1998). *Understanding by design*. Alexandria, VA: Association for Supervision and Curriculum Development.

Wilson, E. (2002). The power of story. *American Educator*, *27*(2), 8–11.

Winzer, M., & Mazurek, K. (1998). *Special education in multicultural contexts*. Upper Saddle River, NJ: Merrill.

Yinger, R., & Nolen, A. (2003). Surviving the legitimacy challenge. *Phi Delta Kappan*, *84*(5), 386–390.

Bonnie Jacobs/istockphoto.com

Selecting Behavioral Supports for All Learners

Contributed by Chan Evans

Establish Learning Goals: Big Ideas for Behavioral Support

Teacher Expectations and Challenging Behaviors

Students with Exceptionalities and Other Diverse Learners

Multiple Meanings of Challenging Behavior

Using Positive Behavior Supports

Assessment of Behavior

Targeting the Behavior

Tracking the Behavior

Recording Behavior

Analyzing Behavior

Methods, Materials, and Resources that Promote Positive Behavior for All Learners

Understanding Terminology

Increasing Appropriate Behavior

Decreasing Inappropriate Behavior

Teaching New Behavior

Maintenance and Generalization

Learning Outcomes

After reading this chapter, you should be able to:

- Describe characteristics of challenging behaviors associated with diverse learners.
- Define challenging behaviors in observable, measurable terms.
- Select strategies to reinforce appropriate behaviors, reduce negative or unproductive behaviors, and teach new behaviors using UDL principles.
- Describe teacher-led and student-initiated mediation.
- Demonstrate understanding of collaboration with parents and colleagues to support generalization of prosocial skills.

Peers and School Personnel
Collaborating with Parents
Culturally Diverse Families

Summary—Putting It All Together

Ms. Cruz has organized her seventh-grade language arts class to run like clockwork. She posted the rules and procedures on her classroom wall and took time to teach specific ones, using both examples and nonexamples. She planned for a high rate of time-on-task, used multiple effective teaching techniques, and offered a safe and nurturing environment to all her students.

But there are still a few students who are not engaged in academic pursuits no matter how interesting Ms. Cruz tries to make the lesson. In first period there are three students who are failing, but not because of intellectual inabilities. Lucy sits at the back and doodles in her notebook. She never volunteers and rarely answers correctly when Ms. Cruz calls on her. Sometimes Lucy appears to be crying. Jamar takes up a lot of time. He is always calling out or poking the boy in front of him, despite Ms. Cruz's verbal reminders. Ms. Cruz is most concerned about Zack, who has just returned to school after being in an auto accident. He used to be attentive to details in his writing and so astute in his observations about characterization and plot development. Now Ms. Cruz hardly recognizes him. He seems angry and agitated, refusing to contribute to discussions or turn in assignments. Yesterday he hit a student for no reason. Ms. Cruz knows it is time to make individual behavior plans for these three students, but how can she do this with 28 students in the class?

In Chapter 10 we discussed creating academic, physical, and social learning environments for all learners. The last three chapters have mainly focused on academic needs. Even when curriculum is mapped out with the whole student in mind, more intensive behavior supports will likely need to be implemented from time to time for some students. In this last chapter, we will talk more about different ways of specifically meeting the behavioral needs of students who require more intensive individualized supports. We feel this is an important chapter as we close this textbook because we know that students with challenging behaviors may be hiding a learning problem. Loud, disruptive students as well as quiet students who never cause trouble may be struggling with academic and social competence at some point in their development. These are important signals for us to identify. We also know that if students are exhibiting challenging behaviors, they are likely not making academic gains. They may also take instructional time away from others. The assessment process for social/behavior skills are as critical (perhaps even more critical) as those for academic skills areas so that interventions can be directly linked to specific behavior skill deficiencies. The more we can know about our learners and how they receive information, express their thoughts and ideas, and how to best engage them, the better we can match interventions that will help them feel safe, valued, and successful. Teachers today must have this knowledge as they strive to build caring communities of learners.

In this chapter, we will first describe characteristics of challenging behaviors that may be associated with diverse learners, including those with exceptionalities. Next, we will recommend methods of defining and tracking specific behaviors that interfere with students' academic and social progress. Then, we will suggest ways to reinforce appropriate behaviors, reduce negative or unproductive behaviors, and teach new behaviors. We will discuss the important transition from modeling teacher-led mediation to student-initiated strategies. Finally, we will review the importance of cultivating an effective and supportive collaboration with parents and colleagues to help students maintain and generalize prosocial behaviors with a variety of people and settings. Throughout the chapter we will apply the principles of UDL.

Establish Learning Goals: Big Ideas for Behavioral Support

Teacher Expectations and Challenging Behaviors

The behaviors of each of the three students in Ms. Cruz's class fall within the outer limits of a range we consider "typical" for early adolescents. Some amount of inattention, silliness, frustration, or anger is to be expected within this age group. But the worrisome behaviors of these students deviate from the norm enough to be of particular concern to Ms. Cruz. The ability of the students to learn and participate has been compromised because of behavioral or emotional factors that have begun to interfere with their academic and social progress.

Before we discuss specific strategies to help individual students, we will describe different types of challenging behaviors. First, let's think of "behavior" as a construct occurring along a continuum. Like Alice in Wonderland after she ate the mushroom, the two extremes of the continuum represent behaviors that are either "too big" or excessive or "too small" or inadequate. Most students, at one time or another, have exhibited too much (e.g., talking out, teasing, movement, rule breaking) or not enough (e.g., lack of social skills, problem-solving strategies, or active participation) of a desirable behavior (Cullinan, 2007). Students like Jamar and Zack are said to exhibit acting-out or **externalizing behaviors**. Other externalizing characteristics include disruptions, antagonizing peers, defiance of authority, and physical aggression. Lucy's crying and passively refusing to participate in class are considered to be **internalizing behaviors**. Withdrawal, social isolation, pervasive sadness, anxiety, or somatic complaints also may be indicators of this type of problem (Achenbach & McConaughy, 1997).

Traditionally, teachers deal with these behaviors in several ways. They may disregard potentially serious problems of withdrawal, depression, or social isolation of some students or consider these problems to be more family oriented than school related (Walker & Severson, 1992). They may ignore students who cause short-lived classroom disturbances or constantly prompt students who are off task. For more serious offenses, they may remove students from the classroom. In this chapter we will offer alternatives to help moderate or alter student behaviors so they will be less like the mercurial Alice and more like Baby Bear's porridge—just right!

Students with Exceptionalities and Other Diverse Learners

When we think of students with disabilities who exhibit disruptive or counterproductive behaviors, those identified with emotional/behavioral disorders may first come to mind. As explained in Chapter 3, students within this disability group exhibit behavior that is markedly different in intensity and duration from their gender- and age-mates. It is important to remember that some students with other types of exceptionalities also may demonstrate challenging conduct. It is just as important to remember that each student has unique strengths and needs and must be assessed individually. Many students with disabilities exhibit behavior well within the "appropriate" range on the behavioral continuum. (Review multiple means of assessment presented in Chapter 7.) Table 14.1 lists several exceptionalities and other types of diverse learners with certain social/behavioral characteristics that may accompany specific individual needs and will require more individual behavioral supports. The table is offered simply as a guide. Some students in these different categories may not exhibit these characteristics.

Some students may have dual exceptionalities and may exhibit a variety of challenging behaviors. Those who are gifted may also have ADHD (Cline & Schwartz, 1999), learning disabilities (Flint, 2001) or another disability (Hallahan & Kauffman, 2005). A student who is academically gifted may daydream or act out in a particular situation because he is bored or impatient with unchallenging academic

Quiet, disengaged students, as well as loud and disruptive ones, may be struggling with academic and/or social skill development.

Cengage Learning/Wadsworth

Table 14.1	Challenging Behavior of Students with Exceptionalities and Other Diverse Learners
Disability	**Potential Indicators**
Autism	• Uses words without attaching meaning to them; repeats certain words • Chooses to be alone; may not participate spontaneously with peers • Does not use social cues, such as eye contact or smiles, to connect with others • May express a need for sameness in surroundings or routine
Asperger Syndrome	• Desires interaction, but does not understand social rules or nonverbal cues • Sensitive to changes; may find comfort in repeating ritualistic behaviors; limited range of interests; continually talks about one idea or thing
Attention Deficit Hyperactivity Disorder	• Inattention; seems not to listen to others; has difficulty completing a task • Fidgets, taps with feet or hands, always in motion • Loud and very talkative; acts before considering the consequences • Impulsive; has difficulty waiting for a turn; calls out, interrupts others
Emotional/Behavioral Disorder	• Difficulty getting along with peers and adults • Defiance or aggression • Unhappiness or depression • Physical symptoms or fears
Learning Disability	• Difficulty speaking in an organized, sequential way • Difficulty reading social cues; may misinterpret social situations • Impulsive or unfocused; may miss directions for activities
Mental Disability	• Difficulty processing oral language or expressing ideas • May feel hurt or confused by misperceived peer interactions • Unable to transfer learned social skills from one setting to another
Speech/Language Impairment	• Omissions, substitutions, or hesitation in pronouncing words • Stuttering, monotone, harsh, breathy, or singsong voice tone • Problems having a two-way conversation with peers • Few social interactions or relationships
Traumatic Brain Injury	• Overestimates own abilities; faulty reasoning; low motivation • Poor impulse control; lowered social inhibitions • Agitation and irritability; acting out
Other Diverse Needs	**Possible Characteristics**
Giftedness	• Inattention; daydreaming; poor judgment • Teasing, silliness; excessive talking • Disorganized, careless; overly emotional
Giftedness & ADHD	• Makes jokes or puns at inappropriate times • Bored with routine and refuses to work • Has difficulty with transitions; difficulty accepting authority
Giftedness & Learning Disability	• Perfectionism, supersensitivity • Unreasonable self-expectations • Distractibility; failure to complete assignments
Ethnically Diverse	• Reticent to work with opposite-gender teacher or peers • Resists studying in cooperative, student-led learning groups • Does not make eye contact when listening or speaking to teacher • Overly loud or aggressive*

*Not all learners within these categories will exhibit any one particular characteristic.
Sources: Adapted from G. Cartledge, L. Tillman, & C. Johnson, Professional ethics within the context of student discipline and diversity, *Teacher Education and Special Education, 24*, pp. 25–37; D. Cullinan, *Students with Emotional and Behavior Disorders: An Introduction for Teachers and Other Helping Professionals*, 2nd ed. (Columbus, OH: Prentice Hall, 2007); L. Flint, Challenges of identifying and serving gifted children with ADHD, *Teaching Exceptional Children, 33*(4), 2001, pp. 62–69; D. Hallahan & J. Kauffman, *Exceptional Learners: Introduction to Special Education*, 10th ed. (Boston: Allyn & Bacon, 2005); H. Parette & B. Petch-Hogan, Approaching families: Facilitating culturally/linguistically diverse family involvement, *Teaching Exceptional Children, 33*(2), 2000, pp. 4–10.

expectations. If written expression is a challenge, another student who is academically gifted may become frustrated if the means of expression is always paper and pencil. However, a student who is gifted with ADHD may daydream or act out because he is lost or confused by academic expectations. The unique combination of giftedness coupled with a disability will require consideration for an individualized plan taking dual exceptionalities into account.

Students from ethnically diverse backgrounds may exhibit behaviors that teachers find unusual, disconcerting, or problematic. These students may appear to be noncompliant or confrontational, when in fact they are responding to teachers and peers in a manner typical of their particular social environment. For example, students from other cultures who have been taught in very formal settings with little, if any, give-and-take with the teacher may be extremely quiet and reticent to participate in interactive classroom learning activities. In contrast, other youngsters may be overly loud and argumentative, appearing disrespectful or verbally aggressive with teachers and peers (Cartledge, Tillman, & Johnson, 2001; Parette & Petch-Hogan, 2000). Teachers need to be aware of strategies to help students who display either type of internalizing or externalizing behaviors that interfere with their academic and social success.

Multiple Meanings of Challenging Behavior

As you know, students express themselves in multiple ways in the classroom. Even though some methods of expression are less socially acceptable than others, teachers should look for the meaning behind the behavior. Just as with academic skills, if we can target a social/behavior skill, establish a specific goal for learning, and select a proven method for intervention, we can move students forward socially and behaviorally one step at a time. Let's begin by examining several common functions for problematic or maladaptive ways of expression (Frey & Wilhite, 2005).

One major function of behavior is communication (see Table 14.2). Students who have cognitive, expressive language, speech, or social skills deficits may use inappropriate actions instead of conventional language to make a point or to acquire a desired object (Saunders, 2001). For example, an elementary-age student with a mild mental disability may push a peer away from a bucket of markers and grab a purple one instead of engaging in the tedious process of conversational give-and-take. His

Table 14.2	Assessment of Challenging Behavior and Strategies for Engagement		
Reason	**Expression**	**Possible Meaning . . .**	**Strategies for Appropriate Engagement**
Communicate	Doodle Grab a pencil	**I'm bored; I need . . . ; I'm tired**	Use cue cards Practice hand raising Use a digital presentation or video Use role play or anchored learning to present Build in response systems (low- or high-tech)
Attention	Call out Interrupt others	**Notice me! Praise me! Help me!**	Work with a peer Pick a time for sharing Increase engagement using classroom response systems Provide opportunities for oral presentations, role plays, reader's theater
Avoidance	Disrupt class Make a joke	**I can't succeed at . . . , so I will . . .**	Task accessibility (give students task they can do easily with success) Make a basic PowerPoint slide show or graphic organizer to pull out critical ideas; use clip art/animation to convey understanding Use digital or anchored learning presentation format
Power	Argue Refuse direction	**You can't make me! I want to make decisions for myself!**	Choice making Help a student at a lower level with a similar task
Fun	Tease a peer Chat in class	**I want to have some fun! Let's play!**	Embed relevance in lesson Active engagement (think-pair-share), classroom response systems Create a rap to go along with content

peers have learned to give in to the student's physical aggression rather than challenge him. His teacher allows this misbehavior because she sees it as less disruptive than a full-blown tantrum that might occur if he were directed to "use his words," ask politely for the marker, and wait patiently for a response.

Another function of challenging behavior is to avoid unpleasant or difficult schoolwork (Zirpoli, 2005). If a student can be sent to the Quiet Corner because he tells the teacher, "Shut up and leave me alone" when she asks him to take his turn reading aloud, he can be spared the embarrassment and agony of the oral reading group.

A third and most common reason students misbehave is to gain attention from peers and teachers. Most teachers expect students to listen to and follow their directions, stay on task, and get along with others (Lane, Wehby, & Cooley, 2006); and therefore they rarely offer praise for the expected (Maag, 2001). Attention from the teacher, whether positive or negative, is reinforcing to most students. The only way some students can attract the teacher's attention is to act out or cause some type of disturbance.

Think about students you have observed and how they get their attention needs met. Let's compare the need to be noticed with different sizes of gasoline tanks. Each student has an internal "attention tank" and each person will find a way to keep his or her tank full (Walker, 2007). Some students have very small, eco-friendly, compact-car-size tanks; others sport ones equipped to run gas-guzzling SUVs. Students with pint-size tanks are content to sit quietly and avoid notice. In contrast, those with huge, possibly even "dual" tanks, will do what it takes, appropriate or not, to acquire a large amount of attention from teachers and peers. As we prepare to discuss ways of observing, measuring, and managing behaviors, keep in mind the "attention tank" and multiple appropriate ways to fill it up.

Using Positive Behavior Support

All the potential meanings of behavior (see Table 14.2) can be simplified to two functions: Students either are trying to get something (e.g., attention, teacher help, friendship, fun) or to avoid something (e.g., nagging teacher, school work that is too hard, too easy, boring) (Artesani, 2001). Students who use maladaptive behaviors to communicate, avoid, seek attention, or express desire for control or fun need more positive support in order to express these needs and have them met using prosocial methods. Most students in your school and classroom use acceptable and effective methods of expression, but a few will need to be taught ways to replace their challenging behaviors with prosocial ones.

Schoolwide **positive behavior support** (PBS) models offer promise for building proactive, effective learning communities in schools. By establishing prosocial methods in schools from the start, academic achievement can improve significantly (Lassen, Steele, & Sailor, 2006). With administration leadership and support, faculty, staff, and families in PBS schools use the same language and training in communicating behavioral expectations to students schoolwide. Everyone teaches, models, and demonstrates desired behaviors in a clear and consistent fashion. Students are acknowledged and rewarded for appropriate behavior. Behavior errors are viewed as learning opportunities and are corrected. Data are collected and used to guide decision making (e.g., number of office referrals, time and place). Parent collaboration and volunteerism at school is encouraged.

There are three levels of support in the PBS model (Sugai & Horner, 2007). All three should involve partnerships with school communities, including families. In the first level, universal supports are offered proactively as preventative measures to all the students in the school. These supports are effective for approximately 80 percent of the school population. There are clear expectations, procedures, and interventions for all students, staff, and settings. These supports may include following procedures for walking in hallways, using restrooms, and addressing others with

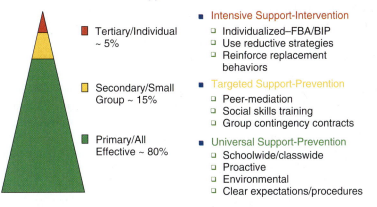

Positive Behavior Support: Prevention and Intervention

- Tertiary/Individual ~ 5%
- Secondary/Small Group ~ 15%
- Primary/All Effective ~ 80%

- **Intensive Support-Intervention**
  - ❏ Individualized–FBA/BIP
  - ❏ Use reductive strategies
  - ❏ Reinforce replacement behaviors

- **Targeted Support-Prevention**
  - ❏ Peer-mediation
  - ❏ Social skills training
  - ❏ Group contingency contracts

- **Universal Support-Prevention**
  - ❏ Schoolwide/classwide
  - ❏ Proactive
  - ❏ Environmental
  - ❏ Clear expectations/procedures

Figure 14.1 **Positive Behavior Support: Prevention and Intervention**
Source: Adapted from C. B. Darch & E. J. Kame'enui, *Instructional Classroom Management: A Proactive Approach to Behavior Management*, 2nd ed. (Upper Saddle River, NJ: Pearson Education, 2006), pp. 220–235; M. Kerr & C. Nelson, *Strategies for Addressing Behavior Problems in the Classroom*, 5th ed. (Upper Saddle River, NJ: Pearson Education, 2006), pp. 42–84.

respect. There may be schoolwide incentives for displaying positive practices that have been clearly articulated and modeling in the school community.

The second level of support specifically and strategically targets students who are at risk for problematic behavior (OSEP, 2007). About 15 percent of the school population needs more direct intervention, small group instruction, and opportunity for positive and corrective feedback. These targeted supports may include social skills or peer-mediation training, and group contingency contracts.

Only about 5 percent of students display high-risk behavior problems and will need tertiary or intensive support (Kerr & Nelson, 2006). These students will require functional behavior assessments and individualized behavior intervention plans to reduce maladaptive behaviors and increase prosocial ones. Figure 14.1 illustrates the PBS model and several prevention and intervention supports for each level.

Assessment of Behavior

In order for Ms. Cruz to help her students who need more than universal support, she will need to examine each of their behaviors more closely. Let's begin with Jamar. Although he exhibits several worrisome behaviors that are starting to affect his academic and social progress, he has many strengths. He is charming, loquacious, bright, and energetic. But he is also disorganized and seldom even brings a pencil, much less completed homework, to school. He impulsively calls out answers, apparently not caring whether they are correct or even on topic. It seems to Ms. Cruz that Jamar interrupts his fellow students at least 50 times during language arts and she finds herself spending a lot of time filling up his attention tank by reacting to his outbursts with comments such as, "Jamar, please wait your turn," "Jamar, please think before you speak," "Jamar, please don't interrupt," or "Jamar, please raise your hand if you would like to answer." None of her verbal reminders seem to make any difference and on most days, the more she prompts him, the more he calls out. Jamar's peers are becoming increasingly exasperated with him, and his lack of impulse control is beginning to also negatively affect his social interactions during nonacademic periods of the day.

Ms. Cruz decided it was time to activate an individualized support plan for Jamar. Even though he exhibited several challenging behaviors, she chose only one to define and target for change. She tracked the behavior by observing and measuring when and how often it occurred. Then she taught and reinforced an appropriate behavior to take the place of the problematic one. Let's examine step by step this process of providing individual support to a student.

Targeting the Behavior

The first step in the process of changing a problem behavior is to create an **operational definition** (Alberto & Troutman, 2009). We name the specific action in order for others, students or colleagues, to observe and measure what we have chosen to target. This is important to ensure that we and others (especially the student!) are accurately measuring only one behavior.

When Ms. Cruz tells her students, "I want you all to be good," they each have a notion of what *being good* is, but the term also leaves room for a lot of ambiguity. The construct of *being good* can be defined differently depending on culture, age, gender, cognition, or prior experience. It may mean one thing to her seventh graders and another to other teachers on her team or the paraprofessional who occasionally helps out in her classroom. By the same token, a clear definition of troublesome behaviors is just as essential. When she remarks to Jamar at the end of class that he was *off task*, he may be unsure to which offense she referred: poking another student, calling out, interrupting peers, or grabbing a pencil from her desk.

Before a student can replace a problematic behavior with an appropriate one, both actions must be defined in terms that are observable, measurable, and repeatable. Alberto and Troutman (2009) referred to this process as "pinpointing behavior" (p. 26). Only one behavior at a time should be chosen for remediation. Also, at first, the time frame should be limited. The goal for Jamar was to decrease calling-out and replace it with hand raising during a 45-minute language arts class. In this instance, *calling-out* was defined as making a statement or asking a question without first raising his hand and being recognized by the teacher. Calling out and hand raising are both discrete behaviors (with specific begin and end points) that can be observed and measured. See Table 14.3 for examples and nonexamples of operational definitions. In the next section, we will discuss how best to track these and other types of behaviors.

Hand-raising is a discrete behavior that can be observed and measured.

Tracking the Behavior

Even though it may seem like a student interrupts, calls out, or gets out of his seat 50 times a day, teachers need to keep a record of the actual problematic behavior as it occurs in its natural state before a new intervention is tried. Collecting these **baseline data** is similar to giving a pretest for an academic skill and is an essential

Table 14.3	**Defining Target Behaviors**

Use action verbs that are observable and measurable to describe what the behavior looks like. When describing prosocial target behaviors, state the behavior in positive terms.

USE	INSTEAD OF
Walking in the hall with hand by sides	Won't hit
Raise hand and wait to be called on	Won't call out
Use nice words (elementary)	Won't tattle
Use appropriate language (middle, high)	Won't curse

VERBS TO AVOID	
Understand	Wonder
Appreciate	Think about
Get along with	Acknowledge
Be sorry	Realize
Feel	Know

step in the process of setting realistic goals for change (Alberto & Troutman, 2006). Although an academic pretest may be given only once, baseline data should be collected for at least five sessions in order to establish a pattern of behavior.

There are multiple ways to track student conduct; the method chosen depends on the type of problem and the circumstances and demands of individual classrooms. A classroom teacher can use direct observation by watching one or more students during designated times of the school day and then recording their behaviors. However, remember Ms. Cruz's concern with her ability to collect accurate and meaningful data for one or two students while teaching the whole class the lesson of the day. We will next describe several types of data collection methods, and we will suggest high- and low-tech ways to record behavior. As you read, try to decide which method would be most appropriate for tracking the calling-out behavior of Ms. Cruz's student, Jamar.

Recording Behavior

Narrative or **anecdotal recording** is typically used as an initial method for investigating academic, social, and behavioral expression of a student who is experiencing challenges in the classroom (Schloss & Smith, 1998). A colleague is needed to help with this type of observation tool. This observer other than the classroom teacher sits in an unobtrusive spot in the room and records all the actions and verbalizations of the target student for a predetermined length of time. It is helpful to establish a set of abbreviations and design an easy-to-use recording sheet before the observation takes place. Sometimes a second student is observed simultaneously and later, a comparison is drawn between the two. Although this method is time-consuming, important information can be gained from this type of data collection (Cooper, Heron, & Heward, 2007).

After the observation, the findings can be transferred to an Antecedent-Behavior-Consequence form (see Figure 14.2) in order to examine behaviors and interactions of the target student. With practice, this form can be used initially in place of the narrative recording method. The ABC method tracks sequential events and records

---

ABC Observation Form

Student: _Zack_ **Date:** _Oct. 31_ **Time:** _8:20 – 8:40_

Setting/Subject/Activity: _Language Arts – independent practice – journal writing_

Observer: _Mr. Harris_

Target Behaviors

On-task: engaged in independent writing, pencil-to-paper, eyes on paper, silently working, hand raising for teacher assistance, asking questions related to assignment
Off-task: doodling/drawing on paper, calling out, talking to peer, out of seat

Antecedent	Behavior	Consequence
Ms. C. assigns journal-writing prompt; models examples & nonexamples on the board; answers students' questions	Z. doodles in his journal, eyes on his paper; looks out the door, calls out to passing student	Ms. Cruz reprimands Z.: "Get back on task, Zack"
Ms. Cruz walks to Z.'s desk, sees his doodling and no written response in journal, redirects him firmly, "Zack it is time to work on your journal response"	Z. "But I don't know what you want me to do. Four pages are too many! It's too hard. I can't write that much"	Ms. Cruz: "It's OK, Zack. Don't be upset. Can you write two of the four pages?"

Figure 14.2 ABC Observation Form

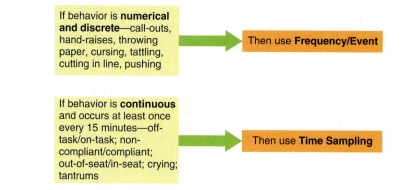

Figure 14.3 Choosing an Observational Method
Source: Adapted from P. A. Alberto & A. C. Troutman (2009). *Applied behavior analysis for teachers,* 8th ed. (Upper Saddle River, NJ: Pearson Education), pp. 88–89.

what happens before (the **antecedent**) and after (the **consequence**) the target behavior (Cooper et al., 2007). The teacher then looks for patterns of predictable behaviors. In planning an intervention, he/she can either change the antecedent or change the consequence in order to break the sequence of problematic behaviors. Read the notes Mr. Harris, the behavior specialist, made as he observed the interaction between Ms. Cruz and Zack during a journal writing activity.

Frequency or **event recording** is another method for data collection (Cooper et al., 2007; see Figure 14.3). It is used when the target behavior is **discrete**—has a definite beginning and ending—and can be easily counted within a specified time frame. It is not an appropriate method, however, for behaviors that occur continuously (e.g., crying, out of seat) or at high rates (e.g., pencil or foot tapping). In most circumstances, the classroom teacher can record behaviors as they happen and continue to teach the lesson. He/she may mark a recording form (see Figure 14.4) each time the target behavior occurs or she may keep track of incidences in other less-conspicuous ways. For example, paper clips can be transferred from one pocket to another as the behavior occurs. Common items like marbles or plastic chips can also be used as counters.

Frequency/Event Recording Form

Student: _Lucy_   **Date:** _Sept. 24_ **Time:** _8:00 – 8:20_

Subject /Activity: _Language Arts/Small Group Discussion_   **Observer:** _Mr. Harris_

Target Behaviors

1. *Appropriate Verbal Response:* Answers the question correctly; after receiving prompts, attempts answer
2. *Inappropriate Verbal Response:* No audible response; responds with negative comments, e.g., "leave me alone," "I don't know," "Stop asking me questions"

Directions: Make a mark in either *Behavior 1* or *Behavior 2* to indicate _Lucy's_ response to _Ms. Cruz's_ questions.

	Day 1	Day 2	Day 3	Day 4	Day 5
Behavior 1 *Appropriate*	##	#	##	##	#
Behavior 2 *Inappropriate*	####	####	########	######	####
Total: *Appropriate Responses*	2/6 = 33%	1/5 = 20%	2/10 = 20%	2/8 = 25%	1/5 = 20%

Figure 14.4 Frequency/Event Recording Form

In some cases, we may want to track more than one student response during a recording session. Remember Lucy, the quiet student in Ms. Cruz's class? Establishing a baseline of Lucy's oral participation is an example of this type of data collection. When Ms. Cruz asks Lucy a question, she may respond in one of two ways. Either (1) she answers with a positive verbal response, or (2) she does not answer or says "I don't know" or other negative responses. Figure 14.4 is an example of a recording form that tracks two responses within the same session. Be sure to read the operational definitions of both of these two global behaviors. The teacher or another observer makes tally marks for either Behavior 1 or Behavior 2 each time Lucy is called on, or if the teacher is keeping track with a counter or PDA, she may write/enter the total number of each response in the appropriate box at the end of the class period.

In order to establish a percentage of appropriate verbal responses, Ms. Cruz will divide the total of Behavior 1 (appropriate response) by the total of Behavior 1 plus the total of Behavior 2 (no/negative verbal response) and multiply by 100. This baseline percentage will be the starting point for increasing appropriate responding behavior.

Another method of tracking student behavior is **time sampling**, a type of interval recording (Cooper et al., 2007). Teachers can record **continuous** (rather than discrete) **behaviors** such as off-task, noncompliance, or disruptions using this method to find a percentage of occurrences of the targeted behavior. To begin this process, operationally define specific behaviors and designate a time period to observe. See Figure 14.5

Student Name Zack
Date Oct. 5 - Oct. 9 Activity Language Arts, independent from 8:30 - 8:40
Observer Ms. Cruz, Language Arts Teacher

On-task: engaged in independent writing, pencil-to-paper, eyes on paper, silently working, hand raising for teacher assistance; asking questions related to assignment
Off-task: doodling/drawing on paper, calling out, talking to peer, out of seat

Directions: Observe ___Zack___ at the end of 1-minute intervals and then mark the grid. Place a (+) in the box if his behavior is *on task*. Place a (0) in the box if his behavior is *off task*. Use this form for 5 days to determine a baseline level of behavior during independent practice.

Day Monday

	1	2	3	4	5	6	7	8	9	10	% On Task
Occur + No occur 0	+	0	+	+	0	+	+	0	0	+	60%

Day Tuesday

	1	2	3	4	5	6	7	8	9	10	% On Task
Occur + No occur 0	0	0	+	+	0	+	0	0	0	+	40%

Day Wednesday

	1	2	3	4	5	6	7	8	9	10	% On Task
Occur + No occur 0	+	0	+	+	0	+	0	0	+	+	60%

Day Thursday

	1	2	3	4	5	6	7	8	9	10	% On Task
Occur + No occur 0	0	0	+	+	0	+	+	0	0	+	50%

Day Friday

	1	2	3	4	5	6	7	8	9	10	% On Task
Occur + No occur 0	0	+	+	0	0	+	+	0	0	+	50%

Figure 14.5 Time Sampling Form

for an example of Ms. Cruz's time sampling recording form for Zack's on-task/off-task behavior during the last 10 minutes of language arts class. Earlier she asked another teacher to observe Zack using the ABC form, but now she wants to investigate his behavior further using time sampling. She reviews the operational definitions of *on task* and *off task* she developed for Mr. Harris and decides they still apply to the expectations for this part of the lesson. Next, she divides the observed time into 10 one-minute segments. She uses a reset timer to remind her to look at Zack at the end of each one-minute segment. At the end of each interval, if he is exhibiting any of the on-task behaviors, she marks a + in the box. If he is not exhibiting on-task behavior, then his actions are considered off task and Ms. Cruz marks a *0* in the box. In order to determine the percentage of Zack's "on-task-ness" (not *number* of on-task behaviors), Ms. Cruz divides the number of occurrences by the total number of one-minute segments (occurrences + nonoccurrences) and multiples the results by 100. She then calculates a percentage of on-task behavior for each session. Ms. Cruz made the right decision to record Zack's on-task behavior in order to focus on increasing his prosocial skills.

We have described a few methods to record discrete and continuous behaviors. See Table 14.4 for a list of more high- and low-tech ways to track, record, and manage this data collection. You may wonder how all the students in the class will react to the sound of a prerecorded beep or another cue. Initially, it may seem that a beep heard every few minutes may be distracting for the class, but most students will learn to ignore it. The wise teacher may instruct all of his/her students to use the beep as a reminder to check their own on-task behaviors, thus beginning the process of classwide **self-management**, which we will discuss later in this chapter. Alternatively, the beeps could be recorded into an MP3 player and an individual student could wear earphones, so only he could hear the beep.

Which method did you choose to track Jamar's calling-out behaviors? If you said, *event recording* you were correct! Ms. Cruz recorded his talk-outs by transferring paper clips from one pocket to another as she taught the language arts lesson. At the end of the class period, she counted the clips and recorded the total number of talk-outs on a data collection form similar to the one she used for Lucy (refer to Figure 14.4). After five days, she discovered that Jamar did not call out 50 times in 45 minutes, but the rate was still too high, a five-day average of nine times per 45 minutes or approximately once every five minutes. Before we discuss ways to decrease talk-outs and other inappropriate or disruptive behaviors, while encouraging and increasing appropriate ones, let's review another important assessment tool for describing student behavior, the functional behavior assessment.

Web Resources

Go to this text's companion website, **www.academic.cengage.com/education/Gargiulo** for links to more behavior management resources, including behavior contract templates and implementation plans, Behavior Report Card generators, and behavior interventions.

Table 14.4	Low-Tech and High-Tech Methods of Tracking and Recording Behavior
Low-Tech	**High-Tech**
Tic marks on chart or clipboard	PDA/laptop/desktop computer with recording template (e.g., Excel spreadsheet,* *Count It* shareware)
Marks on masking tape	Behavior observation system (BOS) software
Paper clips/rubber bands	Data collection assistant (DCA) software
Beads/beans/coins/marbles/tickets/chips	Tape recorder
Golf counter/knitting counter	MP3 player
Egg timer	Headphones
Second hand on wall clock	Electronic timer

*Provide a legend with abbreviations.
Source: Adapted from P. Alberto & A. Troutman, *Applied Behavior Analysis for Teachers*, 8th ed. (Upper Saddle River, NJ: Pearson Education, 2009), pp. 86–88; J. O. Cooper, T. E. Heron, & W. L. Heward, *Applied Behavior Analysis*, 2nd ed. (Upper Saddle River, NJ: Pearson Education, 2007), pp. 88–99; S. Kahng & B. Iwata, "Computerized Systems for Collecting Real-Team Observational Data," *Journal of Applied Behavior Analysis, 31*(2), 1998, pp. 253–261.

Analyzing Behavior

In Chapter 8 you learned about multiple methods of assessing students, including **functional behavior assessments** (FBA) and **behavior intervention plans** (BIP). Special educators use FBAs as a first step in understanding students' motivation for problematic disruptive or disturbing behaviors. Teachers observe, record, and analyze behavior to discover its purpose. They use some of the techniques of indirect assessment and direct assessment we have already discussed. Then the collaborative team develops a BIP for the student in order to help him learn to replace problematic behaviors with prosocial ones. Positive behavioral supports are used to teach and reinforce appropriate behaviors that serve the same purpose (Sugai, Lewis-Palmer, & Hagan-Burke, 2000).

The 2004 reauthorization of IDEA now requires functional behavioral assessment (FBA) and positive behavioral supports to be written and included in the IEPs of students with disabilities whose behavioral problems impede their learning or the learning of others. It is suggested that general education teachers also use FBA procedures to better understand and help any students with problematic behaviors (Arter, 2007; Larson & Maag, 1998). This method is more complex and time consuming than other means of observing and recording behaviors, but the results of using this in-depth assessment have the potential to greatly affect the student and his academic and social growth. The FBA procedure can be a tool that lends itself toward helping all educators become more culturally sensitive if diverse multidisciplinary teams choose and define target behaviors after making a cultural connection with the family (Salend & Taylor, 2002). When gathering information from parents/guardians and students, noting customs, practices, behaviors, or speech that may seem unusual or culturally different from your own may become more apparent. Use this information to customize the design plan for the student to increase its effectiveness.

Functional behavioral assessment is based on two assumptions: (a) all behavior is purposeful and serves a function, and (b) all behavior is contextually defined (Artesani, 2001). For example, Jamar may run around the classroom to attract attention, but he runs around the soccer field to score a goal. Ms. Cruz may wish that Zack would spend more time in silent reading during language arts class, but she worries about Lucy when she reads a book during recess.

As a general educator, you will be one of the members of a multidisciplinary team and may be asked to evaluate one of your students with the FBA protocol. Use the following steps (Artesani, 2001; Kerr & Nelson, 2006) to conceptualize the purpose of your student's challenging behavior, what happened just before and just after the problem occurs:

- Begin with student strengths—Brainstorm a list of academic and behavioral successes.
- Write an operational definition of challenging behavior in observable, measurable terms.
- Identify events, time, and situations when behavior takes place.
- Identify the consequences that reinforce the behavior.
- Develop summary statement or hypothesis.
  - What is the most likely function or reason for the behavior?
  - What is gained by the behavior?
  - When is it most likely to occur; under what circumstances?
  - When is it least likely to occur?
  - What consequences maintain the behavior?
- Collect data to confirm hypothesis.
- Make a plan for positive behavioral support to meet the need with appropriate replacement behavior.

Then use your best professional judgment as to the purpose the behavior serves. This information will be quite helpful to you in devising a support plan for your student. You may choose to use the BIP format that the special educators at your school use in developing your plan. Ask a special educator to be part of your problem-solving team to help you with this. As you read the next section of strategies and supports, remember the fair pair rule: Meet the student's need by teaching and reinforcing appropriate behaviors that replace inappropriate ones (Zirpoli, 2005).

Methods, Materials, and Resources that Promote Positive Behavior for All Learners

We all have an image of "ideal" student behavior. Although there may be variations according to individual temperament, style, or tolerance level, it would be safe to assume that most teachers treasure the same set of positive traits exhibited by students, no matter their age, ethnicity, or grade level. Likewise, some other student behaviors are found to be irritating, disruptive, or counterproductive for academic growth and social well-being of the group and the individual. In this section, we will discuss multiple ways to improve student conduct, including how to:

- Increase desirable and appropriate behaviors;
- Decrease negative and inappropriate behaviors;
- Teach new or underdeveloped behaviors.

Understanding Terminology

Let's begin by clarifying a few basic behavior management terms and concepts. Before we introduce specific strategies and talk about appropriate and inappropriate behaviors, we will define two frequently misinterpreted terms: **reinforcement** and **punishment**.

When a teacher says, "I've used reinforcement but it just doesn't work," know that he/she, like many others, is confusing this term and its function. This mix-up is partly because some words used in behavior management have different meanings in the vernacular. For example, the word *consequences* typically connotes "something bad" in everyday language, but it has a very different meanings when used in the context of classroom management (Maag, 2001).

Remember the ABC recording method (Figure 14.2)? The *C*'s on the form are the consequences—good, bad, or indifferent—that follow the behavior. Before we can help a student change his problematic behavior, we need to establish a functional relationship between it and the consequence that follows. The consequence acts as reinforcement if it *increases* the likelihood of the same behavior occurring in the future under similar circumstances (Cooper et al., 2007). The target behavior is **contingently reinforced** by the consequence. As teachers, we want to only reinforce positive behaviors, so be careful how you react to students' whining or coercive statements. You may be reinforcing problematic behaviors without realizing it. Remember the ABC example of Zack and Ms. Cruz? When Ms. Cruz redirected Zack, he said, "But I don't know what you want! This work is too hard. I can't write four pages!" Then good ole Ms. Cruz, in her attempt to keep him from becoming agitated, responded: "It's OK, Zack. Don't be upset. Can you finish two of the four pages?" What behavior of Zack's was reinforced by Ms. Cruz's response, the *consequence*? Unfortunately, Zack's whining behavior was reinforced and he learned that if he complained enough, Ms. Cruz would cut his assignment by half.

If the likelihood of a target behavior occurring in the future under similar circumstances *decreases*, we call the consequence punishment (Cooper et al., 2007). Maag (2001) suggests that reinforcement and punishment should be thought of as *effects* on behavior instead of specific *things*. In other words, the same consequence can be both reinforcement *and* punishment, depending on the student and the circumstances. For example, Jamar might volunteer more often after Ms. Cruz praises his oral reading skills (*reinforcement*), but Lucy may find the same type of attention too overwhelming and aversive (*punishment*) and refuse to participate the next time she is called on. You can see from this illustration how important it is for you to examine your students' conduct and reaction to consequences before implementing an intervention to either increase or decrease a particular behavior.

Increasing Appropriate Behavior

Let's take a closer look at reinforcement. The first thing to remember is that a consequence needs to appeal to the student in order to function as a reinforcer. McGinnis and Goldstein (1997) suggest several ways to determine if this is the case. If the consequence is serving as a reinforcer, the student will:

- Ask that it be repeated.
- Express contentment at the time of the consequence.
- Seem displeased when the consequence ends.
- Is willing to perform the target behavior in order to earn the consequence.

Students, especially younger ones, may not be aware of what motivates them to increase positive behaviors. If this is the case in your class, spend some time observing the students in order to determine activities or experiences they value. Also, especially at the beginning of the school year, you can simply ask them what they like. You may devise a *reinforcement menu* in order for them to indicate their choices. Preferences will change periodically and from one age group to the next, so be sure to update and vary your reinforcers as needed.

Reinforcers can be categorized into four groups: material, activity, token, and social (McGinnis & Goldstein, 1997). **Material reinforcers** are used frequently in the early stages of a behavioral program. They include edibles and other tangible objects valued by the student. In the beginning, award the material reinforcer immediately after the target behavior is displayed so the student understands that the pleasant consequence is contingent upon a specific behavior. Also remember to *always* pair praise with the reinforcer; the student should be certain what behavior you are rewarding. This reinforcement system is quite easy to carry out and one that students quickly learn. It can be implemented during any of the steps in instruction and works particularly well during independent practice. While circulating through her classroom, Ms. Cruz gives the students who are displaying *appropriate seatwork behavior* a small piece of candy or a sticker as she says, "I like the way you are working on that problem" or "Good job writing the draft."

Activity reinforcement is another type of reward that can be earned by a student after he has exhibited a predetermined target behavior. If, for example, Jamar stays in his seat during the 15-minute silent reading time, he may earn five minutes at the computer or another activity of his choice. Use of the Premack Principle is a variation of this reinforcer (Cooper et al., 2007). In order to participate in a preferred activity, the student must first engage in a less-pleasant task. Ms. Cruz uses this strategy (which she knows as *Grandma's Rule:* First eat the peas, then eat the pie) when she offers Zack an opportunity to try out the new learning games on the laptop computer after he completes his journal writing. By this point, Ms. Cruz also understands Zack is very willing to write *four full pages* if he can use the computer!

Token reinforcers may be traded in for either tangibles or activities. Instead of the teacher giving Jamar an edible each time he raises his hand, she gives him a chip or other object that has no intrinsic value. After accumulating a number of these tokens, he can exchange them for a reward of his choice. Table 14.5 gives examples of material, activity, and token reinforcers.

For most students, positive attention from the teacher is a powerful type of **social reinforcement**. Verbal praise is most effective when it is immediate and

Table 14.5	Examples of Positive Reinforcers	
Material/Tangible	**Activity**	**Tokens**
• Markers	• Line leader	• Chips
• Pens/pencils	• Teacher's helper	• Stamps
• Positive note home	• Computer/Internet	• Marbles
• Poster	• Use laptop	• Play money/checks
• Puzzle	• Board games	• Tickets
• Stickers	• Card games	• Coupons/fast food
• Tapes/CD/DVD player	• Color	• Gift certificates
• Toy	• Lunch with teacher	• Points
• Magazines	• Extra recess time	• Homework pass
• Food/drinks: chocolate milk, juice, soda, raisins, apples, candy, mints, popcorn	• Watch movie	
	• Talking with friends	
	• Library time	
	• Write on board or overhead projector	
	• Art or music project	
	• Water break	
	• Cooking activity	
	• Visit principal	

specific to a target behavior (Darch & Kame'enui, 2004). Teachers can also use non-verbal ways to reinforce positive academic and social behavior. Examples include: a smile, a nod, applause, thumbs-up, handshake, pat on the back, and high five. Below are some verbal praise statements. Be sure to include a behavior with each. Using specific praise such as, "You are very good at setting up these math problems," can help students realize and articulate their own areas of strength and boost confidence.

> You did well
> That's the way
> Much better effort with . . .
> Good thinking
> You're on it now
> Now you figured it out
> You've got it down
> Your hard work shows
> You are very good with . . .
> You're on the right track now
> Way to go
> You remembered how to . . .
> Exactly right
> Keep it up
> You mastered it
> All your effort paid off
> Perfect
> Brilliant
> Super
> Fine
> Wow
> Fantastic
> Great
> Excellent

Seven ways to verbally offer positive corrective feedback include:

- "Good try, but not quite right."
- "You're on the right track."

- "Keep going with that thinking."
- "Think about it, and try again."
- "You're only off by a fraction."
- "That's close, but not the answer here."
- "Your answer shows good reasoning, but it's a bit off the mark this time."

Be sure to choose age-appropriate reinforcers, but don't be too quick to draw a line between activities and items that appeal to elementary and secondary students. Sometimes a ninth grader will work hard to earn stickers (the cool, sparkly ones) and a much younger child might select a car magazine over a carton of chocolate milk.

Some teachers may choose not to use tangible or activity rewards in their classrooms because of the expense or the negative stereotype of students being "bribed" into working or being good in exchange for treats. Use what you feel comfortable with. Maag (2001) reminds us that reinforcement is a "universal principle that occurs naturally in every classroom. Therefore, educators should plan its occurrence to increase appropriate behaviors rather than running the risk of it haphazardly promoting inappropriate behaviors" (p. 175). Effective teachers plan for students to earn privileges by demonstrating appropriate behavior. Other teachers fail to manage behaviors as well because they base their expectations on the assumption that students *know* how to act rather than the observation of what they actually do. Remember that even older and more able students may need to be taught to exhibit socially or academically adaptive behavior.

Decreasing Inappropriate Behavior

Now that you have learned the basics of using reinforcement to increase appropriate behaviors, we will discuss several ways of decreasing inappropriate ones. Keep in mind that reinforcement can also inadvertently increase undesirable actions. As you read on, think about how best to address disruptions, noncompliance, and other troublesome behaviors without reinforcing them with attention. Also remember that we will be using the term punishment to mean a process that *decreases* the likelihood that a behavior it follows will recur in the future (Cooper et al., 2007). Interventions for decreasing negative behavior occur along a continuum. See Table 14.6 for a list of three levels in this hierarchy, from least to most aversive (Alberto & Troutman, 2009; Darch & Kame'enui, 2004; Kerr & Nelson, 2006). In your classroom,

Table 14.6	Using Behavior Reduction Strategies to Decrease Inappropriate Behavior: Hierarchy of Procedures

Level I—Proactive
- Environmental—Consider lighting, sounds/noise levels, temperature, smells/odors, accessibility to materials/technology, seating arrangements, proximity to teacher and other students, proximity to distracters such as wastebasket and windows (see Chapter 9)
- Scheduling/Rules/Procedures—State expectations clearly and in positive terms
- Teach Prosocial Behaviors—Name and define the behavior you want to see
- Vicarious Reinforcement—Reward/praise desirable behavior
- Differential Reinforcement—Encourage behaviors that are different from the inappropriate one
  - DRO—Reinforce other (omission/zero) behaviors (hitting, tantrums)
  - DRI—Reinforce incompatible behaviors (sit in chair vs. out of seat)
  - DRL—Reinforce lower levels of problem behavior (reduce number of tardies)

Level II—Neutral or Mildly Aversive
- Extinction—Removing reinforcement for target behavior
- Inclusion Time-out—removing opportunity for all reinforcement

Level III—Subtracting Reinforcer
- Response Cost—fine for misbehavior
- Exclusion Time-out—remove from immediate area

Source: Adapted from P. Alberto & A. Troutman, *Applied Behavior Analysis for Teachers*, 8th ed. (Upper Saddle River, NJ: Pearson Education, 2009), pp. 266–290; S. Salend, *Creating Inclusive Classrooms: Effective and Reflective Practices*, 5th ed. (Upper Saddle River, NJ: Pearson Education, 2005), pp. 323–330.

you will consider the nature of the challenge and where it lies on the continuum of problems as you decide which strategies to use to encourage and support your students. On the one hand, the behavior may be mildly irritating but worthy of decreasing (e.g., occasional pencil tapping or calling out without hand raising) or alternately, it may be quite disruptive to an individual student and her peers (e.g., physical or verbal aggression or excessive noncompliance). Review Table 14.6 as we describe several types of behavioral reduction interventions within this hierarchy.

You learned about some of the Level I proactive strategies as universal supports earlier in this chapter. Another positive support is called **vicarious reinforcement** (Kauffman, Mostert, Trent, & Pullen, 2006). Teachers may use it as positive strategy during extinction of an inappropriate behavior (see next section). Remember the *attention tank* theory? A student who exhibits negative behaviors is generally seeking teacher attention. During vicarious reinforcement, the teacher chooses an on-task peer in close proximity to the misbehaving one and offers specific verbal praise ("I really like the way you raised your hand before giving the answer.") and possibly a tangible or token reinforcement as well, while ignoring the misbehaving one. The acting-out youngster soon learns that students who are following the prescribed rules of the teacher are rewarded with positive attention and more. The target student will often immediately imitate the student who receives reinforcement.

It is very important for you to reinforce the target student as soon as he or she engages in the desired behavior. Your motto should be *"Catch them being good!"*

Another effective Level I strategy, **differential reinforcement** (DR), can also be used as a positive method for decreasing inappropriate behavior (Zuna & McDougall, 2004). You know from reading the term *reinforcement* that this method is meant to *increase* a behavior. Think "different" when you see *differential* and you will understand the purpose here. DR is a strategy that encourages the occurrence of behaviors *different* from the inappropriate one. There are several ways to differentially reinforce appropriate behaviors while simultaneously discouraging inappropriate actions. When Ms. Cruz wants to limit the number of times Jamar calls out, she uses *differential reinforcement of alternative behavior* (DRA) to reinforce the appropriate hand raising instead of reprimanding (*reinforcing*) the call-outs. *Differential reinforcement of incompatible behavior* (DRI) is used to praise (*reinforce*) a behavior that is impossible to perform concurrently with the undesirable conduct. For example, Ms. Cruz uses DRI when she praises Zack's punctuality rather than nag him when he is tardy. *Differential reinforcement of lower levels of behavior* (DRL) is used to reinforce a gradual decrease in inappropriate behavior. Ms. Cruz doesn't expect Lucy to immediately participate in small group discussions. The first week Ms. Cruz offers Lucy a token when she responds inappropriately only 50% of the time (see Figure 14.4). The following week, Lucy earns the token when she decreases inappropriate verbal responses to 40%, and so on. Teachers should choose DRL for behaviors that can be tolerated at some level. It is not an appropriate intervention for aggressive or dangerous behaviors (Alberto & Troutman, 2009). Finally, Ms. Cruz offers Lucy a token for free time when she sits up and makes eye contact, as opposed to having her head on her desk with eyes closed.

A Level II strategy that goes hand in hand with DR and is considered neutral or mildly aversive is **extinction**. To use this strategy, *all* reinforcement for an inappropriate behavior must be withheld (Kauffman et al., 2006). This is a powerful strategy, but it is only effective if the student with the problematic behavior receives absolutely *no* attention for it over an extended period of time. You can imagine multiple examples of silly or irritating behaviors that you might be able to ignore, but will be very difficult for age-mates to disregard. In elementary school, the class clown might make inappropriate faces or noises with the full intent of cracking up the silent reading group. Older students may use strategies to shock or amuse peers by cursing, joking, or arguing with the teacher. Teachers can encourage students to use extinction by adding powerful reinforcers for *ignoring behavior*.

Time-out from positive reinforcement has been used by teachers for many years (Salend & Gordon, 1987; Skiba & Raison, 1990; White & Bailey, 1990). It involves denying a student access to positive reinforcement from the teacher and peers in classroom activities for a specific amount of time, contingent on display of the target behavior (Alberto & Troutman, 2009). The least intrusive type is called **inclusion time-out** (Ryan, Sanders, Kasiyannis, & Yell, 2007). As its name implies, it can be implemented within whole group instruction in the general education setting. Contingent on misbehavior, reinforcement is temporarily denied, although the student is not required to physically leave the environment. The teacher may turn away or remove materials so the student is not permitted to participate in class activities.

For time-out to have the desired effect, the teacher should make the classroom activity and atmosphere as positive, stimulating, and reinforcing as possible. When this is the case, even a short separation from the main action of the class can act as a punisher.

In **contingent observation**, the student is required to observe the action from a little distance without being permitted to participate for a designated amount of time (White & Bailey, 1990). For example, when Ms. Cruz saw Jamar push another student in the cafeteria line, she instructed him to sit at a lunch table for five minutes while his classmates continued through the line. It is recommended that the number of minutes a youngster experiences time-out should not exceed the number of years of his age (Ryan et al., 2007), and in the case of Jamar and others who need a cooling-off period, just five or so minutes is generally enough time to make the point.

Another, more intrusive type is called **exclusion time-out** (Ryan et al., 2007). Here the student is physically removed from the teaching environment so that he receives no reinforcement from the teacher or peers.

Ms. Cruz decided to arrange the classroom to provide for two exclusion areas. One was the standard *time-out* spot, a three-sided study carrel placed along the back wall. A second seat was placed toward the back of the room facing a side wall. It was separated from the rows of student desks by a high bookcase. This spot was used for what she called *time-in*. She told the students that this area could be used for voluntarily choosing to separate from the group for a cool-down or alone-time break. The students were taught specific expectations for using this seat (e.g., no more than twice a day for no longer than five minutes each time). If they did not follow the time-in protocol, they temporarily lost the privilege to use the area.

Response cost is a Level III strategy that uses the removal of something desirable to decrease inappropriate behavior (Kauffman et al., 2006). Response cost is a system whereby a student is fined for engaging in a negative target behavior. In order for this strategy to be effective, the student must first be allowed to earn tokens or privileges, which can then be partially removed, contingent on the misbehavior. Teachers must be very careful never to fine students more than they have earned. If students do not earn positive consequences early in the program, they will quickly lose faith in it and they will not learn the connection between engaging in appropriate behavior and earning privileges. Teachers must be careful not to appear punitive when executing this strategy. No one likes a fine (or a parking or speeding ticket). The best way to implement response cost is to dispassionately state the offense and the previously agreed upon cost. For example, Ms. Cruz calmly tells Zack, "Because you yelled at Jamar during the transition, you will lose 10 minutes of computer time."

McGinnis and Goldstein (1997) recommend using logical or **natural consequences** as an alternative to punishment. The teacher and students first discuss a variety of cause-and-effect relationships as students are taught to take responsibility for their actions (see below for more information about teaching new behaviors). The consequences for inappropriate choices should meaningfully relate to their behavior and should be carried out consistently. For example, when Jamar and Zack whisper during Mr. Medina's explanation of the math assignment, they don't hear his hints concerning the last word problem. They struggle along trying to

Positive reinforcement is temporarily withheld during exclusion time-out.

Cengage Learning/Wadsworth

figure out the answer well after the others have turned in their papers. Consequently, they miss out on the rousing game of *Uno* that is offered as an activity reinforcer for students who promptly finish their class work.

Teaching New Behavior

Thus far we have discussed ways to increase appropriate behaviors and decrease inappropriate ones. A third option in managing the individual is to teach new or underdeveloped behaviors. Teachers assume (or at least *hope*) that even very young students understand and demonstrate certain basic social and behavioral skills. Unfortunately, that is not always the case. At the beginning of the chapter we listed potential characteristics of students with exceptionalities and other diverse needs (see Table 14.1). Many times these students lack experience interacting with peers and adults and need to be taught basic interpersonal skills, such as engaging in a conversation, taking turns, waiting, or asking for help. Teachers should assess the knowledge and demonstration of appropriate behaviors of individual students with the same intent as they assess reading or math comprehension and performance (Darch & Kame'enui, 2004). After establishing a baseline level of competency, the same effective direct instruction methods used in teaching academics can be applied in instructing students to demonstrate appropriate behaviors.

As we stated previously, verbal and nonverbal positive attention and other rewards act as reinforcers for behaviors we want to increase. As you now know, these are offered *after* the target behavior has been displayed. Any reasonable teacher would not expect a student to be graded on a new math skill *before* she has taught it. Likewise, some behaviors need to be explicitly explained, modeled, and practiced before a student is expected to demonstrate them successfully. Teachers should help students learn and practice appropriate behaviors to take the place of maladaptive ones (Melloy, 2000). For example, as we have already illustrated, some students exhibit noncompliance and disruptions to gain teacher attention or peer approval. These individuals may not be familiar with prosocial alternatives that accomplish the same goal as effectively. In order to improve the behavior of individual students, we need to teach them social skills related to their deficit areas.

Now that we have explained and illustrated behavioral management terminology and concepts, we will discuss specific ways that teachers can assist individual students who are experiencing problematic behaviors. As you now know, there are many strategies the classroom teacher can employ to engage and encourage students who need an extra amount of structure and support. In this section, we will begin by reviewing teacher-initiated interventions. Then we will discuss ways that students can take more responsibility for their own behaviors. By using techniques that encourage independence, decision making, and responsibility, teachers can help students change their view about themselves and others. The **locus of control**, or attribution for negative and positive outcomes, will shift from external to internal as students gain more self-confidence in their ability to have a positive effect on their environment and those in it (Zirpoli, 2005).

See Chapter 10 for a review of the importance of a classroom, schoolwide support, including multiple methods, materials, and resources to use the smooth and efficient operation of day-to-day classroom activities, as well as an effective and well-organized academic lesson. Remember to always state expectations in positive terms, name and define the behavior you want to see, and be consistent following through with both positive and negative consequences. Remember, too, the importance for some students to have a choice in how they engage or respond (Jolivette, Stichter, & McCormick, 2002). For example, if practicing math facts is the goal, you might offer flash cards or a computerized drill. Because UDL is all about offering multiple means of expression and engagement, it comes with a built-in choice system. Next we examine additional teacher tools that help to eliminate, or at least diminish, individual behavioral problems.

The key to teaching and encouraging appropriate behavior, just like with academic instruction, is in the preparation (Darch & Kame'enui, 2004; Maag, 2001). So far we have talked about ways to decrease or correct problematic behaviors after they occur, but now we will discuss *proactive* strategies. Colvin, Sugai, and Patching (1993) suggest a system they call *precorrection*, in which they use functional assessment and advanced planning to counteract predictable problematic behaviors. They suggest changing something in the environment (e.g., moving a talkative young boy's desk away from his buddy and into the middle of a group of studious girls) as one way of preventing, or at least lessening, the chances of misbehavior.

This method can be paired with the strategy called, "Catch them being good" (McGinnis & Goldstein, 1997). Just as its name implies, a watchful teacher finds opportunities for reinforcing socially appropriate behaviors. Ms. Cruz might have to wait quite awhile, but when she finally sees Jamar raise his hand, she should quickly respond with a broad smile and an enthusiastic, "*YES*, Jamar, I see by your raised hand that you have the answer. Good job!" On the other hand, as we suggested earlier, Lucy would find this type of effusive praise punishing. When Ms. Cruz "catches" Lucy engaging in a quiet conversation with the new girl from Puerto Rico, she can simply walk by, nod approvingly, and say, "I'm glad you're getting to know each other." She can also slip Lucy a positive note to reinforce appropriate social interaction.

Proactive strategies can also be used to help avert aggression and noncompliance (Kandel, 2000; Romaneck, 2001). We suggest developing positive alternatives to help your students cope with and express angry feelings in socially appropriate ways. The "time-in" procedure described above is an example of providing a quiet, safe place within the classroom where a student can "chill out" when feeling stressed or upset.

Acting-out behaviors associated with agitation and anxiety can sometimes be circumvented with proactive approaches to the problem. Ms. Cruz has noticed that Zack becomes upset and angry on days when there is a school assembly. After considering the situation and talking with him about it, she realized that it is the change in schedule that is upsetting to him. She encourages him to help her write an alternate "assembly day" schedule, which he can then use to avoid confusion on such days. They use the computer to find the school web page and then turn to the regular daily schedule. Zack shows Ms. Cruz how to use the scheduling program to quickly rearrange the times and activities for what he calls "crazy days." By taking charge and participating in this proactive plan, Zack feels more in control as he learns to advocate for himself.

Ms. Cruz is feeling better about her classroom management style now that she is learning to anticipate certain behavioral problems. She has consistently incorporated positive reinforcement and behavioral reduction strategies into her daily routine. Students seem more engaged in academics and even Jamar has begun to raise his hand in order to receive positive attention. Now Ms. Cruz wonders if her students have become too dependent on her to dispense rewards and reprimands. She would like to help them take the next step in becoming more independent and responsible for their own behavior. She noticed that the strategy she suggested for Zack worked well in easing his anxiety, and just as importantly, in boosting his self-confidence.

Behavioral contracts offer a way to move seamlessly from teacher-controlled to student-initiated expectations and rewards. Scheuermann and Hall (2008) suggest several advantages of this strategy, including the fact that it is based on principles of positive reinforcement. Also, because the student has input in the negotiation process, he or she retains a sense of control of behavior and reinforcement. The behavioral contract is an "if-then" student-teacher deal that states in writing what the student is expected do in order to receive a specific reward. See the elements on page 422 for an example of each.

1. The target behavior must be observable and measurable.

IF Jamar raises his hand and waits to be called on before speaking . . .

2. The circumstances and criteria should be explicitly stated.

80% of the time during the first 40 minutes of Language Arts class . . .

3. The rewards must be clearly defined.

THEN he will receive 10 minutes of computer time at the end of class.

4a. A Penalty Clause must state the consequences for noncompliance.

4b. A Bonus Clause is optional and provides a nice additional incentive.

a. If Jamar does not meet this criterion and talks out without hand raising more than 20% of the time, he may not use the computer during Language Arts activities the following day.

b. For every additional hand raise/correct response, Jamar earns one token to be traded for an activity at the end of the week.

5. A reliable method of record keeping must be used.

Event recording will be used to tally "hand raising" and "talk-outs."

As the student becomes more familiar with the elements of a behavioral contract, he can assume more responsibility for its development and operation. Initially, the teacher will select a target behavior and the student will choose the reward. The teacher should train the student to help with data collection in the early stages of this procedure. At first, he/she and the teacher will review progress and together track daily results. Depending on computer skills' level, the teacher will help the student (or vice versa) use a computer graphing program to enter data each day (Gunter et al., 2002). Gradually, the teacher should transfer to the student the responsibilities of writing behavioral goals, record keeping, and rewarding according to the terms of the contract. This multifaceted activity will help individuals learn important lessons about making and keeping commitments. With practice and encouragement from the teacher, students can next move toward self-management.

When students begin to take responsibility for their actions and the consequences that follow, they are on the right track to developing a strong internal locus of control for self-management. It is our job as teachers to help in this ongoing process. Initially, we offer a consistent, dependable environment where they can feel safe to learn and develop. We structure academic and social lessons to be predictable. We reward appropriate behavior and we discourage inappropriate behavior by our words and actions. Ultimately, however, we want our students to move away from our instruction, evaluation, and reinforcement and become able to regulate, reward, and manage themselves. We need to provide students with tools, practice, and support in this endeavor. Let's review a few strategies that will aid this process.

In order for students to take responsibility for themselves, they need to attribute success or failure to their own talents and deficits. We can encourage this self-awareness in our language of praise and correction. Look back at the examples of statements presented on pages 416 and 417 that emphasize the student's accomplishment, rather than our feelings. When you praise students, avoid making remarks like, "I'm so proud of you" or "You made me so happy." These comments subtly reinforce external locus of control, which is all too common in students with disabilities (Beirne-Smith, Ittenbach, & Patton, 2002). Smith, Salend, and Ryan (2001) agree that students need to receive clear messages that support their learning and their efforts. Statements like, "You really worked hard on this and it turned out beautifully" acknowledge the attempt and payoff.

Research studies have shown improvement in work completion and accuracy, on-task behavior, and positive peer interactions when students used self-management strategies (Brock, 2005; Rock, 2005; Smith & Sugai, 2000). Schloss and Smith (1998) described four components of self-management that can apply to either academic or behavioral goals. We list them here and give behavioral examples for each.

Self-Instruction: Verbally reviewing to oneself the steps of a task. This skill is also an important one for students to see and hear. Teachers should take advantage of occasions to model this process and should explicitly state their intentions. For example, you could talk through the multistepped process of finding your class web page, from turning on the computer to connecting to the Internet to finding the school site. Students with specific behavioral goals can use self-talk to remind themselves of appropriate social interactions, as well. Think about using electronic recording devices to store these step-by-step recordings. Allow students to replay the directions as needed.

Self-Monitoring: Tracking one's own behavior and making choices to discontinue inappropriate actions. Students can track their behavior during class time using a checklist and a beeper. You can help initially by providing a short list of "on-task" behaviors, such as "eyes on my paper; writing; not talking with others." During independent work, the beeper reminds them to review the list and regulate their actions, if necessary. Checklists are also useful in helping a student become better prepared and more independent. He can tape a list to his notebook with reminders of what he needs to bring to class (the *notebook*, homework, pencil and pen, textbook, extra paper). As students become better at self-monitoring, they can catch themselves in annoying or disruptive behaviors and remind themselves that teasing and whispering, for example, are not appropriate and should be replaced with more appropriate ones (check the list for suggestions, if necessary).

Self-Evaluation: At first, teachers should help students with this difficult process of talking about and judging one's own behavior. Give students the vocabulary necessary for this task and model how to reflect on one's actions. Graphing results of a behavioral contract is a good way to begin. Talk about goal-setting and realistic expectations as you review daily results. Remember that self-graphing on the computer can be highly engaging and motivating to students.

Self-Reinforcement: This step logically follows self-monitoring and self-evaluation. Make sure your students are given choices in the classroom for reinforcement opportunities. Trading in tokens for tangible rewards helps them develop decision-making skills. As they move away from material reinforcers, encourage them to use congratulatory self-talk. Congratulatory self-talk phrases can also be programmed into audio recorders for easy access. Students will readily model teachers who use verbal praise. See Figure 14.6 for ways to use self-management strategies as a package intervention to monitor behavior, review performance, and correct or praise efforts.

Maintenance and Generalization

As you now see, managing the behavior of an individual is a complex process with multiple steps. Teachers find rewards in watching their students grow, especially in the latter phases of self-management. Over the months, Ms. Cruz has seen great improvements in the three students who were of most concern. Lucy, Jamar, and Zack have all done much better academically and socially since Ms. Cruz began individualizing her behavior management strategies. There is one more very important phase, however, that mustn't be overlooked. Not only do we want Ms. Cruz's three students to behave well and prosper academically in her first-period class. We want them to also move through their day using their newfound skills to exhibit appropriate, prosocial behaviors at school and in the community. We will now introduce Ms. Cruz to the practices of **maintenance and generalization** (Cooper et al., 2007). These skills go hand in hand and refer to the carry-over of training from one situation to another and from one person to another.

For example, if Jamar's hand-raising behavior is generalized, he will exhibit it in Mr. Medina's math class and Mrs. William's social studies class. Even though hand raising is not as valued in small group work of science lab, if his improved deportment is exhibited in this class as well, we say that his behavior has generalized. Maintenance refers to the continuation of behaviors over time. If after winter break Lucy returns to school and begins the quarter by sitting up and making eye contact, we say that her prosocial behaviors have been maintained over time.

- Self-Instruction/Self-Talk

  ❑ Identify Problem   ⟶

  ❑ Generate a Plan   ⟶

  ❑ Implement the Plan   ⟶

  ❑ Monitor & Evaluate   ⟶

  ❑ Reinforce … or   ⟶

  ❑ Correct   ⟶

- Social or Academic Skills

  ❑ I don't know how to …

  ❑ I think I'll try …

  ❑ First, I need to … then I need to …

  ❑ I'll check off each step as I use it … Is it working?

  ❑ I did great! I earned a …

  ❑ This plan didn't work! Now I need to …

  - Try again.

  - Ask for help.

  - Try another plan.

- Self-Monitoring/Self-Recording
  ❑ Fair Pair = Identify & Define Problem Behavior and Positive Replacement Behavior
  ❑ Use easy recording method
  ❑ Select time to record
  ❑ If-then contract with reinforcers
  ❑ Compare with teacher
  ❑ Reinforce for accuracy

- Self-Evaluation/Self-Assessment
  ❑ Review definition & set goals
  ❑ Decide: How did I do?
  ❑ Meet with teacher to match
  ❑ Did I meet goals? What did I do well? How can I improve?

- Self-Reinforcement
  ❑ Use self-talk to encourage/reinforce
  ❑ Set time for student-chosen reinforcers—activity or tangible

Hand-Raising vs. Calling Out

☺ = I raised my hand.

☹ = I called out and did not raise my hand.

In Seat vs. Out of Seat

- If I am in my seat when I hear the timer, then I check a ☺

- If I am out of my seat, then I check a ☹

How Did I Do?

Total _____ ☺

Total _____ ☹

I did GREAT!
I'm going to work on _____!

Figure 14.6 Individual Positive Support—Self-Management Package
Source: Adapted from P. Schloss & M. Smith, *Applied Behavior Analysis in the Classroom,* 2nd ed. (Boston: Allyn & Bacon, 1998), pp. 299–314.

Peers and School Personnel

Maintenance and generalization rarely occur without training. Most social skills, like academic skills, need to be taught through modeling and practice (Darch, Miller, & Shippen, 1998). Skills that transfer naturally are those used quite often or those found to be naturally rewarding, such as complimenting someone and receiving kind words or a smile in return. In this chapter we have described students who lacked skills relating with peers and teachers. As you help your own students understand, learn, and practice appropriate behavior, you should offer them multiple opportunities to rehearse their new skills within your classroom. Cooperative learning groups (see Chapter 9) provide such an opportunity to work with a few peers at a time on a shared task (Grey et al., 2007). Be sure to change the makeup of these groups periodically so your students have a chance to practice generalizing appropriate peer interactions with as many different youngsters as possible. Initially, you will encourage and reward your students each time you see them using appropriate behaviors within your classroom. Next you can monitor and reinforce generalization of the same prosocial behaviors across different settings in your school, such as the cafeteria, library, auditorium, or playground. In some cases, you might have to be creative to orchestrate opportunities for interactions with students from different grades (easier to accomplish in elementary school than in high school). Cross-grade peer tutoring is always appreciated by other teachers and can be a real confidence boost to students who lack experience with younger children.

When you plan for generalization of behaviors with different teachers, think about the reinforcers you used to teach the skill originally. For example, Ms. Cruz found that Lucy was rewarded more with nonverbal praise, such as smiles and nods, whereas Jamar loved lavish verbal attention. You can share this type of information with your colleagues and subtly prompt them to try the same approach. (Remember, reinforcement is a natural phenomenon. Teachers are susceptible to it, too!) The more practice your students have, the better the chances are that their appropriate behaviors will generalize. Solicit help in this process from other school personnel, as well. Consider using cafeteria workers, bus drivers, custodians, or other members of the school staff who are willing to help your students generalize positive, appropriate, and respectful behavior with a kind word and a smile (and sometimes an extra cookie) and punish reports of misbehavior with extinction, harsh looks, or stern words. Guidance counselors, media specialists, and administrators may also be quite willing to help your students in the process of generalizing prosocial school behaviors.

Collaborating with Parents

When collaborating with parents, always remember that they are the real experts on the students. Express your respect early and often for the parents' knowledge. It is best to contact your parents at the beginning of the school year with good news about their child (Kauffman et al., 2006). Remember that teachers can build rapport with families by stating student strengths at the beginning of conversations. You may have several opportunities later to call to report trouble, so make the initial contact positive. Remember to catch the students being good, make a note to yourself, and pass along the information to mom and dad.

Ms. Cruz decided to set aside one-half hour each evening to make quick parent phone calls or send e-mails. She reaches about five families a night and talks for no more than five minutes to each parent. On the nights she anticipates longer conversations, she limits the number of calls. She keeps accurate phone numbers and e-mail addresses available and shares with her team important information from home that might impact a student's school performance. She is finding using e-mail and her class webpage is reducing some of this investment of time.

You can use a form like Figure 14.7 to keep a record of parent contacts with a few notes as to what was discussed. Naturally, it is easier to help a student in the first stages of behavioral problems, and having a written record facilitates the process.

When you need to contact parents to set up a team meeting, keep the phone conversation short. Be flexible about meeting times; offer to meet early in the morning or during lunch hour to accommodate working parents. Briefly state your concern and treat the parents as equal team collaborators. Ask them to be thinking of suggestions to help the others better understand the student. Keep a hopeful tone and try hard not to pass judgment.

Salend (2005) offers additional suggestions for fostering communication and collaboration with families. They include:

- Ensure parents of the confidentiality of your conversations. Let them know that you will share the information with other team members only. Keep this promise and never gossip about students or their families.
- Structure parent-teacher meetings for comfort and communication. Sit so everyone can see each other, preferably at a round table. Begin with a short report of student progress, and then state your concerns. Ask the parents to join you in brainstorming for solutions. Decide on one or two strategies. End on a positive note and set a time to check progress, either with a phone call, e-mail, or follow-up meeting.

Student _____   *Teacher/Team* _____

Father _____   *Mother* _____

Phone: Work _____ *Home* _____   *Phone: Work* _____ *Home* _____

E-mail _____   *E-mail* _____

Address _____

Other Contact _____   *Relationship* _____

Phone: Work _____ *Home* _____ *E-mail* _____

Type	Summary of Content (attach copies)	Follow-Up
Notes/Letters Date: Date: Date:		
E-mail Date: Date: Date:		
Phone Conversations Date: Date: Date:		
Phone Messages Date: Date: Date:		
Conferences/ School Visits Date: Date: Date:		

Figure 14.7 Record of Parent Contacts

- Collaborate with parents for home-school contracts. Decide on a limited number of behaviors to target. Devise an easy system of communication, such as a home-note to be signed daily. Allow the student to choose the reinforcement. He may prefer to earn a family activity for positive behaviors at school.

Remember the ultimate goal is to help your students become independent and responsible individuals. The parent-teacher collaboration builds on this effort and carries the lessons learned and practiced in your classroom into the home and community.

Culturally Diverse Families

We end this chapter with a few reminders about communicating with culturally diverse parents of exceptional children. The ERIC Clearinghouse on Disabilities and Gifted Education (1991) lists suggestions for honoring ethnic differences while establishing a relationship with family members of your students. Keep in mind the information from the preceding section, and remember that communication and collaboration with culturally diverse parents offers its own set of challenges and rewards. Before your first meeting, consider the following suggestions.

Cengage Learning/Wadsworth

Working toward common student goals with parents can help diverse learners develop responsibility and independence.

First and most importantly, use language that parents can understand. Request a professional interpreter if the parents do not speak English. If possible, send notes in the parents' first language. Keep your messages simple, at an appropriate reading level, and jargon free. Make an effort to find out about the culture of your students and their families, and be aware of different customs and social practices. Here are some guidelines to consider before meeting with culturally diverse families:

- Sharing space: Be aware of different levels of proximity comfort and honor the parent's preference.
- Touching: Different cultures practice varying rules for social touching. Some cultures do not engage in handshaking with the opposite sex, whereas other groups are much more physical.
- Eye contact: Avoiding eye contact is a sign of respect in some cultures, and looking into another's eyes is considered to be a challenge. Take the lead from the parents and try not to appear challenging or threatening.

Don't assume the parents have been well-informed about school procedures or special education matters. Provide them with clear, concise information about your classroom and your behavioral expectations. Be aware that they may not feel comfortable asking questions; so initially offer them basic information about the purpose of the meeting. Be supportive of their efforts to learn how to participate in the system and help them become strong advocates for their children. After establishing an initial relationship, ask if they are willing to work with you in a home-school collaboration. Offer a few suggestions for home strategies that support the effort to generalize behaviors. Set goals for the student together and then decide a time and method of following up with your plan.

Teachers can become more aware of differences in attitudes, verbal responses, and body language by becoming familiar with students' ethnic backgrounds. Encourage students to share information about their culture and cultivate relationships with family members by creating opportunities for them to participate in classroom or schoolwide cultural exchange activities. Observe the interactions of children with their parents to gain insight in familial behavioral expectations and social exchanges (Cartledge et al., 2001; Montgomery, 2001; Parette & Petch-Hogan, 2000).

Summary—Putting It All Together

In this chapter we discussed ways to manage and improve individual student behavior. We began by stating various externalizing and internalizing factors of maladaptive behavior. We paired certain characteristics with specific disability groups and students with other diverse needs. Then we proposed several reasons for inappropriate behavior including efforts to communicate, avoid unpleasant or difficult schoolwork, and gain teacher and peer attention. Next, the importance of operationally defining target behaviors was presented. We illustrated several methods of tracking and measuring the frequency, intensity, and duration and gave examples of different recording methods, including: anecdotal, event, and time sampling. Also, the process of functional behavioral assessment was described.

We discussed three general ways to manage and improve behavior: increase appropriate, decrease inappropriate, and teach new or unfamiliar. We then defined and gave examples of behavioral management terminology. The concepts of reinforcement, consequences, and punishment were illustrated with classroom examples. The use of specific strategies within each area, such as reinforcement, response cost, and time-out were also illustrated.

We described teacher efforts to help individual students take responsibility for their own actions and strengthen their internal locus of control. We also suggested using a behavioral contract as a transitional activity between teacher-led and student-initiated strategies, and we gave examples of the components of self-management.

We emphasized the importance of planning for the generalization of prosocial behaviors after they have been established within one classroom. Cooperation with colleagues and parents is essential in this process and we suggested ways in which students could practice positive interactions at school and at home. Collaboration between teachers and parents was urged, and we closed this chapter by offering suggestions for improving relationships between culturally diverse families and classroom teachers.

The basic principles of UDL are echoed throughout this chapter. Remember that UDL environments can empower teachers and students in multiple settings. They offer choice in representation, expression, and engagement so teachers and students have some control about how they present information, receive it, interact with it, and respond to it. UDL environments focus on organization for success from the start. They establish learning goals, implement ongoing assessment, and select proven methods to ensure appropriateness of instruction, progress and success. They promote safety, clarity, and flexibility. It might be helpful to revisit the ACCESS mnemonic that was applied to social environments in Chapter 10 to help you remember to apply the 3 M's of UDL.

Now let's revisit Ms. Cruz's class and see how she met the challenges of three of her students who needed individualized behavioral supports and other adaptations:

Ms. Cruz has just finished writing her report cards for the first nine weeks. She is pleased that Lucy, Jamar, and Zack are making such good progress. She is glad she asked her colleagues early to help her identify and target these students' challenging behaviors, and they were right there for her. The counselor initially helped organize everyone including Mr. Harris, the special educator. He was instrumental in guiding them through the functional behavior assessment and BIP process for each student. Ms. Cruz was uncertain about her ability to teach the whole class and record behavior, but Mr. Harris helped her see that the observation tools were a lot easier to use than she had originally thought and they really helped target a replacement behavior for each student. She ended up using her PDA for data collection. Ms. Cruz knew that involving families was another key part of each plan, but it was hard to reach some of the parents. The school counselor and social worker made that happen, and the information they contributed was essential in making supportive plans. They discovered Lucy's mom does have access to e-mail, and Ms. Cruz is able to keep in touch with her more easily.

Now Lucy sits near the front of the room and she participates more in group discussions. She even volunteers some answers without prompting! She enjoys using the electronic classroom response system Ms. Cruz checked out from the media center. She can answer questions in class and only she and the teacher know her identification number. This has given her more confidence in responding because she is no longer embarrassed when her answer is incorrect. Ms. Cruz makes sure to smile and nod at Lucy when she responds appropriately. In fact, almost all the adults Lucy comes into contact with at school make an extra effort to smile and nod at her too. All it took was asking them one time! Ms. Cruz chuckled one day when she saw all the positive sticky notes she'd been slipping to Lucy displayed inside the cover of her notebook. The school social worker helped the team learn that Lucy was feeling overwhelmed after school at home. She discovered Lucy was in charge of watching her younger sister and brother after school every day, helping them with homework, and for starting supper. The social worker met with the family and brainstormed solutions. They worked out an arrangement with an aunt who relieved Lucy of some of these duties. Lucy's parents said they didn't realize this was stressing Lucy out so much. Lucy was then able to join an after-school homework group at school herself, which boosted her confidence with class work. She's also made friends with her peer tutor, Katy, who sits near her in class. In fact, Katy has asked Lucy to join an after-school cheerleading club with her, too.

Ms. Cruz knew that Jamar took a lot of her time, and after collecting data and talking it over with the team, she developed positive ways to fill his attention tank. The self-monitoring system using the recorded beeps onto the MP3 player seemed to help him the most. When he realized how often he was calling out, he was surprised. He kept track of his calling out and hand-raising behaviors on the computer every day and was motivated to "beat his score." Once he got a handle on the calling-out behaviors, Ms. Cruz targeted the homework with a contract and a new goal for his self-monitoring. It's amazing that, besides the computer, the reinforcer that worked best for him was simply eating lunch with Ms. Cruz on Fridays. Jamar used to have trouble getting along with peers, but now the other students see him as a positive role model and they think he looks very cool wearing the MP3 player. He is now a peer-buddy to the new student in the class, and he acts as the recorder for a group contract based on the one Ms. Cruz developed for him. He is using a computer template to create a weekly and monthly schedule for himself that he prints out and keeps in his notebook. He is also using a checklist to keep up with materials. These days, Ms. Cruz actually looks forward to spending time with him. Jamar is also enjoying time doing things with his new mentor that the counselor provided for him. Today they are playing basketball together after school and then they will work on a rap they are writing to summarize the story Jamar is reading for homework. Jamar hopes to present it to the class later this week.

Zack has made good progress during this marking period, too. He is regaining some of his writing skills using word processing, word prediction, and graphic organizer software on the computer. Interactive digital books are also helping him with characterization. He is also keeping a daily journal on his laptop to reflect on his positive and negative feelings each day. Sometimes he uses clip art and a drawing program to describe his feelings. Using these technologies has reduced some of his frustration/anxiety with writing and have helped him express his emotions. Ms. Cruz is still concerned about his anger but she can see from her ongoing data collection that the number of Zack's outbursts are decreasing. Zack keeps his daily schedule on his personal PDA that his parents bought for him for his birthday. He keeps a list of his schedule and what he needs every day in his personal study carrel in the classroom. The hand signal they came up (a gesture for "stop") helps everyone in the class recognize when he needs to have some space and regroup. Having that personal study carrel for "time in" has made a huge difference. His other teachers have used the idea also. Ms. Smith, the school's behavioral interventionist, has also helped by doing some role playing with Zack during his homeroom time to help him deal with his anger. She found some cool role-playing software, too. She loaded it on his laptop so Zack can observe and practice what he might do when he finds himself in difficulty situations as needed. Both teachers are thinking they might share some of these role plays with the whole class. When the class reads "Hatchet" next month, for example, they are already thinking about integrating some role play with dealing with loss and adaptation in hard times. Zack's parents have been behind Ms. Cruz 100 percent and are pleased with Zack's progress also. They continue to work faithfully working with the school and Zack's medical professionals since the accident.

Although during the first few weeks of school Ms. Cruz wondered how she would meet the needs of all her students, she now finds that by supporting each student, applying the principles or UDL to positive behavior supports, the whole class benefits!

Thematic Summary

- Inappropriate student behavior falls along a continuum and includes both internalizing and externalizing characteristics. Problematic behaviors serve various functions including communication, avoidance, and attention seeking.
- It is important to operationally define a target behavior in observable and measurable terms before an intervention is planned. An efficient and effective method of recording will help assure the accuracy of the results. Technology facilitates this process.
- Positive reinforcement can be used to increase appropriate behavior. Teachers should catch students being good and offer immediate and specific praise for prosocial actions.
- Teachers can help students become more independent by encouraging their efforts and instructing and modeling specific self-management strategies.
- Generalization and maintenance are important steps in the process of learning new behaviors. School personnel can assist classroom teachers in reinforcing prosocial interactions in different settings throughout the school.

Making Connections for Inclusive Teaching

1. Revisit the pyramid illustration for positive behavior support on page 409 of this chapter and the pyramid used for differentiated instruction on page 272 in Chapter 10. Compare and contrast these two visual representations.
2. Discuss the benefits of collaborative partnerships within the school and home in supporting positive behaviors.
3. Name four externalizing behaviors you have observed and speculate about the reason for each. Name one replacement behavior for each, and suggest one strategy to help reinforce it.
4. List additional learning tools that can be used to target and track problematic behaviors.
5. Discuss how you can use good instructional strategies to teach a social behavior.
6. Help Ms. Cruz develop a behavior intervention plan for Lucy, Jamar, or Zack by completing this worksheet for the collaborative team meeting.

Collaborative Team Worksheet

I. Operational Definition of Challenging Behavior _____
II. Purpose(s) of Behavior _____
III. Name Replacement Behavior(s) _____
IV. What has worked in the past?
  A. What was reinforcing? _____
  B. What was punishing? _____

V. Strategies to Meet the Need: What supports are needed?
   A. Change Environment
   B. Change Antecedents
   C. Change Consequences
   D. Teach Replacement Behavior
   E. Use Self-Management
   F. Build in Generalization

Learning Activities

1. Observe a general education classroom for at least one hour. During the first half-hour, keep a running list of appropriate and inappropriate student behaviors. Then choose one student and one externalizing behavior to track for at least 15 consecutive minutes. Choose an appropriate method of recording, depending on the target behavior. Afterwards, suggest strategies for this student to increase his/her positive behaviors and decrease his/her negative ones.

2. Develop a reinforcement menu survey for either elementary or secondary school-aged students. Make sure the instructions and the choices are age appropriate. List material/tangible, activity, and token reinforcers. If possible, allow students to complete the survey. Afterwards, tally the results and plan how the reinforcers will be awarded.

3. Write a contract for Lucy, Zack, or a student you have observed. Include each of the five elements listed in Jamar's contract.

4. Use one type of differential reinforcement to develop a behavioral support plan for Lucy, Zack, or Jamar, or a student you have observed. First state the operational definition of the problematic behavior. Then state the operational definition of the positive behavior you will reinforce. Include at least two types of reinforcers in your plan.

5. Participate in a role-play activity with half the group representing teachers and the other half playing the part of parents. The teachers will practice calling the parents to set up a meeting about a particularly challenging student behavior. They will have the opportunity to hone their diplomatic skills, as the parents will resist any intimation that there is a problem with their "perfect" child.

6. Attend a community meeting for families with children with disabilities. Note the social and behavioral issues that are discussed. Record problems and potential solutions suggested by the members. Also, record information concerning parents' attitudes toward their children's school and teachers. Suggest ways to improve collaborative efforts. Meeting suggestions:
   a. Council for Exceptional Children (CEC)
   b. Learning Disabilities Association
   c. Association for Retarded Citizens (ARC)
   d. Autism Society
   e. Children and Adults with Attention Deficit/Hyperactivity Disorder (CHADD)

7. Watch a movie in which the main character has a disability. Note the interactions of this person with others. How does he or she relate in social situations? What appropriate or inappropriate behaviors do you see? Make a list of behaviors you would like to increase, decrease, or teach this person. Some movie suggestions: *My Left Foot, Regarding Henry, As Good As It Gets, Children of a Lesser God, Dominick & Eugene, The Other Sister, Nell, What's Eating Gilbert Grape, The Eighth Day.*

Looking at the Standards

INTASC Standards

- *Student Development*. The teacher understands how children learn and develop, and can provide learning opportunities that support their intellectual, social, and personal development.
- *Motivation and Management*. The teacher understands and uses a variety of instructional strategies to encourage students' development of critical thinking, problem solving, and performance skills.
- *School and Community Involvement*. The teacher fosters relationships with school colleagues, parents, and agencies in the larger community to support students learning and well-being.

Council for Exceptional Children

Special educators are to have knowledge of the following:

- GC2K4: Psychological and social-emotional characteristics of individuals with disabilities.
- CC4S5: Use procedures to increase the individual's self-awareness, self-management, self-control, self-reliance, and self-esteem.
- GC4S1: Use research-supported methods for academic and nonacademic instruction of individuals with disabilities.
- CC5S10: Use effective and varied behavior management strategies.
- GC7S1: Plan and implement individualized reinforcement systems and environmental modifications at levels equal to the intensity of the behavior.
- GC8S1: Implement procedures for assessing and reporting both appropriate and problematic social behaviors of individuals with disabilities.
- CC9K2: Importance of the teacher serving as a model for individuals with exceptional learning needs.

Key Concepts and Terms

externalizing behaviors
internalizing behaviors
positive behavior support (PBS)
operational definition
baseline data
anecdotal recording
antecedent
consequence
frequency/event recording
discrete behaviors
time sampling
continuous behavior
self-management

functional behavior assessments
behavior intervention plans
reinforcement
punishment
contingently reinforced
material reinforcers
activity reinforcement
token reinforcers
vicarious reinforcement
differential reinforcement
extinction
time-out from positive reinforcement

inclusion time-out
contingent observation
exclusion time-out
response cost
natural consequences
locus of control
behavioral contracts
self-management
self-instruction
self-monitoring
self-reinforcement
maintenance
generalization

References

Achenbach, T. M., & McConaughy, S. H. (1997). *Empirically based assessment of child and adolescent psychopathology: Practical applications* (2nd ed.). Thousand Oaks, CA: Sage.

Alberto, P. A., & Troutman, A. C. (2009). *Applied behavior analysis for teachers* (8th ed.). Upper Saddle River, NJ: Pearson Education.

Arter, R. S. (2007). The positive alternative learning supports program: Collaborating to improve student success. *Teaching Exceptional Children, 40*(2), 38–46.

Artesani, A. J. (2001). *Understanding the purpose of challenging behavior: A guide to conducting functional assessments.* Upper Saddle River, NJ: Pearson Education.

Beirne-Smith, M., Ittenbach, R. F., & Patton, J. R. (2002). *Mental retardation* (7th ed.). Upper Saddle River, NJ: Pearson Education.

Brock, M. A. (2005). A social-behavioral learning strategy intervention for a child with Asperger syndrome. *Remedial and Special Education, 28,* 258–265.

Cartledge, G., Tillman, L. C., & Johnson, C. T. (2001). Professional ethics within the context of student discipline and diversity. *Teacher Education and Special Education, 24,* 25–37.

Cline, S., & Schwartz, D. (1999). *Diverse populations of gifted children.* Upper Saddle River, NJ: Pearson Education.

Colvin, G., Sugai, G., & Patching, B. (1993). Precorrection: An instructional approach for managing predictable problem behaviors. *Intervention in School and Clinic, 28,* 143–150.

Cooper, J. O., Heron, T. E., & Heward, W. L. (2007). *Applied behavior analysis* (2nd ed.). Upper Saddle River, NJ: Pearson Education

Cullinan, D. (2007). Students with emotional and behavior disorders: An introduction for teachers and other helping professionals (2nd ed.). Upper Saddle River, NJ: Pearson Education.

Darch, C. B., & Kame'enui, E. J. (2004). *Instructional classroom management: A proactive approach to behavior management* (2nd ed.). Upper Saddle River, NJ: Pearson Education.

Darch, C., Miller, A., & Shippen, P. (1998). Instructional classroom management: A proactive model for managing student behavior. *Beyond Behavior, 9,* 18–27.

ERIC Clearinghouse on Disabilities and Gifted Education. (1991). *Communicating with culturally diverse parent of exceptional children.* Reston, VA: U.S. Department of Education.

Flint, L. J. (2001). Challenges of identifying and serving gifted children with ADHD. *Teaching Exceptional Children, 33*(4), 62–69.

Frey, L. M., & Wilhite, K. (2005). Our five basic needs: Application for understanding the function of behavior. *Intervention in School and Clinic, 40,* 156–160.

Grey, I. M., Bruton, C., Honan, R., McGuiness, R., & Daly, M. (2007). Co-operative learning for children with an autistic spectrum disorder (ASD) in mainstream and special class settings: An exploratory study. *Educational Psychology in Practice, 23,* 317–327.

Gunter, P. L., Miller, K. A., Venn, M. L., Thomas, K., & House, S. (2002). Self-graphing to success: Computerize data management. *Teaching Exceptional Children, 35*(2), 30–34.

Hallahan, D. P., & Kauffman, J. M. (2005). *Exceptional learners: Introduction to special education* (10th ed.). Boston: Allyn & Bacon.

Jolivette, K., Stichter, J. P., & McCormick, K. M. (2002). Making choices—improving behavior—engaging in learning. *Teaching Exceptional Children, 34*(3), 24–30.

Kandel, M. W. (2000). When students say "NO!" *CEC Today, 7,* 12–13.

Kauffman, J. M., Mostert, M. P., Trent, S. C., & Pullen, P. L. (2006). *Managing classroom behavior: A reflective case-based approach* (4th ed.). Boston: Pearson Education.

Kerr, M. M., & Nelson, C. M. (2006). *Strategies for addressing behavior problems in the classroom* (5th ed.). Upper Saddle River, NJ: Pearson Education.

Lane, K. L., Wehby, J. H., & Cooley, C. (2006). Teacher expectations of students' classroom behavior across the grade span: Which social skills are necessary for success? *Exceptional Children, 72,* 153–167.

Larson, P. J., & Maag, J. W. (1998). Applying functional assessment in general education classrooms: Issues and recommendations. *Remedial and Special Education, 19,* 338–349.

Lassen, S. R., Steele, M., & Sailor, W. (2006). The relationship of school-wide positive behavior support to academic achievement in an urban middle school. *Psychology in the schools, 43*(6), 701–712.

Maag, J. W. (2001). Rewarded by punishment: Reflections on the disuse of positive reinforcement in schools. *Exceptional Children, 67,* 173–186.

McGinnis, E., & Goldstein, A. P. (1997). *Skillstreaming the elementary school child: New strategies and perspectives for teaching prosocial skills* (Rev. ed.). Champaign, IL: Research Press.

Melloy, K. (2000). Development of aggression replacement behaviors in adolescents with emotional behavioral disorders. *Beyond Behavior, 10,* 8–13.

Montgomery, W. (2001). Creating culturally responsive, inclusive classrooms. *Teaching Exceptional Children, 33*(4), 4–9.

Office of Special Education (2007). What is secondary prevention? Retrieved on August 1, 2008, from http://www.pbis.org/secondaryprevention.htm

Parette, H. P., & Petch-Hogan, B. P. (2000). Approaching families: Facilitating culturally/linguistically diverse family involvement. *Teaching Exceptional Children, 33*(2), 4–10.

Rock, M. L. (2005). Use of strategic self-monitoring to enhance academic engagement, productivity, and accuracy of students with and without exceptionalities. *Journal of Positive Behavior Interventions, 7,* 3–17.

Romaneck, G. M. (2001). Proactive approaches to help students control their anger. *CEC Today, 7,* 1, 9, 13.

Ryan, J. B., Sanders, S., Kasiyannis, A., & Yell, M. L. (2007). Using time-out effectively in the classroom. *Teaching Exceptional Children, 39*(4), 60–67.

Salend, S. J. (2005). *Creating inclusive classrooms: Effective and reflective practices for all students* (5th ed.). Upper Saddle River, NJ: Pearson Education.

Salend, S. J., & Gordon, B. D. (1987). A group-oriented timeout ribbon procedure. *Behavioral Disorders, 12,* 131–137.

Salend, S. & Taylor, L. (2002). Cultural perspectives: Missing pieces in the functional assessment process. *Intervention in School and Clinic, 39*(2), 104–112.

Saunders, M. D. (2001). Who's getting the message? Helping your students understand in a verbal world. *Teaching Exceptional Children, 33*(4), 70–74.

Scheuermann, B. K., & Hall, J. A. (2008). *Positive behavioral supports for the classroom.* Upper Saddle River, NJ: Pearson Education.

Schloss, P. J., & Smith, M. A. (1998). Applied behavior analysis in the classroom (2nd ed.). Boston: Allyn & Bacon.

Skiba, R., & Raison, J. (1990). Relationship between the use of timeout and academic achievement. *Exceptional Children, 57,* 36–46.

Smith, B. W., & Sugai, G. (2000). A self-management functional assessment-based behavior support plan for a middle school student with EBD. *Journal of Positive Behavior Interventions, 2,* 208–217.

Smith, R. M., Salend, S. J., & Ryan, S. (2001). Watch your language: Closing or opening the special education curtain. *Teaching Exceptional Children, 33*(4), 18–23.

Sugai, G., & Horner, R. (2007). SW-PBS & Rtl: Lessons being learned. University of Connecticut & Oregon: OSEP Center on PBIS. Retrieved October 28, 2008, from http://www.pbis .org/files/gsrti2007.ppt

Sugai, G., Lewis-Palmer, T., & Hagan-Burke, S. (2000). Overview of the functional behavioral assessment process. *Exceptionality, 8*(3), 149–160.

Walker, H. M., & Severson, H. (1992). *Systematic screening for behavior disorders* (2nd ed.). Longmont, CO: Sopris West.

Walker, R. (2007). Ten critical behavior management strategies. Retrieved on July 20, 2008, from http://www.volusia.k12.fl .us/ese/Final%20Ten%20Critical%20Behavior%20Mangage ment%20Ron%20Walker%2008-07-07.pdf

White, A. G., & Bailey, J. S. (1990). Reducing disruptive behaviors of elementary physical education students with sit and watch. *Journal of Applied Behavior Analysis, 23,* 353–359.

Zirpoli, T. J. (2005). *Behavior management: Application for teachers* (4th ed.). Upper Saddle River, NJ: Pearson Education.

Zuna, N., & McDougall, D. (2004). Using positive behavioral support to manage avoidance of academic tasks. *Teaching Exceptional Children, 37*(1), 18–24.

Interstate New Teacher Assessment and Support Consortium (INTASC) Standards

1. **Content Pedagogy**
   The teacher understands the central concepts, tools of inquiry, and structures of the discipline he or she teaches and can create learning experiences that make these aspects of subject matter meaningful for students.

2. **Student Development**
   The teacher understands how children learn and develop, and can provide learning opportunities that support their intellectual, social, and personal development.

3. **Diverse Learners**
   The teacher understands how students differ in their approaches to learning and creates instructional opportunities that are adapted to diverse learners.

4. **Multiple Instructional Strategies**
   The teacher understands and uses a variety of instructional strategies to encourage students' development of critical thinking, problem solving, and performance skills.

5. **Motivation and Management**
   The teacher uses an understanding of individual and group motivation and behavior to create a learning environment that encourages positive social interaction, active engagement in learning, and self-motivation.

6. **Communication and Technology**
   The teacher uses knowledge of effective verbal, nonverbal, and media communication techniques to foster active inquiry, collaboration, and supportive interaction in the classroom.

7. **Planning**
   The teacher plans instruction based upon knowledge of subject matter, students, the community, and curriculum goals.

8. **Assessment**
   The teacher understands and uses formal and informal assessment strategies to evaluate and ensure the continuous intellectual, social, and physical development of the learner.

9. **Reflective Practice: Professional Growth**
   The teacher is a reflective practitioner who continually evaluates the effects of his or her choices and actions on others (students, parents, and other professionals in the learning community) and who actively seeks out opportunities to grow professionally.

10. **School and Community Involvement**
    The teacher fosters relationships with school colleagues, parents, and agencies in the larger community to support students' learning and well-being.

Source: Adapted from Council of Chief State School Officers, *Model Standards for Beginning Teacher Licensing, Assessment, and Development: A Resource for State Dialogue* (Washington, DC: Author, 1992).

Council for Exceptional Children Knowledge and Skill Base Standards for All Entry-Level Special Education Teachers

1. Foundations

CC1K1	Models, theories, and philosophies that form the basis for special education practice.
CC1K2	Laws, policies, and ethical principles regarding behavior management planning and implementation.
CC1K3	Relationship of special education to the organization and function of educational agencies.
CC1K4	Rights and responsibilities of students, parents, teachers, and other professionals, and schools related to exceptional learning needs.
CC1K5	Issues in definition and identification of individuals with exceptional learning needs, including those from culturally and linguistically diverse backgrounds.
CC1K6	Issues, assurances, and due process rights related to assessment, eligibility, and placement within a continuum of services.
CC1K7	Family systems and the role of families in the educational process.
CC1K8	Historical points of view and contribution of culturally diverse groups.
CC1K9	Impact of the dominant culture on shaping schools and the individuals who study and work in them.
CC1K10	Potential impact of differences in values, languages, and customs that can exist between the home and school.
GC1K1	Definitions and issues related to the identification of individuals with disabilities.
GC1K2	Models and theories of deviance and behavior problems.
GC1K3	Historical foundations, classic studies, major contributors, major legislation, and current issues related to knowledge and practice.
GC1K4	The legal, judicial, and educational systems to assist individuals with disabilities.
GC1K5	Continuum of placement and services available for individuals with disabilities.
GC1K6	Laws and policies related to provision of specialized health care in educational settings.
GC1K7	Factors that influence the overrepresentation of culturally/linguistically diverse students in programs for individuals with disabilities.
GC1K8	Principles of normalization and concept of least restrictive environment.
GC1K9	Theory of reinforcement techniques in serving individuals with disabilities.
CC1S1	Articulate personal philosophy of special education.

2. Development and Characteristics of Learners

CC2K1	Typical and atypical human growth and development.
CC2K2	Educational implications of characteristics of various exceptionalities.
CC2K3	Characteristics and effects of the cultural and environmental milieu of the individual with exceptional learning needs and the family.
CC2K4	Family systems and the role of families in supporting development.
CC2K5	Similarities and differences of individuals with and without exceptional learning needs.
CC2K6	Similarities and differences among individuals with exceptional learning needs.
CC2K7	Effects of various medications on individuals with exceptional learning needs.

GC2K1   Etiology and diagnosis related to various theoretical approaches.

GC2K2   Impact of sensory impairments, physical and health disabilities on individuals, families, and society.

GC2K3   Etiologies and medical aspects of conditions affecting individuals with disabilities.

GC2K4   Psychological and social-emotional characteristics of individuals with disabilities.

GC2K5   Common etiologies and the impact of sensory disabilities on learning and experience.

GC2K6   Types and transmission routes of infectious disease.

3. Individual Learning Differences

CC3K1   Effects an exceptional condition(s) can have on an individual's life.

CC3K2   Impact of learners' academic and social abilities, attitudes, interests, and values on instruction and career development.

CC3K3   Variations in beliefs, traditions, and values across and within cultures and their effects on relationships among individuals with exceptional learning needs, family, and schooling.

CC3K4   Cultural perspectives influencing the relationships among families, schools, and communities as related to instruction.

CC3K5   Differing ways of learning of individuals with exceptional learning needs including those from culturally diverse backgrounds and strategies for addressing these differences.

GC3K1   Impact of disabilities on auditory and information processing skills.

GC3S1   Relate levels of support to the needs of the individual.

4. Instructional Strategies

GC4K1   Sources of specialized materials, curricula, and resources for individuals with disabilities.

GC4K2   Strategies to prepare for and take tests.

GC4K3   Advantages and limitations of instructional strategies and practices for teaching individuals with disabilities.

GC4K4   Prevention and intervention strategies for individuals at risk for a disability.

GC4K5   Strategies for integrating student-initiated learning experiences into ongoing instruction.

GC4K6   Methods for increasing accuracy and proficiency in math calculations and applications.

GC4K7   Methods for guiding individuals in identifying and organizing critical content.

CC4S1   Use strategies to facilitate integration into various settings.

CC4S2   Teach individuals to use self-assessment, problem-solving, and other cognitive strategies to meet their needs.

CC4S3   Select, adapt, and use instructional strategies and materials according to characteristics of the individual with exceptional learning needs.

CC4S4   Use strategies to facilitate maintenance and generalization of skills across learning environments.

CC4S5   Use procedures to increase the individual's self-awareness, self-management, self-control, self-reliance, and self-esteem.

CC4S6   Use strategies that promote successful transitions for individuals with exceptional learning needs.

GC4S1   Use research-supported methods for academic and nonacademic instruction of individuals with disabilities.

GC4S2   Use strategies from multiple theoretical approaches for individuals with disabilities.

GC4S3   Teach learning strategies and study skills to acquire academic content.

GC4S4   Use reading methods appropriate to individuals with disabilities.

GC4S5   Use methods to teach mathematics appropriate to the individuals with disabilities.

GC4S6   Modify pace of instruction and provide organizational cures.

GC4S7   Use appropriate adaptations and technology for all individuals with disabilities.

GC4S8   Resources and techniques used to transition individuals with disabilities into and out of school and post school environments.

GC4S9   Use a variety of nonaversive techniques to control targeted behavior and maintain attention of individuals with disabilities.

GC4S10   Identify and teach basic structures and relationships within and across curricula.

GC4S11   Use instructional methods to strengthen and compensate for deficits in perception, comprehension, memory, and retrieval.

GC4S12   Use responses and errors to guide instructional decisions and provide feedback to learners.

GC4S13   Identify and teach essential concepts, vocabulary, and content across the general curriculum.

GC4S14   Implement systematic instruction in teaching reading comprehension and monitoring strategies.

GC4S15   Teach strategies for organizing and composing written products.

| GC4S16 | Implement systematic instruction to teach accuracy, fluency, and comprehensive in content area reading and written language. |

5. Learning Environments and Social Interactions

CC5K1	Demands of learning environments.
CC5K2	Basic classroom management theories and strategies for individuals with exceptional learning needs.
CC5K3	Effective management of teaching and learning.
CC5K4	Teacher attitudes and behaviors that influence behavior of individuals with exceptional learning needs.
CC5K5	Social skills needed for educational and other environments.
CC5K6	Strategies for crisis prevention and intervention.
CC5K7	Strategies for preparing individuals to live harmoniously and productively in a culturally diverse world.
CC5K8	Ways to create learning environments that allow individuals to retain and appreciate their own and each others' respective language and cultural heritage.
CC5K9	Ways specific cultures are negatively stereotyped.
CC5K10	Strategies used by diverse populations to cope with a legacy of former and continuing racism.
GC5K1	Barriers to accessibility and acceptance of individuals with disabilities.
GC5K2	Adaptation of the physical environment to provide optimal learning opportunities for individuals with disabilities.
GC5K3	Methods for ensuring individual academic success in one-to-one, small-group, and large-group settings.
CC5S1	Create a safe, equitable, positive, and supportive learning environment in which diversities are valued.
CC5S2	Identify realistic expectations for personal and social behavior in various settings.
CC5S3	Identify supports needed for integration into various program placements.
CC5S4	Design learning environments that encourage active participation in individual and group activities.
CC5S5	Modify the learning environment to manage behaviors.
CC5S6	Use performance data and information from all stakeholders to make or suggest modifications in learning environments.
CC5S7	Establish and maintain rapport with individuals with and without exceptional learning needs.
CC5S8	Teach self-advocacy.
CC5S9	Create an environment that encourages self-advocacy and increased independence.
CC5S10	Use effective and varied behavior management strategies.
CC5S11	Use the least intensive behavior management strategy consistent with the needs of the individual with exceptional learning needs.
CC5S12	Design and manage daily routines.
CC5S13	Organize, develop, and sustain learning environments that support positive intracultural and intercultural experiences.
CC5S14	Mediate controversial intercultural issues among students within the learning environment in ways that enhance any culture, group, or person.
CC5S15	Structure, direct, and support the activities of paraeducators, volunteers, and tutors.
CC5S16	Use universal precautions.
GC5S1	Provide instruction in community-based settings.
GC5S2	Use and maintain assistive technologies.
GC5S3	Plan instruction in a variety of educational settings.
GC5S4	Teach individuals with disabilities to give and receive meaningful feedback from peers and adults.
GC5S5	Use skills in problem-solving and conflict resolution.
GC5S6	Establish a consistent classroom routine for individuals with disabilities.

6. Language

CC6K1	Effects of cultural and linguistic differences on growth and development.
CC6K2	Characteristics of one's own culture and use of language and the ways in which these can differ from other cultures and uses of languages.
CC6K3	Ways of behaving and communicating among cultures that can lead to misinterpretation and misunderstanding.
CC6K4	Augmentative and assistive communication strategies.

GC6K1	Impact of language development and listening comprehension on academic and nonacademic learning of individuals with disabilities.
GC6K2	Communication and social interaction alternatives for individuals who are nonspeaking.
GC6K3	Typical language development and how that may differ for individuals with learning disabilities.
CC6S1	Use strategies to support and enhance communication skills of individuals with exceptional learning needs.
CC6S2	Use communication strategies and resources to facilitate understanding of subject matter for students whose primary language is not the dominant language.
GC6S1	Enhance vocabulary development.
GC6S2	Teach strategies for spelling accuracy and generalization.
GC6S3	Teach individuals with disabilities to monitor for errors in oral and written language.
GC6S4	Teach methods and strategies for producing legible documents.
GC6S5	Plan instruction on the use of alternative and augmentative communication systems.

7. Instructional Planning

CC7K1	Theories and research that form the basis of curriculum development and instructional practice.
CC7K2	Scope and sequences of general and special curricula.
CC7K3	National, state or provincial, and local curricula standards.
CC7K4	Technology for planning and managing the teaching and learning environment.
CC7K5	Roles and responsibilities of the paraeducator related to instruction, intervention, and direct service.
GC7K1	Integrate academic instruction and behavior management for individuals and groups with disabilities.
GC7K2	Model career, vocational, and transition programs for individuals with disabilities.
GC7K3	Interventions and services for children who may be at risk for learning disabilities.
GC7K4	Relationships among disabilities and reading instruction.
CC7S1	Identify and prioritize areas of the general curriculum and accommodations for individuals with exceptional learning needs.
CC7S2	Develop and implement comprehensive, longitudinal individualized programs in collaboration with team members.
CC7S3	Involve the individual and family in setting instructional goals and monitoring progress.
CC7S4	Use functional assessments to develop intervention plans.
CC7S5	Use task analysis.
CC7S6	Sequence, implement, and evaluate individualized learning objectives.
CC7S7	Integrate affective, social, and life skills with academic curricula.
CC7S8	Develop and select instructional content, resources, and strategies that respond to cultural, linguistic, and gender differences.
CC7S9	Incorporate and implement instructional and assistive technology into the educational program.
CC7S10	Prepare lesson plans.
CC7S11	Prepare and organize materials to implement daily lesson plans.
CC7S12	Use instructional time effectively.
CC7S13	Make responsive adjustments to instruction based on continual observations.
CC7S14	Prepare individuals to exhibit self-enhancing behavior in response to societal attitudes and actions.
GC7S1	Plan and implement individualized reinforcement systems and environmental modifications at levels equal to the intensity of the behavior.
GC7S2	Select and use specialized instructional strategies appropriate to the abilities and needs of the individual.
GC7S3	Plan and implement age- and ability-appropriate instruction for individuals with disabilities.
GC7S4	Select, design, and use technology, materials, and resources required to educate individuals whose disabilities interfere with communication.
GC7S5	Interpret sensory, mobility, reflex, and perceptual information to create or adapt appropriate learning plans.
GC7S6	Design and implement instructional programs that address independent living and career education for individuals.
GC7S7	Design and implement curriculum and instructional strategies for medical self-management procedures.
GC7S8	Design, implement, and evaluate instructional programs that enhance social participation across environments.

8. Assessment

CC8K1	Basic terminology used in assessment.
CC8K2	Legal provisions and ethical principles regarding assessment of individuals.
CC8K3	Screening, prereferral, referral, and classification procedures.
CC8K4	Use and limitations of assessment instruments.
CC8K5	National, state or provincial, and local accommodations and modifications.
GC8K1	Specialized terminology used in the assessment of individuals with disabilities.
GC8K2	Laws and policies regarding referral and placement procedures for individuals with disabilities.
GC8K3	Types and importance of information concerning individuals with disabilities available from families and public agencies.
GC8K4	Procedures for early identification of young children who may be at risk for disabilities.
CC8S1	Gather relevant background information.
CC8S2	Administer nonbiased formal and informal assessments.
CC8S3	Use technology to conduct assessments.
CC8S4	Develop or modify individualized assessment strategies.
CC8S5	Interpret information from formal and informal assessments.
CC8S6	Use assessment information in making eligibility, program, and placement decisions for individuals with exceptional learning needs, including those from culturally and/or linguistically diverse backgrounds.
CC8S7	Report assessment results to all stakeholders using effective communication skills.
CC8S8	Evaluate instruction and monitor progress of individuals with exceptional learning needs.
CC8S9	Develop or modify individualized assessment strategies.
CC8S10	Create and maintain records.
GC8S1	Implement procedures for assessing and reporting both appropriate and problematic social behaviors of individuals with disabilities.
GC8S2	Use exceptionality-specific assessment instruments with individuals with disabilities.
GC8S3	Select, adapt and modify assessments to accommodate the unique abilities and needs of individuals with disabilities.
GC8S4	Assess reliable methods of response of individuals who lack typical communication and performance abilities.
GC8S5	Monitor intragroup behavior changes across subjects and activities.

9. Professional and Ethical Practice

CC9K1	Personal cultural biases and differences that affect one's teaching.
CC9K2	Importance of the teacher serving as a model for individuals with exceptional learning needs.
CC9K3	Continuum of lifelong professional development.
CC9K4	Methods to remain current regarding research-validated practice.
GC9K1	Sources of unique services, networks, and organizations for individuals with disabilities.
GC9K2	Organizations and publications relevant to individuals with disabilities.
CC9S1	Practice within the CEC Code of Ethics and other standards of the profession.
CC9S2	Uphold high standards of competence and integrity and exercise sound judgment in the practice of the professional.
CC9S3	Act ethically in advocating for appropriate services.
CC9S4	Conduct professional activities in compliance with applicable laws and policies.
CC9S5	Demonstrate commitment to developing the highest education and quality-of-life potential of individuals with exceptional learning needs.
CC9S6	Demonstrate sensitivity for the culture, language, religion, gender, disability, socioeconomic status, and sexual orientation of individuals.
CC9S7	Practice within one's skill limit and obtain assistance as needed.
CC9S8	Use verbal, nonverbal, and written language effectively.
CC9S9	Conduct self evaluation of instruction.
CC9S10	Access information on exceptionalities.
CC9S11	Reflect on one's practice to improve instruction and guide professional growth.
CC9S12	Engage in professional activities that benefit individuals with exceptional learning needs, their families, and one's colleagues.

| GC9S1 | Participate in the activities of professional organizations relevant to individuals with disabilities. |
| GC9S2 | Ethical responsibility to advocate for appropriate services for individuals with disabilities. |

10. Collaboration

CC1OK1	Models and strategies of consultation and collaboration.
CC1OK2	Roles of individuals with exceptional learning needs, families, and school and community personnel in planning of an individualized program.
CC1OK3	Concerns of families of individuals with exceptional learning needs and strategies to help address these concerns.
CC1OK4	Culturally responsive factors that promote effective communication and collaboration with individuals with exceptional learning needs, families, school personnel, and community members.
GC1OK1	Parent education programs and behavior management guides that address severe behavior problems and facilitation communication for individuals with disabilities.
GC1OK2	Collaborative and/or consultative role of the special education teacher in the reintegration of individuals with disabilities.
GC1OK3	Roles of professional groups and referral agencies in identifying, assessing, and providing services to individuals with disabilities.
GC1OK4	Co-planning and co-teaching methods to strengthen content acquisition of individuals with learning disabilities.
CC10S1	Maintain confidential communication about individuals with exceptional learning needs.
CC10S2	Collaborate with families and others in assessment of individuals with exceptional learning needs.
CC10S3	Foster respectful and beneficial relationships between families and professionals.
CC10S4	Assist individuals with exceptional learning needs and their families in becoming active participants in the educational team.
CC10S5	Plan and conduct collaborative conferences with individuals with exceptional learning needs and their families.
CC10S6	Collaborate with school personnel and community members in integrating individuals with exceptional learning needs into various settings.
CC10S7	Use group problem-solving skills to develop, implement, and evaluate collaborative activities.
CC10S8	Model techniques and coach others in the use of instructional methods and accommodations.
CC10S9	Communicate with school personnel about the characteristics and needs of individuals with exceptional learning needs.
CC10S10	Communicate effectively with families of individuals with exceptional learning needs from diverse backgrounds.
CC10S11	Observe, evaluate, and provide feedback to paraeducators.
GC10S1	Use local community, and state and provincial resources to assist in programming with individuals with disabilities.
GC10S2	Select, plan, and coordinate activities of related services personnel to maximize direct instructions for individuals with disabilities.
GC10S3	Teach parents to use appropriate behavior management and counseling techniques.
GC10S4	Collaborate with team members to plan transition to adulthood that encourages full community participation.

Source: Council for Exceptional Children, *What Every Special Educator Must Know: Ethics, Standards, and Guidelines for Special Educators* (5th ed.) (Upper Saddle River, NJ: Pearson Education, 2005), pp. 54–60.

Glossary

absence seizures   A common seizure disorder that causes an individual to lose consciousness, stop moving, and stare straight ahead.

abstract   The level of learning in mathematics in which students manipulate symbols without the use of concrete objects or pictorial representations.

ACCESS   An acronym for the basic principles of universal design that can be used to assess the classroom setting (Applicable, Capability, Clarity, Expression, Safety, and Size/Space).

accommodation   Service or support that ensures the subject matter and instruction is fully accessible to students.

accommodation plan   Simple, inexpensive, and easy-to-use plan required by Section 504 that includes information necessary to enable the student to have equal access to education and extracurricular activities while also providing an equal opportunity to be successful.

achievement standards   Goals that determine what will be measured (what will be tested) and the level of mastery—along with the "how" and the "when."

acquisition stage of learning   Instructional focus on skill performance. All, most, or some of a skill needs to be learned.

activities-oriented approach   Instruction that begins with real-life discovery learning and inquiry in science and social studies. Student knowledge and understanding are based on these experiences.

activity reinforcement   An activity of choice earned by a student after exhibiting target behavior.

adaptation stage   The highest level of learning. Students independently make discoveries, problem-solve, and make decisions.

adaptive behavior   The ability to cope with the everyday demands and requirements of one's environment.

advance organizer   An outline with prompts for steps or substeps in the concept(s) being taught.

affective systems   Part of the three-part framework of brain processing that impacts the engagement or social interaction of the learner.

algebra   A big idea in mathematics that shows a functional relationship between two or more variables.

algorithm   The steps used to solve a problem in mathematics.

alphabetic principle   Linking sounds to letters, symbols, and patterns.

analytic rubrics   A scoring system used to assign points for responses on an assessment or work sample based on specific predetermined criteria.

anchor   A storyline based in a meaningful context that sets the stage for problem solving.

anchored instruction   An authentic learning approach in which real-life problem-solving situations (e.g., narrative story or case study) are used as an anchor.

anecdotal recording   To record all actions and verbalization of the target student for a predetermined length of time.

antecedent   The events that occur before the target behavior.

aphasia   The loss or impairment of language function.

articulation disorders   Errors in the production of speech sounds.

assessment   An information-gathering and decision-making process to obtain student profile of strengths and needs.

assistive technology device   Any item, piece of equipment, or product system, whether acquired commercially off the shelf, modified, or customized, that is used to increase, maintain, or improve functional capabilities of individuals with disabilities.

assistive technology service   Any service that directly assists an individual with a disability in the selection, acquisition, or use of an assistive technology device.

ataxic cerebral palsy   A type of cerebral palsy that is characterized by poor balance and equilibrium in addition to uncoordinated voluntary movement.

athetoid cerebral palsy   A type of cerebral palsy in which movements are contorted, abnormal, and purposeless.

at risk   Being affected by one or more adverse conditions that severely limit or reduce potential for success in school and later in life.

attention deficit hyperactivity disorder   A persistent pattern of inattention and/or hyperactive impulsivity that is more frequent and severe than is typically observed in individuals at a comparable level of development.

authentic learning   To meaningfully incorporate and connect classroom knowledge into the real world.

authentic literacy   Reading and writing activities that reflect events that happen in people's lives outside of school (e.g., reading newspapers and magazines or writing letters).

autism spectrum disorders   Developmental disabilities significantly affecting verbal and nonverbal communication and social interaction, usually evident before age 3, that adversely affects a child's educational performance; an umbrella term that includes five discrete childhood disorders: autism, Rett's disorder, childhood disintegrative disorder, Asperger's disorder, and pervasive developmental disorder not otherwise specified.

balanced literacy   A combination of the direct instruction of phonics, word study, and decoding, with opportunities to interact meaningfully and holistically with literature, writing, and language.

baseline data   Basic information collected before implementation of an intervention or program that is used to set realistic goals.

behavioral contracts   A written agreement that states what the student will do in order to receive a reward.

behavioral inhibition   The ability to withhold a planned response, interrupt a response that has already been initiated, and protect an ongoing activity from competing or distracting stimuli.

behavior intervention plan   A collection of interventions, techniques, and strategies to assist in supporting specific student's behavior; a plan required by Public Law 105-17 for students with disabilities who exhibit problematic behavior; a proactive intervention approach that includes a functional behavioral assessment and the use of positive behavioral supports.

benchmarks   Short-term objectives, written by teachers, which are only required in the IEPs of students with significant cognitive deficits.

big ideas   The core concepts or principles in the content areas that help learners acquire knowledge across a broad range of experiences.

bilingual education   An educational strategy whereby students whose first language is not English are instructed primarily through their native language while developing their competency and proficiency in English.

biometrics   The study of automated methods for uniquely recognizing humans based on one or more intrinsic physical or behavioral traits.

blind   An impairment in which an individual may have some light or form perception or be totally without sight.

blogs   Web-based writing spaces intended to publish journal entries, research, opinions, artwork, etc.

cause and effect   A big idea in social studies that asks the learner how the development of new ideas and technologies impact people over time.

chunking   To organize material into manageable parts to make it more accessible to learners.

ClassAct Portal   An authentic, web-based learning tool that focuses on a single topic while strategically integrating learning goals.

classroom performance system   A type of computer-based assessment that collects, compiles, and displays student data based on student responses delivered via a response device.

classroom response systems   Systems of handheld devices used to record the responses of a group of students and formatively assess; also known as "clickers."

cleft palate   A birth defect resulting in a gap in the soft palate or roof of the mouth.

clinically derived classification systems   Systems developed by psychiatrists and mental health professionals to describe childhood, adolescent, and adult mental disorders using standardized terminology.

cloze procedure   A technique in which words are deleted from a passage and the student must construct meaning from the text to fill them in.

cluster grouping   Assembling students with similar interests/needs to work on curricular big ideas with differentiated instruction.

collaboration   A cooperative partnership or relationship between two or more individuals who are working toward achieving a mutually agreed-upon goal.

collaborative consultation   A voluntary, focused, and shared problem-solving process in which one individual offers expertise and assistance to another.

color overlays   Colored transparent sheets that are placed over print that may help students see words more clearly.

communication   The exchange of ideas, information, thoughts, and feelings. It does not necessarily require speech or language.

communication aids   Tools designed to assist individuals in language and communication tasks.

community-based learning   Learning experiences that are provided physically or virtually outside the classroom setting to provide background knowledge for learning topics.

comparing and contrasting   A big idea in social studies that asks the learners to discover commonalities and better understand differences in people systems (e.g., political, social, economic, and cultural systems).

complex partial seizure   A seizure disorder that impairs consciousness and often causes a series of motor movements that may appear voluntary but are beyond the person's control.

computation fluency   Accurately and efficiently using operations to calculate numbers.

computer access aids   Tools, devices, or technologies that enable individuals with disabilities to access, interact, and productively use a computer at school or work.

concept maps   Visual organizers for a specific topic or concept used by learners to construct personal meaning and connect new information to prior knowledge.

concrete   The level of learning in mathematics in which students manipulate physical materials (e.g., cubes, blocks, tiles) to find solutions to number problems.

conductive hearing loss   Hearing loss caused by a blockage or barrier to the transmission of sound through the outer or middle ear.

consequences   The events that occur after the target behavior is observed.

conspicuous strategies   Clear, concise, explicit steps that are presented and modeled by teachers to learn content.

constancy, change, measurement   A big idea in science that helps the learner realize how some things continually occur but may change over time. This change can be measured (e.g., weather, plants, animals).

content enhancements   Interventions to help students understand major concepts, ideas, and vocabulary in a manner that is conducive to knowledge acquisition, organization, and retrieval.

content standards   Goals to help teachers define what knowledge and skills need to be taught in a subject.

contingently reinforced   The reinforcer is applied contingent on the demonstration of the target behavior.

contingent observation To require student to observe the action from a distance without being permitted to participate for a designated amount of time.

continuous behavior A student behavior that is constant.

cooperative learning A method that allows learners to work together toward a common goal in small groups or teams.

cooperative teaching An instructional approach in which a special education teacher and a general educator teach together in a general education classroom to a heterogeneous group of students, with each professional sharing in the planning and delivery of instruction.

criterion-referenced tests Tests that provide data useful for instructional planning; student performance on a task is compared to a particular level of mastery.

cues and prompts Signals, hints, or step-by-step supports used to support teaching and guide the learner. These may be verbal, visual, or physical.

culturally and linguistically diverse Pupils whose values, attitudes, norms, folkways, traditions, and belief systems are in contrast to mainstream U.S. culture.

cultural sensitivity An awareness of, respect for, and appreciation of the many factors that influence and shape the values, priorities, and perspectives of both individuals and families.

culture The attitudes, values, belief systems, norms, and traditions shared by a particular group of people that collectively form their heritage.

curriculum A set of learning opportunities for students.

curriculum-based measurement A type of assessment that uses repeated probes to directly measure and systematically chart a student's progress on academic tasks based on curricular materials and activities.

curriculum compacting An instructional procedure that adjusts curricular goals for high-ability students so that work is challenging and interesting.

cytomegalovirus A herpes virus that causes sensorineural hearing loss in children.

daily living aids Devices that increase participation in daily activities such as cooking, bathing, personal hygiene, dressing, and toilet use.

data analysis and probability A big idea in mathematics that asks the learner to collect and analyze data in order to predict future events.

deaf Failure to understand speech; limited or absent hearing for ordinary purposes of daily living.

Deaf community Individuals who are deaf or hard of hearing who see themselves as belonging to a different culture with its own language (sign language), traditions, and values.

decibels Units of sound pressure.

decision-making process A big idea in social studies that asks the learner to identify a situation that requires a decision, gather information, identify options, predict consequences, and take action to implement a decision.

developmental delay A quantitative definition based on standardized developmental assessments applied to children ages 3–9.

differential reinforcement A strategy that encourages the occurrence of behaviors different from the inappropriate behavior.

differentiated instruction An instructional process that offers teachers flexibility in ways to teach students.

digital immigrants Individuals, typically over the age of 30, who spent a childhood without most technology and technological advances.

digital natives Individuals who have spent their entire lives surrounded by technology.

digital storytelling A method of telling stories that uses a variety of multimedia tools, including photos, soundtracks, drawings, animation, and web publishing to communicate and express personal reflection.

diplegia Paralysis (or spasticity) of the legs and partly the arms.

Direct Instruction A specific teaching approach that uses sequenced tasks to teach the learner skills directly and efficiently.

discrete behavior A behavior with a definite beginning and ending.

Dolch sight words A list of 220 frequently used sight words that constitute a large percentage of words encountered by students; first compiled in 1948 by E. W. Dolch.

Duchenne muscular dystrophy An inherited disease that is characterized by progressive muscle weakness from the degeneration of the muscle fiber.

dynamic geometry software Technology used to teach geometrical concepts.

echo reading A technique in which one partner reads a sentence, phrase, or word and the other person repeats it as he/she tracks the print.

education and learning aids Tools, adaptations, software, or devices that reduce or eliminate cognitive barriers to individuals with disabilities (e.g., problem-solving memory skills and software for word prediction). Access tools may include devices such as touch screens and switches as well as mouse access.

electronic dictionary A portable handheld device used to spell check, pronounce, and define words typed into it.

emotional abuse The attack to a child's self-esteem and emotional development resulting from constant criticism, threats, humiliation, and/or the withholding of affection.

emotional disturbance A term sometimes used interchangeably with emotional or behavioral disorders.

emotional or behavioral disorders Conditions exhibiting one or more of the following characteristics over a long period of time and to a marked degree that adversely affects a child's educational performance: an inability to learn that cannot be explained by intellectual, sensory, or health factors; an inability to build or maintain satisfactory interpersonal relationships with peers and teachers; inappropriate types of behavior or feelings under normal circumstances; a general pervasive mood of unhappiness or depression; and a tendency to develop physical symptoms or fears associated with personal or school problems.

English Language Learners Persons with reduced or diminished fluency in reading, writing, or speaking English.

environmental aids   Tools, modifications, alterations, or devices that reduce or eliminate physical barriers to individuals with disabilities; e.g., switch-operated scissors, lowered counters or work spaces, adapted door knobs on cabinets, well-planned activity centers or laboratories with adapted furniture.

epilepsy   A seizure disorder.

ergonomic aids   Tools used to help complete everyday repetitive tasks in a comfortable and efficient manner without causing undue stress to the body.

error analysis   A curriculum-based assessment used to determine how students approach and solve problems. Student mistakes are systematically measured and analyzed to fine tune instruction.

essential questions   The important basic concepts in a lesson or unit in the form of questions that are used to focus and guide student learning.

etiology   Cause of disease or disability.

evidence, models, explanations   A big idea in science that helps the learner explain how things work.

evolution, equilibrium   A big idea in science that considers changes in physical states and the form/function of objects, organisms, and systems over time.

exclusion time-out   To physically remove a student from the teaching environment so that he/she receives no reinforcement from the teacher or peers.

executive functions   Self-directed behaviors.

expressive language   The production (or output) of language that is understood by and is meaningful to others.

externalizing disorders   Behaviors characterized by aggressiveness, temper tantrums, acting out, hostility, defiance, and noncompliance.

extinction   Eliminating the source of reinforcement to extinguish an undesired behavior.

field trips   Authentic learning experiences (face-to-face or virtual) that provide background knowledge for learning topics.

flow lists   Lists of vocabulary terms organized in units or topics used to help students increase their language comprehension.

fluency   The ability to quickly decode words and symbols.

fluency disorders   Problems with the rate, flow, and rhythm of speech.

foldables   3-D, interactive graphic organizers that students create by folding and cutting paper to organize information. May be used for note taking and as study guides.

formal assessment   A type of norm-referenced measure used to compare student performance to the performance of a nationally representative sample of students of the same age or grade.

form and function   A big idea in science that asks the learner to consider the shape of an object and how it relates to what it does. Form changes evolve over time as functions change.

formative assessments   Ongoing, informal assessments that occur during instruction over a specified period of time.

forward and backward chaining   A strategy used to teach either the first step (forward chaining) or the last step (backward chaining) of a task through direct instruction.

framed or masked text   A technique in which text or print of material a student is reading is highlighted or tracked using a card or paper to focus attention on specific text.

frequency   A measure of the rate at which the sound source vibrates.

frequency/event recording   A method for collecting data on a student's target behavior that is discrete and countable within a specified time period.

Fry readability index   One of several formulas available to estimate the reading level of text material.

full inclusion   A belief that all children with disabilities should be taught exclusively (with appropriate supports) in general education classrooms at neighborhood schools.

Full Option Science System   A cooperative learning model that uses discovery learning, cooperative groups, and interdisciplinary activities; teaches scientific language; and promotes the use of related equipment.

functional   Speech and language impairment without an obvious physical basis.

functional behavior assessment   A problem-solving process in which the circumstances that occur around a particular behavior are examined to identify the purpose or function of the behavior.

functionally blind   An educational description in which the primary channel of learning is through tactile or auditory means due to limited or no vision.

generalization   The ability to transfer previously learned knowledge or skills acquired in one setting to another set of circumstances or situation.

geospatial technologies   A group of tools with educational implications, including geographic information system (GIS), global positioning system (GPS), and remote sensing (RS) tools.

gifted and talented   Abilities and talents that can be demonstrated or have the potential for being developed at exceptional levels.

Global Positioning System   A constellation of satellites that orbit the earth and are accessed with receivers for navigation.

goals   One of the four curricular components of UDL; the desired outcomes for learners.

graphic novels   Books similar to comic books but longer in length, often having a complex story that is associated with a novel.

graphing calculators   Calculators that allow the user to view a pictorial representation of mathematical equations or data.

guided discovery learning   An approach learners use to construct knowledge through problem solving and arrive at their own conclusions.

health disabilities   A variety of health conditions that affect an individual's health.

hearing impairment   Disordered hearing.

hemiplegia   Paralysis (or spasticity) of the left or right side of the body.

hertz   Unit of measure for sound frequency.

high incidence disabilities   The group of four disability categories—speech or language impairments, learning disabilities, mental retardation, and emotional disturbance—that accounts for 80 percent of children ages 6–21 receiving a special education under IDEA.

holistic rubrics   A scoring system used to determine the quality of a student's response; relies more on the product or performance rather than on the actual process.

hypernasality   The emission of too many sounds through the air passages of the nose.

hyponasality   The emission of too few sounds through the nasal passage.

inclusion   The movement toward, and the practice of, educating students with disabilities and other learners with exceptionalities in general education classrooms alongside their typical peers with appropriate supports and services provided as necessary.

inclusion time-out   The least intrusive type of time-out used within whole class instruction in the general education setting. Access to positive reinforcement from the teacher and peers in classroom activities is denied for a certain amount of time.

indirect consultation   Suggestions, advice, and insight from parents and/or school practitioners to aid the classroom teacher in teaching specific students.

individualized education program   A document, developed in conjunction with the parent(s)/guardian(s), that is an individually tailored statement describing an educational plan for each learner with exceptionalities.

info murals   Representations of information in the form of large, often bigger than life-size visuals featuring many different types of messages.

informal assessment   A type of norm-referenced measure used to compare student performance to a specific criterion.

informal reading inventory   A reading assessment used to determine general reading skills levels, clues to types of errors made, and a general comprehension level.

inquiry-based instruction   A student-centered teaching method that is guided/facilitated by the teacher. Students investigate real world problems within a broader thematic framework.

integration   The social and instructional incorporation of students with disabilities into educational programs whose primary purpose is to serve typically developing individuals.

interactive whiteboards   A large electronic touch-sensitive board connected to a computer and a projection system or plasma panel display.

interdisciplinary   A model of teaming in which members perform their evaluations independently, but program development and instructional recommendations are the result of information sharing and joint planning.

interest inventories   Student questionnaires used to garner information on the special interests of students to assist in planning instruction to motivate learners.

interindividual differences   Differences between pupils.

internalizing disorders   Behaviors characterized by social withdrawal, depression, phobias, excessive shyness, and anxiety.

intervention assistance team   Group charged with constructing academic accommodations or behavioral interventions for children believed to be at risk for school failure; also commonly called teacher assistance teams, instructional support teams, or child/student study teams.

intraindividual differences   Differences within each child.

judicious review   A principle of curricular design that offers students multiple opportunities to review prior learning to increase retention.

keyword mnemonic   A memory-enhancing technique that combines abstract vocabulary that needs to be learned with words that sound similar and are already known.

KWL chart   A visual representation of what students already know (K) about the subject, what (W) students will learn, what students learned (L).

language   A rule-based method of communication involving the comprehension and use of signs and symbols by which ideas are represented.

large-scale assessments   Local or national assessments used to document teacher, school, and school system record of student progress and proficiency.

lattice multiplication   An algorithm that breaks the multiplication process down into small, manageable steps using a grid.

learned helplessness   A student's excessive dependence on adults, peers, or materials; a tendency to expect failure.

learning preferences   To teach to and through a sensory preference; also referred to as a learning modalities approach.

learning strategies approach   An instructional approach that emphasizes both the attainment of observable skills and behaviors as well as cognitive strategies that go beyond specific content areas.

learning styles inventories   Surveys that can help teachers determine the learning modalities of students.

least restrictive environment   A legal term interpreted to mean that individuals with disabilities are to be educated in environments as close as possible to the general education classroom setting; a concept, not a place.

left to right subtraction   An algorithm for students who are challenged by directionality and/or regrouping in mathematics.

legally blind   A visual acuity of 20/200 or less in the better eye with correction or a visual field that is no greater than 20 degrees.

level of support   Provisions required to effectively function across adaptive skill areas in various natural settings.

limited English proficient   A person with a reduced or diminished fluency in reading, writing, or speaking English.

locus of control   The attribution for negative and positive outcomes.

low incidence disabilities   The group of disability categories (sensory impairments, autism spectrum disorders, physical/health disabilities, and traumatic brain injury) that accounts for about 20 percent of children ages 6–21 receiving a special education under IDEA.

low vision   A visual impairment that interferes with the ability to perform daily activities.

mainstreaming   Dated term, used to describe the movement away from serving children with disabilities in self-contained classrooms.

maintenance   The continuation of behaviors over time.

match-to-sample   A strategy in which the student looks for the object, picture, letter, number, or word that is the same as the one presented on a nearby poster or template.

material reinforcers   Edibles and other objects valued by a student that are used frequently in the beginning stages of a behavioral program.

materials and resources   One of the four components of universally designed curriculum.

math anxiety   An emotion-based, negative reaction to mathematics.

mathematic communication   The ability to associate words with symbols to develop math literacy.

math literacy   The learner's ability to access basic math skills and correctly apply them in appropriate situations.

mediated scaffolding   The personal guidance, assistance, and support that a teacher, peer, materials, or task provides to learners to help them bridge the gap between their current level of performance and the intended goal of independent performance.

mentally ill   A generic term used by many professionals outside the field of special education for individuals with emotional or behavioral disorders.

mental retardation   A disability, originating before age 18, characterized by significant limitations both in intellectual functioning and in adaptive skills.

metacognition   To think about one's own learning or thinking process.

methods   One of the four components of universally designed curriculum; teaching procedures and techniques to increase learner access.

mixed cerebral palsy   Cerebral palsy that consists of combinations of different types (ataxic, athetoid, or spastic).

MMMR Rap   A memory device for remembering the terms mode, median, mean, and range in mathematics.

mnemonic devices   Research-based memory-enhancing techniques that can help students recall facts and see relationships between units of information.

mnemonic letter strategy   A memory-enhancing technique that uses the first letters of a word or phrase to be remembered in acronyms or acrostics.

modeling   To teach by demonstrating the skill to be taught to one or more observers.

modifications   Changes to the subject matter or alterations of the performance level by reducing the content to be learned.

morphology   The rules governing how words are formed from the basic element of meaning.

multicultural education   An ambiguous concept that deals with issues of race, language, social class, and culture as well as disability and gender. Also viewed as an educational strategy wherein the cultural heritage of each pupil is valued.

multiculturalism   The acknowledgment of more than one culture, the basic commonalities among groups of people while appreciating their differences, and the belief that an individual can function within more than one culture.

multidisciplinary   A model of teaming that utilizes the expertise of professionals from several disciplines, each of whom usually performs his or her assessments, interventions, and other tasks independent of the others.

multidisciplinary team   The group responsible for developing an individualized and comprehensive assessment package that evaluates broad developmental domains (cognitive, academic, achievement) as well as the specific areas of concern noted on the referral, such as social/emotional problems or suspected visual impairments.

multimedia inquiry project   A task in which a student uses scanned pictures, Internet websites, digitized video clips, and software to show what they have learned in multiple formats.

multiple disabilities   An individual with two or more primary disabilities or concomitant impairments that cannot be accommodated by one special education program.

multiple intelligences   A theory developed by Howard Gardner that identifies and describes eight intelligence areas in which all individuals exhibit varying degrees of proficiency.

multiple means of engagement   To use a variety of methods to motivate students; one of three qualities of Universal Design for Learning that focuses on affective learning.

multiple means of expression   To provide students with different ways to respond to information received; one of three qualities of Universal Design for Learning that focuses on strategic learning.

multiple means of representation   To provide students with a variety of ways to receive and interpret information; one of three qualities of Universal Design for Learning that focuses on recognition learning.

natural consequence   A logical consequence for inappropriate choices that meaningfully relate to student behavior as alternative to punishment.

neglect   The failure to provide for a child's basic needs.

norm-referenced tests   Standardized tests that compare a pupil's performance with that of a representative sample of children, providing the evaluator with an indication of the pupil's performance relative to other individuals of similar chronological age.

operational definition   The first step in solving a problem behavior. A single behavior is targeted for others to observe and measure.

organic   An identifiable physical cause of speech and language impairments.

other health impairments   Chronic or acute health problems that result in limited strength, vitality, or alertness and adversely affect educational performance.

otitis media   An infection of the middle ear.

overrepresentation   The large number of children from minority groups placed in special education programs than would be anticipated based on their proportion of the general school population.

paraphrasing   To summarize or paraphrase material using a student's own words.

paraplegia   Paralysis (or spasticity) of the legs.

paraprofessional   Individual who provides instructional as well as noninstructional support and assistance to pupils (typically those with disabilities) in the general education classroom and/or a special education setting.

Peer-Assisted Learning Strategies A research-based instructional program that uses explicit teaching and peer tutoring in reading and math to help low-performing students in general education classrooms.

peer buddies/peer tutoring An approach in which a student at the mastery level of learning a skill (or higher) is paired with a learner in the acquisition stage. The mastery-level student explains the process/skill in his/her own words and provides multiple practice opportunities to the other student.

perinatal Occurring around the time of birth.

personal digital assistant A generic term referring to a small mobile handheld device that integrates tools and applications for such tasks as information storage, the Internet, and managing and organizing personal information.

phonation The production of sounds.

phonemic awareness To focus on hearing and using sounds in reading and spelling.

phonics The application of the alphabetic principle to known and unknown words in reading and spelling.

phonology The sounds characteristic of a language, rules governing their distribution and sequencing, and the stress and intonation patterns that accompany sounds.

physical abuse The infliction of bodily harm or injury regardless of intent or source of injury.

physical disabilities A variety of conditions and impairments that results in the inability to physically perform or function.

pinch card A type of response card that lists answer choices. Students "pinch" their answer choice on the card.

podcasting A technology that distributes audio and video files over the Internet using feeds to be downloaded for playback on MP3 players or computers.

portfolios A type of authentic assessment which typically presents a wide range of work examples of a student's emerging abilities and accomplishments. Portfolios may be electronic.

positive behavior supports Proactive, preventative approaches to behavior that identify and support effective, systematic schoolwide practices for desirable behavior up front; teach, model, and demonstrate desired behaviors in a clear and consistent fashion; acknowledge and reward students for appropriate behavior; and view behavior errors as learning opportunities to be identified, targeted, and corrected.

postnatal Occurring after birth.

pragmatics The rules related to the use of language in social contexts.

prenatal Occurring before birth.

prereferral intervention Intervention strategy that occurs prior to initiation of referral for special education services.

preteaching vocabulary A method for helping learners integrate new knowledge by presenting new terms and definitions before a new lesson or unit begins.

primary literacy medium The most frequently used method of reading and writing by an individual.

probes Teacher-created or commercially available measures administered frequently and repeatedly that allow for

instructional planning to collect information that can drive instruction. Results can help teachers match strategies to specific student needs.

problem solving The ability to identify a problem, gather information, list and consider options, consider advantages and disadvantages, and evaluate the effectiveness of a solution.

proficiency The stage of learning in which a skill becomes fluent and accurate; the learning becomes automatic.

progress monitoring To regularly assess student progress and the effectiveness of instruction, and to adjust instruction as needed.

punishment An aversive or unpleasant consequence to a behavior.

pyramid planning A framework for developing the big ideas for a diverse group of learners in a classroom striving to apply differentiated instruction as well as Universal Design for Learning principles.

quadriplegia Paralysis (or spasticity) of all four limbs.

Question-Answer-Response A reading comprehension approach that teaches students to organize four different types of questions and how to go about answering each type.

questioning strategies Strategies used by both students and teachers to plan, organize, explain, and assess knowledge and skills. Adjusting the levels of questions offers flexibility to diverse learners.

RAP A reading-comprehension intervention that involves reading a paragraph or a selection of material, asking one's self what the main ideas are, and putting the main ideas into one's own words.

reading pen A high-tech, handheld device that allows the reader to scan the unknown words or lines of text; the word(s) and definition(s) is/are shown on a LCD screen and pronounced out loud.

receptive language The ability to understand what is meant by spoken communication.

reciprocal teaching An technique in which students model a teacher-student dialogue with each other using teacher-provided prompts.

recognition system The part of the brain used to recognize patterns in received information; part of the three-part framework of brain processing.

regular education initiative Term that advocates restructuring of the relationship between general (regular) and special education toward shared responsibility—a partnership between general and special education resulting in a coordinated delivery system.

rehearsal To practice responses and expressions ahead of time to enhance academic performance.

reinforcement Presenting or taking away stimuli following a behavior that increases the likelihood of increasing or maintaining that rate of behavior in the future.

related services Services that children with disabilities require in order to benefit from their special education (e.g., physical therapy, school bus lift, speech pathologist).

representational A level of learning, sometimes referred to as *semiconcrete*, that moves the learner from the concrete to abstract level. Concrete objects are replaced with pictures or visual displays (e.g., tally marks in mathematics).

residual vision   Usable vision.

resonance   The direction of the sound.

response cards   Engagement tools students can use to respond to teacher questions. Students can have blank cards to write their own answers on or be provided premade answer cards (e.g., true/false; yes/no; A, B, C, D). Answer choices are held up and surveyed by the teacher.

response cost   A Level III strategy that involves removing something desirable to decrease inappropriate behavior.

response-to-intervention   A process used to determine if the pupil responds to empirically validated, scientifically based interventions. Designed to target early, effective instruction to students who are having difficulty learning as well as to serve as a data-based tool for diagnosing learning disabilities.

rubrics   Student- or teacher-created scoring systems used as evaluation tools of a performance-based product.

seating and positioning aids   Tools that assist students with mobility impairments or other disabilities by providing greater body stability, posture, and needed support.

Section 504   A civil rights law designed to prohibit discrimination against individuals with disabilities.

self-instruction   To verbally review the steps of a task to one's self.

self-management   To take responsibility for one's actions and the consequences that follow in meeting both academic and behavior goals. Components include self-instruction, self-monitoring, and self-reinforcement.

self-monitoring   To track one's own behavior and to make choices to discontinue inappropriate actions.

self-monitoring strategies   To observe a certain personal behavior and keep track of the behavior while working using cues.

self-reinforcement   The student delivers a consequence to himself/herself contingent on his/her own behavior after determining whether or not the desired behavior has been met.

semantics   The meanings of words and sentences.

sensorineural hearing loss   Hearing loss typically caused by disorders of the inner ear (cochlea), the auditory nerve that transmits impulses to the brain, or both.

The Sentence Writing Strategy   A strategy for improving writing in which students begin with direct instruction in forming simple sentences with subjects and verbs, progressing systematically to compound and then complex sentences.

service learning   A form of community-based instruction that integrates learning objectives with meaningful community service.

sexual abuse   A form of abuse that involves incest, rape, indecent exposure, inappropriate fondling, and/or sexual exploitation by prostitution or pornography.

shaping   A behavioral technique used to take a close approximation of the desired skill and move it to skill mastery.

slot outline   A technique in which a student fills in the blank lines of a premade outline or presentation summary while the presentation is occurring.

Snellen chart   A clinical measurement of the true amount of distance vision an individual has under certain conditions.

Socratic questioning   A questioning method that logically and sequentially guides students to higher-level thinking through a series of steps.

spaced repetitions   An intervention in which a learner is frequently asked to recall a learning experience or academic information on different days.

spastic cerebral palsy   A type of cerebral palsy in which the person has very tight muscles occurring in one or more muscle groups, resulting in stiff, uncoordinated movements.

specific learning disability   A difficulty in processing information to such a degree that many areas of school performance are negatively affected; a discrepancy between achievement and assumed potential.

speech   The expression of language with sounds; the oral modality for language.

speech or language impairment   A communication disorder affecting, in some instances, the production of speech or a significant limitation in using oral language as a means of communication (e.g., stuttering and articulation).

spiral curriculum   A curriculum in which the basic concepts are taught and subsequently revisited as needed to enable to students to use concepts as a springboard for more-advanced learning.

sports, recreation, and leisure aids   Products that assist people with disabilities to participate in sports, cultural, and social events (e.g., adaptive fishing rods, adapted controls for video games, audio description for movies).

statistically derived classification systems   Systems developed using sophisticated statistical techniques to analyze the patterns or "dimensions" of behaviors that characterize children and youth with emotional or behavioral disorders.

stereotypic behaviors   A variety of repetitive behaviors that people with disabilities may exhibit, including eye rubbing, head weaving, hang flapping, and body rocking.

story maps   Graphic organizers that help students identify and organize the elements of a story (e.g., characters, setting, problem/conflict, and solution); useful for prewriting and postreading activities.

strategic integration   To blend new ideas with the old to help with the transfer of knowledge from one setting/area to another.

strategic systems   The part of the brain used to apply personal meaning to information received, and to sort and classify that information; part of the three-part framework of brain processing.

structured questioning   The sequencing of questions aimed at eliciting student analysis of important problems on a topic, beginning with Level I questions (e.g., who, what, where, when) and followed with questions that probe more deeply to clarify meaning (e.g., how, why).

students with disabilities   Individuals who exhibit mental retardation, hearing impairment (including deafness), speech or language impairment, visual impairments (including blindness), emotional disturbance, orthopedic impairments, autism, traumatic brain injury, other health impairments, or specific learning disabilities.

summative assessments   Assessments that occurs at the end of a program or at the end of the school year.

syntax   The relationships among elements of a sentence.

systems, order, organization　A whole unit that is made up of parts.

task analysis　To analyze and break down a target behavior or skill into sequenced steps.

text messaging　Short messages sent via mobile phones, handheld devices, or computers.

thematic teaching　A method of integrating and linking multiple curricular elements using themes to make learning meaningful, allowing students to see how the parts connect to a bigger idea; students explore many different aspects of a topic or subject.

Think Aloud　A technique in which the teacher explicitly models procedures or steps by speaking while verbalizing his or her own thinking process.

thinking aloud　A technique for learning that is internalized; talking through things to help understand or remember them better.

Think-Pair-Share　A strategy in which teachers give students extra time to frame their response with a partner before actually responding, giving students a chance to find their words. This usually produces higher-quality answers and allows all students to participate.

time-out　To deny a student access to positive reinforcement from the teacher and peers in classroom activities for a specific amount of time, contingent on display of the target behavior.

time sampling　A type of interval recording on which teachers record continuous behaviors to find a percentage of occurrences of the targeted behavior.

token reinforcers　Tangible items given to students when a specified target behavior is performed.

tonic-clonic seizures　A seizure disorder that causes convulsions, loss of consciousness, and stiffness (tonic phase) followed by a jerking (clonic) phase in which the body makes rhythmic jerking motions that gradually decrease.

Touch Math　A multisensory mathematics teaching approach that uses dots or *TouchPoints* to engage students in "hands-on" computation; a research-based supplemental curricular program.

transdisciplinary　An approach to teaming in which team members are committed to working collaboratively across individual discipline lines.

transfer of learning　The application of knowledge and skills acquired by the learner from one problem-solving situation to another.

traumatic brain injury　Acquired trauma to the brain, ranging from mild to significant, that is typically associated with accidents or injury that can impact classroom performance.

twice exceptional　A student who is gifted and talented and also has a learning difficulty.

underrepresentation　The small number of children in a particular category than would be anticipated based on their numbers in the school population.

universal design　The creation of products or environments that are usable and accessible by everyone.

Universal Design for Learning (UDL)　Curriculum and instruction that includes alternatives to make it accessible and appropriate for individuals with different backgrounds, learning preferences, abilities, and disabilities in widely varied learning contexts.

Venn diagram　A visual tool used to compare and contract content material.

vicarious reinforcement　A Level I behavior reinforcement received indirectly by watching another person being rewarded for exhibiting a desired behavior.

visual impairment　A loss of vision that often adversely affects educational performance; includes those who are blind or partially sighted (capable of reading large print); the inability to see or see well, even with correction.

vocabulary　One of the five big ideas in reading; the ability to define words as well as use them in context.

voice disorders　May result from disorders of the larynx or disorders of phonation.

wait time　The thinking time allowed the learner after a teacher poses a question.

WebQuests　Inquiry-based activities during which learners gather information on a topic from the Internet.

whisper-phone　A low-tech handheld device on which students "whisper read" speech sounds/words/passages into the "phone" and hear their own voices back immediately to help them hear the speech sounds (phonemes) in the words they say; also called phonics phones.

wikis　Web-based tools that enable multiple users to work together on the same document or content by adding, removing, or editing content in a seamless manner.

Word Identification Strategy　A strategy developed at the University of Kansas Center for Research on Learning to help readers successfully decode and identify unknown words encountered in reading by identifying prefixes, suffixes, stems, and applying syllabication rules.

word map　A visual organizer that helps the learner analyze a word through its definition, a synonym, an antonym, a mnemonic and the situation(s) in which it might be used; students construct a memory sentence and a mind picture.

zone of proximal development　The area or difference between a person's actual independent level of learning/problem solving and his/her potential level of development of higher-level learning/problem solving.

Index

Italic page numbers indicate material in tables or figures.

AAMR definition of mental retardation, *55*, 55–56
ABC observation form, 409, *409–410*
absence seizures, 106
abstract stage of math, 340
abused children. *See* child abuse and neglect
ACCESS strategy
    physical learning environments, 283–287, *284*
    social learning environments, *289*, 289–293
accommodation
    assessment accommodations, 36
    Rehabilitation Act, Section 504 plans, 44, 46, *47*
    to support UDL environments, 294
    testing accommodations, 225, *226*
acquired immune deficiency, 107
acquisition stage of learning, 235–236, *237*
activity reinforcement, 415, *416*
ADA, 19–20
adaptation stage of learning, *237*, 237–238
adaptation to support UDL environments, 294–295, *295*
adapting learning environments
    science, 392–395, *394*
    social studies, 392–395, *394*
adaptive behavior skills, 56, *56*
ADHD. *See* attention deficit hyperactivity disorder
advance organizer, 348
affective systems, 185
age/grade-appropriate placement, *11*
AIDS, 107
algebra, 335–336
    fostering skills in, 348–349
algorithms. *See* math algorithms
alphabetic principle, 304–305
alternative teaching, *142*, 143, *144*
American Association on Intellectual and Developmental Disabilities, 54
American public education, 2–3

American Speech-Language-Hearing Association, 65
Americans with Disabilities Act, 19–20
analytic rubrics, 220–221
analyzing behavior, 413–414
anchored instruction, 239–241, *240*
anecdotal recording, 409
antecedent, 410
Antecedent-Behavior-Consequence form, *409*, 409–410
aphasia, 66
apprenticeships, 254
Armstrong's checklist for assessing students' multiple intelligences, *214–215*
articulation disorders, 65
Asperger's Syndrome, *404*
assessing learner progress
    behavior rating scales, 218
    curriculum-based measurement, 220
    effective approaches to, 210–218
    formal assessment, 210–211
    formative assessments, 218–219
    functional behavior supports, 218
    importance of, 208–210
    informal assessment, 210–211
    inventories (*see* inventories)
    large-scale assessments, 208–209, *209*
    multiple means of engagement in, 223
    multiple means of expression in, 225–229
    multiple means of representation in, 224–225
    nondiscriminatory assessment, 15
    ongoing assessment, 209–210, 218–219, 222–223
    organizing assessment, 218–220, 222–223
    positive behavior supports, 218
    probes, 220
    recording assessments, 220–222
    rubrics, 220–222
    school records, review of, 210
    standardized tests, 216, 217
    summative assessments, 219

    universal design for learning and, 210
    working collaboratively, 216–217
assessment(s)
    accommodations, 36
    behavior, 407–414
    challenging behavior, *405*
    classroom (*see* assessing learner progress)
    definition of, 37
    functional behavior assessments, 413–414
    of individual differences, 32–33
    information sources, *38*
    literacy skills (*see* literacy assessments)
    mathematics, 337–339
    ongoing (*see* ongoing assessment(s))
    participation in, 25
    for special education, 33, *32–33*, 36–37
    summative (*see* summative assessment(s))
    universally designed curriculum, 280–281, *281*
    See also formal assessment(s); informal assessment(s)
assistive technology
    academic outcomes, 164–165
    communication aids, 161, *161*
    computer access aids, *161*, 163
    daily living aids, *161*, 161–162
    definition of, 160
    "device," definition of, 160
    differentiated instruction and, 166–167
    education aids, *161*, 163–164
    environmental aids, *161*, 162
    ergonomic aids, *161*, 162
    examples of, 160–164, *161*
    functional learning outcome(s), 167
    learner needs/preferences and, 165–166
    learning aids, *161*, 163–164
    leisure aids, *161*, 163
    mobility aids, *161*, 162–163
    positioning aids, *161*, 163
    recreation aids, *161*, 163
    seating aids, *161*, 163

selecting, 167–168, *169*
sensory aids, *161*, 162
"services," definition of, 160
sports aids, *161*, 163
transportation aids, *161*, 162–163
Assistive Technology Act, 160
ataxic cerebral palsy, 103
athetoid cerebral palsy, 103
"at-risk" learners, 114–115
   abuse/neglect and, 118–121
   common factors, *115*
   defining "at risk," 115
   homelessness and, 116–117
   poverty and, 115–116, *116*
   who are, 3–4
attention deficit hyperactivity disorder,
   52–53, 72–73
   American Psychiatric Association defi-
    nition of, 73
   behavioral inhibition, 75–76, *76*
   causes of, 74–75
   characteristics of learners with, 75–76,
    76
   comorbidity and, 76
   DSM-IV-TR diagnostic criteria, 73, *73*
   emotional issues, 76
   environmental factors, 75
   executive functioning and, 76
   giftedness and, *404*
   hereditary factors, 75
   indicators of, *404*
   intervention strategies, 257, *260*
   literacy skills, 325–326
   neurological dysfunction and, 74–75
   number of learners with, 74
   social issues, 76
authentic learning, 239
   anchored instruction, 239–241, *240*
   ClassAct Portal, 241
   WebQuests, 242–243
authentic literacy, 304
autism spectrum disorders, 69, 97–98
   causes of, 99–100
   characteristics of learners with, 100
   definitions of, 98
   DSM-IV-TR diagnostic criteria, 98, *99*
   as federally recognized disabilities, 4
   indicators of, *404*
   number of learners with, 99

backward chaining, 243
balanced literacy, 304
baseline data, 408–409
behavior
   analyzing, 413–414
   assessment of, 407–414

challenging behavior, 403–407
disorders (*see* emotional or behavioral
   disorders)
externalizing, 403
internalizing, 403
intervention plans, 218, 413
peers and, 424–425
rating scales, 218
recording, 409–412
school personnel and, 424–425
targeting, 408, *408*
tracking, 408–409
behavioral contracts, 421–422
behavioral supports, 402, 428–430
   "big ideas, 403–407
   challenging behaviors, 403–407
   collaborating with parents, 425–426
   culturally diverse families, working
    with, 426–427
   diverse learners, 403–405, *404*
   exceptional students, 403–405, *404*
   externalizing behaviors, 403
   internalizing behaviors, 403
   maintenance and generalization, 423
   positive (*see* positive behavior
    supports)
benchmarks, 40–41
"big ideas," 238, *251*, 269
   behavioral supports, 403–407
   in literacy instruction, 303–307
   in mathematics instruction, 333–337
   in science instruction, 368–370
   in social science instruction, 370–371
bilingual education, 111, 112
biometrics, 154
blindness, 94–95
   definition of, 94
   as federally recognized disability, 4
   functionally blind, 95
   See also visual impairments
blogs, 170
Bloom's taxonomy of educational objectives, 186–187, *187*, 188
*Board of Education of the Hendrick Hudson
   Central School District v. Rowley*, 13
Boerum's portfolio design format, *229*
Braille, 94
brain-based research, 184–185
brain injury. *See* traumatic brain injury
brainstorming with a graphic organizer,
   375, *376*
*Brown v. Board of Education of Topeka,
   Kansas*, 11, *13*
Bruner's spiral curriculum, 189
Burke Reading Inventory,
   307–308, *308*

Cabri, 353
CAP strategy, 349, *353*
cause and effect, 371
*Cedar Rapids Community School District v.
   Garret F.*, *14*
cerebral palsy, 103, *103*
change (science), 369
child abuse and neglect, 118–121
   causes of, 119–120
   reporting, 121
child/student study teams, 34
chunking, 247
circle map for math vocabulary, 344, *345*
ClassAct Portal, 241
classroom assessments. *See* assessing
   learner progress
classroom response systems, 250–251
classroom Websites, 260–261
cleft palate, 66
cloze procedure, 318
cluster grouping, 253–254
cognitive impairments, 54
   intervention strategies, 252–253, *259*
   See also mental retardation
cognitive/social learning theories,
   185–189
collaboration
   classroom assessments, 214
   with culturally/linguistically diverse
    families, 134–136
   definition of, 128
   effective collaboration, 128–129, 148
   between general and special educators,
    129–130
   literacy, 326
   in mathematics instruction, 359
   with paraprofessionals, 130–132
   with parents/families, 132–136, 148,
    425–426
   science instructions, 395–396
   social studies instruction, 395–396
   UDL environment planning, 296–303,
    303
collaborative consultation, 136–137
   effective consultation, *139*
   planning form, *138*
collaborative planning
   science, 395
   social studies, 395
collaborative teams. *See* teaming models
color overlays, 324–325
communication
   definition of, 64
   mathematics ideas, 334, 342–344
communication aids, 161, *161*
community-based learning, 385

community support
    science, 396
    social studies, 396
comparing and contrasting, 371
complex partial seizures, 106
computation fluency, 335
computer access aids, *161,* 163
computerized assessments, 222–223
concept maps, 171
concrete stage of math, 339
conductive hearing loss, 89
consequences, 410
conspicuous strategies, use of, 243–246,
    251. See also intervention strategies
constancy (science), 369
content enhancements, 243–244
content standards, 276
contingently reinforced behavior, 414
contingent observation, 419
continuous behaviors, 411–412
cooperative learning, 258
    science, 388–389
    social studies, 388–389
    use of, *11*
cooperative teaching, 140–141
    advantages/disadvantages of options,
        144
    alternative teaching, *142,* 143, *144*
    one teach, one observe, 141–142, *142*
    one teach, one support, 142, *142*
    options, 141–143, *142, 144*
    parallel teaching, *142,* 143, *144*
    research support, 144
    station teaching, *142, 142, 144*
    suggestions for building successful
        arrangements, 144, 146, *146*
    team teaching, *142,* 143, *144*
co-teaching
    science, 395–396
    social studies, 395–396
court cases, 11–12, *13–14*
CPS software, 339
criterion-referenced assessment, 37
criterion-referenced tests, 210
cues and prompts, 248–249
culturally diverse families
    behavioral support from, 426–427
    collaboration with, 134–136, 148
culturally diverse learners, 110–111
    multicultural education, 111
    overrepresentation, 113
    and special education, 112–113
    underrepresentation, 113
    who are, 3
cultural sensitivity, 135–136
culture, 111

curricular design principles
    "big ideas," 238, *251*
    conspicuous strategies, use of,
        243–246, *251* (*see also* intervention
        strategies)
    in intervention selection, 238–252
    judicious review of learning, 250–251,
        252
    learning goals, integration of,
        239–243, *251*
    mediated scaffolding, application of,
        246–249, *252* (*see also* mediated
        scaffolding)
    prior knowledge, activation of,
        238–239, *251*
    UDL curriculum (*see* universally
        designed curriculum)
curriculum-based measurement, 220
curriculum compacting, 253
curriculum planning
    intervention selection, use of princi-
        ples in, 238–252 (*see also* curricular
        design principles)
    UDL curriculum (*see* universally
        designed curriculum)
cytomegalovirus, 92

daily living aids, *161,* 161–162
Daniel R.R. v. State Board of Education, 14
data analysis, 337
    fostering skills in, 357–358
deafness, 89
    as federally recognized disability, *4*
    See also hearing impairments
decibels, 89–90
decision-making process, 371
developmental delays
    as federally recognized disabilities, *4*
    mental retardation (*see* mental
        retardation)
Diana v. State Board of Education, 13
differential reinforcement, 418
differentiated instruction
    assistive technology and, 166–167
    social studies, 376–377, *377*
    universal design and, *199,* 199–200,
        272
digital immigrants, 155–156
digital natives, 155–156
digital storytelling, 171–172
diplegia, 103, *103*
Direct Instruction, 246–247
disabilities, students with, 3
    ADA, 19–20
    ADHD (*see* attention deficit hyperac-
        tivity disorder)

"at-risk" learners (*see* "at-risk" learners)
culturally diverse learners (*see* cultu-
    rally diverse learners)
federally recognized disabilities, *4*
high incidence disabilities, 52, *81* (*see
    also* emotional or behavioral disor-
    ders; learning disabilities; mental
    retardation; speech and language
    disorders)
linguistically diverse learners (*see* lin-
    guistically diverse learners)
low incidence disabilities, 88, *121* (*see
    also* autism spectrum disorders;
    hearing impairments; physical/
    health disabilities; traumatic brain
    injury; visual impairments)
technological tools for, 158–160 (*see
    also* assistive technology)
disciplining students, 23
discrete behavior, 410
Dolch sight word lists, 309
DRAW strategy, 341
Duchenne muscular dystrophy, 104
due process, 15, 23–24
dynamic geometry software, 353–354

echo reading, 313
education aids, *161,* 163–164
educational placements, 6–7
    contemporary challenges, 8
    evolution of options, *10*
    full inclusion, 10, *11*
    inclusionary practices, 10–11
    instructional programming and, 37, 39
    least restrictive environment, 5–6, *6,* 9,
        14
    mainstreaming, 8–9
    regular education initiative, 9–10
educational reform, 20. *See also* standards-
    based education
Education for All Handicapped Children
    Act. *See* IDEA
electronic dictionaries, 314
emotional abuse, *120. See also* child abuse
    and neglect
emotional or behavioral disorders, 67, 69
causes of, 71
    classification of learners with, 69–70
    clinically derived classification systems,
        69–70
    definitions of, 69
    as federally recognized disability, *4*
    indicators of, *404*
    intervention strategies, 257–258, *260*
    learning characteristics of learners
        with, 71

emotional or behavioral disorders
(*continued*)
literacy skills, 325
number of learners with, 70–71
social characteristics of learners with, 72
statistically derived classification systems, 70
engagement, multiple means of, *192,* 195–196, *196*
in assessment, 223
science, 388–390, *390*
social studies, 388–390, *390*
universally designed curriculum, *280*
English as a Second Language (ESL) programs, 113
English Language Learners, 112
environmental aids, *161,* 162
environments. *See* learning environments
epilepsy, 105
equilibrium, 369
ergonomic aids, *161,* 162
error analysis, 338, *339*
essential questions, 270, *270,* 376–377
evaluation of students, 24–25
Rehabilitation Act, Section 504, 44
See also assessing learner progress
event recording, 410, *410*
evidence (science), 369
evolution, 369
exceptional students. *See* gifted and talented learners
exclusion time-out, 419
explanations (science), 369
expression, multiple means of, *192,* 196–198, *198*
in assessment, 225–229
science, 391–392, *393*
social studies, 391–392, *393*
universally designed curriculum, *280*
expressive language, 65
expressive language disorders, *68*
externalizing behaviors, 403
extinction, 418

families. *See* parents/families
Federal Register
autism, definition of, 98
blindness, definition of, 94
deafness, definition of, 89
emotional disturbance, definition of, 69
learning disabilities, 61–62
multiple disabilities, definition of, 101–102, *102*

orthopedic impairment, definition of, 101, *102*
other health impairment, definition of, 101, *102*
speech and language impairment, definition of, 64–65
traumatic brain injury, definition of, 102, *102*
feedback, 223
field trips, 385
FLEAS strategy for timed tests, *257*
flow lists, 245
fluency
computational, 335
disorders, 65
with text (*see* fluency with text)
fluency with text, 305
increasing, 312–313
"foldables," 316, *317*
formal assessment(s), 210–211
literacy assessments, 307
mathematics assessments, 337–339
science assessments, 373–374, *374*
social studies assessments, 373–374, *374*
form and function, 369
formative assessments, 218–219
forward chaining, 243
FOSS, 388–389
framed text/print, 324
Frayer Model, 344, *344*
free appropriate public education, 14, 44
frequency recording, 410, *410*
Fry readability index, 323, *324*
full inclusion, 10, *11*
Full Option Science System, 388–389
functional behavior assessments, 413–414
functional behavior supports, 218
functional causes of speech/language disorders, 66
functionally blind, 95

Gallon Man, The, 355, *355*
Gardner's "multiple intelligences," *189,* 189–190
generalization
of behavior, 423
skills, 253, *259*
stage of learning, 236, *237*
Geometer's *Sketchpad,* 353–354
geometry, 336
fostering skills in, 352–354
geospatial technologies, 172–173
gifted and talented learners, 52–53, 77
behavioral supports, 404–405, *404*

causes of "giftedness and talent," 78–79
characteristics, 79, *79, 80*
definitions of "giftedness," 77–78
indicators of "giftedness," *404*
intervention strategies, 253–254, *259*
literacy deficits, 302–303
literacy skills, 326
number of, 78
twice exceptional students, 302
who are, 3, 77–78
Global Positioning System (GPS), 356
data collection sheet, *387*
lesson plans, 377, *378,* 382–383
goals. *See* learning goals
grand mal seizures, 106
graphic novels, 171–172, *172*
graphic organizers, 375, *376*
graphing calculators, 172
guided discovery learning, 247

Hands-On Equations, 349, *354*
handwriting skills, 306–307
assisting learners with, 317–321
health disabilities. *See* physical/health disabilities
hearing impairments, 89
academic achievement and, 93
causes of, 92
characteristics of learners with, 93
classification of learners with, 89–90, *90–91*
conductive hearing loss, 89
definition of "deafness," 89
as federally recognized disabilities, 4
impact on learning, *90–91*
indicators of, *92*
intervention strategies, 259
language skills and, 93
number of learners with, 91
psychosocial development of learners with, 93
sensorineural hearing loss, 89
sensory aids, *161,* 162
speech skills and, 93
hemiplegia, 103, *103*
hertz, 89–90
high incidence disabilities, 52, 81. *See also* emotional or behavioral disorders; learning disabilities; mental retardation; speech and language disorders
"highly qualified" special education teachers, 22–23
historical overview, 2–3

HIV-infected learners, 107
Hobson v. Hansen, 13
holistic rubrics, 221
homelessness, 116–117, *117, 118*
consequences of, 117–118
definition of, 117
indicators of, *118*
origins of, 117
"homeschool" attendance, *11*
"hunt-and-peck" method, 248
hyperactive learners. *See* attention deficit
hyperactivity disorder
hypernasality, 65
hyponasality, 65

IDEA, 3
1955 Education for All Handicapped
Children Act, 12, 14-16
1966 Education for All Handicapped
Children Act, 15–17
1970 Amendments, 16–17
1977 Amendments, 17–18
1984 Improvement Act, 21–25, 62
autism, definition of, 98
blindness, definition of, 94
deafness, definition of, 89
emotional disturbance, definition of, 69
highlights (1955–1984), 24
key features of, 17–18, *19*
learning disability, definition of, 61–62
mental retardation, definition of, 54,
56
overview of, 14
Rehabilitation Act, Section 504, compared, *19*
speech and language impairment, definition of, 64–65
identification of individual differences,
32–33
IEP(s), 15, 38–41
benchmarks, 40–41
components/elements of, 39, *41*
meaningful IEPs, 39
parents' right to participate, 39
related services, inclusion of, 42–43
IEP process, 21–22
immersion programs, 113
inclusionary practices, 10–11
inclusion time-out, 419
inclusive education strategies, 147–148
indirect consultation, 137
individualized education program(s). *See*
IEP(s)
Individuals with Disabilities Education
Improvement Act. *See* IDEA
infectious diseases, 107

info murals, 171, *171*
informal assessment(s), 210–211
literacy assessments, 309–310, *310*
mathematics assessments, 337–339,
338
informal reading inventories, 309–310
inquiry-based instruction/activities, 384
instant messaging, 171
instructional support team, 34
integration, 8–9
intellectual disability, 54. *See also* mental
retardation
interactive whiteboards, 169–170
interdisciplinary teams, 139, *140*
interest inventories, 211, *212*
interindividual student differences, 32–33
internalizing behaviors, 403
internships, 254
intervention assistance team, 34
intervention plan(s), 218, 413. *See also*
intervention strategies
intervention selection, 234–235
curricular principles in, 238–252
learning stages, consideration of,
235–238
intervention strategies
attention deficit hyperactivity disorder,
257, *259*
classroom response systems, 250–251
cognitively impaired learners,
252–253, *259*
content enhancements, 243–244
emotional or behavioral disorders,
267–258, *260*
flow lists, 245
forward and backward chaining, 243
generalization skills, 253, *259*
gifted and talented learners, 253–254,
259
hearing impairments, 259
keyword mnemonics, 244
language and speech disorders,
254–255, *259*
learning strategies approach, 243
match-to-sample, 244–245
memory improvement strategies (*see*
memory improvement strategies;
mnemonic devices)
motivating students, 258
organizational skills improvement
strategies, 255, 257, *259*
physical/health disabilities, 258–259,
260
questioning strategies, 245, *245*
response cards, *250,* 250
selection of (*see* intervention selection)

social disorders, 257–258
Socratic questioning, 245
spaced repetitions, 250
study skills improvement strategies,
255, 256, *259*
test-taking skills improvement strategies, 255, 256, *257, 259*
Think Aloud, 245–246
visual impairments, 258–259
intraindividual student differences, 33
inventories, 211
informal reading, 309–310
interest, 211, *212*
learning styles, 211, 213, *213*
math interest, 338, *338*
multiple intelligence, 213–214,
214–215, 216
reading interest, 307–309, *308*

Jacob K. Javits Gifted and Talented Students Education Act, 77
judicial decisions, 11–12, *13–14*
judicious review of learning, 250–251, *252*

keyword mnemonics, 244
KWL chart, 239, *239*
for GPS lesson, 380, *384*

language
components of, 65, *66*
definition of, 64
disorders (*see* speech and language
disorders)
diversity (*see* linguistically diverse
learners)
expressive, 65
hearing impaired learners, 93
receptive, 65
language cues, 248
language disorders. *See* speech and language disorders
large-scale assessments, 208–209, *209*
Larry P. v. Riles, 13
lattice multiplication method, *347,*
347–348
Lau v. Nichols, 13
learned helplessness, 294
literacy skills, 303
learning aids, *161,* 163–164
learning disabilities, 58–60
behavioral characteristics of learners
with, 63–64
causes of, 63
definitions, 60–62
as federally recognized disabilities, *4*
and giftedness, *404*

learning disabilities *(continued)*
  identifying students with, 22
  indicators of, *404*
  learning characteristics of learners
      with, 63–64
  number of learners with, 62
  response-to-intervention, 62
  See also specific disability
learning environments
  science, 392–395, *394*
  social studies, 392–395, *394*
  UDL environments *(see* universally
      designed learning environments)
  See also physical learning environment;
      social learning environment
learning goals
  integration of, 239–243, *251, 273,* 273,
      276
  mathematics, 333–337
  in science instruction, 368–370
  in social science instruction, 370–371
learning preferences, 190–192, *191*
  universally designed curriculum, 278
learning stages
  acquisition stage, 235–236, *237*
  adaptation stage, *237,* 237–238
  generalization stage, 236, *237*
  intervention selection, consideration
      in, 235–238
  maintenance stage, 236, *237*
  proficiency stage, 236, *237*
learning strategies approach, 243
learning styles inventories, 211, *213,* 213
learning toolbox, 243, *243*
least restrictive environment, 5–6, *6,* 9, 14
left-to-right subtraction, 346–347
legally blind, 94
leisure aids, *161,* 163
lesson plans
  GPS lesson plans, 377, *378, 382–383*
  mathematics, *350–351*
  multiple ways to present content,
      193–194, *194*
  UDL plan, 281, *282*
  writing skills, 318–320 *319, 320*
Levine's All Kinds of Minds, 216
limited English proficient, 112
LINCS strategy, 343
linguistically diverse learners, 110–111
  bilingual education, 111, 112
  enrichment programs, 113
  ESL programs, 113
  immersion programs, 113
  instructional options for, 113
  maintenance programs, 113
  overrepresentation, 113

sheltered English, 113
and special education, 112–113
transitional programs, 113
underrepresentation, 113
who are, 3
literacy assessments
  formal, 307
  informal, 309–310, *310*
  ongoing, 310
  reading interest inventories, 307–309,
      308
literacy skills, 302–303
  assessments *(see* literacy assessments)
  attention deficit hyperactivity disorder,
      325–326
  authentic literacy, 304
  balanced literacy, 304
  "big ideas" in instruction, 303–307
  collaboration, 326
  comprehension *(see* reading
      comprehension)
  eliminating the reading requirement
      entirely, 321–322
  emotional or behavioral disturbances,
      325
  fluency with text, 305, 312–313
  gifted and talented students, 326
  handwriting skills, 306–307, 317–321
  learned helplessness, 303
  math literacy, 334
  methods, materials, and resources,
      310–321
  modifying the reading level, 322–323
  modifying the text format, 322–323
  modifying the text's presentation,
      323–325
  motivational challenges, 325–326
  phonemic awareness, 304–305,
      311–312
  phonics, 304–305, 311–312
  science, 385–386
  social disorders, 325
  social studies, 385–386
  spelling skills, 306–307, 317–321
  struggling readers, 302–303, 321–325
  UDL applications, 321–325
  visual impairments, 325
  vocabulary, 305–306, 313–314
  word recognition, 304–305, 311–312
  writing skills, 306–307, 317–321
literacy technology, 171–173
locus of control, 420
logical consequences, 419–420
low incidence disabilities, 88, *121. See also*
      autism spectrum disorders; hearing
      impairments; physical/health

disabilities; traumatic brain injury;
      visual impairments
low vision, 95
LRE, 5–6, *6,* 9, 14

mainstreaming, 8–9
maintenance
  of behavior, 423
  stage of learning, 236, *237*
masked text/print, 324
match-to-sample, 244–245
material reinforcers, 415, *416*
math algorithms, 335
  lattice multiplication method, *347,*
      347–348
  left-to-right subtraction, 346–347
math anxiety, 338
mathematical algorithms, 335
mathematics, 332
  abstract stage of, 340
  algebra, 335–336, 348–349
  assessment of, 337–339
  "big ideas" in instruction, 333–337
  collaboration in instruction, 359
  common errors in, *339*
  communication of ideas, 334, 342–344
  concrete stage of, 339
  concrete stage of representational
      stage of, 339
  CPS software, 339
  data analysis, 337, 357–358
  error analysis, 338, *339*
  geometry, 336, 352–354
  learning goals, 333–337
  lesson plans, *350–351*
  measurement skills, 336, 354–356
  methods, materials, and resources,
      339–358
  numbers and operations, 334–335,
      344–348
  probability, 337, 357–358
  problem-solving skills, 333, 341–342
  progress monitoring, 339
  representational stage of, 339–340
math interest inventories, 338, *338*
math literacy, 334
measurement
  mathematics, 336, 354–356
  science, 369
media literacy tools, 171–173
mediated scaffolding, 246
  chunking, 247
  cues and prompts, 248–249
  Direct Instruction, 246–247
  guided discovery learning, 247
  modeling, 247

peer tutoring (*see* peer tutoring)

self-monitoring strategies, 247–248

shaping, 248

task analysis, 248

memory aids, 255

memory improvement strategies, 257, *259*

   CAP strategy, 349, *353*

   DRAW strategy, 341

   LINCS strategy, 343

   RIDE strategy, 341

   social studies, 386–388

   STAR strategy, 348–349, *352*

   See also mnemonic devices

mentally ill, 69

mental retardation, 53–54

   behavioral characteristics of learners with, 58, *60*

   causes of, 57–58, *59*

   classification of learners with, 57

   definitions of, 54–57

   as federally recognized disability, 4

   indicators of, *405*

   intelligence-based classification of, 57, *57*

   learning characteristics of learners with, 58, *60*

   level-of-support classification of, 57, *58*

   number of learners with, 57

   traumatic brain injury, distinguishing, 57

mentorships, 254

metacognition, 185

Mills v. Board of Education, District of Columbia, 13

mixed cerebral palsy, 103

MMMR Rap, 357–358

mnemonic devices, 244

   letter strategy, 244

   "RAP" a paragraph, 315, *315*

   science, 386, *386*

   social studies, 386, *386*

mobility aids, *161,* 162–163

modeling, 247

models (science), 369

modifications to support UDL environments, 294–295

morphology, 65, *66*

motivating students, 223

   intervention strategies, 257–258 (*see also* intervention strategies)

multicultural education, 111

multiculturalism, 111

multidisciplinary teams, 37, 138–139, *140*

multimedia anchors, 322

multimedia inquiry projects, 227, *227*

multiple disabilities, *102,* 104

as federally recognized disabilities, 4

See also physical/health disabilities

multiple intelligence assessment profile, *216*

multiple intelligence inventories, 213–214, *214–215,* 216

multiple intelligences, 189–190

   universally designed curriculum, 278

multiple means of engagement, *192, 195–196, 196*

   in assessment, 223

   science, 388–390, *390*

   social studies, 388–390, *390*

   universally designed curriculum, *280*

multiple means of expression, *192, 196–198, 198*

   in assessment, 225–229

   science, 391–392, *393*

   social studies, 391–392, *393*

   universally designed curriculum, *280*

multiple means of representation, *192,* 193–195

   in assessment, 224–225

   universally designed curriculum, *280*

muscular dystrophy, 104

narrative recording, 409

National Council for the Social Studies (NCSS), 370

national social studies standards, *370*

Nation at Risk, A, 115

natural consequences, 419–420

natural proportion at the school site, *11*

neglect, *120. See also* child abuse and neglect

No Child Left Behind Act, 20–21, 208–209

nondiscriminatory assessment, 15

norm-referenced tests, 37, 210

note-taking improvement strategies, 255, *256*

numbers and operations, 334–335

   foster skill development in, 344–348

Oberti v. Board of Education of the Borough of Clementon School District, 14

one teach, one observe, 141–142

one teach, one support, 142, *142*

ongoing assessment(s), 209–210

   computerized assessments, 222–223

   high-tech materials, 222

   literacy assessments skills, 310

   low-tech materials, 222

   methods for, 222–223

   planning for, 218–219

operational definition, 408

order (science), 368

organic causes of speech/language disorders, 66

organizational skills improvement strategies, 255, 257, *259*

organization (science), 368

orthopedic impairments, *103,* 103–104

   cerebral palsy, 103, *103*

   as federally recognized disabilities, 4

   muscular dystrophy, 104

   spina bifida, 104

   See also physical/health disabilities

otitis media, 92

overrepresentation, 113

parallel teaching, *142,* 143, *144*

paraphrasing, 315

paraplegia, 103, *103*

paraprofessionals

   collaborating with, 130–132

   qualifications of, 130–131

   responsibilities of, 131, *132*

   teachers' responsibilities, 131–132, *133*

   training of, 131

   who are, 130

parent contacts, record of, 425, *426*

parents/families

   collaborating with, 134–136, 148, 425–426

   culturally/linguistically diverse, 134–136

   IEP participation, 39

   parental participation, 15

   reactions to disability, 133–134, *134*

   record of parent contacts, 425, *426*

PDAs, 173

peer instructional models, *11*

peers and behavior, 424–425

peer tutoring, 249

   science, 389–390

   social studies, 389–390

Pennsylvania Association for Retarded Children v. Commonwealth of Pennsylvania, 13

personal digital assistants, 173

petit mal seizures, 106

phonation disorders, 65

phonemic awareness, 304–305

   fostering, 311–312

phonics, 304–305

   fostering, 311–312

phonics phones, 313

phonology, 65, *66*

physical abuse, *120. See also* child abuse and neglect

physical cues, 249

physical/health disabilities, 100
  causes of, 107–108
  characteristics of learners with, 108–109
  conditions associated with, 102–107
  definitions of, 101–102, *102*
  infectious diseases, 107
  intervention strategies, 258–259, *260*
  multiple disabilities, 104
  number of learners with, 107
  orthopedic impairments (*see* orthopedic impairments)
  "other health impairment," 4, 53, 101
  school performance, impact on, *108*
  seizure disorders, 105–106
physical learning environment, 282–283
  ACCESS strategy, 283–287, *284*
  design considerations, 283–288
Piaget's stages of development, 186, *186*
pinch cards, 392
placements. *See* educational placements
podcasting, 173
portfolios, 228–229, *229*
POSE strategy, *228*
positioning aids, *161*, 163
positive behavior supports, 218, 293–294, 406, *407*
  decreasing inappropriate behavior, 417–420
  increasing appropriate behavior, 415–417
  methods, materials, and resources, 414–428
  self-management, 422–423, *424*
  teaching new behaviors, 420–423
  See also reinforcement
poverty, and at-risk learners, 115–116, *116*
PowerPoint multimedia inquiry project rubric, *229*
pragmatics, 65, *66*
prereferral intervention, 33–34
prereferral intervention plan, *35*
preteaching vocabulary, 254
primary literacy medium, 95
probability, 337
  fostering skills in, 357–358
probes, 220
problem-solving skills, 333
  fostering, 341–342
  mathematics, 333, 341–342
  social studies, 370
proficiency stage of learning, 236, *237*
progress monitoring, 339
punishment, 414
pyramid planning, 271–272, *272*

quadriplegia, 103, *103*
QAR strategy, primary song, *317*
Question Answer Response strategy, 316, *316, 317*
questioning strategies, 245, *245*

"RAP" a paragraph, 315, *315*
reading comprehension, 306
  building, 314–317
  charting reading accuracy, 220, *221*
  questionnaire for, 307–308, *308*
  See also literacy skills
reading interest inventories, 307–309, *308*
reading interest survey, 211, *212*
reading pens, 314
reading skills. *See* literacy skills; reading comprehension
receptive language, 65
receptive language disorders, *68*
reciprocal teaching, 253, 322–323
recognition system of the brain, 184, *185*
recording assessments, 220–222
recording behavior, 409–412
record of parent contacts, 425, *426*
recreation aids, *161*, 163
referral for special education, 34, 36
  Rehabilitation Act, Section 504, 44
reforms in education, 20. *See also* standards-based education
regular education initiative, 9–10
Rehabilitation Act, Section 504, 18, 43–44
  accommodation plans, 44, 46, *47*
  eligibility, determination of, 45–46
  free appropriate education, 44
  IDEA, compared, *19*
  key features of, 18, *19*
  students covered by, 44
rehearsal, 389
REI, 9–10
reinforcement, 414
  activity reinforcement, 415, *416*
  contingently reinforced behavior, 414
  differential reinforcement, 418
  material reinforcers, 415, *416*
  self-reinforcement, 423, *424*
  token reinforcers, 415, *416*
  vicarious reinforcement, 418
reporting child abuse and neglect, 121
representation, multiple means of, *192*, 193–195
  in assessment, 224–225
  universally designed curriculum, *280*
representational stage of math, 339–340
residual vision, 95
resonance disorders, 65

response cards, *250*, 250
response cost, 419
RIDE strategy, 341
rubrics, 220–222
  science, 372, *372*
  social studies, 372, *373*

Schaffer v. Weast, 14
schizophrenia, 69
school personnel and behavior, 424–425
school records, review of, 210
science, 366–367
  academic learning environment, 393–395
  adapting learning environments, 392–395, *394*
  assessing content areas in, 371–375
  "big ideas" in instruction, 368–370
  challenges for diverse learners in, 367–368
  collaboration in instruction, 395–396
  collaborative planning, 395
  community-based learning, 385
  community support, 396
  content enhancements, 386
  cooperative learning, 388–390
  co-teaching, 395–396
  field trips, 385
  inquiry-based instruction/activities, 384
  lesson preparation, 379–384
  literacy skills, 385–386
  memory strategies, 386–388
  methods, materials, resources, and tools, 377–379, *380*
  mnemonic devices, 386, *386*
  multiple means of engagement, 388–390, *390*
  multiple means of expression, 391–392, *393*
  peer tutoring, 389–390
  planning instruction, 375
  representation ideas for, *388*
  rubrics, 372, *372*
  service learning, 385
  social learning environment, 392–393
  story maps, 387, *387*
  thematic teaching, 375
  universally designed learning assessments, 373–374
  Venn diagrams, 387, *387*
  vocabulary, 385–386
scientific notation, 349, *353*
seating aids, *161*, 163
seizure disorders, 105–106
self-instruction, 423–424, *424*

self-management, 412
self-monitoring, 390, 423, *424*
    strategies, 247–248
self-reinforcement, 423, *424*
semantics, 65, *66*
sensorineural hearing loss, 89
sensory aids, *161, 162*
sensory challenges. *See* hearing impairments; visual impairments
Sentence Writing Strategy, 318
service delivery options, 5–8, *7. See also* educational placements
service learning, 385
sexual abuse, *120. See also* child abuse and neglect
shaping, 248
sheltered English, 113
site-based management, *11*
"sky writing," 321
slot outlines, 318
Snellen chart, 94
social disorders
    intervention strategies, 257–258
    literacy skills, 325
social learning environment, 288–289
    ACCESS strategy, *289,* 289–293
    positive behavior support, 293–294
    science, 392–393
    social studies, 392–393
    technology tools, *293*
social software tools, 169–171
social studies, 366–367
    academic learning environment, 393–395
    adapting learning environments, 392–395, *394*
    assessing content areas in, 371–375
    "big ideas" in instruction, 370–371
    challenges for diverse learners in, 367–368
    collaboration in instruction, 395–396
    collaborative planning, 395
    community-based learning, 385
    community support, 396
    content enhancements, 386
    cooperative learning, 388–390
    co-teaching, 395–396
    differentiated instruction, 376–377, *377*
    field trips, 385
    inquiry-based instruction/activities, 384
    lesson preparation, 379–384
    literacy skills, 385–386
    memory strategies, 386–388

methods, materials, resources, and tools, 377–379, *380*
    mnemonic devices, 386, *386*
    multiple means of engagement, 388–390, *390*
    multiple means of expression, 391–392, *393*
    peer tutoring, 389–390
    planning instruction, 375
    representation ideas for, *388*
    rubrics, 372, *373*
    service learning, 385
    social learning environment, 392–393
    story maps, 387, *387*
    thematic teaching, 375
    universally designed learning assessments, 373–374
    vocabulary, 385–386
Socratic questioning, 245
sound frequencies, 89–90
spaced repetitions, 250
spastic cerebral palsy, 103
spatial sense, 336
    fostering skills in, 352–354
special needs learners
    number of, 5
    service delivery options, 5–8, 7 (*see also* educational placements)
    See also "at-risk" learners; disabilities, students with; gifted and talented learners
speech
    definition of, 64
    disorders (*see* speech and language disorders)
    diversity (*see* linguistically diverse learners)
    hearing impaired learners, 93
speech and language disorders
    articulation disorders, 65
    causes of, 66
    characteristics of learners with, 66–67, 68
    classification of learners with, 65
    definitions of, 64–65
    as federally recognized disabilities, 4
    fluency disorders, 65
    indicators of, *405*
    intervention strategies, 254–255, *260*
    number of learners with, 66
    voice disorders, 65
spelling inventory score sheet (elementary), *310*
spelling skills, 306–307
    assisting learners with, 317–321
spina bifida, 104

spiral curriculum, 189
sports aids, *161,* 163
stages of learning. *See* learning stages
standardized tests, interpretation of, 216, 217
standards-based education, 20
    No Child Left Behind Act of 1981, 20–21
STAR strategy, 348–349, *352*
station teaching, 142, *142, 144*
story maps, 387, *387*
structured questioning, 391
student feedback, 223
study skills improvement strategies, 255, 257, *259*
summative assessment(s), 219
    science assessments, 373–374, *374*
    social sciences assessments, 373–374, *374*
Supreme Court decisions, 11–12, *13–14*
syntax, 65, *66*
systems (science), 368

talented learners. *See* gifted and talented learners
"talking" dictionaries, 314
targeting behavior, 408, *408*
task analysis, 248
Tatro v. State of Texas, 13
teacher assistance teams, 34
teaming models, 137–138
    characteristics of, *140*
    components of, *140*
    interdisciplinary teams, 139, *140*
    multidisciplinary teams, 37, 138–139, *140*
    transdisciplinary teams, 139–140, *140*
team teaching, *142,* 143, *144*
technology, 154–155
    active learning through, 168–169
    assessments, use in, 222, 225, 226
    digital immigrants, 155–156
    digital natives, 155–156
    disabilities, for people with, 158–160 (*see also* assistive technology)
    literacy tools, 171–173
    myths and facts, 156–158
    ongoing assessments, use in, 222
    opportunities through, 173–174
    organizational skills, use for improving, 257
    social learning environment access, *293*
    social software tools, 169–171
    student expression formats, 226–229, *227*

technology *(continued)*
    study skills, use for improving, 255
    testing accommodations,
        225, *226*
testing accommodations, 225, *226*
test-taking skills improvement strategies,
        255, 257, *257*, *259*
text messaging, 171
"think alouds"
    algebra skills development, 349
    Think Aloud, 245–246
thinking aloud, 315
thinking map to aid scientific notation,
        349, *353*
Think-Pair-Share, 254
time-out from positive reinforcement, 419
time sampling, 411–412, *411*
token reinforcers, 415, *416*
tonic-clonic seizures, 106
toolbox for learning, 243, *243*
TouchMath, 344–345, *346*
tracking behavior, 408–409
transdisciplinary teams, 139–140, *140*
transition cues, *293*
transportation aids, *161*, 162–163
traumatic brain injury, 57, 102, 105
    characteristics of learners with,
        108–109, *109*
    definition of, *102*
    as federally recognized disability, *4*
    indicators of, *405*
twice exceptional students, 302

UDL. *See* Universal Design for Learning
underrepresentation, 113
Universal Design for Learning,
        25–26, 180
    3 M's of, *192*
    applications in society, 182–183
    architectural background of, 181
    brain-based research, 184–185
    classroom assessments and, 210
    classroom implications, 182–183
    cognitive/social learning theories,
        185–189
    concept of, 181–183
    curriculum (*see* universally designed
        curriculum)
    development of, 183–192

    and differentiated instruction, *199*,
        199–200, *272*
    flexible options, benefits of, 200–202
    learning environments (*see* universally
        designed learning environments)
    learning implications, 190–192
    learning preferences, 190–192, *191*
    lesson plan, 281, *282*
    math applications, *350–351*
    multiple intelligences, 189
    multiple means of engagement, *192*,
        195–196, *196*
    multiple means of expression, *192*,
        196–198, *198*
    multiple means of representation, *192*,
        193–195
    principles of, 182, *182*
    qualities of, *192*, 192–198
    reading in content areas, 321-325
    science assessments, 373–374
    social studies assessments, 373–374
    teaching implications, 190–192
    writing applications, *320*
universally designed curriculum
    assessments, 280–281, *281*
    "big ideas," 269
    components of, 268–269
    content standards, 276
    essential questions, 270, *270*
    goals, 269–276
    materials and resources, 277–278, *278*,
        288
    methods, 278–280
    multiple means of engagement, *280*
    planning, 271–272
    preplanning guide, *271*
    pyramid planning, 271–272, *272*
    sample unit organizer, *274–275*
    strategic integration of goals, *273*, 273,
        276
universally designed learning
        environments
    accommodations to support, 294
    collaboration in planning, 296–297
    modifications to support, 294–295
    physical environments, 281–288
    social environments, 288–294
U.S. Supreme Court decisions, 11–12,
        13–14

VARK Questionnaire, 213, *213*
Venn diagrams, 387, *387*
vicarious reinforcement, 418
visual cues, 248–249
visual impairments, 94
    academic achievement and, 96
    causes of, 95–96
    characteristics of learners with, 96–97
    classification of learners with, 94–95
    definitions of, 94
    emotional development of learners
        with, 96
    as federally recognized disabilities, *4*
    indicators of, *96*
    intervention strategies, 258–259
    literacy skills, 325
    number if learners with, 95
    orientation and mobility, 97
    sensory aids, *161*, 162
    social development of learners with, 96
    stereotypic behaviors, 97
visual literacy tools, 171–173
vocabulary, 305–306
    developing, 313–314
    math vocabulary, circle map for, 344,
        345
    preteaching, 254
    science, 385–386
    social studies, 385–386
voice disorders, 65
Vygotsky's zone of proximal development,
        185

wait time, 254
Web-based learning tools, 170
WebQuests, 242–243
Web tools, use of, 260–261
whisper-phones, 313
Wiki technology, 170
Word Identification Strategy, 312
word maps, 313, *314*
word recognition, 304–305
    fostering, 311–312
writing skills, 306–307
    assisting learners with, 317–321
    lesson plans, 318–321, *319*, *320*

zero rejection, *11*
zone of proximal development, 185